1 MONTH OF FREE READING

at

www.ForgottenBooks.com

By purchasing this book you are eligible for one month membership to ForgottenBooks.com, giving you unlimited access to our entire collection of over 1,000,000 titles via our web site and mobile apps.

To claim your free month visit:

www.forgottenbooks.com/free909691

ISBN 978-0-265-91903-3
PIBN 10909691

This book is a reproduction of an important historical work. Forgotten Books uses
state-of-the-art technology to digitally reconstruct the work, preserving the original format
whilst repairing imperfections present in the aged copy. In rare cases, an imperfection in
the original, such as a blemish or missing page, may be replicated in our edition. We do,
however, repair the vast majority of imperfections successfully; any imperfections that
remain are intentionally left to preserve the state of such historical works.

The City Club Bulletin
Published Weekly by the City Club of Chicago
A Journal of Active Citizenship

VOLUME XI   MONDAY, JANUARY 7, 1918   NUMBER 1

Next Thursday at Luncheon

Experiences of Two

Chicago Boys at the Front

—Field Ambulance Service in France—

Told By Themselves

SPEAKERS:

LOUIS G. CALDWELL, sous-chef S. S. U. No. 65. In service on the Chemin des Dames, May to October, 1917.

Mr. Caldwell was a member of the City Club before he went to France.

THOMAS B. POPE, driver of the Glencoe, Illinois, ambulance. In service on the right of Verdun, May to October, 1917.

Mr. Pope is a nephew of Henry Pope of the City Club.

The City Club Bulletin
A Journal of Active Citizenship

PUBLISHED WEEKLY BY THE
CITY CLUB OF CHICAGO
315 Plymouth Court   Telephone: Harrison 8278

DWIGHT L. AKERS, Editor

OFFICERS OF THE CLUB

FRANK I. MOULTON, President
EDGAR A. BANCROFT, Vice-President
ROY C. OSGOOD, Treasurer
CHARLES YEOMANS, Secretary
GEORGE E. HOOKER, Civic Secretary

EDITORIAL BOARD

HERBERT H. SMITH, Chairman
FREDERICK D. BRAMHALL   S. R. WATKINS
C. COLTON DAUGHADAY   PAUL R. WRIGHT

$1.00 per Year   -   -   -   -   10c per Copy

Entered as second class matter, December 3, 1917,
at the postoffice at Chicago, Illinois, under the act of
March 3, 1879.

> The purpose of the Club is to bring together in
> informal association those men who are genuinely
> interested in the improvement of the political,
> social and economic conditions of the community
> in which we live.

THE Legislative Committee of the Woman's City Club is trying to find out why the wheels of justice in Chicago grind so slowly—particularly in those courts which are devoted to the enforcement of laws having a social bearing, such as the compulsory education law, sanitation laws and the factory inspection act. The committee in a report printed in the January issue of the Woman's City Club Bulletin refers to the excessive number of continuances in many cases. On this point it says:

"The onlooker is filled with curiosity as to why, on December 12, three cases against Mr. Brady, which involve such simple things as the supplying of ash cans and garbage receivers, and which have already been continued eight times, are again put off by the prosecuting attorney until January 9, 1918. In an incomplete review of the cases in court on December 5 and 12 we find two cases which have been continued twelve times (one from January, 1917, the other from May, 1917); one case had eleven continuances; three, eight continuances; three, six continuances; four, five continuances. Of these ninety-seven continuances on thirteen cases, only seventeen were due to inability to secure a jury."

THE LISTENING POST

FRED A. GROW is going to France for service with the Y. M. C. A.

DOCTOR CHANNING W. BARRETT is in France with Base Hospital Unit No. 36.

FRANK L. VENNING of Lowe and Bollenbacher, is in the Camouflage Service of the Quartermaster's Department.

THE FOLLOWING PERSONS joined the Club last week: William K. Hodges, The Northern Trust Company, and Oliver M. Burton, President, Burton-Dixie Corporation.

ONE OF OUR STENOGRAPHERS has left us to do war work. Anyone who knows of a reliable, efficient stenographer to take her place will confer a huge favor by notifying Miss Corbyn in the office.

ARTHUR MANHEIMER has been commissioned Second Lieutenant in the Signal Reserve Corps. He expects to leave for France shortly as Supply Officer of the 415th Railway Telegraph Battalion.

THE DUES NOTICES for the coming quarter bear a war tax of $1.25, including 50c for the two months of the last quarter during which the tax was in effect. Those who paid war taxes on dues incurred prior to November 1st will now have a little pin money coming their way. The government has rescinded its former ruling imposing a tax on such dues and these members now have a credit on the club books.

THE SOLDIERS' AND SAILORS' Entertainment Committee is asking members to impose upon themselves a voluntary tax of at least $1.00 each to assist the committee in keeping the Club house open for enlisted men at week ends. This is payable with Club dues. "Your dollar," says the Committee, "will help to provide attractive club facilities for thousands of young enlisted men most of whom are from distant parts of the country and entire strangers to the city."

It's war work. It will cost very little if every member does his duty. What's a dollar?

CITY FATHERS TACKLE MONEY PROBLEM

Make Tentative Cuts in Expenditures
Preparatory to Request for Legislation

Mr. Rufus 'Rastus Brown
What's you goin' to do
When de rent comes 'roun'?

THE City Hall choir has been fervently chanting this refrain now for many weeks and Rufus is at last down to brass tacks. The City Council last week tentatively lopped off $3,657,799 from city expenditures as compared with last year. Estimates of the number of employes laid off vary because a number are absent on military leave and their positions have not yet been filled.

The passage of this measure, determining the operations of the city until the annual budget is framed, is an attempt by the city authorities to meet the recommendation of the civic organizations, including the Public Affairs and the Public Expenditures Committees of the Club, that before further taxes are voted by the legislature, the city should in its annual budget make retrenchment in departments where this is possible so that the people may know what relief is necessary to take care of vital and indispensable activities. Several organizations have pointed out that the amount of relief asked for would depend upon the economy and efficiency moves which the council would stand for in laying out the work of the city for 1918.

Some of the special economies recommended were adopted in whole or part:

FEWER STATIONS—MORE COPPERS

1. *The number of police stations was reduced.* The superintendent of police last April recommended that the 45 police stations of the city be consolidated into 22. The present action of the council is not so thorough-going but twelve of the stations are to be eliminated at an estimated saving of $170,000 for overhead expenses and with the result of placing on beat 300 additional policemen now doing useless station duty. In his letter on the subject last April the superintendent of police stated that the elimination of 23 stations would save about $850,000 annually and put about 750 men on beat. He said:

"Contrary to the prevalent idea, police stations themselves do not afford protection to the citizens. The only effective manner in which police protection is furnished is by placing policemen on the streets. In my judgment there should not be more than twenty-two stations, four on the north side, eight on the west side and ten on the south side, and two of these stations should be reserved exclusively for women."

"RISE UP SO EARLY IN DE MORN"

2. *City Hall employes will be required to work eight instead of seven hours per day.* It is reported that one person opposed to this action charged that the City Hall employes were being unjustly treated, that 26 years ago the working day was changed from six hours to seven hours and that now it is proposed to lengthen the long day still more.

3. *Extra holidays for city employes were abolished.* A report of the Chicago Bureau of Public Efficiency recently pointed out that the closing down of city bureaus on primary and election days involves a heavy financial loss to the community and much inconvenience.

JOINT COMMITTEE ACTS

The special joint committee of members of the City Council and of the State Legislature, appointed to find a solution for the city's financial dilemma, last Thursday adopted a resolution favoring a special session of the General Assembly. It recommended legislation to enable the city to levy an additional tax of fifty cents on a hundred dollars for a period not to exceed two years and to permit the licensing of certain kinds of business not now subject to license. The committee also proposed the appointment by the legislature of a committee to consider a comprehensive re-organization of the city government of Chicago, including therein legislation for a survey of the city's finances to meet requirements for a ten-year period. The committee gave no consideration to the suggestion for an immediate re-organization of the city government along the lines of the manager plan, proposed by the Chicago Bureau of Public Efficiency and endorsed by various civic organizations including committees of the City Club. (See City Club Bulletin of last week.) The idea of a financial survey, also backed by civic organizations, was endorsed but the committee proposes additional legislation in 1919 before starting on this survey.

FEWER ELECTIONS—SHORTER BALLOT

Two proposals advocated by the Club's Committee on City Manager Plan were also approved by the joint committee for favorable action by the Legislature in the event of a special session, namely, those:
1. To make the offices of City Clerk and City Treasurer appointive by the City Council.
2. To extend the term of office for Aldermen from two to four years with the right of re-call.

THESE DIDN'T GET BY

The City Council has not seen fit to adopt a number of recommendations made by the civic organizations affecting the efficiency of the city departments, namely:
a. Abolition of ward lines as a basis of administration of Bureau of Streets activities.
b. Standardization of employment in the law department and in the offices of the Clerk and Bailiff of the Municipal Court.
c. Centralized and standardized purchasing, testing, inspection and stores.
d. Consolidation of visual inspections.
e. Reduction of the number of yards, etc.
f. Consolidation of the Bureaus of Sewers and Compensation with the Bureau of Streets.
g. Consolidation of license, permit and plan examination bureaus.
h. Centralization of pay-roll divisions in the Comptroller's office.

The possible savings from the various economies suggested above, including those recommended to and adopted by the City Council are estimated in the Woman's City Club Bulletin for January at $2,530,-000. Estimated new revenues and proceeds of economies already instituted are listed at around $770,000. Together these would net a saving of approximately $3,300,000.

It is reported in last Saturday's papers that the Woman's City Club will oppose the calling of a special session.

"At present we are opposed to the calling of a special session of the legislature,"

(Continued on page 6)

A New Year's
Resolution

for a City Club Member

I resolve—

TO SECURE at least one new member for the Club—the sooner, the better,

TO "BOOST" the City Club loyally and enthusiastically among my business and social associates,

TO SEND to the Membership Extension Committee the names and addresses of friends and acquaintances who should become members;

Because—

MORE CIVIC-MINDED men should share the advantages and support the ideals of the Club,

MORE NEW MEMBERS are needed to fill the places of those who have and others who will enter military service,

MORE DOLLARS must be secured to meet the expenses of the Club inasmuch as members entering service are exempt from dues, and cost of operation has increased.

Information, Literature, Co-operation upon application to the

MEMBERSHIP EXTENSION COMMITTEE

CHICAGO EFFICIENCY PLAN FAVORED

"Mayor-Manager" Unification Scheme, Endorsed by Club Committee, Is Advocated for Los Angeles

W E used to read in the Sunday School books about the little acorn that became a mighty oak. The Chicago Bureau of Public Efficiency last winter planted a little seed of an idea and has been watering it and watching over it and hoping that some day it would become a fine young tree. Now it finds the idea sprouting up in an altogether unexpected place.

TOO MANY GOVERNMENTS

Los Angeles County is in somewhat the same situation as Chicago in respect to her local governments. There are all sorts of little governments, each running around on its own job and bumping into other little governments, getting in their way and making a general nuisance of itself—besides costing a lot of money. There are 187 school districts, thirty-eight distinct municipalities, thirty-four lighting districts, thirty-three road improvement districts, three waterworks districts and two protection districts—each with power to raise and spend money. There are enough of these little drops to make a respectable puddle if they could all be brought together—and that's what the California Taxpayers' Association proposes to bring about. Knowing that Chicago had proposed the most thorough-going plan anywhere for the re-organization and simplification of local governments in a large city, they sent for George C. Sikes to show them how to tinker up their machine, with the result that they have adopted and are backing up for Los Angeles some of the best features of the plan of the Chicago Bureau of Public Efficiency.

WHAT'S TO BE DONE

The re-organization which they propose is along two lines, which they state as follows:

1. "A re-organization of the machinery and tools of government along simple lines, with as little indirect transmission of power as possible and with a minimum of platings to box in and conceal from view the actual workings of the machinery when installed.

2. "Consolidation of governments which lie within a natural metropolitan area and the consequent substitution of one local government for the many."

You can almost see the horns and cloven hoof of George C. Sikes and smell the brimstone and sulphur of the Chicago Bureau of Public Efficiency in this. Wait a minute and you'll see the devil himself.

WANTED—A MANAGER

The most original contribution in the Efficiency Bureau's plan is their scheme for getting around the difficulties ordinarily urged against the city-manager plan as applied to large cities. Hitherto the city manager has been a sort of tail to the "commission-government" dog and everybody thought that tail wouldn't wag unless that particular dog was there to wag it. Now commission government is ordinarily very good for a small town but there are many reasons why it wouldn't do for Chicago. On the other hand the city-manager plan has its points for a large city and the Efficiency Bureau came to the conclusion that by a very slight operation the tail could be removed and grafted onto a reorganized and simplified council government based on ward representation. The idea is finding a great deal of favor, not only in the City of Chicago, as applied to our own conditions, but elsewhere. It is an integral part of the plan for reorganizing the government of Los Angeles County.

A REAL MAYOR

Both the Chicago and Los Angeles adaptations of the city-manager plan, however, give the manager a special dignity and authority—which he does not always possess in the commission-governed city. Although elected by the City Council and removable by them he will retain the title of mayor and will in fact be a "manager-mayor." The Los Angeles report on this point says:

"There is danger, especially in large cities, of regarding the person bearing the title of manager as merely a high-grade foreman or chief clerk, whose main function is to look after details. That is not the proper conception. The need of cities is for executives of training and experience in public affairs, with broad grasp of municipal problems, and capable of furnishing leadership in solving problems. Instead of being a mere detail man—a manager in a narrow sense—the executive of a large city should supervise and plan, leaving to subordinates selected for the purpose the actual work of administration.

What Council Will Do

"The function of the council under such an arrangement is to select the executive and in a very general way to direct his activities, upholding him when he is right, and offering the corrective of responsible group judgment for the peculiarities that any single individual is liable to develop. The council should determine the broad questions of policy. Instead of administering, however, it should act through its executive agent, in whom responsibility should be centered. It probably would be better for Los Angeles to style such an executive the mayor, rather than manager, as the term mayor would be more likely to signify to the public mind the type of executive needed."

The Los Angeles plan and the Chicago plan involve many other important points relating to the size of the council, the number and character of elections and so on which the eager reader, interested in details, should follow out by getting the reports.*

Will Save Cash

The Taxpayers' Association figures that Los Angeles can save over $2,600,000 annually by a complete consolidation. Los Angeles is a much smaller city that Chicago. In these times of financial stress for our city government, with a money-famine at the city hall and with frantic appeals in the air for new taxing powers, the City ought at least to look into the proposals of the Bureau as a means to permanent future economies.

This has already been suggested to the Special Joint Committee of the City Council and the State Legislature by the City Club Committee on City Manager Plan (City Club Bulletin, Vol. X, No. 21) and by other organizations which have endorsed the idea.

* The report of the Chicago Bureau of Public Efficiency can be had upon application at the office of the Bureau, 315 Plymouth Court. The Los Angeles report is on file in the City Club Library.

Chicago's Financial Dilemma
(Continued from page 4)

Miss Sears is quoted as saying. "We do not feel that the council assures us of effecting the economies suggested in our recommendations to it. If we could get true assurance of fundamental economies, including the riddance from the city service of superannuated and inefficient help and practical curtailment of expense, we might be convinced that the methods suggested in the appeal to the legislature are sincerely made."

PERMISSION to graze live stock in the national parks "during the period of the war" is being urged upon Congress by western grazing interests. The Conservation Department of the General Federation of Women's Clubs has just issued a statement opposing this use of the parks. It says:

"At the preent time the use of our national parks for grazing is inexcusable. Sheep ruin parks for the use of people. They destroy one of the greatest attractions of the outdoor world—the wild flowers. But the sheep isn't to blame. It is his nature to eat wild flowers, and not only the blossoms, but the plants and then the roots. At Crater Lake National Park there isn't a wild flower to be seen. Years ago sheep grazed within the boundaries, and although they have not been in the park for years, the ground is barren of flowers."

The park area available for grazing is limited, according to this statement. On the other hand there are large unused areas in the public domain suitable for nothing else. The parks can contribute but little to the food production of the country. Why, then, asks the Federation, should we allow them to be despoiled? It urges that letters be sent to Congressmen opposing this effort.

THE CUT USED IN THE dining room ad this week was shamelessly purloined from the Bulletin of the St. Louis City Club.

PREPAREDNESS FOR THE PERIOD of readjustment following the war will be the keynote of the convention of the Vocational Education Association of the Middle West to be held January 24-6 at the Morrison Hotel.

At the Sign of the Book

Wild and Wooly

REPORT OF THE DIRECTOR OF THE NATIONAL PARK SERVICE, for the fiscal year ending June 30, 1917.

JUST as the small boy loves to stick a feather in his hat and pursue imaginary Indians into the hayloft, the grown-up boy in the city once a year loves to shove his chair under his desk, dress like backwoodsmen and with pack on his back tramp up hill and down dale over the wild places of the earth. Even if the impulse for adventure doesn't lurk in so primitive a form, he probably likes to oil up his rusty Ford or get his Packard Twin-Six from the garage and roll around in state among the rugged peaks and primeval forests.

BETTER THAN GOLD

We have never particularly cared for that type of park propaganda which has given so much emphasis to the commercial side of these great natural resources. It is undoubtedly true that the parks "keep money at home that might otherwise be spent on travel abroad"—and if that type of argument convinces a certain type of mind it is legitimate to use it. But the commercial side of the nation's great parks is incidental as compared with their immense spiritual and recreative values.

The Director of the National Park Service has just issued his report for last year. The National Park Service is of very recent origin and it is particularly fortunate that the man selected to organize it and through it to administer and develop our great wilderness playgrounds was one who approached his work with more than official interest, one who had tasted the wilderness life, roamed the woods, climbed rugged peaks, slept in the snow and developed a love of outdoor life as part and parcel of himself—our former vice-president, Stephen T. Mather.

PARKS ARE POPULAR

The Director's Report is a convincing demonstration of the immense value of these national play spaces. They were visited last year by nearly a half million people and were entered by over 55,000 private automobiles. But the appropriation for their administration, protection and improvement—although having a combined area of over six and a quarter million acres—was but little in excess of a half million dollars. This covers not only trail and road building and the general operation of the parks but the dissemination of information about them—a task which the National Park Service is doing in a large scale.

The American people can congratulate themselves that with the organization of the new park service the parks are at last being efficiently organized and directed. Until recently they were administered as individual units by various and sundry departments of the government. Under such conditions they were generally considered side-issues. Their consolidation under a bureau whose sole purpose is their development and use as national playgrounds is a measure which park advocates long argued for. It has now been practically accomplished although the Yellowstone Park and some of the national monuments still remain under the Secretary of War or of Agriculture—a defect in existing legislation which ought to be corrected.

MORE PARKS WANTED

The Park Service recommends an extension of the national parks by the addition to the system of the Grand Cañon—now a national monument—the extension of the Sequoia National Park by the inclusion of the Kings and Kern River Cañons and the crest of the Sierra and the addition to the Yellowstone Park of a part of the famous "Jackson Hole region."

Glimmerings From the Past

EIGHTH ANNUAL REPORT OF THE BOARD OF SUPERVISING ENGINEERS, CHICAGO TRACTION, Covering the Fiscal Year Ended January 31, 1915. Published by the Board, Chicago, 1917.

THIS book, which came to our desk hot off the press a few days after Christmas, is a volume which every citizen interested in his city's past should possess. In these days of whirling events, when one tires of Russian revolutions, "peace drives," and exhortations to buy smokes for Sammies, it is soothing to turn the leaves of this attractively covered volume to the income account of the Chicago City Railways Company for the year before the war or to read over Mr. Arnold's statement in reply to Barrow, Wade and Guthrie, May 14, 1914. There is nothing of the seething outer world in this and the reader may rest assured that he will encounter no mention of bolsheviki, General Haig or the government operation of railways.

It is this which we like about the book. We doubt if we would be sufficiently interested in an up-to-date account of our transportation system, but the antiquarian interest in us is sufficiently strong to make us almost want to read this from cover to cover. We are glad that the cloistered clerks who produced it did not hurry to put it on the press for we are sure that it would have thereby lost much of its classic charm.

Three years is not too long to wait for a volume of this sort. We are almost afraid the infectious spirit of an office devoted to "rapid transit" may seize upon the authors of this volume and force them to publish the report for the year just ending before it is normally due, New Years, 1921.

Please Note That

E VERY day the librarian brings to our desk a collection of interesting literature just received. It may be seen in the library by anyone interested. Just to mention a few items received recently:

The Avenue, Vol. I, No. 6. Official Bulletin of the Fifth Avenue Association, New York. Contains discussion of the limitation of building heights on Fifth Avenue. Of interest particularly to members of the City Planning Committee.

Report of the Work of the Bureau of Education for the Natives of Alaska, 1915-16. Sounds dry, but has interesting pictures. Describes pioneering educational work among the Esquimaux and Laplanders.

Forty-eighth Annual Report, West Chicago Park Commission, 1916. The pictures in this report are numerous and attractive. We suggest as a desirable war economy the omission of the 100-page list of vouchers—nearly 10,000 in number—issued by the Commission in 1916. Good financial summaries in adequate detail are, of course, essential, but there is a limit to the extent which a public body needs do its bookkeeping in public.

Housing Problems in America. Proceedings of the Sixth National Housing Conference, Chicago, October 15, 16 and 17, 1917. A bulky volume of live material

on a subject of great and immediate national importance. A number of the papers relate to the housing emergency created by the war. The Association deserves the thanks of the public for getting the volume out while the papers are still up-to-date and of live interest.

"What Is a House?—Our National Obligation." By Frederick L. Ackerman. Published by the Journal of the American Institute of Architects. Described on the cover as "the story of England's colossal work in building workmen's houses as a prerequisite to maximum output of war munitions, and as a part of her program of social and economic reconstruction after the war." The most satisfactory account of the English housing program that we have seen so far. It is to be supplemented by articles which will appear in future issues of the *Journal.*

A membership in the City Club comes nearer being a privilege bestowed upon a prospective applicant than any favor you might wish to show him.

The material side of the club, as to meals, service and prices is beyond comparison. How about it?

mr. jack horner

sat in a corner

  when suddenly he had a

  bright idea:

  this christmas pie stuff

  is all right for a

  nursery rhyme, he said

    —as he reached for his hat—

but for genuine grub

I'll go to the Club

  and try that new pastry

  cook's pie.

The City Club Bulletin
Published Weekly by the City Club of Chicago
A Journal of Active Citizenship

VOLUME XI   MONDAY, JANUARY 14, 1918   NUMBER 2

THIS WEEK'S EVENTS

Next Thursday, January 17, *at luncheon*

"What Is the Matter with the New Gas Ordinance"

DONALD R. RICHBERG, Special Counsel for the City of Chicago, Gas Litigation Case.

Luncheon from 11:30.   Speaking promptly at 1:00.

Next Saturday, January 19, *at luncheon*
Ladies' Day (see below)

NORMAN ANGELL of London
"Success in Our War Aims"

MR. ANGELL'S MANAGER SAYS:

"Mr. Angell was one of the earliest advocates of American participation in the war and he is in the country at the present time with the full consent and approval of his government. His object is to contribute towards the formation of such a foreign policy that Allied victory will really have those political results for which the war is being fought."

CITY CLUB LADIES' DAY—Many requests come in from time to time that members' wives be invited to noon-day discussions By special arrangement, therefore, ladies are cordially invited for luncheon and Mr. Angell's talk. For luncheon come not later than 12:45! Mr. Angell will speak in the lounge—not the dining room—at 1:30.

Luncheon from 11:30. Speaking promptly at 1:30 in the Lounge.

Ghe City Club Bulletin

A Journal of Active Citizenship

PUBLISHED WEEKLY BY THE

CITY CLUB OF CHICAGO

315 Plymouth Court   Telephone: Harrison 8278

DWIGHT L. AKERS, Editor

OFFICERS OF THE CLUB

FRANK I. MOULTON, President
EDGAR A. BANCROFT, Vice-President
ROY C. OSGOOD, Treasurer
CHARLES YEOMANS, Secretary
GEORGE E. HOOKER, Civic Secretary

EDITORIAL BOARD

HERBERT H. SMITH, Chairman
FREDERICK D. BRAMHALL   S. R. WATKINS
C. COLTON DAUGHADAY   PAUL R. WRIGHT

$1.00 per Year   -   -   -   -   10c per Copy

Entered as second class matter, December 3, 1917, at the postoffice at Chicago, Illinois, under the act of March 3, 1879.

The purpose of the Club is to bring together in informal association those men who are genuinely interested in the improvement of the political, social and economic conditions of the community in which we live.

THE LISTENING POST

DR. DAVID KLEIN has received the Commission of Captain in the Sanitary Corps.

OSCAR M. WOLFF is in Washington with the Food Administration, connected with the Division of Enforcement.

WE REGRET TO NOTICE the report in the newspapers of last week that Thomas D. Jones, who has been serving on the war trades board at Washington, has resigned on account of ill health.

IF THE MEMBER who wrote President Moulton an anonymous letter the other day on the theme, "Live bait catches the fish," will make himself known to Mr. Moulton, the directors will be glad to take up with him the suggestion therein contained.

CHARLES R. CRANE, scheduled to speak here last Saturday, was prevented by the big storm from keeping his engagement. The large crowd which braved the blizzard was not disappointed, however, for, by rare good fortune, S. S. McClure and T. P. O'Connor were present and talked in his stead. The meeting lasted till nearly 3:00 o'clock. A full account will be printed in next week's Bulletin.

DR. FRANK BILLINGS was appointed last week as chairman of the State Commission which is to investigate the subject of working hours for women.

WILLIAM HOSKINS is on the Board of consulting chemists to the Director of the United States Bureau of Mines, one of the most important boards for chemical research in connection with the war activities.

THESE ARE LAST WEEK'S additions to the Club's Roll of Honor:

Joseph W. Northrop, First Lieutenant, 335th Field Artillery, Camp Pike, Ark.

S. L. Orwall, aviation service.

R. D. Donovan, Lieutenant, Camp Logan, Houston, Tex.

EVERY NOW AND THEN some member asks if the Club has a notary. Sorry that we haven't, but Miss Bertha Freeman in the office of the National Conference of Social Work (sixth floor of the club house) has a commission and will be glad to render special notarial service for members. She is on hand at the lunch hour until 1:15.

BION J. ARNOLD, according to a dispatch received last week from Washington, will leave soon for France to assume charge of an important undertaking with the American Aviation Service. Mr. Arnold holds a Commission as Lieutenant-Colonel. While Mr. Arnold is known chiefly for his work as a street railway expert, it is stated that he has made a study of aviation for twenty-five years and was associated with Chanute, one of the aviation pioneers, in his experiments with flying machines.

WELCOME TO OUR MIDST! These are new members of the Club, who joined last week: Roy L. Griffith, Editorial Staff, Chicago Evening American; Rev. James B. Haslam, Field Secretary, Commission on Social Service; F. S. Hickok, Ridgway Dynamo & Engine Company; Charles D. Loper, Mullen & Co. (Woolens); T. A. Lorenz, Jr., Hill Binding Co.; L. D. H.

(Continued on page 16)

PLUG WATER LEAKS, SAYS BUREAU

Urges Universal Metering to
Stop Waste and Save Money

CHICAGO is the most inveterate user of water of any city in the world. We wish that we could assure the Anti-Saloon League that this is due to the growing consumption of water in our city as a beverage and is a product of their efficient and vigorous campaign. We would like to believe that it is due to the excessive predilection of our people for baths and shampoos. But, alas, the Bureau of Public Efficiency, after a characteristically thorough investigation, disappoints us by concluding, in a report issued last week,* that we simply waste it—shamelessly and needlessly waste it. It slips from the pumps, it leaks from the pipes, it drips from the faucets. Two hundred and fifty-nine gallons every day are pumped for each man, woman and child in the city and of this 60 per cent is lost through leakage and waste.

NEW YORK A BAD SECOND

It would probably amaze the New Yorker who looks at our city for the first time to know that although we have less than half the population of his city we use fourteen per cent more water. We waste so much that in some parts of the city or at certain periods of the year, the pressure is often inadequate for fire protection or good service to the upper floors of apartment houses.

Just because we are so spendthrifty in our use of water, there is a constant race between the supply and the equipment with which to pump it. Next to air, we regard water as about the freest of the necessities of life. With Lake Michigan at our front door we forget that it costs us money. We think that we can simply turn on the faucet and that Lake Michigan, which has stood by us all these years, will do the rest. And just because we have this fantastic and erroneous idea, it is costing us about $500,000 a year to pump water which is later wasted or which leaks away. We are also year by year needlessly digging new tunnels, needlessly building new pumping stations and needlessly adding new equipment to the water system. Three and a half million dollars is being spent each year on additions to equipment, according to the Bureau. The water system earns about 3.6 per cent on the investment but this is more than eaten up by these unnecessary expenditures.

We wonder why people who kick about taxes, never worry about the water waste.

WORTH DOING

The water consumption in Chicago, the Bureau estimates, can be reduced to 125 gallons per day per person if effective waste control measures are undertaken. But merely Hooverizing on water is not likely to produce results. · There must be a real stimulus to save. The Bureau, therefore, recommends universal metering as the biggest single step toward economy in our use of water.

Metering has already proved its practicability in many places. The prejudice against it, the Bureau points out, is in communities where it has not been tried. It is feared that meters will mean larger water bills. Furthermore, plenty of water is needed for sanitation and health and anything that reduces legitimate consumption is bad. "Experience has demonstrated, however," replies the Bureau, "that where meters have been introduced they neither restrict the use of water nor increase water bills. . . With practically every consumer exercising care to eliminate waste, water can be furnished so cheaply that no one need think of restricting the amount of which he can make any use."

WILL CUT WATER BILLS

To show that water bills would not be increased by metering, the Bureau points—to mention but one of its illustrations—to our next door neighbor, Oak Park. Thousands of small houses in Chicago pay a flat rate for water of $5.64 a year; two flat buildings a rate of $10.38 per year. In Oak Park, which is metered and where nobody will deny that water is used lavishly, three-fourths of the population, at

* Copies of this report, a document of over 200 pages, may be obtained on application at the office of the Chicago Bureau of Public Efficiency, 315 Plymouth Court.

the Chicago meter-rate, would pay less than five dollars a year. Chicago pays practically double.

The Bureau arrives at the following interesting conclusions: "If waste and leakage are brought under effective control during the next ten years the pumpage of the Chicago Water Works can be reduced to 425,000,000 gallons per day by 1928, as compared with 645,000,000 gallons per day in 1916; and further, *the daily pumpage can be kept considerably below the 1916 figure as late as 1950.* This reduction in pumpage will make possible an immense saving in expenditures for water works plant. *It will mean that additional tunnels, cribs, and pumping stations will not be needed for thirty-three years.* The reduced pumpage will also effect very large savings in operating and maintenance costs. . . . The total saving which will result from universal metering will aggregate $135,000,000 between now and 1950."

THIS SHOULD BE DONE

The Bureau therefore recommends that the City Council adopt a policy of universal metering, retaining for the present the existing meter rates of 6¼ cents per thousand gallons. The meters should be owned by the city and installed and maintained free of charge. The cost of installing the meters would average about $900,000 a year, during the first ten years, and thereafter $200,000 per year.

Incidentally the Bureau condemns severely the practice of diverting, under one pretext and another, money from the water fund for ordinary corporate expenses.

THE LIBRARIAN HOPES that the members will not be impatient if their favorite magazines fail to appear on the reading room table on schedule time. We are informed by our magazine agent that the government has placed embargoes on second class matter so that whole wagon loads of magazines have been refused in the post office or, if accepted, are in many cases forwarded by freight.

WHAT IS YOUR BOY doing "over there"? If you have a son at the front who has been having any interesting experiences, tell us about it. Other members of the Club will be interested in what he is doing.

Continue Ogden Avenue Planning, Urges Club Committee

WAR has laid its heavy hand not only on many industries but upon public improvements. Everybody agrees that many such improvements will have to be postponed until after the Germans have decided to give it up as a bad job and go home, but is that any reason why we shouldn't plan *now* for the time when the boys come back from the trenches and we can invest our pennies in city improvements instead of liberty bonds? The City Planning Committee of the City Club thinks that now is the time to *plan* these improvements, although of course they can't be carried out right away. Last week, the Committee sent a letter to the City Council Committee on Home Defense urging continuance of the planning for the proposed Ogden Avenue extension. The latter Committee had before it a proposal to discontinue this work. This paragraph from City Planning Committee's letter sums up its position:

"While the primary efforts of all must now be concentrated on the successful prosecution of the war, and while large expenditures should not be made at this time unless the object for which they are made is urgently required, it would be unwise and unfortunate to discontinue the active planning of work of such real importance and consequence to our city as the Ogden Avenue extension. We therefore trust that your honorable committee will decide to continue the preliminaries in connection with this improvement so that when, after the war, the favorable opportunity arrives to make the expenditures required for the acquisition of the necessary properties and for the structural work, this can then proceed to early completion."

The letter was signed by R. F. Schuchardt, chairman of the City Planning Committee.

THE CLUB DEPARTS from precedent in opening its dining room to ladies at the lunch hour in connection with next Saturday's address by Norman Angell. The very special character of the event is the occasion of this modification of the rule.

UNDER FIRE STORIES BY CHICAGO MEN

*Ambulance Drivers Tell Club Audi-
ence of Experiences "Over There"*

TWO men from Chicago who have been in the ambulance service on the West Front told their experiences to a Club audience last Thursday at luncheon. Louis G. Caldwell, who served on the Chemin des Dames from May to October, 1917, was a member of the City Club until he left the U. S. A. for his little flier abroad. Thomas B. Pope, who drove an ambulance donated by the village of Glencoe, was in service on the right of Verdun also from May to October. He is a nephew of Henry Pope of the City Club.

PLEASE GO 'WAY—LET ME SLEEP

We gather from the stories told by both Mr. Pope and Mr. Caldwell that there is plenty of variety and excitement in the ambulance driver's life, certainly enough to keep it from being one of dull routine. The usually methodical Germans, according to Mr. Pope, whose post was only a few miles from Verdun, had a bad habit of not keeping office hours and would send bombing planes over at any time of the night to disturb sleepy American ambulance drivers and force them to scurry from bed to shelter. On one night in particular, which Mr. Pope described, the aeroplanes came whirring along several times, dropping bombs, doing considerable damage to the windowpanes and killing a number of horses. Fortunately nobody was hurt in this raid but another bombing raid at a near-by hospital had a less fortunate result. German machines flew over this hospital and dropped bombs at intervals of about fifteen minutes. The wounded were carried out to a near-by field to keep them from the bombs, but the German machines then turned their attention from the hospital and swept these rows of wounded men with the fire of their machine guns.

On one occasion when a German bomb-plane flew over, a squad of German prisoners was marched around as a target. Unfortunately the first bomb which was dropped killed the French guard of these men. On another occasion, through a mistake, when bombs were dropped into a German prison camp, the French on the following day had a great celebration.

PRAISE FOR THE POILUS

Mr. Pope praised the poilus for the grim courage with which they bore their wounds. There were very few "olalas" (or "humming birds" as they were called in Mr. Caldwell's section). The wounded men would for the most part smoke their cigarettes in silence, although their faces would be drawn with pain.

Mr. Pope saw many German prisoners brought in. Comparatively few of them, he said, were within the limits of the draft age in America. Hundreds of them appeared to be not more than seventeen years of age and there were also many older men. Most of them were a sorry sight after their service in the trenches.

Mr. Pope's section was cited for its work and five of its members received individual citations. Mr. Pope mentioned one member of the section in particular, who when the section was aroused hurriedly one night to dig around for wounded men in the ruins of some buildings which were being shelled, got into action clad only in shoes, a part of his pajamas and an overcoat. This was mentioned in his citation.

"SOUS-CHEF"

Mr. Caldwell served only a few weeks as a driver, being promoted to the position of *sous-chef* for his section. Contrary to the opinion of one of our members who thought a *sous-chef* must be the fellow who serves the drinks to the section, the position is one of responsibility. Mr. Caldwell served in the Chemin des Dames sector. This famous old "road of the ladies," he said, according to a joke of the French, "is no longer fit for the ladies" but is merely a mass of shell holes.

Mr. Caldwell's post was located at the little town of Vendresse and the headquarters for the section was about five miles behind the lines. The road to the post lay along the Ainse river, passed through a wood used as an ammunition depot, crossed the river to the little town of Bourg, then through another wood filled with artillery, across an open space and into town. The road was often choked with the traffic of troops and supply trains passing in both directions and it was, on this account, sometimes almost impassable for the ambulances.

DEEP DOWN IN THE CELLAR

The post was located in the wine cellar of an old chateau. On other floors were a dressing station, operating room, etc., and the place was often filled with desperately wounded men or men suffering from gas attacks. This cellar was the scene of some thrilling and amusing episodes. Probably the most exciting night there was that of July 31, during the drive of the Crown Prince to take some of the neighboring heights. At that time the Germans broke through to within a quarter of a mile of the post. Two cars belonging to the section were smashed and three times the telephone connections were out. During the night, many Germans were brought in. One who had become lost and thought that he was still within his own lines, came in, and not recognizing in the dim light that he was among his enemies, asked them to telephone his company that he was safe. When he came to, he was scared stiff, but perhaps not more so than the others who thought that the Germans were already upon them. A German officer who was slightly wounded, gave a cordial invitation to the men to visit him in his home in Prussia after the war.

GENTLEMEN OF COLOR

Mr. Caldwell encountered many Senegalese soldiers. They are an interesting lot of men, he said. Huge, black as coal, their fingers covered with rings, their faces gashed, they are impressive soldiers. In an offensive with their long knives they are very devils, but are no good in the trenches. They are childishly curious about Americans. One of the boys in the ambulance section volunteered to give them a lesson in English. "Bow wow wow!" he taught them, meant "Come here," and thereafter, whenever one of them said "bow wow wow" all the Americans would come running. "Moukahi" was another "American" word that he taught them and which they used with great enjoyment.

WHERE THE POPPIES BLOOM

Mr. Caldwell was for a short time on that sector of the front which was the scene of Hindenburg's famous strategic retreat. The place was devastated, he said. It was strewn with old barbed wire and wrecks of the German occupation but already this is being covered over by the brilliant crimson poppies of France.

The section to which Mr. Caldwell belonged was also cited for its work. It was the youngest section to receive a citation, having been in service at the time only three weeks.

PROCEDURE IN LIBRARY TEST IS ISSUE

Efficient Methods and Expert Examining Board
Urged as Means of Selecting Legler's Successor

IS Chicago to maintain its front rank among the library cities of America? The answer depends in a considerable measure upon the examination for public librarian, to fill the position vacated by the death of Henry E. Legler, announced for January 22nd. Mr. Legler put us on the library map by the carrying out of his far-visioned scheme of making the library a popular institution. It is agreed by everybody that his successor should be a man of ability and standing whom Chicago can trust to carry on the program of generous library expansion which Mr. Legler initiated.

UNITE ON RECOMMENDATIONS

The Association of Commerce and the Special City Club Committee on Public Librarian, sensing the importance of this examination, have suggested to the city administration a line of procedure, similar in essential respects, to that followed in the selection of Mr. Legler, by which it is hoped that a librarian of the highest professional standing will be secured to fill the position. The recommendations of the Association of Commerce were contained in a letter addressed last week by the President of the Association, Mr. O'Leary, to the Mayor, and its position was strongly supported in a letter last Saturday from the Special City Club Committee on Public Librarian to the Civil Service Commission.

A feature of these recommendations was that the board of examiners which chose Mr. Legler, made up of some of the foremost librarians in the country, the Librarian of Congress and the librarians of the John Crerar and the Brooklyn Public Libraries be re-appointed for the coming examination and that these appointments be made public as soon as possible to relieve the uncertainty in the mind of the public as to the action which the Commission will take. The City Club Committee's letter says in part:

ESSENTIALS

"The great success of the former examination was due very largely to the choice of the examiners, the ample notice of the date for filing applications, the material information furnished each applicant in such form that he could work out his thesis without coming to Chicago for his material, and the additional important assurance that he would not be embarrassed by undue publicity.

"Such methods produced a Henry E. Legler; we believe their repetition will result in securing another like him, if he is in the country and available.

A CHANCE WORTH WHILE

"This is an opportunity to demonstrate what a Civil Service examination can accomplish when the highest motives and the best intelligence are backing it. It is up to your Commission to respond to such an opportunity and give Chicago a librarian worthy to carry out the plans and ideals of Mr. Legler."

The Committee also suggests an extension of time from January 22nd, which would seem too short to reach the best available material for the place. The letter is signed by Charles M. Williams, chairman.

GOOD CANDIDATES WANTED

Local residence has been waived for this examination and the Committee is writing to a number of the most competent library people in the country urging them to take the examination. It will be "unassembled," so that candidates will not have to come to Chicago to participate.

THE CITY CLUB OF ST. LOUIS prints the following items in its December Bulletin:

The civic influence of the club is one of the most potent factors for advancement that has ever come into the life of St. Louis.

Intellectually, the open forum arranged by the Public Affairs Committee is little short of a University Extension Course.

Your duty as a member of the City Club is to see that no desirable applicants are overlooked. Tell everyone whom you think fills the qualifications what he is missing.

At the Sign of the Book

LISTENING POST

(Continued from page 10)

Doctor Favill

HENRY BAIRD FAVILL, 1860-1916. A Memorial Volume—Life, Tributes, Writings, Compiled by His Son and Privately Printed, 1917.

ABOUT three weeks before his death, Dr. Favill addressed the Harvester Club of Chicago. His plea to his hearers was for "an outside interest," by which he meant particularly a larger participation in the affairs of the community, a broadening of vision, a better understanding of public issues and an active sharing of time and energy in their solution. A well-rounded scheme of interests, he pointed out, contributes not only to the public welfare but is itself essential to a good life for the individual. Dr. Favill in this address, stood for the measuring of citizenship in terms of community service, an idea which the City Club, whose president he was for several years, in particular represents. And it was, in fact, the foundation upon which his own life was built.

This book preserves to the community, so far as that can be done in print, nearly every phrase of the doctor's intense preoccupation with the affairs of the community. Through its pages, one discerns the variety of his interests, extending beyond the practice of his profession to public medicine, education, social legislation, the wellbeing of working people and civic and political endeavor in many directions. Through it also one discerns not only the practical judgment and large sympathy which marked the doctor's attitude toward every matter which he touched but the strong, virile humanity which made him so effective as a leader of community life. Dr. Favill's son has rendered us a service in compiling this record of the activities and the thoughts of one of Chicago's most devoted and useful citizens.

CHARLES YEOMANS has donated three books of Bairnsfather's cartoons of trench life for the amusement of the soldiers and sailors who visit the Club at week-ends. If you haven't seen these cartoons and want a huge laugh, look at these books some day in the Club lounge.

Weld, Commercial Research Department, Swift & Co.; W. C. West, Special Metal Products—Manufacturers Representatives.

WALTER LIPPMAN WRITING in *The New Republic* of Mr. Norman Angell, who is to address the City Club next Saturday, said in reference to his previous visit to the United States: "I do not know what the British Government will do with him, whether it will order him to sweep up mines or run an automobile, or become a clerk in a munition factory. But if there is one jot of wisdom in that government, it will invite Mr. Angell to the Foreign Office, give him a quiet room with a desk and order him to think. To use a man with a brain like his in anything less than its highest capacity would be downright idiocy. . . . The question has never been put more eloquently or more impressively than by Mr. Norman Angell in this published address. It is done with a skill and good humor and damaging logic unequalled I believe by any propagandist in the English-speaking world."

GOVERNOR LOWDEN last week announced the membership of the new Illinois Commission on Health Insurance, organized under an act drawn by the Illinois Committee on Social Legislation, actively supported by the City Club Committee on State and Local Charities and passed at the last session of the legislature. It consists of: William Beye, attorney, Chicago; William Butterworth of Moline, plow manufacturer; Miss Edna Foley, head of the Visiting Nurse Association; Dr. Alice Hamilton, Chicago; John E. Ransom of the Central Free Dispensary; Miss Mary McInerney of the Bindery Woman's union; Mathew Woll of the International Photo Engravers' organization; M. J. Wright, a farmer from Woodstock, and Dr. E. N. Cooley of Danville, president of the Illinois Medical Association.

The commission will make a study of the subject and report its recommendations to the next session of the legislature. It has an appropriation of $20,000. Commissions have been appointed in Connecticut, Ohio, Pennsylvania and Wisconsin.

The City Club Bulletin

Published Weekly by the City Club of Chicago

A Journal of Active Citizenship

VOLUME XI   MONDAY, JANUARY 21, 1918   NUMBER 3

COMING THIS WEEK

Ladies' Night, Wednesday, January 23 at 8:00

"Over the Rocky Mountain Divide and A Trip to the Mesa Verde"

Illustrated by Lumiere Autochrome slides from natural color photographs

FRED PAYNE CLATWORTHY, of Estes Park, Colorado.

> Mr. Clatworthy's slides are *not* hand-colored. They are original photographs in natural colors, according to a method which marks a great advance in photography.

> Regular evening dinner service. Those coming for dinner well please make reservation in advance.

Thursday, January 24, *at luncheon*

"What Is the Matter with the New Gas Ordinance"

DONALD R. RICHBERG, Special Counsel for the City of Chicago, Gas Litigation Case.

Luncheon from 11:30.   Speaking promptly at 1:00.

THE CLUB WILL BE OPEN ON MONDAYS AS USUAL

The City Club Bulletin
A Journal of Active Citizenship

PUBLISHED WEEKLY BY THE

CITY CLUB OF CHICAGO

315 Plymouth Court   Telephone: Harrison 8278

DWIGHT L. AKERS, Editor

OFFICERS OF THE CLUB

FRANK I. MOULTON, President
EDGAR A. BANCROFT, Vice-President
ROY C. OSGOOD, Treasurer
CHARLES YEOMANS, Secretary
GEORGE E. HOOKER, Civic Secretary

EDITORIAL BOARD

HERBERT H. SMITH, Chairman
FREDERICK D. BRAMHALL   S. R. WATKINS
C. COLTON DAUGHADAY   PAUL R. WRIGHT

$1.00 per Year - - - - 10c per Copy

Entered as second class matter, December 3, 1917, at the postoffice at Chicago, Illinois, under the act of March 3, 1879.

The purpose of the Club is to bring together in informal association those men who are genuinely interested in the improvement of the political, social and economic conditions of the community in which we live.

THE LISTENING POST

THE FUEL ORDER does not affect clubs, according to a ruling from Washington, and the City Club will be open on Mondays as usual.

JOHN S. VAN BERGEN is going to France for the Red Cross.

DR. FRANK S. CHURCHILL has been commissioned in the Medical Reserve Corps.

JOSEPH H. DEFREES is with the Chamber of Commerce of the U. S. A. at Washington.

LIEUT. NORRIS W. OWENS is in the aviation service with the American Expeditionary Force in France.

WE REGRET TO REPORT that S. S. Van Der Vaart, a member of the Club for the past five years, died January 16, 1918.

THE CITIZENS' ASSOCIATION and the Woman's City Club have added their influence to the request upon the city administration by citizens' organizations for the adoption of efficient methods and the appointment of qualified library experts as an examining board for the test for the librarian of the Chicago Public Library. Both organizations have sent communications on this subject to the administration. The letter on this subject from the City Club Committee on Public Librarian was quoted in last week's Bulletin.

FRED PAYNE CLATWORTHY, who is to show his autochrome slides of the Rocky Mountains at the Club next week, will take the audience with him on a trip from the Rocky Mountain National Park over the Continental Divide to Grand Lake, where is located the highest Yacht Club in the world. The return is made by Andrews Glacier and Lochvale, one of the wildest and most beautiful spots in the Rocky Mountain country. Side trips are taken to the interior of Hallet Glacier and the summit of Long's Peak, 14,255 feet. The first color plates ever taken of a sunrise from this famous Peak are shown.

From the Rocky Mountain Mr. Clatworthy journeys to Mesa Verde National Park in southwestern Colorado, a few slides en route being shown. The story of the pre-historic Cliff Dwellings as evidenced by the wonderful remains of their many roomed homes is told, and illustrated by recently made color plates.

In conclusion a number of slides are shown of the Pueblo of Taos and its inhabitants, who are, in all probability, the direct descendants of the Cliff Dwellers.

Mr. Clatworthy's collection of autochromes is reported to be the finest exhibit of its kind ever shown in the east. He has presented them before to the National Geographic Society, the American Museum of National History, New York, and many other places.

THE EMPTY GARBAGE PAIL, these days, is a badge of patriotism. During the first ten months of 1917, the amount of garbage collected by the city was only 84,078 as compared with 109,726 tons in the corresponding period of 1916, a decrease of 25,648 tons.

CLUB COMMITTEE PRESENTS MILK CASE

Shows Producers' Cost Estimates Too High—Food Administration Plans Special Inquiry on Distribution

ERNEST S. BALLARD, attorney representing the City Club Milk Committee in its inquiry into milk production costs, went before the Milk Commission early last week with his witnesses and was still presenting his evidence at the writing of these lines. There have been two teams at work for the committee in the gathering and presentation of the evidence, one with Francis X. Busch, as counsel, dealing with possible economies in the distribution of milk, the other represented by Mr. Ballard, dealing with the problems of milk production. Both Mr. Busch and Mr. Ballard, who have devoted practically their entire time to this work for a number of weeks, and the others who have co-operated with them, have served without compensation, considering their work as essentially a war service.

It was originally understood that the Milk Commission would deal with both production and distribution from a constructive standpoint. It developed, however, that the Commission's authority which was fixed by an agreement between the producers, the distributors and the Food Administration, did not extend beyond the fixing of an immediate price to producers and distributors and that no modifications of existing arrangements would be made. When this fact became known, the Committee, which had accumulated a mass of evidence tending to show the possibility of reducing materially the cost of distributing milk through better methods of distribution, took up the matter with the Food Administration at Washington and with Mr. Harry A. Wheeler, its local representative. Mr. Wheeler suggested the creation of a new commission to be appointed after the present commission has finished its work, to go into the more constructive possibilities of the question and this plan was agreed upon. The Committee will not, therefore, present the evidence on distribution to the present Commission but will reserve it until the new commission is appointed.

The testimony produced by Mr. Ballard and his witnesses tends to show that the costs of milk production submitted to the commission by the producers' witnesses are too high, that these results are arrived at by wrong accounting methods, and that by application of proper charges to the feeding formulas introduced by the producers' witnesses would show a much lower cost of production.

C. S. Duncan of the Department of Political Economy of the University of Chicago, was the first witness for the Committee. After his direct examination the producers, represented by Governor Deneen, turned their artillery loose and kept up the cross-examination for over a day, but when the Governor was through, his cross-examination had greatly strengthened Prof. Duncan's direct testimony. Other witnesses examined were Edward E. Gore, certified public accountant, of the firm of Wade, Guthrie, Barrow & Co., and Prof. W. F. Handschin, of the University of Illinois. Mr. Ballard also recalled for cross-examination Prof. F. A. Pearson of the University of Illinois, who had testified early in the proceedings.

The essential issue which is being debated is whether in making up the costs of production, feeds and other dairy materials raised upon the farm should be charged in at market price or at the cost of producing them. It is the contention of the producers that the former method should prevail. Mr. Ballard and his witnesses contend to the contrary, and substantiate their claim by citing the accounting practice in other industries. They point also to the fact that some of the important feeds and other items entering into dairy costs are essentialy by-products of the farm and have no market value.

The commission has been holding hearings since December 3 and will probably finish its work within a short time.

CLARENCE J. PERFITT, Sergeant in Base Hospital Unit No. 11, not yet called into service, has been called to Washington to assist Major P. L. Doane in the Sanitary Division of the U. S. Shipping Board until his unit receives mobilization orders.

MAKE WAR-TIME CHANGES PERMANENT

Experiments Forced by War Show Ways to
Social Betterment, According to Dr. Bartlett

IS the war to be a dead loss, just so much destruction of life and property, or is there a measure of compensation in the fact that we are being forced to do things for our own benefit which we should have had the foresight and sagacity to do in times of peace? Some of the by-products of the war, according to A. Eugene Bartlett, of Brooklyn, who spoke here last Monday, we should endeavor to make permanent. He mentioned five in particular:

1. *The restriction on the use of alcoholic beverages.* "I am more hopeful of Russia," said Dr. Bartlett, "than are many people. When a man can think clearly, he is likely sooner or later to be able to strike hard and Russia's great experiment of the abolition of the liquor traffic will help her people to think, and to think clearly. In that is Russia's hope. France, too, is awakening to this. It has been estimated that before the war France had a drinking place to every eighty-three people, but she is beginning to understand that she must drive out alcohol. And America must follow the example of these other countries."

2. *The human repair shops brought into being for the care of the disabled.* "The repair shops for the soldiers of France," Dr. Bartlett explained, "are among the most wonderful institutions in the world. Armless, legless men are rehabilitated and trained so as to be able to return to their occupations as useful, productive citizens. Europe, by reason of her losses, needs every returning soldier in her industries. Canada has been following in her footsteps and so must the United States when our own boys come back from the firing line.

"But why should we maintain these human repair shops for war time only. How do we care for the thousands of workers injured in industry in America every year. We allow them in many cases to become burdens upon charity or even to slip into the criminal class. Should we not maintain our human repair shops in peace as well as war and send these men back to occupations at which they can maintain themselves!"

3. *The building of new ships.* "If America had had the ships," said Dr. Bartlett, "Italy would now be in Austria. Italy needed food and steel but we couldn't send them because we didn't have the ships. If America had had ships enough the war would now be over. After the war the American flag should fly from ships in every harbor in the world and the building of American ships should continue so that we may be able to meet any world emergency of the future."

4. *Conservation.* "The women of the country have been urged to practice economies. That is good, but the business men must practice them too. It's time to make our profiteers keep time with the boys in the trenches.

"We have been wasteful. It is estimated, for instance, that fifty per cent of our fruits and vegetables are wasted through rotting, etc. We ought to have government dehydrating plants to squeeze out the water and preserve these foods. About 70 per cent of fruits and vegetables are water. Not only would they be preserved by the dehydration but they could be shipped in smaller weight and bulk, and cans and jars could be dispensed with."

5. *Our army camps.* "The cantonments should be made permanent. I have been converted to universal military service. I hope that there will be an international police force after the war but in any case we shall need an army. At the cantonments I saw young men converted into fine physical specimens. The young men should be trained too for service in time of peace. We should give them advantages of changed environment and why not send them out for national service in peace time, in such work, for instance, as reclaiming the deserts and the marshy places of the country."

THE GOVERNMENT OF QUEBEC is proposing legislation for the creation of a provincial department for municipal affairs. The purpose of the department would be to check up the administration of local communities—particularly on the financial side.

BIG MEETING HELD DESPITE BLIZZARD

Speaker Missing—S. S. McClure and T. P.
O'Connor Fill Gap with Talks on War Issues

THERE have been many explanations of the big storm, but some of us are convinced that Nicholas Romanoff sent it over here from Siberia on purpose to gum up our meeting of a week ago Saturday. We believe it, because Charles R. Crane was to talk about Russia and nothing would have been more in keeping with this foxy Romanoff than to pull off a sly trick of this sort. When the large crowd which had braved the blizzard to hear Mr. Crane had been warmed up with a good dinner and leaned back comfortably in their chairs, there was a mutter of disappointment when Toastmaster Walter Fisher announced that the speaker was stuck "somewhere in St. Louis" by the storm and would not be present.

SENT FROM HEAVEN

The next moment, however, the skies cleared for it so happened that two Irishmen, S. S. McClure and T. P. O'Connor, had been sent to the club house by the Angel Gabriel to take Mr. Crane's place. And rarely in the City Club has there been such a dazzling combination of speaking talent. The oratorical festivities lasted till nearly three o'clock.

Returning again for a moment, however, to Cousin "Nicky," let it be known that he was the end frustrated, for Mr. Crane did finally reach the city and on Thursday last he had his say before the Club. A report of his address is on another page.

S. S. McClure talked first. In addition to having founded McClure's Magazine, and organized the first press syndicate in America and writing a book, just published, called "Obstacles to Peace," Mr. McClure has knocked around the world more than most of us, knows diplomats by their first names and has an inside story of the diplomatic intrigues before the war that is very important and interesting. He told a part of this story in his City Club address.

CARVING THE TURK

The friction between the powers led to war, he said, came about largely through their differences with reference to Asiatic Turkey. To Germany, it was not only the key to her Mesopotamia ambitions but a strong, naturally fortified military position from which she could flank the English route to the East and by taking the Suez and Egypt cut the British Empire in two. This concerned not only England but Russia, for it conflicted directly with her aims with reference to the Bosphorus. It was about the knottiest problem which European diplomacy had to solve.

In March 1916 Mr. McClure was travelling from Berlin to Constantinople. By accident, he met Dr. Jaeckh, who knew more perhaps about the problems of Asiatic Turkey than any other person. In a long interview, he gave a complete story of the Anglo-German and Franco-German treaties with reference to Turkey which preceded the war. An understanding had been reached between England and Germany that the terminus of the Bagdad Railway should be 40 miles up the river from the Persian Gulf, so England would not be menaced from that direction. The irrigation projects of Persia would be operated on a "fifty-fifty" basis. The treaty with France provided that France should have Palestine and make numerous developments there. Her position there would prevent Germany from cutting off England's route to the East. By these treaties, England had yielded a great deal and had indicated a sincere desire to keep the peace. The treaties were printed in 1914 but were not published.

Mr. McClure having pieced together his information on these treaties, presented a statement regarding them to Herr Zimmerman at Berlin. The statement was returned to him with a few pencil correetions, evidently inserted to make the treaties appear in a better light to Germany's ally, Turkey. Bethmann-Hollweg also mentioned them in an address and they are also mentioned by other German authorities.

WAR PARTY FORCES KAISER'S HAND

Why, then, Mr. McClure asks, assuming that the Asiatic Turkey questions had been settled by these treaties, did Germany break the world's peace to carry out her ambitions in this territory. Mr. McClure is inclined not to hang the blame on the Kaiser personally. Bethmann-Hollweg, who is practically the Kaiser's spokesman, has had to defend himself from the most virulent attacks of the war-party because he delayed mobilization for three days to keep the peace with England—a delay which they charge lost Germany the war. In a speech which Bethmann-Hollweg delivered in the Reichstag in November, 1916, to defend himself, he made public a telegram which he had sent to Vienna during the last days which preceded the war, urging with the utmost emphasis that Austria should submit her claims to arbitration. Mr. McClure concludes that the Kaiser and Bethmann-Hollweg, his spokesman, did not want the war but that it was forced by the military party.

Now or Never

The reason for the haste of the latter in plunging Germany into war was probably, Mr. McClure said, due largely to the fact that France had just loaned a huge sum of money to Russia for the building of strategic railways on the German frontier and that France had herself adopted a three-year service act. The experts said that in 1917 France and Russia would be ready while Germany could not materially increase her resources. They believed that the war should come at once, that in any case it wouldn't last more than three months, that it could be paid for by the levy of huge indemnities, and that Asiatic Turkey could be had outright without any treaties.

The French army, they asserted, was in bad shape—it wasn't even adequately equipped with shoes, according to revelations made in an investigation by the Chamber of Deputies. Russia was not equipped to fight and England wouldn't —or if she did her little army wouldn't make any appreciable difference.

So they were sure that the war would be over in three months. By putting a thin screen of troops on the French frontier and throwing an army through Belgium they could turn the French left and execute another Sedan on a huge scale. If France held on and wouldn't surrender they would take Paris and by razing one section of the city after another force France to her knees.

Why did the Germans fail in their plan? "I am told," said Mr. McClure, "that at the battle of the Marne the Germans' supply of munitions was so low that they couldn't continue their enveloping movement and that this was the reason they were forced to retire to their prepared positions —which they regarded as only temporary. It is said that Von Moltke was removed for his failure to have this ammunition ready. Germany had developed her huge war machine, had built up her armies and planned her equipment for enormous bodies of men, but she had failed to keep her manufacture of ammunition co-ordinate with the rest of her equipment. All this was left to the experts and in Germany nobody went behind the expert. *Germany lost the war in her ordnance department.* Talk about German efficiency! French efficiency has far outstripped it.

Another Bouquet for France

"Nothing but a miracle can explain how France held back the enemy. With ninety percent of her iron ore gone, 70 percent of her iron mills and 68 percent of her coal in the hands of the enemy, she has displayed resources and inventive genius, particularly in the field of artillery, with which 'German efficiency' cannot compare. Germany lost the war in her ordnance department. *France won the war in her ordnance department.* This is the lesson which America should take to heart.

"When England found out the importance of this work she put the most 'doing man' in the Empire at the head of it. In England, 80 percent of the manufacturing is wholly for the war and the immense output of all these factories is for the armies occupying only one-third of the front!"

Mr. McClure described the war economies which the people in the other warring countries have adopted. "I have seen more automobiles in Los Angeles," he said, "than in European capitals aggregating 15,000,000 people."

Erin Go Bragh

After Mr. McClure's talk, T. P. O'Connor took the floor. He was in a blarney mood and the Irish flowed trippingly from his tongue.

Mr. O'Connor gave the English parliamentary system a sound spanking. "France," he said, "has the only really effective and democratic form of parliamentary government in the world. Every department has a parliamentary commission of twenty-five

(Concluded on page 24)

RUSSIA VAST EXPERIMENT GROUND

Charles R. Crane Tells of Conditions in Revolutionary Russia

"RUSSIA will probably try every kind of social experiment before she is through," said Charles R. Crane, speaking before the City Club at luncheon today. "Russia is a large country, so I wouldn't be surprised if there should be a break-up and each division should try out its own experiment." Mr. Crane, who is a charter member of the City Club, returned recently from Russia, via England and the west front. He was a member of the Root Mission to Russia and spent five months there during some of the most stirring events.

UNDISCOVERED COUNTRIES

"In my travels this year," said Mr. Crane, "I have discovered two new countries—Russia in revolution and America in evolution. Returning from Russia I feel that I am a traveller here and I am going around trying to get acquainted with the new America.

"The first revolution with which I ever came in contact was that of the Young Turks. Everybody was very enthusiastic about it at the time. It looked like the millennium for Turkey. But the government under the Young Turks was worse even than under Abdul Hamid. Espionage was stricter and in killing Armenians, Abdul Hamid was a novice in comparison. Two years ago there were 2,000,000 Armenians—now there are hardly 500,000. Turkey has never been squeezed so tight economically and the country is óf course now practically sold out to the Germans.

"THE NEW FREEDOM" IN RUSSIA

"The revolution in Russia is in some respects similar. It was a swing from the extreme right to the extreme left, but in some respects the change was not so great as might have been expected. There is no greater freedom of the press than before. The Bolsheviki have seized the paper supply and the printing offices. The Fortress of St. Peter and St. Paul is just as full of political prisoners as ever and some of the best people in Russia have been imprisoned there.

"When the revolution started, Russian exiles returned from all over the world. Many of them from this country brought back bad stories about America. Petrograd is much like a western mining camp. There is something doing all the time and there are no precedents to go by. Old time diplomacy can make no headway under such conditions.

MAKING IT WARM FOR FRANCIS

"The Russian people are of course illiterate but they like to talk. The streets are full of speakers and there are processions constantly. There has been a great deal of inflammatory, anti-American talk and on one occasion a speaker got the crowd very much excited by asserting that an 'Italian' anarchist by the name of 'Munie' was to be executed by the United States. The crowd then started for the American embassy with the intention of cleaning it out. The government was unable to cope with the mob for the Bolsheviki controlled the town but it 'phoned a warning to Mr. Francis, the American Ambassador. Mr. Francis was having a dinner party. The guests left at once but Mr. Francis declined to leave. What happened afterwards I heard from an old colored servant of Mr. Francis when I arrived a few minutes after it was all over.

"Mr. Francis sent this man upstairs for his revolver and had it loaded. A little later the 'black flag' crowd was heard coming down the street. They broke in the door and the leader said: 'Your government is going to execute "Munie."' Mr. Francis said: 'I don't know anything about it.' The leader said: 'We are going to clean out the embassy.' 'You keep back,' replied Mr. Francis. 'This is American soil. The first man that crosses this threshold will be killed. Back up there.' They looked at one another and at the ambassador and decided to back up.

MARCHING AROUND

"The news got around and the next day and for four or five days processions kept marching to the embassy—processions of wounded soldiers, of women, of school children carrying American flags—and called for Mr. Francis to come out so they could salute him.

"We are fortunate that the American ambassador, Mr. Francis, is a man not of diplomatic experience but of very wide political experience. If he had been an old-time diplomat he would have been tired of his job long before this, but as it is he is enjoying his work over there very much. And he has been able to get more information as to what is going on than anybody else."

English Are Steady Fighters

If there is pessimism in England about the outcome of the war there is none at the front, according to Mr. Crane. He spent about a week on his return from Russia inspecting conditions on the western front. "I was proud of my Anglo-Saxon blood," he said, "when I saw the sturdiness and confidence of the men in the face of the ferocious German war-machine. The further I got from London and the nearer I got to the trenches, the stronger I found the note of confidence. I told some English officers of the pessimism I had found among some of the members of Parliament and one of them said, 'Yes I hear that they do feel that way. Sometime we'll have to take a week off and clean *them* up too.'"

The French Artillery

The French artillery service, Mr. Crane said, is the last word in warfare. He told of the taking of a certain ridge, of the long advance preparation, the photographing of every detail of the topography by the aeroplanes. Two thousand guns were brought up and each assigned a definite objective. When the signal was given to go ahead and guns broke loose, the ridge, says Mr. Crane, "was anything but a health resort." The aeroplanes hovered on three levels, so it was impossible for German machines to live in the air. Photographs were taken to show the progress of the bombardment, whether the ridge was sufficiently pitted for the advance.

Good Work by the Secret Service

"The infantry advance was ordered for 6:45. Somehow the Germans got news of the order. But the French intelligence department somehow found out that the Germans had the news and the advance was started at 6:15—a half hour early! The Germans kept retreating for three days and the French captured three times as much territory as was comprised in the original objective. And although the French were on the offensive their losses

were only 7,000 as compared with the German losses of 30,000. I was over the ground within a few days after it was taken.

"Then I came home. I had left America heading one way and on my return found her heading exactly the opposite way. It is an inspiring thing to see. I am glad that we are able to show to Russia that we can go full speed ahead in this direction as well as in the opposite direction."

T. P. O'CONNOR

(Continued from page 22)

members appointed to it, made up in strict accordance with the principles of proportional representation. These commissions have the right of supervising the work of their respective department, to demand all documents, to summon the minister, etc. The hearings are secret.

"In the English parliament, before the war, there was very little discussion of foreign affairs and it was generally to nearly empty benches. I remember one occasion when the foreign affairs of the Empire were under discussion there were about forty members in the house. At promptly 8:15 foreign affairs were dropped, the house filled up and the private bills were taken up. The question at issue was the right of a certain water company to take more than a certain amount of water from a stream. Over this question the house became eager almost tumultuous. Two evenings and a part of a third till 11:00 were filled up with this wrangling."

Mr. O'Connor's account of English parliamentary government reminded us how close together we Americans and English are in some things.

Restore Alsace-Lorraine!

Mr. O'Connor backed up France vigorously in her demand for the restoration of Alsace-Lorraine. "Every man interested in the progress of science and art," he said, "must regard France almost as his second Motherland. To reduce her to the position of an inferior power would be a deadly blow to all civilization and all righteousness. Alsace-Lorraine is a symbol of what Prussianism means to the world, a symbol of the triumph of might over right, of the false gospel of the soldier. Accursed be the peace that fails to give back their liberty to the people of this oppressed land!"

The City Club Bulletin

Published Weekly by the City Club of Chicago

A Journal of Active Citizenship

VOLUME XI   MONDAY, JANUARY 28, 1918   NUMBER 4

TWO EVENTS THIS WEEK

Thursday, January 31, at Luncheon
"Club Day"

Belgium's Part In the War Since the Battle of the Yser

ALBERT MOULAERT, Belgian Consul in Chicago.

Luncheon from 11:30.   Speaking promptly at 1:00.

Friday, February 1, at Luncheon
The Fuel Crisis

EARL DEAN HOWARD, Deputy Federal Fuel Administrator for Illinois.

Luncheon from 11:30.   Speaking promptly at 1:00.

THE CLUB WILL BE OPEN ON MONDAYS AS USUAL

The City Club Bulletin
A Journal of Active Citizenship

PUBLISHED WEEKLY BY THE
CITY CLUB OF CHICAGO
315 Plymouth Court   Telephone: Harrison 8278

DWIGHT L. AKERS, Editor

OFFICERS OF THE CLUB

FRANK I. MOULTON, President
EDGAR A. BANCROFT, Vice-President
ROY C. OSGOOD, Treasurer
CHARLES YEOMANS, Secretary
GEORGE E. HOOKER, Civic Secretary

EDITORIAL BOARD

HERBERT H. SMITH, Chairman
FREDERICK D. BRAMHALL   S. R. WATKINS
C. COLTON DAUGHADAY   PAUL R. WRIGHT

$1.00 per Year - - - 10c per Copy

Entered as second class matter, December 3, 1917, at the postoffice at Chicago, Illinois, under the act of March 3, 1879.

> *The purpose of the Club is to bring together in informal association those men who are genuinely interested in the improvement of the political, social and economic conditions of the community in which we live.*

THE LISTENING POST

THE MONDAY "heatless holiday" is a holiday for the printer but not for the editor. The fuel order makes it necessary for the Bulletin to go to press on Saturday instead of Monday.

LETTERS COME BACK quite frequently from former Club employes who are in military service. The other day a letter came from Holden, our former storekeeper, now at Camp Custer, Battle Creek. He likes soldiering.

THERE WAS A GOOD audience present last Wednesday night to hear Fred Payne Clatworthy and to see his collection of Lumiere Autochromes. Those who came saw something unequalled in color photography. The infinite variety and exact reproduction of color shading would not have been possible a few years ago. We commiserate the unfortunates who staid away.

Mr. Clatworthy's pictures were of the Mesa Verde cliff-dwellings, the Indian village of Taos and of the Rocky Mountain National Park.

It was Ladies' Night.

THE CITY CLUB is still stirring up the milk situation and the Bureau of Public Efficiency is trying to plug the holes in the water system. Here's to cheap milk, cheap water and plenty of both!

THE NUMBER OF reservations for the dinner preceding the Clatworthy talk last Wednesday night was *nineteen*. The number who came for dinner was *one hundred and twenty*.

The manager takes a great deal of pride in the service and if he has a little advance notice, by which he can gauge the size of the party, he can lay in enough food and employ help to take care of everybody. As it was, everybody was fed with a good dinner, but the service was slow and a matter of some criticism by those who did not understand.

In the future, on such occasions, will not the members please make advance reservations?

THE LIST GROWS! We are glad to report these new members and to extend a glad hand of welcome into the Club: J. M. Chaplin, Accountant and Department Manager, Swift & Co.; C. T. Crossland, Attorney; L. A. Dozois, Building Manager, W. W. Kimball Company; Stanley P. Farwell, Efficiency Engineer, Arthur Young & Co.; Norman J. Fellows, Secretary Flanner-Steger Land & Lumber Company; Howard M. Frantz, H. W. Johns-Manville Company; August Gatzert, with Rosenwald & Weil; F. A. Lorenz, Jr., President Hill Binding Company; E. A. Mann, Assistant Purchasing Agent, Mark Manufacturing Company (Machinery); R. W. Martindale, Manager Central Division, Martindale American Law Directory; Alvin C. McCord, President McCord Manufacturing Company (Railway Supplies); Thomas H. Morrison, Manager Robert O. Law Co. (Book Manufacturers); R. G. Rosenbach, Engineer, Warren Webster & Co.; Charles H. Smith, President, Smith, Barnes & Strohber Co. (Manufacturers of Pianos); George E. Traub, Dellman Waist Company; James R. Wolfenden, Vice President and Secretary, Smith, Barnes & Strohber Co.

"SUCCESS IN OUR WAR AIMS"

Norman Angell Describes to Club Audience the Conditions of a Democratic Peace

"A DEMOCRATIC peace," "a peace with the people of Germany, not with her rulers," are phrases which have entered much into the vernacular of war-discussion lately. To many, those phases have not been entirely convincing because they have conveyed no clear picture of how the thing could be done. Norman Angell of L o n d o n, speaking at the City Club Saturday afternoon, January 19, sketched the outlines of a parliament on peace terms, selected by the legislatures of the various states and representing the various parties on a proportional basis. This he said, should be the first of our war aims, a condition of all the others. We should devote ourselves now to this problem of how the peace negotiations should be organized, for if we drift till the end of the war, we will be unprepared and may lose in the settlement what we have gained on the field. If intelligent people refuse to use their brains during the war on the theory of "win first, talk afterwards," the Germans may catch us napping at the peace conference.

President Wilson's advocacy of an international league to guarantee the security of nations was warmly endorsed by Mr. Angell. Without such a guarantee, he asserted, it will be very difficult to dispose of the conflicting territorial aims of the powers so far as they are based on the requirements of national defense.

Mr. Angell is best known probably as the author of "The Great Illusion," pub-

NORMAN ANGELL

lished in 1910, a work on the futility and waste of war, which is said to have been translated into nearly twenty different tongues, including Chinese, Hindu and Bengali. He was general manager of the Paris *Daily Mail* from 1905-14 and his pamphlets, articles and books on international p o l i - ties have been widely circulated a n d read. Since the beginning of the war he has published the following books: "The Foundations of National Polity," "Prussianism a n d I t s Destruction," "The W o r l d ' s H i g h w a y," and "T h e Dangers of Half Preparedness." His address at the City Club is printed herewith in full:

"By way of clarifying some of the issues with which we have to deal, may I make a confession of political faith with reference to the war?

FAVORED AMERICAN PARTICIPATION

"I was an early advocate of American participation in the war, of the abandonment of American neutrality, on the ground that the outcome of the war would be more truly democratic if America were a participant than if she were not. Neutrality, in a war of this character, is an impossible position for a great people who want to take their part in organizing the world and making it safe. I am not in favor of a 'patched up' peace; I have never spoken a word in favor of an early peace, not because that is not important—no one but a homicidal maniac would want to prolong the war a day beyond the point necessary for our purposes—but because I believe that the results which the war achieves are more important than the date at which it finishes; I believe that it is absolutely necessary to defeat and thoroughly discredit German militarism, and that until that institution is destroyed the world will never be safe. And the war that America is waging to that end, a war in which she will obtain nothing that cannot equally be shared by all mankind, is an inexpressibly inspiring, noble and hopeful spectacle.

"Yet, sincerely as I believe all that, I am also convinced that it is not enough, and that victory, whatever the efficiency and sacrifice of the soldier, will be impossible, or would finally be misused and rendered futile if it were possible, unless the civilian does his part in devising the right policy. Nothing that I shall urge in that respect is proposed as a substitute for or an alternative to the active prosecution of the war, but as an aid thereto—an essential part of it, matters which we must consider if we are to wage war successfully.

Civilians May Decide War

"The President hinted the other day that if the policy of the Allies towards Russia on the morrow of the Revolution had been somewhat different, if they had made a clear declaration of revised aims, as Kerensky desired, Bolshevik and German forces would not have been able to trade on Russian suspicion as they did, and Russia might still be fighting on the side of the Allies. Suppose this implication of the President is sound. The case furnishes a striking proof of the fashion in which civilian policy may have vast military consequences, consequences measured in terms of whole armies and years of war; of the way in which civilian policy may add enormously to the soldiers' burden, or lighten it. No increase of merely military preparedness would have prevented this disaster; it might have made it worse. If the material now ready for shipment had reached Russia, we might be faced by the possibility of its actually being used against us. For victory depends not alone upon guns and munitions, but upon the direction in which the guns shoot. And that depends upon policy, upon us civilians. We have only to make a few more mistakes like those which may have marked the relations with Russia to find the Grand Alliance going to pieces, during or after the war, and that would give the victory, ultimately, to

Germany, however well our soldiers may have done their work.

"The danger of our ultimate failure, not from military but from political causes, bringing about the disintegration of the Alliance, is a real one. The story of most military victories of the past in Europe is that the results which might have been secured by them have been sacrificed at the peace table—generally by the disintegration of the military alliances that won the victories. And America might contribute to that catastrophe, or perhaps render it inevitable, by a wrong line with reference to the Alliance after the war.

Conflict of Allies' War Aims

"Why did the Allies fail to make that statement of aims which in the President's view might have kept Russia in the war? We now know that among other causes certain Italian claims, which not only might have been regarded by Russia as 'Imperialistic' but which came into conflict with the claims of certain other allies, made such a statement difficult. This is no reflection whatever upon Italy, for she made those claims from motives which must come first with every nation—motives of national self-preservation. In a world in which nations can only depend upon their own strength for security, a world of shifting alliances, and armament competition, and unstable balance of power, she had to look to her future strength, and so had to command the Adriatic, and so needed the Dalmatian Coast Island in the Aegean, even though that did collide with the aspirations of Greece and Serbia.

"But suppose the Allies had been able to say to Italy: 'The old Europe of shifting alliances and international anarchy, of struggle for power one against the other, is not going to be re-established after this war. We really are going to create this League of Nations that President Wilson talks about. You do not need to command the Adriatic because our whole naval force will be available for your defense.' If they had been able to say that, Italy would not have made, and Italian public opinion sanctioned, claims that threatened the solidity of the Alliance, and have actually resulted in making a great breach in it.

"Why could not the Allies make that proposal in terms of the League of Nations? Because public opinion is not ready

(Continued on page 38)

RICHBERG BLOWS UP GAS COMPANY

Charges Violation of Faith in Asking
Utilities Commission for Rate Increase

DONALD R. RICHBERG had his pockets full of "T.N.T." or some other high explosive when he came to the City Club last Thursday to discuss the new gas ordinance. Mr. Richberg prepared the original draft of the ordinance. He is attorney for the city in the gas litigation.

COMPANY BREAKS CONTRACT

Declaring that the Gas Company, in applying to the State Public Utilities Commission on January 17 for a 22% increase in rates over those fixed in the ordinance, had acted in direct violation of its contract and without even consulting the city, he asserted that if contracts with public utility companies had no more sanctity than this, there is an end to such contracts. The Gas Company, in accepting the ordinance, had specifically agreed to recognize the city's regulatory power over its business. If such violations of contract are to be sanctioned, Mr. Richberg said, there is nothing for the city to do but to abdicate its functions.

The Company, Mr. Richberg charged, quickly took advantage of the provisions of the new ordinance allowing a change from a candle-power to a heat unit basis, but it has flatly violated both of the essential provisions designed to protect the consumer, namely, the readjustment of appliances before the reduction of candle-power, and the pledge not to seek a change of present rates for a year.

THE QUESTION AT ISSUE

The application of the Gas Company, Mr. Richberg stated, proposes an increase of the rate to the average consumer to 88c, eight cents more than was charged for the old high-candle power gas. "I am not interested," he continued, "in the claims which the Company sets up to justify its application or to prove that it is entitled to an increase. I am interested in the bearing this has upon the sanctity of contracts between public utility companies and the city. The Company has asked the Public Utilities Commission to use its authority to impose upon the City of Chicago a direct violation of a contract into which the Company had voluntarily entered. That is

an extraordinary position, I think you will admit."

The situation has its humorous aspects, said Mr. Richberg. The officials of the Gas Company are rare comedians. "In the manner of violating its present contract with the City and applying to the Utilities Commission for increased rates," he said, "the Gas Company officials have exhibited characteristic humor. To understand the joke a little ancient history should be briefly reviewed:

TAKING CARE OF OGDEN GAS

"In 1895 Roger C. Sullivan and his friends acquired the Ogden Gas franchise. In 1901 the president of The Peoples Gas Light and Coke Company made an affidavit in the Circuit Court of Cook County charging 'that said Ogden Gas Company, through certain of its officers and stockholders, made certain unconscionable demands upon said People's Gas Light and Coke Company, threatening said last named Company with corporate destruction, unless said demands were complied with.' It appears that these 'unconscionable demands' made in the fall of 1900 were successful, because in November 1900 the Ogden Gas Company sold its property to The Peoples Gas Company for $7,000,000. In 1907 The Peoples Gas Company leased the property of the Ogden for a rental of about $600,000 per year for thirty-eight years and assumed payment of $6,000,000 Ogden Gas Company bonds. In September 1913 The Peoples Gas Company paid the Ogden Company $5,000,000 in lieu of the $600,-000 annual rental under the previous lease, agreeing in addition to pay $300,000 per year for the remaining thirty-three years of the lease.

BUILD PLANT FROM TAXES?

"This brief summary indicating how much money it has cost the Gas Company in order to insure Mr. Roger C. Sullivan and his friends a handsome profit on their investment in Ogden Gas shows one reason why the Company now complains that it has not the money necessary to build a new gas plant. The Company therefore asks that an additional tax of over $11,000,000 be levied on Chicago gas consumers during the next three years, in order that the Company may finance the building of the new plant.

MR. SULLIVAN, GENTLEMEN!

"The Gas Company officials, with a fine sense of humor, notified the people of Chicago of this unconscionable demand through Mr. Boetius H. Sullivan, the son of Mr. Roger C. Sullivan. With keen irony the Company put Mr. Sullivan forward to present its demand as a physical presentation of the reasons for the Company's lack of cash. It was as though the Company said to the people of Chicago: 'You will recollect it cost us so much money to buy up Mr. Sullivan's Ogden Gas Company that you will understand why we cannot raise the money to build this new gas plant, but must tax the people with increased rates to make up the price we paid for Ogden Gas.'

"This manner of presenting the Company's demand for increased rates may not appear tactful to serious minded people, but it must appeal to all persons with a sense of humor as being very funny."

IF PEOPLE PAY, SHOULD OWN

If the people are to pay for this plant, Mr. Richberg said, the people ought to own it. The company should certainly not be allowed to capitalize and charge the consuming public interest on an investment for which they, the consumers, have paid.

The ordinance provides, Mr. Richberg continued, for a profit sharing arrangement under which, after certain charges and a 4% profit to the company are paid, the balance is divided with the consumer. The Company's application to the Public Utilities Commission asks for a 6% return upon the capital stock, much of which is watered.

ORDINANCE ITSELF O. K.

Mr. Richberg defended the terms of the new ordinance. It provides specifically, he said, against the conditions against which the complaints by consumers have been lodged. The consumers are not getting poor gas under the new ordinance, they are getting poor gas service, due to the failure of the Gas Company to carry out its contract obligation to readjustment appliances before reducing candle-power below sixteen.

The change from a candle-power to a heat unit basis, Mr. Richberg said, was prompted not only by the fact that the latter is more economical, but that the manufacture of gas on the former basis required the use of large quantities of gas oil, rapidly increasing in price and needed by the government in the manufacture of explosives. It was pointed out by Prof. Bemis at the time that Chicago was using as much of this oil in the manufacture of gas as was used in the entire United States Navy. There was danger, too (a forecast which has come true in the case of companies in other cities where no such change was made), that the government would sooner or later force the change in order to secure the oil for its own use.

⸱ PLAYING BOTH ENDS

There have been requests upon the government, said Mr. Richberg, to help gas companies build new plants for the sake of the by-products needed in the manufacture of explosives. It would be interesting indeed if the Gas Company, having obtained permission to tax the people of Chicago for the construction of its plant, should get the government to pay for it.

ALDERMANIC LOG-ROLLING will get a crack in the ribs if the City Council carries out the plan of its Finance Committee, adopted last Monday, for the abolition of ward lines as administrative boundaries for street cleaning and waste disposal. The annual tug-of-war among the aldermen, for a larger share of the city's revenue for their respective wards will fade away into history along with the First Ward Ball and other ancient political institutions.

The plan, if adopted, will be the second big item in the 1918 budget program of the civic organizations to be realized. The first was the consolidation of police stations and the reduction of their number by ten. Among the organizations recommending these two measures was the City Club Committee on Public Expenditures. This reorganization of the street bureau's activities was also recommended by the "Merriam Commission" on City Expenditures a number of years ago.

The Finance Committee is now at work on the 1918 budget, plans for a further appeal to the Governor for a special session of the Legislature to consider financial relief legislation having been abandoned for the time being.

TOO MUCH "BUTTER FAT" IN MILK COSTS

Counsel for Club Committee Files Brief
Showing Producers' Figures Too High

ERNEST S. BALLARD, counsel for the City Club Milk Committee on the production side of its case, last week applied his separator to the cost figures submitted by the milk producers and was able to show just how much cream the latter have been getting from their business since December, when present prices became effective. If he made a correct diagnosis of producers' costs in his brief filed with the Chicago Milk Commission costs last Thursday, they have had to worry along with a profit of only 33 1/3 per cent. Their profit at the higher price prevailing in November was slightly better—a little over 40 per cent. Mr. Ballard's recommendations would cut the latter figure about in half.

WHAT MILK COSTS

The filing of this brief marks the close of the Committee's case so far as production costs are concerned. Mr. Ballard shows that under a proper accounting system, the cost of production per hundred pounds of milk would range, according to the feeding formula used, from $2.17 to $2.83. He recommends that the average of these figures, $2.42—which also corresponds almost exactly with the figure produced by three of the six formulas considered—be adopted by the Commission.

RAISE PRICE OR LOWER IT?

Mr. Ballard arrives at what he considers a fair profit to be added to the cost of production by averaging retailers' profits for eight different food commodities. This average, 21.3 per cent, applied to cost of producing milk, would yield a price of $2.94 per hundred—28c below the present price. If distributors' prices should remain unchanged, this would mean a reduction of about six-tenths of a cent per quart to the consumer. It has been estimated that if the claims of producers and distributors were allowed, the price to the consumer would have to be raised to about 15c per quart. Other briefs were filed by Charles S. Deneen for the producers; Frederick W. Pringle and A. B. Williams for the distributors; John Dill Robertson for the Department of Health of Chicago, Nicholas Michels for the State's Attorney and Wallace Ingalls for the Illinois Ice Cream Manufacturers Association.

DISTRIBUTION EVIDENCE WAITS

The Milk Committee made no recommendations to the Commission affecting charges for milk distribution. It did, however, present to the Commission a critical analysis prepared by Edward E. Gore, accountant, of the firm Barrow, Wade & Guthrie, of the cost figures submitted by the distributors. The constructive suggestions of the Committee as to distribution contemplate a reorganization of delivery service, a matter with which, it became apparent during the hearings, this Commission has no authority, to deal. As announced in last week's Bulletin, a new Commission is to be appointed with full power to effect constructive improvements. The "team" which has been at work for the Club Committee on this phase of the question—Francis X. Busch, as counsel; C. S. Duncan, Charles K. Mohler and F. S. Deibler—will therefore continue its inquiries.

ACKNOWLEDGMENT

The closing of the Committee's case on production costs calls for an acknowledgment of the services of men who have conducted this feature of the inquiry for the Committee. Mr. Ballard, Professor Duncan and Mr. Gore entered upon their work as a war service and have devoted their energies to it without remuneration. Mr. Ballard has given practically his entire time since he took up the case, a month ago, in analysis of producers' testimony and the presentation of the case. Professor Duncan worked with him and also gave up a major portion of his time. Mr. Gore, who was assigned by the Illinois Society of Certified Public Accountants, has also contributed generously in analyzing the cost figures submitted by the producers and the distributors.

The City Club Milk Committee is composed of W. B. Moulton, chairman; Samuel Dauchy, F. S. Deibler, Carl S. Miner, and Thomas W. Allinson.

At the Sign of the Book

¶ *Efficiency in the Parks*

SEVENTH ANNUAL REPORT of the Civil Service Board and Superintendent of Employment of the West Chicago Park Commissioners for the Year 1917.

A FEW weeks ago we expressed our admiration of the Report of the Board of Supervising Engineers, Chicago Traction, 1914 (then just issued) as a document of the highest interest to the student of history. Here we have a contrast. That a public body should make the results of its work known within two weeks after the year has closed savors almost too much of modern business efficiency to be characteristic. And yet the date stares you in the face—January 15, 1918. We wondered if other civil service bodies were as expeditious as the West Park Board and found, on inquiry, that the latest report of the City of Chicago's Civil Service Commission is two years old. The 1916 report, however, will be issued within a few weeks so the Commission will then be only a year behind.

TRIALS

The contents of the report also interested us. Last year, the merits of the "trial before removal" clause of the civil service law were debated very hotly at Springfield with the result that that clause in the state civil service law was trimmed down to practically nothing. The report of the West Park Board shows that, under the "trial" method during 1917, a year during which there was a political change, only twelve of the Board's 1200 employes were discharged.

CUTS DOWN THE "TEMPORARIES"

The record of the board in the granting of temporary appointments is highly commendable. Temporary appointments have been used by civil service commissions from time immemorial to camouflage evasions of the law. It is not possible to compare the record of the West Park Civil Service Board in this respect with that of the City of Chicago because of the absence of data about the latter. The Civil Service Reform Association in 1915, published figures showing that in the city service from May 1 to September 1, 1915, 9163 grants of authority for temporary appointments were made in a total service of 20,000 employes or approximately one for every two positions. In 1917, the West Park Board made 67 such grants including renewals, in a service of 1200 or one for every nineteen positions. There were two periods of thirty-nine days each during which there were no persons in the park service employed on temporary authority.

One of the abuses of temporary authorities has been the renewal of these grants time after time. In this way, political favorites are kept in positions without examination, or at least until they can bring up their experience rating so as to head the eligible list after examination. The average duration of employment in each temporary position in the West Parks was forty-one days. There were only seventeen renewals.

DATA COMPLETE

Appended to the report of the Superintendent of Employment is a table which shows the name of the appointee, the position filled, the pay, the period of the grant, the time employed, the reason for employment and other data with reference to each position filled by temporary appointment.

The West Park Civil Service Board is composed of John F. Smulski, chairman; Jens C. Hansen and Fred G. Heuchling, secretary. Mr. Heuchling as Superintendent of Employment, is the executive in charge. Mr. Heuchling was reappointed to this position last July for a six-year term.

THE CLUB DINING ROOMS have been doing a capacity business on "talk days" lately. The attendance when Caldwell and Pope, the ambulance drivers, spoke was 340. When Charles R. Crane spoke, the attendance was 415, the largest noon crowd ever served.

THE INVITATION TO LADIES to attend the Club luncheon, when Norman Angell spoke, a week ago last Saturday, met with an excellent response. This invitation was a departure from the usual rule, due to an oft-repeated request by members that women be given an opportunity to attend some of the noon meetings. A large number of women were present.

"HOLD HOME LINES" IS SLOGAN

Chicago Welfare Agencies Unite in Big
Drive to Rouse Public to Home Needs

"HOLD the Home Lines" will soon be a familiar phrase in Chicago. It stares at you from the billboards, it greets you in the elevated trains as you swing to and fro on your strap, it says "Good morning," as you open your paper at the breakfast table. Soon it will give you a knowing wink from the screen at the "movies." The reason is that the public welfare agencies of Chicago want you to understand that in spite of the war, poverty, sickness among the poor, helpless old age, juvenile delinquency, and other social ills have to be met and coped with in Chicago. And instead of competing with and cutting under each other, they have organized this joint publicity campaign, which has the backing of the State Council of Defense, the Chicago Association of Commerce and the Central Council of Social Agencies.

NEEDS OF THE HOUR

Along with the campaign, the agencies are making a survey of the field to determine exactly the activities and needs of each, particularly in view of the emergencies created by the war. To mention a single case, this was the situation which they found confronting the children's institutions and societies of Chicago: These agencies in 1917 housed and cared for more than 10,000 dependent and neglected children—"a small city of great potential human strength." A report upon an inquiry among thirty-five such institutions states that:

CHILDREN'S AGENCIES IN WAR TIME

"Since war was declared, there is shown an increase of from 25 to 100% in the number of applications received by the institutions for the temporary care of children. The average increase is 36%. Think of adding one-third to the expense of feeding, clothing and caring for 10,000 children. Parents and relatives responsible for these cases are now unable to pay as great a proportion of this expense as in the past, on account of increase in living expenses.

"The periods of care, in these temporary cases, pending the ability of parents to again assume their responsibility, have increased in length about one-third compared with one year ago.

CHILDREN OF SOLDIERS

"One-half the agencies reported an added responsibility owing to the admission of many children from soldiers' families; the Red Cross assists in part of the financial care but cannot cover overhead and supervision in all cases.

"War added new and changed forms of work to the programs of these institutions and Societies:

FEWER ADOPTIONS

"A large child placing society declared: A decrease in applications from families desiring to assume the care of a child or children, especially older children; such applications are about 40% of normal. This means more care in the institution or at board in families. It also reports the return of many older children by foster families, whose economic condition has become uncertain in the stress of war conditions.

MORE WORKING MOTHERS

"Practically all questionnaires point out a new type of need from families of young hard working parents in which the rise in cost of living necessities has compelled the mother to leave home for employment to supplement the husband's income, the children being cared for by a children's agency during this period of stress. In one instance this new form of need added one-fourth to the expense of the organization's department dealing with temporary care. Nurseries have been recently established by two institutions to take care of children while their mothers are employed, heroically endeavoring to meet the almost prohibitive high costs of life.

WAR ILLEGITIMACY

"Cases of 'War Illegitimacy' are already beginning to demand attention, and one agency points out an extended department for maternity care and placement of the infants.

"Special relief to sick and defective children of families now unable to meet the cost of necessities is reported as a new feature by one agency.

MORE WORK—INSUFFICIENT MONEY

"The foregoing new and changed forms of urgent needs are overcrowding the capacities of institutions, and taxing the human service of visitors and investigators, so that many agencies point out the dire need of additional buildings, equipment and workers but *cannot provide these because of financial stringency.*"

If this truly represents the increased burden, it is not surprising that all but two of these agencies reported financial deficits for the year.

Reports have also been submitted showing the situation which the settlements and the correctional, legal and reform agencies are facing. We hope to make fuller mention of these later.

GROUP MEETINGS

One feature of the campaign to "Hold the Home Lines" is a series of group meetings which is being held at the City Club on Tuesday and Friday afternoons. Four meetings have been held so far and these have been well attended. Next Tuesday afternoon, January 29th, the discussion will be devoted to relief and personal service agencies. The speakers will be Eugene T. Lies, General Superintendent of the United Charities; Charles W. Folds, Ella Boynton, President School Children's Aid Society; Judge Henry Horner, representing the Jewish relief agencies; Father Edward F. Rice, of the St. Vincent De Paul Society; David R. Forgan and John W. O'Leary.

Other programs arranged for are as follows:

Friday, February 1—Hospital and Medical Agencies.

Tuesday, February 5—H o m e s f o r Working Women and Girls.

Friday, February 8—Old P e o p l e ' s Homes.

The meetings are at four o'clock and are open to the public.

F. EMORY LYON has an article on "The Housing of Prisoners" in the January issue of the Journal of Criminal Law.

DO THE SOLDIER AND SAILOR BOYS who come here on Saturdays and Sundays enjoy the Club? If you doubt it, read the following story turned in by one of our members who was at the Club a week ago Saturday, about two sailors who came in:

"They had been in the service at the Naval Training Station but five weeks. Three weeks had been spent under quarantine observation. A 'shot in the arm' varied the regular routine. One was from down in Ohio—the other from up near Detroit. It was their first leave—12 hours to see Chicago. They had seen the sights. 'You can't keep going to the movies all the time,' they said.

"One played the phonograph—he picked out the ones with plenty of 'pep' and swing. The other wrote a letter and read awhile before the fire in the Lounge. 'Well, we know where to drop in when we're in Chicago,' they said. 'We appreciate your taking us in.' "

"IN March, 1915, there was created in the Municipal Court of Chicago a special branch for hearing all causes involving not more than $35. In this branch, with the consent of litigants, trial procedure was reduced to the minimum necessary to adjudicating on the facts and the law. All the frills and time-consuming melodrama were omitted. The judge elicited the facts in a few minutes and announced his decision as soon as he reached it.

"This informal trial procedure proved so successful that before the close of the year the scope of the branch was extended to causes involving $50 or less. In 1916 the jurisdictional limit was raised to $100 and two judges were assigned to this work. Recently another horizontal raise has been made and a judge has been assigned to the trial of causes involving more than $100 and not more than $200. The fact that appeals from these branches are rare and juries are seldom called for proves their entire success. In them justice does not cost more than it is worth. All this illustrates what can be done by a court which has reasonable administrative control and is compelled by the responsibility resting upon it to devise economical methods of operation."—*Journal of the American Judicature Society, December,* 1917.

CLUB MEMBER TAKES TO WINGS

T. W. Osborn, Learning to Fly,
Writes Letter to His Club Friends

TEN or twenty years hence we suppose it will be as common to jump into our private aeroplane and have the pilot drive us over to Evanston or Oak Park as it is now to bring our tin Lizzies out of the cigar-box garage in the back yard and spin down the boulevard on a like errand. But just now there is a thrill in the idea and we wonder how it feels to be sailing around in three dimensions with nothing but a couple of thousand feet of air underneath.

A letter came to our desk last week from a member of the Club who is in the American flying corps and is just learning to navigate the upper spaces. Read it and decide for yourself if you want to enlist. The letter is from Thomas W. Osborn and is written from Rich Field, Waco, Texas. Mr. Osborn says:

THE REAL THING

"Our advent into Rich Field was a vast disappointment to us. We were pampered and spoiled 'stage' soldiers when we came here, but it was soon taken out of us. We were ordered to take off our officers' clothes and put on the garb of privates, not to put on so much 'dog' when we came in contact with enlisted men. In other words, we were ordered to become a part of Uncle Sam's army. It did us all good, I'm sure.

"Our quarters at ground school were too perfectly appointed and everything was made too easy for us physically—here this is not so. But we are kept in good condition, have no mental labor, and are really better off than we were at our ground school.

"Today a new flying list was posted (owing to lack of planes there are quite a number of men not yet on flying) and the names of several Illinois men were on it. I was one of the lucky ones, and we were ordered to report for flying duty at 1 o'clock. Needless to say we were not late for that formation.

"As each man awaited his turn he kept saying 'I hope she doesn't miss' (the engine), or 'I hope the "prop" holds up,' the 'prop' being the propeller. Each man was so anxious to go up and asked all sorts of foolish questions of the enlisted men and mechanics. (Just a word here—never, if you are in the army as a candidate for a commission, ask an enlisted man anything which you do not understand and he does. They shrivel you with a glance. The general effect is that of speaking to a woman whom you thought you knew and having her tersely explain that you are mistaken.)

"To resume—As each man came down, instead of raving about their experience they all tried to assume a nonchalant air which was evidently forced. For even to us in our excited condition, it was very apparent that they were just burning to relate their experiences.

UP WE GO

"At length our turn came. My pilot gave me a few instructions and we started off 'taxi-ing' across the field. The motor opened up with a sudden roar and instead of bumping along as we had been doing, it became suddenly smooth. I was watching my pilot's right hand for signals so intently that I didn't even look over the side. When I did I found that we were about one hundred feet above the ground. That was the first intimation I had that we were really flying, but when I saw it I returned my glance quickly to the pilot's hand to see his signals and took a little firmer hold on the 'joystick' (control lever).

LOOKING DOWN

"For about five minutes I saw nothing but the pilot's hand, the wires in a gray background (it was cloudy), but finally I gathered nerve enough for a good long look over the side. It certainly was wonderful to see everything so far below you (we were then about 2000 feet high), but I was interrupted by a violent wig wag of the pilot's hand and an awful tipping of the 'ship' and moved my control lever to right it, but had to exert considerable force to right it. It is queer, but you cannot realize that you are in the air. You feel as though this were not happening to you but to some one else, but this is what the instructors want, for if you think too much about yourself you are apt to commit that crime of crimes, and freeze the controls (grip them so hard out of sheer fright), so that your instructor cannot move his controls.

"When the pilot shuts off his engine and noses the ship down, most fellows get dreadfully nervous and afraid. With our pilot it was different. I breathed freely for the first time, for in the air he had taken both hands off the controls to show me that I actually had my life in my own hands, and I would much rather have had it in his hands—they seemed more efficient. But on the landing, I drew the first decent breath I'd taken since I left the ground, and looked all around me. We approached the ground at a terrific angle, but you didn't think of that, you were too busy taking in all the scenery which you had no time to glance at before.

"After a perfect landing we set foot on the solid earth, but only to realize that we were victims of aeroplane fever and could not recover nor reconcile ourselves to walking as a means of locomotion.

"My regards to my friends of the Club and especially to my old friends of the Eleventh Base Hospital Unit.

"Yours truly,
THOMAS W. OSBORN.

Mr. Osborn adds a postscript saying that he would be glad to hear from his friends at the City Club.

JOHN S. VAN BERGEN, who is going to France, as we announced in last week's Bulletin, is going not with the Red Cross but with the Y. M. C. A.

A MEMBER of the editor's family in business in Calcutta recently received from a native the following application for a job:

"Most Honored Sir:

"Understanding there are several hands wanted in your honour's department, I beg to offer my hand as to adjustment.

"I appeared for the matriculation examination at Dota-camud, but failed; the reason for which I shall describe; to begin with, my writing was illegible. This was due to climatic reason, for having come from a warm to a cold climate found my fingers stiff and very disobedient to my wishes. Further, I had received great shock to my mental system in the shape of death of my only fond brother—besides, most honoured Sir, I beg to state that I am in very uncomfortable circumstances, being the soul support of my fond brother's seven (7) issues, consisting of three (3) adults and four (4) adultresses, the latter being bain of my existence owing to my having to support my own two (2) wives as well as their issues, of which by God's misfortune, the feminine gender predominates. If by wonderful good fortune, these humble lines meet with your benign kindness and favorable turn of mind, I, the poor menial shall pray for the long life and prosperity of yourself as well as your Honour's post-humour olive branches."

EXAMINATION METHOD BRINGS PROTEST

Citizens Conference Urges Examining
Board of Library Experts—Plea Is Denied

THE recommendation of a number of civic organizations, including the Special City Club Committee on Public Library, of which C. M. Williams is chairman, that the City Civil Service Commission reappoint, as an examining board to conduct the forthcoming examination for librarian, the same committee which conducted the examination when Mr. Legler was chosen, has not been carried out by the Commission. Mr. Herbert Putnam, Librarian of Congress, was appointed but one of the other members of the board, is a member of the City Civil Service Commission, the other a member of the library board.

It was the belief of the organizations which recommended the appointment of the previous board that the examiners should be men of the highest standing in the library world, so that men of high professional attainments would know that their qualifications would be properly passed upon and would be more ready to take the examination.

When the personnel of the examining board was announced, a conference of citizens representing various organizations was called by the City Club Committee on Public Librarian. It was held at the Club last Monday. It was agreed at this conference that another effort should be made to secure the appointment to the board of two additional librarians of high professional standing. A letter to the Civil Service Commission urging these additional appointments and also urging a two-weeks postponement of the examination was drawn up and presented to the Commission by a delegation. These recommendations, the letter urged "are reasonable, practical and based on sound business policy, are in accord with the spirit of the law, and besides are 'good politics.' "

The letter was signed by J. C. M. Hanson, University of Chicago; Mrs. Edwin T. Johnson; Chicago Woman's Club; Mary E. McDowell, University of Chicago Settlement; John F. Lyons, President, Chicago Library Club; James B. Haslam, Secretary, Social Service Commission, Episcopal Church; Mary Anderson, Woman's Trade Union League; Olive Sullivan, Secretary, Woman's Trade Union League; Mrs. A. H. Schweizer, First Vice-President, Chicago Political Equality League; Mrs. Kenneth Rich, Woman's City Club; Dr. Graham Taylor, Chicago School of Civics and Philanthropy; George E. Carman, Director of Lewis Institute; Thomas W. Allinson, Henry Booth House; Julius Stern, Citizens' Association of Chicago; Mary Eileen Ahern, Editor "Public Libraries"; Charles M. Williams, Chairman of City Club Committee on Public Librarian; Charles M. Moderwell, Union League Club.

The Civil Service Commission refused to accede to the recommendations of the conference and the examination is being held with the examining board as previously announced.

The Club's Committee on Public Librarian, as announced in a previous issue in the Bulletin, sent letters to a number of librarians in various parts of the country urging them to take the examination. Affirmative replies, with applications to be filed in their behalf were received from several of these.

JOHN P. LENOX last week, brought into the office an interesting souvenir of the war, a paper cutter manufactured out of British, French and German bullets, sent by his nephew, Elmer Roberts, who is in the X-Ray room of the Northwestern University Hospital Unit in France. Mr. Roberts is a son of E. E. Roberts of Oak Park. On the side of the paper cutter is mounted a German coin, which was taken from the pocketbook of a captured officer. This officer had been asked to help carry a stretcher and had refused saying, "German officers do not carry stretchers." The stretcher bearer knocked him down—and the officer carried the stretcher. Before they reached the dressing station, however, a shell exploded killing or severely wounding all but this one stretcher bearer, who later turned over to Mr. Roberts the pocketbook which had been taken from the German officer.

NORMAN ANGELL

(Continued from page 28)

for it, does not believe in it. And that is true not only of Europe, but of America. People are not hostile to it—they just don't believe in it. Everybody is willing to approve the idea 'in principle.' Even the German Chancellor approves the general idea; in fact he says Germany is ready to lead a League of Nations. If he really thought it possible, he would bitterly oppose it, for it would be the end of the German system. Nobody approves it because nobody believes it will come.

"We say: 'We do not believe in it because it is not practical.' But the truth is that it is not practical because we do not believe in it. If we all believed in it and were determined to bring it about, that fact of itself would make it not only practical but inevitable.

THE IMPORTANCE OF "TALK"

" 'Win the war first and then talk.' That advice is usually given by folk who do an immense deal of talking that does not help to win the war. We cannot win the war if we don't hold together, and policies like those pursued with reference to Italy and Russia are bound to drive us apart. And governments adopted them because public opinion made impossible the only alternative policy. And public opinion was of that kind because none of us likes to be called upon to do a little serious thinking, to revise our old ideas, and because it is easy to dismiss any invitation so to do, as 'talk.'

"Popular support of the League of Nations is necessary, not only for preventing the disunity of the Alliance, it is necessary for preventing the continued unity of the enemy. We have proclaimed—very rightly —as our main object the 'destruction of German militarism.' But we have never told the German how his country is to be protected when we have destroyed its military power, and until we do so he will go on fighting just to preserve some means of defending himself.

MUST DEFINE AIMS CLEARLY .

"At the present time the enemy governments are trying to persuade their peoples that defeat for Germany must mean the destruction of German nationality and the economic opportunity of her future children. Against such a fate any people, good,

bad or indifferent, savage or civilized, will fight to the end. This effort of the enemy governments to stiffen the resistance of their people, we are directly aiding by our refusal to state clearly what we mean by the destruction of German militarism. Does it mean that Germany is to be manifestly inferior in power, and that we are to have no responsibility for her protection? Then whatever the responsibility for the beginning of the war, the Germans are fighting for the right to defend themselves. Such a situation undoes the work of the blockade. We hope by pressure upon the civil population to produce readiness for peace—and undo the effect by furnishing the German people with the strongest possible motive which any nation can have for continuing a war. That aid to the enemy governments must be withdrawn. Until the safety of Germany is assured, German militarism will be supported by the German people, and however we may crush them, be a constant menace to the rest of Europe. Germany is a criminal nation, but the way to deal with the criminal is not only to punish him if he breaks the law—that is certainly necessary—but also to undertake to protect him if he observes it. Unless that is done the criminal will always be taking the law into his own hands as a measure of defense, and continue to be a common menace.

MUST GUARANTEE SECURITY

"If the German people are to be brought to see that they are not fighting a war of defense, if the support which they give their government is to be undermined, if Germany is to be democratized, if the way is to be prepared for territorial concessions necessary for better Europe, it must be made plain that the Allied policy offers to a democratized and law-abiding Germany a security greater than that which she can enjoy under a militarist and autocratic regimen. That cannot be done by a mere general diplomatic declaration of ultimate intention. As the President has most truly said, war aims, when stated in general terms, seem the same on both sides. The plans of the Allies for post bellum security must take shape sufficiently to form a recognizable policy; to strike the imagination of the German people, and to be, themselves, obviously of democratic inspiration and promise.

"Another of our battle cries—and a very

good one too—is 'No peace with the Hohen-zollerns.' I take it to mean no peace with a government not responsible to its people. But secret diplomacy—which has been universal in Europe in the past—means that in foreign affairs all governments were able to commit the nation to all sorts of courses—courses involving war—which the people not only did not sanction, but of which they were even ignorant. The old methods of diplomacy made all governments pure autocracies in foreign affairs, however democratic they might be at home. And we might abolish the Kaiser and make Germany in home affairs as democratic as you like and still leave the people without any real control over her foreign policy, unless we make an organic change in the at present universal method of managing international affairs; unless, that is, we take them out of the hands of diplomats responsible only to foreign offices or executives, and treat those things as what they are, a legislative function, and not the proper work of executives.

AN INTERNATIONAL PEACE PARLIAMENT

"If, after peace, we are to talk to the German people instead of to the German government, the Peace Conference must be made more in the nature of an International Parliament, and much less in the nature of a secret meeting of diplomats, than have been past Peace Conferences.

"A proposal has been made that the Peace Conference should consist of two bodies, a smaller one composed, as in international Congresses of the past, of the delegates or nominees of the governments participating, and a larger body representing proportionately the component parties of the respective parliaments.

"The smaller body should act as the initiating and drafting committee, their proposals being subject to amendment, approval or rejection by the larger body, before being finally ratified by the constituent states of the Congress.

WOULD WIN LIBERAL GERMANS

"That is to say, under such a principle at the Peace Conference the real power of representation in the case of Germany would rest not with diplomats appointed by the Kaiser, but with delegates from the Reichstag, mainly the Social Democrats. By that simple device we should have democratized Germany, by taking power in the most important acts of the State—and those

acts with which we are most concerned—out of the hands of the rulers and putting into the hands of the people; resting power on the country's parliamentary institutions. And if we announced that as our policy now, we win to its support all the forces in Germany now fighting for parliamentary institutions. For those forces would realize that the acceptance of this item of our peace terms would win their battle.

"All this does not mean that we have not got to defeat Germany; it means that the defeat cannot be complete until we have added wise political management to the military effort.

SHOULD DEVISE PLAN NOW

" 'Win the war first and then will be time enough to talk of the policy that this country is to pursue afterwards.' Then would be too late. Take the most important point of all—the kind of Conference that shall settle the terms of peace. The constitution and composition of the Conference would be the very first thing to decide in order of time. It is one of the most important 'terms of peace' itself. But the people can play no part in determining it unless it is discussed before the peace comes. If no attention is paid during the war to the form of Conference, it will to a certainty take the form with which the men who now constitute the governments of Europe are familiar. Yet, if, after the war we are to discuss settlement with the German people instead of the German Government; if we are to treat with the stable and moderate as well as with the extremist sections of the Russian people, the peoples of the western democracies must during the war demand that the settlement is not made by the old methods of Peace Congresses of the past. The governments of the European Allied nations are themselves for the most part no longer representative. They have been chosen largely for their administrative fitness for the purpose of carrying on the war. But there are elements in most the presence of which are due to the suspension—the very proper and necessary suspension—of democratic machinery. However desirable for the purposes of the war, they could by no stretch be called democratically representative. They were not selected by the people for the purpose of making a peace which might settle the destiny of the world for generations. Yet, if nothing better is devised during the war it is precisely they who would fix the peace terms and determine the general character of the settlement.

THE DANGER OF DRIFT

"Very shortly now—in a few months perhaps, or a year or two at most—the nation will be faced by these problems, vaster, more difficult, containing more possibilities of disastrous mistakes, than any which have heretofore confronted the statesmanship of the world. It is our duty to see, if our people are not to have fought in vain, that we do not drift to that decision unprepared, our statesmen unguided by any unformed opinion, or worse still, harassed by one that is fickle and unstable, with understanding clouded and power of thought submerged by momentary passion, crude herd instinct, or the momentum of old prejudices and obsolete conceptions."

Mr. Angell's audience, which was large, was of an inquiring frame of mind. After the address a number of questions were asked bearing upon his argument. Would Mr. Angell favor a direct popular vote in the choice of representatives to a peace parliament, was one of these questions. It would be difficult to state the issues for a general election, Mr. Angell replied. Furthermore, a popular campaign might result in the selection of representatives whose appeal had been to mass patriotism and chauvinism rather than to statesmanship. On the whole, in Mr. Angell's opinion, a selection by the parliamentary bodies, in which already there is an alignment of parties on war issues would be preferable.

LINCOLN STEFFENS' ADDRESS last Friday will be reported in next week's Bulletin.

HAROLD R. HOWES who has been wintering at Camp Grant expects to leave within a few days for France. He is with the 311th engineers as first lieutenant.

THE MONEY ROLLS IN gradually for the soldiers' and sailors' entertainment fund. Members have been asked to remit a dollar or more for this fund with their quarterly dues, now payable. If you have forgotten to send in your dues, don't wait for a second notice. And don't forget the extra dollar to help us give the soldiers and sailors a good time at their week-end visits to the Club.

The City Club Bulletin

Published Weekly by the City Club of Chicago

A Journal of Active Citizenship

VOLUME XI MONDAY, FEBRUARY 4, 1918 NUMBER 5

THREE IMPORTANT MEETINGS

Wednesday, February 6, at Luncheon:

"The World's Lowest Death Rate for Children —How New Zealand Won It." Illustrated

DR. F. TRUBY KING, New Zealand. Dr. King inaugurated the methods which produced this record. He has been called to England, and is on his way, to inaugurate those methods there. Miss Lathrop of the Children's Bureau wishes this country to learn of Dr. King's achievements.

Friday, February 8, at Luncheon:

"Home Fires For the Training Camps"

ALLEN D. ALBERT, special representative of the War and Navy Department Commissions on Training Camp Activities. His theme is: Recreation and "a place to go" for soldier and sailor when off duty. Mr. Albert is past president of the International Association of Rotary Clubs. He comes to Chicago from a tour of the camps.

Saturday, Feb. 9, at Luncheon—Ladies' Day:

"The Manufacture of High Explosives—and the Health of the Workers"

DR. ALICE HAMILTON, investigator of occupational diseases, U. S. Department of Labor. Dr. Hamilton has just completed a survey of occupational diseases in war industries.

LADIES INVITED—The Club dining room is open to ladies for luncheon hereafter every Saturday. Ladies are invited to the luncheon to hear Dr. Hamilton

Luncheon from 11:30 Speaking at 1:00

The City Club Bulletin
A Journal of Active Citizenship

PUBLISHED WEEKLY BY THE
CITY CLUB OF CHICAGO
315 Plymouth Court   Telephone: Harrison 8278

DWIGHT L. AKERS, Editor

OFFICERS OF THE CLUB

FRANK I. MOULTON, President
EDGAR A. BANCROFT, Vice-President
ROY C. OSGOOD, Treasurer
CHARLES YEOMANS, Secretary
GEORGE E. HOOKER, Civic Secretary

EDITORIAL BOARD

HERBERT H. SMITH, Chairman
FREDERICK D. BRAMHALL   S. R. WATKINS
C. COLTON DAUGHADAY   PAUL R. WRIGHT

$1.00 per Year - - - 10c per Copy

Entered as second class matter, December 3, 1917, at the postoffice at Chicago, Illinois, under the act of March 3, 1879.

> *The purpose of the Club is to bring together in informal association those men who are genuinely interested in the improvement of the political, social and economic conditions of the community in which we live.*

Club Committee Calendar

Tuesday, Feb. 5 to Monday, Feb. 11.

Tuesday—
  City Planning Committee . . 12:30
Wednesday—
  House Committee 12:15
  Wartime Committee . . . 12:30
  Editorial Board 12:00
  Membership Extension Committee 12:30
Thursday—
  Club Activities Committee . . 12:15
Friday—
  Admissions Committee . . . 1:00
Saturday—
  Committee on Public Education 12:30
Monday—
  Committee on Public Utilities . 12:30
  Committee on Public Affairs . 1:00

THE CASTLE, ORPHEUM, Bijou Dream and Lyric "Movie" Theaters on State St., are co-operating with the City Club in entertaining soldiers and sailors by showing slides calling the attention of the men to the City Club privileges and giving explicit directions for reaching the Club from each theater.

THE LISTENING POST

THE CLUB last week welcomed the following persons into its membership: Dr. Lee A. Bacon, Dr. William S. Harvey, Raymond Kelly, Chicago Manager, Security Life Company; Frederic Leake, Secretary, Bon Air Coal & Iron Corporation; Herbert N. McCoy, Chemist.

W. S. REYNOLDS, a member of the City Club, was the successful candidate in the examination last Monday for the position of Chief Probation Officer in Cook County, left vacant by the resignation of Joel D. Hunter. Mr. Reynolds is at present superintendent of the Illinois Children's Home and Aid Society.

IT'S "COLONEL" NATHAN WILLIAM MACCHESNEY no longer. Gentlemen, allow us to introduce *"Brigadier-General,"* or for the sake of brevity *"General"* Nathan William MacChesney of the United States Army! General MacChesney's new commission was announced last Thursday. Congratulations!

A NUMBER OF OUR MEMBERS on the War Service List have been promoted. Some of the majors would suffer a horrible shock if they came home and found themselves listed as lieutenants. For that reason, will members who know of any errors in the military list which is posted in the lobby, please notify the editor by letter or by dropping a notice in the "Listening Post" box? This applies particularly to the anonymous member who gave us the tip.

CHARLES D. WATERBURY, of Pond and Pond, is another addition to the City Club delegation in Washington. "I came very suddenly," he writes, "all arrangements being made by telegraph and I did not know what my duties were to be until after I reported. They've started me as assistant chief of drafting room in the Cantonment Division, Quartermaster's Department and as there are 30 or 40 projects on hand, some of them costing well into the millions, there is plenty to keep me busy."

OGDEN AVENUE PLAN SUGGESTED

Club Committee Recommends Modification of Big City Planning Project

The City Club City Planning Committee has evolved a modification of the Ogden Avenue extension project which it believes would not only solve some of the present difficulties in the way of the plan and increase the usefulness of the street but would save many thousands of dollars to the city. The ideas of the Committee are outlined in a letter transmitted with maps to the Chicago Plan Commission last Thursday. The letter is signed by R. F. Schuchardt, chairman.

The essence of the Committee's plan is that instead of carrying Ogden Avenue through to the intersection of Wisconsin and Clark streets, as at present proposed, it should be carried through only to Cleveland Avenue and at this point traffic should be diverted to existing streets—light vehicles north on Cleveland Avenue to Fullerton and thence on Lake View Avenue and Sheridan Road or other north streets; street car traffic and heavy vehicles to Sedgwick Street and north to Clark.

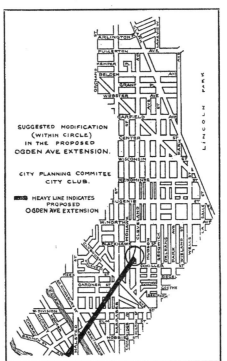

SUGGESTED MODIFICATION (WITHIN CIRCLE) IN THE PROPOSED OGDEN AVE. EXTENSION.

CITY PLANNING COMMITTEE CITY CLUB.

■■■ HEAVY LINE INDICATES PROPOSED OGDEN AVE EXTENSION

The advantages of this plan may be summarized as follows:

1. By establishing the street car terminal near Sedgwick and Clark streets instead of at Wisconsin and Clark, the possibility of further increasing the traffic at this already badly congested point would be avoided.

2. By this diversion of traffic, both street cars and vehicles would reach Lincoln Park at points nearer the places where the majority of people desire to go, namely, the bathing beach and the animal houses.

3. The new diagonal street would be shortened approximately one-fifth of its proposed length, thus reducing the amount of property necessary to purchase and thereby saving expense to the city. This saving would take place at that section of the proposed route where values are the highest.

As an incidental feature, the committee suggests a public square at the intersection of Cleveland Avenue with the new street. (See plan.)

Don't forget to register your guests in the big book by the door.

The Club library on the fourth floor is a reference collection of books on civics. It is at the disposal of members.

The special 40c lunch in the Club's restaurant is very popular.

The House Committee is glad to have suggestions for the improvement of the service.

COMMITTEE BACKS CENTRAL PAYROLLS

Supports Plans for More Efficient and
Economical Payroll Check by City

IT sometimes takes a good, new idea from five years to a generation to get "across." It is very interesting these days, when the City is worrying over its depleted money-bags and counting its nickels, to see the rejected ideas of the past coming to the front as life savers. It was so with the proposal to abolish ward lines in the administration of the Bureau of Streets, proposed a long time ago by the Merriam Commission and now approved by the Finance Committee. So also with the proposal for a centralization of city payrolls advocated by the city Efficiency Division in 1913 and now resurrected and urged as a means of municipal economy. Promoters of "lost causes" can perhaps take a little satisfaction from the manner in which their ideas "bob up" after years of innocuous desuetude.

Club Committee Endorses Idea

The central payroll idea is advanced by the Woman's City Club in its list of suggested city economies for next year. The City Club Committee on Public Expenditures backs up the proposal and in a report forwarded to the Finance Committee last week, in response to an invitation for an expression of its views, urged its adoption. The Committee said in part:

"Centralization of payroll preparation permits the elimination of much of the payroll work (in the case of New York City a saving in services of approximately 73% has been accomplished) and of much of the expense of printing, books and records in the several departments.

Could Use Efficiency Devices

"Improved time saving mechanical devices for efficient handling of payroll work are available, the cost of which would be prohibitive were they provided for each individual department, but which, for a central division would result in large saving in labor and supplies, in less frequent errors and in simpler and more uniform procedure. The system used in New York City includes the use of these mechanical devices which makes the work of writing all payrolls and checks from the same plates and the performance of the functions of the auditing office and payroll checking by the civil service commission automatic, for the greater part.

"Such a centralized payroll system should be designed and placed in operation by a competent body of experts, such as the efficiency staff of the Committee on Finance.

Would Make Saving

"The expense involved in the purchase of the equipment and the preparation of standard payroll and check forms will reduce the possible maximum saving the first year, but not thereafter. Even with this reduction, however, the estimated saving, for the first year, of $20,000 indicated in the Woman's City Club recommendation, appears to be reasonable in the light of the results obtained elsewhere. The savings through centralized and co-ordinate service should correspondingly increase after the first year."

CHARLES F. GREY, 2nd, has gone to San Antonio for service training in the Ordnance Department.

SEES WORLD IN REVOLUTION

Russian Turmoil Beginning of Universal Upheaval, Says Steffens

"THE Bolsheviki peace talk is camouflage," says Lincoln Steffens, speaking at the City Club last Friday. "The Bolsheviki are not pacifists. They are not for peace at any price. What they want is *The Revolution*—not simply the Russian revolution, but a world-wide revolution of the proletariat. They want it in Italy, they want it in Germany, in France, in England and in all the other countries of the world.

MUST HAVE GERMAN REVOLT

"Suppose, however, the Revolution should come in the allied countries but not in Germany. Italy was on the verge of a revolution but it was checked by the Germans when they made their last big drive. France is only waiting until after the war. The Bolsheviki understand that if the revolution should come in these countries but not in Germany, German imperialism would win. They know that they *must* get a revolution in Germany."

Mr. Steffens traced back the causes of the present world turmoil to underlying social and economic conditions. "Back of this war," he said, "is the social war—the war that we will all be fighting when this one is over." Throughout his investigations of corrupt city governments, of labor troubles, of the I. W. W., the MacNamara case, the Mexican revolution, he had found, he said, the same underlying disease, special privilege. And he had found it in Russia. "I am not against this war," he said, "except as I am against poverty, disease and other social ills. It's the next war that I'm against and that war cannot be stopped except by the solving of social problems."

PRIVILEGE PROVOKED OVERTURN

The Russian revolution, Mr. Steffens said, was provoked by the government. "All autocratic government," he said, "is representative government—it represents the privileged interests. In Russia the power of the Czar was controlled by the great nobles and landlords and the others whose interest was in breaking the laws."

Persons high in political power, Mr. Steffens charged, sold out the Russian army to Germany. It is the universal belief in Russia that the German high command bribed certain persons in the Russian high command to march the Russian troops into traps, where whole armies were annihilated. This has not been proven but it is expected that it will be revealed in certain trials to be held shortly.

THE FIGHTING ENDS

"After the revolution, the word came back to the army 'The Revolution is here'! and the peasants and the workingmen turned from fighting to look at the dawn. They didn't say, 'We won't fight'—they just stopped. To them it wasn't the *Russian* revolution—it was *The* revolution. It was for the Germans, too.

"And so along the eastern front workmen and peasants sat down and talked. They asked themselves what the war was about and had to confess that they didn't know. The Russians thought that since the revolution they were fighting for democracy and liberty and against imperialism. And the German soldiers thought they were fighting against imperialism too—British imperialism.

SECRET TREATIES HARM ALLIES

"They asked why they couldn't have peace. The German high command sent word down to be passed along to the Russians that the reason why they couldn't have peace was that Russia was bound to the allies by imperialistic secret treaties. The Russian soldiers didn't believe it. But they sent committees back to Petrograd to find out and they found that it was true. Today you can hardly mention Constantinople to them—it means to them Russia's own perfidy. A million soldiers left the front and went home carrying the conviction that there was something wrong on their own side.

"Milyukov said that maybe these treaties were wrong, but that Russia should abrogate her contract. He went down holding to this principle. Kerensky said, 'I can arrange the matter.' He thought he could arrange a conference of the allies for a revision of war aims. But the allies would have none of it and Kerensky went down and the Bolsheviki, a minority party, came into power.

MOB IS HERO OF RUSSIA

"But the Bolsheviki do not really rule Russia. The Russian people rule. The Russian mob is the hero of the revolution. So stupid, so sincere, so conscientious— these mobs, not the provisional government or its leaders, are the rulers of Russia.

"When the revolution came Milyukov and others of the Constitutional Democrats assumed that they were to be leaders and appointed themselves as a cabinet. But they soon found that they didn't govern at all. They announced decrees but no one knew it. Milyukov decided that some socialists ought to be put in the cabinet but he couldn't find anybody who wanted to be in the cabinet. Everybody was too busy. They were on their own problem—the economic conditions of the country. The Russian people tolerate the provisional government because it seems to represent and express what they wish. Neither Milyukov nor Kerensky, whom the people loved, was forced out by the Russian mobs. They fell simply because nobody would listen to them. The moment the Bolsheviki cease to represent the thought of the people, the people will turn from them.

DEMOCRACY OF NEW SORT

"The mobs pay little attention to laws. If they are good laws, the people will obey them; if they are bad laws, they will ignore them. They didn't abolish the Duma. 'It may pass some good laws,' they reasoned, 'and if it does the people will obey them.' The fact is that they take their new democracy seriously and literally and they are more interested in the real thing than in the machinery.

"The Russian mob is gentle. It does not kill, it does not loot. The killings, about which we have read, were by soldiers and sailors, who had been armed and taught to kill—not by the mobs. We newspaper men would hear a mob coming down the street and would stop and interview it. 'Where are you going?' we would ask. 'We don't know.' 'What is the matter?' 'We don't know—we simply heard that there is something wrong and we have set out to make it right.' That is the spirit of

the Russian mob—stupid, simple, sincere. It is the key to the revolution.

THE GOLDEN RULE IN RUSSIA

"Once some police fired upon a mob from a roof. The mob simply moved down the street out of range and sent a committee to get them. To get to the roof they had to go up a narrow stair and they made their way up over the bodies of dead and wounded comrades. They took the policemen and handed them over to the mob. What did the mob do? It might have been expected to kill them, but it didn't. 'That's what the government would have done,' they said. 'We musn't.' Kerensky, not really a leader but an expressor of the Russian people, at a conference in Petrograd, spoke these words, which should be a motto for all democratic peoples: 'We, the people, must not do to others any of the things that have been done to us. The Revolution is not for revenge but to establish justice and liberty.' The Russian mob has been the most consistent statesman in Europe and is compelling the other governments of the world to come to its views.

FOR ALL MANKIND

"The Russian revolution is the beginning of the international mind. The Russian democracy is not patriotic, not moral, not political, but sees the solution of social problems in economic changes. And it wants nothing for itself that it cannot have for all the world. Not once while I was in Russia did I hear the advocacy of a separate peace. The people talked always in terms of a 'general' peace, every term of which would be the same for every country in the world."

BRITISH LABOR BACKS WILSON

Mr. Steffens called attention to the reception of President Wilson's "peace terms" as an evidence of the international attitude of labor. "When the President sent his radical message," he asked, "from whom did he get his answer? From British labor. British labor said: 'Yes, that's right. We are willing to accept the terms and to apply them not only to Germany but to Great Britain.' And they named India, South Africa, and Asia."

LIEUTENANT VICTOR R. ANDERSON is with the 314th Field Artillery at Camp Lee, Virginia.

PEACE NOW WOULD PERIL BELGIUM

Consul General Fears German
Trickery Would Divide Country

"Peace talk at this time is dangerous—particularly to Belgium," said Albert Moulaert, Belgian consul-general, in an address at the City Club last Thursday. Mr. Moulaert warned against a possible repetition in the peace negotiations of German methods at Brest-Litovsk.

CAMOUFLAGE AT PEACE MEET

"The Germans," he charged, "will endeavor to talk Belgium out of her independence. They have been endeavoring to break up Belgium by exploiting the long standing lack of friendship between the Flemish and the Walloons. They will say that Belgium must be broken up because the so-called 'Council of Flanders,' a body of seven men, appointed it is said by 200 men whose names we do not even know, has declared for a Duchy of Flanders. Germany has nothing to back her claim but the names of these seven traitors, who were so much under German influence that they even asked for safety assurances, knowing that if the Germans ever got out of the country, they would be hanged. Peace now would be inconclusive. We must first have victory and our independence back."

REBUILDING THE ARMY

"The Belgian army," Mr. Moulaert said, "re-equipped and recruited to 200,000 men stands ready today to go on." He described the gallant stand of the almost exhausted army for fourteen days at the battle of Ypres, its recuperation and re-equipment in France and its services in various theatres of the war. The army originally had a strength of 117,000 men but at the end of October, 1917, after the battle of Ypres this was reduced to 60,000. The army had no more shells, the majority of the guns and rifles were out of order owing to the unceasing firing, the uniforms and equipment were torn and useless. The government at once took steps, in spite of enormous difficulties, to repair the army. Shops were opened but so great was the congestion that leather repair shops had to be located in the holds of cargo boats. The

Belgian government established in France and England, employing only Belgian workmen, repair shops for guns, rifle shops, powder and ammunition factories. The work of reconstructing the army personnel was also marvellously executed.

CONQUEST OF EAST AFRICA

Mr. Moulaert's account of the Belgian conquest of German East Africa was a story of the conquering of apparently insurmountable difficulties. A division of 12,000 men had to be formed with the police troops as a nucleus. "Equipment, guns, shells, food," he said, "had to be brought over from England and France. After the long voyage on the ocean and up the Congo River, for the last 360 miles everything had to be carried by native porters. Several hundred thousands boxes and packages were forwarded in that way." Once started in the first half of 1916, the campaign went on without a hitch and in a short time German East Africa had been cleared of Germans.

The passive resistance of the civilian population, Mr. Moulaert asserted, is as wonderful as the active resistance of the army. He described the exactions and atrocities and the stripping of the country not only of its wealth but of its man power. "There are more orphans in Belgium of men who have been deported," he said, "than of men killed in the war."

STIRRING UP TROUBLE

"The Germans have endeavored to stir up enmity between the Walloons and the Flemish. But while these two in peace times were not on the best of terms they are united against the external foe. One of the first things the Germans did was to re-establish the Flemish University of Ghent. Although this had been one of the dreams of the Flemish people, when it was offered by German hands the people didn't want it. The Germans could find only about 150 people who would sign the petition, although in 1912 a petition for the re-establishment of the University contained 125,000 names. They also encountered great difficulty in getting students. There are today about 100 professors in the institution but not an equal number of students. They went to the prison camps and offered young Belgian prisoners their freedom if they would enter, but out of 20,000 prisoners they could find only thirty.

"Having failed in this, they hit on the plan of administrative division of the Flemish and the Waloons. They set up independent governments but a great many of the officials resigned. I have heard that 50,000 municipal and government officials and employes have resigned. That is the way Belgium answered."

Belgium's ability to maintain her morale in the face of such circumstances, Mr. Moulaert ascribed in part to the inspiring and democratic leadership of King Albert and Queen Elizabeth and in part to the solid foundation of centuries of freedom. "The word 'liberty' is engraved in us," he said, "and if we cannot have our liberty we would rather die."

Mr. Moulaert has asked us to announce that in order to get Belgium's story more clearly understood by the public he will be glad to accept other engagements to speak. His headquarters are at the Belgium consulate, 108 North State St.

THE SOLDIERS AND SAILORS who come here at week-ends are gathered from the four corners of America. Saturday, January 26, for instance, those who registered —and this includes only a part of those who came—hailed from Hutchinson, Minn., Bicknell, Ind., Delhi, La., Buffalo, N. Y., Enid, Mont., Clinton, Iowa, Omaha, Nebr., Kansas City, Mo., Cincinnati, Ohio, Earlsboro, Okla., Flint, Mich., St. Louis, Mo., Salt Lake City, Utah, Bayfield, Wis., New Orleans, La., Detroit, Mich., Milwaukee, Wis., St. Paul, Minn., Rochester, Minn., Ft. Dodge, Iowa, Isle of Luzon, New York City, Everitte, Texas, Gilbert, Pa., Johnstown, Pa.

The following members are in charge of the Soldiers and Sailors Entertainment next Saturday and Sunday:

Saturday, February 9: S. Bowles King, H. Daughaday, T. N. Bishop, C. W. Andrews and A. B. Hall.

Sunday, February 10: J. R. Ozanne, R. H. Clark, George Gordon, and George K. Reed.

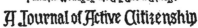

The City Club Bulletin

Published Weekly by the City Club of Chicago

A Journal of Active Citizenship

VOLUME XI   MONDAY, FEBRUARY 11, 1918   NUMBER 6

"TALK DAYS" THIS WEEK

Thursday, Feb. 14, at Luncheon—"Club Day":

"What I Saw in Roumania." Illustrated

DR. H. GIDEON WELLS, member Red Cross Mission to Roumania. Luncheon from 11:30. Speaking at 1:00.

Saturday, Feb. 16, at Luncheon—Ladies' Day:

"Should Chicago and the Nation Go Dry?"

OLIVER STEWART and GEORGE C. SIKES

Everybody knows these two speakers. They present opposed views. Come early. Luncheon from 11:30. Speaking at 1:00.

Wednesday Evening, Feb. 13—Woman's City Club Meeting:

Members of City Club of Chicago invited.

"Chicago's Financial Difficulties"

By Six Chicago Aldermen Who Know Them.

Those wishing dinner, $1.00, should reserve by Tuesday, Feb. 12
Dinner at 6:00. Speaking at 7:00.

FURTHER INFORMATION INSIDE

The City Club Bulletin
A Journal of Active Citizenship

PUBLISHED WEEKLY BY THE
CITY CLUB OF CHICAGO
315 Plymouth Court   Telephone: Harrison 8278
DWIGHT L. AKERS, Editor

OFFICERS OF THE CLUB
FRANK I. MOULTON, President
EDGAR A. BANCROFT, Vice-President
ROY C. OSGOOD, Treasurer
CHARLES YEOMANS, Secretary
GEORGE E. HOOKER, Civic Secretary

EDITORIAL BOARD
HERBERT H. SMITH, Chairman
FREDERICK D. BRAMHALL   S. R. WATKINS
C. COLTON DAUGHADAY   PAUL R. WRIGHT

$1.00 per Year - - - - 10c per Copy

Entered as second class matter, December 3, 1917,
at the postoffice at Chicago, Illinois, under the act of
March 3, 1879.

*The purpose of the Club is to bring together in
informal association those men who are genuinely
interested in the improvement of the political,
social and economic conditions of the community
in which we live.*

THE LISTENING POST

ANDREW R. SHERIFF, of the law firm of Sheriff, Gilbert & Krimbill, has been appointed chairman of the City Club Committee on State Constitution. The passage at the last legislature of a resolution for a state constitutional convention and the statewide vote on that question next fall will make the work of that committee of unusual importance in the coming months.

THE ROSTER of the new Club members for last week is as follows:

Clarence Arnold, Salesman, Commission Lines.

Elbert Beeman, Wilson & Co., Advertising and Publicity.

Dr. T. A. Broadbent, Dentist.

E. J. Buffington, President, Illinois Steel Company.

George H. Ellis, Vice-President, Diamond Red Paint Manufacturers.

Louis Frank, Copp & Frank, "Simplex System."

Ernest W. Hunt, Agency Director, New York Life Insurance Co.

Frank D. Loomis, Secretary War Recreation Board of Illinois.

H. A. Parkin, Lawyer, Tenney, Harding & Sherman.

Henry R. Pebbles, Lawyer.

Fred Rawitser, Chairman, Employment Committee for the Handicapped.

Fred Uhlmann, Secretary, I. Rosenbaum Grain Company.

CAPT. JOSEPH S. WRIGHT is athletic officer, 33rd Division, N. A.

KARL D. LOOS, formerly listed in the U. S. Marine Corps, is now First Lieutenant, Small Arms Division, Ordnance Reserve Corps. He is at Washington, D. C.

THE decision of the Chicago Milk Commission reducing the price the farmer is to be paid for his milk and increasing the share to the distributor has started a row.

The fixing of the retail price of 12c leaves the consumer no worse off than before, as he might have been, if the evidence presented to the commission had been allowed to pass unchallenged.

The distributor is better off—much better off than he should be, according to some persons who have watched the testimony. Until next June he will receive a share of retail price much in excess of what he has been receiving.

The producers on the other hand feel much injured at the decision. They resent, they say, not only the actual cutting down of their prices but the method which the commission used in arriving at its conclusions. They have appealed to the Food Administrator against the decision.

The Commission which has just adjourned, while without power to deal with the matter, has given its approval to the program of unifying milk deliveries as a means of effecting economies in distribution—a program which the City Club's Milk Committee is promoting. It says in its report: "Unification should be effected as rapidly as possible. The Commission believes that overlapping deliveries and uneconomic methods result in expenses which the consumer should not be called upon to assume. An immediate step should be taken to eliminate these factors of cost."

Another Commission will be appointed by the Food Administration shortly with power to deal with this matter.

THE MONEY QUESTION ONCE MORE

City's Financial Snarl is Again Subject of Communication from Club Committee

THE City Club Committee on City Manager Plan has replied to the request of the joint legislative and city council committee (see Bulletin, January 7, 1918) for support in its endeavor to secure increased taxing powers for the city. "The things that are essential to the safety and health of the people of Chicago ought not to be neglected or omitted from lack of funds," says the Club Committee, "and we feel sure that the taxpayers of the city of Chicago will cheerfully agree to additional taxation if it is clearly and positively shown to be necessary to carry on those necessary functions in an economical manner.

"We respectfully suggest, however, that everything has not yet been done which the taxpayers may rightfully and properly expect to demonstrate and exhibit the necessity of additional funds, and exactly the disposition to be made of them. The completion of an actual budget, with the best possible distribution of the existing resources of the city, with a parallel column showing exactly and conclusively the application to be made of additional funds, accompanied by an explanation of the need, will we believe enable the taxpayers to form an intelligent and just conclusion upon the questions involved.

CITY FINANCE NOT EFFICIENT

"We respectfully suggest, further, that the public is thoroughly satisfied that the financial administration of the city's affairs is not and has not been either economical or efficient, and that little patience is likely to be shown toward a request for more funds that is not accompanied by proposals for cutting out future waste and increasing future efficiency. Certain of such proposals are contained in the resolutions accompanying your letter,* and we are in hearty accord with the policy of extending the length of the aldermanic term (with

---

* In its resolutions asking for a special session of the legislature, the joint committee had endorsed a number of measures for municipal economy, including a reduction in the number of municipal elections, through an extension of the term of alderman and the appointment of the City Clerk and City Treasurer, now elective.

the recall) and making the City Clerk and City Treasurer appointive officers. It seems to us, however, that these do not go far enough, either to meet the necessities of the situation or take full advantage of the opportunities of the proposed special session, nor do they in our judgment satisfy the demands of public opinion.

NON-PARTISAN ELECTIONS FIRST STEP

"The City Council has repeatedly gone on record in favor of non-partisan elections for all elective municipal offices, and we believe that should be the beginning of any program of reform.

"The proposal for the four-year term, and the appointment of the City Clerk and the City Treasurer, properly co-ordinated with other arrangements will decrease the number of elections and afford an immediate economy.

REORGANIZE ADMINISTRATION

"Further than that, however, and vastly more important, is the question of the reorganization of the executive end of the city administration. We all know that great private businesses everywhere in the world are organized upon the principle of a comparatively small body which legislates and determines policy (the board of directors), and that this body elects a chief executive to exercise full authority and undivided responsibility. There seems no good reason why the plan which is universally employed in private business, and which is the only plan that works, should not, with necessary modifications of detail, be applied to public business. And there is ample experience in the history of other municipalities to sustain that conclusion.

APPROPRIATE TIME FOR SETTLEMENT

"We respectfully submit that a special session, if one be held, and especially when held under the stress of war and the resulting necessity and demand for economy in all directions, affords a peculiarly appropriate opportunity for dealing with this question, and we believe that the voters and taxpayers are not likely to approve action by their representatives at this time involving further taxation and increased public expenditure unless it is accompanied by a full and satisfactory program for future economy and efficiency."

The letter was sent on January 26 to Alderman W. F. Lipps, chairman of the joint committee, and was signed by Joseph Cummins.

M. V. L. Endorses Plan

The Municipal Voters' League in its annual pre-primary review of aldermanic activities, made public last week, also urges the program outlined in the committee's letter. It says in part:

"A recognition of the need of reorganization of local government is a forward step which might appropriately be followed by effective action at the proposed special session, if one be held. There would seem to be no reason except political ones why the special session should not deal with the matter comprehensively so as to afford the city relief from enormous election expenses and create an executive organization for the city that would correspond with sound business practice, and that should and probably would eliminate much of the waste and inefficiency resulting from the present political administration of the executive departments."

Budget Is Due

The City Council, as this Bulletin goes to press, is about to vote upon the municipal budget for 1918. If it adopts the recommendations of the Finance Committee, it will bring about a number of very important administrative changes recommended by civic organizations, in addition to those already put into effect by the Council. The proposed changes are:

1. Elimination of ward lines in administration of bureau of streets.
2. Centralization of city purchasing, testing, inspection and stores.
3. Reduction in the number of sinecures in the law department. A number of "investigators" are dropped from the payroll.

Changes which the City Council has already put into effect are the elimination of ten unnecessary police stations, the abolition of extra holidays, such as primary and election days, and the establishment of an eight-hour day for city hall employes. The proposal to centralize payroll divisions in

Continued on page 55

Saving the Next Generation —New Zealand's Experience

ALREADY statesmen are beginning to learn that if the nations of the world are to maintain their efficiency after the war, they must be less wasteful of child life than in the easy-going peace times before 1914. The terrible decimation of man-power in the war must sooner or later arouse them to a consciousness of their dependence upon the next generation. Reports that Germany is sanctioning so-called "lateral marriages" as a means of encouraging her birth rate are only an extreme illustration of the recognition of this dependence. Everywhere the necessity of protecting motherhood, of reducing the number of preventable deaths among children and of conserving the vitality of those who pass the critical period of infancy, is beginning to filter into the consciousness of nations. England feels this and has called from New Zealand, to institute infant welfare work there, the man who is chiefly responsible for making New Zealand the safest place in the world for babies.

The experience of a country which can lay claim to such a record is worth learning about. New Zealand's death rate for children under one year of age is fifty per thousand; Chicago's is from 100 to 106 per thousand. Even fifty babies are worth saving, and if this could be multiplied for every thousand babies born here in a year, Chicago would be well paid for instituting a real baby saving campaign.

New Zealand's pre-eminence as a safe place for babies is the result of hard sustained effort—not of accident. The campaign of child-saving was under the direction of Dr. F. Truby King, whom England is now drafting for a similar enterprise. Dr. King is traveling to his new field by way of the United States, and the City Club was fortunately able to arrange for a meeting with him last Wednesday and to hear his story.

Those who expected to learn from Dr. King of some new sleight-of-hand by which New Zealand turned the trick were disappointed. *Education,* universal education of motherhood, so far as that could be brought about by a vigorous and strongly supported

Continued on page 56

FUEL ORDER MAY CLOSE PLANTS

Deputy Fuel Administrator Says Priority
Clause   May   Shut   Down   Industrials

"IF the present fuel situation continues, somebody will have to do without coal," said Earl Dean Howard, Deputy Fuel Administrator for Illinois, in an address at the City Club, Friday, February 1st. "The saving in coal by the shut-downs of business ordered by the Fuel Administration has been offset by the lesser production and the transportation difficulties owing to adverse weather conditions. In January we lost nearly a week's production of the Illinois mines.

To Distribute Burden

"The orders of the Fuel Administration were made so as to distribute the sacrifice as equitably as possible. If the existing conditions had been allowed to continue somebody would have had to do without coal anyway, many plants would have had to close down and the domestic consumer—particularly the poor—would have suffered. We will get back to normal conditions as soon as the safety of the domestic consumer is assured.

"Probably the most important feature of the fuel order, and the one least understood, is the priority section, by which the order of delivery is determined. It may be necessary to shut off the shipments to industrials until the more necessary demands of other consumers are filled."

Why Coal is Short

The coal shortage, Mr. Howard said, is due to a variety of causes, namely:

1. Inadequate transportation. Fuel cannot be stored at the mines; it must be loaded directly into cars. There has been a continuous wail from the coal producers that they couldn't get cars. Investigations seem to indicate that there have been enough cars, but that they were not moved fast enough. The railroads were in a tangle. If the routing of cars had been rationalized, Mr. Howard said, it is probable that the fuel administration would have been unnecessary except as a regulator of prices.

2. Inadequate coal reserves. One reason for this was that dealers last summer were advised to wait until prices were fixed before placing their orders. So at the time when coal is ordinarily being stocked up, but little was moving.

3. Unusually large consumption, partly on account of the extreme weather conditions, and partly, in the case of industries, on account of the increased production due to the war.

Diverted from Chicago

4. Diversion of coal from Chicago to other points. Chicago coal consumption has been adapted largely to the burning of smokeless coal, Pocahontas from the West Virginia mines and anthracite, also from Eastern fields. This involves a cross-haul, with incidental congestion and delay. The government is trying to eliminate this cross-haul. It is a question of whether this eastern coal should be retained in the east for supplying our shipping or sent west to Chicago. The former, of course, means a sacrifice on Chicago's part, for our furnaces have been adapted to other than Illinois coal, which is uneconomical and smoke producing.

There has also been a diversion of coal from Illinois fields to other points—never before supplied. This has been done upon orders from Washington, so there is no help for it. Shipments of anthracite from the east have been seized by the government.

Should Have Been Plan

Much of the shortage, Prof. Howard contended, could have been avoided if attention had been paid to warnings and an adequate plan worked out for meeting the emergency. "This is one thing," Mr. Howard said, "that we must learn from our enemy—the importance of anticipating emergencies and planning for them."

The local situation was made more acute, Mr. Howard said, by the lack of authority of the local officials of the fuel administration. When the big storm came, it was evident that, if an effort were made to move the cars containing coal to the consignees, it would be days, in the face of the bad weather conditions, before deliveries could be made. Mr. Durham, the county administrator, according to Mr. Howard, did a courageous and revolutionary act, and saved the situation. He decided, with the assurance of the coal dealers that they would back him up, to disregard the claims of the owners and pool the coal supply. He had no legal authority to do this, but the thing was done and on the next day the coal was moving on the streets.

The Illinois fuel administration, Mr. Howard said, was in a very difficult position after the Garfield order owing to the necessity of interpreting the order—e. g., in cases where several kinds of business were conducted in the same place—and the lack of any such authority. The administration assumed the authority but labored under the difficulty of having conflicting interpretations come from Washington, perhaps several days after a decision had been made.

Mr. Howard made a plea for economy in the use of coal. "Every man who has coal which he can't use before March," he said, "ought to be sent back to the dealer. It is pretty certain that before March there will be enough. If well-to-do people would recognize that the coal they get from dealers today is taken away from the poorer wards, there would be less clamor to have their orders filled."

Contract System Is Obstacle

The contract system of supplying coal, Mr. Howard asserted, is one of the chief difficulties in the way of a satisfactory handling of the situation. In times past, if there was shortage, the price would be raised and consumption would decline. Those who relied for deliveries upon the open market and couldn't afford the higher prices, or who did have the right connections with the dealer—usually the less prosperous customers—would not be able to get coal. It was seen that under present conditions such a system would not be satisfactory, and it was to meet the new situation that the Fuel Administration was organized.

Dr. J. R. Gerstley has received a commission as First Lieutenant in the Medical Reserve Corps.

Francis W. Parker is in France in Y. M. C. A. work.

H. C. L. Increases Charity Burden

SIXTEEN public and private relief and personal service agencies had a meeting at the City Club the other day to talk things over among themselves and to find out why it is so hard to keep swimming these days. Eugene T. Lies, general superintendent of the United Charities, reported some very illuminating facts which he had uncovered by inquiries among these agencies. They had spent last year for *material relief* alone—this does not cover a great many other very important activities—$900,000. Nine-tenths of a million dollars is a big amount of money, but the interesting fact is that *one-fourth* of this, $225,000, is chargeable—not to increased activities—but simply to the increased *cost* of necessities of life.

Inability on the part of hundreds of families to meet war prices on peace incomes, Mr. Lies said, is reported to be the cause of many applications for aid. The cost of relief supplies has mounted 25 per cent to 35 per cent within the year.

No Able Bodied Adults

"It is a striking fact," said Mr. Lies, "that practically no able bodied adult men are found in the poor families that are being dealt with by the distinctly relief agencies, and this has been true for a year. The fit men are at work but there are plenty of unfit men in these poverty stricken homes."

The relief organizations of the city want to carry out this year a big offensive against poverty and its allied social ills. For this they need a larger army of workers and plenty of ammunition. Several agencies, if funds were available, would add more visiting housekeepers just now when food conservation and proper food preparation are matters of special importance.

A Menace to National Vigor

"Behind the simple appeal for food and fuel," said Mr. Lies, "there are usually found conditions which menace the vigor of the nation. They are illness, unemployment, accident, inefficiency, exploitation and injustice, personal delinquency, carelessness, bad housing, intemperance, low wages, maladjustment to prevailing conditions, child labor, misery, hopelessness, feeble-mindedness, old age, sheer misfortune, deaths of breadwinners.

"To work out the oft times complicated problems, the enlightened agencies realize that they must give more than material relief. . . . They know they must get away from wholesale, stereotyped ways of dealing with the poor and apply individual cures, each to fit as accurately as possible the ascertained difficulty. Trained personal service among the poor is needed pre-eminently at this time of distraction and stress.

"Furthermore, enlightened relief agencies of Chicago realize clearly enough that the cost of looking after the destitute is great, but they know also that any radical reduction in that cost can come only if the causes of poverty are attended to. They stand for prevention, but they also believe that while there is want and misery in our midst, there is called for an application of wise sympathy, relief and personal service."

THE ASSIGNMENTS of club members for duty on Soldiers and Sailors days, next Saturday and Sunday, are as follows:

Saturday, February 16, Morris L. Greeley, V. M. Gaspar, Dr. Bayard Holmes, J. B. Freeman, J. B. Weart.

Sunday, February 17, E. F. Hiller, James Melville Hart, H. J. Kaufman, Richard Pride, Julian Roe, N. T. Yeomans.

SHALL WE CORK THE BOTTLE?

What shall we do with old King Booze? Shall he go the way of the Romanoffs and the Hohenzollerns— not yet but soon—or will he be allowed to maintain a mild sort of sway under strict constitutional limitations? George Sikes and Oliver L. Stewart will go on the mat on this subject next Saturday at luncheon. Members who like a good boxing match will be there to see. Mr. Stewart is an old-time heavy weight champion for the drys. He wants to give King Alcohol the "knock-out absolute." George Sikes, as everybody around the City Club knows, is something of a fighter himself. He thinks there are things to be said on the other side. By mutual arrangement of the fighters, no brass knucks will be used.

Members who want to increase the cheering for their side may bring their wives.

Remember the date—next Saturday at luncheon.

Continued from page 52

the comptroller's office, endorsed by the Public Expenditures Committee of the City Club, was referred to the efficiency staff of the Finance Committee with instructions to work out a plan.

The Finance Committee has also approved the policy of water metering fathered by the Chicago Bureau of Public Efficiency, whose report on the subject was reviewed in the Bulletin several weeks ago, and has requested the City Engineer and the Bureau of Efficiency to prepare tentative ordinances for putting such a system into effect. If the metering policy is finally adopted, the Bureau contends it will make unnecessary the construction of the proposed $3,500,000 William Hale Thompson pumping station and other such stations, cribs, tunnels, etc., for a long time to come.

ROUMANIA

DR. H. GIDEON WELLES who speaks on "Roumania" at the "Club" day luncheon next Thursday, spent several months in that unfortunate war-stricken country as a member of the Red Cross Commission. He was there on an errand similar to that of Dr. Frank Billings in Russia, whose interesting account of conditions there our members had the good fortune to hear several weeks ago.

Dr. Welles is a distinguished scientist, professor of pathology and dean in medical work at the University of Chicago and Director of Medical Research for the Sprague Memorial Institute.

He has a large collection of slides to help his hearers visualize the conditions which he describes.

MONEY MAGIC

Have you given Chicago's financial difficulties up as too badly scrambled for any outsider to understand? We hope not, for next Wednesday evening the Woman's City Club is to have a meeting, to which we are all invited, at which six of the City Council's financial experts will endeavor to unscramble this complex situation for the benefit of those present. If you enjoy seeing a magician pick a white rabbit from a high hat, you will be interested in seeing the city fathers trying to produce several million dollars from—apparently—nowhere. And it is important to you that the million dollars should be produced and that you should know whether it is to come from new taxes or from economies which the city might make if it would.

The speakers are Aldermen John A. Richert, chairman of the Finance Committee; William F. Lipps, chairman of the special joint committee of the City Council and the legislature which has been trying to solve the city's financial troubles; A. A. McCormick, John C. Kennedy, Oliver L. Watson and Otto Kerner.

The meeting is to be at our clubhouse and we are invited. If we come to dinner, which is at 6:00 o'clock, we will get one of the chef's best dinners, for only a dollar. Please reserve. The speaking is at 7:00.

Continued from page 52

campaign, backed in part by government money, has been responsible for her success.

The education of mothers in New Zealand, according to Dr. King, has not been confined to the poor. It is of even more national importance, he argued, that the self-reliant and better-off nine-tenths of the population should be properly educated in these matters than that submerged tenth should be taken care of—however important from a humanitarian standpoint that may be. There must be a higher conception of maternity among those classes capable of spreading it throughout the community.

The educational campaign in New Zealand took the form of direct instruction, lectures, popularly written pamphlets on the care and feeding of children, newspaper publicity, e. g., a weekly column in the newspapers throughout the island, having a combined circulation of about a million. Every agency in New Zealand was working harmoniously toward the end of bettering the conditions of life for the children.

The methods which worked so successfully in New Zealand ought to produce good results in the United States, Dr. King said, although there are special difficulties on account of the size of the country and the heterogeneous character of the population. New Zealand's experience ought to be well considered by the social agencies of the country.

The City Club Bulletin

Published Weekly by the City Club of Chicago

A Journal of Active Citizenship

VOLUME XI   MONDAY, FEBRUARY 18, 1918   NUMBER 7

War-Stricken Roumania Is "Club Day" Topic

We have heard very little of internal conditions in Roumania since her disastrous entrance into the war. Occasionally we hear of conflicts with the bolsheviki and of possibilities of a separate peace with Germany but we have little notion the background of conditions prevailing there.

Dr. H. Gideon Wells, who speaks on "Roumania" at the "Club Day" luncheon next Thursday, spent several months in that unfortunate, war-stricken country as a member of the Red Cross Commission. He was there on an errand similar to that of Dr. Frank Billings in Russia, whose interesting account of conditions there our members had the good fortune to hear several weeks ago.

Dr. Wells is a distinguished scientist, professor of pathology and dean in medical work at the University of Chicago. He has a large collection of slides.

THIS WEEK'S EVENTS

Thursday, Feb. 21, at Luncheon— "Club Day"

What I Saw in Roumania (*Illustrated*)

DR. H. GIDEON WELLS, University of Chicago, Member American Red Cross Mission to Russia.

Saturday, Feb. 23, at Luncheon— Ladies' Day

The Revolutionary Aims of the Jugo-Slavs—and the Cause of the Allies.

DR. H. HINKOVIĆ, Ex-member Croatian Parliament and Member of the Jugo-Slav Committee of London.

Luncheon from 11:30   Speaking at 1:00

Austrian Disruption Threatened by Subjects

The President's "peace" offensive makes doubly important just now the possibility of a disintegration of Austria through the breaking away of her subject peoples. The chance of a revolution by the Jugo-Slavic population of Austria, composed of Serbians, Croatians and Slovenians, looms large as a possible factor of great importance in the outcome of the war.

Dr. H. Hinkovic, formerly a member of the Croatian Parliament and of the Servian War Mission to America and now a member of the Jugo-Slav Committee of London, is to be a guest of the Club at luncheon next Saturday and is to forecast the probabilities of a revolt by the Jugo-Slavic peoples. Dr. Hinkovic helped to draw the new declaration of Croatia for union with Serbia and Slovenia.

Don't miss this! Ladies' Day!

The City Club Bulletin
A Journal of Active Citizenship

PUBLISHED WEEKLY BY THE
CITY CLUB OF CHICAGO
315 Plymouth Court   Telephone: Harrison 8278
DWIGHT L. AKERS, Editor

OFFICERS OF THE CLUB
FRANK I. MOULTON, President
EDGAR A. BANCROFT, Vice-President
ROY C. OSGOOD, Treasurer
CHARLES YEOMANS, Secretary
GEORGE E. HOOKER, Civic Secretary

EDITORIAL BOARD
HERBERT H. SMITH, Chairman
FREDERICK D. BRAMHALL   S. R. WATKINS
C. COLTON DAUGHADAY   PAUL R. WRIGHT

$1.00 per Year   -   -   -   10c per Copy

Entered as second class matter, December 3, 1917,
at the postoffice at Chicago, Illinois, under the act of
March 3, 1879.

> The purpose of the Club is to bring together in
> informal association those men who are genuinely
> interested in the improvement of the political,
> social and economic conditions of the community
> in which we live.

The City Club "Liberty Loaf" is a triumph of baker's art.

So much superior is it to the ordinary "baker's bread" that requests have come to the House Committee from members to be allowed to buy it for home use.

Members may purchase the "Liberty Loaf" by ordering it from the cashier a day in advance.

Prices according to size

THE LISTENING POST

THESE MEN HAVE JUST JOINED the Club: Nathan C. Rockwood, Editor "Rock Products"; Charles E. Reed, Assistant Secretary War Recreation Board, State Council of Defense; J. M. Simpson, Lamson Bros. (Brokers); D. H. Ellsworth, Chandler, Hildreth & Co. (Brokers); H. A. Stark, Secretary W. S. Bogle & Co. (Coal); James E. Greenebaum, Greenebaum Sons' Bank & Trust Co.; J. W. Ryan, Accountant, Lyon & Gary Co. (Bankers); John Coenen, Chief Clerk and Superintendent, Chicago Great Western R. R. Co. We are very glad to welcome these men into membership.

WEDDING BELLS RANG on Saturday, February 9, for James Max Hart. He married Miss Gertrude Foreman.

CAPTAIN CHARLES E. MERRIAM, of the Aviation Examining Board, is stationed at present at Camp Beauregard, Alexandria, La.

GUY L. JONES has been promoted from First Lieutenant to Captain of Field Artillery. He is commanding a motor company of the 311th ammunition train.

THE WARTIME COMMITTEE has inaugurated a series of Sunday evening parties at which some of the fundamental war problems are being talked over. The subject assigned for yesterday evening's discussion was "How can the President's Political Offensive be made more Effective."

ERNEST L. BALLARD left for France last week to take charge of the operation of a line of railroad between a port and a military base. He had just completed his volunteer service as attorney for the City Club's Milk Committee. Prior to his departure, President F. I. Moulton, for the directors, wrote him a letter of appreciation. "The chairman of our committee," Mr. Moulton said, "speaks in the highest terms of your skill and tireless devotion in this exacting piece of work and of its decisive influence in the case. I congratulate you upon the splendid undertaking upon which you are about to enter."

(Continued on page 64)

John Masefield Talks on War

"IMAGINE a strip of earth thirty miles wide by four hundred and fifty miles long. It is without any green, growing life, just a brown strip of dead earth. From an aeroplane it looks like a lunar picture. It is spotted with gigantic holes, which fill up with water and look like the eyes of dead men staring upward. Scattered about are broken men, dead mules, smashed rifles, unexploded shells, bits of iron and other litter in the utmost confusion. Here and there are little piles of brick which mark the spots where once were human habitations. One big town which I visited was so completely gone that the oldest inhabitant could not have told where any dwelling had been.

SIGHTS AND SOUNDS UNHOLY

"There are endless sounds of explosions and of hissings like steam. And with every 'bang' a column of yellow or green smoke rises and dances in the air. At night the sky is lit up with flashes and a red haze. You know that you are among men because of the fighting. But you don't see any men. If you go along you will come presently to a gash in the earth in which are strange men in gas masks, who call on you and ask you for news of the war."

This is the French front as described to members of the City Club last Wednesday by John Masefield, English poet of the seas and author of "Gallipoli" and "The Old Front Line." The readers of "Dauber" and "Salt Sea Ballads" were not disappointed, for Mr. Masefield's address was sprinkled with the brilliant descriptions which they expected and bedecked with anecdotes of one of England's best writers of narrative.

THIS "LOVELY" WAR

How do the men in the trenches like their jobs? "It is attractive to them in various ways," said Mr. Masefield. "Many of those who return to England want to go back after a time. The sense of comradeship with men whom they know would be ready to die for them is particularly uplifting. And there is always something going on—often something very romantic. The war is very delightful to adventurous young men." "I don't know what I'll do when this *lovely* war is over," he quoted an English soldier, "I've enjoyed every minute of it."

Mr. Masefield praised particularly the bravery of the carriers. "Nearly everything needed in the front line," he said, "has to be carried by hand—across the mud. That mud is at times more terrible even than quicksand. Many who have tried to cross it have been actually swallowed up. Crossing it with a heavy load under fire is even worse than standing in the trenches for *there* at least is some protection."

THE THREE "D's"

"The war is damned dull, damned dirty and damned dangerous" is a soldier's phrase quoted by Mr. Masefield. "You may become a casualty at any time," he said. "A shell may drop on you at any minute, or you may hear a little bird's piping that turns out to be a bullet or you may lie in a trench and listen to a whirring two or three miles overhead until you hear a crash—or maybe you don't hear it. You may be killed accidently back of the lines by an unexploded bomb or shell. There are many of these scattered about and the soldiers gather them and build fires under them just to make them go 'bang.' "

LIES AGAINST THE ENGLISH

"The enemy, not being able to beat us in the field, has spread many lies about us," said Mr. Masefield. "He has said that we are slothful, decadent people, with no conception of state service. The answer is that 5,400,000 men volunteered for army service, not including three million more who were rejected as too old, needed elsewhere or disqualified for some other reason.

"The enemy has also said that we are letting others fight for us. England could have kept out of the war but she went in and has lost two and a half million of her best men in killed, wounded and missing. She is to-day holding a third of the line in France, about a fourth of the line in Italy, most of the line in Serbia and all of the

line in Mesopotamia. The charge that we
have let the colonials do all the fighting is
untrue. We know how magnificently they
have done their part, but for one Colonial
who has been killed nine Englishmen have
died.

Is America Starving?

"They say that we are asking America to
starve so that we may be well fed. I have
searched in vain here for any evidence of
starvation. England has had practically
no white bread for a year. The submarine
menace, however, cannot beat us. The land
in England is being so cultivated that even
if the submarine should double or treble
its effectiveness they could not starve us.

"They charge that we will profit from
the war. No belligerent country will
profit. But we will have saved our own
souls and we will have learned that all
mankind is one body and ought not to be
split into a number of competing bodies.
If we have learned that lesson the war
will have been worth while.

England's Sacrifice

"I know my nation's faults and I believe they are faults of the head and not
the heart. There is a graveyard in France
a hundred and thirty miles long where
lie thousands of simple Englishmen who
have died in every conceivable kind of
agony. Many of the graves are unmarked.
These men didn't know what Belgium is
or Germany is but only that one big country
had taken another little country by the
throat. And they went out into the mud
and died by the thousands, by the million.
They went to help their fellowmen in
trouble and were here by their own
choice."

Mr. Masefield mentioned among the
causes of the war, the irresponsible auto-
crat, the adventurous spirit, the lack of understanding between nations and the self
interest of those who profit commercially
from war. "It should be our aim," said
Mr. Masefield, "to provide against the possibility of any more wars on this scale. I
don't know whether we can hope to abolish
war altogether. There is always evil in
the world and wherever it exists there will
be free men who will take it by the throat
and say, 'You shall not do that—My God,
You shall not do that!'

"The evil things of the world have
proved not to be inevitable but simply results of obsolete thinking. Only a little

while ago, there were pirates on the seas
and yellow fever ports. The pirates were
hunted from the seas and the scientists
have hunted down the yellow fever. There
is practically nothing that men cannot do
if they have the mind and the will.

"Man's inventions have outgrown his
social institutions. After the war, the nations must set to work to reorganize their
social institutions. If there is another great
war, civilization may cease for with the
progress of science within the next twenty
or thirty years a nation may be able to
destroy another by touching a button. After this war, we will know that the evil of
the war is a grim devil which eats the nation wholesale. I speak for the common
man and woman whose blood and tears
pay for the war. I have seen the bodies
of French, English, Turkish and German
soldiers lying out in the rain and I know
that every one had some woman weeping
for him. It is because man still suffers
from the war fever.

"When this war ends, I hope that the
three countries which have done the most
for democracy, your country, France, and
my country will have the deciding voice
as to the way in which the spirit of man
shall grow in the years to come. I hope
that they may be able to work together to
make a social system that will be worthy of
man's place in the universe."

Watch the Bulletin every Tuesday
for news of all affairs at the Club.

Speak to the other men at your
luncheon table. You'll feel better—and so
will they.

"TALK DAY" LUNCHES

Here's another forward step in the
City Club dining room!

The House Committee announces
that on "talk days" hereafter, instead
of a set 60c lunch, lunches at 40c, 50c
and 60c, with a wide selection a la
carte will be served.

On occasions when an usually
large attendance is expected, a set
lunch will be served as heretofore in
order to expedite the service.

And don't forget that all these
lunches are of the new kind the City
Club is now serving.

ROUT RED PLAGUE IN ARMY

*Fighting Efficiency Increased and Citizenship Im-
proved by Protection of Soldiers' Leisure Hours*

A T Camp Funston, among 32,000 men, a month ago there were but six cases of venereal disease contracted within thirty days. At army posts in peace times the number of such cases have ranged from 240 to 350 for every thousand men. "There has been a greater social step forward in ten months in the American army," asserted Allen D. Albert, who gave these facts in his City Club address, February 8, "than has been taken by all the other armies of the world in four thousand years." Mr. Albert, formerly president of the International Association of Rotary Clubs, represents the War and Navy Department Commissions on Training Camp Activities. He had just completed a tour of the camps.

WITH AID OF SCIENCE

"Venereal contagion," said Mr. Albert, "has usually produced a greater loss in physical efficiency than all the other forms of disease combined." He ascribes the remarkable accomplishment of the new National Army to the present effort by the United States "to employ modern social science to develop and increase the power of our thrust against the Germans." In the effort the President and the Secretaries of War and of the Navy aimed:

"First. To increase the efficiency of our armies by reducing the 'sag,' particularly the loss of time and spirit through venereal contagion.

"Second. To return the men to civil life symmetrically benefited by military training; and

"Third. To fulfill the special responsibility of the government to families of the drafted boy."

THE GOVERNMENT'S PROGRAM

The government's program includes both restrictive and positive measures.* On the positive side, the government "has undertaken to provide wholesome recreation under competent leadership within the camp and to produce an effective substitution of American hospitality for the old exploitation of the soldier outside the camp."

*Lack of space forbids an account of the restrictive measures mentioned by Mr. Albert.

Inside the camp, not only are the men better paid, better fed, better washed, better quartered than any other army in history, but a variety of recreation is provided, so "the day is filled with rounded, balanced, wholesome employment and comes to its close with boys admirably disposed for dreamless sleep."

EDUCATION IN CAMPS

"Among the million and a quarter of men with the colors three months ago, it is probable that there were 72,000 who could not read or write a sentence in any language. Most of these boys are now learning to read and write English. There are probably 60,000 boys, not largely the same group of illiterates, who do not know English. These are all learning the speech of their government, and literally scores of thousands of boys are learning colloquial French."

THE SOLDIER ON LEAVE

Outside the camps, difficulties were greater: "One day's leave," said Mr. Albert, "may undo all the gain in physical efficiency produced by unparalleled expenditures of time and money in the camp." To offset this possibility "the uniform must be accepted as an evidence of unusually good conduct; the soldier must be given abundant opportunity for grown-up, whole-hearted masculine relaxation not destructive in quality; good women must deliberately and tactfully substitute themselves for the old corrupting associations; the communities close to the camps must enter upon a program of social enterprise reflecting the most advanced methods of supervised public recreation.

"In nearly every city which is the focus of interest for one of the new camps these amazing results have been achieved: Not one of the forty-six larger towns now has a red light district; clubs have been builded; swimming pools opened; dances organized; open-air games arranged; dinners given in churches, clubs, schools, and hundreds of thousands of private homes; theatre parties given; welcomes sustained at stations; families of officers given suitable rooms; 'town' turned from a place of maddening roar and personal insignificance into a place of helpfulness and hospitality."

The activities are encouraged by the War and Navy Commissions in Training Camp Activities who work through specialists of the American Playground Association. "They have wrought wonders," said Mr. Albert, "in pioneering work of almost baffling difficulties."

A TEST OF SUCCESS

The success of the work is evident from a comparison of results at camps where the activities are not so well organized. At a small station located near a town of about 125,000, not well organized, there have been among 1,800 boys twenty times as many new cases of venereal disease within the same months as among the 32,000 at Camp Funston.

ARE WE PROUD OF THIS?

The work inside the camps has been more generously supported than that outside. Sixty million dollars has been subscribed for the former; only $4,000,000 for the latter. "Two jurisdictions in the Union have been unhappily conspicuous," said Mr. Albert, "for making those who do the work within their borders pay the cost of it also and for permitting citizens of other jurisdictions to pay for the care of their boys in camp elsewhere. These two jurisdictions are Illinois and Chicago." The War Recreation Board is now campaigning to raise $500,000 for this work in Illinois.

Mr. Albert congratulated the City Club upon the work which it is doing in opening its club house to soldiers and sailors at the week ends.

LOOK IN THE elevator for the announcement of committee meetings.

"WHEATLESS DAYS" strike no terror to the hearts of Club members. The Club's baker makes wheat substitutes that make your mouth water.

DO YOU FILE YOUR COPY of the Bulletin? Why not keep it as a record of social work in Chicago? If you wish, the Bulletin Office—phone Harrison 8278—will reserve another copy for you, one each week for the small sum of 50 cents. Please pay in advance. Money may be left with the Club cashier when you pay your check.

MUNITION WORKERS RISK DEATH

Insidious Poisons Prey Upon the Makers
of High Explosives, Says Dr. Hamilton

IN the days of real sport, before the "Sane Fourth" became a national institution, small boys used to make the early morning hideous with toy cannon. The writer of these lines had one made from the barrel of an old pistol and mounted in a heavy block of wood. Loaded with powder and paper wadding and exploded by a firecracker fuse, it made a glorious racket under the windows of unpatriotic would-be-sleepers. From this cannon he derived his first knowledge of high explosives, closing one brilliant holiday with a face full of black powder and a visit to the doctor. Gunpowder has always remained to him the most dangerous and effective of all high explosives. When Dr. Alice Hamilton, at the City Club, February 9, told of the new forms of explosives by which the Allies and the Kaiser are trying to blow each other off the map, he wondered what would have happened to him if his cannon had a charge of "trinitrotoluol," picric acid or "dinitrobenzine."

THE REAL "SAMMY-BACKERS"

Dr. Hamilton has been going about as a representative of Uncle Sam among the places in this country where the explosives are made, to find out how the men and women behind the "man behind the front" are faring. She was commissioned to inquire, not about accidents from these explosives, but about the more insidious and quite as terrible results through poisoning. On this mission she visited nearly every high explosive plant in the United States.

Before the war, Dr. Hamilton said, we manufactured in this country only gunpowder, nitroglycerin and fulminate of mercury. None of these in the process of manufacture is very dangerous, although workers in nitroglycerin plants may have so-called "powder headaches" and workers with fulminate of mercury in cartridge plants may be affected with a sort of itch. It is among the explosives which we started to manufacture after the beginning of the war that the really terrible poisons occur.

Here are some of the facts as Dr. Hamilton gave them:

All of these explosives are nitrated compounds. In some of the higher explosives, 100 per cent nitric acid is used. In the making of guncotton, for instance, the chief danger is from the orange or nitrous fumes. If the worker breathes these too deeply his lungs become blistered and he may be actually drowned in his own fluids. Or he may contract pneumonia. The effect of breathing nitrous fumes is similar to the "gassing" of the men in the trenches, but the fumes are not so choking and the effects are not always apparent immediately.

The guncotton may be converted to smokeless powder. Women are employed in this process. The worker may get a so-called "ether-jag," may become hysterical, laughing, quarrelling, then drowsy. He is allowed to sleep it off. There are no other effects.

DEATH MADE EASY

The chief high explosive used by the French is picric acid. We make quantities of this. It can be made so simply that in some of the largest plants only the crudest equipment is used; it may be made in open pots and the workers subjected to great danger from nitrous fumes. In the better equipped factories, the nitrating takes place in "fume-tight" vessels.

"T. N. T." (trinitrotoluol) is manufactured in closed vessels by the nitrating of "toluol." The danger is not in the manufacturing process but in the loading of the shell. "T. N. T." is a slow poison. Its effects do not appear at once. The British have formulated rules for the protection of "T. N. T." workers, which require caps fitting the head like a helmet, close fitting collars, gloves with gauntlets, etc. Stockings are inspected every morning and others furnished if holes are found. "The application of these rules to American workmen," said Dr. Hamilton, "will be difficult. Can we expect them to work through a hot New Jersey summer dressed in this manner? It is too easy in these times to get other jobs."

The government, Dr. Hamilton said, is endeavoring to bring about better conditions in the explosive plants. It has no power except in the letting of its contracts. A committee appointed by the government and headed by Dr. W. A. Evans of Chicago has formulated standards, but if these are to be effective they must be supervised. It is the intention of the committee to have the inspection done by the federal Public Health Service.

Many women are working in explosive plants. "There is no reason," said Dr. Hamilton, "why they should not be employed there on an equality with men, except in positions which would be more harmful to them than to men. They are more susceptible to lead poisoning for instance, but not more susceptible to nitrous fumes."

Dr. Hamilton is now making a second survey of conditions. New plants are going up all the time, she said, and the work of education must be repeated with each new establishment.

THE LISTENING POST

(*Continued from page 58*)

PROFESSOR JAMES A. FIELD, according to press reports, left Washington recently with the Shipping Commission appointed to study British methods and is on his way to England. Professor Field has been in Washington since October, aiding the Shipping Board in the collection of statistics on the ship building industry.

LEWIS C. CONANT, Quartermaster, Camp Paul Jones, Great Lakes, was a visitor at the Club Saturday, February 2nd. Subsequently we found this note in the Listening Post Book:

I wish to express my appreciation of the marked hospitality and thoughtfulness your club has shown toward myself and others in the United States Navy.

LEWIS C. CONANT.

NOT ALL THE SAILOR BOYS who come here Saturdays and Sundays are just learning to get their sea legs.

John W. Israel of Nashville, Tenn., one of our guests on several occasions, has been a sailor for many years, has served aboard French and Italian square rigged ships, was shipwrecked on the Portuguese coast in an Italian bark, served for a time in the British navy and until recently, injured by the recoil of a gun during target practice, has been in the U. S. convoy service on the destroyer *Chester* and the cruiser *Charleston*. He tells a stirring tale of an engagement with a German submarine while he was a gun captain on the *Charleston*. He is now on the naval reserve ship *Commodore* awaiting examination for re-enlistment in the navy.

OUR "WASHINGTON COLONY" seems to have trouble in getting the right sort of "smokes." Ed McCarty, who manages the cigar department of the Club, has received this letter from Clarence J. Perfitt, who is with the U. S. Shipping board, acknowledging the filling of an order for his special brand:

"Thank you so much for your promptness in complying with my request for my 'real' cigarettes.

"I hope that Sergt. Vance read my letter to you as this explained my situation here in Washington. It's truly a wonderful city at this time and makes you violently aware of the fact that war is on in earnest. My work as secretary for the Department of Health and Sanitation under the direction of my superior officer, Major Doane, promises great interest in the near future.

"If you think that the H. C. L. is high in Chicago you should try it in Washington. Restaurant prices here make the Blackstone look like an automat. *How I miss the good old City Club with its little comforts and conveniences.*"

Club Committee Calendar

Tuesday, Feb. 19 to Monday, Feb. 25.

Tuesday—
Public Utilities Committee . . 12:30
Wednesday—
Editorial Board 12:00
House Committee 12:15
Wartime Committee 12:30
Friday—
Admissions Committee 1:00
Saturday—
Education Committee 12:30
Monday—
Public Affairs Committee . . 1:00

The City Club Bulletin

Published Weekly by the City Club of Chicago

A Journal of Active Citizenship

VOLUME XI   MONDAY, FEBRUARY 25, 1918   NUMBER 8

Will He Tell Us How?

"Win the Next War Now" is the title which Prof. Theodore G. Soares has given to the address which he is to make before the City Club at luncheon next Wednesday. Killing two birds with one stone is something of a feat, but winning two wars —this one and the next—simultaneously, sounds almost like the Arabian Nights.

Prof. Soares has written several books, contributed many articles to periodicals and has lectured extensively throughout the country. Last week he was a principal speaker at the conference of the Council of National Service. He is not only a brilliant speaker but a man whose thinking on affairs of the day is particularly sane and vital. He is professor of religious education at the University of Chicago.

The title which Prof. Soares has given to his address indicated that his suggestions have a forward look, that he has constructive ideas for the future to put before us. Our members cannot afford to miss this significant address.

DON'T EAT YOUR LUNCH in silence. Your neighbor is a fine fellow.

"TALK DAY" LUNCHEONS

Wednesday, February 27

"Win the Next War Now"

PROF. THEODORE G. SOARES, University of Chicago

Thursday, February 28

"America's Food Problem in the Great War"

PROF. H. C. SHERMAN, Columbia University

Tuesday, March 5

"With the Serbian Army in the Great Retreat"

MRS. ST. CLAIR STOBART, "The Lady of the Black Horse," Major in the Serbian Army

Fuller notice of Mrs. Stobart's address on page 72

What Science Says

The war has lifted the discussion of food problems out of the technical high-brow press and the women's magazines and put it on the front pages of the daily newspapers. In the old days, when Providence and the grocery man supplied flour, sugar and meat regularly and without stint, we were satisfied to leave food science to the housewives and the professors. But now everybody has become interested in this most vital of subjects.

The City Club has arranged for an address on this subject at luncheon next Thursday by H. C. Sherman, Professor of Food Chemistry at Columbia University, a man who has made the study of food problems his life specialty. Prof. Sherman has conducted nutrition investigations for the United States Agricultural Department. Since 1912 he has been research associate in the Carnegie Foundation.

We have the opportunity of hearing Prof. Sherman through the kindness of the Institute of Medicine of Chicago. He comes to Chicago especially to address that body at a meeting at Recital Hall, Fine Arts Building, on Wednesday evening.

The City Club Bulletin
A Journal of Active Citizenship

The purpose of the Club is to bring together in informal association those men who are genuinely interested in the improvement of the political, social and economic conditions of the community in which we live.

PUBLISHED WEEKLY BY THE

CITY CLUB OF CHICAGO

315 Plymouth Court   Telephone: Harrison 8278

DWIGHT L. AKERS, Editor

OFFICERS OF THE CLUB

FRANK I. MOULTON, President
EDGAR A. BANCROFT, Vice-President
ROY C. OSGOOD, Treasurer
CHARLES YEOMANS, Secretary
GEORGE E. HOOKER, Civic Secretary

EDITORIAL BOARD

HERBERT H. SMITH, Chairman
FREDERICK D. BRAMHALL   S. R. WATKINS
C. COLTON DAUGHADAY   PAUL R. WRIGHT

$1.00 per Year - - - - 10c per Copy

Entered as second class matter, December 3, 1917, at the postoffice at Chicago, Illinois, under the act of March 3, 1879.

THE LISTENING POST

ONE OF THE MEMBERS of the City Club the other day sent in a check for $50 for the fund for the entertainment of soldiers and sailors. Have you forgotten to send in your dollar? More money is needed by the committee for this excellent piece of war work.

SAMUEL A. GREELEY is on his way to the Pacific Coast. He is on an assignment from the government to report on the sanitary condition and the water supply of the ship yards. Mr. Greeley has been a generous contributor of his time and technical ability to the City Club, particularly in matters relating to city planning.

MEMBERS WHO HAVE WIVES, sisters, cousins or friends who would like to come to the Club occasionally on Sundays to sing or play piano accompaniments for soldiers and sailors singing, will confer a favor by notifying C. Yeomans, 231 Institute Place, Superior 9200. Songs should be light in character with English words.

F. H. CENFIELD, chief of the efficiency division of the City Council Finance Committee, has a captain's commission in the army. Mr. Cenfield was a member of the City Club Committee on Public Expenditures.

P. JUNKERSFELD, engaged in directing cantonment, hospital, etc., construction in the war department at Washington under Gen. Littell, has been promoted from Major to Lieut.-Colonel.

HERBERT FLEMING, one of our members, has been appointed secretary of the Illinois Pension Laws Commission. This Commission, of which George E. Hooker is chairman, is making an investigation of the pension systems for public employes in Illinois and will make a report on that subject to the next Illinois Legislature. Mr. Fleming is associated with the accounting firm of Arthur Young & Co. and is editor of the Civil Service News, a weekly publication devoted to the interest of civil service employes. He was formerly on the editorial staff of the Chicago *Daily News,* investigator for the Merriam Commission on City Expenditures and later secretary of the Chicago Civil Service Reform Association.

NEW MEMBERS OF THE CLUB who joined last week were F. A. Newton, Ivan Ringheim, Charles A. Logan, George S. Albaugh, Edwin W. Eisendrath.

Mr. Newton is cashier for Bonright & Co., investment securities. He is a brother of Harold J. Newton, also a member of the Club.

Mr. Ringheim is also in the investment business. He is assistant cashier for Powell, Garard & Co.

Mr. Logan is an attorney, associated with Wilson, Moore & McIlvaine.

Mr. Albaugh is president of the Albaugh-Dover Co.

Mr. Eisendrath is superintendent of the tannery of the Monarch Leather Co.

IF YOU DON'T SEE IT IN THE BULLETIN perhaps it's your fault! Give the editor the benefit of personal, publishable facts about fellow members. There's a box for such items just under the Bulletin Board.

WHEN LUNCHING AT THE CLUB, why not introduce yourself to your neighbor? Be clubby!

PLEAD FOR STARVING RUSSIA

Russian Commissioners Tell of Condition of People in New Republic

HAS Russia gone back economically to medieval times? Her money system has apparently broken down and trade is on a basis of barter. People are starving in the towns because they do not have the manufactured products for which alone the peasants will exchange their grain. This was the message from Russia which was presented to the City Club last Monday by three representatives of the Russian people. They were:

Prof. George Lomonosoff, commissioner from the Milyukoff government to the United States. Prof. Lomonosoff was in charge of Russian ways of communication under the early revolutionary government.

Constantine Fabian, representing the All-Russian Peasants' Council (coöperative societies) and the Moscow District Supply Committee.

Leonidas Vtoroff, representing the All Russian Railway Employes' Union. These men are members of a committee of seven Russians who are endeavoring to procure supplies for the Russian people.

Mr. Fabian and Mr. Vtoroff left Petrograd in November.

"I have been deeply touched," said Prof. Lomonosoff, "when my country has been called treacherous by your newspapers. When Italy broke the Triple Alliance, the Allies applauded, but when my people, bleeding from their many wounds, had to stop we were called traitors.

STARVATION IN PETROGRAD

"In Petrograd there is very little bread to be had and almost no meat or milk. There are only four eggs a month for each child under six years of age. In this country you have three pairs of shoes a year but in Russia there is only one pair of shoes for ten men in a year.

"The ideals of the Revolution are in danger if hunger continues in Russia. If those ideals mean anything to you, you must hurry up. If you fail to help Russia you are pushing her into the arms of Germany and her markets will be taken by the Germans.

"Since President Wilson has spoken, everybody admits that it is right to help Russia, but how? In going into economic relations with Russia, it is not necessary to enter into relations with any particular government. Relations can be established with the strong economic organizations which exist there. President Wilson has suggested on more than one occasion that it is possible to have relations directly with a people rather than with its government. The commodities most needed in Russia now are shoes, agricultural implements and locomotives. Shoes may be sent to the organizations of workmen and peasants and to the supply committees. Agricultural implements can be sent to the agricultural organizations and the locomotives can be sent to the railroads.

THE RISK?

"As to the financial risk: The sooner you help Russia the less will be the risk. But there are times when you don't think of returns. When you talk of helping Belgium or Serbia do you consider the risk?

"Is there danger that your supplies will get to Germany? I can assure you that if you send shoes to Russia they will not get to Germany. You would have to knock the peasants down to take the shoes away from them. The locomotives could not possibly be used on German railways. But suppose Germany does succeed in getting some of these supplies. Would you for a similar reason keep back ammunition from the French because the Germans might capture some of it?

THE KAISER AND TROTZKY

"Forgive my frank words. I believe you are afraid of the Bolsheviki. I am not one of the Bolsheviki, but if I had to choose between William and Trotzky I would choose Trotzky, for I realize that the world is moving in the direction of the Bolsheviki ideals rather than toward those of the Prussian Junkers. The fate not only of the Russian democracy, but of the democracy of the world is in your hands. I am sure the United States will remain true to itself, but you cannot hesitate; you must decide—time does not wait!"

Mr. Fabian explained the organization

of the Moscow District Supply Committee, which he represents. This committee unifies 27 supply districts in central Russia, 16 of them purely agricultural and 11 partly industrial. It endeavors to supply the economic needs of about fifty million people. It arranges for the exchange of agricultural and manufactured products.

A RETURN TO BARTER

"At present," said Mr. Fabian, "it is practically impossible to buy grain for rubles in Russia, for the peasants will not exchange it for money but only for manufactured products. The Moscow District Supply Committee has at its disposal over five hundred million rubles, deposited by the local committee. It has its factories, work-shops and grain mills. It has agents everywhere in Russia to find out where supplies can be had. The committee is an economic and social organization solely. It is popularly organized and non-political.

"It is a mistake to say that Russia does not have grain. She has the grain but does not have the manufactured products which the peasants will take in exchange for it. If America can send us the manufactured products she would thus give bread to the starving people."

Mr. Vtoroff described the organization of the railway employes which he represents. This organization includes superior as well as subordinate employes, and every member has the same rights. It is in control of the Russian transportation system. It provides for the disposition and supply of necessities to its members. It has a common capital and is trying to provide for the needs of every person, officials and workmen. It has its supply committee, stores, etc. Its capital amounts to over two hundred million rubles.

SHALL GERMANS GET FOOD?

"We come not to ask donations," said Mr. Vtoroff. "We ask your help in a difficult moment. You must not let Russia drop into the hands of Germany. Germany's first treaty of peace is with the Ukraine, where there are stores of grain. It is not too late to prevent this grain from getting into the hands of Germany. Germany understands that the Russian peasant will give up his grain only for manufactured products and is promising to provide the peasants with such goods. The Russian market is there and you can take it. You need not worry about the Bol-

sheviki. You can work through the economic social organizations which are able to take up this question."

ORGANIZATIONS NON-POLITICAL

In reply to a question concerning the relation between the Bolshevik government and the economic organizations, all the speakers agreed in saying that the latter have nothing to do with politics, that only by keeping entirely away from politics can they do their work. "The fact that the Bolsheviki had not appointed a minister of transportation," Prof. Lomonosoff said, "indicates that they do not intend to interfere with the transportation system. They understand they had better not meddle with the transportation question and they have turned it over to the railway union."

Prof. Lomonosoff explained the supply committees are made up from all political parties. "There are certain things," he said, "shoes for instance, which the people of all parties need. The committees are made up of Bolsheviki, Mensheviki and all the other 'vikis,' meeting together to obtain for themselves necessities of life."

All the speakers used the Russian language and their addresses were translated to the audience.

Following the address, Mr. Cyrus McCormick, who had lately returned from Russia, took the floor at the suggestion of the chairman. Every American who has gone to Russia, Mr. McCormick said, has come back with a firm faith in Russia. We ought to assist her in every possible way, study the situation and not be too careful about the dollars.

WET-DRY ISSUE DEBATED AT CLUB

Fate of "Demon Rum" Discussed by
Oliver W. Stewart and George C. Sikes

OLIVER W. STEWART and George C. Sikes crossed swords on the Wet-Dry issue at the City Club, Saturday, February 16. It was a skirmish preliminary to the big fight which will occur this spring when the question is submitted to the voters. The subject of the discussion at the City Club was, "Should Chicago and the Nation Go Dry?"

Mr. Stewart assailed the saloon as an outlaw, a breeder of poverty and crime, a waster of national resources in food and fuel at a time of great national emergency. He predicted that the nation would go dry and urged Chicago to get into the bandwagon.

Mr. Sikes did not attempt to defend the saloon. He did, however, charge that the leadership of the "drys" is, in the main, fanatical and intolerant, and that reforms accomplished under the influence of an emotional wave do not represent the sound judgment of the community. The question, after all, he said, is one of administration, and prohibition, even if it is enacted into a constitutional amendment, would be ineffective unless the people are sincerely behind it. The dry leaders in pursuit of their fixed idea, he charged, have been very easy-going in respect to the character of the men whom they have supported for office, going so far at times as to back —perhaps ignorantly—men with crooked political records. They are trying to subvert the principle of home rule and the jury system.

CHEWING GUM AND PRUNES

"If chewing gum or eating prunes conduced to crime, insanity, economic waste and political corruption," said Mr. Stewart, "and if the men engaged in the business of supplying the public with chewing gum or prunes were organized to combat with all their strength any effort to lessen their grip on governmental machinery, this meeting would be discussing the problem of chewing gum or prunes as well as the liquor question."

The statistics of arrests for drunkenness prove nothing as to the results of prohibition, according to Mr. Stewart. They may merely indicate the conditions existing in the police department. Equally unreliable are conclusions drawn from statistics about relative tax rates in "wet" and "dry" communities. "But the average citizen knows," he said, "that 6,000 saloons doing a business sufficiently large to permit each to pay $1,000 for its license, must grind out a grist of drunkenness, industrial and economic waste, crime, distress and misery, which inevitably will cost the community more than the six million dollars it collected in license fees.

POCKET MONEY FOR CHICAGO

"If we assume that the saloons of this city take in but $10,000 apiece, as an average—which would be but $2 an hour running 16 hours out of the 24 and only six days out of seven—the drink bill of this city amounts to more than sixty million dollars per annum. Who is there who believes that it runs much, if any, below 100 million? It is difficult to conceive what it would mean to this city if that money were put into the legitimate channels of trade.

"It may be objected that the law cannot be enforced. The law can be enforced and will be enforced to as great an extent as laws generally are which have to do with vicious and criminal classes. More than that, no man has a right to ask of a prohibition law.

WASTING OUR RESOURCES

"We face a world war, with a food shortage that affects every tribe and clan,— every man, woman and child. No amount of money which the liquor traffic may offer in return for the right to exist, could begin to compensate for the loss of food thus entailed. He is a rash man who would gamble on our chance of winning the war by wasting our grain and food-stuff in the manufacture of alcoholic liquor, at a time when the victory remains to be achieved. If anything in economics ever were plain; if anything in industry ever were sure, it is that we are fighting the war with one hand strapped to our side by the liquor traffic.

"The waste of fuel by the liquor traffic

has made the problem one of the most acute our people have ever faced. It is estimated that the manufacture, transportation and retail of alcoholic liquors, require the consumption of coal to the amount of eighteen million tons per year.

Why Nation Will Go Dry

"The nation is going dry because the average man knows that his drunken neighbor is a menace. He knows that the drinker is decreasing his efficiency and failing in his duty. He knows that the liquor traffic is an economic monstrosity and that the hour has come for it to slough off and allow the nation to go on its upward way. This explains why states and cities so rapidly are abandoning the saloon to its fate. It explains why communities, heretofore hopelessly wet, are putting themselves in the dry column; why states already are ratifying the federal amendment, or are starting their campaigns for the election of legislatures which will ratify. Once put prohibition into the federal constitution and the liquor traffic will be as dead as human slavery."

Is Prohibition Only Remedy?

"Liquor is the cause of much human misery and the saloon is a disturbing factor of importance in politics," began Mr. Sikes. "It by no means necessarily follows," he continued, "that complete prohibition of the liquor traffic is the proper remedy for these ills. What is wise in a given case depends to a large degree upon what public opinion will permanently back up, rather than upon what can be enacted into law—constitutional or statutory—under the influence of a temporary wave of emotional enthusiasm.

"Have the Constitution worshippers so soon forgotten the fate of the Fifteenth Amendment, intended to give black men the vote in the South, put into the Constitution by the familiar alliance of hysterical fanaticism and political hypocrisy?

"It is the sheerest folly to undertake to write into a Constitution—especially into our federal Constitution—a specific solution of a continuous administrative problem. The attempt to control or even to suppress the liquor traffic must be regarded as such a problem.

"It is one thing to attempt prohibition by legislation that can be modified to meet changing public opinion. But it is a radically different matter to utilize a fanatical wave to put prohibition into the federal Constitution, which is very difficult to amend. Suppose public opinion after a time veers away from prohibition, as it may do, and suppose an active minority opposes the plan to take the dry amendment out of the Constitution. The result simply will be more disrespect for law, of which we already have too much, in large part because fanatical minorities insist upon keeping on the statute books laws that do not represent public opinion.

"As a war measure, the manufacture of strong drink has already been forbidden. When the existing supply of whiskey shall be exhausted, which should be within a year or two, the nation will be upon a light wine and beer basis. Why not try the new régime out, instead of hastening to apply the extreme, fanatical, knockout remedy, from which an extreme reaction will be likely?

Fanaticism in Dry Movement

"The leadership of the present prohibition movement in Chicago and in the United States is fanatical in the extreme. The 'dry' leaders insist that we must take their remedy and nothing else. And they want to apply it regardless of conditions and do not hesitate to subvert the government to their propaganda. Periods of fanaticism are always marked by political demoralization. Following the free silver craze of 1896, privilege was enthroned at Washington as it had not been before in years.

Playing With Crooks

"Dry leaders blame all the evils of government upon the liquor interests. But the prohibitionists, when following fanatical leadership, also commit serious political wrongs. Some of the very worst men in the Illinois legislature sit in that body because of 'dry' backing." Mr. Sikes mentioned the case of State Senator Pemberton, whom he described as "a brazen member of one of the worst political gangs that ever infested the state legislature." Because he professed to be "dry" and on one occasion had gavelled a local option bill a step further on the calendar, he was, Mr. Sikes said, supported by the Anti-Saloon League and "Billy" Sunday. The Legislative Voters' League, which opposed Pemberton on the ground of general unfitness, was denounced throughout the district as a "booze" organization. Pemberton was later indicted for bribery in the Lorimer scandal. " 'Billy' Sunday," Mr. Sikes said, "in helping to put the disgraceful Pemberton in office, meant no wrong of course. He acted on emotional impulse and offered advice to voters without knowing the facts."

"The drys are trying to override the principles of home rule and trial by jury," said Mr. Sikes. This was denied by Mr. Stewart, who said that in not one of the twenty-seven states which are "dry" at present has such a thing taken place. Mr. Sikes explained that he referred to the use of the injunction in enforcing liquor laws. Violation of these laws is made an offense against the court and the defendant may not demand a jury. North Dakota and other dry states have such a system, he said.

"WETS TO BLAME"—STEWART

In answer to Mr. Sikes' contention that we should not move so fast in adopting the constitutional amendment, Mr. Stewart said, "The wets in the Senate put in a seven-year limit for the adoption of the amendment. Time runs against us. The wets have put us in that position. We are not hurrying into prohibition recklessly. For a hundred years we have been studying and investigating. Every other imaginable plan has been tried. We are now ready to adopt the last and final way.

"It is true that prohibition is a continuous administrative problem. But legislation is the expression of the people's will as to the course which administration shall follow.

GET RID OF THE ISSUE

"By putting prohibition in the constitution, we put it beyond dispute. When Mr. Sikes goes to Springfield, he finds a 'wet-dry' fight in the way of the legislation he is interested in. The best way to get the question out of the way is to settle it finally.

"Mr. Sikes says that our leaders are fanatical. I suppose that any reform will draw fanatics to it. But after a long acquaintance with the leaders of this movement, I do not find them to be as Mr. Sikes describes them. The American people have not been swept into the 'dry' camp by a fanatical leadership but because they find the arguments for prohibition everywhere about them."

Mr. E. J. Davis, speaking from the floor, answered the charges relating to Senator Pemberton. "Every organization may make mistakes," he said. "The Legislative Voters' League supported 'Bob' Wilson, also indicted later in the Lorimer scandal. The Anti-Saloon League has been successful because it has stood by its friends. I san say confidently that the legislature is safe in the hands of the men supported by the Anti-Saloon League."

T HE CITY CLUB now has an "engineering staff." It consists of Charles K. Mohler, who worked with us several years ago and who recently returned to Chicago from Los Angeles. We drafted him at once for service on the Milk Committee and arrangements have now been made whereby he is to give a part of his time regularly to those phases of our public work which require technical attention. He has been made a member of the City Planning and the Public Utilities Committees.

Mr. Mohler was formerly engineer for the Loop Protective Association of Chicago and made for that organization a valuable report on traffic conditions on the union loop and another on the use of creosote wood block paving. For the City Club he prepared a report, which was published, on "Passenger Subway and Elevated Railway Development in Chicago." He compiled much of the original data and many of the maps on railway development in Chicago for the City Club's Transportation Exhibit, a part of which was published in the book "Through Routes for Chicago's Steam Railways," a City Club publication. He also made other valuable studies for the Club on specialized transportation subjects. This work was of a volunteer character, and represented Mr. Mohler's "patriotism of peace" contribution to the progress of Chicago.

He left Chicago in 1912 to take the position of Chief Engineer of the Public Utilities Commission of Los Angeles. We are glad that he is with us once more.

AN HOUR IN THE LOUNGE of the Club once in a while keeps you in touch with all the current magazines.

BE SOCIABLE—tell your table neighbor your name. Your action will improve the flavor of the lunch for both of you.

"The Lady of the Black Horse" Will Speak to the City Club, Tues., Mar. 5

WE are to hear one of the most thrilling personal stories of the great war. On Tuesday, March 5, at luncheon, Mrs. St. Clair Stobart, a major in the Serbian Army, is to tell her experiences in the great retreat.

Mrs. Stobart is known throughout Serbia as "The Lady of the Black Horse." She was the first woman in the history of the world to take command of a field hospital in war time. She was the founder of the Women's Convoy Corps and commanded a detachment of this corps—the first women's hospital unit—with the Bulgarian army in Thrace in the first Balkan war in 1912-13.

When the present war broke out, she organized, in 1914, in both Belgium and France, women's hospital units, being in charge of one of these units at Antwerp during the bombardment when the wounded were rescued under shell fire. She was taken prisoner by the Germans, imprisoned at Aachen and condemned to be shot as a spy. She escaped by what seemed to be a miracle, returning to England. Later she established a hospital at Cherbourg in France.

Then when the outbreak of typhus came in Serbia, she organized a hospital unit composed entirely of women and started for Kragujevatz, the military headquarters of the Serbian army. She was honored by the military authorities with the appointment of commandant of a column and invited to accompany the army to the front. From then on until the retreat began in December she ministered to the wounded and dying soldiers and the needs of the civil population.

Later as Commander of the Flying Field hospital column at the front, with the rank of Major in the Shumadia division of the Serbian army, she led her column, pursued by Germans, Austrians and Bulgarians, still carrying on hospital work, through Serbia and over the mountains of Montenegro and Albania to the coast—a journey of 800 miles, to Scutari.

The date of the lecture is Tuesday, March 5.

ENTER THIS ON your desk pad: On Saturday, March 9, at luncheon, Robert Sterling Yard, of the National Park Service, will address the Club on a subject relating to American scenery. This will be "Ladies' Day."

MARK EVERY THURSDAY on your desk pad as "City Club Day."

CIGARS, BIG OR LITTLE, and your own brand of coffin nails are on sale at the cashier's desk.

CLOSE UP THE RANKS!

We yet require more new members to fill the places of those gone to the Service.

141 of them! And 500 more to give us the number we need to make our membership fully effective.

About a quarter of a new member to each present member.

Don't be a fraction of a man. Bring in one new member, and then another!

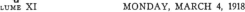

The City Club Bulletin

Published Weekly by the City Club of Chicago

A Journal of Active Citizenship

VOLUME XI   MONDAY, MARCH 4, 1918   NUMBER 9

THREE "LUNCHEON TALKS"

TUESDAY, MARCH 5

"With the Serbian Army in the Great Retreat"

MRS. ST. CLAIR STOBART, Major in the Serbian Army.

THURSDAY, MARCH 7, "CLUB DAY"

"Men and Events in England"

S. K. RATCLIFFE, of London.

SATURDAY, MARCH 9, "LADIES' DAY"

"Our National Parks" (*Illustrated*)

ROBERT STERLING YARD, National Park Service, Washington, D. C.

Mrs. Stobart's story is one of the most thrilling of the war

The Political Whirligig in England

We have been so obsessed with the tumultuous happenings of the Russian revolution that our eyes have been only partly open to the tremendous political changes which have been taking place in the British political system. "There will be no revolution in England," said John Masefield to a group of City Club members recently, "because the revolution has already taken place."

Next Thursday at luncheon S. K. Ratcliffe of London will speak on "Men and Events in England." It is expected that he will discuss the great political issues in that country.

Mr. Ratcliffe is known internationally as an interpreter of the social and political currents of the time. He is secretary of the Sociological Society of London, of which Lord Bryce was the first president, and lecturer for the London University Extension Board. As an editorial writer, he has contributed to the *London Daily News* and the *New Statesman*. He has lectured extensively throughout this country and has twice before spoken to City Club audiences.

Members who remember Mr. Ratcliffe's interesting talk before the Club a year ago, will be glad to have his view of English politics in the changed perspective of a year of great events.

The City Club Bulletin
A Journal of Active Citizenship

The purpose of the Club is to bring together in informal association those men who are genuinely interested in the improvement of the political, social and economic conditions of the community in which we live.

PUBLISHED WEEKLY BY THE
CITY CLUB OF CHICAGO
315 Plymouth Court   Telephone: Harrison 8278
DWIGHT L. AKERS, Editor

OFFICERS OF THE CLUB
FRANK I. MOULTON, President
EDGAR A. BANCROFT, Vice-President
ROY C. OSGOOD, Treasurer
CHARLES YEOMANS, Secretary
GEORGE E. HOOKER, Civic Secretary

EDITORIAL BOARD
HERBERT H. SMITH, Chairman
FREDERICK D. BRAMHALL   S. R. WATKINS
C. COLTON DAUGHADAY   PAUL R. WRIGHT

$1.00 per Year   -   -   -   10c per Copy

Entered as second class matter, December 3, 1917, at the postoffice at Chicago, Illinois, under the act of March 3, 1879.

Mountain Pleasure Grounds a Wartime Necessity

Germany, it is reported, has allowed piano manufacturing to be continued during the war as a "necessary industry." The Germans are a musical people and music, presumably, would help to support the national morale.

The United States Government believes that the recreational opportunities of the country should be developed rather than retarded in wartime. It is not closing the national parks but is, on the contrary, encouraging their use.

Our fellow-member, Stephen T. Mather, is Director of the National Park Service at Washington. One of his right hand men, Robert S. Yard, is to speak to us about the national parks, at luncheon next Saturday. Mr. Yard prepared the wonderful portfolio of National Park pictures with which many of our members are familiar. He is to show a large collection of slides. This meeting is open to the ladies!

MAYBE IT HAS NEVER occurred to you to drift into the billiard room after lunch. The jolly click of the balls will cheer you up, if business worries are on your mind.

THE LISTENING POST

FIVE NEW MEMBERS joined the Club last week. They are:

H. W. Coolidge, Treasurer Crowe Name-Plate & Engraving Co.

Prof. Harold G. Moulton, Department of Political Economy, University of Chicago. Prof. Moulton is Secretary of the Western Economic Society. Our members will remember his able paper before the Club several months ago on "Industrial Mobilization."

John E. Ransom, Director Central Free Dispensary. Mr. Ransom is a member of the Health Insurance Commission recently appointed by Gov. Lowden.

H. E. Shepherd, Rosenwald & Weil.

J. A. Walker, Vice-President, Blue Valley Creamery Company.

WE CONGRATULATE Washington upon its choice of Captain Charles E. Merriam to organize and take charge of the government propaganda bureau at Rome. The purpose of this bureau is to disseminate correct information about American war aims and war activities and offset the German propaganda, which aided the drive into Italy. Captain Merriam will sail shortly.

"JOY RIDES FOR JACKIES!" Do you want to give some soldiers or sailors a good time? Bring your car down to the City Club some Saturday or Sunday afternoon and give him a ride around the boulevards. They are probably from out of town and want to see our fair city. Even if they don't they are sure to like a spin in the fresh air.

ALLAN J. CARTER has been appointed chairman of the City Club Committee on Public Order. This is the committee that deals with all questions relating to crime, policing and the administration of criminal justice. Mr. Carter is associated with the law firm of Montgomery, Hart, Smith & Steere. As a member of the last General Assembly, he led the fight for such important legislation as the woman's eight hour bill and the bill to prohibit the sale of liquor in dance halls.

ROUMANIA'S TRAGEDY IS TOLD

Member of Red Cross Commission Tells Plight of Defeated Nation

THERE are few countries in the world about which we know so little as Roumania. There was a brief moment during the great war when she flashed upon the center of the world's stage, but after the failure of the Russian support and the smashing drive by General Mackensen, she retired again into the shadow. Since then very little news has come to us concerning her condition. The story of her plight during the terrible months which followed her defeat by the German armies, was told at a meeting of the City Club February 21, by Prof. H. Gideon Wells of the University of Chicago. Prof. Wells was a member of the American Red Cross Commission which spent several months in Roumania to learn the needs of her population and to arrange, if possible, ways of helping her.

A NATION UPROOTED

"After Roumania's defeat," said Prof. Wells, "she was thrown back into the province of Moldavia. To a population of two and a half or three million in this territory, there were added about three quarters of a million of refugees, many of whom had traveled from twenty to thirty days, cold and hungry, about four hundred thousand Roumanian soldiers and a million Russian soldiers. The population thus was doubled, but fuel, food, clothing and housing and hospital accommodations were lacking. An epidemic of cholera appeared but through efficient vaccination was checked.

"Then a new and worse disease appeared, typhus. Under the terrible conditions which prevailed, this disease (which is carried only by lice) spread rapidly. People died in the streets. They were picked up dead in the railway stations. The railroad trains were full of people trying to escape and were sometimes so crowded that the dead were packed in with the living. Not less than a hundred thousand and probably two hundred thousand people died, which means that about a million, or one person in five of the population, had the disease. Not until several months had passed was it overcome.

"There has been a great deal of starva-

tion in Roumania. The people have lived principally on a corn diet. There have been many of the so-called 'deficiency diseases,' resulting not from a lack of food in quantity but from a lack of some of the essential elements of a diet.

"Clothing is lacking. Wealthy women are wearing their fine clothes on all occasions because they have no others left. When those are worn out they will have to wear the rags."

AMERICA'S PART

What America should do and what she can do to help Roumania are two different things, according to Dr. Wells. Roumania is isolated among her enemies. She can be reached only through Russia, and what we can do depends upon the clearing up of the Russian situation.

The Roumanians, said Dr. Wells, are descendants of Roman colonists. They show a surprising similarity to the north Italian. They have been isolated among peoples of other races and have been trampled upon by all nations. Roumania has been invaded nine times by Russia alone. Belgium and Roumania have been the cock-pits of Europe.

WHY ROUMANIA WENT IN

"Roumania's entry into the war," according to Dr. Wells, "has often been ascribed to sordid reasons. She did go into the war partly for material reasons, but for very justifiable ones. The Roumanian kingdom does not correspond geographically with the Roumanian people. It has been the desire of Roumania to annex the oppressed Roumanian populations outside her national boundaries. After the declaration of war, fifty to seventy-five thousand of these fled from Transylvania across the Carpathians into Roumania, bringing harrowing stories of persecution by the Magyars. It was the desire of Roumania to take in all of the Roumanian peoples.

"Roumania could not escape the war. Both sides threatened her. Both Germany and Russia wanted her supplies, but there was no question as to which side she would join. She was betrayed by the crowd at

Petrograd. She was unable to defend her long frontier with her small army, the promised Russian assistance did not make good, the Allied offensive from Saloniki was too late and the terrible military disaster followed."

"Even under the terrible conditions which prevailed," said Dr. Wells, "there was no talk of peace, and even now, with the Bolsheviki as well as the Germans against them, they are standing out against it. If they are forced to sign an unwilling peace, it should be torn up at the settlement in justice to a sorely tried ally."

Shall We Cork Up Our Through Streets?

A NY plan for Chicago's development will provide for liberal street traffic access to all parts of the city. Chicago is even now considering a proposal to cut a great artery, costing several million dollars, from the west to the north side along Ogden Avenue extended. It is common sense, therefore, to keep for traffic purposes, the main thoroughfares which now exist.

Chicago's development has followed her section and half-section line streets. It is a well-recognized principle in Chicago that such streets, wherever possible, must be kept for business and for traffic circulation. But every now and then a proposal is made which tends to block one of them up and divert it from its logical purpose. The latest of these is a proposal for the boulevarding of that part of Addison Street, a half-section line artery, between Kedzie and Cicero avenues. The boulevarding of this two mile section of an eight and a half mile street would mean the exclusion of street car lines and ordinary street traffic.

This proposal is opposed on principle by the City Club Committees on Highways, Bridges and Garbage Disposal and on Public Utilities. Last week they sent a joint letter to the City Council Committee on Streets and Alleys, before which the proposal was pending. Addison Street, they urged, will, with the development of the district, naturally become necessary as a business thoroughfare. Eventually there will be a need for a street car line on it. "Addison Street," reads the letter, "is one of the natural arteries that will serve as a means of access to the Lake Front for the people living on the west side. This access cannot be truly effective without a through car line."

The Committee on Streets and Alleys did not see the force of this argument and the ordinance was recommended to the Council for passage.

Your Money for a Good Cause!

"It is all the same to the Kaiser whether an American soldier is put out of the running by a German bullet or by the evil influences in a war camp city."

T HE campaign of the War Recreation Board of this state for a war chest of $400,000 for the entertainment of soldiers and sailors on leave from the camps is in full swing. Illinois is the last state of the Union to come across with its share. An appeal has come to the City Club for its support in this campaign.

The activities to be supported from contributions to this fund are directly in line with the purpose of the City Club in opening its Club house to enlisted men. Our members who heard Allen D. Albert talk the other day, or those who read the account of his address in the Bulletin, will realize how directly service of this sort contributes to the efficiency of the fighting forces.

The Board has its offices at 120 W. Adams Street and will take checks of any kind or size. They should be made out to John J. Mitchell, Treasurer. The sky is the limit!

HOUSEWIVES MAY TAKE HEART!

Hoover Rations Make Better
Diet, Says Food Scientist

IF American housewives thought they were exercising Spartan economy by observing Mr. Hoover's rules, they were undeceived by H. C. Sherman, Professor of Food Chemistry, Columbia University, who spoke last Thursday afternoon before the City Club.

"In order to obtain sufficient meat, wheat, fats and sugar to send to our Allies," said Prof. Sherman, "it is necessary to reduce our consumption of these articles about one-third. It is my contention that we can do this without detriment to our nutrition—even to its advantage. We have been extravagant in the use of these foods in the past.

Too Much Meat

"We have, for instance, been consuming meat in quantities which would be expected in a pioneer grazing country like Australia or Argentine where comparatively little labor is required to produce it. Even if we reduce our meat consumption a third, we will be consuming twice as much as France and three times as much as Italy before the war. We consume twice as much sugar as France and more than twice as much as Russia, before the war.

"Because we use more of these foods, we consume less of perishable foods, such as vegetables, fruits and milk, which are more 'fussy' to handle and transport; if we would eat more of these perishables, a better balanced diet would result—particularly for our children.

Corn or Hogs?

"The substitution of corn for wheat does not mean a sacrifice in nutritive value. Nine-tenths of our corn crop is fed to animals which give back only from 3 to 30 per cent of its food value. We ought to consider carefully whether we should put corn through a process which sacrifices so much in nutritive value or should consume it directly. Even if we should decide to make bread half of corn and half of wheat, we should lose nothing essential. We would merely have to revise our ideas as to color, flavor and texture.

"Meat and sugar are conspicuously one-sided foods. Sugar serves as fuel but as nothing else. Meat serves as fuel and also supplies protein. Until the science of nutrition was better understood, meat seemed to be an all-sufficient food, but now we know that it is lacking in mineral elements, particularly in lime. Milk is very rich in lime. By reducing meat and increasing milk consumption, therefore, we better our diet.

Food Values in Milk

"A larger percentage of the money spent by the ordinary family for food should go for milk. We consider a quart of milk roughly equal in nutritive value to a pound of steak and it costs much less, even at present high prices. An increase in milk prices is very unfortunate in any community, because it tends to decrease consumption. The unwillingness of consumers in New York to pay increased prices has had a bad reaction against milk production and is resulting in a reduction of dairy herds."

Prof. Sherman said that we need have little fear that German food supplies would be materially increased this year by a Russian peace. There are no great stores of grain in Russia at the present time, he said. If Germany has a chance to extend her railroads, however, and exploit the country, she can increase her food supplies very considerably in later years.

Dr. J. R. Gerstley has been called to Camp Custer to act as assistant to the Major in charge of medical work there. He has been commissioned as a Lieutenant.

Captain James A. Britton has been made division tuberculosis specialist at Camp Wheeler, Macon, Georgia. Another of our doctors, Major L. W. Bremerman, is Director of Field Hospitals at Camp Custer, Battle Creek, Mich.

Dr. F. R. Green is an ex-captain in the army. He has been promoted to a majorship.

The literature which is put upon the counter under the Club Bulletin Board is for your consumption. Help yourself!

Smash German Plans or Fight Later, Warns Dr. Soares

"WE can have peace with Germany to-day, we can have it on very satisfactory terms—and Germany will be free to get ready for the next great war," said Prof. Theodore G. Soares of the University of Chicago in an address at the City Club last Wednesday. Dr. Soares sketched the outlines of a vast German conspiracy for world control, beginning with the crushing of Russia and France and the cementing of a grand alliance among her present allies, followed by a crushing defeat of the British Empire and culminating in a conquest of the Western hemisphere. "Germany has completed the first stage of her world conquest," he asserted, "and desires a peace through which she may recoup her losses and with the vast resources of the Central Alliance at her command, build a navy such as the world has never seen. She will then be ready to fight the next war. The British Empire is the second line of trenches, and we are the third."

"The German conspiracy," said Dr. Soares, "rests on an idea which has been growing in Germany for twenty-five years —the idea that world supremacy rests with the Germans. There is only one way to destroy that idea and that is to crush the foundation on which it rests. Germany must be shown that the nation which draws the sword for the purpose of burglarizing its neighbors is doomed."

"THE DOUBLE CROSS."

"How did Germany propose to cement the Great Pan-American Alliance? Not by conquest," said Dr. Soares. "She was more astute than that. She saw that by uniting them in a war, as the German States were united in the Franco-Prussian war, and by keeping the kings and princes on the throne, she could keep her allies permanently under the financial, industrial and military domination of Berlin."

"The first stage of the German conspiracy has been completed. If you leave Germany nothing but her allies, she has won. What are these people, now under her domination, to us—the Czechs, the Jugo-Slavs, the Armenians, Syrians, Arabs, Palestinian Jews and so on? These peoples are the barrier to German supremacy.

When they are freed we can build the ramparts of our own civilization."

"When the Germans get together in their own territory," concluded Dr. Soares, "free their subject peoples and learn to be neighbors we will give them the hand of fellowship. But we must keep our eyes on the next war—*we must fight the next war now!*"

The Mail Pouch

Wants More Friendliness

To THE EDITOR: The little notes I have been seeing lately in the Bulletin about introducing one's self to one's neighbor and speaking to the other men at the table seems to me to have great possibilities.

Since joining the City Club about three years ago, I have received a lot of benefit from it, and while I do not belong to many clubs, and do not care to, I think this is the last one I would part with.

But the one defect that has always been sticking out is the lack of sociability in the dining room. At the Association of Commerce luncheons, no one ever thinks of starting the meal without introducing himself to his neighbor. One day last week, when our Russian friends talked, I spoke to the man at my right and he said it was the first time that anyone had ever addressed him in his year and one-half membership. I confessed to him that he had nothing on me, for in my three years' membership it was I who had always taken the initiative.

I believe your notes are all aimed in the right direction and I sincerely hope that the propaganda you have started will be carried through to a great improvement along these lines.   E. E. H.

THE ASSIGNMENT of Club members for duty at Soldiers' and Sailors' "open house" this week-end are as follows: *Saturday, March 9,* J. P. Petrie, Julian Roe, V. M. Gaspar, H. C. Edmonds, W. S. Reynolds. *Sunday, March 10,* W. S. Monroe, A. S. Fielding, Spencer Gordon, L. J. Kempf, Jens Jensen, A. E. Taylor.

AT THE BULLETIN BOARD in the lobby, there is a box for items for the "Listening Post." Give us an item now and then, even if it has to be about yourself.

Hit Germany Through Austria!

Revolutionary Spirit of Subject Peoples
Makes Her Weak Spot in Alliance

"The Allies have hitherto underestimated the importance of the Balkan front," said Dr. H. Hinkovic, member of the Jugo-Slavic Committee of London, at a City Club meeting, Saturday, February 16. "Austria is Germany's weakest spot. A vassal state herself, her population is composed in part of subject nations, who are rebellious against the system which is exploiting them. You would be welcomed by them as a liberator and would have their support."

A Revolutionary Leader

Dr. Hinkovic is a Croatian, formerly a member of the Croatian parliament and a delegate to the Hungarian parliament. From his early youth he has been a revolutionary leader among the Jugo (South)-Slavic peoples. In 1908 he defended fifty-two of his countrymen indicted for treason as a result of the outbreaks which took place following the annexation of Bosnia and Herzegovina to Austria. He was one of three representatives of the Croatian people at the conference last summer at Corfu which drew up the plan of union for the South Slavic peoples, the Serbs, Croatians and Slovenians—a plan is now officially recognized by the Serbian government.

"The South Slavic peoples," said Dr. Hinkovic, "have been the bridge over which in times past the invasions from Asia have passed. Now there is a reverse invasion from Germany and, stationed as we are in southeastern Austria, Serbia and Montenegro, we are again in the path of the invader."

A War for Extermination

"The war was in its beginning a war against the South Slavic peoples. It was a war for our extermination. Our young men have been forced to fight in a fratricidal war—or worse, a war against themselves. We have lost twenty per cent of our population in the war and unspeakable atrocities have been committed against us.

"A revolution against Austria is not easy to start under present war conditions. All our young men have been enlisted and only the old people, women and children are left. In spite of this there have been many courageous acts by those who remained at home and many have had to escape from the country or be put in prison. During the war, thousands of our boys in the army deserted to the allies.

Should America Sign Peace

"There is talk of a separate peace with Austria. Austria will make a separate peace only on the basis of her territorial integrity and this would perpetuate the rule of the Germans and the Magyars over our people. You cannot have a permanent peace that way. America ought to speak directly to our people, to encourage the revolutionary spirit among them, not to deal with Count Czernin, who represents only the dynasty and the ruling races—a feudal empire which treats its people like cattle. When your great president, who proclaimed the principle upon which we base our hopes of independence—the right of self-determination of nations—says to us: "We have followed your struggles; we understand your dream of liberation; we will support you," it will bring the greatest moral support to the cause of the Allies and I believe will mean the shortening of the war.

"Our aims are also yours. We are all—small and great—fighting for the liberation of the world. We are your allies and I implore you not to underestimate our co-operation."

Our former member, Allen Burns, was in the city last week and paid us a visit.

Albert O. Anderson, one of our members in the 33rd ward, upset the plans of Fred Lundin's organization at the Republican primaries last Tuesday. He surprised Lundin by racing in several hundred votes ahead of the City Hall candidate.

Two members of the City Club are pitted against each other in the 3rd ward aldermanic fight—Ulysses S. Schwartz, the present alderman, on the Democratic ticket, and Felix A. Norden, Republican.

In the Mirror

WE have been "written up" in the *Daily News*. A writer from that paper visited our Club house recently in company with an artist, gave it the "once over," liked it and wrote a special article which appeared last Wednesday.

"In the midst of the 'bustle and din' of the busy down town," he said, "one comes unexpectedly on Plymouth court. Nestled in between State and Dearborn streets, running south from Jackson boulevard, it offers an oasis of peace and quiet in the turmoil of motor horns and street car bells."

He found the exterior of the building "most attractive." "The quiet location," he said, "makes the site a distinctly desirable one for a club wherein conferences and public speaking play such important part."

Within the building, he found the Lounge particularly interesting. "Great dignity," he said, "is to be found in this room, but dignity in no way opposed to comfort. The huge fire-place with comfortable davenports grouped around it makes an attractive center of interest. Less intimate, less gracious than the Lounge, the dining room has all the charm of the former coupled with the necessary formality of a dining room."

"An interesting experience it was for me—to visit this club," he concluded after describing the Club in detail. "It is so peaceful, so restful, so cheerful. My note book was bulging with notes when I left. I stepped out into the rain again. The bustle of the city greeted me as I turned up Jackson boulevard. It was hard indeed to adjust myself to State street after quaint Plymouth court! And I was sorry that the adjustment had to be made."

The article is accompanied by an interesting pen sketch of the Lounge by Harry A. Hueser.

ONE evening last week a young man from Winnetka dined at the City Club with his family. They had:

CREAM OF TOMATOES

RIPE OLIVES   MIXED PICKLES

ROAST TENDERLOIN
OF BEEF WITH MUSHROOMS

AU GRATIN POTATOES

HEAD LETTUCE

CITY CLUB DRESSING

CHOCOLATE ICE CREAM

HOME MADE COOKIES

COFFEE

Price per plate 75c. No tips —good service.

—And since then he's been a kind of walking advertisement for the place.

Won't *you* join our "advertising club"?

H. M. DARLING has been commissioned as Captain in the Signal Service Corps. He is connected with the Air Craft Board at Washington. Mr. Darling has been very active for the City Club in promoting short ballot reform.

MANY MEMBERS SAY the next best thing to attending a Club luncheon is reading the reports in the Bulletin—but you can't thus get the personality of the speaker.

"GERMANY LOST THE WAR in her ordnance department," said S. S. McClure at the City Club recently. She lost the battle of the Marne, he said, through the failure of her ammunition supply. Will Chicago, the relief agencies of the city are asking, fail to hold her "home lines" against poverty, disease and crime by a failure in her ammunition and equipment. These agencies stand equipped with a splendidly trained army of workers, but they insist that they must have supplies, and more and more supplies, if the battle is to be won. "This is a time of sacrifice but not the sacrifice of the helpless," said Governor Lowden. That is why the "Hold the Home Lines" campaign, under the direction of the Central Council of Social Agencies, a superior war council for the allied public welfare agencies, has been launched.

The City Club Bulletin

Published Weekly by the City Club of Chicago

A Journal of Active Citizenship

VOLUME XI   MONDAY, MARCH 11, 1918   NUMBER 10

"TALK DAYS" THIS WEEK

Wednesday, March 13	Friday, March 15
## S. K. Ratcliffe	## Maj. S. M. J. Auld
of London	Chemical Adviser British Military Mission
Subject: "Men and Events in England"	*Subject: "Chemistry in War"*

Luncheon from 11:30   Speaking at 1:00

British Military Adviser to Be Club Guest

. The age of chemistry is upon us. Already it is fighting our battles on the west front. Behind the lines, the leaders of chemical science in every country are at work on problems of the great war. The nation which can invent the most powerful explosive or the most deadly gas will possess a marked superiority in the battle line.

"Chemistry in War" is, therefore, a fascinating subject in itself. The City Club is very fortunate in being able to hear it discussed by Major S. M. J. Auld, who has come to this country with the British Military Mission, as Chemical Adviser. Major Auld will be our guest next Friday at luncheon.

Major Auld is a leader in chemical science in England. He is professor of agricultural chemistry at University College, Reading, and is the author of several important scientific works.

S. K. RATCLIFFE of London, who was scheduled to address the Club last Thursday on political events in England, very kindly allowed us to change the date to Wednesday of this week, in order that the Club might hear Dr. Simon Flexner. Mr. Ratcliffe, as we said in last week's Bulletin, is a keen observer of political and social movements. Members should hear his interpretation of the great political upheaval which is going on in England.

The City Club Bulletin
A Journal of Active Citizenship

The purpose of the Club is to bring together in informal association those men who are genuinely interested in the improvement of the political, social and economic conditions of the community in which we live.

PUBLISHED WEEKLY BY THE

CITY CLUB OF CHICAGO

315 Plymouth Court   Telephone: Harrison 8278

DWIGHT L. AKERS, Editor

OFFICERS OF THE CLUB

FRANK I. MOULTON, President
EDGAR A. BANCROFT, Vice-President
ROY C. OSGOOD, Treasurer
CHARLES YEOMANS, Secretary
GEORGE E. HOOKER, Civic Secretary

EDITORIAL BOARD

HERBERT H. SMITH, Chairman
FREDERICK D. BRAMHALL   S. R. WATKINS
C. COLTON DAUGHADAY   PAUL R. WRIGHT

$1.00 per Year - - - 10c per Copy

Entered as second class matter, December 3, 1917, at the postoffice at Chicago, Illinois, under the act of March 3, 1879.

THE LISTENING POST

THESE MEN JOINED the Club last week:

H. P. Albaugh, General Agent, Square Turn Tractor Company.

Allen D. Albert. Mr. Albert is promoting the work of the War Recreation Service. He addressed the City Club recently on this subject. He was formerly president of the International Association of Rotary Clubs.

J. A. Beidler, Ludowici-Celadon Company (credits).

Arthur B. Jones, Treasurer, C. & N. W. Railway Company.

J. Edward Kearns, Manager Lighting Department, General Electric Company.

Simon A. Kohn, Secretary-Treasurer Lukone Tailoring Company.

Nahum Miller, Lawyer, Winston, Payne, Strawn & Shaw.

Arthur P. Stanley, Local Manager Kohrs Packing Company of Davenport, Iowa.

THESE MEMBERS ARE ON SENTRY DUTY at the Club House for the soldiers' and sailors' entertainment this week-end:

Saturday, March 16.—N. T. Yeomans, J. D. Clancy, R. M. Cunningham, G. O. Fairweather, P. J. Templeton.

Sunday, March 17.—J. J. Forstall, V. S. Yarros, C. P. Parker, T. N. Bishop, G. L. Weaver, W. J. McDonough.

DR. JOHN FAVILL, First Lieutenant in the Medical Reserve Corps, has been ordered to leave immediately for active service at Camp Lee, Petersburg, Va. He will be on temporary duty until Base Hospital Unit No. 14, of which he is a member, is mobilized.

TWO HUNDRED NEIGHBORS of Captain Charles E. Merriam gathered at the Hayes Hotel last Wednesday evening at dinner to bid him farewell. He left Friday morning for the East and will sail shortly for Rome where, as stated in the Bulletin last week, he is to be in charge of the American Propaganda Bureau. His task there will be to interpret to the Italian people America's war aims and the contribution which America expects to make to the Allied cause.

THE SOLDIERS' AND SAILORS' Entertainment Committee last week distributed copies of a new poster advertising the City Club's "open house" for Soldiers and Sailors on Saturday and Sunday. These posters are being sent to the Great Lakes Station, Fort Sheridan, the Municipal Pier, and other points in and near the city where soldiers and sailors are quartered or which they frequent. They are also being placed in State Street and Madison Street stores.

The poster was designed and manufactured without cost to the City Club, as a war contribution. The drawing was made by Claude K. Brown, who is a member of the Club, the plates were made by the Federal Engraving Company and stock and printing furnished by D. F. Keller & Co. J. R. Ozanne, a member of the committee, prepared the copy and secured the co-operation of the donors. The Soldiers' and Sailors' Entertainment Committee takes this opportunity of expressing its appreciation and thanks.

If any Club member happens to think of a place where the posters can be displayed to good advantage and will undertake to place them, he can get copies on application at the office.

A Woman at the War Front

Mrs. St. Clair Stobart Tells Experiences in Great Serbian Retreat

THE burden of war, it has often been said, falls upon women with even more crushing weight than upon men. Out of the mass of suffering inflicted upon women in this war and out of the personal sacrifices demanded of them, there have arisen many instances of individual heroism and devotion which history will never forget. The name of Edith Cavell will be remembered as long as the war itself.

It was the good fortune of the City Club to have as its guest last Tuesday one of the women heroes of the war, Mrs. St. Clair Stobart, of England. Her story has already been briefly told in the City Club Bulletin. Those of our members who failed to hear Mrs. Stobart's story from her own lips should read it in her book, "The Flaming Sword in Serbia," published in 1916.

A PACIFIST AT WAR

Mrs. Stobart admitted to her audience that she is a pacifist, that she believes that it is particularly woman's task to put an end to militarism and war, but that if women are to do this they must know war as it is and not at second-hand. It was with this belief that she organized the Woman's Sick and Wounded Convoy Corps which served with the Bulgarian Army in Thrace in 1912-13, the first unit composed entirely of women which had served in any war.

Mrs. Stobart was first awakened, she said, to the real nature of Germany's military mania after the declaration of war and following a trip to Brussels to arrange for her hospital unit. The city was taken by the Germans. and in endeavoring to leave Belgium she was arrested as a spy, marched through the streets guarded by a squad of German soldiers, and taken before a German officer. In a snarling, insulting tone, he refused even to examine her papers showing that she was an accredited representative of the Red Cross, and said, "You are an Englishwoman and whether you are right or wrong, this is a war of annihilation." Mrs. Stobart was condemned to death and narrowly escaped the

fate of Edith Cavell. She was finally released and soon thereafter brought her woman's hospital unit to Antwerp. This unit served during the heaviest bombardment of the city and escaped to Holland just before the bridge was destroyed.

A DYING NATION

It was in Serbia, however, that the most remarkable chapter in Mrs. Stobart's history was enacted. After a few months' service in France, she went to Serbia in command of a woman's unit, to care for typhus victims. In the region where this unit was established, there was not one doctor to help check the spread of infectious disease among the civilian population. In two weeks, no less than 32,000 people passed through the hands of the unit. A graveyard near headquarters contained the bodies of four thousand victims of typhus alone.

Then came the great Austro-German and Bulgarian drive and Mrs. Stobart was asked to go to the front in command of a flying field hospital unit, with the rank of Major. "Mrs. Stobart," says a recent article, in the *Contemporary Review,* "was probably the first woman to be made responsible with executive rank for the conduct, movements and discipline of a body of soldiers engaged in operations of the field and on the march." Mrs. Stobart's unit was composed of twelve English women doctors and nurses, six chauffeurs and over sixty Serbian soldiers, orderlies and transport drivers.

THE FLIGHT OF SERBIA

The three-months' retreat of the defeated Serbian army, fighting a constant rear-guard action, was a sombre chapter in Serbian history. Mrs. Stobart's unit worked night and day to an accompaniment of groans from the wounded and the sound of the German guns. "The retreat," said Mrs. Stobart, "was not the retreat of an army, it was the retreat of a nation. Old men, women and children swelled the procession and added to the difficulties of the march. As we approached the mountains, the roads became constantly worse. We had to saw our wagons in two and finally abandon them and travel on foot. In the mountains we had to make our way through snow and ice, over boulders, through mud holes and across rivers—with the sound of the German guns always in our ears. As the physical difficulties increased, the food began to give out. We passed thousands of men dead and dying by the roadside but we could not stay to help them. It will probably never be known how many thousands died from hunger, cold and fatigue in this march." The unit under Mrs. Stobart's command was constantly on the march, car-

ing for the sick and wounded, breaking camp at a moment's notice to escape the oncoming armies of the enemy.

The Germans, Austrians and Bulgarians committed terrible atrocities against the Serbs, Mrs. Stobart charged. Women and children were driven into buildings and the buildings burned. Prisoners were shot and buried, some of them still living. "Of Serbia's four million people," said Mrs. Stobart, "about a million and a half remain." "It is possible that Serbia may exist," according to a Bulgarian newspaper, which she quoted, "but there will be no more Serbs."

At the Sign of the Book

"WIDOWS' PENSION LEGISLATION." Municipal Research, No. 85. Issued by the Bureau of Municipal Research and Training School for Public Service, New York, 125 pages.

Twenty-eight states have "mother's pension" legislation. Among them is Illinois. Under the Illinois law, which has been on the books since 1911, Cook County is providing regularly for about 800 families and about 500 more are on the waiting list. The monthly payroll for "mother's pensions" is about $22,000.

The New York Bureau of Municipal Research has made a survey of the operation of mother's pension laws in the various states and of the manner in which problems arising under them have been met. Its findings are published in this report. Summarizing the results of the law in New York the Bureau says: "It has not been very successful in bringing about the transfer of children from institutions which it was hoped it would facilitate. It has, however, awakened widespread interest both on the part of the people and of public authorities in the problems of the dependent child and in the standards of normal home treatment."

For those who are not familiar with the principle underlying mother's or widow's pensions, the following statement from the report will be illuminating: "Neither the endowment of motherhood, nor indemnity for widowhood, nor the relief of need, im-

portant as is the role played by all of these motives, explains adequately the public purpose sought in all of this highly experimental legislation. It is rather *the conservation of childhood as a public asset,* and the discovery of a new method of committing dependent children whereby they are given home care under the guidance of a real mother, that must be regarded as the supreme motive which explains the legislative purpose of widows' pensions and should guide the administration in their execution and the legislator in the further amendment and perfection of the present tentative statutes."

THE TWO CITY CLUB committees which are opposing the proposed boulevarding of Addison Street, sent a joint letter to the City Council last week renewing their objections. Readers of last week's Bulletin will remember that the boulevarding was opposed on the ground that it is unwise to block up our section and half-section line streets from street car and ordinary street traffic. The committees, in their letter to the Council, say further: "If the portion of Addison Street in question is designated a boulevard, it will not form a link of any use or importance in the boulevard system of Chicago, nor is it apt to do so through any future extension of the system. Instead it will be a restricted traffic pleasureway leading from one business street, namely, Kedzie Avenue, to Cicero Avenue, which is also a business thoroughfare."

The letter is signed by F. G. Heuchling, Chairman Committee on Highways, Bridges and Waste Disposal, and Clifton R. Bechtel, Secretary Committee on Public Utilities.

A Broadside by the Woman's City Club

THE Civil Service Committee of the Woman's City Club is on the warpath. It claims to have found conditions at the Municipal Tuberculosis Sanitarium which are against the interest of the public and a detriment to the proper care of the patients at that institution. On November 1, 1917, the Committee reports, the payroll of the Sanitarium showed 310 temporary appointees out of approximately 550 employees.

"What does this mean?" asks the Committee. "It means that the safeguard of Civil Service voluntarily established by Dr. T. B. Sachs has been effectually broken down. It means that jobs are given for a period of 60 days. While business organizations are devising ways to reduce the 'labor turn over' the Municipal Tuberculosis Sanitarium has devised a way to increase the 'turn over' and that in the delicate and intricate business of caring for the sick. . ."

"Abuses exist under the temporary employee system," the Committee charges. "*The pay rolls of the Department of Health show ambulance surgeons who hold no license to practice and who are not graduate physicians.* The pay rolls show internes in the Contagious Disease Hospital who at the time of employment were students in a medical college, were not graduates, and were not licensed to practice." The Committee cites a number of such cases, with specifications, and then concludes: "These instances were discovered in a very cursory review of the Department of Health pay rolls. What might be discovered among the 310 temporary employees of the Municipal Tuberculosis Sanitarium is a matter of conjecture. Are the men and women listed there as such all accredited physicians? Are the nurses all graduate nurses? Have we in that department men giving medical advice who are not equipped to do so, and nurses entering homes dressed as nurses but in reality lay people masquerading as nurses?"

The Committee has laid out a very interesting and profitable line of investigation. The public certainly ought to have answers to all those questions. We hope that further investigations by the Committee will furnish them.

THE STATE CONSTITUTION COMMITTEE of the Club is getting ready for its big spring and summer drive. "The present committee will be reconstructed and much enlarged," said Andrew R. Sheriff, its chairman, in a letter addressed to a number of members of the Club last week. It is necessary that it be a strong working force of men able in campaign management, and familiar with the subject of state constitutions.

"By action of the last legislature," he continued, "the electorate of the State will be required at the next November election, to decide whether a constitutional convention shall be called. The future welfare of the State urgently demands a revising of the constitution; but the great task, in the first instance, will be to make this clear to the voters, and move them to call a convention. The campaign for this purpose throughout the State will be controlled by a state-wide organization created specially for this campaign; in Chicago the City Club provides a most competent agency, through its above-named committee, to do the work, in this locality, in connection with the general organization."

No committee of the Club has more important work ahead of it than the Committee on State Constitution.

RAYMOND ROBINS is still in the cyclone center of Russia. This dispatch from Petrograd is printed in the Chicago papers of March 6: "Raymond Robins, head of the American permanent Red Cross mission to Russia, with a contingent of Red Cross workers, and Roger C. Tredwell, the American consul, returned to Petrograd last night. They express the determination to remain on Russian soil as long as possible."

Graham R. Taylor, another member of the City Club, is also in Russia.

A Jolt for Lawyers

RESPECTED and conservative members of the bar have long argued for a simplification of legal procedure. But for Prof. John R. Roos, of the University of Michigan, who writes in the March issue of the *Illinois Law Review,* half-measures are too mild. "Throw pleadings and procedure to the winds," he urges. "They never assisted in arriving at practical justice and have been the tools and instruments of technicality, delay and defense against just claims since the days of King Edward I."

Prof. Roos bases his contention in part upon a study of cases in one of the Circuit Courts in Michigan. He endeavors to show how justice is defeated for the mass by the costliness of the procedure. He estimates that the average expense to taxpayers and to parties in litigation for a day in court is $943.16—"in most cases more than the difference between the parties." The causes of the expense, he lists as follows:

"1. The number of persons required to make a decision, and that they must assemble at one time and place and wait each other's turn. These persons are judge, reporter, clerk, sheriff, jury, attorneys, parties, and witnesses.

"2. The right of parties to be heard in person or by attorney at each step, to produce, examine, and cross-examine witnesses, and accumulate evidence without limit so long as it has any relation to the controversy.

"3. The number of steps and processes required to reach a decision: Complaint, plea, demurrer, hearings, repleadings, appeals, and new trials."

If all this complicated machinery is to be eliminated, how is public justice to be conducted? "Take from the parties," says Prof. Roos, "the right to be heard in person or by attorney or to have anything to say as to how the trial shall be conducted, what or how many witnesses shall be examined, or what or how many questions shall be asked. This will strip the case of unessentials and expedite the conclusion. Instead of an army solemnly assembled at one place at an expense greater than the amount in controversy, let two persons, the referee and jury, go about visiting the witnesses to ascertain the facts and law and report them to the court, and the administration of justice will take on new life. People will take their differences to the court for settlement. Do these things, and public justice will be cheap and fair to rich and poor alike."

The lawyer who reads this article will feel as if he had been spending a few pleasant minutes in an electric chair. However, the human race likes to be shocked and lawyers are no exception.

The Mail Pouch

ONE EVENING RECENTLY the manager of the Club was startled by the unexpected arrival for dinner of seventy-five members of the American Chemical Society. Through a misunderstanding he had not been notified in advance. By the time the guests were ready to sit down, however, the food and the waiters were on hand. This prompt service received recognition from the society last week in the following letter:

GENTLEMEN: Am writing this letter to convey to the City Club the appreciation of the Chicago Section of the American Chemical Society for the very prompt and efficient manner in which the Club handled the last meeting of the Chicago Section, of which, through some misunderstanding, the Club had not been notified in advance.

The members of the Section expressed to me, many times during the evening, their very great appreciation of the action of the Club and the very satisfactory manner in which the Club had met the situation.

Yours respectfully,
(Signed)   L. M. TOLMAN,
Chairman, Chicago Section, American Chemical Society.

LAST WEEK we printed a letter from one of our members urging more sociability in the dining room. The Bulletin welcomes such letters from the members of the Club. It is glad to have your ideas in letter form on any subject which you think ought to be put before the members. Letters should preferably be no more than 150 words long.

We will not print anonymous contributions, but we will keep the writer's name a dark secret if he so desires. We also reserve the right to censor any matter which appears to be libelous, scurrilous or otherwise likely to get the editor into trouble.

SCIENCE CONQUERING ARMY DISEASES

Makes Big Contribution to Efficiency of Fighting Forces, Says Head of Rockefeller Institute

WARS have in the past always been associated with plagues of disease. Medical science in this war, however, is mitigating many of the diseases which have played havoc with armies in the past, according to Dr. Simon Flexner, Director of Rockefeller Institute, who addressed the City Club at luncheon last Thursday. Several new diseases have arisen on the fighting fronts, the result of the peculiar conditions of trench warfare, but these, also, are being brought under control.

FIGHTING THE UNSEEN ENEMY

"In spite of the enormous size of our modern armies," said Dr. Flexner, "the percentage of cases of disease to those of wounds has been reduced to a minimum. This result is due to a better understanding of the causes of disease. Efforts are being made to reduce this ratio further and so prevent the throwing out of service of men who are at the front."

Dr. Flexner is one of America's most eminent men in medical research. As head of the laboratories of the Rockefeller Institute since 1903, he has explored the frontiers of medical science and has added much to our knowledge of diseases and their cure. His visit to Chicago at this time was for an inspection of conditions at the Great Lakes Naval Training Station.

ROUTING DISEASE FROM ARMY

Typhoid in the army, said Dr. Flexner, discussing the contributions of medicine to the war, has been much reduced by vaccination. Dysentery and cholera, while not so successfully met as typhoid, have been also much lessened in amount by the chlorination of water supplies. The conditions which favor the spread of meningitis in an army are well understood but are hard to control because they involve such common habits among the men as spitting, sneezing and coughing. Pneumonia has now been resolved into several different diseases, each caused by a different organism, and medical laboratories here and abroad are working upon methods of producing a neutralizing serum for each type. Pneumonia is very prevalent in armies and this problem, according to Dr. Flexner, is one of the most serious of the war.

NEW FORMS OF DISEASE

But the conditions of trench warfare have introduced new forms of disease. A new form of jaundice among the men in the trenches puzzled medical scientists for a long time. The puzzle was solved through a Japanese scientist, who discovered the organism responsible for a similar infection local to Japan. The results were given to Dr. Flexner, then in Japan, and recognizing in this disease a similarity to the jaundice which had developed in the trenches, he forwarded the information to the French and English war offices. Within a month the same organism was traced down in the laboratories of these countries. In a similar manner the rat was discovered to be the carrier of this organism and the method of treatment is now approaching a successful solution.

GAS GANGRENE

Gas gangrene is another disease developed by the war. Thousands of men have died from it. It is a wound infection. The tissues around the wound die—it is, in fact, a form of local death. This infection, it has been discovered, is caused by a micro-organism which is found in the dejecta of domestic animals. The fields of France and Belgium have been under intensive cultivation in a long time and when earth gets into the wounds the conditions are favorable for "gas gangrene." The Rockefeller Foundation has developed an anti-toxin for it, which has proved successful on animals, and Dr. Bull of that institution is now in France preparing for its use by the fighting men. This anti-toxin may be administered to a wounded man in the same way and at the same time as tetanus anti-toxin. It is expected that many lives will be saved through its use.

KEEPING THINGS DARK

"It is an interesting ethical question," said Dr. Flexner, "whether new medical discoveries should be kept a secret from our enemies. It has been our idea that medicine is in essence a humanitarian science. Up to the present there has been no secrecy on our part. I wish that as much could be said for our enemy. In the early part of the war, no German medical publication was allowed to pass outside the boundaries of the country. This was modified because of protests from the journals, who feared perhaps that their pre-eminence in medical science would be lost if they were cut off from the world. German medical publications may now circulate outside Germany but they are subject to strict censorship."

Is the City Healthy?

Dr. Flexner disputed the common belief that men who joined the army from the country are in better condition physically than those from the city. "The city man is, on the whole," he said, "much less subject to common diseases. For instance, there is much less measles and—as measles predispose to pneumonia—less pneumonia among city men. The same is true of mumps and meningitis. Where men have been accustomed to associate in large numbers there is apparently less predisposition to these diseases and they are less severe when they do occur. However, conditions in the camps are being so changed that ultimately the country boy will have as good a chance as the city boy."

CARL B. RODEN, whose appointment, through civil service, as librarian of the Chicago Public Library was announced last week, has been a member of the City Club for the last ten years. Mr. Roden assumes his official duties this week. He has the heartiest congratulations and best wishes of his City Club friends.

"It shall be my policy to carry out the plans inaugurated by Mr. Legler," Mr. Roden told a representative of a morning paper last week. "Just as rapidly as the money becomes available we shall establish more regional branches and make it our business to carry the books to the people. The present capacity of the library is 6,-000,000 a year. In ten years I hope that it will be twice the number."

City Club members will remember the action of various civic organizations—in which the special City Club Committee on Public Librarian, Charles M. Williams, chairman, took a leading part—urging the appointment of a qualified board to conduct the examination.

IF THE MAN AT YOUR ELBOW at dinner is a clam, don't give him up! If the weather doesn't interest him, baseball bores him and he's sick of war talk, try something else on him. Maybe he's a shark at billiards, reads Browning or has just been to the Follies. If you strike his major interest, you have hooked him.

VERY OFTEN THERE ARE interesting announcements on the Bulletin Board. Get the habit of looking!

SOME OF THE BRIGHTEST IDEAS of all time originated at the dinner table. Try yours on your neighbor.

The City Club Bulletin

Published Weekly by the City Club of Chicago

A Journal of Active Citizenship

VOLUME XI   MONDAY, MARCH 18, 1918   NUMBER 11

KEEP THESE DATES FREE!

Thursday, March 21

George H. Cushing

Editor "The Black Diamond"

Subject: "The Coal Program for the Coming Year"

Saturday, March 23

—Ladies' Day

Edward H. Forbush

State Ornithologist, Massachusetts

Subject: "Birds — A Wartime Asset." Illustrated with slides

Luncheon from 11:30   Speaking at 1:00

PUT YOUR MORNING "GROUCH" in your old kit bag when you come to the Club for lunch.

"TALK DAY" ADDRESSES are an intellectual treat. And—if you will excuse the bromide—they are really *both* entertaining and instructive.

Harbingers of Spring

THE long cold winter on Plymouth Court is drawing to a close. The snow hummocks along the sidewalks have vanished and the haberdasher around the corner is loading his windows with spring neckties and gorgeous shirts appropriate to the season. The barber shop next door is doing a land office business.

A little of the infectious spirit of the season has crept into the Public Affairs Committee and they have provided us this week with a program of springtime events.

LOOKING AHEAD

Every member of the Club who sat in a cold office on the fuelless days last winter will agree that our first thought this spring should be our next winter's coal supply. So the committee, with true civic foresight, has made this the first subject on the spring program. It has arranged with George H. Cushing, editor of *The Black Diamond*, official organ of the coal trade, to address the Club at luncheon next Thursday in "The Coal Program for the Coming Year." Mr. Cushing is known throughout the country as one of the best informed men on the coal situation.

"IN THE SPRING, TRA-LA!"

On Saturday, however, the committee abandons itself completely to the spirit of spring. The subject for the luncheon that day will be "Birds," and the speaker will be Edward Howe Forbush, state ornithologist of Massachusetts. Massachusetts is the first state in the Union to recognize the importance of bird life to the extent of having a paid guardian for the birds. Mr. Forbush has made birds his life study, is the founder of the Massachusetts Audubon Society and the author of several books on birds. He believes that birds have an eco-

The City Club Bulletin
A Journal of Active Citizenship

The purpose of the Club is to bring together in informal association those men who are genuinely interested in the improvement of the political, social and economic conditions of the community in which we live.

PUBLISHED WEEKLY BY THE

CITY CLUB OF CHICAGO

315 Plymouth Court   Telephone: Harrison 8278

DWIGHT L. AKERS, Editor

OFFICERS OF THE CLUB

FRANK I. MOULTON, President
EDGAR A. BANCROFT, Vice-President
ROY C. OSGOOD, Treasurer
CHARLES YEOMANS, Secretary
GEORGE E. HOOKER, Civic Secretary

EDITORIAL BOARD

HERBERT H. SMITH, Chairman
FREDERICK D. BRAMHALL   S. R. WATKINS
C. COLTON DAUGHADAY   PAUL R. WRIGHT

$1.00 per Year   -   -   -   10c per Copy

Entered as second class matter, December 3, 1917, at the postoffice at Chicago, Illinois, under the act of March 3, 1879.

nomic importance to the country which contributes to the efficiency of our food production and so to the prosecution of the war. He will have slides. Ladies are invited to this luncheon.

OUR THANKS!

The arrangements with Mr. Forbush are made by courtesy of the Illinois Audubon Society, under whose auspices he is to speak at Central Music Hall at 2:30 Saturday afternoon. Mr. Forbush's address is one of a series which concludes with a lecture Saturday, March 30, at the same hour and place by Louis Agassiz Fuertes, "the greatest bird artist of this or any other country."

DID IT EVER OCCUR TO YOU that every time you bring a new member into the Club you are not only building up the man-power of the Club, but are contributing the equivalent of $30 a year to the Club treasury?

THE WARTIME COMMITTEE and the Public Utilities Committee of the Club meet every week. The committees which meet frequently are generally the best attended.

THE LISTENING POST

If you have anything "on" a fellow-member, whisper it in the editor's ear. Listen as hard as he can from his advanced post in "no-man's-land" the editor cannot learn all the interesting gossip about the "doings" of members.

The editor wants every kind of information about them: Weddings, business changes, arrival of offspring, war service, awards of the Croix de guerre, election or appointment to office, and so on ad infinitum.

Call Harrison 8278 and ask for the editor of the Bulletin. Or drop your item in the box in the lobby.

THE ANNUAL MEETING of the City Club for reports and for the election of officers and directors for the ensuing year will be held on Saturday, April 20th. The directors last week, in accordance with the by-laws of the Club, appointed a Nominating Committee, consisting of Philip S. Post, Chairman, W. D. Herrick, F. B. Johnstone, S. R. Watkins and Horace J. Bridges. This committee will submit nominations for officers and for four new directors. They are required to post these nominations by April 1st.

NEW MEMBERS are coming in at the rate of about one a day. These men joined last week:

Charles L. Byron, Patent Attorney, Wilkinson & Huxley.

H. T. Cartlidge, Agency Superintendent, National Fire Insurance Co.

J. P. Davis, Purchasing Agent, Belden Mfg. Co.

Peter J. Dunne, Superintendent, Rothschild & Co.

Irving Herriott, General Attorney, C. & N. W. Ry. Co.

I. Horween, Leather Manufacturer.

Thomas H. West, Marks & Clerk, Manager.

IF THE FRIEND who lunches with you at the City Club enjoys himself, don't deny him the opportunity of becoming a member. The waitress will get you an application card.

(Continued on page 94)

What the City Club Means to One Member

What does the City Club mean to you?
A member who prefers to be anonymous,
brought to us last week this expression of
his feeling about the Club:

LIFE in a city like Chicago has very grave disadvantages—recognized and admitted by any one who is discriminating. It also has compensations—in fact, sufficient compensations to justify spending a major part of our very limited and uncertain time above ground, among its appalling noise, dirt and general stridency, its hideous maladjustments, its debasing amusements. Perhaps you read Hackett's comments in the *New Republic* a few weeks ago. Against all this you must weigh the compensations.

THE EXPERIENCE OF LIVING

You get something here that is so stimulating, that is so profoundly nutritious and constructive and provocative of thought and emotion—of *generous* thought and deep emotion—that once having experienced it you can't live without it, and gladly pay the price for it.

Among these things—among these priceless things, is this City Club—for $30 a year! Not as a convenience and a comfort—which are as nothing compared with its value as an educational force—but as an absolute essential to a man's intellectual life.

With no effort on our part, with no intrusion on our time, in fact, what do we get, simply handed to us with our lunch. Well, may I just recall a very few things, occasions when the whole year's dues would be too little to pay for that single event?

GIANTS OF THEIR RACE

Booker Washington, for instance, a perfectly astonishing person, standing there in the dining room, the man in whose plans and purposes all the bewildering problems of the Negro in America is bound up, and a little later, Mr. Du Bois, with his exquisite English, expounding the tragedy of the colored man's isolation. There you are—the whole range, Washington, the statesman, DuBois, the poet!

And do you by chance remember the singing of the Hampton Quartette? Do you know where you can find singing like that anywhere at all, singing that comes directly out of the red soil, the only indigenous American music?

STIRRED FROM OUR COMPLACENCY

Then there was Thomas Mott Osborn. How can a man measure the value to himself of such a talk as that, altogether the most impressive and the most illuminating words that have ever been said in our hearing on that subject, the subject of the prison and the prisoner, and the deadly complacency of polite society—your society and mine.

But why go on, even if there were space to go on? Every Club member has felt this presence of the big soul, of the genius, of the uncompromising champion, the knight errant, the lover of liberty and justice.

A PROCESSION OF PERSONALITIES

Since the war, think of the people who have given their best thoughts and their nervous energy to us absorbent, smoky, lunch eaters. Captain Ian Hay Beith, General Gorgas, T. P. O'Connor, Simon Flexner, Mr. Ratcliffe, and that English officer with no legs who toiled painfully up the aisle to say a few words, also John Masefield, the greatest of living poets, and women of high distinction beginning with Jane Addams.

Can we repay the City Club for these experiences with $30 a year?

THE INTIMATE TOUCH

Moreover, we are allowed to enter into the life of the City, to get behind the scenes and see how democracy carries on its business, and to suggest and assist in improvements. We can work as well as listen. We can find expression for any craving to make some little mark on our times and to register our conviction that a man's life does not consist in the accretiveness of a business career, to which most of us are condemned.

In other words, the City Club, when recognized, when appropriated to the uses

Soldiers & Sailors

welcome at the City Club of Chicago, 315 Plymouth Ct

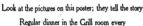

Every Saturday and Sunday from 2:30 p. m. until 11 p.m. the Club rooms are open to all enlisted men

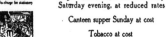

Free use of pool and billiard tables, club stationery, magazines, telephone

Look at the pictures on this poster; they tell the story

Regular dinner in the Grill room every Saturday evening, at reduced rates

Canteen supper Sunday at cost

Tobacco at cost

Make this your club every Saturday & Sunday

Poster Design—Soldiers' and Sailors' "Open House"

of our best life, is one great compensation and consolation for the rigors of our city residence, the sordid meannesses of traffic, the shallowness of amusements, the remoteness of the clean and sweet open country with its stately procession of seasons passing in beauty and in peace.

Meantime we get older, and it is not at all out of place to apply to our general experience in this Club the devout words of Tagore: *"When I go hence let this be my parting word, that what I have seen here is unsurpassable."*

(Signed.) A CLUB MEMBER.

DON'T COMPLAIN if your committee has been inactive. Appoint yourself a sub-committee of one to put a little ginger into the chairman.

ONE OF THE BEST WAYS to get acquainted in the City Club is through the civic committees. You miss this opportunity if you fail to attend the meetings of your committee.

 # At the Sign of the Book

HERE are some additions to the Club library which will be of interest to our members:

FOREST PRESERVE DISTRICT OF COOK COUNTY. Second Annual Message of Peter Reinberg, President, Board of Forest Preserve Commissioners, January 7, 1918.

A review of the year's work toward saving Cook County's forest regions. During the year the Board acquired title to 6,642 acres. With land previously acquired and additional land contracted for the estate of the Forest Preserve District amounts to 9,393 acres—the total cost of which is $3,475,946. The report describes briefly the areas acquired and the steps which have been taken for their protection and care and to make them available for recreation. Plans for the propagation of wild life in the preserves—birds and animals that formerly inhabited them—are under consideration, says the report.

HEALTH INSURANCE—A POSITIVE STATEMENT IN ANSWER TO OPPONENTS. American Labor Legislation Review, Vol. VII, No. 4, December, 1917.

The American Association for Legislation, which publishes this book continues to be not only the foremost advocate of health insurance but perhaps the most satisfactory source of information on the subject. This is essentially a "reply brief" to the arguments submitted in opposition to health insurance. It analyzes and presents in readable form the information and conclusions reached in recent studies of health insurance, particularly by the various state investigating commissions. To the person who is interested but who can't afford time to wade through the mass of literature which is being produced on this subject this book will be very useful.

The subject headings suggest the scope of the book: "The Sickness Problem in America," "Possible Methods of Meeting the Sickness Problem," "Methods of Applying the Insurance Principle," "Scope and Benefits of Health Insurance," "Administration of Health Insurance," "Cost of Health Insurance," "Health Insurance and Social Welfare."

A Picture of British Politics

S. K. RATCLIFFE, the luncheon-hour speaker of March 13, gave a rapid survey of men and events in present-day England and discussed the outlook as regards the Lloyd George war government. Members of the Club remembered Mr. Ratcliffe's keen observations on English political life when he addressed the Club in 1915 and 1916 and a large audience was present to hear him.

"Fifteen months have passed," he said, "since Mr. Asquith gave way to Mr. Lloyd George, who in framing his new war cabinet of five members made the most adventurous of experiments in constitutional change. It came in as a victory government, but the high hopes entertained a year ago had not been fulfilled. The Russian revolution, the Italian reverses, the indecisive operations on the Western front have combined with the ravages of the submarine to make a war situation which, now that America is in a position to use her military force, is vastly different from the situation foreshadowed by both statesmen and generals a year ago.

FOOD SITUATION GRAVE

"It is necessary to say that the food situation in England is grave. The supplies of all necessaries, except bread, are extremely short; and, after a winter marked in all the large cities by lines of people standing in line for hours outside the provision stores, the country is now entering upon the stage of government rationing by means of sugar and food cards. The moral for industrial America lies in the one word *Ships*. The imperative need of the Allies and especially of Great Britain, is more ships, and necessarily the progress of American shipbuilding is watched with the keenest anxiety.

"In England today, absorbed as the country is in the stupendous task of war, nothing is more remarkable than the fact that Parliament and people should be working toward laying the foundations of a new political and social structure. The new Franchise Act, just passed, is the longest step ever taken toward complete political democracy. It embodies the principle of manhood suffrage and confers the vote upon some six million women, and this greatly enlarged electorate will probably be called upon within the next few months to pronounce judgment upon the government's war record and to give Mr. Lloyd George, or withhold from him, a mandate in the direction of settlement and reconstruction."

THE TURN OF THE WHEEL

In estimating the probabilities, Mr. Ratcliffe said that if any turn should come in the war situation which was seriously unfavorable, the result might be a dramatic tightening of executive control and possibly a dictatorship. A favorable alternative would be a remodeling of the existing Cabinet by the appointment of statesmen more representative of the people than Curzon and Milner and possibly the addition of Mr. Asquith and a few of his colleagues of the last coalition. Or again, if the election should be held under constitutional conditions, it was conceivable that a democratic majority in the new House of Commons might, in view of the advancing strength of organized labor and its progressive allies, bring England to the point of having a labor government.

"Lloyd George," concluded Mr. Ratcliffe, "is still, as he has been since before the war, the most challenging figure in British politics, and his future presents the most fascinating personal problem. He stands now in a position unlike that of any preceding prime minister, in that having left his old party, the liberals, and not linked himself to any other, he is a leader without party backing, a party machine or funds. Accordingly he stands upon his record, and on the eve of a general election would rely upon his command of political strategy and upon his extraordinary and oft-repeated power of leadership and faculty of stirring the enthusiasm of the multitude."

THERE IS A CITY CLUB in each of the following cities: Baltimore, Md.; Berkeley, Cal.; Boston, Mass.; Chicago, Ill.; Cincinnati, Cleveland, Ohio; Hartford, Conn.; Indianapolis, Ind.; Kansas City, Mo.; Los Angeles, Cal.; Memphis, Tenn.; Milwaukee, Wis.; New Rochelle, N. Y.; New York City; Philadelphia, Pa.; Portland, Ore.; Rochester, N. Y.; St. Johns, N. B., and St. Louis, Mo.

THE LISTENING POST

(*Continued from page 90*)

Thomas T. Jones adds another star to our military list. He is leaving for service in the medical corps.

Alfred Yeomans is "back to town" again after a visit of several months to the Pacific Coast.

Capt. Guy L. Jones has been transferred from Camp Grant to San Antonio, Texas, on special duty.

The entertainment committees for the Soldiers' and Sailors' days this week-end are as follows:
Saturday, March 23, F. E. Plowman, H. Daughaday, S. B. King, J. R. Bibbins, A. B. Hall.
Sunday, March 24, H. J. Kaufman, George W. Gordon, J. B. Freeman, Morris L. Greeley, G. K. Reed, F. T. Hennessy.

The marriage of Robert T. Mack to Miss Jeanette Steele has been announced. Mr. Mack is serving at Washington in connection with the government army insurance program. He recently received a commission as 2d lieutenant.

Laird Bell leaves for the East on March 27, as the first step in a journey to France. He will be in the Red Cross field service. Mr. Bell was secretary of the City Club in 1912-1913 and was until recently chairman of the Club's Committee on Political Nominations and Elections. His many friends here wish him the best of luck!

Last Thursday's papers contained the announcement that the 149th Field Artillery, composed principally of Chicago men, participated in a raid on the German lines March 5. Noble B. Judah, Jr., a member of the City Club, holds a commission as Major commanding the Second Battalion of this unit.

The Club library is a storehouse of material on current civic questions. It should be a workshop. Get busy, you committee members!

"Camp Logan, Houston, Tex., March 12.—(Special.)—Major Abel Davis of the First battalion of the One Hundred and Thirty-first infantry and in charge of the trench system and its accompanying schools, has been placed in command of the One Hundred and Thirty-second Infantry.

"Major Davis replaced Col. Houle of the regular army, who has been in command of the regiment since Col. J. J. Garrity went to school at San Antonio.

"This is the third responsible position Major Davis has held since coming to this camp. He was first put in command of a provisional regiment, in which he saved 3,000 supposedly useless men from discharge, and next was given charge of the trenches. He is a Chicago banker and lawyer. He has been in the One Hundred and Thirty-first infantry since 1898, having enlisted in that regiment—then the Illinois national guard—as a private in the Spanish-American War."—Press item.

The Mail Pouch

Does the use of advertising space in a billboard which defaces a boulevard injure the prestige of the advertiser in the eyes of the public? This interesting point is raised in a letter addressed to the Bulletin by one of our members. We have taken the liberty of "painting out" the names. He says:

"Apropos of the defacement of Sheridan Road with bill boards, I am in receipt of the following letter from the advertising manager of the X Association.

I am in receipt of yours of the 26th. Some weeks ago we instructed the Y Company to paint out the boards painted for our account which were located on Sheridan Road and we were under the impression that this had been done.

"It has been represented to X that a great number of people in Chicago seriously object to having Sheridan Road defaced with billboard advertising. The Y Company has not painted out the billboards; it looks as though they were bolstering their business by retaining a high class establishment on their bill boards contrary to its wish. It is unquestionably derogatory to X's reputation; perhaps an action for damages would lie."
(Signed)   G. I. J.

Scenery Is National Asset

So Says . Representative from National Park Service in Club Address

"AMERICA possesses the greatest amount and variety of scenery accessible to tourists existing in any part of the world," said Robert Sterling Yard of the National Park Service at the City Club Saturday, March 9th. "It requires little imagination to realize what can be made of this not only as a great educational and spiritual resource but as an economic asset. Switzerland, up to the time of the war, realized an income of one hundred million dollars a year from the sale of her scenery. To develop this she spent about a million dollars a year in advertising it. Canada by exploiting the scenic resources of her Rockies has stimulated tourist travel to such an extent that it now ranks in fourth place among the sources of her national income."

A PROGRAM FOR PARKS

The program of the National Park Service, for the immediate future, Mr. Yard said, covers some very interesting projects:

"1. The Park Service is urging the repeal of the provision in the Rocky Mountain National Park act, which limits the annual expenditure for that park to $10,000. With that amount it has been possible to employ only about half the rangers needed, to maintain the present trails and to lay out a very few new ones.

"2. It is advocating the development of the Sequoia Park and its extension to include the King's and Kern River cañons and the wonderful High Sierra mountain region around Mount Whitney.

"3. It is asking that the Grand Cañon, now a national monument, be made a national park. As a park it would have the opportunity for much greater development as a national scenic resource and as the greatest exhibit of erosion in the world.

"4. It is urging, finally, the inclusion of the beautiful 'Jackson Hole' country and the Teton range lying just to the south of the Yellowstone Park as a part of that park."

Mr. Yard exhibited a large number of beautiful slides of Glacier National Park and the proposed Greater Sequoia Park. Glacier Park he described as the "Canadian Rockies painted in Grand Cañon colors." "It is accessible," he said, "at times when the Canadian Rockies are inaccessible." The Greater Sequoia Park, by adding to the wonderful Sequoia groves the mountain wonderland behind them, would mean the union of two superlatives.

The national parks, according to Mr. Yard, are being used to protect the wild animals. "In the parks," he said, "there is no game, there are only animal friends. The only animals that are not protected are the mountain lion and wolves which prey upon others. The animals under these conditions are becoming very tame." Mr. Yard showed an interesting series of animal pictures.

CHIEF OF STAFF

Mr. Yard is an assistant to Stephen T. Mather, formerly vice-president of the City Club and now at the head of the National Park Service. Mr. Mather's accomplishments at the head of this bureau are a matter of much pride to his friends in the Club. Mr. Yard paid him a high tribute. "He has had to fight," he said, "against ignorance, indifference and red tape. This fight has required great persistence and strength. His victory has secured a firm foothold for the national park idea."

PROF. HORACE SECRIST, of the department of economics, Northwestern University, a member and until recently chairman of the Club's Committee on Public Expenditures, left last Thursday for Washington to take a position as statistician with the Shipping Board. Prof. Arthur E. Swanson, also of Northwestern University and a member of the City Club, preceded him to Washington and is engaged in the same task. Their work is to assist in ascertaining the amount of tonnage of various classes available and the possible reductions in exports and imports to make the tonnage available for war purposes.

The City Club Bulletin

Published Weekly by the City Club of Chicago

A Journal of Active Citizenship

VOLUME XI   MONDAY, MARCH 25, 1918   NUMBER 12

THIS WEEK AND NEXT

Wednesday, March 27, at Luncheon

DR. ISAAC J. LANSING

Pastor Collegiate Churches, Ridgewood, N. Y.

"THE PERILS OF A PREMATURE PEACE"

Dr. Lansing has been speaking under the auspices of the National Security League to large and important audiences in New York, Chicago and other cities, on problems relating to the war.

Thursday, March 28, at Luncheon

GEORGE H. CUSHING

Editor, "The Black Diamond"

"THE COAL PROGRAM FOR THE COMING YEAR"

Mr. Cushing's address was postponed from last Thursday. Now is the time to think about next winter's coal problems.

Monday, April 1, at Luncheon

CHARLES H. WHITAKER

Editor, Journal American Institute of Architects

"OUR WARTIME HOUSING EMERGENCY." (*illustrated*)

Congress has appropriated fifty million dollars to build houses for shipyard workers. How will this money be spent? How should it be spent? The shipbuilding program is dependent on houses. "This is one of the biggest war emergency problems before the American people," says Mr. Whitaker. "Millions of money and months of time have already been wasted." Mr. Whitaker has been working on this problem for over a year.

Wednesday, April 3, at 8:00 p. m.—Ladies' Night

"FIRST AND ONLY SPRING MUSICALE"

Trio: Amy Emerson Neill, violin; Vera Poppe, 'cello; Mary Cameron, piano. Soloist: Hector G. Spaulding. Program on page 104.

"Put away gloom and forget the winter of discontent," urges the Music Extension Committee of the Club, which is arranging for the Musicale.

Every person who comes will chip in 15c toward expenses.

There will be the usual dinner service with 75c and $1.00 table d'hote—but please reserve not later than Tuesday, April 2.

Ghe City Club Bulletin
A Journal of Active Citizenship

The purpose of the Club is to bring together in informal association those men who are genuinely interested in the improvement of the political, social and economic conditions of the community in which we live.

PUBLISHED WEEKLY BY THE
CITY CLUB OF CHICAGO
315 Plymouth Court　　Telephone: Harrison 8278

DWIGHT L. AKERS, Editor

OFFICERS OF THE CLUB
FRANK I. MOULTON, President
EDGAR A. BANCROFT, Vice-President
ROY C. OSGOOD, Treasurer
CHARLES YEOMANS, Secretary
GEORGE E. HOOKER, Civic Secretary

EDITORIAL BOARD
HERBERT H. SMITH, Chairman
FREDERICK D. BRAMHALL　　S. R. WATKINS
C. COLTON DAUGHADAY　　PAUL R. WRIGHT

$1.00 per Year　-　-　-　-　10c per Copy

Entered as second class matter, December 3, 1917, at the postoffice at Chicago, Illinois, under the act of March 3, 1879.

THE LISTENING POST

The successful operation of Plan No. 2 adopted by the directors for meeting the Club deficit depends upon your co-operation. Please send your check immediately so the books may be closed March 31st with the balance on the right side!

THESE MEN JOINED the City Club last week: Oliver S. Brown, salesman, iron and steel; Burt A. Crowe, lawyer; E. G. Krumrine, real estate; Wm. A. Stewart, Stewart & Ashby (tea and coffee importers).

H. T. KESSLER, who has been on a vacation in Florida for the past month, will return this week.

EDWARD B. DE GROOT is in France helping the Y. M. C. A. organize recreation among our fighters. Mr. De Groot was formerly superintendent of playgrounds for the South Park Commission and moved to San Francisco several years ago to direct recreation in the public schools of that city.

He has maintained a non-resident membership in the City Club in Chicago. While a resident of Chicago, he was a member of the Board of Directors of the Club.

THE SOLDIERS' AND SAILORS' Entertainment Committee has had cards printed directing soldiers and sailors how to reach the Club House. Members may obtain these from the cashier for distribution to soldiers and sailors. The printing was done gratis by James E. Bell. The Committee desires to express its appreciation through the columns of the Bulletin.

EVER NOTICE the silent little group of chess fans that foregathers every noon in the east end of the reading room? The other day "Pa" Williams said "Checkmate" and someone accused him of being a chatterbox.

THESE MEMBERS OF THE CLUB will act as reception committees for the soldiers and sailors next Saturday and Sunday:

Saturday, March 23. F. E. Plowman, H. Daughaday, S. B. King, J. R. Bibbins.

Sunday, March 24. Geo. W. Gordon, H. J. Kaufman, Morris L. Greeley, G. K. Reed, F. T. Hennessy, J. M. McVoy.

MRS. ST. CLAIR STOBART, who recently addressed the City Club, is the lecturer at Orchestra Hall Friday night, April 5, for the benefit of the Serbian Red Cross. Mrs. Stobart will for the first time in Chicago, display new photographic scenes of the extraordinary work of the hospital division under her command.

ANOTHER OF OUR MEMBERS is going "over there" for the Y. M. C. A. Prof. Allan Hoben is the latest recruit. Prof. Hoben told a newspaper reporter the other day, "I do not know what my work will be, but I've heard I may begin as a physical instructor. Yes, I've played baseball and football and have done a good deal of gym work. I'm told that this is a fine way to get into close touch with the soldiers, and I welcome this opportunity to do something for a big cause."

SOME OF OUR MEMBERS have forgotten what the Club looks like. Why not give us the "once-over" again?

AFTER LUNCH, a half-hour session in the reading room, with a magazine will put you in mental trim for the business of the afternoon.

Farmer in War Against Starvation

Handicapped by Labor Shortage
and Other Farm Conditions

"THE war against starvation is being fought over here. Never before has such a responsibility rested on any people as rests upon the American farmers today," said F. B. McLeran of Minnesota, who addressed the City Club on "The Farm Crisis" last Thursday. Mr. McLeran owns and operates a farm near Duluth. He is vice-president of the Minnesota State Dairyman's Association and an extension lecturer for the Agricultural College of the State University.

THE FARM EMERGENCY

The farmer, Mr. McLeran said, is struggling against very great odds in his effort to meet the requirements of the government in food production. "The farmer is patriotic but he must have men, money and machinery. He cannot make bricks without straw." So serious is the situation that "if food is to win the war, the war is in danger of being lost." Mr. McLeran read from a recent issue of the Literary Digest reports from seventeen agricultural states, showing the existence of serious labor shortage on the farms and a probably decreased production on that account.

Mr. McLeran does not believe that the labor of men and boys, or even of women, from the cities is to be discredited as of little use on the farm. "There is no reason why the city man cannot learn to use a pitchfork as well as a bayonet. It is reported that there are 125,000 women at work on the farms in England. The greatest obstacle in this country to the use of women on the farms is the prejudice of farmers against it." Mr. McLeran endorsed the programs for boys' and women's working reserves and for farm vacations for city men. The contacts of the farm, he urged, would be of greatest benefit to the city dweller.

DAIRYING IN DANGER

The dairying business in particular is in serious danger, according to Mr. McLeran. It is estimated, he said, that there is a world shortage of 28,000,000 dairy cattle. In some parts of the United States, herds have been reduced fifty per cent. Among the dairymen in his state association the reduction has been about 20 per cent. "The question of the future," he said, "is going to be, where can you get milk, not how much you will pay for it. The farmer is not trying to starve the milk consumer in the city, he is trying to save an industry." Mr. McLeran criticized the findings of the Chicago Milk Commission which allowed, from the 12c per quart to be paid by the consumer, less than half to the farmer and the remainder to the distributor. The only response which the farmer has had to his efforts to help himself through his associations has, he said, been opposition and the indictment of officials of his associations by the government.

POTATOES

Another branch of farming which is in danger at the present time is potato culture. "You are paying," said Mr. McLeran, "$1.20 per bushel for potatoes. I receive for them thirty cents per bushel and the freight to Chicago is fifteen cents. Who is getting the balance—the seventy-five cents? The potatoes are handed from one middleman to another, each of whom takes a profit, and adds so much to the cost. Don't think that the farmer is getting rich by raising potatoes. Last year I raised forty-seven acres of potatoes and didn't realize enough from them to pay the labor cost."

The difficulties which the farmer meets make it difficult for him to get the credit which he needs. "If I want to borrow money on my potato or dairy business," Mr. McLeran said, "the banker who knows the conditions turns me down. If I want to borrow on my wheat crop, however, the case is different, for the government guarantees me $2.20 per bushel at the Chicago market." Mr. McLeran said that the farmers would be "tickled to death" with a guaranteed 10 per cent margin above cost of production.

"There is a 'no-man's land' of prejudice between the farmer and the city dweller now," said Mr. McLeran. "It is hard for

The City Club Bulletin

either to get an audience with the other." This mutual distrust and suspicion, he urged, should be put aside and a better understanding, a greater reciprocity established between them in matters affecting them in common.

Last week the Farm Service Division of the U. S. Employment Service announced its plans for recruiting labor for the farms. The announcement is interesting in connection with Mr. McLeran's address. Special agents are being sent into farm districts where an acute labor shortage exists to devise ways of meeting the most pressing needs. Publicity is obtained through posters, newspapers, local organizations, etc. Third and fourth class postoffices are made local clearing agencies for farm labor. The Farm Service Division is establishing offices in nearly one hundred centers for gathering information and developing ways and means of meeting calls for labor. The announcement concludes:

THE SOURCES OF SUPPLY

"The sources of farm labor lie this year in the local unemployed farm labor, single and married men in cities who are available for farm work, boys between 16 and 21, and those former farm workers who, having drifted to cities, are now desirous of a return to the land. There are many thousands of former farm hands who want to return, and an enrollment campaign to find and list all these in a reserve of not less than 250,000 will shortly be opened by the Public Service Reserve and pushed to early completion. The Boys' Working Reserve expects to enroll 250,000 boys between 16 and 21 to aid in farm work this year; and in many States these boys have for weeks been given practical training by farmers in preparation for their summer's work.

"The Department of Labor's study has convinced it that while there is today a severe shortage of farm labor, there is sufficient available labor to meet the demands of agriculture if the farmers co-operate by outlining the demands with definiteness and in time. It is suggested that this can most readily be done by asking the rural carrier or postmaster for a blank and filling it at once."

LADIES MAY USE THE FACILITIES of the Club after 5 P. M. On Saturdays, they may come to the Club luncheons.

GEORGE C. SIKES, in an article on Chicago transportation conditions in the March *Review of Reviews*, says: "Inefficiency of terminal facilities constitutes the main defect of the Chicago railroad situation. That inefficiency affects the transportation welfare of the entire country. It is hard to remedy because of the deep-seated conditions growing out of the conflicting interests of diverse private ownership. I had supposed, like many others, that taking over of the railroads by the Government was to mean an end of these diverse interests for the time being; that the Government was to treat the railroads, terminals and all, as one property. Inquiries among railroad men in connection with the preparation of this article soon developed another point of view. The railroad properties should not be so thoroughly 'scrambled' while in the possession of the Government, it was said, that they could not be 'unscrambled' again. That is, the individual properties must be kept so separate that they can be returned to their owners intact when the war is over.

"It is by no means certain that the Chicago terminal problem can be solved properly, even for the period of the war, on such a theory."

THIS IS ONE ON US: Thomas T. Roberts, who has gone to France, broke into this column last week under the name of "Jones." Nobody else will accept the responsibility so it must be on the editor. There are thirteen members of the distinguished Jones family in the Club and the editor cannot afford to offend them by apologizing to Mr. Roberts. However, we regret the mistake.

Another recent slip-up for which we are sorry was in misprinting the name of one of our new members, Mr. Nahum Morrill, of Winston, Strawn and Shaw.

JACK SMITH, the other day, brought George Brown to the City Club for lunch. It was "talk day" and George heard a speaker from Russia who told a lot of interesting inside "stuff" about conditions there which George had never heard before. George thought the lunch and the service were superfine. He would have joined the Club, if Jack had spoken the word, but it didn't occur to Jack to ask him. Thus Jack lost an opportunity of serving the Club and doing a friend a good turn.

At the Sign of the Book

No Nonsense

1917 REPORT OF THE DOMESTIC RELATIONS BRANCH OF THE MUNICIPAL COURT OF CHICAGO, with a special report on its organization and operation, with suggestions and recommendations of needed legislative and administrative measures to increase its value and efficiency. By Judge John Stelk.

"No red tape, no dilly-dallying, no nonsense." These phrases, each dignified with a paragraph on page 26 of the report, represent Judge Stelk's ideas on the conduct of the court over which he presided until last December. Judge Stelk particularly distrusts "nonsense." On page after page you see him pursuing it with a sharp stick, and whatever form it assumes the judge is never in doubt as to its identity. Nonsense is nonsense, just as a spade is a spade.

SWATS "REFORMERS"

The judge objects violently, for instance, to "reform ideas and so-called humane philosophy" in the treatment of prisoners. He is for the rock-pile, for "hard-driving" and even speaks with some favor of the lash as a cure for wife deserters. "There is no room outside of four walls for human panthers of the Bill Sykes type." He objects to having prisoners "molly-coddled" with "orchestral, vocal and vaudeville entertainments." "Short-haired women and long-haired men should not be allowed to play at the game of fuss and feathers in their efforts to exploit their maudlin sympathy, dawdling away the time of the prisoners and the guards."

And yet Judge Stelk is far from hardhearted. These ideas should not be "mistaken as the sentiments of an old Scrooge," he warns us. And in another place: "There was no 'Bloody' Jeffrey irascibility in the proceedings." He regards the Domestic Relations Court as essentially a humanitarian institution. "It is the Triple Alliance of the three great powers, Love, Sympathy and Help," he says in his "Salutation."

It must not be assumed either that the judge is in any sense a reactionary. He is against "nonsense," but he has many advanced ideas of his own which are discussed at length in characteristic Stelkian English

—vigorous, picturesque and cocksure. The book is liberally sprinkled with the judge's observations on human life and character and with his common-sense advice on everything from household economy to birthcontrol.

Judge Stelk's experience on the bench has given him a low estimate of loafer husbands. He says: "It is unfortunate that the courts have not the authority to compel a certain breed of loafer husbands to dress in petticoats and do their duty as domestic servants. They would look well humped over washtubs, the dishpan, making beds or swinging scrub brushes. Indeed, I doubt whether washtubs and scrub brushes would work in harness with them or be seen in their company. The most humble feminine drudge holds an imperial station compared with the shiftless ilk of so-called men to whom reference has been made."

A TIP TO "FRIEND WIFE"

Not that the men are always to blame. "Many men," says the judge, "are naturally bad beyond all hope of redemption, but again, I insist that the great majority, as I have observed them in my court, would be as pliable as putty in the hands of their wives if only they had proper handling—not to be coaxed, wheedled and made babies and 'boobs' of—but guided and treated as ordinary human beings. Given a square deal and a 'show for his white alley' the average man, as in the case of the average woman, will not be found lacking in the ordinary decencies of life, and may be depended upon to come up to reasonable expectations, if not 100 per cent to the good."

PROCEEDINGS OF THE FOURTH ANNUAL CONVENTION OF THE ILLINOIS MUNICIPAL LEAGUE, December 6-7, 1917, University of Illinois Bulletin Vol. XV, No. 16, 152 pages.

"The Illinois Municipal League" is formed for "the improvement of municipal conditions in Illinois." Its members include 48 cities and villages of Illinois, public officials, civic and commerce associations and just plain citizens. In its meetings problems of Chicago and of "downstate" cities are discussed. The proceedings of the last conference, just issued, contain a dozen papers on a variety of subjects. The president of the League is Mayor H. J. Rodgers of Jacksonville.

The Mail Pouch

Haag's Wood Carvings

To the Editor: It is not unjust or inconsiderate to say that the uncertainty of Chicago as to matters of Art—its inability to decide between what is vital and what is merely imitative and stale, is sufficiently illustrated by the general attitude toward such work as Charles Haag has done in the carvings now at the Art Institute called "The Spirits of the Wood."

The pity is that the Art Institute itself does not encourage this sort of thing and gives it only a grudging space in its corridors. Because it cannot possibly be denied by any critic of discrimination that this work of Haag's is so much more interesting—so much more artistic—so much closer to the real heart of beauty and mystery and tragedy in all affairs on this planet, that the usual exhibit in the Art Institute must take a very inferior place—especially the usual exhibit of Sculpture.

These statuettes are not negligible things at all. They are very profound things. They correspond to the creations of all great artists of this or any time in their simplicity and subtlety. It makes no difference what kind of a person Haag is, or whether he has succeeded so far in impressing Art Institutes or the public anywhere. It is the business of lovers of beauty to *recognize* beauty and to acclaim it, and celebrate it, and honor it. And it is because Art Institutes are rarely above the popular standards in their tastes and are always, therefore, timid and gregarious, that they encourage art very little indeed, and our sterility continues in spite of our self-advertisement.

If you wish to test yourself in the domain of imagination,—and of artistic response,—if you want to decide whether you have or have not a response to the under-tones and over-tones of the scale—just subject yourself honestly and frankly to the spell of Haag's "Spirits" and accept the verdict. But go more than once and stay long enough. It is not a moving-picture show.   Edward Yeomans.

The Club library has not yet reached its peak load of use. It stands ready to serve you.

In the reading room are the magazines you like. There are literary eclairs such as Life or the Saturday Evening Post, if you like 'em. And there are also the more serious periodicals for those who want the mental stimulus.

Are you a member of the Club for "patriotic reasons" only? Are you one of those who believe in the Club and support its public work, but who have never become accustomed to its use as a Club? If so, you should get acquainted with the Club and with its opportunities to be of use to you.

Slams

These comments are taken from replies by members to the Director's letter about the Club deficit:

"The City Club is a necessity and a low priced one."

"I should consider making the annual dues $40 beginning with the Fall quarter. This is not an unreasonable amount for the facilities of our Club."

"I am a strong believer in the City Club and am willing to co-operate in whichever plan is decided upon."

"I have never been in the Club and joined and continue my membership because I believe it does good work and is entitled to the consideration of the public."

"The City Club has become a necessity rather than a luxury."

"I believe the City Club should be operated as a club first, and if there is any surplus it could be spent in gratifying the whims of otherwise idle members who are burdened with the cares of everyone else and have an inborn desire to reform them."

"I wouldn't continue to belong if I didn't feel that it was a sort of civic duty. I miss the great proportion of club events, and wish there were talks in the late afternoon or on Saturday; but, continuing to be democratic, I see that the club must serve the large group and not a lone individual."

"I appreciate my individual duty to pay my individual share. An argument: those at home are helping in the dues of those on and going to the front. The least we can do. There is a warm feeling of patriotism in it that salves the act of 'coughing' when my throat is so dry. Vive le City Club!"

Chemistry Plays Big War Role

May Be Decisive Factor, Says
Member of British War Mission

"IT is no clap-trap to say that this is a chemists' war and that it may be won in a laboratory," said Major S. M. J. Auld, Chemical Advisor of the British Military Mission, in his address at the City Club last Thursday. "There is always, for instance, the possibility of a gas being discovered against which there is no protection under conditions which prevail in the field. The side which does this first has pretty nearly won the war. Both sides are striving for this and it is work for your best chemists.

FIGHTING WITH GAS

"Gas has come to stay in this war," said Major Auld. "Few persons not at the front realize the extent to which it is used. Nearly one-fourth of the German shells are gas shells. Fifty thousand of such shells were fired into one town in a few hours one night. The French estimated that a million of them were fired against a few miles of their front within a month."

England did not at first appreciate her chemists, according to Major Auld. Many of them, he said, were allowed to go to the front when they should have been kept at home for research. After the development of gas warfare, a body of chemists was organized to go into the trenches to do the gas fighting, but it was soon discovered that it was work for plumbers, not for chemists. "Chemists now, however, are not taken to the front except for scientific work that must be done in the field or just behind the lines. There are laboratories, for instance, where German shells are examined in order that we may know at all times what the Germans are up to. A chemical advisor is attached to each headquarters staff."

CAREFUL WORK

Major Auld described the work of English chemists in meeting the constantly changing methods of gas attack by the Germans. He paid a compliment to the work already achieved by American chemists along these lines. "The work," he said, "requires men of the highest standing and character. The least drop in standards may mean a loss of life. Also in the manufacture of gas the utmost care is required. If the work is not carefully done the gas may be ineffective. In one bombardment, thirty per cent of the German tear-shells were ineffective because they were not prepared correctly."

America, Major Auld said, realized at once the importance of her chemists. She has provided for calling them out of the national army for service along scientific lines. "Most of our important chemical work," he said, "is done at home. In your case, however, since you are several thousand miles from the front, it will be necessary to maintain a larger force of chemists on the field."

HOW TO WIN

Major Auld gave this word of warning to Americans: "Settle down to the war as if it were a life work. If you consider the war as a temporary thing which may be over any time, you cannot get the best results from your efforts. The war will reach its climax when America has become capable of putting forth her full strength."

CHARLES H. WHITAKER, who is to speak at the Club Monday, April 1, on the great national housing emergency, has been studying housing problems for twenty years in all civilized countries of the world. He has been working for almost a year on the problem in this country as it relates to the crisis of the war. He is editor of the *Journal of the American Institute of Architects,* and is joint author of a book "The Housing Problem in War and in Peace," just coming off the press.

Mr. Whitaker will speak with illustrations of what England has done, of what France is proposing to do and especially of how both of these nations are studying the housing emergency in war with a view to making its solution a vital factor in the new industrial fabric of the future. With these new industrial fabrics in Europe the United States will have to contend in world commerce.

YOU who haven't tried it yet; who are still skeptical or cautious, or procrastinating—a lot of your old friends are lunching here regularly again.

Even some former members who had dropped out have come back into the club because the food is so good here now!

How much longer are you going to deprive yourself of this added benefit of the City Club?

The Spring Musicale

The "first and only spring musicale" which is to be given in the Club Lounge Ladies' Night next week, Wednesday, is going to be distinctly worth while. The Music Extension Committee makes this announcement:

"Come to this spring musicale. The music is to be Russian and French. Melody, charm and beauty are to have the occasion all to themselves.

"Put away gloom and forget the winter of discontent. Come and bring your family and friends—for all need cheer and inspiration.

"The price of admission, including war tax, will be only 15 cents. *Reason: We want a crowd.*

"Dinner—the now famous City Club Table d' Hote dinner at 75c and $1.00 a plate—will be served in the dining room. Make reservations early, not later in any case than the evening of Tuesday, April 2."

This is the program announced by the committee:

1. Trio for Violin, 'Cello and Piano......
   ....*Rachmaninoff*
   (In three movements)
   AMY EMERSON NEILL, VERA POPPÉ AND MARY CAMERON

2. Group of Songs......HECTOR G. SPAULDING
3. Violin Solo, Caprice..............*Guiraud*
   AMY EMERSON NEILL

4. Piano Soli—
   (a.) The Return of the Muleteers..*de Severac*
   (b.) Reflections in the Water..} ....*Debussy*
   (c.) Prelude, A minor........}
   MARY CAMERON

5. 'Cello Soli—
   (a.) The Minstrels Song........*Glazounoff*
   (b.) Orientale....................*César Cui*
   (c.) At the Fountain..............*Davidoff*
   VERA POPPÉ

"LABOR PROBLEMS under War Conditions," is the subject of a national conference to be held at the Hotel La Salle next Wednesday, Thursday and Friday under the joint auspices of the Society of Industrial Engineers and the Western Efficiency Society. On Wednesday afternoon and evening and on Thursday morning, the subject will be "Women in Industry." Thursday afternoon the subject will be "Mechanical Equipment—Its Function in Replacing Men." The evening program for Thursday is devoted to "Men Remaining—Securing Their Maximum Production." The same subject will be taken up at the Friday morning session and on Friday afternoon the topic will be "After the War—Readjustments to Take Care of Those Returning, Including Disabled." Friday evening there will be a banquet. The announcements state "that all interested are cordially invited."

In connection with the conference there will be an exhibit of labor saving factory equipment and modern office devices, also an educational exhibit comprising organization charts, standardized instruction forms, planning and dispatching sheets, lay-outs, employment forms, stores' control systems, etc.

"THE FIRST THING I DID when I came in," said one of the Jackies who visited the City Club at one of its week-end openings, "was to dig into the wash-room and use a towel for each ear." The story was told by Allen D. Albert, who talked at the Club Friday, Feb. 8, on War Camp Community Service. "Ours is the first army in history," Mr. Albert said, "that has had a chance to wash and it is doing it on every conceivable opportunity. The City Club is doing a wonderful service in opening its club-house to the men."

THE CLUB'S LOW DUES are no measure of the service it renders.

The City Club Bulletin

Published Weekly by the City Club of Chicago

A Journal of Active Citizenship

VOLUME XI   MONDAY, APRIL 1, 1918   NUMBER 13

KEEP YOUR MIND BRIGHT BY HEARING WHAT MEN "ON THE INSIDE" SAY ABOUT BIG AFFAIRS OF THE DAY

Monday, April 1, at Luncheon
CHARLES H. WHITAKER
Editor, Journal American Institute of Architects

"OUR WARTIME HOUSING EMERGENCY." *(illustrated)*

Congress has appropriated fifty million dollars to build houses for shipyard workers. How will this money be spent? How should it be spent? The shipbuilding program is dependent on houses. "This is one of the biggest war emergency problems before the American people," says Mr. Whitaker. "Millions of money and months of time have already been wasted." Mr. Whitaker has been working on this problem for over a year.

Wednesday, April 3, at 8:00 p. m.—Ladies' Night
"FIRST AND ONLY SPRING MUSICALE"

Trio: Amy Emerson Neill, violin; Vera Poppe, 'cello; Mary Cameron, piano. Soloist: Hector G. Spaulding. Program on page 106.
Every person who comes will chip in 15c toward expenses.
There will be the usual dinner service with 75c and $1.00 table d'hote—but please reserve not later than Tuesday, April 2.

Thursday, April 4, at Luncheon
PROF. HORACE M. KALLEN
University of Wisconsin

"THE PLACE OF PALESTINE IN THE SETTLEMENT OF THE WAR"

The capture of Jerusalem by the Allies brings nearer to realization the dreams of many generations of Jewish leaders for the re-establishment of a national home in Palestine. Dr. Kallen is a member of the Executive Committee for General Zionist Affairs. He is professor of Philosophy at the University of Wisconsin and a contributor to several leading periodicals.

Monday, April 8, at Luncheon
SAMUEL N. HARPER
Lately returned from Russia

"THE RUSSIAN SITUATION"

Mr. Harper is Assistant Professor of the Russian Language and Institutions at the University of Chicago. He has made several visits to Russia.

PUT AWAY GLOOM AND COME TO NEXT WEDNESDAY'S MUSICALE

The City Club Bulletin
A Journal of Active Citizenship

The purpose of the Club is to bring together in informal association those men who are genuinely interested in the improvement of the political, social and economic conditions of the community in which we live.

PUBLISHED WEEKLY BY THE
CITY CLUB OF CHICAGO

315 Plymouth Court   Telephone: Harrison 8278

DWIGHT L. AKERS, Editor

OFFICERS OF THE CLUB

FRANK I. MOULTON, President
EDGAR A. BANCROFT, Vice-President
ROY C. OSGOOD, Treasurer
CHARLES YEOMANS, Secretary
GEORGE E. HOOKER, Civic Secretary

EDITORIAL BOARD

HERBERT H. SMITH, Chairman
FREDERICK D. BRAMHALL   S. R. WATKINS
C. COLTON DAUGHADAY   PAUL R. WRIGHT

$1.00 per Year   -   -   -   10c per Copy

Entered as second class matter, December 3, 1917, at the postoffice at Chicago, Illinois, under the act of March 3, 1879.

PROGRAM FOR THE SPRING MUSICALE

This is the program announced for the musicale next Wednesday evening:

1. Trio for Violin, 'Cello and Piano........
.... *Rachmaninoff*
(In three movements)
AMY EMERSON NEILL, VERA POPPÉ AND MARY CAMERON.

2. Group of Songs......HECTOR G. SPAULDING
3. Violin Solo, Caprice.............*Guiraud*
AMY EMERSON NEILL

4. Piano Soli—
(a.) The Return of the Muleteers..*de Severac*
(b.) Irish Tunes from County Derry........
.... *Grainger*
(c.) Concert Study................*McDowell*
MARY CAMERON

5. 'Cello Soli—
(a.) The Minstrels Song........*Glazounoff*
(b.) Orientale ....*César Cui*
(c.) At the Fountain..............*Davidoff*
VERA POPPÉ

Dinner—the now famous City Club Table d' Hote dinner at 75c and $1.00 a plate—will be served in the dining room. Make reservations early, not later in any case than, the evening of Tuesday, April 2.

GET THE HABIT of using the Club.

THE LISTENING POST

NEW MEMBERS LAST WEEK:

Henry A. Dreffein, Flinn & Dreffein Company (mechanical engineer).

Nathan Klee, Klee, Rogers, Wile & Loeb (insurance).

D. C. Kreidler, Western Manager, F. A. Owen Publishing Company.

R. L. Murphy, General Contractor, East St. Louis, Ill.

Milton Morgenthau, Morgenthau Bros. (manufacturers of clothing).

William E. Sparrow, Jr., Babcock & Wilcox Company.

J. WILLARD BOLTE has moved from Chicago to Indianapolis, but will maintain a non-resident membership. Mr. Bolte is one of several of our members in the advertising profession who have been writing those interesting advertisements in the Bulletin about the new deal in the Club dining room.

PROF. H. A. MILLIS has been appointed secretary of the State Health Insurance Commission, created under act of the legislature at its last session and recently appointed by Governor Lowden. It is to make an investigation of the subject of health insurance and to report to the General Assembly at its next session.

ON DUTY FOR SOLDIERS' AND SAILORS' days this week:

Saturday, April 6: H. E. Hudson, R. L. Megowan, T. W. Allinson, Richard Pride, W. R. Smith.

Sunday, April 7: C. Fantozzi, A. H. Reynolds, D. R. Kennicott, J. J. Forstall, Herbert Harley, James M. Hart.

ORNO B. ROBERTS is a flying cadet at Fort Omaha, Nebraska. He writes: "I wish you all the success in the world and hope the City Club will continue its good work."

LEROY K. SHERMAN, civil engineer, left last week for Washington to serve in the department which is to construct workmen's houses for the Shipping Board.

BURT A. CROWE and William E. Sparrow joined the Club recently. Sing willow, tit-willow, tit-willow!

World's Coal Needs, U.S. Problem

Must Mine Millions of Tons for Our Allies, Says Cushing

AMERICA before the war, in spite of her great coal deposits, was not an exporter of coal in great quantity. Now, according to George H. Cushing, editor of "The Black Diamond," the official organ of the coal trade, in his address last Thursday, the whole world relies upon America for coal. The deposits in Belgium, in Northern France, and in Western Russia are in the hands of Germany, deposits in other parts of the world are inadequate or, as in China, are not sufficiently developed to meet the needs. America must fill the gap. Her coal production is no longer merely a matter of domestic concern but rises to the dignity of an international problem—on which has an important bearing on the winning of the war.

NEXT YEAR'S DEMAND

America's coal production for its own consumption next year, said Mr. Cushing, will have to be about 720,000,000 tons or 2,400,000 tons per day for 300 days in the year. This is about 90,000,000 tons more than we produced last year. Besides this amount we must place about 25,000,000 tons in the hands of the State Department "to put a little punch into its diplomacy." Our factory consumption now, particularly because of increased demands of war industries, about equals our coal consumption before the war.

If every coal car in the country moved with clock-like regularity in transporting this coal, the carrying capacity would be about 2,500,000 tons. The mining capacity of the country for 300 days of the year with no allowance for strikes, disasters or other interruptions, is about 2,600,000 tons. These estimates are based on ideal conditions and the factor of safety in either case is small.

THE ZONING REGULATIONS

On April 1st the new zoning regulations applied by the Fuel Administration to the coal industry go into effect. Under these rules, according to Mr. Cushing, coal mined in the eastern zone will be used there and coal mined in other zones will be moved to meet the consumption requirements as understood by the Fuel Administration. The Fuel Administration, he said, has no machinery for gathering the data for coal consumption and relies entirely upon unchecked statistical information furnished by one man in the Geological Survey. It is a risky experiment to try to reorganize on such slight data the entire coal industry of America.

BUY COAL NOW

"The time to force the mines and the railroads to their limit of capacity," Mr. Cushing said, "is in the summer months. That puts the problem up to the consumer and you know human nature. We buy things in season when they need them." He urged that every consumer get in his coal at once so far as possible.

"The one big hopeful thing," Mr. Cushing concluded, "is that beginning April 1 the coal men will do nothing but move coal. After that time we will not spend an hour in arguing about policy or haggling over prices. We are going to devote 100 per cent of our energy to the simple job of getting out 2,400,000 tons of coal every blessed day."

ANOTHER SLAM!

DID YOU READ the "Slams" in last week's Bulletin? Here is another from one of our members:

"I wish to take this opportunity to express my approval of the action of the Club in opening up the Club House to enlisted men at week-ends and also to compliment you on the excellent showing made in operating cost during previous year as explained in your statement. While you have kept the cost within 5 per cent of the previous year, the same standard of excellence has been maintained—and even considerably improved in the dining room.

"I have no doubt that the membership of the Club sufficiently appreciates the privileges furnished, the economical management, splendid civic and patriotic war work carried on by the Club."

A New Plan for Club Committees

A BETTER organization of civic committees is contemplated in a plan which has just been approved by the Board of Directors. It was proposed by the special Committee on Club Activities, which has been making a survey of this field with a view to increasing the Club's effectiveness. "Normal civic work," says the committee in its report to the Directors, "is naturally affected by and must be modified because of war conditions. But these conditions bring with them the danger of undesirable happenings in local matters which now attract little hostile attention because every one is absorbed in the war. This makes it all the more necessary that those who are not actually in war matters be particularly watchful. The new attitude of the public mind resulting from an awakened conscience brought about by the war should be taken advantage of in the furtherance of desirable movements.

COMMITTEE WORK

"The civic committee's activities," says the Committee, "are interesting and moderately effective and have resulted in some real monuments to the credit of the Club. However, as at present conducted, there are unnecessary limitations to the effectiveness of the work."

"The various committees at present work more or less independently, and the spur to action must come from within. The absence of a stimulus has resulted in a condition in which a number of the committees are entirely inactive or meet very seldom. . . . Theoretically the Public Affairs Committee has supervision over the committees, but this is in general applied only to the finished product as it is turned out by the committee, in the form of reports on definite public subjects. Civic committee work should be actively directed at all times and the Club should be kept informed of what is being done by the Committees." At present, the Committee also points out, there is no contact except on special occasions between committees although their fields may at times overlap.

Under the new plan, the Public Affairs Committee will be reconstituted to consist of five members, with the president of the Club as a member *ex officio*. The civic

(Continued on page 117.)

NEW HOUSE RULES

The House Committee has adopted and the Directors have approved the following revised house rules for the City Club:

1. The clubhouse is open every weekday from 9 o'clock a. m. to 10 o'clock p. m., except on such holidays as the House Committee shall direct.

2. The main dining room is open from 11:30 a. m. to 2:30 p. m. The grill room is open from 11:30 a. m. until 5 p. m.

3. Private dining rooms may be reserved by members for either noon or evening use upon application to the management of the Club.

4. Dining rooms may be reserved for meetings of six or more members of outside organizations at a minimum price of 75 cents per person at noon or $1.00 in the evening.

5. Rooms may be reserved for meetings, without dining room service, at a nominal charge, varying with the size of the room at the discretion of the House Committee.

6. Parties and banquets may be arranged through the courtesy of a member. Information concerning arrangements for private rooms, meetings, and dinners may be secured by application to the manager.

7. All checks for service must be signed by members only and shall be paid at the desk in the lobby before leaving the clubhouse.

8. No member shall take from the clubhouse any article belonging to the Club, nor from the library or reading room, any book, pamphlet or newspaper, nor mark or in any way mutilate the same.

9. No member or guest shall give any fee or other gratuity to any employe of the Club.

10. No article shall be exposed or advertised for sale in the clubhouse, nor any subscription solicited, unless authorized by the President or Directors.

11. Employes shall not be sent out of the clubhouse by members for any purpose.

12. Persons when accompanied by a member may be extended the privileges of the Club without a guest card. Members introducing guests in this manner are, however, requested to register them in the Club guest book each time a guest is so introduced. Upon application by a member the secretary may issue a guest card to a non-resident for a period not exceeding two weeks. A guest card may be issued to members of City Club in other cities with which reciprocal membership relations have been established for the same period upon presentation of membership credentials.

(Continued on page 116.)

New By-Laws for City Club

*Will Be Voted on at Annual Meet-
ing, April 20. Read Them Over!*

THE directors have framed a new club code. It will be voted upon by the members at the annual meeting, Saturday, April 20. The old by-laws are the result of much patchwork and tinkering and are incomplete in several important particulars.

The directors have endeavored to build a more systematic and complete structure by bringing together under one head all related matter, by adding such articles and sections as are necessary to make the by-laws conform to state statutes and by incorporating a few changes to increase the efficiency of the Club. Other changes are mere modifications of phraseology and arrangement.

The changes, other than which are merely formal, are as follows:

(a) *Art. II, Sec. 4.* Gives the Board of Directors power to change the initiation fee from time to time. At present it is fixed definitely in the by-laws.

(b) *Art. III, Sec. 2.* Makes the President *ex officio* a member of all standing committees.

(c) *Art. VI, Sec. 1.* Changes the date of the annual meeting from the third Saturday to the third Friday of April. It has been found difficult to get members to attend the annual meeting on Saturday afternoons in the spring of the year. Also provides the number that shall constitute a quorum at an annual or special meeting of the Club. This provision is required by the statute.

(d) *Art. VII, Sec. 1, Par. (d).* Provides that the Finance Committee shall be a regular standing committee of the Club, instead of as heretofore a committee appointed by the Board of Directors, without any specific provision in the by-laws. It also provides for the introduction of the budget system in the financial affairs of the Club.

(e) *Art. VII, Sec. 1, Par. (e).* Provides for a Social Committee as a regular standing committee of the Club. Heretofore the Board has been in the habit from time to time, without any definite plan, of appointing an Entertainment Committeee. By providing for such a committee as a regular standing committee of the Club, this phase of the Club's activities will, it is thought, receive greater attention.

(f) *Art. IX, Sec. 1.* Provides for the manner of election of officers and directors, especially in case there is more than one candidate. This section is necessary in view of the provision for nominations under Section 1, Article V.

(g) *Art. IX, Secs. 2 and 3.* Provides for the method of amending or changing the Articles of Association and by-laws. These sections are introduced to meet the requirements of the statutes.

The proposed by-laws are printed in full below. If you have any amendments to offer, send them at once to President Frank I. Moulton, care of the City Club, so they may be published before the annual meeting.

BY-LAWS OF THE CITY CLUB OF CHICAGO

PREAMBLE

The object for which it is formed is the investigation and improvement of municipal conditions and public affairs in the City of Chicago, and the establishment and maintenance of a library and other facilities of a social club for the use of men who desire to co-operate in the accomplishment of this purpose by non-partisan and practical methods.

ARTICLE I.

MEMBERS

SECTION 1. Any male person who has manifested an interest in the objects of this Club as stated in its Charter shall be eligible to a resident or non-resident membership.

SEC. 2. Resident members shall be such persons as reside or have their place of business in the City of Chicago or within fifty miles of the City of Chicago.

SEC. 3. Non-resident members shall be such persons as do not reside or have their place of business within fifty miles of the City of Chicago.

SEC. 4. The election to membership in the Club shall be by vote of the Committee on

Admissions. Elected persons shall upon acceptance by them, be enrolled as members.

Sec. 5. Any member or member-elect may become a life member upon payment of Four Hundred Dollars. Life members shall not be subject to the payment of dues but shall have all the rights and privileges and shall be subject to all the obligations of a resident member. The number of life members shall not exceed forty.

ARTICLE II.

Dues and Initiation Fees

Section 1. The dues of resident members shall be Thirty Dollars per annum, $1.00 of which is for one year's subscription to the City Club Bulletin, payable quarterly in advance on January 1, April 1, July 1 and October 1 of each year.

Sec. 2. The dues of non-resident members shall be Ten Dollars per annum, $1.00 of which is for one year's subscription to the City Club Bulletin, payable semi-annually in advance on April 1 and October 1 of each year.

Sec. 3. The dues of new members shall begin with the quarter whose commencement is nearest the date of their enrollment.

Sec. 4. The initiation fees of resident members and non-resident members shall be Ten Dollars, subject to the right of the Board of Directors to change the amount of initiation fee of either or both classes of membership from time to time at their discretion, upon giving thirty days' notice of the proposed change to the members of the Club.

Sec. 5. Any member who shall fail to pay his dues for a period of seventy-five days from the first day of the quarter when the same became due and payable, shall thereupon forfeit his membership in the Club.

The Treasurer shall cause to be sent to each member a bill for dues on the first day of each quarter. At the expiration of thirty days thereafter he shall send a notice to each delinquent that he will be posted on the bulletin board of the Club if his dues are not paid within fifteen days thereafter. If any delinquent shall not have paid such dues within said fifteen days, his name and the amount due shall thereupon be posted on the bulletin board of the Club. If, at the end of sixty days from the first day of the quarter, the dues of any member shall remain unpaid, a notice shall be sent such delinquent that his membership will be forfeited if the indebtedness is not paid within fifteen days from that time.

The posting and forfeiture of membership hereunder shall be effective automatically without further notice at the expiration of the periods named.

A member thus forfeiting his membership may be reinstated within three months there-after by a vote of the Board of Directors and upon payment of all arrears. Any person whose membership shall have been forfeited hereunder shall not be eligible to re-election to membership in the Club until all moneys owing by him to the Club are fully paid.

ARTICLE III.

Officers

Section 1. The officers shall consist of a President, Vice-President, Secretary and Treasurer.

President

Sec. 2. The President shall preside at the meetings of the Club and of the Board of Directors and shall perform the duties usual to his office. He shall be ex-officio a member of all standing committees. At the annual meeting of the Club he shall make a report of the proceedings and activities of the Club during the preceding year.

Vice-President

Sec. 3. In the absence or disability of the President the Vice-President shall act and perform the duties of the President.

Secretary

Sec. 4. The Secretary shall keep a record of the proceedings of all the meetings, shall attend to the correspondence of the Club and keep same on file. He shall be ex-officio a member of the Committee on Admissions, and shall act as its Secretary. He shall notify members of their election, keep a roll of members, issue notices of all the meetings of the Club called as hereinafter provided. He shall have custody of the seal, and perform such other duties as may be provided by the Board of Directors.

Treasurer

Sec. 5. The Treasurer shall collect and disburse the funds of the Club. He shall be custodian of all bonds and securities of any kind whatsoever belonging to the Club. He shall present a monthly report to the Board of Directors of all monetary transactions and shall make a report to the members at the annual meeting, which shall be verified prior to such meeting by public accountants. He shall deposit the moneys of the Club in any bank in the City of Chicago approved by the Board of Directors. He shall keep proper books of account in books which shall belong to the Club, which shall at all times be open to the inspection of the Board of Directors. At the expiration of his term of office he shall within ten days deliver to his successor all moneys, securities, books or documents of any kind in his possession belonging to the Club. For the faithful performance of his duties he shall furnish a bond in such an amount as may be determined by the Board

(Continued on page 118.)

IF THE BRITISH LINE SHOULD BREAK!

America's Future at Stake in Conflict
on Western Front, Says Dr. Lansing

"I have been under the influence of five men, Alexander the Great, Julius Caesar, Theodoric the Second, Frederick the Great, and Napoleon Bonaparte. Each of these men dreamed a dream of world empire. They failed. I am dreaming a dream of the German world empire, and my mailed fist shall succeed."—Wilhelm II. 1892.

"I shall stand no nonsense from America after this war."—Wilhelm II to Ambassador Gerard.

"IN the great struggle on the Western Front, the life of America and everything that we hold sacred is involved," said Dr. J. Lansing of Ridgewood, N. J., in his address last Wednesday. "Germany does not want 'a place in the sun,' her purpose is world domination and America is in her scheme of conquest." Dr. Lansing is pastor of the Collegiate churches of Ridgewood, N. J., and was formerly pastor of the famous Park Street Church in Boston.

Dr. Lansing was scheduled to speak upon the "Perils of a Premature Peace." Because of the crisis on the west front, however, he spoke instead upon the "Perils of German Conquest to America," and of America's lack of preparation to assume her share of the world's task of defeating Germany.

OUR UNPREPAREDNESS

"After four years of war," he said, "we are still being defended—we are not defending ourselves. The revelations in the Senate yesterday show that we are far behind with our preparations. Our program of 2,000 aeroplanes has shrunk to thirty-seven which we can deliver by July 1st. Our soldiers in the camps are almost as much in need of defense as our women and children, for men cannot fight without adequate equipment.

"We are challenged and threatened by the German purpose to subjugate and dominate the world," said Dr. Lansing. "The Central Powers long ago openly resolved to conquer, to enslave, and to despoil the world; to bring it by conquest under their absolute control, to reduce under their will all men, nations and races; and to seize of what we have, whatever they choose, without our consent.

"If the conceited aspirations of those two strange yet very influential characters, the Kaiser and Crown Prince, have been theirs alone, no one would have feared. But the profoundest thinkers and most influential citizens of Germany have endorsed the idea of the German domination of the world. Through the German system of education, these ideas have been implanted in the minds of the people.

"What does America stand to lose by a German mastery of the world? We would lose our liberty. We would become slaves as Belgium has been made a land of slaves. What else are Belgians than slaves when they are dragged from their homes and forced to work for a master who is driving them to a task which they hate?

THE WILL TO POWER

"The Germans are ready to take away our ideas of morality. There is no morality in the theory of the Germans, there is none in their actions, there is only a 'will to power.' Without moral restraints there can be no society of nations. We are fighting today for a moral world.

"The Germans, too, are out for plunder. The Huns in Belgium and France stole the underclothing of the women and little children; the mattresses from the beds, the bed blankets; destroyed all farm implements; sent the machinery in the Belgian and French factories to Germany and then blew up the factories. They expect to win this war without paying one cent for it by levying upon the defeated nations. Germany's financiers would never have supported the war if they had not believed this."

WHAT MAY AMERICA EXPECT?

America, Dr. Lansing said, can expect no better treatment at the hands of the Germans than our allies have received. The plans of Pan-Germania embrace the domination of America. "It is said on high authority that the Germans have transferred their direct hatred from England to America."

THE CITY CLUB AND MUSIC

The spring musicale for next Wednesday evening is one of several such affairs in the history of the Club. On a previous occasion one of our Chicago newspapers editorialized as follows:

"Man does not live by bread alone. Neither does a civic organization. The City Club, busy as it is with housing, garbage, traction, terminals, and other important but prosaic topics, surrenders itself for one evening to the charms of music. It announces its second annual spring musical. We note, by the way, that in giving the joy, constitution and reinvigoration of music to its own members it doesn't forget the community at large. It has organized a new committee, called the music extension committee, to aid in carrying music into quarters, circles and homes not now sufficiently cultivated by our many excellent musical organizations.

"The City Club, slightly misquoting Shakespeare, warns us not to trust the man that hath no music in his soul. Perhaps we may add that the club or organization that hath no music in its collective soul is likewise to be viewed with distrust. A poet and critic has said that to make or complete a home two things are necessary—a fireplace and music. To make a civic organization complete and effective, social intercourse, friendliness and a genial atmosphere, as well as music, are more and more regarded as necessary. The University Club, the Sunday Evening Club and other such organizations give musicals to members and guests. A touch of nature makes us kin, and music makes us more genial in our civic struggle. Would the militant suffragettes resist a course of musical treatment in and out of prison? Soldiers march to music; civic soldiers will work better, perhaps, if subjected to the mollifying influence of music."

THERE IS A STORY of a new member who on his first tour of the Club paid a visit to the lounge. It was after lunch and on every couch on the outer rim of the room was the reclining figure of a Club member, relaxing after a hearty lunch. And from every place there rose to the ceiling a thin column of blue smoke from an after-dinner cigar. He gazed about him and said, "My God! It's a hop joint!"

BOOKWORMS PLEASE NOTE!

The Chicago Public Library has put on deposit in the City Club reading room fifty volumes of light fiction. They cannot be withdrawn for home use, but they will be on deposit for the next three months so you may have plenty of opportunity to use them in your idle half hours after lunch or dinner. The books are as follows:

Baldwin—Holding the Line.
Barbusse—Under Fire.
Bennett—The Honeymoon.
Daviess—The Heart's Kingdom.
Dawson, C.—Carry On.
Dowd—Polly and the Princess.
Empey—First Call.
Field—The Little Gods Laugh.
Greene—The Grim.
Grey—The U. P. Trail.
Howard—Breathe and Be Well.
Hueston—Sunny Slopes.
Lincoln—The Nameless Man.
London—Burning Daylight.
Mackenzie—The Man Who Tried to be It.
Marquis—The Cruise of the Jasper.
Norris—The Story of Julia Page.
Norton—The Unknown Mr. Kent.
Oliver—Ordeal by Battle.
Oppenheim—Mr. Crex of Monte Carlo.
Oyen—The Snow-Burner.
Parker—The Money Master.
Poizetto—Pacific Shores from Panama.
Porter—Miss Billy—Married.
Prouty—Bobbie General Manager.
Rice—Calvary Alley.
Richmond, G.—Red Pepper Burns.
Roche—The Sport of Kings.
Seltzer—Vengeance of Jefferson Gawne.
Sinclair—The Belfry.
Sinclair—King Coal.
Sinclair—The Tree of Heaven.
The Sturdy Oak—A novel by fourteen American authors.
Sullivan—The Inner Door.
Tagore, Rabindranath—The Hungry Stones and Other Stories.
Tarkington—Seventeen.
Trask—The Invisible Balance Sheet.
Turczynowicz—When the Prussians Came to Poland.
Vance—The False Face.
Van Schaick—A Top-Floor Idyl.
Wallace—Kate Plus 10.
Wells—Mr. Britling Sees It Through.
Wharton, E.—Summer.
Wylie—The Hermit Doctor of Gaya.

EVERY MEMBER of the Club who signed the dry petition ought to get a copy of the Bureau of Efficiency's report of Water Waste. It can be had for the asking. The Bureau has its offices on the sixth floor of our club house and any member may call for a copy when he comes to lunch.

At the Sign of the Book

THE NEW YORK STATE LEGISLATIVE BUDGET for 1917. Municipal Research, No. 86. 140 pages.

The New York Bureau of Municipal Research reviews the activities of the governor and the legislature in framing the 1917 budget. The science of budget making is the Bureau's long suit and this report is done in characteristically thoroughgoing fashion. The book offers a fund of information on budget-making technique and some interesting side lights on legislative methods.

EIGHTH REPORT OF THE TENEMENT HOUSE DEPARTMENT, CITY OF NEW YORK. For the years 1915 and 1916.

The period, covered by this report, is a milestone in housing history in New York. It marks a general shift in emphasis to preventive measures. In 1915, the Department reports, the fight to eliminate dark rooms in tenements was successfully completed. When the Department was organized in 1902, there were at least 300,000 inadequately lighted rooms in New York tenements. "This condition," says the report, "has been remedied and now practically all tenement rooms are ventilated and lighted to the full extent that the law requires." This, with the elimination of the old yard school-sink, the Department considers its two most substantial contributions to the hygiene of the city. The Department believes that in the future more of its attention should be directed to fundamental educational work, among the tenants, rather than to rely too exclusively upon coercive measures.

In July, 1916, the Building Zone resolution was adopted for New York. To quote the concise summary in this report: "It regulates and limits the height and bulk of buildings hereafter erected and the area of yards, courts, and other open spaces; it also regulates and restricts the location of trades and industries and the location of buildings designed for specific uses, establishing boundaries of districts for said purposes." The adoption of this resolution was a step toward the prevention of the evils against which the tenement house department has been struggling for over a decade and a half. It is the application of scientific city-planning to the housing problem. It will be interesting to see New York grow year by year into a better housed city under the guidance of its new zone regulations. The next legislature ought to empower Chicago to apply similar regulations to guide its own growth and to insure better living conditions for its people.

The Mail Pouch

From a Sailor and His Mother

SECRETARY CITY CLUB: Kindly allow me to thank you and the City Club for the privileges which you have extended to the enlisted men. As one, I am more than indebted to you for your kindness.

It is a great sense of satisfaction to be able to walk into the City Club and feel as though you were either in your own Club or home, and the friendly spirit with which your members greet us, removes any doubt that may lurk in your mind as to your welcome. Your generosity in only charging the boys the nominal sum you do for meals is also noteworthy and I wish to take this opportunity to thank you and the City Club for the courtesies extended.

I am enclosing a part of a letter which I received from my mother in which she also expresses her appreciation. Wishing you and the City Club all the good luck in the world, I am,

Sincerely yours,
LEONARD L. LAIRD.

Co. F, 3d Reg., Camp Dewey, Great Lakes, Ill.

The letter from Mr. Laird's mother reads in part as follows: "I noticed in your letter of Sunday that you went to the City Club. It certainly is fine of them to offer their club and its privileges to you enlisted boys. Nobody but a mother can tell what it means to her to know that her boy can go to a place such as the City Club and know that he is in good company with such fine surroundings."

HAVE YOU AN AUTOMOBILE BLUE BOOK which you would like to give to the City Club? It doesn't have to be the latest edition. We can find good use for it here.

In Russia

Lincoln Steffens, speaking before another Chicago audience on the evening of his City Club address, told this story:

The owner of a manufacturing plant on the outskirts of Petrograd, came into his club one evening and said: "What do you think they did to me today? The workmen held a shop meeting and decided to take over the plant. They sent for me and asked me to bring in all the books. They told me that they did not know much about financial management and since they liked me wanted to have me take charge of things for them. They asked me how much salary I would want. I told them that I could not estimate that and they then asked me how much I had paid myself last year. I did not like to tell them how much I had really earned and I told them about 35,000 rubles. 'That is too much,' they said. 'You have always told us that a man could live and support a family on four rubles a day.' " It is in this simple, literal way, Mr. Steffens said, that the Russian people interpret their new democracy.

The following day, Mr. Steffens said, the proprietor of this factory again came into his club and said: "Well, what do you think they did to me today?" He said that the workmen had now decided to take over his house. He had told them, he said, that he could not maintain his house on the salary which they wanted to pay him and they had taken literally and decided to make use of the house for a club.

Mr. Steffens said that the industries are being organized along syndicalistic lines; that while syndicalism had not been much thought of before the revolution, the taking over of an industry by the workers in that industry seemed to be the easiest and most natural course of procedure.

THE MAN WHO SITS at your elbow in the office is a potential member of the City Club. Why not bring him around some day, treat him to a good dinner, and then shove him an application card? It works.

THE SOLDIERS AND SAILORS continue to come to the Club in large numbers on Saturdays and Sundays. The Club is fulfilling a real need by opening the Club house to these men.

What Birds Can Do in the War

Massachusetts Ornithologist Says
They Are Doing Their Bit

IT has been said that food will win the war, that ships will win the war, that sundry other things will win the war. Nobody yet has suggested that birds will win the war, but Edward H. Forbush, in his address on Saturday, March 23rd, said that birds can help in many ways. Mr. Forbush is the state ornithologist of Massachusetts.

Here are some of the ways in which birds have helped and are helping according to Mr. Forbush:

GAS DETECTORS

Canary birds are used in the trenches to aid in detecting poison gas. They are more sensitive to it than men and when they become uneasy the men know that it is time to put on their masks.

In great battles, when ordinary communications are shattered, carrier pigeons are often the only means of sending back word for reinforcements. The Germans try to shoot them but 95 per cent of them make their way back safely. They have undoubtedly saved thousands of lives.

Sea gulls are submarine detectors. They are being fed from submarines so they will follow the enemy U-boats and reveal their presence. Flying overhead they can see the submarine even when submerged for a considerable depth.

Certain kinds of wild fowl will help to augment our food supply if we will have the wisdom to protect them in the spring.

PROTECT FOOD SUPPLY

Birds help in many ways to protect the food supply. Fishhawks destroy other birds which prey upon domestic fowl. Even the hawks and owls help in one way by killing rats and mice. Birds eat caterpillars and worms, insects which injure crops—crickets, grasshoppers, etc.

Farmers hate crows. Crows do a great deal of mischief but they should not be exterminated. In 1879 in Massachusetts nearly all of them were killed off as a result of the offering of bounties. The next year, however, there was a plague of caterpillars which did great damage to the crops.

Woodpeckers and other birds protect our forests from tree insects.

Mr. Forbush showed pictures of corn fields which had been attacked by the armyworm. One of these fields was shown to be completely devastated and the crops ruined. In a near-by field which was protected by birds a full crop was raised.

A cranberry farmer of Mr. Forbush's acquaintance lost several successive crops through worms. Finally he put up boxes for birds to nest in. Within a year or two these were occupied by birds and his crops are now amply protected.

Mr. Forbush illustrated his appeal for bird conservation by some very interesting slides showing close range pictures of birds feeding their young on the destructive insects of the fields and forests,

---

THE LIBRARY COMMITTEE has received a request that a New York paper be added to the reading room files and another request that we subscribe for an Australian newspaper. The Committee wants to know if there are others who also wish these papers. If you do, drop a note to Frederick Rex, Chairman Library Committee, City Club.

Absolute knowledge I have none
But my aunt's washerwoman's sister's son
Heard a policeman on his beat
Say to a laborer in the street
That he had a letter last week
Written in the finest Greek
From a Chinese coolie in Timbuctoo
Who said the niggers in Cuba knew
Of a colored man in a Texas town
Who got it straight from a circus clown
That a man in Klondike heard the news
From a gang of South American Jews
Of somebody in Borneo
Who heard a man who claims to know
Of a swell society female rake
Whose mother-in-law will undertake
To prove that her husband's sister's niece
Has stated in a printed piece
That she has a son who has a friend
Who knows when the war is going to end.
—*Chicago Commerce.*

New House Rules

(*Continued from page* 108.)

13. Any member introducing a guest shall be responsible for the conduct of such guest and for any debt or liability to the Club incurred by him.

14. Guest privileges may be terminated, extended or controlled at the discretion of the House Committee.

15. Guests are not permitted to introduce any person to the Club or to give any entertainment in the clubhouse except as may be specifically authorized by the House Committee.

16. The privileges of members as to the use of the clubhouse may be suspended at the discretion of the Board of Directors.

17. The Club is not responsible for the loss of any property sustained in the clubhouse by members or guests.

18. No game for a wager nor gambling in any form is permitted in the Club.

19. No member or guest in his individual capacity shall date or address from the Club, or on Club stationery, any communication intended to appear in any newspaper, periodical or other publication.

20. Property of the Club broken or injured by members or their guests must be paid for by the members responsible for same.

21. Complaints, requests, or suggestions should be addressed in writing to the House Committee.

22. It is the duty of every member of the Club to report in writing to the House Committee any known violations of the foregoing rules and of the constitution and by-laws.

23. Membership in the City Club constitutes an introduction to any other member.

24. The solicitation of business at the clubhouse from fellow members is not considered to be consistent with the spirit of the Club.

25. The privileges of the Club may be extended to ladies related to, or friends of, members, at such times and under such circumstances as the House Committee may authorize.

26. Members and guests are requested not to reprimand the employes. Should any cause for complaint arise, the attention of the House Committee should be immediately directed thereto.

27. No member or guest shall make unreasonable use of any telephone in the Club. All tolls must be paid for by the person incurring the same before leaving the clubhouse. The manager shall have full authority to enforce this rule.

28. Pursuant to the by-laws of the Club,

the consent of the House Committee must be obtained for the holding of all meetings in the Club rooms by outside persons and organizations, for any purpose.

29. A copy of these rules shall be kept posted in a conspicuous place on each floor of the clubhouse.

30. No resident of Chicago shall be permitted to be a guest of the Club oftener than once in 30 days.

(Sd.)　HOUSE COMMITTEE,
Bradford Gill, Chairman.

Making Laws in New York

"Writers have frequently pointed to the fact that our legislatures are not performing the functions of a representative body. With individual initiative and our standing committee system, each standing committee in effect is a small specialized legislature. Bills are referred to them. Hearings are conducted, and in so far as there is any planning, this is done by the committee. Any attempt at co-ordination must be made in the committee room. Measures which have backing are committee measures. No one can be held accountable to the state-wide electorate, each chairman becoming the pilot of his measures through the stage of enactment. The legislature is thus is reality a conglomeration of fifty-nine "little legislatures" each enacting the bills consigned to it.

"After the appropriation and taxation committees have drafted the bills and brought them before the house the consideration given to the measures is usually a perfunctory character. Ninety per cent of the bills enacted by the legislature are passed under the short or the party roll-call. During the closing days of the session when procedure is swift and ruthless, the power over the enactment of the appropriation and tax bills is wielded in reality by the committees which draft and introduce them. The bills reach the third reading calendar and are called up one after the other and pass so fast that a moment's inattention puts even the alert legislator completely at sea. He loses his place in the calendar and bills escape him for several minutes before he can get track of their course again. By means of the short or party roll-call bills are passed with amazing speed."

The quotation is from a report by the New York Bureau of Municipal Research on "The New York State Legislative Budget for 1917."

Daylight Saving

THE passage by Congress of the so-called daylight saving bill will make of particular interest the following statement of the advantages of the plan, prepared by the Boston Chamber of Commerce:

A. HEALTH, MORALS AND SOCIAL WELFARE

1. One hour or more for outdoor recreation. Recreation is a national asset, an immense force for health and moral well-being.

2. Working mothers and fathers obtain an extra hour for outdoor play with their children, both summer and winter.

3. One hour less for bad lights in tenements.

4. Lessened eye-strain for workers and school children due to the use of artificial light.

5. Smaller risk of accident in industrial establishments, because there will be a light hour instead of a dark one at the end of the working day at the time of greatest fatigue and more frequent accident.

6. Lessened risk of accident due to transportation and traffic conditions, because the afternoon rush will fall in daylight instead of in darkness.

7. Working girls will be on the way home in the daylight instead of in the dark in winter.

8. Our last hour of sleep will be sounder and more beneficial than it is under present conditions, because there will be less light.

B. EFFICIENCY

1. General efficiency will, of course, be increased by any improvement in the health, morals and social welfare of the workers and others.

2. In summer a cool hour in the morning is substituted for a hot one in the afternoon.

3. In winter a light hour at the end of the day is substituted for a dark one. This is especially valuable, coming as it does at the time of greatest fatigue, and is peculiarly valuable in some industries where accurate eyesight is essential.

4. Efficiency is lowest in the later afternoon, the time when accidents are more frequent.

C. ECONOMY.

1. There will be the greatest of all savings—that of human materials, as pointed out above.

2. Immediate saving in form of reduction of expense for light and heat.

3. Ultimate saving in the conservation of coal and other sources of light and heat.

4. Possible reduction in the cost of living of those who like to work in their gardens, utilizing the extra outdoor hour for the purpose.

New Committee Plan

(*Continued from page* 108.)

committees will be divided into four groups, Public Safety, Public Works, Government, and Finance, each group consisting of several committees. For each of the groups there will be a head, a member of the Public Affairs Committee, who will give general direction and stimulus to its work and bring about co-operation.

SOME OTHER SUGGESTIONS

The Survey Committee makes the suggestion that the appointment of committees should be for one year only. It suggests also that the Public Affairs Committee should outline for each committee at the beginning of the year some of the work which it should undertake. Present committees, says the report, should be combined wherever desirable in order to reduce the number. These suggestions and others the Directors have referred to the Public Affairs Committee.

The chairman of the Committee on Club Activities is R. F. Schuchardt, chairman of the City Planning Committee of the Club. Other members are C. P. Schwartz, chairman of the Committee on Immigration and Citizenship, Walter A. Shaw, chairman of the Committee on Water Supply, Henry P. Chandler, formerly Secretary of the Club, Paul Steinbrecher, a member of the Board of Directors, and Fred G. Heuchling, chairman of the Committee on Highways, Bridges and Waste Disposal.

Any member who has a suggestion about the activities of the Club ought to write to Mr. Schuchardt or to the Public Affairs Committee.

New By-Laws

(Continued from page 110.)

of Directors, which bond shall be approved by the Board of Directors and which shall be paid for by the Club.

ARTICLE IV.

DIRECTORS

SECTION 1. The Board of Directors shall consist of the officers of the Club and eight other members to be elected as hereinafter provided.

SEC. 2. The Board of Directors shall have the general control and management of the activities and property and affairs of the Club.

SEC. 3. The Board of Directors shall meet during the second and fourth weeks of each month, except the months of July, August and September, at the pleasure of the President, who shall give, so far as he can, at least two days' notice of the time of such meetings.

Special meetings of the Board of Directors may be called at any time by the President or by any three Directors, provided the call gives twenty-four hours' notice of the time and object of such special meeting.

ARTICLE V.

NOMINATIONS

SECTION 1. A nominating committee of five members of the Club shall be selected by the Board of Directors on or before March 15th of each year. This committee shall nominate a list of candidates for officers and directors, which list shall be prominently posted in the Club House on or before April 1 of each year.

Any twenty members may by petition posted at least ten days before the date of the annual election, nominate their candidates for officers and directors. Notice of all nominations for officers or directors shall be given as required by Section 1, Article VI, of these by-laws.

SEC. 2. At the regular annual meeting of the Club each year there shall be elected the officers of the Club for a period of one year and four directors to hold office for the term of two years, as well as directors to fill the unexpired term of any director who may have resigned or whose office may have become vacant for any reason.

SEC. 3. Whenever a vacancy shall occur in any office, or in the Board of Directors, it shall be filled by a majority of the remaining members of the Board of Directors by a majority vote of the members present at any regular meeting or special meeting of the Board called for that purpose. Persons so elected shall hold office until the next annual meeting.

ARTICLE VI.

MEETINGS—QUORUM

SECTION 1. The regular annual meeting of the Club shall be held at the Club House or some other designated place in the City of Chicago, on the third Friday of April in each year at such hour as may be determined by the President. For the purpose of transacting business at any annual or special meeting, thirty members shall constitute a quorum. At least ten days' notice of the time and place of the annual meeting shall be given to all members of the Club by the Secretary. Such notice shall contain the names of all nominees for office.

Special meetings of the Club may be called (a) by the Board of Directors, (b) by the President, or (c) upon the petition of twenty members in writing to the Secretary, who in either instance shall mail to the members of the Club notice of such meeting at least five days before the date fixed for such meeting, which notice shall state the time, place and purpose for which the meeting is called. The day and time for such special meeting shall be fixed by such person or persons at whose instance the same may be called.

ARTICLE VII.

COMMITTEES

SECTION 1. The Board of Directors shall annually appoint the following standing committees:

(a) A *Committee on Public Affairs,* which committee shall have charge of the investigation and discussion of public affairs by the Club, and of informal meetings of the Club.

(b) A *House Committee,* which shall have charge of the employes, club rooms, furniture and equipment of the Club and the management of the restaurant.

(c) A *Library Committee,* which shall have charge of the selection and purchase of books, newspapers and periodicals, and management of the library.

(d) A *Finance Committee* of five members, of which the Treasurer shall be a member, which committee shall prepare and submit to the Board of Directors at the earliest date practicable after appointment a budget of receipts and expenditures for the coming year, and from time to time, at its discretion, submit to the Board of Directors recommendations in reference to the Club's finances and management.

Such budget upon approval and adoption by the Board of Directors shall be controlling upon all officers and employes and committees of the Club, and no expenditures in excess of the amount appropriated in the budget shall be made or liabilities incurred in excess of the amount appropriated in the budget, by them, except by authority of the Board of Directors.

(e) A *Social Committee,* which shall have charge of entertainments of a social nature, and shall especially be charged with the duty of introducing new members and fostering a feeling of good-fellowship among the members of the Club.

(f) A *Committee on Admissions,* to consist of nine members of the Club who are not members of the Board of Directors, except the Secretary of the Club, who shall be ex-officio a member.

All proposals for membership in the Club shall be submitted to the Committee on Admissions and acted upon by them under such regulations as the Board of Directors may from time to time prescribe, and upon the election of each new member the committee shall forthwith give notice of the same to the Secretary.

All of the foregoing committees shall consist of such number of members as the Board of Directors may from time to time determine, except as otherwise herein provided.

The Board of Directors may, at its discretion from time to time, appoint additional standing committees and directly or through the Public Affairs Committee, appoint and provide for such civic committees as it may deem wise and expedient.

All committees shall be subject to the control and direction of the Board of Directors.

ARTICLE VIII.

House Rules

Section 1. Members shall be privileged to introduce as guests, residents of the City of Chicago and adjoining territory under regulation of the Board of Directors. Non-residents may be accorded the full privileges of the Club for a period of two weeks, upon notice to the Secretary in writing by the member introducing such non-resident, and upon such member guaranteeing all charges incurred by such non-member.

Sec. 2. The club rooms may be used as places of meetings by outside persons and organizations with the consent of the House Committee.

ARTICLE IX.

Elections and Amendments

Section 1. Officers and directors shall be elected at the annual meeting each year by viva voce vote, except should more persons be nominated for the position of director than there are vacancies, or should more than one person be nominated for the office of either President, Vice-President, Secretary or Treasurer, then the election shall be by ballot, and the polls shall be kept open from 12:00 m. to 5:00 p. m. on the day of election.

Sec. 2. The Articles of Association may be changed, modified or amended by a two-thirds vote of members present at any annual meeting, provided ten days' notice by mail of the proposed change, modification or amendment has been given to all members of the Club by the Secretary.

Sec. 3. These By-laws may be modified, altered or amended at any annual meeting of the Club, or at an adjourned session thereof, by a majority vote of the members present, provided that a notice stating the time, place and objects of the meeting shall have been sent to the members at least ten days prior to the date of the meeting. All by-laws not herein contained are hereby repealed.

THE SURVEY last week contained this appreciation of Carl B. Roden, recently chosen librarian of the Chicago Public Library. It is in an editorial referring to the examination through which Mr. Roden was appointed: "At the head of the list of the six eligibles stood Carl B. Roden, with a grade of 92.50. In the previous examination, he stood next to Mr. Legler, and he has since served as assistant librarian. For thirty-two years, since he started as page when a lad of fifteen, Mr. Roden had been continuously in the library's service. To the use he has made of the library he attributes his promotion from one position to another, and his choice as librarian. Not only has he the most thorough acquaintance with the contents of the library and all its operations, but he is recognized to be widely versed in the history of literature. He also studied law and has been admitted to the bar. Thoroughly devoted to the policy and to be credited with the success of the Legler administration next to Mr. Legler himself, Mr. Roden's appointment is greeted with great satisfaction, and the success of his management is considered to be assured in advance."

"I HAVE NEVER USED THE CLUB" is a reason frequently given by members who resign. Many of them have never tried to use it and don't know what the Club has to offer them. Give the Club a trial and you will never again consider dropping your membership on that account.

IT'S HARD TO BE INTERESTED in anything but the war. But the home fences must be mended. There is need for activity on the part of every club committee.

CITY CLUB BOOK WEEK

For Soldiers and Sailors

This is "clean-up week" for your bookcases. The books which you have read and which serve now only as "backs" in your library are needed by the soldiers and sailors. The Library Committee of the Club has set this week for its spring offensive for books for the men in khaki and blue.

WHAT YOU CAN DO

You can pass on the books you have enjoyed but will not read again.

You can give them some of the books you like best—books you would like to keep. They will like them, too.

You can send novels, tales of adventure, detective stories and standard fiction; up-to-date books on civil, mechanical and electrical engineering, the trades, business, the professions and agriculture; recent textbooks on military subjects, mathematics, the sciences, and foreign languages; books of travel, history, biography, poetry and the present war; dictionaries and new encyclopedias; interesting books in foreign languages.

Make it your duty to examine your library for suitable books tonight. You should deem it a privilege to pass on to the men in khaki the books which you have enjoyed.

WHERE TO LEAVE BOOKS

When you have laid out the books you have decided to give, bring them to the City Club and leave them at the desk; or, if more convenient, leave them at the nearest branch or delivery station of the Public Library. They will be forwarded to the camps.

This is a simple service within the means of every member to perform.

LIBRARY COMMITTEE.
Frederick Rex, Chairman.

Why Not Do Your Cigar Buying at the City Club?

The high cost of tobacco has not raised cigar prices at the City Club. McCarty can sell you cigars at prices from a nickel up. He can get you any brand.

Box purchases save you at least 15 per cent. You can buy a box and leave them in the humidor at the Club for use as desired.

The cigar department is maintained for your benefit.

The City Club Bulletin
Published Weekly by the City Club of Chicago
A Journal of Active Citizenship

VOLUME XI   MONDAY, APRIL 8, 1918   NUMBER 14

Monday, April 8

AT LUNCHEON

Prof. Samuel N. Harper
University of Chicago

"The Russian Situation"

Prof. Harper has been in Russia several times before and during the war. A member of the Red Cross Mission said of him: "He was one of the few men in Russia to whom almost everybody was willing to talk because he was known to be disinterested." Prof. Harper teaches the Russian language and institutions at the University.

Friday, April 12

AT LUNCHEON

Dr. E. V. McCollum
Johns Hopkins University

"Nutrition and the War"

Have you ever heard of "vitamenes"? If you talk in terms of "calories" only you are several jumps behind the procession. Dr. McCollum is the discoverer of "vitamenes." Through his experiments, it is said, "the knowledge of scientific feeding has been advanced a decade." Dr. McCollum will discuss the nutrition problem up-to-date in its bearing upon the war.

Tuesday, April 9

AT LUNCHEON

Raymond Hitchcock
will speak on

The Third Liberty Loan

An Interesting and Stirring Message for all Loyal Americans.

Wednesday, April 17

AT LUNCHEON

H. Charles Woods
Lecturer Lowell Institute 1917-1918

"The Near East and Pan-Germanism"

Mr. Woods has travelled extensively in the Balkans and in Asia Minor, making special studies of the Dardanelles, of the country surrounding Salonika and of the Bagdad Railway. He has acted as special correspondent of the London *Times* and military and diplomatic correspondent of the London *Evening News*. He is personally acquainted with M. Venizelos and all the leading Balkan statesmen.

Saturday, April 20, at Luncheon
THE ANNUAL MEETING OF THE CLUB

The annual Club meeting will be held in the main dining room at 1 p. m., Saturday, April 20. The business before the meeting will be the consideration of the revised by-laws, reports of officers and standing committees, and election of officers for the coming year. The following nominations have been posted by the Nominating Committee:

For President—George H. Mead.
For Vice President—Charles M. Moderwell.
For Treasurer—Roy C. Osgood.
For Secretary—Charles Yeomans.

For Directors (for a term of two years):
Arthur L. Hamilton.
Alfred L. Baker.
Bradford Gill.
Harris S. Keeler.
(Sd.) CHARLES YEOMANS, Secretary.

At All Meetings : Luncheon from 11:30—Program at 1:00

Ghe City Club Bulletin
A Journal of Active Citizenship

The purpose of the Club is to bring together in informal association those men who are genuinely interested in the improvement of the political, social and economic conditions of the community in which we live.

PUBLISHED WEEKLY BY THE
CITY CLUB OF CHICAGO
315 Plymouth Court   Telephone: Harrison 8278
DWIGHT L. AKERS, Editor

OFFICERS OF THE CLUB
FRANK I. MOULTON, President
EDGAR A. BANCROFT, Vice-President
ROY C. OSGOOD, Treasurer
CHARLES YEOMANS, Secretary
GEORGE E. HOOKER, Civic Secretary

EDITORIAL BOARD
HERBERT H. SMITH, Chairman
FREDÉRICK D. BRAMHALL   S. R. WATKINS
C. COLTON DAUGHADAY   PAUL R. WRIGHT

$1.00 per Year - - - 10c per Copy

Entered as second class matter, December 3, 1917, at the postoffice at Chicago, Illinois, under the act of March 3, 1879.

LOYALTY COMMITTEE

THE DIRECTORS have appointed a "Loyalty Committee." It is to have charge of the Liberty Loan campaign so far as the City Club is concerned. Its members will *not* buttonhole you either at the Club or at your office, but the committee will provide every convenience by which you can make your subscription through the Club. There will, for instance, be a table in the lobby at which you can sign up for as many bonds as your pocketbook can afford—and more.

The first help you can give the committee is to come to the Tuesday luncheon. *Raymond Hitchcock is to speak and the committee wants to make this a bang-up meeting!*

The chairman of the committee is M. H. Cowen and its members are: Robert M. Cunningham, Edwin H. Cassels, T. O. Bunch, H. P. Chandler, Walter J. Hamlin, F. E. Reeve, F. J. Reichman, Almer Coe, George W. Dixon, J. J. Forstall, Richard T. Fox, T. K. Webster, Jr., Malcolm D. Vail, Victor Yarros, Henry G. Zander, Albert B. Cone.

MAKE YOUR DOLLARS WORK FOR THE WAR!

THE LISTENING POST

JOHN S. VAN BERGEN has gone to France as a worker for the Y. M. C. A.

MAJOR DEAN D. LEWIS is director of Base Hospital Unit No. 13, which left Chicago for the East a few days ago on the first leg of its journey to France.

ELBERT BEEMAN left last week for the East. He will sail shortly with about twenty other men who are going to France for the Red Cross Bureau of Personnel.

JOHN D. JACKSON has arrived "over there," according to official advices received at the Club last week. Jackson ran a "lift" at the City Club prior to his enlistment.

CORRECTION. HOUSE RULE No. 2, printed in the last issue of the Bulletin, should have read as follows:

2. The main dining room is open from 11:30 a. m. to 2:30 p. m. The grill room is open from 11:30 a. m. until 8 p. m.

NEARLY EVERY WEEK some member of the City Club joins the drift to Washington. The latest recruit is Allan J. Carter. He left last week to serve as attorney with the War Trade Board. Mr. Carter is chairman of the City Club committee on Public Order.

FOUR NEW MEMBERS joined us last week. They are:

William S. Miller, Attorney and Vice-President, Northern Trust Company.

Maurice Shulze, Secretary-Treasurer, Reliance Manufacturing Company.

F. William Simpson, Simpson Manufacturing Company.

Ludwig Simon, Physician.

CAPTAIN WILLIAM S. TAUSSIG of the 114th Engineers, who has been stationed at Camp Beauregard, Alexandria, Louisiana, since last September, visited the City Club the other day. He returns to his post in a few days to continue his work of training the contingents from southern Arkansas and Louisiana to become good members of the engineering corps.

"MAC" SELLS YOUR FAVORITE BRAND of cigars. At the cashier's desk!

City Club Ambulance at Front

*Letters from Driver Tell of Service
Near "World's Most Famous Town"*

LAST summer, the members of the City Club, by $2 subscriptions, raised a fund for the purchase of a field ambulance to serve on the western front. The car went into service last October, with Rembert C. Anderson of Los Angeles as its driver, but until last week no definite news had come about its movements. Letters from Mr. Anderson written in December and January were forwarded to us from Los Angeles last week by his sister. They tell some very interesting experiences and indicate that the little Ford car (S. S. U. 13, No. 40) has been doing its bit.

THE AMBULANCE POST.

Mr. Anderson at the time these letters were written was stationed at a post "in a large old building that was formerly a seminary, and within a stone's throw of the most famous town of the war." "The shells are making such a noise," he says in his first letter, "they sound uncomfortably close." Some interesting excerpts from his letters are printed herewith.

"December 6.

"We work three posts; one artillery post to which two cars are sent. Besides that artillery post, we work two other posts from what is called the taxi-stand (an abri where the ambulance drivers wait for

REMBERT C. ANDERSON
Driver of the City Club Ambulance on the West
Front

telephone calls.) It is a Post de Secours in what was formerly a little village—there is not a wall now standing as high as the first floor. This is my second trip out and I am at the taxi-stand. One of us—it was I today, being the first on the alphabetical list—goes to the front post and waits for a load.

DEAD HORSE A GUIDE.

"I went to the post at noon. The road had been shelled in the morning, and it was covered with dirt and rocks. I had not been there before, and the direction given me was to follow the road until I came to a dead horse on the side of the road, and the post was one hundred feet further. I went up there about 1 o'clock and no blessés appeared until 4 o'clock. That post is a short tunnel that runs into the side of a hill off the road and slopes gradually downward into the hill. It is only about twenty feet long and very narrow, and as there were about five Frenchmen in it—the lieutenant and brancardiers —I stayed outside and walked back and forth. It was awfully interesting listening to the shells. At one time the Germans dropped about a dozen shells into the road half a mile further on.

"I stayed up there this afternoon until 4 o'clock, when an officer, a captain, came down through the communication trench and they sent me on in with him. He was sick. I brought him here to the taxi-stand and then took him to the hospital.

DRIVING IN THE DARK.

"Coming out from dinner it was dark as pitch for a little while, and I couldn't find my car; soon my eyes became accustomed to the dark and I could distinguish things. It is quite a strain driving through traffic though, on a narrow, rough road with no lights, and traffic—mostly horse-drawn wagons—moving in both directions. As soon as it becomes dark you know, the supply and ammunition trains start out, and the troops are moved.

• • • •

"We are busy tonight. This is no work for a nervous person, especially at night. There is a shell hole in the middle of the road on the way to the front post. I dodged and straddled every dark spot on the way up and missed it. Guns were booming in the distance, and a couple of Boche shells landed right near me. It was so dark that I wasn't sure that I saw the dead horse, and not seeing the post when I thought I should, I had the queer feeling that I had passed it and was on my way to the German trenches. However, I soon spied it, turned around on the narrow road, went into the abri, and found that they had one couché (lying down case), a man that had been shot in the side, and two assis. Coming down I missed seeing the shell-hole and a back wheel went into the side of it with a terrific bump. I thought it broke the spring, but it didn't. I'll sure hand it to the Fords for standing rough work. The poor couché probably cussed me out. I went in low the rest of the way.

AT THE TAXI-STAND.

"The blessés are brought down from the front post as fast as they come in, and are brought in here to the taxi-stand where the wounds are looked at and tagged. They are not sent on down to the hospital, however, from here, until there is a load, unless they are bad off or happen to be an officer. We are going to have a busy night. Since dark there has been a load waiting each time a car has gone up.

• • • •

"Was called again. It is now 25 minutes to 2. I have made two trips since I wrote the above. They were coming in so fast, the Médecin Chef had to call one of

the cars from the other post. This is sure nerve-racking work.

"Next morning. I crawled into a bunk and put a couple of dirty, muddy blessé blankets over me and went to sleep. I may have gotten lice but I did not care then. I woke up at 6 o'clock, cold and feeling rotten, as the air in here is terrible. Went out and warmed my motor, then came back and climbed into my bunk again.

"At 7 I was called to go out to the front post. It was light then—had two cups of delicious coffee—also took a man up with a big bucket of coffee for the brancardiers at the post. I passed the dead horse—the guide—but did not see the post. While I was at the post yesterday afternoon I saw about twelve big shells drop on the road a quarter or half a mile on up. The first thing I knew I found myself at the place—some sort of a post, with shell-holes all around, fresh ones—and men at work filling them. I saw three dead horses piled on one side of the road, and began to think I was getting over in the Boche trenches—you can bet that I got out of there in a hurry—nearly killed my motor turning around on the narrow road.

UNDER FIRE.

"Later. I had to make another trip to the front post, where I am now writing, and German shells are falling all around. They seem to be shelling a hill between here and the taxi-stand. Gee! The French batteries are shooting three or four a second now, just over the hill. It is wonderful—I can hear the whistle of the German shells gradually get louder and then break right across the road, one hundred yards away.

"This is a very disconnected letter, but it is written under and in between the French and German shells. I wish they would hurry up and come, so that I can get out of here. This little abri at the front post is full of Frenchmen eating, so I am standing without in the runway leaning against piles of rocks."

A GERMAN BOMBARDMENT.

"December 11.

"We have been working hard since we came here. I work 24 hours at a poste, then off 24 hours, then on call again for 24 hours. I was at the poste Sunday afternoon, night, and Monday morning. There

(Continued on page 126)

City Club Election Coming!

SATURDAY, April 20, is the day on which members exercise their rights of suffrage at the City Club. A complete new set of officers and four new directors will be elected at the annual meeting—the former for a one-year, the latter for a two-year term.

The nominating committee, last Monday, April 1, as required by the by-laws, posted its list of nominees, printed on the first page of this Bulletin.

The by-laws provide that other nominations must be posted at least ten days before the election, so on next Wednesday, April 10, the lists will be closed. Nominations may be made on petition of twenty members.

The nominating committee this year consisted of Philip S. Post, chairman; Horace J. Bridges, Walter D. Herrick, F. B. Johnstone, and S. R. Watkins.

Below is the Bulletin's "impartial review of the nominees":

For President. George H. Mead, University of Chicago. Prof. Mead is now a member of the Board of Directors and chairman of the Public Affairs Committee of the Club. He is President of the Vocational Guidance League; Treasurer of the University of Chicago Settlement; Vice-President of the Immigrants Protective League and of the Public Education Association of Chicago, and Chairman of the Section on Social Problems of the War and Reconstruction, National Conference of Social Work.

From 1908 to 1914, Prof. Mead was chairman of the Club Committee on Public Education and, in 1909, of the special committee which investigated conditions at the Public Library and made a report which brought about its reorganization. He was also chairman of the special committee which prepared the volume on "Vocational Training in Chicago," published by the Club in 1912.

Prof. Mead has been on the faculty of the department of philosophy at the University since 1894.

For Vice-President. Charles M. Moderwell, President C. M. Moderwell & Co. Chairman Political Action Committee, Union League Club. Member Executive Committee, Association of Commerce. Member Committee on Coal Production, Council of National Defense. Special assistant to Illinois Fuel Administration in coal shortage emergency last winter. Formerly President Illinois Coal Operators' Association.

Mr. Moderwell was a member of the Board of Directors in 1915.

For Treasurer. Roy C. Osgood, Trust Officer, First Trust and Savings Bank. Present treasurer of the Club. Elected secretary last year but resigned to fill unexpired term of treasurer. President Legal Club of Chicago. Treasurer Gads Hill Center. Member Board of Governors, Investment Bankers' Association.

For Secretary. Charles Yeomans, Secretary Yeomans Bros. Co. Present secretary of the Club. Chairman Soldiers' and Sailors' Entertainment Committee. Secretary City Club Committee on Public Health.

For Directors.

Arthur L. Hamilton, President International Tag Company. Member Board of Trustees, Chicago Ethical Society.

Alfred L. Baker, President Alfred L. Baker & Co. A charter member of the Club and one of its incorporators. President 1912-14.

Bradford Gill, Fred S. James & Co. Chairman, House Committee of the City Club.

Harris Keeler, Director Chicago Bureau of Public Efficiency. Member Public Affairs Committee of the City Club.

President Frank I. Moulton retires after serving two terms. Edgar A. Bancroft retires as vice-president and Shelby M. Singleton and Paul Steinbrecher as directors.

THE SPRING MUSICALE last Wednesday evening was a delightful affair. The music was by Miss Vera Poppé, 'cellist; Miss Mary Cameron, pianist; Miss Ruth Miller, violinist, and Mr. Hector Spaulding, who sang a group of French songs.

A REPORT OF PROF. KALLEN'S interesting talk before the Club last Thursday will be printed in next week's Bulletin.

THE ADDRESSES AT LUNCHEON once or twice a week furnish a liberal education on affairs of the day.

On the West Front

(Continued from page 124)

was a terrific artillery bombardment from 2:30 to 7:30 in the morning. The poste is right in the middle of the 75s, 105s and 155s. One big German shell, a 210, dropped in front of the abri about 20 feet from our cars. The cars were covered with mud. Another piece of shell lit in front of our door to the abri—shot it open and broke it. Woke me up and scared me to death. One shell dropped into an abri where some men (artillery) were sleeping, buried two of them up to their waists. They were brought in in a couple of hours and we took them down to the hospital.

"This section is nearly all artillery fighting on account of the hills. There is practically no rifle shooting here. We, of course, work right in the way of the big guns, and are therefore right in the thick of it.

AIR BATTLES.

"Sunday afternoon I counted 15 aeroplanes in the air—six of them were Boche. We saw a Boche plane fall over the hill, hit by a machine gun. That afternoon six French planes were brought down. One of our boys carried two of the dead aviators—they were burned to a crisp. Fitzpatrick, who carried them, said it was a terrible sight. The day before that the French brought down 12 German planes.

"Our French Lieutenant said tonight at dinner that the Médecin Chef of our division told him today that we have been doing excellent work; that we are the best ambulance section that they have ever had.

"Two of our cars have been wrecked lately at night, it is so dark.

RED CROSS FIRED ON.

"January 7, 1918.

"We had a bit of excitement yesterday. Four of our ambulances were deliberately fired on as they stood in front of our front poste, which is in sight of the German trenches. One car is supposed to be there all the time. The Boche started yesterday morning at 8 o'clock and began dropping them in, tearing the body of the car to pieces and blowing out three tires. The second car came up and while the boys were trying to change the tires, more shells dropped; the boys dropped flat on the ground and then ducked into the abri; after a dozen shots the boys went out again. The Germans saw them and began firing

again. That kept up all morning, the two cars being smashed all to pieces.

"The phone wire was out of commission so they could not call another car for more tires. Finally, at 11 o'clock, the third car brought the food up from the taxi-stand poste for the brancardiers at the front poste. He had no more than turned his car around and lined it up with the others when the shells began to come again. The driver ducked for the abri, a shell burst six inches out of the opening, went up through the body, knocked the soup, food and can of wine in all directions.

"After lunch the first car of the relief went up and it, too, was shot up pretty badly.

CLEARING THE WRECKAGE.

"After dark the cars were all brought out with the aid of the wrecking crew from here headed by our mechanic. The boys who had been trying to change tires laid their overcoats on the bank beside the road. The coats were riddled with holes and in tatters from the éclat from the shells. There are no batteries near that poste and there was nothing but that blessé poste with its Red Cross flag in front in the whole valley. The shells were not stray ones, but were fired directly at the ambulance. The boys surely had a close call."

———

LAST WEEK YOU RECEIVED with your dues notices a request from the War Department for gifts of photographs, drawings and descriptions of bridges, buildings, towns and localities now occupied by German forces in France, Belgium and Luxemburg and likewise in that part of Germany lying west of a line running north and south through Hamburg. This data is to be used for intelligence purposes. Send it to Mr. Harry Gay, American Protective League, 120 W. Adams, or, if more convenient, bring it to the City Club marked for Mr. Gay and we will deliver it.

MR. SHERLOCK HOLMES is on the trail of the thief who took from the Club reading room the following books belonging to the Chicago Public Library: "Miss Haroun Al-Raschid," by J. F. Kernish, and "Moonbeams from the Larger Lunacy," by Stephen Leacock. If the books are returned at once, the borrower's name will be suppressed.

House Shortage Is War Problem

U. S. Must Extend War Housing Program, Says Whitaker

THE $50,000,000 appropriated by Congress for the housing of workers in the ship-building industry is but a fragment of what the government will have to spend for this work, if the war continues very long, according to Charles H. Whitaker, editor of the Journal of the American Institute of Architects, in an address at the City Club last week. England, he said, has spent over $700,000,000 already.

BIG LABOR TURNOVER.

Mr. Whitaker said in part: "War is a supreme test of the imagination. When we went to war we started to build new plants and stimulate the production of war supplies, but no one had the imagination to look at the social side of the problem. It is easy enough to build plants, but what will you do with the workmen? We haven't in this country been able to mobilize our social imagination.

"There came a tremendous shortage of housing in the ship-building industry. The result was a tremendous turnover of labor. At least 100,000 workmen have come to the Atlantic seaboard for jobs in the ship yards and have gone home within a few days because they have been unable to find a decent place for their families to live in.

PRIVATE CAPITAL NOT IN MARKET.

"Why did not private capital come to the rescue? The cost of building is very high and after the war nobody knows what will happen to the houses that have been built. Private builders faced with this uncertainty will not take the risk and the banks will not loan money on such an enterprise.

ENGLAND'S GREAT ACCOMPLISHMENT.

"France, at the beginning of the war, with the major part of her coal fields in the hands of the Germans, was practically put out of the industrial field, and the burden of war production fell upon England. How she responded on the production side is well known but what she did in a social way is not so well understood. In making plans for the housing of the workers she had to begin with certain machinery already estab-

lished. Under the Housing and Town Planning Act any town had power to initiate housing projects, and many such projects were in operation when the war broke out. England at first relied upon these communities for her war-housing, but it was soon demonstrated that this would not work because of competition between towns for labor and materials delayed through haggling over terms, etc. So the government took over the whole program and put it in charge of Raymond Unwin, one of the foremost city planners of England, and instructed him to do what was necessary in the housing line to get the supply of munitions flowing.

TEMPORARY OR PERMANENT?

"The question of temporary versus permanent construction came up immediately. Very naturally, at the beginning, the tendency was to build temporary structures, but it was soon seen that this would not do. The workingmen would not stay in temporary structures and the turnover increased. Also, when it was considered that the cost of improvements, layout of streets, sewers, water supply, etc., remains the same, it was found that the difference in cost between temporary and permanent houses did not warrant the building of the temporary structures. England saw that the only thing to do was to provide decent houses for all the workers in the munitions industries.

"In building these new communities the English government has done more than simply construct houses. She discovered that houses alone would not solve the problem, that provision must be made for the amenities of life, and so she has built in each of these communities, halls, recreation places, churches, hospitals, moving picture theatres and everything that is necessary to community life.

A COLOSSAL UNDERTAKING.

"England is said to have spent between seven and eight hundred million dollars on this work. Even under the pressure of war conditions she has built towns which are

COM' ON OVER

The young man in this cartoon is not a member of our Club, but he had luncheon with us in the main dining room the other day and since that time he has been advertising us very consistently; and we feel that his enthusiasm is a good example to present to other members who eat here and go back home without a word to a living soul.

STATEMENT OF THE OWNERSHIP, MANAGEMENT, ETC., REQUIRED BY THE ACT OF CONGRESS OF AUGUST 24, 1912,

Of CITY CLUB BULLETIN published weekly at Chicago, Illinois, for April 1, 1918. State of Illinois, County of Cook, ss.

Before me, a notary public in and for the State and county aforesaid, personally appeared Dwight L. Akers, who, having been duly sworn according to law, deposes and says that he is the editor of the CITY CLUB BULLETIN and that the following is, to the best of his knowledge and belief, a true statement of the ownership, management, etc., of the aforesaid publication for the date shown in the above caption, required by the Act of August 24, 1912, embodied in section 443, Postal Laws and Regulations, to wit:

1. That the names and addresses of the publisher, editor, managing editor, and business managers are: Publisher, City Club of Chicago, 315 Plymouth Court, Chicago. Editor, Dwight L. Akers, 315 Plymouth Court, Chicago. Managing Editor, None. Business Managers, None.

2. That the owners are: The City Club of Chicago, a corporation organized under the laws of Illinois. No stock. Frank I. Moulton, President, 110 S. Dearborn St., Edgar A. Bancroft, Vice President, 606 S. Michigan Ave., Roy C. Osgood, Treasurer, 1st Trust & Savings Bank, Charles Yeomans, Secretary, 231 Institute Place.

3. That the known bondholders, mortgagees, and other security holders owning or holding 1 per cent or more of total amount of bonds, mortgages, or other securities are: None.

4. That the two paragraphs next above, giving the names of the owners, stockholders, and security holders, if any, contain not only the list of stockholders and security holders as they appear upon the books of the company but also, in cases where the stockholder or security holder appears upon the books of the company as trustee or in any other fiduciary relation, the name of the person or corporation for whom such trustee is acting, is given; also that the said two paragraphs contain statements embracing affiant's full knowledge and belief as to the circumstances and conditions under which stockholders and security holders who do not appear upon the books of the company as trustees, hold stock and securities in a capacity other than that of a bona fide owner; and this affiant has no reason to believe that any other person, association, or corporation has any interest direct or indirect in the said stock, bonds, or other securities than as so stated by him.

                                    DWIGHT L. AKERS.

Sworn to and subscribed before me this 28th day of March, 1918.
    [SEAL]   BERTHA A. FREEMAN.
        (My commission expires Sept. 18, 1918.)

not surpassed by those which were built before the war. The largest of these is at Gretna. At this point a great explosives plant was built, stretching in one direction ten miles. To house the workers of this plant, two communities were built. These towns, laid out upon the open prairie, were built within less than a year. There are other government housing enterprises at Wellhall and about fifty other places in England. At the present time there is before Parliament an after-the-war house-building program, backed by the Labor Party, involving the erection of 100,000 houses, 10,000 to be built each year. This program provides a priority of labor and materials for housing work. It is well understood in England that there will be no more slums.

"England in these undertakings has recognized the truth that there will be no

solution of the housing problem until the land question is solved. She provided that all land taken for housing purposes should be acquired at its pre-war value and that surrounding land should also be maintained at this value. So nobody gets any increment of land values from this government work. This is understood at Washington in connection with the Shipping Board's housing projects, and already plans for two of the developments are being worked along similar lines."

Charles B. Ball, Chief Sanitary Inspector of Chicago, speaking at the same luncheon, said that Chicago has an over-supply of houses. "We have probably enough empty houses in Chicago," he said, "to take care of 30,000 families." He suggested that these houses might be brought into use if factories manufacturing war materials were established in convenient locations."

The City Club Bulletin

Published Weekly by the City Club of Chicago

A Journal of Active Citizenship

VOLUME XI   MONDAY, APRIL 15, 1918   NUMBER 15

A Letter from the President

To the Members of the City Club:

The Annual Meeting, which ought to be the most important meeting of the Club, and the most largely attended, has usually had the smallest attendance of any of the club meetings, and has, in a measure, led the officers to feel that there was a lack of interest in club affairs.

The meeting this year should be of interest to members and be assured of a full attendance.

We are to vote up by-laws submitted by the Directors, and upon certain amendments which have been proposed by members.

The proposed amendments, if adopted, will radically change the plan of procedure as heretofore followed by the club, and should have the mature consideration of all of our members. It would involve the commitment of the club in the public mind on contentious questions, which has been avoided under our present method of public discussion and committee action.

The proposed amendments are printed in this issue of the Bulletin, the by-laws prepared by the Directors having been published in the Bulletin of April 1st.

The Annual Meeting will be held in the Lounge of the Club House, Saturday, April 20th, at 2 p. m.

Reports of the various officers will be submitted, adoption of the by-laws considered, and officers elected.

I respectfully urge members to attend this meeting.   F. I. MOULTON,
Président.

No NEW NOMINATIONS for Club officers and directors were made last week and there will accordingly only be one ticket. But there promises to be a lively discussion of the new by-laws. Read Mr. A. B.

Wednesday, April 17

AT LUNCHEON

H. Charles Woods

Lecturer Lowell Institute 1917-1918

"The Near East and Pan-Germanism"

Mr. Woods has travelled extensively in the Balkans and in Asia Minor, making special studies of the Dardanelles, of the country surrounding Salonika and of the Bagdad Railway. He has acted as special correspondent of the London *Times* and military and diplomatic correspondent of the London *Evening News*. He is personally acquainted with M. Venizelos and all the leading Balkan statesmen.

Luncheon from 11:30   Speaking at 1

Saturday, April 20

2:00 P.M. IN THE LOUNGE

The Annual Meeting of the Club

Our yearly gathering next Saturday promises to be interesting as well as important. Even if you dislike annual meetings on general principles you ought to be there to help in the important decisions which are to be made. Make your attendance an evidence of loyalty to your Club. Read President Moulton's letter printed on this page.

Notice the hour and place announced above. They were incorrectly stated in last week's Bulletin.

Cone's letter on another page of this Bulletin.

A DINNER WITHOUT CONVERSATION is a poor dinner, no matter how good the cooking may be.

The City Club Bulletin

A Journal of Active Citizenship

PUBLISHED WEEKLY BY THE

CITY CLUB OF CHICAGO

315 Plymouth Court   Telephone: Harrison 8278

DWIGHT L. AKERS, Editor

OFFICERS OF THE CLUB

FRANK I. MOULTON, President
EDGAR A. BANCROFT, Vice-President
ROY C. OSGOOD, Treasurer
CHARLES YEOMANS, Secretary
GEORGE E. HOOKER, Civic Secretary

EDITORIAL BOARD

HERBERT H. SMITH, Chairman
FREDERICK D. BRAMHALL   S. R. WATKINS
C. COLTON DAUGHADAY   PAUL R. WRIGHT

$1.00 per Year   -   -   -   -   10c per Copy

Entered as second class matter, December 3, 1917,
at the postoffice at Chicago, Illinois, under the act of
March 3, 1879.

THE LISTENING POST

Here is a test of your loyalty to the Club: Give up that game of golf, Saturday, the 20th, and attend the annual meeting in the Lounge at 2 p. m. We ask this only once a year.

AT A MEETING last Wednesday, the Directors adopted a resolution expressing their appreciation of the opportunity of serving under President Moulton during the last year and of his able and progressive conduct of the affairs of the club during his administration.

FIVE NEW MEMBERS last week. They are:

John T. Booz, lawyer.

Rev. Carl D. Case, First Baptist Church.

W. deF. Curtis, Secretary, Estate of Mrs. George M. Pullman.

Thomas J. Mercer, Editor Music Trade Indicator.

Roy F. Perkins, Cashier Peter Schuttler Co.

AFTER APRIL 21, the Sunday "open house" for soldiers and sailors will be discontinued and the club house will be closed. Since the establishment of the Army and Navy Club, the lack of accommodations downtown for soldiers and sailors on leave has been met. It was to supply such accommodations that the "open house" was established by the City Club. The club, we believe, rendered a real service in this, for the club house was used on each of these days by from one to two hundred men. Men in uniform will be welcome on Saturday afternoons and evenings as heretofore.

A LETTER from Elmo C. Lowe who has been doing Y. M. C. A. war work in the East informs us that he expects to leave within a few days for France in charge of a group of twenty-five men and women who are going over seas for special work with the Y. M. C. A. Accompanying him will be Joseph Hudnut of New York, whom many of our members will remember as having been associated with our Neighborhood Center committee as assisting architect in the summer of 1915.

Our Attitude Toward Russia

Fail to Understand Meaning of
Revolution, Says S. N. Harper

A MERICANS have not succeeded in interpreting rightly the forces which are at work in Russia and the spirit and meaning of the Revolution, according to Prof. Samuel N. Harper of the University of Chicago in his address last Monday. We have been unimaginative and "stiff-necked" in our attitude, he asserted. Professor Harper teaches the Russian language and institutions. He has been in Russia several times, before and during the war and has come into close touch with the leaders of affairs. He said in part:

FRIEND OR TRAITOR?

"Many Americans, since the revolution, look upon Russia frankly as having betrayed our cause. Many of us have become accustomed to regard her simply as a place from which comes sensational, nerve-tingling news.

"When the war came, we were Pro-ally, but in spite of Russia. We could not see the forces of liberation that were at work, and that Russian liberals regarded this as a war for Russian freedom. Our representatives there dealt exclusively with the agents of the autocracy and gave no encouragement to the forces working for a stronger Russia.

TO AVOID SEPARATE PEACE

"The Revolution startled us because we did not understand this under-current. Our first question was, Does it mean a separate peace? That proves how little we understood the revolution. The aim of the revolution was, in fact, to prevent a separate peace. The old regime was working for it and was bringing about disorganization and anarchy that must ultimately result in a separate peace. If the revolutionists of March had not acted, Russia would have been out of the war in 1917. Nevertheless, we have complained in whining tones that Russia had no right to have a revolution in wartime.

"One of the first things which the revolutionists did was to ask the Allies for a statement of their war aims. They prefaced this by giving their own. The revo-

lutionary formula was crude enough—no annexations, no indemnities and self-determination—but it was not understood by our people. We interpreted it simply as German intrigue. All that they demanded has since been advocated by Lloyd George, President Wilson, and the British Labor Party. One of the most powerful weapons of the Bolsheviki against the Kerensky government was the failure of the Allies to respond to Russia's appeal for a statement of war aims.

EXPLAINING AMERICA

"Americans in Russia tried to explain America's position in the war, but the importance of interpreting America to Russia was not sufficiently recognized at home. America's attitude was misrepresented by German agents and revolutionists who had returned from America and whose knowledge of this country was confined mostly to the East side of New York. But Americans in Russia who tried to give a better interpretation of our position were left without the necessary information about what was going on in this country. Fortunately this publicity work is now being adequately organized and a full telegraph service has been established.

"During the first few months of the revolution the order was remarkable in Russia although there was no police force. Hearing of the propaganda of extremists and of German agents, Americans demanded repressive measures. But the revolutionary government could not exert repression, even where it was needed, because it had been so long the weapon of the autocratic classes that even the words 'order' and 'discipline' had become discredited.

NAPOLEON NOT WANTED

"We called not only for order but for a new Napoleon, a strong man who would save Russia. We should have known that a Napoleon could play no part in a democratic revolution. And when we did not see a strong man we became worried. We did a lot of whining and worrying about conditions in Russia when we should have been helping.

"The Bolsheviki came into power partly by taking advantage of the economic distress and partly through the unwillingness of the government to bring about further chaos and sacrifice of life by standing out against them. I do not approve of the Bolshevik program, but I must say that they did contribute something of value to our cause in the negotiations at Brest-Litovsk. They showed up Germany's war aims as they have never been disclosed before. By giving them credit for this we do indeed help their position in Russia, but we are in this dilemma because of our stiff-neckedness and our lack of imagination, which has allowed these fanatics to steal our moral thunder. The principles which the Bolsheviki used at Brest-Litovsk were not Bolshevik principles but the principles of the Russian revolution.

OUR ATTITUDE NOW

"Our present attitude toward Russia shows still a lack of understanding. A month ago, President Wilson sent a message to Russia saying that America would support her, but there was a regrettable lack of response on the part of the American press, and even of the liberal non-socialists. Alexander Berkman from prison sent a message to Lenine, urging him not to talk peace with Germany and to recognize President Wilson's sincerity. Morris Hillquit sent to Lenine a message supporting the President's position but the liberals of this country failed to back up the President in this in any effective way.

"Economic distress is to a large extent at the bottom of Russia's trouble. Appeals have been made to us to help relieve this distress. Germany is pushing into Russia. If she should go in in a spirit of helpfulness to relieve Russia's distress, Russia will feed Germany. While we are, of course, forced to give our first attention to the West Front, we ought so far as possible to allow Russia to buy from us the supplies which she needs."

Dramatic Column

R AYMOND HITCHCOCK appeared before the club last Tuesday noon in a new sketch entitled: "The Liberty Loan, or Watch Me Get Your Dollars." He arrived just before the hour for the speaking and a committee was on the point of visiting the John Crerar Library or the Billy Sunday Tabernacle in search of him when he appeared, escorted by M. H. Cowen, chairman of the City Club Loyalty Committee.

Prussianism never got a harder "strafing" than it got from Mr. Hitchcock. But what really did the business, we believe, was the battery of good stories he brought along. Raymond is a psychologist and knows that a laugh creates a feeling of expansiveness and prosperity which opens the pocketbooks and gets the dollars. His stories, we are sure, sold several good-sized bonds.

DOES THIS HIT YOU?

"Any man who can't spare two dollars a week for a fifty-dollar bond ought to hang out the suicide sign," Hitchcock said. "Why, you men spend more than that for liquor!" We saw Lorado Taft and George Hooker wince under that, but Raymond didn't really know who he was talking to, so we let it pass.

The Loyalty Committee of the Club did a land office business after the meeting. Over $11,000 was subscribed by our members. We were the first Chicago Club to get into action, according to a letter from the captain of the division on clubs, printed on another page.

The committee has a desk in the Club lobby and a man in charge each noon hour to take your subscription. Why not make your subscription through the Club?

The committee asks that you make it a point to file your subscription today!

CHANGE IN PROPOSED BY-LAWS

The directors have made two changes in the proposed by-laws to be voted on at the annual meeting, next Saturday, April 20, at 2:00 P. M., viz.:

Art. VI. Sec. 3. The third sentence should read: "At least *seven* days notice of the time and place of the annual meeting shall be given to all members of the Club by the Secretary."

Art. IX. Sec. 2. Add the following: "Members whose dues are in arrears to exceed 30 days shall not be privileged to vote."

IN LAST WEEK'S Bulletin it was erroneously stated that Paul Steinbrecher retires from the Board. Mr. Steinbrecher's term extends to April, 1919.

Member Attacks By-Laws

SOME amendments to the proposed new by-laws have been presented by Albert B. Cone and will be considered at the annual meeting, April 20. Mr. Cone has sent out letters to a large number of members in support of his amendments and had asked for proxies for the annual meeting. His letter called for a meeting of members to be held at a down-town hotel last Wednesday. The letter follows:

Dear Sir: At the last annual meeting of the City Club I offered by-law amendments providing; (1) For a referendum plan, enclosed. (2) For direct primary nominations. (3) For cumulative voting for directors. The opposition succeeded in referring these to the directors. In debate they conceded no argument could be made to these in their substance, but thought the directors could improve their form. My supporters offered a motion which was unanimously carried, instructing the directors after considering these measures to call a special meeting of members and report their recommendations to it for its action. Legally, I believe such instructions are mandatory but directors have permitted eleven months to pass without complying.

Now they offer for vote of members new by-laws which contemptuously ignore these suggestions and in other particulars are even less democratic than the old ones. Members now do have express right to inspect minutes of meetings of the club and board; this privision is omitted. They have by statute the right to amend by-laws at any annual meeting; the new draft attempts to abridge that statute right. I've been sitting on the doorstep for nearly a year waiting for the directors to do something—and they have! Again it's up to me to do something or lie down and be stepped on.

I've proposed these measures again as amendments to the offered by-laws. I am sending out this rally call at my own expense, a call for votes, a call for a caucus of all members who will support the main issue, the referendum measure. The caucus is for those who will support that; the other measures, and any other matters, I leave in their hands. Whether five or five hundred appear, I place this issue and whatever supporting proxies I receive in their hands, and join them in the ranks, yielding the initiative which has been forced upon me to whatever leadership may be developed.

There's no neutral ground on this issue. If you are against it I can't stop now to convert you. If you are with me in spirit don't stop there. I ask definitely:

Firstly—Telephone me at once. I can tell you then where the caucus will be held. . I am calling it for Wednesday, April ten, at some downtown hotel. Plate luncheon 12:15 sharp. Tell me you will be there; or if engagements prevent will try to send a personal representative to act for you; or will at least send a terse message by wire or mail.

Sign enclosed proxy and mail now or bring to the luncheon. Do this even though you EXPECT to attend the annual meeting. We will want to know at the caucus what votes are with us. Leave the proxy line blank so the steering committee can attend to voting it.

Thirdly—Be at the annual meeting if at all possible. Reclaim your proxy, vote for yourself and help with motions and debate.

Finally—Read "firstly" again and phone me now, before you lay this down. I must know how many covers to order. Harrison four six eight seven from nine to five. Ravenswood one one one one evenings till midnight.

There's nothing radical in this referendum. It's merely advisory, not mandatory. It gives members no new power—only a voice. I suspect that the opposition to it would disappear if it were fitted with a device something like a casement window fitting whereby it could be manipulated and controlled from the INSIDE. One suggestion in that direction was made at the last meeting.

Yours sincerely,

ALBERT BENJAMIN CONE.

Associate Editor American Lumberman. Member (sometime chairman) Committee on Publicity and Statistics, City Club.

Mr. Cone's proposed amendments are as follows:

Article III, Section 4, in the second line after the words "all the meetings" add "of the Club and of the Board of Directors" as in the old By-Laws. At the end of the section add the following, "The record of proceedings of meetings of the Club and of the Board of Directors and the roll of members shall at all times be open to the inspection of members at the business office of the Club."

Add the following as a new Article IX, Section 1, headed "Initiative and Referendum,"—"Upon resolution of the Board of Directors, or upon petition of any twenty members in writing to the Board of Directors, any question relating to the affairs or activities of the Club shall be submitted to referendum letter ballot of the members; and the returns when duly canvassed by the Board of Directors or by such committee as it may appoint for the purpose shall be spread upon the minutes of the Board of Directors and communicated to the members of the Club."

In the present Art. 9 renumbered as 10 add to Section 1, "Members may if they so desire, cast their votes for Directors in accumulative manner."

Section 2, Art. IX, I propose to have transferred to the articles of association where it belongs.

Section 3, Art. IX, to be renumbered Section 2, cut out the word "provided" and all following words down to the last sentence which retain.

I also offer the following amendment to the articles of association as an addition to numbered paragraph 3, "Nominations of candidates for officers and directors to be voted upon at the annual meeting shall be by direct primary as further provided in the By-Laws."

Amend Article V, Section 1A by addition of the following which follows the old By-Laws: "This committee shall have no power to commit the Club to any policy or opinion with respect to public affairs or questions."

Is Your Diet Right?

BUY no meat till you have a sufficient supply of milk! Cereals, roots, meat, the muscle tissues to which we are accustomed, in any possible combination lack essential elements of food value, including one of the substances—popularly known as "vitamines"—whose exact nature is unknown but which are found in the leaves of plants and more particularly in milk. This is the latest word of science on the subject of diet, brought to the City Club last Friday by Dr. E. V. McCollum of Johns Hopkins University.

Dr. McCollum's remarks have immense practical bearing on a situation of national importance. The national vitality requires the maintenance of our present standard of milk consumption, but the production of milk, according to Dr. McCollum, is being curtailed by inadequate returns to the dairy industry. Americans must be educated to buy milk at a price which will afford adequate compensation to the producer. Dr. McCollum said in part:

A Lack in the Diet

"Experiments in feeding have amply demonstrated that it is impossible to induce growth in a young animal by a diet of seeds, in any possible combination. An adequate diet consists of proteins, sugar, fats, inorganic elements and certain unknown elements—the so-called 'vitamines.' The absence of one of these elements is indicated in eye trouble, blindness and ultimately death.

"In striking contrast to the seed diet is a combination of the seed with leaves. Seeds consist of the germ tip and the endosperm, the latter of which is the reserve food for the seed and is not living matter. The leaf on the other hand is living matter and contains the elements lacking in the seed.

"A diet of potatoes, sweet potatoes and other roots (essentially 'storage foods') is also deficient in certain necessary elements. So are the muscle tissues of meat. There is no combination of seeds, roots or meats which will keep an animal alive and in health.

"There are only two classes of what we may call protective foods—'protective' because they contain the vital elements lacking in other foods. They are (1) milk and its products and (2) the leaves of plants.

Milk is the most important. You may combine it with seeds, with roots or with meat and get a fairly satisfactory diet.

"There are some nations—for instance Japan and China—which use but little milk in the diet, but if they have maintained their vitality it is because they have eaten leafy foods in large quantities. It is not an exaggeration to say that only those peoples who use dairy products are strong and virile, with low infant mortality and a long span of life.

Peril to Milk Supply

"The dairy industry is today in a precarious condition. The number of dairy cows which are being slaughtered is alarming. Consumption is going down and producers cannot make a profit at present prices and with the present cost of feed. Thousands of city children are underfed, not through a lack of quantity in food but through the lack of the vital food elements which are found in milk. We cannot permit the health of the nation to be jeopardized by a decrease in our standards of milk consumption."

In the discussion which followed Dr. McCollum's address, he elaborated some of his points in answer to questions. He said:

Milk in Cooking

"Many people can't take milk as a beverage, but our system of cookery has been built up on the use of milk. Our foods should be prepared with milk. There is no appreciable harm to the vital elements in the process of cooking, except where soda is used."

"Condensed or evaporated milk is almost as good as fresh milk, although inferior in taste. Butter does not fill the place of milk and the importance of milk in the diet is no argument against the substitution of vegetable fats for butter. Skimmed milk contains probably enough of the vital elements of milk to carry the user along, but all the constituents of milk are needed."

Some members are not acquainted with the facilities of the Club above the third floor. On the fourth floor, is a good library on civics. Also a shower bath!

The Jewish People and the War

Restoration of National Home Under League of Nations, Advocated by Professor Kallen

THE progress of the British armies in Palestine, culminating in the capture of Jerusalem, has the most intense dramatic interest for Jew and Gentile. Something of the glamour of the Crusades is brought down to the twentieth century. But for many people of the Jewish race this twentieth century conquest of Palestine has more than a romantic or military interest. It brings nearer to realization their dreams of a reunited Jewish people in the old national homeland of Palestine.

The Zionist program as it relates up to the great democratic programs for reconstruction after the war was the subject of Prof. H. M. Kallen's address at the City Club at luncheon, April 4. Dr. Kallen is professor of philosophy at the University of Wisconsin, author of "The Structure of Lasting Peace," and "In the Hope of a New Zion"—both soon to be published.

EUROPE'S RECONSTRUCTION

Prof. Kallen prefaced his statement of the Zionist position with a discussion of the reconstruction programs which Europe is facing. He said in part:

"Today the whole world is considering the problems of the future after the war, from the point of view not simply of a recovery of losses but of the reorganization and development of the whole social structure. There are, in general, two programs, one the democratic program of the laboring classes; the other, the program of the ruling classes, embodying not only various ameliorative measures, but their economic ambitions, their desires with reference to foreign markets, colonies, the economic penetration of undeveloped countries, etc. In the interest of an international peace program for the benefit of capital, there has been held in Switzerland an international conference of capitalists to discuss the future after the war.

"The other program is that defined in President Wilson's speech of January 28. It is a program which the interallied conference of labor has endorsed and which in general the masses of the allied countries are backing as against the classes and even in some cases against their governments. The most significant point in this program is the proposed league of nations and the machinery for avoiding future wars.

"The comment of the press in this country and abroad on President Wilson's speech indicates a sharp division of thought regarding these points. Clemenceau has sneered at the whole scheme for a league of nations and some members of the British Government have passed it over very politely. The league of nations has, however, become for America, fundamental to any treaty of peace which we can enter into. In backing it President Wilson, our most liberal statesman since Lincoln, has become the spokesman for the labor groups who represent the masses of men in all the allied nations, rather than of those frightened vested interests represented by such men as Lord Lansdowne. The investing classes generally are opposing the league of nations because it would mean that in the future their foreign investments would no longer be insured by the blood and power of the nation.

THE AMERICAN POSITION

"The American position then is the position of international democracy and the foundation of any settlement for us must be the establishment of the league of nations to prevent future wars. The exact form of the league has not been defined by President Wilson, but its general principles have been laid down—the principles of democracy and of nationality.

"The conception of democracy is changing. We no longer hold to the eighteenth century formula that the equality of individuals means their similarity. Democratic movements have in the past been corrective rather than creative—attempts to recover for the mass rights and privileges which have been taken from them. The newer conception of democracy is creative and implies opportunity for the free development of the individual. And as we realize that this development proceeds by an ever widening association of the individual with new groups, we grasp the principle that democracy must now be interpreted in terms of free groups rather than of individuals. These fall into two classes—natural and artificial. Nationalities are natural groups; states, nations, vocational or religious associations are artificial. The history of democracy has become the struggle for the liberation of groups—of nationalities. Nationality is to the group what personality is to the individual. The need is that there should be a guarantee of law that each social group shall be free to develop its group personality according to its own inner quality. This can only be accomplished through a league of nations.

THE JEWS AS A NATION

"The Jewish people are the great historical incarnation of the principle of nationality. They have maintained their historic continuity through generations. Against all types of imperialism—the religious imperialism of the middle ages and the political and cultural imperialism of the dynastic state of today—represented in its most vicious form by Germany—the Jew has been a protestant. So the recognition of the Jewish people as a cultural group becomes inevitably a part of the democratic peace program.

"The idea of the re-establishment of the national integrity of the Jewish people was first endorsed by the British Labor group and later by the British Government. It is indicated as one of our war aims in President Wilson's speech of January 8. It has been endorsed here by the Alliance for Labor and Democracy. America, England, France, Italy, Russia and Belgium have made it a part of their program for the reconstitution of Europe.

THE FUTURE OF PALESTINE

"Inevitably the place chosen for the Jewish national home was Palestine, for the Jewish people throughout history have had before them the thought of the ultimate recovery of the promised land. It has been suggested in England that Palestine should be the seat of the proposed league of nations.

"Following the conquest of Palestine by the British, a civil government has been established under a Zionist commission. Its present . purpose is to develop agriculture behind the lines, for in retreating before the British, the Turks have devastated the country, driving the cattle before them and destroying the countryside. The immediate restoration of the colonies to activity will relieve much shipping and the Zionists are gathering a Restoration Fund for that purpose.

"The program of the Zionist is intended to establish fundamental social justice based on the traditions of the Jewish people. They propose to establish, first of all, economic democracy, for that implies political democracy, though the converse is not necessarily true. We would establish in Palestine an experiment for the avoidance of social evils and the promotion of social justice. It would, we hope, be the center of constructive rather than of the protesting democracy of history."

CITY CLUB FRIENDS of John S. Van Bergen had a surprise the other day when Mr. Van Bergen walked into the Club, after having started for France for the Y. M. C. A. about two weeks before. Mr. Van Bergen explained that he had just received a new commission as First Lieutenant in the construction division, Quartermaster's Corps. He left again for Washington last Wednesday.

First Into Action

THE CITY CLUB was the first Chicago Club to get into action for the Liberty Loan. Following the Raymond Hitchcock meeting last Tuesday over $11,000 was subscribed by our members through the Club and up to the time this Bulletin goes to press over $20,000 has been raised.

M. H. Cowen, chairman of the City Club Loyalty Committee, received this letter last Wednesday from R. S. Ripple, Captain of the subdivision on clubs, Liberty Loan Committee:

MY DEAR MR. COWEN:

I am taking this opportunity to offer my heartiest congratulations to the members of the City Club who so gallantly responded to their country's call by subscribing to the Third Liberty Loan on Tuesday.

The City Club was the first club in Chicago to report its subscription to me on Tuesday in the amount of $11,200. This should be especially gratifying to the Loyalty Committee and to every member of the Club. Since that time I am glad to say that nearly all of the other clubs have come into line.

Assuring you of my sincere appreciation for what you have done in making this loan a success, and trusting you will keep this good work up, I remain,

Very sincerely yours,
(Signed) R. S. RIPPLE,
Captain Subdivision of Clubs No. 7.

9

The City Club Bulletin

Published Weekly by the City Club of Chicago

A Journal of Active Citizenship

VOLUME XI   MONDAY, APRIL 22, 1918   NUMBER 16

THIS WEEK

Luncheon from 11:30   *Speaking at 1:00*

Wednesday, April 24

"National Insurance for Our Fighting Men"

HON. CHARLES F. NESBIT

Commissioner in Charge of Claims, Bureau of War Risk Insurance,
Washington, D. C.

The United States Government has launched upon a great scheme of social insurance. It has already written insurance amounting to about $14,000,000,000—more than four times as much as is carrried on the books of the largest ordinary insurance company in the world. The War Risk Bureau also has charge of allotments to dependents of soldiers and sailors.

Mr. Nesbit is at the head of one of the most important divisions of this service.

Friday, April 26

An Interpretation of Russia

PROF. EDWARD A. ROSS

University of Wisconsin

Prof. Ross returned from Russia the last of January. During his trip he covered 20,000 miles of Russian territory, reaching as far down as Turkestan. He has talked to all classes of Russians.

Wednesday, May 1, at Luncheon. James Weldon Johnson
"The Negro Soldier in the War"

The City Club Bulletin

A Journal of Active Citizenship

The purpose of the Club is to bring together in informal association those men who are genuinely interested in the improvement of the political, social and economic conditions of the community in which we live.

PUBLISHED WEEKLY BY THE

CITY CLUB OF CHICAGO

315 Plymouth Court   Telephone: Harrison 8278

DWIGHT L. AKERS, Editor

OFFICERS OF THE CLUB

GEORGE H. MEAD, President
CHARLES M. MODERWELL, Vice-President
ROY C. OSGOOD, Treasurer
CHARLES YEOMANS, Secretary
GEORGE E. HOOKER, Civic Secretary

EDITORIAL BOARD

HERBERT H. SMITH, Chairman
FREDERICK D. BRAMHALL   S. R. WATKINS
C. COLTON DAUGHADAY   PAUL R. WRIGHT

$1.00 per Year - - - -   10c per Copy

Entered as second class matter, December 3, 1917, at the postoffice at Chicago, Illinois, under the act of March 3, 1879.

JOSEPH Z. UHLIR
Died April 13, 1918

JOSEPH SCHAFFNER
Died April 19, 1918

THE LISTENING POST

VICTOR A. REMY has been appointed to a post with the Aircraft Board, Washington, D. C.

CHARLES H. PRINDEVILLE has been commissioned lieutenant in the Construction Division, Quartermaster Reserve Corps, with headquarters at Washington.

CLIFTON R. BECHTEL expects to sail shortly for France where he will act in a secretarial position in connection with the Y. M. C. A. He left Chicago for the East April 15.

DR. J. H. HESS has been commissioned as Major in the Medical Reserve Corps. He entered upon active service at Ft. Riley April 10.

WE ARE GLAD TO WELCOME these new members into the Club: Julius Goettsch, Assistant General Superintendent, Graham, Anderson, Probst & White (architects); Richard L. Huehne, Crescent Engraving Company; Frank W. Smith, Secretary Corn Exchange National Bank.

THE DIRECTORS have just completed arrangements for an exchange of courtesies with the New York Civic Club. Members who are visiting New York may have the privileges of their clubhouse at 14 W. Twelfth Street by presenting a membership card, which can be obtained from the City Club office. The Civic Club is an organization similar to our own City Club except that it does not undertake organized work.

PROF. ANDREW C. MCLAUGHLIN of the Department of History, University of Chicago, has gone to England at the invitation of the University of London and other English universities to deliver lectures on English and American relations, the causes of America's entrance into the war, and allied topics. Prof. McLaughlin goes as a representative of the National Board of Historical Service. He will deliver lectures at the Universities of London, Oxford, Cambridge and other great universities, before historical societies and other groups.

DO YOU EXPECT to visit any of these cities: Baltimore, Boston, Cincinnati, Kansas City, Milwaukee, Philadelphia, Portland, Ore., St. Louis, Duluth? If so apply to the club office for one of the new cards which certifies your membership in the City Club of Chicago and you will then be entitled to the privileges of any one of the following clubs:

City Club of Baltimore.
Boston City Club.
City Club of Cincinnati.
City Club of Kansas City.
City Club of Milwaukee.
City Club of Philadelphia.
City Club of Portland, Ore.
City Club of St. Louis.
Duluth Commercial Club.

Annual Meeting Held

Officers Elected—Frank I. Moulton, Re-
tiring President, Reviews Club Work

The annual meeting of the Club was held last Saturday. President Frank I. Moulton surrendered the gavel after two terms of active service for the Club and Prof. George H. Mead was elected to succeed him. The officers and directors elected at the meeting were:

OFFICERS (FOR A TERM OF ONE YEAR)
President—GEORGE H. MEAD.
Vice-President—CHARLES M. MODERWELL.
Treasurer—ROY C. OSGOOD.
Secretary—CHARLES YEOMANS.

DIRECTORS (FOR A TERM OF TWO YEARS)
ARTHUR L. HAMILTON. BRADFORD GILL.
ALFRED L. BAKER.   HARRIS S. KEELER.

The new by-laws submitted by the directors and printed in the Bulletin April 1 were adopted with some amendments which will be printed in the next issue of the Bulletin.

THE PRESENT TASK

President Moulton's review of Club activities showed that during the last year the Club has been principally occupied with matters relating to the war. "The immediate future," he said, "will be pregnant with world-wide social, economical and governmental questions, pressing for consideration and determination. Their final determination lies with the electorate. No greater service can be rendered the community than to aid in arriving at a correct solution of these problems. This is a service the City Club has rendered in the past, and must continue to render, by providing a forum for the frank discussion of these questions."

The effect of the war upon the activities of the Club was described by Mr. Moulton as follows:

OUR FINANCES

The fiscal year 1917-18 has been one of difficulty in financial matters. It was believed the readjustment made in 1916-17 would enable us to carry on the ordinary operations and public work of the Club during the present year, without the usual appeal for public-work funds becoming necessary. In this we have been disappointed. The number of our members who have been called to the service in the Army and Navy and who have taken Government positions at lowered salaries, together with those whose incomes have been depleted by war conditions, has so far reduced our income as to compel a financial appeal to our membership. The response has justified the statement which has been made "that the people are just beginning to learn how to give." *Notwithstanding our difficulties, we have paid every bill at maturity and availed ourselves of every cash discount offered.*

PUBLIC WORK AND THE WAR

War conditions have also affected committee work. Our Civic Secretary has given a large share of his time since early last July to the work of the exemption board in the Hull House district, where his wide acquaintance with the people and local conditions has been of special value to the Government. Many of the most active workers on various civic committees have been among those called to the military or civil service.

The situation has also called into being additional committees, and led to new fields of activity. The War-Time Committee, created to deal with subjects which were being neglected, or not fully covered by other organizations, has been one of our most active and efficient committees.

DOING OUR BIT

The Loyalty Committee was organized at the request of the Liberty Loan Campaign Committee, to assist, not only in the Third Liberty Loan Campaign, but to be an intelligence corps in the Club for all Government financial matters for the duration of the war. It has secured subscriptions to the Third Liberty Loan from sixty-six members and fifteen employes of the Club, amounting to $28,800.

Concretely, the Club's interest in the war is represented by 160 members in the Army and Navy; a number in Y. M. C. A and Red Cross work; memberships on various war boards; the contribution of an ambulance now on the firing line in France; the opening of our Club House and its privileges Saturday and Sunday afternoons to men of the Army and Navy; the securing of subscriptions to the Liberty Loan; the releasing of Mr. Hooker, our Civic Secretary, and at times some of the office force, for service on the exemption board. The grateful letters which have been received from men in the Army and Navy, and from their parents, for the privileges of the Club House which have been extended to them, have fully repaid the expense and trouble of that enterprise.

A RECONSTRUCTION PLAN

During the year, Mr. Moulton said, the directors have dealt with two concrete problems: One, to increase the efficiency of committee work; the other, related to it, to keep our members better informed about club activities. A committee appointed by the directors and composed of members who have been active in the public work of the Club, reported a plan of committee reorganization, as previously noted in the Bulletin. This plan provided that the committees should be grouped into four divisions of related subjects, each group to be represented on the Public Affairs Committee, that semi-annual reports should be made by committees to the club membership and that appointments to civic committees should be for a term of one year, thus securing an annual reorganization of committees. The Directors adopted that part of the report relating to the committee groups and referred the other recommendations to the attention of the Public Affairs Committee. Discussing these points, Mr. Moulton said:

• A Grave Defect

I have been convinced for some time that a grave defect exists in the plan under which our civic committees have been operating, in that it has not provided for more frequent accounting to the full membership of the Club of their activities. The intimate touch that there should be between the members and our committees is lost under the present methods. I believe that a definite requirement that the civic committees shall make semi-annual reports would incite the committees to greater effort, and serve to keep alive interest of Club members in committee activities. Whether the committees are doing little or much, the fact would be disclosed by more frequent reports.

Keeping Up Interest.

The recommendation of the special committee that appointments to civic committees should be made definitely for one year ought also to give new life and vigor to the committees. It has been found that where the membership of committees has been continuous from year to year, some of them have gradually frayed out, because of members moving or losing interest and not enough attention has been given to drafting new men to fill these vacancies. There is a great reservoir of ability in the membership which has not been drawn upon, and from which we should be able to get a constant renewal and reinvigoration of our committees. There is ample scope in our various civic committees for the exercise of the talent of all of our members.

A Publicity Plan

The other matter considered by the Board of Directors, Mr. Moulton said, was the desirability of greater publicity for the work being done by the various committees and for Club activities in general.

To effect this purpose, the Bulletin was changed from a publication at irregular intervals to one appearing definitely each week. By securing second class mailing privileges and by utilizing the Bulletin for the announcement of meetings, the saving in postage has approximately equaled the increase of expense incident to changing to a weekly publication. The Bulletin is now published under an editorial board which brings to the service of the Bulletin varied talents and qualifications for the work. Through the Bulletin our members are kept constantly informed of all discussions and addresses at our noon meetings, and of the results of the activities of our various civic committees.

Mr. Moulton reviewed the work of various civic committees, which will be summarized in the next issue of the Bulletin. He spoke also of the unusually interesting program of luncheon talks which the Club had last year and of the accomplishments of the House Committee in improving the service in the dining room.

Finding a Middle Ground

"In considering the field work of the City Club," Mr. Moulton concluded, "it seems to me some middle ground must be found between pure idealism and mere privilege and corrupt and inefficient administration of public affairs. This was possibly in the mind of the founders of the City Club when they wrote into its charter the desire to accomplish the purposes stated in the charter, 'By non-partisan and practical methods.' Dreams are of small value unless they can be made to come true. The Club should strive to formulate its ideals into a concrete program, and endeavor by all practical methods to carry the program into effect. To this end we must enlist all of our forces; and there should be cooperation with such other agencies and organizations as will travel with us the whole or any part of the way.

Toward the Goal

"If 'Lyf so short, the craft so long to lerne,' is true, so may it be said of betterment in civic matters, that the journey is long and the goal still far distant. It was many years after the battle for civil service reform, and the merit system began, before the fruits of the agitation were realized; and it has been a constant struggle since to hold the ground gained. This is true of every local advantage gained by those sincerely interested in the improvement of civic conditions. The struggle will continue, and there is yet work to be done by the City Club, and a justification for its being."

The report of Roy C. Osgood, treasurer of the Club, is printed elsewhere in this issue.

Efficiency Plan for City Purchases Proposed by Club Committee

A MERICANS are learning rapidly these days from events at Washington the importance of those tedious words "co-operation" and "centralization" as applied to the affairs of government. Democracy must have her battle cry of freedom, but she must also do a little prosaic thinking from time to time on the problems of managing her household efficiently.

The City Club Committee on Public Expenditures has been doing some hard thinking on one of these problems of organization in our city government. It is the problem of how the city should do its buying. The City Comptroller last fall announced a plan for centralizing all city purchasing in the hands of the comptroller. The Public Works Department approved the centralized purchasing idea but favored the Public Works Department as the purchasing agent. The City Club Committee on Public Expenditures after a thorough examination of the merits of the proposals, made some suggestions of its own on the subject, which were transmitted last week to the City Comptroller.

The committee believes thoroughly in the principle of centralized purchasing. "Centralizing of purchases of supplies and materials," it says, "is in line with the movement for centralization of administrative services which are common to all departments and is now recognized as essential for responsible and effective service and for economy of operation."

The plan of organization proposed by the committee contemplates the organization of a separate purchasing department rather than the centralization of purchases in any existing department. At the head of the new department would be a commissioner of purchasing appointed by the Mayor. The committee outlines the general duties of the new department—which include the preparation of standard specifications as well as the operations of buying—proposes certain methods of operation and suggests the procedure by which the civil service employes of the present department of supplies, which would be abolished under the revised plan, should be transferred to the new department.

Briefly stated, the following are the major suggestions which the committee believes should be incorporated in an ordinance providing for the purchasing of supplies and materials:

(1) There should be one administrative head of the department, a Commissioner of Purchasing, unfettered by subordination to a board (as recommended in the report) intermediate between him and the appointing power and thereby interfering with a direct line of authority and exact location of responsibility. The Commissioner of Purchasing should be appointed by the Mayor, without submission for approval to the City Council.

(2) The committee believes that a centralized plan of purchasing supplies and materials should include purchasing, storing, distribution of and accounting for supplies as well as preparation of standard specifications and testing and inspection of commodities purchased.

(3) The Committee is of the firm opinion that the bureau of standards, inspections and tests should be located in the proposed purchasing department and not in the Comptroller's office, as recommended in the report. This also would look toward definite location of responsibility as opposed to a diffusion of responsibility.

(4) Standard specifications should be prepared in the bureau of standards, inspections and tests, in consultation with a technical advisory board consisting of the head of the bureau of standards, inspection and tests, a technical representative of the department requisitioning the commodity to be purchased and a member of the technical staff at present attached to the Committee on Finance of the City Council.

(5) The proposed central purchasing department should not let contracts for a construction of public improvements, but the letting of these contracts should be left in the respective departments.

(6) The central warehouse should be under the control of the proposed purchasing department as recommended in the Comptroller's report, but the "capital account" method of financing, purchasing, storing and distribution of supplies and materials should be abolished, the funds for these purposes should be replenished by annual appropriation and not by payments from other departments. Under this plan the amount charged the several departments for commodities purchased will be the actual cost of the items and delivery to the city, whether the point of delivery be the warehouse or the point of use. This will discourage the storing of commodities in the warehouse except for the purpose of buying advantageously and holding for inspection or testing. It will end the practices of unnecessarily purchasing and holding goods in the warehouse and of cumulative charges of warehouse overhead to other departments. It also will encourage the practice of obtaining prices f. o. b. warehouse and f. o. b. point of use before ordering so that cost of delivery by the city from the warehouse to the point of use may be calculated in and the buying done in the more economical way.

(7) The present ordinances giving sundry departments the right to contract independently for purchases in excess of $500 should be repealed and the proposed purchasing department should be authorized to contract for such purchases without referring them to the City Council for approval.

(8) Going farther than the points covered by the Comptroller's report, after the proposed central purchasing department is created, with a Commissioner of Purchasing at its head, the present office of Business Agent should be abolished and the staff of civil service employes in the present Department of Supplies should be transferred to the new department, together with such civil service employes in other departments whose major duties consist of work in connection with purchas-

ing. Where the work of these employes at present includes duties other than those of purchasing, re-adjustments of the duties should be made, but from each of the larger departments at least the proposed central purchasing departments should obtain the services of employes sufficient to maintain its work.

The committee believes that it is desirable to present and adopt a complete plan for the organization of a central purchasing department at this time rather than to try piecemeal methods. The latter, it pointed out, resulted in the experience of the present Department of Supplies which was organized twenty years ago as a "first step" toward central purchasing but which has never functioned as such.

"With the changes herein briefly outlined," the letter concludes, "the Committee on Public Expenditures endorses heartily the broad central purchasing plan and ex-presses the hope that it may be installed in the city government. The committee believes it to be a long step in progress toward business-like management in city affairs and hopes it ultimately will result in a centralization of purchasing for all purposes of local government, when consolidation of local taxing bodies shall have been brought about."

The letter is signed for the committee by J. L. Jacobs, acting chairman.

MEMBERS' DAUGHTERS may buy City Club cigars for their gentlemen friends at members' rates!

THE NEW TABLE LAMPS in the grill give a touch of color which adds greatly to the attractiveness of the room.

Treasurer's Report
Year Ended March 31, 1918

The Treasurer's Report for the year ended March 31, 1918, is appended hereto and consists of the following Statements:

Statement of Assets and Liabilities as at March 31, 1918.
Income and Expenses for the year ended March 31, 1918.
Surplus Account for the year ended March 31, 1918.
Departmental Accounts for the year ended March 31, 1918.

Respectfully submitted,
(Signed) ROY C. OSGOOD, Treasurer.

Statement of Assets and Liabilities

ASSETS.

LEASEHOLD BUILDING AND EQUIPMENT AT
  Cost $173,719.98
FURNISHINGS:
  Furniture and Fixtures 7,796.69
  Kitchen Equipment 1,978.60
  Crockery and Utensils 2,576.20
  Silverware 1,661.43
  Linen 451.48
  House Linen 40.61
                                      $14,505.01
INVENTORIES:
  Provisions ....$ 1,232.46
  Cigars 991.02
  Dining Room Supplies 49.50
                                      $2,272.98
ACCOUNTS RECEIVABLE:
  Unpaid Dues ....$ 1,753.75
  Unpaid Restaurant and Cigar Checks... 289.75
  Rents Receivable 59.14
  Subscriptions to Deficiency Fund..... 3,699.25
  General Accounts 115.77
                                      $5,917.66
SUNDRY PREPAYMENTS:
  Leasehold Ground Rent ....$ 845.80
  Insurance Premiums 850.20
                                      $1,696.00
CASH IN BANK AND ON HAND............$ 1,231.21
DEFICIENCY 5,598.41
                                      $209,941.25

LIABILITIES.

FIRST MORTGAGE LEASEHOLD 5% BONDS,
  Authorized Issue, Due 8-1-1941.$200,000.00
  Bonds Issued $182,000.00
  Scrip Issued (secured by deposit of
    $3,900 City Club Bonds with Northern
    Trust Company) ....$ 3,650.00
                                      $185,650.00
NOTES PAYABLE, NATIONAL CITY BANK.
  (Secured by deposit of $14,000 of City
    Club Bonds) 14,000.00
ACCOUNTS PAYABLE 3,648.81
RESERVES:
  Dues paid in Advance................$ 590.00
  Bond Interest Accrued 3,871.73
                                      $4,461.73
UNEXPENDED BALANCES SUNDRY FUNDS:
  Christmas Fund ....$ 303.32
  Quarter Section Publication 554.13
  Educational Research Bureau 18.41
  Terminal Publication 35.51
  Housing Exhibit Publication 49.40
  Publication Fund 663.64
  Neighborhood Center Publication Fund.. 64.35
  North Side City Planning Study Fund.. 48.00
  Chamber of Music Fund 97.97
  Ambulance Fund 235.45
  Posterette Fund 1.50
  Soldiers' and Sailors' Entertainment
    Fund 111.03
                                      $2,182.71
                                      $209,941.25

Income and Expenses

EXPENSES.

FIXED CHARGES:
Leasehold Ground Rent $10,150.00
Taxes 5,832.25
Fire and Employers' Liability Insurance. 537.12
Interest on Bonds and Loans........... 10,065.98

$26,585.35

BUILDING MAINTENANCE AND HOUSE EXPENSE:
House Employes' Wages $10,510.16
House Employes' Meals 2,370.60
Electric Power 1,609.80
Electric Light 848.35
Fuel 1,794.86
Building Repairs, Etc................... 874.42
Uniforms 372.74
General House Expense 1,402.48
Laundry 603.61

$20,387.02

ADMINISTRATION EXPENSES:
Office Salaries ....$ 4,438.49
Stationery and Printing 907.65
Postage 761.40
Telephone 955.15
Newspapers and Periodicals 405.96
Premiums on Surety Bonds 73.50
Entertainment 73.75
Membership Extension Expense 158.87
General Expense 323.46
Membership in Organizations 18.00
Art Exhibit 5.00

$8,121.23

DEPARTMENTAL ACCOUNTS:
Restaurant Operating Loss ....$ 4,515.26
Add Depreciation on Equipment:
Kitchen Equipment 600.00
Crockery and Utensils 1,051.98
Linen 646.25
Silverware 39.70

Total Loss on Restaurant..............$6,853.19
Profit on Cigars $627.70
Profit on Billiards 342.54   970.24

$5,882.95

CLUB HOUSE DEPRECIATION:
Furniture and Fixtures ....$ 1,080.00
House Linen 100.00

$1,180.00

CHRISTMAS FUND:
Distribution Amongst Employes.......... 1,644.80

PUBLIC WORK:
PROVIDED FROM GENERAL FUND: Miscellaneous:
Salaries of Civic Secretary and Assist-
ants $4,143.11
Sundry Expenses 1,682.07
Symposium 157.70
Bulletin 3,200.65
Library 683.25
Milk Investigation 618.89
General Investigation 31.00

$10,466.67

PROVIDED BY SPECIAL CONTRIBUTIONS:
Quarter Section Publication ....$ 7.52
Terminal Publication .... .60
Publication Fund 36.14
Chamber Music 352.45
Ambulance Fund 1,718.55
Soldiers' and Sailors' Entertainment
Fund 655.55

$2,770.81

$13,237.48

$77,088.83

INCOME.

MEMBERS' DUES $54,529.50
RENTS 3,708.00
PROFIT ON RENTAL OF STEREOPTICON....... 38.13
PROFIT ON UMBRELLA RENTALS 7.00
CHRISTMAS FUND, Donations transferred to
cover Expenditure per contra........... 1,644.80
SPECIAL CONTRIBUTIONS TO SPECIFIC ITEMS
OF PUBLIC WORK to cover Expenditures as
per contra 2,770.81
LOSS FOR THE YEAR, carried to Deficiency
Account 14,340.59

$77,038.83

Departmental Accounts

RESTAURANT.

CREDITS:
Receipts from Members and Banquets...$48,822.15
Guests and Symposium 916.10
Employes' Meals 2,370.60

$52,108.85

CHARGES:
Provisions Used $30,347.50
Kitchen Wages 9,682.88
Kitchen Expense 2,212.79
Dining Room Wages 8,958.30
Dining Room Expense 2,289.16
Manager's Salary (Proportion) 1,450.22
Cashier's Salary (Proportion) 1,185.00
Electric Light (Proportion) 498.26

$56,624.11

OPERATING LOSS FOR THE YEAR BEFORE CON-
SIDERING DEPRECIATION OF EQUIPMENT....$4,515.26

CIGARS.

CREDITS:
Receipts from Members $5,784.80
CHARGES:
Stock Used ....$ 4,472.10
Wages 660.00
License 25.00

$5,157.10

PROFIT FOR THE YEAR......................$627.70

BILLIARD ROOM.

CREDITS:
Receipts from Members ....$ 856.95
CHARGES:
Wages of Attendant 480.00
Supplies 34.41

$514.41

PROFIT FOR THE YEAR......................$342.54

Surplus Account

CHARGES.

LOSS FOR THE YEAR ENDED MARCH
31ST, 1918 ....$14,340.59
DUES, FOR PERIODS PRIOR TO APRIL
1ST, 1917, CHARGED OFF........$920.00
LESS: RECOVERIES ON DUES PRE-
VIOUSLY WRITTEN OFF.......... 30.00
                                         890.00

$15,230.59

CREDITS.

BALANCE APRIL 1ST, 1918.................$ 9.14
DEFICIENCY FUND 7,838.04
CONTRIBUTIONS TO PUBLIC WORK FUND, for
year ended 3/31/17, received during cur-
rent year 155.00
INITIATION FEES, appropriated to deficiency
account the year ended March 31st, 1918 1,630.00
BALANCE AS AT MARCH 31ST, 1918......... 5,598.41

$15,230.59

We hereby certify that we have audited the Books of Account and Vouchers of the City Club of Chicago for the year ended March 31, 1918, and that in our opinion the foregoing statements of Assets and Liabilities, Income and Expenses and Departmental Accounts accurately exhibit the Club's financial condition as at March 31, 1918, and the result of its operation during the year ended that date. A detailed report showing the extent to which we were able to verify the Contributions to the Special Funds has been submitted to the Directors as of even date.

ERNEST A. RECKITT & Co.,

April 19, 1918.　　　　　　　　　　Certified Public Accountants.

THE NEAR EAST AND PAN-GERMANISM

The allied governments must resist Germany's efforts at domination in the Near East, even if a satisfactory settlement could be arranged in the West, according to Mr. H. Charles Woods, of London, who addressed the City Club last Wednesday. A continuation of German intrigue there, he said, would mean continued unrest and the disturbance of the peace of the world. Mr. Woods is a close student of problems of the Near East. He has traveled extensively in the Balkans and Asia Minor, as correspondent for the *London Times* and the *London Evening News*. He was lecturer for Lowell Institute last winter. Mr. Woods said in part:

"The German infatuation for domination in the Near East dates approximately from the accession of the present emperor to the throne. The Kaiser's carpetbagging expeditions to Turkey in 1889 and 1898, the dropping of Bismarck in 1890 and the reversal of his policy, the German military mission to train the Turkish army, the intrigues of Baron Marshall von Bieberstein, the sowing of the seeds of unrest in the Balkans to prevent the consummation of a Balkan League were all part of a definitely conceived plan for German supremacy.

"Since the outbreak of the war, events such as the enforced disappearance of the German fleet from the high seas have compelled Germany to turn her attention even more definitely in a direction where she does not need to rely upon sea power, i. e., the East. It is this particularly which has led her to seek peace with Russia and Roumania—with the former to remove a menace on the north, with the latter in order to facilitate her communications with the east. The possibility of using this opportunity depends in part upon the attitude of the Russian Black Sea fleet toward Germany, in part to the resistance offered by the Armenians in the Caucasus.

"When England, unexpectedly to the Germans, joined in the war, German policy in the East had to be changed so that military operations might be conducted against the British in Egypt, Mesopotamia and Persia. To bring this about Germany had first to get Turkey into the war, which she accomplished largely through an understanding with the Ottoman Committee on Union and Progress, which is the secret government of Turkey. She had then to establish communications with Turkey by bringing Bulgaria and Roumania into the war. Failing to bring Roumania to her side, Germany probably through Pan-German influence in Russia, pushed her into the war on the side of the allies, preferring her as an enemy rather than as a neutral, and then easily accomplished her defeat.

"The Bagdad Railway has been the backbone of the plans of Pan-Germany in the East. Of the fifteen hundred miles from Constantinople to Bagdad, about twelve hundred may now be accomplished by train. This railway has been of great military profit to Germany and to Turkey for it has enabled them to bring troops not only to the Mesopotomian front but to the Caucasus and Syrian fronts as well."

The success of Germany's diplomacy in the East was probably due, Mr. Woods said, to the fact that its brutality was better understood by the peoples of the near East than was the straightforward diplomacy of the allies.

9

The City Club Bulletin

Published Weekly by the City Club of Chicago

A Journal of Active Citizenship

VOLUME XI   MONDAY, APRIL 29, 1918   NUMBER 17

AT LUNCHEON

WEDNESDAY, MAY 1

"The Negro Soldier and the War"

JAMES WELDON JOHNSON

Field Secretary, National Association for the Advancement of Colored People

The negro soldier played an inspiring part in the Civil War. What is he doing in the present crisis?

Mr. Johnson, who is to speak to us on this subject, represents the national organization which is trying to secure a "square deal" for the black man. He was formerly in the U. S. consular service. Mr. Johnson is the author of several books, the latest a volume of verse entitled, "Fifty Years and After."

FRIDAY, MAY 3

"Unemployment— Before the War and After"

HORNELL HART

Helen S. Troutstine Foundation, Cincinnati, Ohio

What will happen when the war is over and our soldiers come marching home? Will there be jobs for them? Will there be jobs for the hundreds of thousands of war workers, whose occupations will be gone? How shall we re-absorb our first and second lines of defense into civilian occupations?

Mr. Hart has been making a special study of these questions for the Troutstine Foundation. He was formerly secretary of the Milwaukee City Club.

SPEAKING AT 1:00

THE LISTENING POST

SAMUEL H. HOLLAND, attorney, joined the Club last week.

THEODORE T. REDINGTON is in Army Y. M. C. A. work at Camp Dodge, Iowa.

SEIZE EVERY OPPORTUNITY to enlist your friends as members of the City Club.

R. E. SCHREIBER is serving in the Construction Division, Contracts Branch, Quartermaster's Corps, at Washington.

ELMER S. BATTERSON leaves today (Monday) to serve as a secretary of the American Y. M. C. A. with the army in Italy.

THERE WERE SIXTY-EIGHT luncheon addresses last year, according to the report of the Public Affairs Committee, submitted at the annual meeting of the Club. Fifty of these were devoted to aspects of the war.

EUGENE T. LIES left last Friday for Washington to assume charge of the new department of investigation under the Division of Military and Naval Insurance in the War Risk Bureau. It will be his task to organize 25 or 30 district offices in the more important cities of the country, to secure and train a group of investigators and to secure the co-operation of social agencies in promoting this service. It is not only an important piece of war work but a new type of social service of the highest order. Mr. Lies takes with him the best wishes and the confidence of his many friends in the City Club.

A RESTFUL EATING PLACE on a quiet street in the loop! The City Club.

The City Club Bulletin
A Journal of Active Citizenship

The purpose of the Club is to bring together in informal association those men who are genuinely interested in the improvement of the political, social and economic conditions of the community in which we live.

PUBLISHED WEEKLY BY THE
CITY CLUB OF CHICAGO
315 Plymouth Court   Telephone: Harrison 8278

DWIGHT L. AKERS, Editor

OFFICERS OF THE CLUB
GEORGE H. MEAD, President
CHARLES M. MODERWELL, Vice-President
ROY C. OSGOOD, Treasurer
CHARLES YEOMANS, Secretary
GEORGE E. HOOKER, Civic Secretary

EDITORIAL BOARD
HERBERT H. SMITH, Chairman
FREDERICK D. BRAMHALL   S. R. WATKINS
C. COLTON DAUGHADAY   PAUL R. WRIGHT

$1.00 per Year - - - - -   10c per Copy

Entered as second class matter, December 3, 1917, at the postoffice at Chicago, Illinois, under the act of March 3, 1879.

Hail and Farewell!

Frank I. Moulton is a modest man, but he must have felt not a little puffed up at the resolution of appreciation adopted by the members at the annual meeting April 20 for his two years of service as president of the Club. The resolution reads:

In view of his large measure of service and unselfish devotion of time, labor and thought to the City Club, be it unanimously resolved that the members in their annual meeting assembled render to Frank I. Moulton by a standing vote their appreciative thanks.

To Mr. Moulton, said Prof. Mead, should be given the chief credit for two important accomplishments, the placing of the Club on a firmer financial foundation and the execution of the plan for a weekly publication of the Bulletin—"a policy," he said, "which I am sure has won the hearty approval of the members." Continuing Prof. Mead said:

"The City Club is under obligation to play its part at this time in the affairs of the city. Because of our absorption in the war, we are in danger of forgetting the task near home. It is the duty of the City Club to meet this obligation and I am sure that during the coming year it will fully realize and undertake this responsibility.

"Related to this is our own attitude to the war. This is a war for democracy, and democracy is bound to conquer if we at home are conscious of the issue. But to be conscious of the issue we must be democratic ourselves. There is no moral athletics more invigorating than the exercise of democracy at home. This attitude the City Club should exemplify in all its affairs."

Freed from the cares and responsibilities of office, Mr. Moulton left last Friday evening for a six weeks holiday in California.

Loaves and Fishes

AT the annual meeting of the Club, Saturday, April 20, Bradford Gill, chairman of the House Committee, told of the efforts of his committee to satisfy the inner animal of the Club members last year in the face of "war prices, war delays and war prohibitions." The House Committee was faced at the beginning of its term with an alarming decrease in the patronage of the dining room and an increasing loss. It decided on radical alterations of policy, with results which patrons of the dining room know.

FEEDING THE MULTITUDE

The new practice was to put into the service every possible touch to make it attractive to the eye and palate. New dishes were served and the old ones made more attractive. A baker was employed so that our breads and pies might be made to our own taste. The present neat uniform of the waitresses was adopted. Various other touches were made to increase the attractiveness of the service. Then the committee, with the aid of a special advertising committee consisting of Fred J. Stebbins, J. R. Ozanne, Claude K. Brown, Oliver Gale, E. S. Brandt and J. Willard Bolte, through the columns of the Bulletin endeavored to acquaint the members with these changes.

HOW THE MONEY ROLLS IN!

The result Mr. Gill described as follows:

"In December we started to see light in a recovery in the number of patrons at each meal, in fact, there were enough new customers to offset the losses of war and other things, but the losses were still bad. It was in February that we nearly had heart failure when we balanced up to find a loss in that one little month of only twenty open days of over $800. March

(Continued on page 151.)

Uncle Sam, Insurance Agent

Provision for Soldiers and Sailors Makes U. S. A.
the World's Greatest Insurance Corporation

WHEN the United States government went into the insurance business for its soldiers and sailors last fall, the most sanguine advocates of the plan had no idea of the colossal scale upon which the venture would work out. Their wildest dreams, according to Judge Mack, author of the insurance act, did not contemplate the insurance of more than 75 per cent of the men in service for an average policy of about $6,000 each. Within five months, 92 per cent of the men have been insured with average policies of over $8,000. The total insurance written is more than $14,000,-000,000—almost twice the combined totals of the first three liberty loans. The government is also, under the same bill and through the same administrative machinery, supervising allotments of pay by soldiers and sailors to their dependents, providing allowances for these dependents and compensation in case of death or disability.

THE WAR RISK BUREAU

The administration of this plan, the world's greatest experiment in social insurance, is in charge of a War Risk Bureau under the Treasury Department. Charles F. Nesbit, Commissioner of Military and Naval Insurance, in charge of one of the two great divisions of that bureau, in an address at the Club last Wednesday told of the perplexing problems of organization and policy which that bureau is facing. With him at the speaker's table sat Judge Julian W. Mack, author of the bill, a former member of the Board of Directors of the City Club, and Eugene T. Lies, also a member of the City Club, who has been selected as head of the newly created department of investigation under the bureau, and who left last Friday to take up his duties at Washington.

"FIFTY-FIFTY"

The "allowances" by the government to the dependents of soldiers and sailors are substantially on a "fifty-fifty" basis, according to Mr. Nesbit. They are made on the condition of a substantially equal allotment of pay by the soldier and sailor whose family is concerned.

"Compensation" for death or disability is on a much sounder basis than the old-time service pension, said Mr. Nesbit. "Since the Civil War, most states have adopted plans for workmen's compensation and it would be most unfair for the government to take a man from an occupation in which he is entitled to compensation in case of accident and to enroll him in the more hazardous enterprise of war without provision for fair and adequate compensation in case of death or disability. It was the aim of those who proposed the bill that the compensation should be in the first instance liberal and that there should then be no further compensation. Otherwise, pension legislation would inevitably become a political football as it did after the Civil War."

GOVERNMENT INSURANCE

The principle behind the insurance features of the plan Mr. Nesbit described as follows: "When the government takes a man into the service, it destroys his insurability. That is fair enough, for the insurance companies are handling trust funds—your money and mine—and there is no way by which they can compute the risk. The American people could hardly afford to penalize military and naval service by forcing the men to pay higher premiums for their insurance.

"The cost of government insurance is about $80 a year for a $10,000 policy. The demand for this insurance among the men in service has been far beyond expectations. In the five months since the act went into operation, fourteen billion dollars of insurance has been written. In 1916, all the insurance companies in the United States wrote only five and one-half billion. The total insurance on the books of all the companies in the United States—about thirty-three billion dollars, twice the amount of insurance elsewhere in the world—is only a little more than twice the amount which the government wrote in five months."

The act went into operation immediately and machinery had to be improvised at once for its administration. Mr. Nesbit said "It was like building a dam with the water running over us." During the first five months of its existence, the Bureau handled 1,672,000 applications for allotments and allowances, each of which required at least eleven operations, a mistake in any one of which might cause serious difficulties. The sources of confusion in dealing with such an enormous clerical task can hardly be estimated—e. g., in the duplication of names, difference in spelling, etc.

Problems of policy in respect to individual cases have frequently been very knotty. Fraudulent claims have to be guarded against and the government must take steps to insure that the allotments and allowances go to the person entitled to them. The investigation service, of which Mr. Lies has been put in charge, will have to meet and solve many of these difficult problems.

The Russian Ferment

THE key to the events which have followed the Russian revolution, according to Prof. Edward A. Ross, of the University of Wisconsin, who addressed the City Club last Friday at luncheon, is to be found in the balked desires of the people under the autocracy. When the obstacles were removed, people began immediately to do the things which they had formerly been prevented from doing. They began to express their opinions. There was a furor for public meetings. All day long the ears of the people were filled with new doctrines, as they tried to acquire in a few days political wisdom which we have had a lifetime to acquire. Discipline was relaxed and people refused to obey rules whose purpose they did not understand. The subject nationalities which had chafed under Romanoff rule began to pull away from Russia, although the reason for their disaffection had disappeared with the revolution. Groups of working people tried to better their economic conditions, to get higher wages and shorter hours; the peasant demanded lower rentals. But in spite of all, there was little disorder because of the innate reasonableness of the Russian people. The unreasonable demands of which we have read in the papers are the extreme demands among a people of 150 million.

Prof. Ross spent several months in Russia. During his stay, he traveled 20,000 miles, visited all classes of the people and interviewed leaders of all factions. He returned to America last January.

BACKWARD RUSSIA

Russia is backward, said Prof. Ross, but for reasons which do not reflect on the Russian character. For two hundred and forty years her people were under the yoke of the Mongols. Then until the time of Peter the Great, her people were prevented

from cultivating the rich black soil belt because of raids by the Tartar tribes. About the time of Queen Elizabeth, Russia began to tie the peasants to the soil. For a long time outright slavery existed and white people were sold in the slave markets. About one hundred years ago the slave markets were suppressed and it was not till the sixties that Czar Alexander freed the 23,000,000 serfs. The people have been bowed down by the oppression of the autocracy.

THE RUSSIAN PEOPLE

"I believe," said Prof. Ross, "that the Russian people have as high natural gifts as any people in the world. They are a friendly people. I have never seen human beings more responsive to others or more instinctively democratic. Russians are not militaristic; they do not believe in the glory of war, although at one time Russia was the most dangerously militaristic power in Europe. You must learn to think of the Russians as a fundamentally pacific and democratic people which has had erected upon it a Germanic government with a Prussian spirit.

THE MILLSTONE

"For from two to three generations, the autocracy had been a millstone around the neck of the Russian people. As the more enlightened and liberal spirits drew away from it and rebelled against it they were by thousands sent to prison and to Siberia. The autocracy organized the dregs of society into the infamous 'black hundred' to crush out men of liberal sentiments and sowed the seeds of discord among the subject nationalities to keep them in subjection.

"In Russia, I was struck by the concentration of wealth. I saw evidences of the

(Continued on page 150.)

Direct Primary and "I. and R." Proposals Bring Lively Contest

THE NEW BY-LAWS proposed by the directors and printed in the Bulletin of April 1, with some amendments, were adopted at the annual meeting April 20. The discussion of these by-laws was enlivened by the debate over two proposals submitted by A. B. Cone—one an amendment to the Articles of Association which would provide a direct primary method of electing officers and directors, the other an amendment to the by-laws providing for the initiative and referendum in the determination of Club policies.

THE DIRECT PRIMARY

The direct primary, Mr. Cone asserted, is of the City Club's own political stock of merchandise. The City Club advocates this principle in public, he said, "but when its members appear to choose the officers who are to 'represent' them they are handed a ticket with a single candidate for each office." The argument that efficiency requires expert knowledge and experience and a consistent control from year to year is plausible but "out of step with the basic principle of democratic government. . . . There is no room on our soil for any government by rulers with power to choose their own successors."

Mr. Cone's charge that the present method of electing Club officers is undemocratic was denied by Herbert J. Friedman, chairman of the directors' sub-committee which drafted the proposed new by-laws. Under the old by-laws and under those now proposed, he said, any twenty members could by petition nominate candidates in opposition to those proposed by the nominating committee—a method of nomination which is easier and more liberal than that of a direct primary.

THE "I. & R."

The proposal for the initiative and referendum on matters of Club policy was advocated by Mr. Cone also on the ground of its fundamental democracy. The committee which drafted the new by-laws had for a time considered such a proposal favorably, Mr. Friedman answered, but had altered its position when the dangers of dividing the Club on controversial issues

were pointed out. At the present time, the public work is conducted by committees and the Club as a whole is not committed by their action. Among those who spoke in favor of Mr. Cone's plan was Robert M. Buck, among those who spoke against it, Prof. George H. Mead and Henry P. Chandler.

There was no debate as to the principle of the initiative and referendum. The issue between those who favored Mr. Cone's proposal and those who opposed it narrowed down in the last analysis to the advisability of committing the Club as a whole to one side or another of public questions. That has not been the policy of the Club in the past and the members by a large majority voted not to change from the present system of committee action.

PUBLICITY

Mr. Cone's proposals were both defeated by considerable majorities when put to a vote. Another amendment proposed by Mr. Cone and published in the Bulletin of April 15 provided that the proceedings and membership roll of the Club should be open to the inspection of members. Mr. Friedman stated that this provision from the old by-laws had been omitted by oversight and the amendment proposed by Mr. Cone was accordingly accepted as a part of the original draft and adopted with the by-laws. It reads as follows:

ART. III. SEC. 4. At the end of the section add the following: "The record of the proceedings of meetings of the Club and of the Board of Directors and the roll of members shall at all times be open to the inspection of members at the business office of the Club."

VOTING BY MAIL APPROVED

An amendment proposed by R. F. Schuchardt, providing for voting by mail under certain conditions, was adopted unanimously. It reads:

ART. X. SEC. 1. Add: "In case of illness or absence from the city, members may also submit their ballots by mail and such ballots shall be counted if received at the City Club before noon of the day of election. Such ballot shall be written on plain paper and may be enclosed in a plain envelope without identification marks and then enclosed in an outer envelope which shall bear the name of the member sending the ballot.

The changes in the proposed by-laws printed on page 132 of the Bulletin of April 15 were embodied in the draft presented by the directors for ratification.

THE RUSSIAN FERMENT

(*Continued from page* 148.)

most lavish scale of expenditure in the cities, but when I came to the villages I found the most complete destitution. The people lived in one and two room cabins. Villages with 8,000 or more population had no amusements—no. pleasure animals, no moving pictures, no amusements of any kind. There was nothing to absorb the nickels because there were no nickels to absorb.

"Russia is in reality a rich country but the methods of siphoning the wealth from the places where it was produced to the pockets of the wealthy privileged classes were more efficient than anything which we have evolved in this country. The Romanoffs and their bureaucracy, their secret police, *agents provocateurs,* nobility, landed estates, cossacks, etc., produced this result.

THE LAND QUESTION

"The land question was most acute after the freeing of the serfs, for instead of giving to the serfs the land which they had formerly tilled for themselves and instead of paying them to work upon the land which they had tilled for the landlord, they were compelled to buy the land on installments at inflated values, payments continuing for a period of 49 years. One-third of the land of Russia was left in the hands of a few thousand nobles.

"The Bolsheviki are now nationalizing the land. They have adopted the principle that no man shall have more land than he can till. If he has so much land that he needs to employ a hired man, a part of the land will be lopped off and given to the hired man. The idea is to do away completely with the system of exploiting labor upon the land.

"Before the revolution, the workingman received about one-third the 'real wages' which the workingman in this country received. And I have been assured that before the revolution 20 per cent was as common a return upon capital in Russia as 10 per cent was in the United States. Thus millions of rubles that under American institutions would have stayed in the pockets of labor went to the capitalists. This was possible because labor was not allowed to organize, because strikes were outlawed, because ignorance was deliberately fostered among the people."

Prof. Ross, referring to the present situation, said: "The Bolsheviki are planning to nationalize the factories. Trotzky has stated that the factories would not be confiscated, that the owners would be paid probably 5 or 6 per cent. Their operation would be controlled by committees but they would be run for the benefit of society as a whole. No factory, he said, would be allowed to retain trade secrets and no factory would be closed because it failed to produce a profit so long as its product was needed by the people.

THE SOCIAL REVOLUTION

"The Bolsheviki differ from other parties in that they wish to keep the working class in a position of dictatorship. The revolution of March was a political revolution. The Bolsheviki revolution of November was a social revolution—a revolution different from any that the world has ever seen. The soviets are the rulers of Russia and the idea behind their government is that everybody shall have a share in the government except the propertied classes.

"I do not believe that Lenine and Trotzky are German agents. They are more interested in the class war than they are in national war and they wanted peace so as to preserve the working classes who were being destroyed by the war. I do not at this time see any power in Russia capable of overthrowing the present broad-based government of the soviets. In the end the peasants will decide, for they are the large majority of the people.

THE SOVIETS

"The soviet government is now a 'fifty-fifty' arrangement between the peasants and the workmen. If it were on a strict basis of representation the ratio would be about 85-15, but the workmen are at present better organized and more class conscious."

Prof. Ross stated that prohibition had come to stay in Russia. It has been continued under the revolution. Wine cellars in the Winter palace and in hotels in Petrograd have been destroyed by revolutionaries. "One reason," he said, "why the revolution was so free from gigantic horrors was that the liquor traffic had been suppressed."

ON "TALK DAYS" 40c, 50c and 60c table d'hote with wide selection à la carte.

YOU CAN HELP YOUR DIGESTION and that of your neighbor by starting a little table talk.

Wasteful Economy

By GEORGE L. ROGERS,

Chairman City Club "North Shore Committee."

ARE the American people indulging in wasteful economy? Last year considerable effort was made in promoting war gardens. Wide publicity was given the movement, and a great deal of enthusiasm aroused, largely among those who had little or no experience in such work.

The North Shore Committee of the City Club has undertaken the investigation of last year's garden efforts on the North Shore and has reports of the results in nearly all of those communities. Last week a conference was held at the Club to which were invited the leaders of the work in Chicago. There were present J. H. Prost of the State Council of Defense, Mrs. Tiffany Blake, who is promoting the Woman's Land Army Movement, Mrs. W. D. Richardson, well known for her excellent work on vacant South Side properties, Mrs. Edward Gudeman, chairman of the Garden Committee of the Woman's City Club, Dudley Grant Hayes of the Board of Education and Alfred B. Yeomans, in charge of the executive work for Mrs. Pelham. Many interesting facts and experiences were developed at this conference and from these reports that are deserving of serious consideration.

HIGH COST GARDENS

On the North Shore, under the spur of patriotic duty, many engaged in garden work who had not before done so. Having large plots of ground but little knowledge of the secrets of the soil, they employed men to do the work at salaries as high as $75 a month. Many such gardens did not yield $50 in food during the season. Common barnyard fertilizer was purchased at $9 a load. Potatoes costing $4.25 to $4.50 a bushel were encased in clay soil and imprisoned under newly turned sod. Weeds were encouraged to mature and spread their devastating seeds where only grass had grown before. Many other similar mistakes were reported.

The Community Gardens appear to have been another error of judgment, and practically every municipality reports that as a result of last year's experience, these will be abandoned. The principal mistake seems to have been the belief that men would volunteer their labor to produce vegetables to be sold to others under the market price. After these gardens were planted it became necessary to employ help to cultivate and harvest the crops, most communities reporting a loss on this account. At one place a $700 canning outfit was installed, although but few vegetables were canned and some of these spoiled. In some places the men in charge of the work were inexperienced and in others experienced men were hampered by an amateurish advisory committee.

On the other hand, many small individual gardens, worked by the owners, were a decided success.

The conference was a most enthusiastic meeting. Each of the parties present is heart and soul in the work. It developed, however, that each knew little of the work being done by the others, and the State Council of Defense is endeavoring to remedy this condition by having its department act as a clearing house for all other groups and organizations.

SOME HINTS

The following suggestions may assist those contemplating the planting of a garden this spring:

1. Don't be in too much of a hurry to get your garden in. May 10th is sufficiently early for ordinary vegetables in this climate.

2. Wait until your ground is crumbly before plowing. You will ruin your garden for several years if you work the wet clay.

3. Plant vegetables that can be stored and will keep during the winter.

4. Do not employ help, but do your own gardening. One man can cultivate 40 acres on a farm. He cannot earn his salary with a hoe. It is not economy and you do not increase the food supply by withdrawing needed help from the farms.

5. Club together and purchase fertilizer by the car. One community did this last year at a cost of between $2 and $3 a load.

6. Study the seed catalogues.

(*Continued from page* 146.)
brought hope with the abolition of heatless Mondays, a rather general reduction in prices and slightly decreased portions. We enjoyed an increasingly good and profitable patronage of our facilities by outside parties in the evenings. And now, much to our joy, we are able to report a profit of about $550.00 for March."

Mr. Gill praised the co-operation of Mr. Joseph Palise, manager of the Club, and of the entire staff. Mr. Palise was promoted to his position last year, following the resignation of the former manager.

Open House for Enlisted Men

A STATEMENT BY THE SOLDIERS' AND
SAILORS' ENTERTAINMENT
COMMITTEE.

Beginning December 8, 1917, the Club
has been open every Saturday and Sunday
afternoon and evening to enlisted men of
the army and navy. The War Recreation
Board of the State Council of Defense and
a committee of the Woman's City Club co-
operated in making arrangements, and the
Canteen Service of the American Red Cross
undertook to furnish and sell light refresh-
ments on Sundays when the club kitchen is
not running. Club members donated phonograph records, posters and announcement
cards, and have been on hand regularly at
the Club to receive the men and to explain
the facilities available.

To defray the expense involved in keeping the clubhouse open on Sundays, which
amounts to from $25.00 to $35.00 per
Sunday, a special fund was raised from
members. Receipts and disbursements to
date have been as follows:

Receipts.............................$766.58
Disbursements—
    Fuel 212.20
    Light 57.00
    Wages 328.50
    Laundry 19.50
    Printing 42.75
    Sundries 38.30

                      $698.25

Balance April 18, 1918.................$ 68.33

All food and tobacco have been sold at
cost and no charge has been made for use
of the pool and billiard tables.

The maximum attendance on any one
day has been about 200, and many of the
soldiers and sailors have expressed their
appreciation of the club privileges.

CLOSED ON SUNDAYS

Owing to the recent opening of the Central Soldiers' and Sailors' Club on W.
Washington St. and to the falling off in
attendance with the approach of warm
weather, the committee has thought it unnecessary to continue the Sunday "Open
House" after April 21, but enlisted men
will be welcome as heretofore on Saturdays. The balance of the fund remaining,
after deducting expenses for Sunday, April
21, will be applied to extra telephone service
and other incidentals.

(Sd.) CHARLES YEOMANS,
Chairman.

Death's Valley

"IF the German offensive should succeed,
and the Germans should get to Calais,"
said Charles W. Whitehair, speaking at the
City Club, Saturday, March 20, "we need
not be surprised to see fighting on our own
coasts within two months." Mr. Whitehair as a representative of the Y. M. C. A.
has traveled over the whole British front
—the training camps, the hospitals, the
prison camps, the front trenches. He was
at the front line when "the big push" was
made last September.

THE LONESOME ROAD

What does a soldier do and how does
he feel under fire? "The stories of men
going into battle laughing, singing and
whistling are a pack of lies," said Mr.
Whitehair. "Don't think that the men
like to go 'over the top.' The most lonesome road a man ever travels is that road.
But I have never yet seen a man who
wanted to turn his back on that hell. The
men are ready to go in and to die rather
than to submit to a dishonorable peace.

"I asked our American boys for a message to take back to America. They said,
'Tell them over there that we would like
to come home—but we won't come home
till the show is over!' They are living in
barns, in haymows and chicken coops, but
I heard less complaining from them than
I have heard here in America over wheatless and meatless days, etc."

THE HUMAN SACRIFICE

Will the world ever fully understand
the tremendous human sacrifice that has
been made in this war? The smallest loss
in any one month's fighting on the British
front last year, according to Mr. Whitehair, was 30,000 men and boys. "I went
over the battlefield of the Marne," he said,
"and there were times when I could not
get my feet off the graves. I visited Verdun and the hills were thick with graves.
I am sick of the talk that 'food will win
the war' and 'liberty bonds will win the
war.' These are necessary to victory but
the war will be won by the human sacrifices of the boys in blue and khaki. In
the face of what they are giving, can any
sacrifice here at home be considered too
great? The man who hoards his money
at this time is not a slacker, he is a traitor
to his country."

Buy Liberty Bonds from the City Club.

The City Club Bulletin
Published Weekly by the City Club of Chicago
A Journal of Active Citizenship

VOLUME XI   MONDAY, MAY 6, 1918   NUMBER 18

LUNCHEON TALKS THIS WEEK

WEDNESDAY, MAY 8

"Illinois War Work"
SAMUEL INSULL
Chairman Illinois State Council of Defense

FRIDAY, MAY 10

"Prussia and Our Schools"
CHARLES H. JUDD
Director School of Education, University of Chicago

"The Elementary Schools of the United States," says Prof. Judd, "borrowed their plan of organization and the general definition of their course of study from Prussia. For more than half a century, we have harbored this borrowed institution and have tried to use it for the purposes of a democracy. We have failed conspicuously."

LUNCHEON FROM 11:30   **SPEAKING AT 1:00**

Pershing Boys at Club

FIFTY-TWO of our members joined the "Plus Club" at last Thursday's luncheon and subscribed $4,600 more to the Liberty Loan. The total so far subscribed through the Loyalty Committee of the Club is $40,400.

A variety of missionary talent was on hand at the luncheon and talent of a sort which held the audience fast in their seats a half hour beyond the usual quitting time. First came the Jackies' Band. After their appearance, conversation ceased except among the shouters. After weeks of campaigning the boys had apparently lost none of their wind and the bass drummer's pitching arm was in splendid trim.

Fred Dale Wood was the speaker. He won instant approval for his plan for ending the war, namely, to tie Kaiser Bill and his generals to a persimmon tree and *let them pucker to death*. The war, Mr. Wood said, is not only for democracy's sake but

The City Club Bulletin
A Journal of Active Citizenship

The purpose of the Club is to bring together in informal association those men who are genuinely interested in the improvement of the political, social and economic conditions of the community in which we live.

PUBLISHED WEEKLY BY THE

CITY CLUB OF CHICAGO

315 Plymouth Court   Telephone: Harrison 8278

DWIGHT L. AKERS, Editor

OFFICERS OF THE CLUB

GEORGE H. MEAD, President
CHARLES M. MODERWELL, Vice-President
ROY C. OSGOOD, Treasurer
CHARLES YEOMANS, Secretary
GEORGE E. HOOKER, Civic Secretary

EDITORIAL BOARD
HERBERT H. SMITH, Chairman
FREDERICK D. BRAMHALL   S. R. WATKINS
PAUL R. WRIGHT

$1.00 per Year   -   -   -   -   10c per Copy

Entered as second class matter, December 3, 1917, at the postoffice at Chicago, Illinois, under the act of March 3, 1879.

THE LISTENING POST

for the humanization of the world. It must bring back the condition of civilized living among nations which existed before the rape of Belgium. For this no sacrifice is too great and the man who buys his bonds without some personal sacrifice has not met his full obligation.

Then came the surprise—something not on the program! Two of Pershing's doughboys—Corporal Merle Skinner and Albert Montgomery—walked in—tin hats and all —and, with the band blowing like a Kansas cyclone, marched up the aisle to the front table. Both had served in the front trenches, lived with the rats and the other little animals which infest Northern France, slept in mud and water and had finally gone over the top. Both indicated that they would rather do all those things than talk to an audience, but they got away with it and were enthusiastically cheered. At the end, Montgomery gave a demonstration of the use of a gas mask. Aren't you sorry you missed this meeting?

DON'T WAIT TILL CHRISTMAS to send a box of cigars to a soldier. We will ship to any address.

THE SAFE ARRIVAL in England of Prof. Andrew C. McLaughlin was announced in last week's dispatches.

LIEUTENANT GEO. J. ANDERSON, formerly chairman of the City Club committee on vice conditions, has been appointed head of a new section on vice and liquor control in the reorganized law enforcement division of the commission on training camp activities. Lieutenant Anderson has been closely identified with the law enforcement work of the Committee of Fifteen. It is expected that a closer supervision of Chicago conditions will be the result of the appointment.

THE MANY CITY CLUB FRIENDS of Major Abel Davis congratulate him upon his promotion to the rank of Lieutenant Colonel. The press dispatches state that his promotion to the rank of Colonel is expected shortly. He is with the 132d Infantry, at Camp Logan, Houston, Texas.

THE PUBLIC UTILITIES COMMITTEE of the Club has the banner record for staying on the job. The committee had fifty-two meetings last year with an average attendance of nine.

BE A MIXER! You will find that your neighbor at the table is a cordial "good fellow" after you have thawed his icy exterior.

JAMES WITKOWSKY has entered the service of the Enforcement Division of the Food Administration and will travel through the Northwest.

PROFESSOR C. S. DUNCAN of the University of Chicago, who assisted the City Club Milk Committee in the preparation and presentation of its case before the Chicago Milk Commission, has written an article on "The Chicago Milk Inquiry," which is published in the April number of the Journal of Political Economy.

CAPTAIN PATTERSON, a Canadian chaplain, recently returned from the front and now a volunteer speaker in the Liberty Loan Campaign in this section, has visited the Club recently on several occasions. He has seen service on the western front and in Africa.

Our Industrious Committees

WHAT did our civic committees do last year to justify their existence? Not every committee which has a low score in number of meetings or attendance loafed on the job. Some were shot to pieces by the war. Some found little or nothing to do in their respective fields, again often because of war conditions. Many of the committees can point to a very creditable year of activity and accomplishment. The following information is gathered mainly from the report of the Public Affairs Committee on civic committee work for the year just ended:

AT SPRINGFIELD

Several of the committees, according to that report, found their chief field of operations in the state legislature which closed its fiftieth session last June. By brigading their efforts with those of other organizations, they assisted in bringing about the passage of several very useful bills. The Committee on State and Local Charities, for instance, gave its support to the bill for the licensing and regulation of "loan sharks," the bill authorizing the establishment of a state penal farm colony to replace the vile county jails of our state as places for the commitment of offenders, and the enabling bill for the establishment of a municipal farm colony—all of which passed. The Committee on Public Health supported the bill for a state commission to investigate the subject of health insurance—a commission now at work.

The committees, however, were not successful on all fronts: The woman's eight-hour bill, a measure which was endorsed by the Club Committee on Labor Conditions, was defeated after one of the hottest and most prolonged contests of the session.

TAKING ONE TRENCH

The bill for non-partisan municipal elections favored by our Committee on Political Nominations and Elections, failed to pass but made progress over previous sessions by securing the endorsement of the House Committee on Elections. It may take several sessions to put this bill "across," but some of the most important legislation on our statute books has been put there only after persistent effort, continued from session to session. So the committee was not down-hearted by that defeat.

A bill for the "zoning" of cities, supported by our City Planning Committee, came so close to passage that its friends were confident it could not be defeated. A surprise attack upon the bill at the eleventh hour threw it back to a defeat. Another attempt will surely be made at the next session to get legislation along these lines.

CAMOUFLAGE

Two bills, the alleged object of which was to secure the development of Calumet Lake as a harbor in connection with certain arrangements for filling in adjacent land and changing title thereto, were passed by the legislature. Examination of these bills by our Club Committee on Harbors convinced that committee that these bills were undesirable and a communication was sent to the Governor pointing out the objectionable features. The Governor vetoed both bills. The committee was not so successful in its opposition to another bill which it considered objectionable. This was a bill granting to the Iroquois Iron and Steel Co. certain submerged lands in Lake Michigan near 95th street under conditions and at a rate of compensation which the committee considered unfavorable to the State.

The State Constitution Committee of the Club supported the proposal for a constitutional convention and is planning to back the resolution strongly when it comes before the voters for approval next November. The committee wrote to the Governor in favor of legislation allowing this resolution to be incorporated in the party columns, but this legislation failed of passage.

A MAJOR ATTACK

The Public Affairs Committee went into action on its own account in an effort to secure the validation of certain county taxes which had been declared invalid by the courts. The validation bills were opposed by certain firms of attorneys (including that of which the Attorney-General of the State had been a member) who had collected large fees for services in securing exemptions from these taxes. The bill validating the 1916 taxes was passed, but that relating to the 1915 taxes was defeated.

The civic committees in addition to their maneuvers at Springfield last year carried on a number of local operations of considerable importance. The work of the Milk Committee has been so frequently cited in the Bulletin that no further recital of its efforts is necessary. The committee is still on the job and is gathering further ammunition for a renewal of its attack on this problem.

LIBRARY POLICIES

Following the death of Henry E. Legler, fears were entertained that the public library might be thrown into politics and that the position of librarian might be filled by some person not inspired with the standards of efficiency and library expansion which had characterized Mr. Legler's administration. At the memorial meeting for Mr. Legler, under the auspices of about a dozen Chicago organizations but arranged largely through the activity of our Committee on Public Education, the ideals of library development for which Mr. Legler had stood were put very prominently before the public. The Education Committee later used its best efforts to secure the appointment of a non-political library board and jointly with the Civil Service Committee urged the adoption of methods in the examination to fill Mr. Legler's position which would secure the competition of the best library talent in the country. It is impossible to weigh accurately the influence of these activities, but they probably helped the situation very materially. The choice of Carl B. Roden for the position has been universally commended.

THROWN FOR A LOSS

The Health Committee of the Club on grounds of health and safety opposed the ordinance legalizing the use of the subbasement of Mandel Brothers' store as a salesroom. A similar ordinance opposed by the committee had previously been defeated, but on this occasion the ordinance was passed.

The Committee on Public Expenditures has a couple of deep notches in its stick:

1. It joined with other civic organizations in opposing a special session of the legislature to increase the city's taxing power until certain economies in city administration had been accomplished and the need for additional revenues demonstrated. A number of these economies have been brought about.

(Continued on page 158)

NEWS FROM RUSSIA

A RECENT news dispatch from Petrograd says that "the only Americans remaining in Petrograd are Graham R. Taylor of Chicago and Arthur Bullard." Advices through Washington, however, apparently of later origin, indicate that Mr. Taylor has been transferred to Moscow. He is a son of Prof. Graham Taylor and has been for many years a member of the City Club of Chicago.

ASSISTANT TO AMBASSADOR

Mr. Taylor has been in Russia for about two years as special assistant to the United States Ambassador. Before the declaration of war with Germany he was assigned as a representative of this government to the oversight of German prisoners in Russian internment camps, with headquarters at Orenberg. The United States as a neutral was at that time acting on behalf of the German government in the administration of relief funds in these camps and in caring for the needs of prisoners—a work which has now been taken over by the government of Sweden. Mr. Taylor's work covered the entire Ural Mountain region, a territory as large as all France. He made trips sometimes as long as thirteen or fourteen hundred miles on wheels or runners, sleeping frequently in the huts of peasants.

IN MOSCOW

When Mr. Taylor was relieved of this work, after the declaration of war, he made an interesting trip through Turkestan and the Caucasus and then returned to Moscow, where for a time he was attached to the American Consulate. He was in that city during the week of terror in November when street fighting was so intense and had some thrilling experiences.

COUNTERACTING GERMAN INTRIGUE

Last December he was transferred to Petrograd and put in charge of the United States publicity work in that city to assist in counteracting German intrigue and propaganda. This was done through communications to the Russian press and through the use of billboards. One hundred thousand posters, some large enough to contain President Wilson's message, were displayed.

DON'T WAIT FOR THE OTHER FELLOW to start the conversation.

Preparedness for Peace

Make Plans Now for Unemployment Crisis at Close of War, Urges Hornell Hart

"WHEN the war is over," said Hornell Hart in his address at the City Club last Friday, "an unemployment crisis of unprecedented severity is likely to sweep over the country unless preventive steps are taken now by the government. From 2,000,000 to 5,000,000 soldiers and perhaps as many war industry workers will be thrown out of work by the declaration of peace. Abnormal expansion such as we are now passing through is always followed by reaction." Mr. Hart has been making special studies of this subject for the Helen S. Trounstine Foundation of Cincinnati. He was formerly civic secretary of the Milwaukee City Club.

AFTER THE WAR

Measures to prevent the unemployment of our defenders when they return should be, according to Mr. Hart:

Plans to give returning soldiers access to the 60 per cent of our tillable land which is now idle, and which should be producing food for a famished world;

Plans for extending and improving the railways, with specifications ready to let contracts immediately when peace is declared;

Plans to push public buildings, highways, waterways and other public projects immediately after the war;

Plans for adequate housing for American workmen, to be put into action when demobilization commences.

UNEMPLOYMENT CYCLES

"Severe unemployment crises have occurred about every six years," said Mr. Hart. "The years 1902, 1908, and 1914-15 each saw from three to seven million city workers out of a job. In January, 1915, nearly one man out of every four in American cities was unemployed. Intelligent planning ahead by the government could largely avoid such social catastrophies.

"Nearly 2,000,000 women and farm workers have been drawn into industry by the recent intense demand for labor. At the same time, a million and a half have constantly been unemployed, due to seasonal fluctuations, changing from one position to another, strikes, sickness, and general lack of organization of the labor market. A government monopoly of the employment business would greatly reduce this unemployed margin of labor.

"The peak of demand for labor seems to have passed. Ordinary building fell off tremendously in 1917, and other peace industries ceased the rapid expansion which went on in 1915 and 1916. War demands are now filling gaps left by the falling off of normal business.

SEASONAL OCCUPATIONS

"Seasonal changes cause wide fluctuations every year in the demand for labor. The demand is usually greatest in October and least in January. Transportation and building employ two millions more men in summer than in winter, while school teaching, coal mining, and amusements occupy a million more in winter than in summer. Retail and wholesale stores have two busy seasons —one in spring and one in fall.

"The number of children working in industries other than agriculture has decreased in recent years at the rate of about 20,000 annually.

IMMIGRATION

"Although immigration has practically ceased, the number of foreign born workers in cities of the United States is still 7,500,-000 as compared with 7,700,000 three years ago. If normal immigration had continued, we should now have 8,400,000 foreign workers."

DOWN DEEP IN THE CELLAR is the billiard room. Why don't you submerge some day and "shoot a few."

OUR INDUSTRIOUS COMMITTEES

(Continued from page 156)

2. It prepared a plan for centralized city purchasing which has been submitted to the City Comptroller and the Finance Committee of the City Council as an alternative to the plan proposed by the Comptroller. It is too early to estimate results.

DRAINAGE AND STREETS

The Harbors Committee has gone on record in favor of the request of the Sanitary District to be allowed to take more water from the lake through the drainage canal by reducing the outflow at other points. The Highways Committee opposed the ordinance for the boulevarding of Addison street—a half-section line street which the committee believes should be reserved for general traffic and business development. The City Planning Committee has suggested to the Chicago Plan Commission a modification of the proposed Ogden avenue extension.

A NEW JAIL?

Chicago needs a new county jail, but when the County Board failed to give assurance in submitting the jail bond issue to the voters last November that the new building would embody modern ideas of jail construction the Club Committee on State and Local Charities, coöperating with other civic organizations, advised a negative vote. The bond issue was defeated, as similar propositions had been on previous occasions.

Through a special committee appointed for the purpose, the Club has coöperated with other organizations in getting public attention to the proposal of the Chicago Bureau of Public Efficiency for fundamental changes in the government framework of the city, including the adoption of the city manager plan.

Representatives of the Club have participated in several important conferences on the coal problem.

The WARTIME COMMITTEE

The Club has recognized the fundamental concern of all citizens in the problems of the war by organizing a Wartime Committee, which has been meeting weekly. It was through this committee that the Club's milk inquiry was instituted.

THE ILLINOIS FEDERATION of Women's Clubs will celebrate the admission of Illinois into the Union with a great pageant to be given at the Auditorium Theatre Saturday, May 11, afternoon and evening. The pageant is largely the work of Wallace Rice, the official pageant writer for the state, appointed by the Illinois Centennial Commission. There will be 2,000 persons in the caste from the ages of 6 to 80 years. History will be told in pantomime, tableaux, music and dancing. The Chicago Fire will be featured in an immense ballet. The proceeds of this pageant are to be devoted to the work of the Commission on Training Camp Activities.

THE LEAGUE TO ENFORCE PEACE, of which Hon. William Howard Taft is President, is to hold a convention in Philadelphia May 16 to 18. The object of the convention, as stated in the announcement, is: "To sustain the determination of our people to fight until Prussian militarism has been defeated, confirm opposition to a premature peace, and to focus attention on the only advantage the American people are holding to gain from the war—a permanent peace guaranteed by a League of Nations."

BOYS IN THE TRAINING CAMPS must have thousands of new magazines. The Collegiate Periodical League is conducting a campaign to secure this sort of reading matter for them. At least 5,000 magazines are needed at the Great Lakes station every week. As soon as you have finished reading your magazines will you either take them to the Chicago Public Library or leave them at any branch library marked, "For the soldiers and sailors"?

The Club Arsenal

Up on the fourth floor of the Club house, next to the office, is the powder magazine and arsenal for civic committees. Here is stored quantities of ammunition in the form of data—books, magazines, pamphlets, special articles, etc., on practically every subject in which a committee is interested. The Library Committee at the annual meeting of the Club, reported that the library contains about 3,500 books and 15,000 pamphlets. Think what a lot of "damage" that ammunition could do if the civic committees would only get busy and load their guns with it.

A New Idea in Zoning

SENATOR EDWARD J. GLACKIN is preparing a new bill, to be introduced in the Illinois legislature of 1919, for the "zoning" of Illinois cities. Last Tuesday he met with the City Planning Committee of the Club to discuss its provisions.

Senator Glackin's proposal differs radically in two particulars from zoning legislation heretofore proposed or adopted in American cities. The New York plan now in operation and the plan embodied in the Chicago bill defeated by eleventh-hour opposition at the last session of the Illinois legislature, are based upon the power of the community—commonly known as the police power—to promote the health, comfort, safety, and welfare of the people. The community in securing such conditions is under no obligation to pay compensation to any vested interest which might be adversely affected.

SENATOR GLACKIN'S PLAN

The theory underlying Senator Glackin's proposal is that the creation of such a building zone or district would be a local public improvement, similar, for instance, to a street-paving or street-widening operation. Property prevented by the districting regulations from attaining its most profitable use would be compensated by damages, while property benefited by the restrictions would be assessed. The city would perhaps contribute from general taxes in cases where the improvement is of more than local importance. Senator Glackin provides in his plan for hearings of all parties interested before the board of local improvements, for the veto of a districting plan or of a change from a plan already adopted by a petition of 40 per cent of the property frontage, for the approval of districting ordinances by the City Council and for opportunity for property owners to file objections to the assessment roll in the courts.

There is another fundamental difference between Senator Glackin's plan and that, for instance, which New York has adopted. The New York districting regulations are conceived fundamentally as a city planning enterprise. The major part of the city is districted according to a zoning plan, the relations of one district to another being carefully worked out in advance. The Glackin plan leaves the initiative largely in the hands of local property owners and an adverse petition by 40 per cent of the frontage owners in any community would effectually prevent the formation of a "district."

SOME QUESTIONS

Senator Glackin's plan is a departure from accepted theories of "zoning." What would be the practical effect of its adoption? The property owners would be more amply protected. Would he be too well protected? Would a minority of local property interests, armed with a veto power upon any proposal for the formation of a district, be able to check regulations needed for the benefit of adjoining districts or of the city as a whole? Would this veto stand in the way of a comprehensive zoning plan for the city and bring about only a "spotty" regulation? Would the penalty of having to pay an assessment to keep his neighbor from erecting an objectionable structure deter many property owners—particularly those of small means—from agreeing to a desirable districting plan?

The Glackin plan, as at present worked out, provides no procedure by which the boundary lines of a proposed district would be determined. And yet the character of the regulations—in fact the question of whether or not a protesting minority might block the plan entirely—would depend upon the boundary lines arbitrarily drawn by the Board of Local Improvements or by local petitioners.

PERFECTING THE DETAILS

Senator Glackin's bill is still in an embryonic stage. Some of the difficulties suggested in the above questions, if they are difficulties, can probably be met without changing the fundamentals of the plan. Other difficulties may be more vital. In any case Senator Glackin has some brand new ideas on the subject, ideas which are of more than local interest and which ought to have the earnest consideration of public officials, city planners and "average citizens" everywhere.

Senator Glackin asserts that in his opinion the plan proposed at the last session can not be passed, that the more conservative proposal which he outlined would stand a better chance of adoption.

Negro Soldier Praised

Drawing of Color Line Against Black
Men Is Condemned by Club Speaker

THE negro, as a bearer of arms in America's struggle against Prussianism, is displaying no new attitude, according to James Weldon Johnson of the National Association for the Advancement of Colored People, who spoke at the Club last Wednesday. He has a military record, Mr. Johnson said, which has never been stained by disloyalty and of which he may well be proud, reaching from Bunker Hill to San Juan. Over 200,000 negro soldiers served in the Civil War. But in spite of the negro's high contribution to American military success, in spite of his eager response to his country's call at this crisis, there has been evidenced against him in some quarters, Mr. Johnson said, an ugly spirit of prejudice, which is endeavoring to put him in a separate class from his white countrymen.

Negro Workers Segregated

At the great Hog Island shipyard many thousands of negro workers—skilled and unskilled—are employed in the service of their government and for a long time there was a common democracy with the white men. But a certain Senator visited Hog Island and in a few days came an order for segregation. Signs were put up saying that colored men should eat at one place, white men at another. "It seems a small thing," said Mr. Johnson, "but I want the American people to see that the prejudice of which this is an illustration not only is a violation of the common democracy which should exist in such a place but a hindrance as well to the efficiency of the negro workers. Fortunately, the segregation order has been rescinded."

Prejudice Shown Blacks

Mr. Johnson told the story of a young negro officer, traveling in the uniform of the United States, who was ordered by the conductor of his car to go into "the car for niggers" and upon his refusal was ejected, thrown into jail and fined. In another instance, men in a colored division were told not to apply for admission at places of amusement where their presence would cause resentment. "Can't you see," asked Mr. Johnson, "the dampening effect of an order like that on men who are willing to pay the last full measure of devotion to the cause of liberty?" He pleaded that we should apply in our treatment of the negro here the same democratic principles for which we are fighting "over there."

A Chance for the Negro

"The war has already set in motion," Mr. Johnson said, "forces affecting greatly the future of the negro. The negro exodus from the South to fill the vacuum created by the return of immigrant labor to Europe at the beginning of the war is having profound effects. The negro in the South had been robbed of his civil rights although he possessed a fairly assured economic status. In the North, however, where his political rights were more fully recognized, his chance to earn a living in competition with white labor was much restricted. For the first time, now, the negro has the opportunity to live in the free states of the North and to earn his bread in the industrial centers by the side of the white man. It means much for his economic, social and intellectual progress.

"This shift of negro population has also improved the condition of the negro in the South. The people of the South are more inclined to listen to the demands of the negro, to provide him with good schools, to insure him a better chance in the court and better police protection."

WHY TAKE A BATH AT HOME in a tub when the City Club has an excellent shower bath free to its members?

49

Prof.Davi ... ...,

Commerce Urbana,
Ill.

UNIVERSITY OF ILLINOIS LIBRARY

OCT 23 1918

The City Club Bulletin
Published Weekly by the City Club of Chicago
A Journal of Active Citizenship

VOLUME XI   MONDAY, MAY 13, 1918   NUMBER 19

NEXT FRIDAY, MAY 17TH, AT LUNCHEON

A Story of the Invasion of Belgium
—————————— BY ——————————
MLLE. SUZANNE SILVERCRUYS

Mlle. Silvercruys is the 18 year old daughter of the Chief Justice of Belgium. She came to this country two years ago as a refugee. At that time she could not speak a word of English but has since developed into an unusually gifted speaker. In her address she tells what she saw and experienced during the German invasion.

Mlle. Silvercruys has addressed large audiences in the East.

SPEAKING PROMPTLY AT 1:00

"Made in Germany"

OUR eight-year elementary schools, devoted to rudimentary education, are an imported institution, according to Prof. Charles H. Judd, of the School of Education, University of Chicago, in his address at the City Club last Friday. What is worse, they are an adaptation of a wholly undemocratic system of education, developed in Prussia in the interest of the aristocratic classes. The Volkschule, the school for the common people of Germany and the institution on which our elementary schools are modeled, gives only the most rudimentary instruction, suited to the station in life to which its pupils are expected to graduate and to which they are bound by class restrictions. Prof. Judd demands for the later years of elementary education an enrichment of the school course, which would afford opportunity for varied types of development for the children of the common people. Prof. Judd spent a part of 1913 in Germany, studying the Volkschule. (*Continued on next page.*)

The City Club Bulletin
A Journal of Active Citizenship

The purpose of the Club is to bring together in informal association those who are genuinely interested in the improvement of the political, social and economic conditions of the community in which we live.

PUBLISHED WEEKLY BY THE
CITY CLUB OF CHICAGO
315 Plymouth Court   Telephone: Harrison 8278
DWIGHT L. AKERS, Editor

OFFICERS OF THE CLUB
GEORGE H. MEAD, President
CHARLES M. MODERWELL, Vice-President
ROY C. OSGOOD, Treasurer
CHARLES YEOMANS, Secretary
GEORGE E. HOOKER, Civic Secretary

EDITORIAL BOARD
HERBERT H. SMITH, Chairman
FREDERICK D. BRAMHALL   S. R. WATKINS
PAUL R. WRIGHT

$1.00 per Year   -   -   -   -   10c per Copy

Entered as second class matter, December 3, 1917, at the postoffice at Chicago, Illinois, under the act of March 3, 1879.

NEW MEMBERS
A. E. Cooke, Western Trunk Line Committee.
Alexander J. Resa, Lawyer.
King C. Thorn, American Posting Service.
John W. Williams, Sec.-Treas. Harris Safe Deposit Co.

(Continued from preceding page.)
Germany's undoubted influence on the school systems, not only of America but of Europe and Japan, Prof. Judd ascribed to the fact that Germany had a well organized system of education earlier than any of the other great nations.

NATIONAL EDUCATION
Germany before this war, said Prof. Judd, knew better than any other country how to relate education to industry. She also realized that education is the most potent instrument of government, the one instrument through which people may most easily be brought to a sense of loyalty to the state. America, however, has had no national policy of education. In our constitutional convention there was no recognition of education as a national question. Our Bureau of Education today is only a small bureau without authority. We have one educational system in Illinois, another in Indiana and another in Wisconsin.

ARISTOCRACY AND PEOPLE
"If we examine the history of education," Prof. Judd continued, "we find that the early schools were for the training of the sons of the aristocracy. In Germany today such training has a definite part in the system of education. Only from the Gymnasium, the institution for the aristocracy, can a student enter the University. Only the boys from the Gymnasium may be officers in the army. There is no access to the Gymnasium or to the University for the common man.

"The institution from which 92 per cent of the German people receive their education is the Volkschule. Schools for the common people always begin with religious instruction—as a missionary enterprise—and in Germany, the Volkschule teaches religion as its most fundamental subject. The Volkschule is an institution absolutely distinct from the Gymnasium. It is a free school which admits both girls and boys. Its teachers are especially trained for this work and never come in contact with the Gymnasium or the University.

"The Volkschule has a fundamentally different course of study from that of the Gymnasium. Only the rudiments are taught. In the Gymnasium everything is opened up—in the 4th grade the boy begins his Latin, in the 6th grade his French. He is recognized as one of the chosen few, to be trained for the higher professions. No boy who fails in the Gymnasium can hope for a social career. But 92 per cent of the people are denied these privileges. In 1913 only 178 students entered the Gymnasium from the Volkschule.

"THE DEESTRIK' SCHOOL"
"From 1800 to 1830, the district school was the typical school for the common people in America. Years after Chicago was incorporated, the district schools remained, with local autonomy and a variety of courses of study. Some of the district schools held for a few weeks only, when boys were not needed on the farms, very few held for more than five months. The course of study depended very largely on what the teacher knew and was in most cases restricted to the must rudimentary subjects—the three Rs.

(Continued on page 168.)

Illinois in the War

HOW is Illinois as a state meeting the test of the present crisis? The official body appointed by the governor to organize Illinois war activities is the State Council of Defense. Its chairman, Samuel Insull, addressed the Club at luncheon last Wednesday. His talk was in part an exposition of the work of the Council and in part a reply to a letter sent him by the War Time Committee of the City Club.

REPRESENTS ENTIRE CITIZENSHIP

"The State Council," Mr. Insull said, "has among its members a wide representation of interests and points of view. At various times, some of them would be looked upon with great favor and others would be looked upon with disfavor by the membership of the City Club. There are representatives of labor, of capital, of agriculture, of the banking interests and the learned professions. Notwithstanding the diversity of the point of view, no decision has failed to be unanimous."

The appointment of the State Council, Mr. Insull said, was in obedience to the request of the President that such bodies be formed in the various states for the assistance of the federal authorities in the prosecution of the war and for the conduct of such affairs within the state as might from time to time be necessary as a part of war operations. "Our policy," he stated, "has been to follow the instructions of the federal authorities—not to branch out on lines of our choosing. Our attitude is necessarily more or less a waiting attitude. We have guarded ourselves against falling into a habit very common among bodies that do not have the full responsibilities of office, of general criticism of those who are charged with responsibility."

LOYALTY PROPAGANDA

Mr. Insull described a number of the important activities and accomplishments of the State Council. "About the first activity in which we engaged was the endeavor to bring the entire citizenship of the state into full accord with the government's war policy. A year ago there was no such unanimity of feeling as exists today. Some of our citizens were slow to realize the situation and the call of the blood temporarily overcame the call of the plighted word. I am glad to say that with rare exceptions, the entire citizenship of the state is now, we feel, strongly back of the government.

"In bringing home to the people the fundamental principles governing our entry into this war, the agency which has probably been more effective than any other connected with the State Council, is the Woman's Committee presided over by Mrs. Joseph T. Bowen. That committee has 15,000 active, volunteer officers in the state and over 700,000 women registered and subject to call for war work. In connection with the patriotic propaganda, we also organized a thousand local neighborhood committees through the state. The propaganda through these two agencies has had a great deal to do with bringing the state to a point where it is 100 per cent behind the government, whereas I doubt whether it was forty per cent behind the government when the war started."

THE COUNTY AUXILIARIES

The State Council has also, in all but three counties of the state, auxiliary committees which deal with problems of food, fuel, conservation, etc. Typical of the work of these bodies, said Mr. Insull, is their response to the appeal for aid in raising funds for the War Recreation Board. With their co-operation and practically without expense, the fund was oversubscribed by 40 per cent within a few weeks. The county organizations have also been very active in liberty loan work.

Among other activities of the State Council, Mr. Insull mentioned the assistance rendered the federal authorities in the fuel crisis last winter. He spoke also of the work of the conservation committee in stimulating food production. That committee has, in every county, a subcommittee which works with the local auxiliary. Last January, an investigation showed that the Mississippi Valley as a whole was in very bad need of seed corn. The situation was serious. "We organized the whole state to look for seed corn. The agricultural department of the state university co-operated by testing samples of corn to see if they were good for seed. It was necessary for us to get financial assistance in order to provide the farmers of Illinois

with seed corn, to finance the operation
from the time the seed is purchased until
it is paid for by the farmer. Two or three
of the leading bankers of Chicago promptly
provided us with a fund of a million and
a quarter dollars. That is now making
possible in Illinois a corn crop that would
have been impossible without it.

A FOOD PROGRAM

"In a conference between the agricultural staff of the state university and experts representing the State Council a food
production program was mapped out. This
program has the widest circulation not
only in Illinois but in a great many of the
other states of the Mississippi Valley.

"The State Council organized a food
show to teach our people how to shop and
to cook economically. That food show has
been copied all over the United States
and the recipe book has an international
circulation.

MAKING FARMERS

"We thought we were going to be short
of farm labor," said Mr. Insull. "The
shortage is not as great as we at first an-
ticipated it might be, although it may be considerably increased by the new draft. To
help the farm labor situation and to co-
operate with the federal authorities in their
plan for a Boys' Working Reserve, we got
the various educational authorities of the
city and state to join with us in a plan to
educate the boys for farm work. As a
result we have a series of high school lessons
of such a character that if all the farmers
of the state would get a copy and read it,
they would be better farmers during 1918
than they were in 1917.

"We took up the subject of war gardens
and we are told that the movement is being handled in Chicago with greater intelligence and in a more practical way than
elsewhere in the country."

"When the National Guard was mus-
tered in as a part of the federal forces,
the state of Illinois was left absolutely without any form of military protection. The
Governor, in case of riot, would have been
dependent upon assistance from the federal
authorities, at a time when the federal
authorities would need every soldier that
they could muster. The State Council of
Defense through its Military Committee,
which is presided over by Lieutenant Governor Oglesby and Mr. Speaker Shanahan,
took up the subject and legislation was
passed at Springfield empowering the Governor to create certain new militia regiments and militia reserve regiments. The
State Council of Defense was authorized to
organize volunteer training corps. As a
result of that operation we have provided
the state with about 20,000 men.

"In all the various activities our keynote is patriotic propaganda. All of them

(*Continued on page 166.*)

Over-Seas for Uncle Sam

Forty-two members of the City Club are in over-seas military or other war service or are on the way, according to our club records. Except as indicated, they are in France. The following list is probably incomplete and there have undoubtedly been some promotions. Will any member who knows of additions or corrections which should be made to this list please notify the editor?

Field Artillery
MAJ. NOBLE B. JUDAH, JR.
LIEUT. WHEATON AUGUR
LIEUT. EARL O. BLAIR
LIEUT. MARSHALL G. SIMONDS
LIEUT. WALTER B. WOLF
LIEUT. H. S. MARSH
CORPORAL F. O. MASON
K. K. RICHARDSON, Field Artillery School of Instruction.

Engineer Corps
LIEUT. HAROLD R. HOWES
CAPT. JOHN B. JACKSON
CAPT. FRANCIS W. TAYLOR

Aviation Service
LIEUT. NORRIS W. OWENS
LIEUT. J. C. BOLLENBACHER
LIEUT.-COL. BION J. ARNOLD
GALE WILLARD

American Red Cross
RAYMOND ROBINS, Chairman Permanent Red Cross Mission to Russia—Moscow.
ELBERT BEEMAN, Bureau of Personnel
LAIRD BELL, Field Service
PAUL E. WILSON
ERNEST ·P. BICKNELL, Director of Red Cross Work, Belgium
WILLIAM R. DICKINSON
RUSSEL TYSON

Medical Service
MAJOR CHANNING W. BARRETT, Base Hospital Unit No. 36

Quartermasters Corps
LIEUT. A. K. ATKINSON
LIEUT. CHARLES B. BENJAMIN
CAPT. PERRY M. SHEPHERD

Ambulance Service
J. ARNOLD SCUDDER
H. M. CONARD

Y. M. C. A.
ELMO C. LOWE
CLIFTON R. BECHTEL
ALLEN HOBEN
EDWARD B. DEGROOT
FRANCIS W. PARKER
FRED A. GROW
JOHN K. SIMONS

Signal Corps
LIEUT. ARTHUR MANNHEIMER

War Risk Bureau
CAPT. WILLIAM J. MACK
SERG. LEON LEWIS

U. S. Shipping Board
PROF. JAMES A. FIELD, Statistical Service
National Board of Historical Service
PROF. ANDREW C. MCLAUGHLIN, England

Diplomatic Service
GRAHAM R. TAYLOR, Assistant to American Ambassador, Moscow, Russia.
CAPT. CHARLES E. MERRIAM, Chairman U. S. War Propaganda Bureau, Rome, Italy.

The Listening Post

FRANK T. HENNESSY is now a member of the National Army, stationed at Fort Jefferson, St. Louis, Mo.

As PREDICTED IN LAST week's Bulletin, "Major" Abel Davis, after enjoying for a few days only his new dignity as Lieut. Colonel, has been promoted to the rank of Colonel.

JOHN A. LAPP VISITED the Club last week. Mr. Lapp is known to many of our members as former legislative reference librarian for Indiana. He is now the secretary of the health insurance commission of the state of Ohio.

WHEN THE DOG DAYS COME, you will be glad of that shower on the fourth floor.

ILLINOIS IN WAR WORK

(Continued from page 164.)

tend distinctly to increase the patriotic fervor of the people engaged in the work and by example and reflection the patriotism of the whole people of the state.

WORK BY VOLUNTEERS

"Except in one or two rare instances the entire service to the State Council of Defense is by volunteers. We have between 50,000 and 75,000 men in the state engaged in public work because they want to do it and without any expectation of reward. Don't you think that the effect of this will be felt beyond the period of the war and that many of these men, after the struggle is over, will realize the duties of citizenship and instead of being mere critics of government will pull the laboring oar in public affairs?"

The latter part of Mr. Insull's address was in reply to questions propounded in the letter of the City Club's Wartime Committee. The letter asked, first:

ARE WE GETTING RESULTS?

"Is satisfactory progress in your opinion being made in Illinois in the production of food, ships, coal, munitions, the provision of transportation, the necessary conversion of industrial plants, the determination of priority between essential and non-essential industries, and the elimination of wastes? Are the material resources and the six million people of Illinois doing all they might toward winning the war quickly?"

In reply Mr. Insull said: "The answering of that question is a very big contract. I can't answer it without getting into an attitude of either praise or criticism of the people from whom I get my instructions —the federal authorities. A great many of those questions have no possible connection with my work. If I should see something which ought to be done in connection with such a question I wouldn't try to do it myself because I would be throwing a monkey wrench into the machinery. I would draw it to the attention of the people at Washington.

"The production of food is within our sphere of operations. I believe that everything possible is being done with relation to that but if not we would like to get the advice of people who think they can do it better. But if they come around with advice they are very likely to be put to work, for we are a little impatient with the fellow who comes around and just criticizes.

"Ships I know little or nothing about. When the shipping board asked us to enroll men we went to work and in the course of a couple of weeks had enrolled 30,000 men, although Washington had asked us for only 20,000 or 25,000.

NEXT WINTER'S COAL CRISIS

"In my judgment we will have more trouble with coal next winter than we had last winter. In proportion to the amount of material to be moved, steam railroads will have fewer cars this coming winter than last. Illinois will have very little anthracite coal and very little high class bituminous coal from Kentucky and Virginia. We will have to rely mainly upon our own production. Everything possible should be done to arouse our people to the necessity of storing coal during the summer months. Everybody ought to store coal and persuade his neighbor to store it—to store more than he needs and place it at the disposal of the fuel administrator for distribution among the poor classes when the pinch comes next winter."

The second question asked by the committee was:

COORDINATING WAR EFFORT

"How far is it possible for the State Council of Defense to serve as a central agency for stimulating co-ordinating and controlling the effort of citizens in the state."

"I disclaim," replied Mr. Insull, "any desire on the part of the State Council to control the citizens of the state. If we have not succeeded in stimulating and co-ordinating their efforts we have failed in the purposes for which we were created. We have probably done more of this outside of Chicago than in the city. We are now trying to bring the various organizations in Cook County into one central body."

The committee's third question was:

SHOULD WE HAVE CLEARING HOUSE?

"Would it not be advisable to establish a clearing house of information as to war activities of all sorts of organizations in the state and in connection with it to hold conferences either of special groups of persons or upon special problems for the benefit both of the Council itself and of the public?"

Mr. Insull replied: "It is very desirable to have information on those things but we haven't the money to establish an expensive organization. Whenever there is a specific subject needing consideration we have a conference on that subject, but the officials of the council are too busy to deal with anything but live immediate issues. We think it would be wasted effort on our part to discuss a program of theoretical subjects—so many volunteer agencies are doing that at this time. It is impossible to lay out a program of our work. We have to do largely as we are told. Every morning I open my mail looking for the next subject that Washington wants us to deal with."

The last question asked by the committee in its letter was:

SOME SPECIFIC PROBLEMS

"How is the State Council of Defense now dealing with the following important subjects? (a) *The promotion of shipbuilding in Illinois.* (b) *The question of industrial relations.* (c) *The application of industrial labor according to the priority demanded by war needs.* (d) *The prompt conversion of industrial plants where necessary to meet such priority demands.* (e) *The elimination of waste of man power and material resources in the production of luxuries or other non-essentials or in non-productive advertising or other forms of competitive wastes, whether in respect to production for war purposes or for essential civil needs.* (f) *The question of demobilization, so that we may be able to insure wise action in that regard when the time shall come."*

"The promotion of ship building in Illinois," Mr. Insull replied, "I think is coming along very well.

"The conversion of industrial plants is being looked after by the federal authorities and is not within our control. We are sometimes asked by a department at Washington to look for various establishments just as we are asked to find men for the various departments there.

BUSINESS AS USUAL?

"The elimination of waste of man power and material resources by the stoppage of non-essentials is a subject upon which all we can do is to preach. And we get into a great deal of trouble with our citizens when we do preach it. We are told that business should go on as usual, but I think that when public opinion is fully aroused that situation will very largely take care of itself.

"The question of demobilization will have to be taken up as a federal proposition and we will have to join with the federal authorities in helping and assisting in that work but we are more concerned now with helping to get the men and to get them over there than we are at this moment

with bringing them back. The time for us to consider demobilization is later on when we will be ready to carry the burden that our allies have carried for three years past.

"As to whether the six million people of Illinois are doing their part, whether their services are being availed of to the best advantage, that is a personal question for every citizen to answer. The first duty of a citizen is to see that his services are being availed of to the fullest possible extent in connection with the great work we have in hand."

The purpose of the questions which the War Time Committee presented to Mr. Insull is indicated in the following quotation from the letter:

OUR MAXIMUM EFFORT

"Our committee feels very keenly the importance of affording a wider and better opportunity for the zeal and devotion of great numbers of persons to find scope, and a chance for such persons to understand and to help forward the war efforts of Illinois. We feel that the enlargement of such opportunities is vital to the maintenance of the public morale in this crisis and still more to the realization of the maximum powers of the people of Illinois toward a quick victory.

"Speaking not only for ourselves, but, as we believe for other organizations as well, we believe that the State Council of Defense should be the center of all war activities in this state and we should like therefore to be able to look to the Council for information, advice and guidance in our own activities."

ARE YOU A MAGAZINE HAWK? A magazine hawk is a bird who pounces down on three or four of the latest periodicals, gathers them under his wing and goes to roost for an hour on an easy chair. You can see him occasionally in the Club lounge. He is usually surrounded by three or four hungry-looking members.

Another unpopular bird in our Club ornithology is the one who takes his after-dinner nap without troubling to remove the magazines or afternoon newspapers from the couch where careless members have left them.

IN THESE TIMES of high prices, be thankful for the City Club's low dues.

"MADE IN GERMANY"

(Continued from page 162.)

"Another American educational institution of this period was the academy. In the academy was taught anything that the teacher could possibly teach. It represented the demand of the democracy for more training and greater opportunities.

"The interesting fact about the district schools and the academies was that they articulated. There was no aristocracy and the academies were open to the common people from the district schools. In Germany, when a boy goes to the Volkschule at six years of age, he knows just where he is going. If he enters the Gymnasium, also at six, he knows that he is in the school for the aristocracy. But in America we created a unified continuous school system, without class distinctions.

IMPORTING OUR SCHOOLS

"In the thirties, Horace Mann and several other Americans interested in education were greatly disturbed by the lack of uniformity and standards in our schools, so they packed their grips and went to the place where they could find a good school system—to Prussia. When they came back they brought home with them this Prussian Volkschule which I have described, and gave it to us. And because the Volkschule had an eight-year course and was restricted to the rudiments, our children in this country have been studying the rudiments for eight years. Now there is nothing to prove that eight years is the time needed for mastering the rudiments. The eight-year period exists in the Volkschule because the child is confirmed into the church at the age of fourteen and the school is intended to prepare the child for confirmation. But that fact has determined the form and character of our elementary schools.

TOO MUCH ARITHMETIC

"In 1830, when school kept at the most about five months of the year, perhaps it was proper to teach arithmetic for eight years. Under those conditions, perhaps, there was enough arithmetic to last, but as the length of the school year has extended, it has been hard to find enough to go around. Attempts have been made to bring a little algebra and geometry from the higher grades, but these efforts have generally been resisted. What we need in these higher grades is to give the children new types of study and of experience.

"Another result of having adopted the eight-year course of the Volkschule is that our boys enter the professions about two years later than those in Europe. A student who is going into one of the professions must mark time for two years in the 7th and 8th grades.

"It is time that American communities should recognize that in the schools they have the most potent influence for the development of the next generation. The Volkschule doesn't need to teach anything about self-government. Religion is taught and after that loyalty to the Kaiser. But in America we must put something into the schools to train the children to take their part in government. When we have done that we will have the type of nationalism appropriate to a country where 100 per cent of the people make up the aristocracy. If we are to have a school system appropriate to our democracy we must get away from the Prussian system.

"We should develop beyond our sixth grade a highly differentiated educational system. We have offered equal opportunities of education but have insisted that they should be offered to all in the same way. In the higher grades, differentiated opportunities of the richest types should be given. After the war we must determine for ourselves the kind of democracy we are to have and must develop a type of educational organization appropriate to our way of thinking."

IT MUST HAVE BEEN a new and exquisite sensation for the "drys" who sat in the gallery of the City Council last Monday to hear the impassioned oratory of the wets in favor of suspending the special bar permit ordinance. They harked back in memory to those not distant days when the wets refused them even the "littlest" concession toward stricter regulation. But now, thanks apparently to Secretary Daniels and the "five-mile zone" order, the debate narrowed down to an issue between a mere suspension of the ordinance for the period of the war and its complete repeal. The suspension won out but the drys do not seem seriously downcast or suffering over their defeat. Many of them expect to see the national prohibition amendment in the federal constitution before the special bar permit can be resurrected as a Chicago institution.

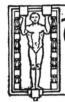

The City Club Bulletin

Published Weekly by the City Club of Chicago

A Journal of Active Citizenship

VOLUME XI   MONDAY, MAY 20, 1918   NUMBER 20

NEXT THURSDAY AT LUNCHEON — MAY 23

The Present Situation and Prospects in Russia

VICTOR S. YARROS

The first interpretation of the Russian Revolution to the City Club was given by Mr. Yarros over a year ago. Since then a second great revolution and other events of world significance have taken place in Russia. Many different interpretations of Russia have been brought to us.

Mr. Yarros will round up this complex subject for us and interpret Russian conditions in the perspective of the year's developments.

SPEAKING PROMPTLY AT 1:00

A Daughter of Belgium

"WAR as we saw it over there, how the Germans took our towns and killed our people" was the story told to a large City Club audience last Friday by Mlle. Suzanne Silvercruys, twenty-year-old daughter of the Minister of Justice of Belgium. Mlle. Silvercruys was clad in her country's colors—"Red," she explained, "for the blood that had been shed, black for her country's sorrow and gold for the glory that would be Belgium's in the end."

Mademoiselle told how the war had fallen upon Belgium as from a clear sky. A few days before, not dreaming of what was to come, she with her father had gone to their country home, near Liege. It was there that the news of Germany's threatened invasion reached her and it was there that messengers came in the night, knocking upon the doors and calling upon the men, in the name of the king, to join the army. Her brother had gone and was among the defenders of Liege. At that time a sixteen-year-old girl, she was playing in the garden with her dogs when the first sound of guns reached her ears.

But it was at Brussels, she said, to which she had returned immediately with her father, that she first fully realized the war. "When you see the boys going away you

The City Club Bulletin

A Journal of Active Citizenship

PUBLISHED WEEKLY BY THE

' ⌐ CITY CLUB OF CHICAGO

315 Plymouth Court   Telephone: Harrison 8278

DWIGHT L. AKERS, Editor

EDITORIAL BOARD
HERBERT H. SMITH, Chairman
FREDERICK D. BRAMHALL   S. R. WATKINS
PAUL R. WRIGHT

$1.00 per Year - - - - 10c per Copy

Entered as second class matter, December 3, 1917,
at the postoffice at Chicago, Illinois, under the act of
March 3, 1879.

NEW MEMBERS

J. Esten Bolling, Chief Engineer, Drying Systems, Inc.

N. B. Hodskin, Barrett Cravens Co. (Trucks.)

Victor E. Russum, Associate Editor, "The National Underwriter."

don't know. Even when you hear the guns you don't know. But when you see the wounded coming in, covered with blood and mud, then you *do* know."

Too Young!

Sixteen-year-old Mademoiselle volunteered at once for hospital service but was refused because of her youth. Pursuing an unswerving resolution to be of use, however, she found a place in the kitchen of a large hospital, peeling onions and potatoes and washing dishes. Later she was promoted to a ward, where she worked as a nurse for the soldiers.

She told of the arrival of the Germans, of the steady stream of gray-clad soldiers that marched for two days through the streets on their way to the south, of German insolence and tyranny and of the indomitable spirit of resistance and of long-suffering among the Belgian people. "We were not beaten," she said, "we have not been beaten, we never will be beaten!"

Cruelties of the Germans

Mlle. Silvercruys told some hideous stories of massacre and deportation, whose authenticity she guaranteed. "The Germans seem to enjoy making people suffer,"

(*Continued on page 176*)

THE LISTENING POST

PRESIDENT MEAD last week appointed the following standing Committees of the Club:

House Committee: Bradford Gill, Chairman; Fred J. Stebbins, Morris L. Greeley.

Finance Committee: A. B. Hall, Chairman; Allen B. Pond, Bradford Gill, Roy C. Osgood.

SOME OF OUR MEMBERS are actively promoting at this time the work of the National Association for the Advancement of Colored People. Among them are Judge E. O. Brown, Robert McMurdy, William T. Chenery and T. W. Allinson.

WALTER L. FISHER has been appointed by the ship-building labor-adjustment board as its representative for the Great Lakes District, which extends from Buffalo to Duluth. This board has jurisdiction over wages, hours and other labor conditions in all ship yards having contracts with the emergency fleet corporation and the navy. The board was formed under an agreement between the navy department, the emergency fleet corporation and the American Federation of Labor.

URBAN A. LAVERY is in charge of work for the American Protective League, operating under the direction of the Department of Justice at Washington. Victor Elting is one of the national directors of this League.

MANY OF THE SOLDIERS and sailors who use the Club house at week ends, repeat from week to week.

WITH THE INFLUX of negro workers and their families from the South, there is an increased demand for nursery care of the children of colored working mothers. In spite of this demand, however, the two nurseries caring for colored children have had to close their doors. A special committee of the Chicago Association of Day Nurseries has been formed, with Mrs. Emil Levy as chairman, to promote a plan for the creation of three new nurseries to meet this need.

Americanization

"FOR the sake of national unity and for all practical purposes, English should be the common language." This is the first plank in the Americanization platform of the Committee on Foreign Born Women, Council of National Defense, a committee of which Miss Mary McDowell of Chicago is chairman. The committee urges national legislation making the use of the English language compulsory in all elementary education.

CAN'T SPEAK ENGLISH

The instruction of non-English speaking adults in this country is a problem of very great magnitude. In 1910, according to a bulletin of the U. S. Bureau of Education, there were in this country, over two and one-half million foreign born white persons, 21 years of age and over, unable to speak English. Of these only 1.3% were in school and the report, published in 1916, concludes that "practically no aliens are making any systematic effort to acquire the English language."

English should be taught, according to the committee above quoted, both as a means of accomplishing national unity and as a protection and aid to the foreign born workers themselves. They are easily deceived and exploited by the unscrupulous and have little chance for advancement. They become victims of unprotected machinery and fire because they cannot heed the warning given in print or by word of mouth.

INTEREST DECREASING

But how is our language to be taught to this legion of the foreign born, many of whom have already passed the age when learning is easy? A pamphlet on this subject just issued by Mr. Max Loeb of Chicago, says that the attendance in the evening schools in large cities is actually decreasing in spite of many ingenious plans to arouse interest. In four years, he says, the registration in the elementary classes of evening schools in Chicago has shrunk from 18,000 to 8,000.

What explains this indifference? The Committee on Foreign Born Women points to some considerations which explain it perhaps to some extent. Wages "have not been equal to the growing American stand-ards of the family. The unskilled worker wants a home of his own and tries desperately to meet the monthly payments. In the struggle his wife often has to go to work either at night or in the day time and the children are neglected. Can we wonder why they do not flock to our evening schools to learn English after long days of monotonously ugly work. . . . We have not considered good housing, good industrial conditions and recreational facilities are fundamental to Americanization."

POOR TEACHING A CAUSE

Another reason for the failure of the evening schools to realize their full potentialities in the education of the immigrant is the inappropriateness in many cases, of the teaching. In Cleveland recently, an investigator found a class (which was typical of others) in which husky laboring men were engaged in copying "I am a yellow bird. I can sing. I can fly. I can sing to you." The Committee on Foreign Born Women urges that the instruction "must be simple but with a content which will appeal to the intelligence of the adult." English related to the every day life of the working people—their food, clothing, shelter and work—will be of the greatest practical value to them. Later, lessons in civics should be given.

VOLUNTEER OR COMPULSORY METHODS?

Mr. Loeb, in the pamphlet which has been referred to, concludes that "volunteer methods" of training our foreign born having failed, we must resort to compulsory methods. "Every adult, able-bodied and between the ages of 16 and 45 should be compelled to learn to read and write English." He suggests certain methods of bringing this about, including the utilization in modified form, of our present truancy machinery.

Whether the futility of the "volunteer system" has been finally demonstrated is a point on which there is apparently a difference of opinion. "Until there is a friendly response from the neighborhood people themselves," says the Committee on Foreign Born Women, "the time is not ripe to begin further work." The Committee proposes, not compulsion, but more attractive types of instruction, the better training of teachers and larger opportunities for school attendance, including free classes in factories on company time.

The Committee does not sympathize with the extreme view that foreign people should be denied the right to retain their native customs and language. "In their first years in this country, our language cannot feed their minds." "Culture is a possession that grows best by handing its life roots from one generation to the other. If the first generation Americans are cut loose from the culture of the past of their parents, they start their young lives in our country without nourishment for the higher sides of their nature."

The Mail Pouch

Glackin Zone Plan Criticized

RECENTLY we published an article referring to a new zoning bill which is being prepared by Senator Edward J. Glackin. In that article we raised certain questions about the bill, which seemed fundamental. An answer to some of these questions comes this week in the form of a letter from Herbert S. Swan, Executive Secretary of the Zoning Committee of New York. This is the committee which has put into operation the New York zone plan, the most ambitious and comprehensive plan yet adopted by any American city. Mr. Swan condemns the idea underlying Senator Glackin's proposal and says that it would be "a calamity to zoning if this method should be followed generally." His letter is as follows:

New York, May 15, 1918.

Dear Sir: In a clipping from the City Club Bulletin, which I obtained a few days ago from Mr. Clinton Rogers Woodruff, I note that Hon. Edward J. Glackin, a senator in the Illinois Legislature, is preparing a zoning bill. According to the information which I have this bill will follow in its general outline the one passed a couple of years ago in Minnesota. This bill provides for the creation of industrial and residential zones through the assessment of benefits and damages. I think it would be a calamity to zoning if this method should be followed generally. I do not

think it is at all possible for Chicago or any other city to obtain the most satisfactory results under the condemnation method. Zoning in order to be practical and useful will have to be sustained under the police power of a state, not under the power of eminent domain. It is very unlikely that a city could be zoned as a comprehensive whole under the condemnation method. In all probability it would mean piecemeal zoning. Each piece zoned would be zoned without reference to other neighborhoods and, of course, many would not be zoned at all.

I do not know Senator Glackin's address or I would write to him, too. If there is any aid that I can give you in this matter, kindly let me know.

Yours very sincerely,
(*Signed*) HERBERT S. SWAN.

Learning About Russia

DO CITY CLUB MEMBERS realize what a rounded view of the situation in Russia they have been getting at the noon meetings? Soon after the Revolution, Victor Yarros, who is thoroughly conversant with the background of life and political conditions in Russia, gave us an interpretation of events. We have since had the benefit of hearing a series of men who have had the most recent personal contact with events in Russia: Charles R. Crane, a member of the "Root mission" to Russia; Dr. Frank Billings, chairman of the relief mission sent by the Red Cross; representatives of the Russian Peasants Council and of the All-Russian Railway Union, direct from Russia; Prof. Edward A. Ross of the University of Wisconsin, who traveled 20,000 miles through the Empire studying the conditions among all classes of people since the Revolution. These men have been personally acquainted with the Russian leaders, some of them have participated in Russian events as more than mere observers. They have been able to translate Russia's aspirations and picture her distress to us from first-hand acquaintance with conditions.

Next Thursday Victor Yarros who gave us our first interpretation of the Revolution over a year ago is to speak about Russian conditions today.

IN THE BILLIARD ROOM: Rates for billiards, 40 cents per hour; for pool, 60 cents per hour.

Light on the Gas Controversy

DONALD R. RICHBERG, special counsel for the city in its ten-million-dollar gas litigation, won the first round last week in his controversy with Corporation Counsel Ettelson. This controversy, one of the most bitter in recent City Hall history, involves the conduct of the City's suit to enforce the gas rates fixed by the City Council in 1911. Mr. Richberg charged that Mr. Ettelson had interfered with his conduct of the case and was playing into the hands of the gas company. Mr. Ettelson answered by "discharging" Mr. Richberg and Richberg countered by denying Ettelson's authority to do so.

THE LITIGATION COMMITTEE

The gas litigation for two and a half years has been in charge of a special Gas Litigation Committee of the City Council, with Mr. Richberg as its attorney. This Committee was appointed by the Mayor in fulfillment of a pre-election pledge. The Law Department of the city, until recently had not participated in the litigation, which so far, has been largely a battle for positions. Mr. Richberg claims that the technical points have now been settled, that the city is in possession of all the high ground and is ready for a trial of the case on its main issues.

THE SUTTER CASE

The dispute between Mr. Richberg and Mr. Ettelson arose over a suit filed in the Municipal Court by a consumer, apparently to test the validity of the 1911 ordinance. The law department, according to Mr. Richberg, without consulting the Gas Litigation Committee or its counsel, into whose hands the city had given entire control of the gas litigation, joined in this new suit—the so-called Sutter suit—and also joined with attorneys of the People's Gas Light and Coke Co. in a request to the Circuit Court for a postponement of the original litigation.

"COLLUSIVE AND FICTITIOUS"

Mr. Richberg claims that the Sutter case is "collusive and fictitious," that the issues have been inadequately presented and that the prosecution of the case at this time would endanger the ground won by the city in its litigation so far. Mr. Ettelson's former affiliation with a law firm employed by the gas company is given by Mr. Richberg as an additional reason which should bar him from participation in the case.

"DILATORY AND POLITICAL"

Mr. Ettelson replied that Mr. Richberg has been dilatory in his conduct of the litigation and extravagant with the city's money. The Sutter case, he claims, offers opportunity for an earlier conclusion of the litigation. He charges that Mr. Richberg has prolonged the case for the benefit of the fees involved and for political reasons. Mayor Thompson in his annual message supports Mr. Ettelson as against Mr. Richberg, whom he calls "a political ally of Charles E. Merriam."

ROUND ONE

The controversy is now before the City Council and Mr. Richberg has won the first encounter before that body. On Saturday, May 11, the Gas Oil and Electric Light Committee, a standing committee of the Council—not to be confused with the special committee on Gas Litigation—approved a resolution directing the Corporation Counsel, pending further investigation, not to interfere in the conduct of the litigation and directing Mr. Richberg to continue in charge. "The Corporation Counsel," says the resolution, "has not made public any adequate justification of his sudden and arbitrary attempt to remove the attorney in charge of the City's interests in a critical time of litigation between the city and the gas company, following the winning of substantial victories for the city by this attorney before the State Utilities Commission and in the Circuit Court." This resolution is now before the City Council for consideration.

IN "STATUS QUO"

At its meeting last Monday, the Council by a vote of 56 to 11, adopted an order which directs that pending consideration of the resolution presented by the "G. O. L. Committee," neither Mr. Ettelson nor Mr. Richberg should take any action contrary to the terms of the resolution. Mr. Ettelson has however pursued his intention of displacing Mr. Richberg from the suit by appearing in court before Judge Torrison to prevent recognition of Mr. Richberg as the city's attorney.

The "G. O. L. Committee" last week approved another resolution designed to place the conduct of the litigation exclusively in Mr. Richberg's hands. The outcome of the controversy will evidently depend upon whether the city council has legal authority to employ special counsel independent of the city law department.

THE NEW COMMITTEE

The special committee on gas litigation for the present Council year has not yet been appointed. Bound up with the Richberg-Ettelson controversy is the question of whether the Litigation Committee should be appointed by the Mayor, as heretofore, or by an amendment of the rules, made a standing committee of the Council. A resolution to make it a standing committee and nominating as its members, Aldermen Capitain, Nance, Richert, Lipps and Littler, has been approved by the Judiciary Committee of the Council and will probably be voted upon at the Council Meeting May 20.

 ## At the Sign of the Book

Education Outdoors

The United States Bureau of Education has published a book on "Open Air Schools" by our friend and former member, Sherman C. Kingsley, now of Cleveland, in collaboration with Prof. F. B. Dressler of Nashville, Tenn. It is a comprehensive treatment of the whole movement in its various manifestations in the United States, Germany, England, France, Switzerland, Sweden, Hungary, Holland, Canada and Australia.

KEEPING THEM WELL

The open air school has developed out of our increasing consciousness of the effects of adverse physical, economic and environmental conditions upon the intellectual attainments of the child in school. "Indoor schools," says the report, "have for the most part grown and developed under the idea that teachers had to do with the minds and not with the bodies of the children, while open air schools are based on the conception that the first essential to a worthy education is sound bodily health."

The first open air school was established in Providence, R. I., in 1908. For so recent an institution, they have gained an important place in the American educational system. There are now more than 1,000 open air classes in 168 cities in 32 different states.

FOR NORMAL CHILDREN TOO

While the open air school has been so far primarily for the physical sub-normal child, recognition of its advantages for normal children is increasing. There are already open air schools for normal children in 30 cities.

The open air school is much more than a school in the open air. Children are given the best medical attention and proper feeding. An investigation of 598 children in Chicago open air schools, as reported in Mr. Kingsley's book, indicates that—

43 per cent had tonsils removed.
40 per cent had adenoids removed.
74 per cent had teeth corrected.
62 per cent had eye defects corrected.
38 per cent had ear defects corrected.
29 per cent had nose defects corrected.

PERMANENT RESULTS

The results of such attention upon the later life of children are inestimable. "The immediate purpose of the open air school," Mr. Kingsley's report concludes, "will be realized only when all debilitated children now in the regular schools have a chance for fresh air, sufficient food and a general hygienic life."

The National Federation of Settlements which meets in Chicago this week will be glad to have members of the City Club attend any of its meetings. They will be held at Bowen Hall, Hull House, Thursday at 8 p. m., Friday and Saturday at 10 a. m. and Sunday at 10:30 a. m. and at the City Club at 8 p. m. Friday and Saturday. The two meetings at the Club would probably be of chief interest to our members:

1. On Thursday evening Prof. John R. Commons will speak on "New Industrial Problems," and Horace Bridges on "The British Labor Party and Its New Program."

2. The Friday evening session will be on the topic, "Immigration and Americanization." The speakers have not yet been announced, but good ones are guaranteed.

"NATION PLANNING"

To avoid and remedy the irregularities and wastefulness of ill-directed growth in our cities, the science of "city planning" has been formulated. But is not the principle of orderly growth that underlies "city planning" equally applicable to the development of national resources and the organization of industry? The pooling of the railroads, which has for the first time allowed our transportation problem to be considered in terms of what Zueblin calls "national strategy," has already resulted in the elimination of some competitive wastes and a more effective adjustment of the railway system to its task.

A Reconstruction Plan

In various countries programs have been prepared for reconstruction after the war. Some of these programs contain very interesting suggestions for nation-wide industrial reorganization. One of these, proposed by the coal conservation sub-committee of the Reconstruction Committee in England, is a plan for the centralization of electric power production under a national board of electrical commissioners. The 600 different companies for the supply of electrical power would be eliminated and the country divided into sixteen districts, in each of which should be erected a large power station for the supply of that area.

These stations would be located at strategic points outside the boundaries of dense population and would be equipped with the most modern appliances for saving fuel and reclaiming by-products—fertilizers, crude oils, etc. "By locating either the main or supplementary plants in or near the collieries," according to the committee, "much coal that is now wasted or left in the pits could be profitably utilized and coal which would otherwise be burned to transport the coal used would also be saved." Another advantage claimed for the plan would be a more economical distribution of the "load" as a large plant of this sort would serve many different types of consumers.

Saving the Nation's Coal

Fifty-five million tons of coal, the Committee estimates, could be saved annually under this plan. With other economies and with the profits from by-products it is believed that the plan would bring a net annual return of about £100,000,000. The scheme has social implications also. "To those interested primarily in the cleanliness and healthiness of the towns and cities," says E. W. Marchant, writing of the plan in the Town Planning Review for April, 1918, "this scheme foreshadows the beginning of that time when the dirt and squalor of the town, due primarily to the smoke from the house and factory chimneys, will disappear."

The plan of the English coal conservation committee is an example of how the science of planning may be applied to industry as a whole. A similar plan has been embodied in the elaborate reconstruction program of the British Labor Party.

CHILDRENS' YEAR

During the year special efforts are to be made throughout the country to save the lives of 100,000 of the 300,000 children who die annually in the United States and to promote better conditions for the development of child life. A national program for the year has been mapped out by the General Medical Board, Council of National Defense, by the Federal Children's Bureau and by the Child Welfare Department, Woman's Committee, C.N.D. As outlined in the Woman's City Club Bulletin for May it includes:

1. The complete registration of births.
2. Prenatal instruction for every mother and adequate care by doctor and nurse at confinement, and afterward.
3. Weighing and measuring of all children under six years of age.
4. A campaign of publicity and education in child hygiene.
5. Children's conferences where well babies can be taken periodically to be weighed and examined, and clinics where sick children may be given medical attention.
6. Public health nurses throughout the state.
7. The guarding of the milk supply, that every child may have his quota of clean, pure milk.

McCarty tells us that he will sell cigars to members by the box at very favorable prices.

The Boston City Club has over 5,000 members. It has $15 dues. If we had 5,000 members, we could have $15 dues. We ought to have more members.

To Help Win This War

This Club, at the request of the U. S. Food Administration, has disregarded its own interests by
voluntarily agreeing to serve no Wheat in any form
until the present wheat shortage is relieved.

Each one must save if our army and the nations
associated with us are to be fed.

You Can Help Win This War

by supporting those eating places which are undertaking to make this sacrifice. You will have good
food and a better conscience.

UNITED STATES FOOD ADMINISTRATION

A Daughter of Belgium

(Continued from page 170)

she said. Men have been forced to dig
their own graves. In Dinant, they shot
people down with machine guns, and of
the six hundred killed, two hundred were
small children. Men deported to Germany from Louvain were forced to stand
four days in cattle cars—in one train seventy-five were dead at the end of the journey.

The unconquerable spirit of the Belgians
is nowhere better shown than in the secret
publication, during the last four years, of
a Belgian newspaper. The Germans have
never been able to locate its place of publication. It circulates secretly among the
people and is then destroyed, for severe
penalties are attached to the possession of it.

For several months Mlle. Silvercruys
was in charge of the feeding of a group of
about 250 children. Later she managed to
leave Belgium, went through Holland to
England and came finally to this country.
She is speaking under the auspices of the
Belgian Relief.

HERE IS ONE of Raymond Hitchcock's
stories told at the Club's Liberty Loan
luncheon the other day: An old lady met
a Tommy in a London street. One of his
legs was gone, one arm was in a sling and
he had only one eye left. "My poor man,"
said the lady, "I do sympathize with you.
Your experiences in the trenches must have
been terrible indeed. Tell me your most
agonizing moment so that I may grieve with
you." "Lidy," answered the Tommy, "h'it
was this wy, H'I was four dys in the
trenches with water up to me chest, h'and
not a drop to drink. The Boches were
shootin' at us h'and we couldn't get h'awy.
So there we stands with water h'up to 'ere
and not a drop to drink. Finally we was
sent back to rest, h'and first thing we
knows we comes to a saloon. H'I goes up
to the saloon, puts me 'and on the door
knob and there H'I was—four dys in the
trenches, and not a drop to drink—and one
of those bloody German shells comes h'over
an' blows the saloon right out o' me 'and.
That was me most hagonizin' moment,
ma'am—four dys in the trenches and not
a drop to drink!"

Commerce

The City Club Bulletin

Published Weekly by the City Club of Chicago

A Journal of Active Citizenship

VOLUME XI   MONDAY, MAY 27, 1918   NUMBER 21

NEXT WEDNESDAY, MAY 29, AT LUNCHEON

The Censorship of Moving Pictures

Should the Proposed New Ordinance Pass?

Clarence Darrow   Harriet Vittum

The new ordinance which vests the censorship of moving pictures in a board of eleven instead of in the second deputy superintendent of police, promises to be one of the most hotly contested measures before the City Council. It was recommended for passage by the Judiciary Committee of the Council last Tuesday.

SPEAKING AT 1:00

Regulating the Movies

THE Judiciary Committee of the City Council last Tuesday approved the Maypole ordinance changing the methods of censorship of moving pictures. Indications are that the ordinance will bring a lively contest on the floor of the Council. The purpose of the new ordinance, according to its proponents, is to do away with the existing "one-man censorship." Its opponents charge that its purpose is to "get" Major Funkhouser and that its effect would be to lower the standards of censorship now maintained by the office of the second deputy superintendent of police.

At present the second deputy is charged by ordinance "with the censoring of moving public pictures and public performances of all kinds." He is assisted by a board of censors, which has, however, no ordinance powers, and whose decision is not final. No picture may be shown without a permit from the police department and the department is directed to refuse a permit for the exhibition of any picture which is "immoral or obscene or portrays any riotous, disorderly or otherwise unlawful scene or has a tendency to disturb the public peace." The new ordinance transfers the censorship to a board of eleven whose decision is reviewable by the courts.

The City Club Bulletin
A Journal of Active Citizenship

The purpose of the Club is to bring together in informal association those men who are genuinely interested in the improvement of the political, social and economic conditions of the community in which we live.

PUBLISHED WEEKLY BY THE
CITY CLUB OF CHICAGO

315 Plymouth Court   Telephone: Harrison 8278

DWIGHT L. AKERS, Editor

EDITORIAL BOARD
HERBERT H. SMITH, Chairman
FREDERICK D. BRAMHALL   S. R. WATKINS
PAUL R. WRIGHT

$1.00 per Year   -   -   -   -   10c per Copy

Entered as second class matter, December 3, 1917, at the postoffice at Chicago, Illinois, under the act of March 3, 1879.

Gray Says

that full many a flower is born to blush unseen and waste its fragrance on the desert air.

We Don't Propose

to blush unseen or waste any of the City Club luncheons on the desert air of an uninformed or unenlightened membership.

For Your Sake

we are going to keep on telling all of you what there is here for you until you get out of the rut of eating elsewhere and come here.

CITY CLUB
HOUSE COMMITTEE

THE LISTENING POST

LAST WEEK Charles T. Jeffrey and Dr. James C. Gill joined the Club.

THE CLUB SUBSCRIBES for sixty periodicals. It receives others in exchange.

R. LEE MEGOWEN has received a commission as captain in the National Army.

THE CLUB HOUSE will be locked and barred against all comers next Thursday, Decoration Day.

IF THE CITY CLUB means anything to you, remember that your friends will enjoy it too. Give them the opportunity to join.

CAPTAIN WILLIAM J. MACK, formerly of the War Risk Bureau in France, has been promoted to the rank of major and assigned to the Judge-Advocate's department.

LOUIS W. MACK, who was formerly associated with the Division of Films under the Committee on Public Information, is now in the Quartermaster General's Department, Washington, D. C.

COMMONPLACE MEALS are no longer served at the City Club. If that is the reason you are staying away, get wise to the new conditions.

DON'T MISS THE DISCUSSION next Wednesday on the "movie censorship."

HOMEWARD BOUND! Raymond Robins, according to reports from Russia, has left Moscow in company with other representatives of the American Red Cross and is on his way home.

A SPECIAL CABLE from Captain Charles E. Merriam, Rome, Italy, was printed in the *Daily News* last Friday, "Italian Day." Captain Merriam is organizing the United States Propaganda Bureau in Italy. His message was a tribute to the Italian people for their ideals and sacrifices in the war.

IF YOU HAVE A DRESS SUIT, you can change into it after business hours at the City Club. There are lockers in the shower room.

"Diplomacy of the Red Cross"

Sustains Civilian Morale in Europe, Says Prof. Robert Herrick

"THE Diplomacy of the Red Cross" was the subject of Prof. Robert Herrick's address at the Friday luncheon last week. He said in substance:

I was in Italy when war was declared. Italy's attitude toward the war has been much misrepresented in this country. What swayed Italy was not a desire for additional territory. The upper classes and the aristocracy were against the war. The socialists were cynical of all national wars and the hard working peasants were also opposed. It was very largely the intellectual, middle and lower-middle classes who realized the menace of Germany and supported the demand for war.

Italy entered the war in the expectation that it would soon be over. Her troops were not well prepared or equipped for a long war. I was in Italy again about a year ago. At the time of my second visit Italy's loss in man power had been less perhaps than that of any other country, but she was evidently staggering. The spirit of the people was much lower than when they went into the war.

THE BREAKING POINT

The war has shown that when any nation gets to a point of misery which they can no longer sustain, they break. That is what happened in Russia. Italy, being closer to the allies than Russia, was saved then from the danger of social collapse, but she is not yet out of that danger nor will she be until the end of the war.

One of the means by which the spirit of Italy was sustained when the break came was the Red Cross, which rushed supplies to her, took care of the refugees and entered upon the social work of reconstruction behind the lines. That work behind the lines is of vital importance if Italy is to be kept in the war, and she must be kept in the war if the allies are not to lose the entire Eastern Mediterranean. Italy needs coal, iron, food, medical and other supplies such as are furnished by the Red Cross. The supplying of these needs, it seems to me, is not sentiment but business. Italy's man power is still to a great extent untouched. We can draw upon that man power if we will equip it and look after the condition of the people behind the lines.

IN FRANCE

The story in France is more complex. France has suffered under the war more than any other country and it is small wonder that the structure of her civilization is cracking. A civilization is not made of buildings and roads, but of customs and habits, family relationships, the spirit of the people and their attitude toward their lives. There can be no question but that these things have been subjected to a terrible strain—indicated by an increase in tuberculosis, alcoholism, acute depression, lowered morale, etc. When I was in Paris the spirit was at a low ebb. Fortunately we believe the worst days are over but in France, as well as in Italy, the spirit of the people has been sustained by the civilian aid such as the Red Cross is giving. Even before the war America gave generously to France. When we entered the war there were 400 American charities registered in Paris. These different agencies have now been taken over by the Red Cross—not without some dissatisfaction among organizations which were superseded, but with a great gain of efficiency.

AMERICA'S REPUTATION

In 1915 the reputation of America in Europe was at a low ebb. It seemed that we were getting the blood of Europe in the profits of our war industries. We had a long way to go to make up our reputation. The American Red Cross ambulances were then our best symbol for the American spirit and the work of the American Red Cross has immensely increased our moral prestige in Europe.

In Europe I met few people who did not believe that war was eternal, but Americans, except those among us who are cynics, do not believe that war is inevitable. We entered the war with a feeling of faith and hope for the future. America has a great part to play in the war, not only in a military way but spiritually. We must have the deciding voice in peace. Liberal opinion in Europe regards President Wilson as the saviour of mankind and looks to him for the realization of a just settlement. What that settlement is to be depends upon what we stand for. Europe believes that if we stand for the dollar, we have little power but if they understand that our motives are unselfish our influence in the settlement will be greatly increased. An institution like the Red Cross which increases our moral prestige in Europe and our reputation for disinterested motives will add strength to our cause.

ETTELSON vs. RICHBERG

THE Richberg-Ettelson controversy, outlined in last week's Bulletin, involves issues of great importance to the gas users of Chicago. It is very much more than a personal contest between the two men for control of the gas litigation. Mr. Ettelson claims that the course of action which he has taken in backing the "Sutter suit" will procure a more expeditious and less costly settlement of the litigation in favor of the city. Mr. Richberg claims that the Sutter suit is "collusive and fictitious" and that in it defenses are raised by the Gas Company which it is prevented from making in the Circuit Court. Mr. Ettelson's participation in this case, he charges, tends to jeopardize the chances of the gas consumers to recover the ten million dollars of excess charges under the rates fixed by the Council in 1911.

At the City Council meeting last Monday, Mayor Thompson vetoed the order passed at the previous session, directing Ettelson and Richberg to take no action in conflict with the pending resolution of the "Gas-Oil Committee." That resolution directs Ettelson not to interfere with the litigation and retains Richberg as counsel pending investigation. The order was promptly passed over the Mayor's veto by a vote of 52 to 15. Later in the session, the Council, after eliminating the clauses containing criticisms of Mr. Ettelson, passed the resolution.

Another resolution of the "Gas-Oil Committee" is now before the City Council and will probably be discussed Monday, May 27th. It appointed Mr. Richberg special attorney for the city in the gas controversy, thus making the record of his employment by the City Council clear. If this resolution is adopted, the outcome of the controversy will depend upon the decision of the Court as the right of the City Council to employ special legal assistance outside the Law Department of the city.

MORALE

"ONE of the very remarkable things in this war is the preservation of the morale, both in the field and at home, of the countries in the war—if perhaps we make an exception of Russia. All of the communities have risen to a level of morale which has not been reached I think, for evenness and lack of break, in any past war which may in any sense be compared with this. One of the explanations for this, I think, is to be found in the fact that this war is being conducted by the peoples, not simply in the sense that we have conscription—conscription of men, conscription of capital, of incomes and even possibly of labor—but that it involves the intelligent activity of the entire community.

"You are all familiar with that, but I do want to emphasize the fact that we can all get into this war, into the conduct of it, in some sense; that we are not simply called upon to give—give our life and give our money—but that we can actually help to take part in it. That is responsible for the fact that the nations all over the world have stood up as they have. It is a bit of psychology that only in those causes in which you can be yourself active can you be continuously and uniformly interested."—GEORGE H. MEAD, at the City Club, May 8, 1918.

IT IS THE PENALTY of those who do not come to the noon meetings of the Club that they often miss some unusually interesting things which lack of space prevents us from publishing in the Bulletin.

THE LOW DUES OF THE CLUB are maintained in order that the membership may be on as broad and democratic a basis as possible.

COMMITTEE MEMBERS! The City Club library has a large collection of material on your special subject.

Bolshevik Power Rests on Force

*Must Hold National Election and Surrender
Dictatorship to Gain Allies' Support, Says Yarros*

THE soviet government in Russia is holding its power at the point of the bayonet, said Victor Yarros in his address at the Club last Thursday. It is a self-appointed government, representing only a minority of the Russian people. It is to have the support of America and the Allies, it must show that it really stands for freedom and democracy by putting itself to the test of a national election.

TOO MUCH SENTIMENTALITY

There is as great danger today of sentimentalizing about Russia, Mr. Yarros said, as here was a few months ago of exaggerating her so-called "treason" to the allies. We should by all means win Russia for the allies, for not to do so would be to push her into the arms of Germany and of Czarist reaction. We should do this, however, not by flattery or by a recognition of the bolshevik minority, but by a perfectly candid exposition of what Russia must do as a condition of our support. We should send to Russia representatives who really understand democracy, who can explain that we are against counter-revolution but that Russia, to gain our support, must establish real freedom and democracy.

"PEACE AND BREAD"

The Russian "revolution" of fourteen months ago, Mr. Yarros said, was not in fact a revolution, it was—quoting a writer in the *English Nation*—simply a gigantic, national riot for peace and bread. The Russian people had come to the point where human flesh could no longer stand the strain. It was not a people's war. The people were not consulted about it and many of them didn't know whom they were fighting or why. When the first provisional government was formed, there were only two demands in the platform of the Russian people—peace and bread. Russia, it has often been said, does not think in political but in economic terms. Famine in Russia has been chronic and when the people demanded "bread" they wanted not soup-kitchens, but permanent relief. That meant a settlement of the land question.

The new provisional government was not able to satisfy the demand for "peace and bread." The government felt bound to the allies and would have considered it treachery to make a separate peace. It would take years to bring about a settlement of the land question. The government failed to command the confidence of the people because it was composed almost entirely of men belonging to the bourgeois classes whom the people blamed for existing conditions. The provisional government had an amazing record of constructive achievements, but it could not give the people "peace and bread" and the restless intellectuals and socialists brought about their downfall.

KERENSKY

The one man who commanded the support of the radicals and was yet sufficiently moderate to hold the confidence of the more conservative elements was Kerensky. Kerensky's platform was substantially that of the first provisional government. He at no time even considered a separate peace, but his plan for a general peace conference at Stockholm was misunderstood by the allies and interpreted as "treason." The allies couldn't understand why Kerensky didn't put the "peace talkers" in jail or "shoot them down." But Kerensky knew that he couldn't do this. It was one of the tragic misunderstandings of history. Kerensky couldn't give the people "peace."

In the settlement of the land question and in summoning a national assembly, Kerensky did not act with sufficient promptness. The setlement of the land question meant the taking of the land for the peasants without compensation and Kerensky felt that this should await the action of the national assembly. He, in common with many of the leaders in the struggle for Russian democracy,—for instance, Kropotkin and Catherine Breshkovsky,—begged for patience, but the people wouldn't wait.

All the time, a new power was rising, the power of the soviets, the councils of workmen's and soldiers' deputies. They were irritating to the government. They made all sorts of charges against it. The

government felt that it could beat the bolsheviki, represented in the soviets, and then
go ahead with its reforms, but Kerensky had
failed to get "peace and bread" for the
people and in the end he was overthrown.

Whom did the new government represent?
There are several types of socialism in
Russia. There is a national and an international socialism. National socialism involves no break with Russia's past but a
building up on the foundation of Russian
institutions. It has been said that the Russian people are born socialists for they already have their village communities. The
new government represented not national,
but international socialism. It had no respect for the old institutions and was ready
to destroy the village communes. It classed
the small proprietor with the large proprietor, among the bourgeoisie. It wanted to
establish, first of all, a socialist state and
then hand down such measure of local self-
government as it considered expedient.

THE BOLSHEVIK PEACE

On the question of peace, the bolsheviki
stood for the program of the people. It
opened negotiations. But even the bolsheviki didn't want a separate peace.
Trotsky postponed the meeting at Brest-
Litovsk as long as possible, hoping to induce
the allies to join in the negotiations. He
said that although Russia did not want to
make a separate peace, it might be forced
to make one. And that was what happened.

The land problem was an easy one for
the bolsheviki. They simply issued paper
decrees saying, "The land is yours, take it."
They said, "See, we have given you peace
and land."

But they have delivered only on paper.
Has Russia peace today? There is fighting
going on in every part of Russia. Trotsky
has told Germany that if her invasions of
Russian territory do not cease, Russia
might have to raise a new army. In some
cases the peasants have taken the land but,
on the whole, the paper decrees have been
just paper decrees.

The actual government in Russia today
is the old local self-government of the peasant. The peasant is taking things into his
own hands. The power of bolshevik
government rests upon force alone. It is
taking no step toward a final settlement
of these great problems. Why? Because
it knows that it does not represent the people and it doesn't dare to go ahead. Many
of the champions of Russian liberty have
been imprisoned, papers have been suppressed, the constituent assembly has been
dissolved because the bolsheviki were so
clearly in the minority. They have defended this use of force on the ground that
it was for the benefit of the people not of
a Czar.

SOVIETS MUST SURRENDER POWER

As long as there was danger of a counter-revolution, we could tolerate almost
anything from the bolsheviki. But there is
no such danger now—and the bolsheviki
may be thanked for having made that clear.
But if the bolsheviki are for freedom and
democracy why are they afraid to put themselves to the test of a national election?
They call their government "a dictatorship
of the proletariat," but any kind of a dictatorship is inconsistent with a democracy.
The soviet are self-appointed bodies. How
do we know, without an election, that they
represent the people? The fact is that they
know they are a minority and that if they
are put out of power Russia's problems will
not be settled their way. The only ray of
light is that the leaders are now showing
some signs of moderation and willingness to
make concessions. They must put into
power with them men from other parties,
for all the brains and ability in Russia are
needed for the solution of her problems.
Until they are ready to do these things
there is no reason why we should recognize
them.

CAMPAIGNING AGAINST INDUSTRIAL EVILS.
Report of the Consumers' League of the
City of New York, 1917.

Among its other useful activities, the
League last year carried on an agitation
against "the returned goods evil." Here
are a few facts it gathered: "Twenty-five
per cent of the goods purchased at the retail stores of New York City are returned.
One-fifth of your purchases have already
been purchased by somebody else. It costs
25c to deliver a package. It costs the same
amount, minus the price of the wrapper,
when a purchase is returned." The elimination of this waste is urged by the League
as a patriotic duty.

SHAKE OFF THE INERTIA which has
kept you away from the Club and pay
us a visit. You will be surprised at the
advantages which are offered for the low
dues.

"The Postal Breakdown"

THE New York Merchants' Association has just made public the results of a nation-wide inquiry by postal experts into delays in the United States mails. The percentage of delayed letters is astonishing, says the Association. In response to letters sent to business associations in all parts of the United States, answers came from 119 different cities and towns that mail service is less prompt and efficient than formerly. "Many of them severely condemned the present service, alleging that delays are constant and protracted." In February and March, the Association sent 9,612 test letters to 82 different railroad points and of these 54 per cent were delayed for periods of from 4 to 48 hours.

CUTTING DOWN SERVICE

In locating the causes of these delays, the Association states that, concurrently with a large increase in postal business, postal facilities have been greatly reduced. Between July 1, 1916 and December 31, 1917 postal car service was withdrawn from or greatly reduced upon 44.23 per cent of the total line mileage and 25.32 per cent of the trains. This curtailment was made as an incident to the introduction of the "terminal postal station" system which the department claims is equally efficient and cheaper. The sorting of large portions of the mail in these terminal stations, the Association says, has resulted in the serious detention of mails in the terminals. Consolidation of mails into minimum space rather than frequent dispatch and continuous movement became the paramount consideration. Under the former conditions, the railroads were paid according to weight of mail, under the new conditions on a basis of floor space occupied.

The result of the new policy, says the report, is two-fold:

"(a) In some cases a reduction in the number of mail trains in order to consolidate the mails in a minimum of space, with a corresponding increase in the intervals between dispatches and corresponding delay to mails.

"(b) Insufficiency of space to provide for mails awaiting transportation at large stations. . . . It frequently happens that several trains having no mail space pass before one arrives upon which the mail can

be taken, and in some instances the delay has extended to days. . . .

"The transfer, in large part of the function of sorting the mails from railway postal cars to terminal postal stations has materially diminished the celerity of mail movement. Mail arriving unworked must remain in the terminal while being worked and must in many cases be subject of a delay of several hours."

Inferior classes of mail are particularly subjected to delays. The Association cites as an example of delays because of "unworked mail" a train from Washington to New York which during eleven days in December brought in daily from 50 to 584 packages of "unworked" mail.

"Post-office officials in Chicago and in Boston have attributed belated deliveries to the defective operation of the railway post-office branch. In Chicago the excuse was given that the postal clerks were unable to work up the mails in time to make proper distribution at Cleveland. That is to say, that the clerks on the trains east of Cleveland could not complete the separation of the Chicago mail which was therefore carried into Chicago unworked."

NOT DUE TO RAILROAD CONGESTION

The Department has endeavored to charge the delays, the Association says, to the congestion of the railroad system. Train delays, however, it asserts as a cause of delayed movement of mails has been seriously exaggerated. Eighty-two per cent of the mail trains during November were substantially on time. Many of the delays, moreover—on some trains more than 50 per cent—were due to methods of handling mail.

The Association, therefore, concludes that "insufficiency in the number of postal cars, their withdrawal from a great number of routes throughout the United States and reduction of the crews of railway postal cars appear to be the main causes of the conditions shown."

The Merchants' Association has requested Congress to create a special joint congressional committee to make a comprehensive investigation of postal methods with a view to causing such improvement therein as may be found necessary and practicable.

At the Sign of the Book

Some Library Acquisitions

DIRECT COSTS OF THE PRESENT WAR. By
Ernest L. Bogart, Professor of Economics, University of Illinois. No. 5 of Preliminary Economic Studies of the War,
published by the Carnegie Endowment for
International Peace, 1918. 43 p.

A statistical study of the money outlay
of the various belligerent countries for the
purposes of war. The author estimates
that up to December 31, 1917, the total of
such expenditures was $117,831,000,000.
The indirect costs, through destruction of
property, etc., is probably as much again.
On the other hand, the author says, the
expenditures are not all loss. In some
cases, as in the building of railways and
merchant marine, they are positively productive. It is also quite obvious, the author says, that a partial explanation of the
growing cost of the war lies in the depreciation of the money unit.

VOCATIONAL REHABILITATION OF DISABLED
SOLDIERS AND SAILORS. Letter from the
Federal Board for Vocational Education
with report. Senate Document No. 166,
65th Congress, 2nd Session, 1918. 112 p.

The nature of the problem dealt with in
this report is indicated by this statement:
"There are at present 13,000,000 wounded
and crippled soldiers in the belligerent
countries of Europe, including 3,000,000
cases of amputation." The number of disabled men for whom America will have to
care will depend of course upon various
factors which cannot be computed, including the length of the war. This report estimates fully 100,000 such men will be returned during the first year of fighting.
Vocational education of these men is
needed to insure economic independence,
avoid vocational degeneration, prevent exploitation, conserve trade skill, insure national rehabilitation, adjust the supply of
labor to the demand, and to develop new
vocational efficiency. The report discusses
the need of such education, measures
adopted by the various belligerent countries and suggestions for the work here.
The dimensions of the problem are indicated by the 35-page "bibliography of the
war cripple" at the end of the report.

Government Houses

LAWRENCE VEILLER, Secretary of
the National Housing Association,
writes in the *Architectural Record* for
April about the policy of the government
in respect to the housing of war workers.

METHODS OF FINANCE

"The policy of the Housing Administration, as thus far announced," he says,
"is to encourage the formation in each locality of a responsible housing corporation,
organized and financed by the leading
business men of that community, and to
loan to that corporation a very considerable proportion of the funds needed for
the building of workingmen's dwellings; as
a rule, the Government plans to lend 80
per cent of the total capital required.
While the Housing Administration expects
to function chiefly in this manner it also
recognizes that there will be cases where
it will be necessary for the Government to
do all the work itself; for, there will be
communities where there are isolated plants
and where there is no possibility of local
capital being interested or secured.

"Under whatever system it operates the
Housing Administration has recognized the
following principles:

HOUSING STANDARDS

"*First*: That in order to attract and
hold the right kind of skilled worker it
must build houses of an attractive type;
houses that will not only provide the essentials of light and air, shelter, warmth and
convenience of living, but also be reasonably
attractive.

"*Second*: That in order to protect the
Government's investment in the property
the houses must be built substantially and
well.

"*Third*: That in order to have the
property of use after the war the houses
must similarly be built substantially and
attractively.

"For all of these reasons the Housing
Administration has been hard at work for
some months past formulating 'Standards of
Types of Houses for Permanent Construction,' which it expects to have followed
where houses are built with Government
money." The *Architectural Record* publishes, as a supplement to Mr. Veiller's
paper, the complete text of the government's housing standards.

Commerce.

The City Club Bulletin

Published Weekly by the City Club of Chicago
A Journal of Active Citizenship

VOLUME XI   MONDAY, JUNE 3, 1918   NUMBER 22

No Luncheon Meetings This Week

NEXT WEEK

Monday, June 10, at Luncheon

Rescuing the Children of the War Zone

"The Infantile Mortality Situation in France"

DR. PAUL F. ARMAND-DELILLE,
Public Health Service, France, and Major in the
French Army.

"Child Welfare Work in France"

DR. WILLIAM P. LUCAS,
Chief Children's Bureau, American Red Cross, in France.

One of the saddest features of the European struggle has been the suffering inflicted upon the helpless children of the war zone and upon other children throughout France made fatherless by the great war. The infant mortality rate, always high in France, has been greatly increased. The American Red Cross has been doing an extensive work in caring for the war orphans, including the children from the evacuated towns.

Major Armand-Delille and Dr. Lucas who have been engaged in this work came to this country from France only last month.

How IS THIS, you City Club members? The Secretary has just received a letter from a *non-member,* which says: "I am enclosing my check for $5.00, made out to the City Club of Chicago, to express my appreciation in a small way of the fine action of the Club in opening its doors to the enlisted men during the week ends."

CHARLES D. WATERBURY, formerly of Pond & Pond, has been commissioned captain in the Quartermaster's Corps of the National Army. He has been assigned to duty in the Engineering Branch, Construction Division, where he has been in service for several months past. Mr. Waterbury is stationed at Washington.

The City Club Bulletin
A Journal of Active Citizenship

The purpose of the Club is to bring together in informal association those men who are genuinely interested in the improvement of the political, social and economic conditions of the community in which we live.

PUBLISHED WEEKLY BY THE

CITY CLUB OF CHICAGO
315 Plymouth Court   Telephone: Harrison 8278

DWIGHT L. AKERS, Editor

OFFICERS OF THE CLUB
GEORGE H. MEAD, President
CHARLES M. MODERWELL, Vice-President
ROY C. OSGOOD, Treasurer
CHARLES YEOMANS, Secretary
GEORGE E. HOOKER, Civic Secretary

EDITORIAL BOARD
HERBERT H. SMITH, Chairman
FREDERICK D. BRAMHALL   S. R. WATKINS
PAUL R. WRIGHT

$1.00 per Year - - - - 10c per Copy

Entered as second class matter, December 3, 1917, at the postoffice at Chicago, Illinois, under the act of March 3, 1879.

THE LISTENING POST

MAJOR CHARLES H. PRINDEVILLE is at Washington as assistant to the office in charge of the Engineering Branch of the Construction Division, National Army.

F. L. DAILY has entered military service and is stationed at Camp Wheeler, Ga.

ANOTHER MEMBER OVERSEAS not included in the recently published list is Dr. Ralph C. Hamill. He is in Italy in Red Cross Service. Dr. Hamill has the rank of Major.

DR. HARRY E. MOCK has just been promoted to the rank of Lieutenant-Colonel. He is assistant director of the Division of Reconstruction which is planning the system of care for returning disabled soldiers. Dr. Mock will address the Third Annual meeting of the American Association of Industrial Physicians and Surgeons, of which he is secretary, at the Congress Hotel, Monday, June 10th, at 2:45 p. m. The subject of his address will be: "Lessons from the Reconstruction of the War Disabled, Applicable to the Industrial Army."

ERWIN R. LILLARD now has the rank of Lieutenant. He is stationed at Camp Grant.

DR. B. M. LINNELL, Major M. R. C., has been ordered to active duty in the Base Hospital at Camp Jackson, Columbia, S. C.

WE REGRET TO LEARN of the death of Mr. D. C. Prescott, a member of this Club since 1916.

FRED A. GROW, who has been engaged in Y. M. C. A. work in France for the past few months, has returned to Chicago.

LAWRENCE VEILLER, Secretary of the National Housing Association, visited us last Saturday.

NEWTON H. CARPENTER, business manager of the Art Institute, died last Monday night. Mr. Carpenter had been a member of the City Club for the last six years. He had been connected with the Art Institute since its founding, forty-two years ago. He was president of the American Association of Museums and of the Association of Art Museum Directors.

MAX LOEB AND O. E. GRIFFENHAGEN were elected vice-presidents of the Chicago Civil Service Reform Association at its annual meeting last Tuesday.

MAJOR WILLIAM B. JACKSON, Quartermaster's Corps, is stationed at Camp Merritt, N. J.

SPENCER GORDON is attending the United States School of Military Aeronautics at Champaign, Ill.

R. W. MILLER is another new recruit for overseas service with the Y. M. C. A.

YOUR PALATE and your "tummy" are the two chief objects of concern in the City Club kitchen.

ARE YOU "LOGGY" about business after a heavy feed in the middle of the day? The City Club's forty-cent lunch will satisfy your appetite without "crowding" you.

The Censorship of "Movies"

Clarence Darrow and Harriet
Vittum Debate New Ordinance

A NEW ordinance for the censorship of moving pictures, drawn by Alderman Maypole and approved by the Judiciary Committee, was considered by the City Council, Monday, June 3, and referred back to the Committee for further examination. Under the present ordinance, the censoring is done by the second deputy superintendent of police. He has been assisted in this by a paid board of censors, selected by civil service.

The new ordinance takes away the censorship powers of the second deputy and lodges them in the hands of a board of twelve. It provides also that if, in case of a refusal of a permit, the applicant should take the case into court and the court should find the picture not to be within the prohibitory provisions of the ordinance, a temporary permit shall be issued pending an appeal.

The case for and against the new ordinance was discussed by Clarence Darrow and Harriet Vittum at the City Club luncheon last Wednesday. Mr. Darrow said:

CRIMINAL OFFENCE NOW

"The proposed ordinance would make a change in two particulars only. As the ordinance stands now, and as it will stand if the proposed amendment is passed, it is a criminal offence to exhibit pictures which are obscene or which depict riots, disturbances, or scenes of that sort. The state and federal laws also make such an exhibition a criminal offence. So even if a picture which violates the law gets by the censor, the person who shows it may be arrested and the exhibition stopped.

"The present city ordinance provides that one man and one man only shall decide whether a picture should be exhibited or not. Of course this censoring is done in the name of the child. Whenever anybody wants to put something across, he always does it in the name of the widows and the orphans.

"The new ordinance proposes that the censoring power be left with a board of twelve. Such a board already exists. Its members are selected by civil service. The board looks at the pictures but if the Second Deputy of Police wants to overrule them he can do so and he does. The present censorship board is purely ornamental.

"Except for the placing of the censorship in the hands of a board instead of one man, the only other change from the present ordinance is that when a picture finds its way into court and the court says that the picture does not violate the law, a temporary permit shall be issued pending an appeal. That seems to me to be in accordance with every principle of law and right, for without it one man can prevent a picture from being shown until it is out of date.

"The people are very much agitated about this question and false issues have been raised, but there is only one issue and that is whether the pictures shall be passed upon by a representative board made up of men of different creeds, races, political opinions, etc., or by one man. Less than 10 per cent of the population of the United States live under censorship today, and in every other city of any size where censorship exists, the censoring is done by a board. Here alone we say that one man shall decide whether a particular picture contains an attack on some religion, nationality, creed, or code of morals.

ANY CENSORSHIP BAD

"To be frank, I do not believe either in the present ordinance or in the proposed new ordinance. One is simply worse than the other. The censorship itself is a medieval institution and Chicago is the most provincial city in the country in this regard. The theory of our constitution has been to leave people free to speak or to publish what they choose, holding them responsible for any abuse of this right. It is true that evil may come of this freedom, but I believe that more evil would come if we should do away with it. There are many things which ought not to be printed in the newspapers, but we don't submit our papers in advance either to a board of censors or to one man. Many people make foolish speeches, but the constitution leaves them free to talk, holding them responsible for what they say. It is an anomaly in a free country to guarantee freedom to speak, to publish, or to put anything upon the stage and to single out the moving pictures as subject for censorship."

Miss Vittum spoke in favor of the ordinance: "I did not understand," she said, "that we had come here to discuss the general subject of the censorship, but rather to consider the ordinance which is before the City Council. The people of Illinois and Chicago have gone on record in favor of censorship.

AN EDUCATIONAL ASSET

"I believe that motion pictures ought to be an important educational and social asset. I know their importance and value, particularly in a foreign neighborhood. They are a universal language. No matter what country a person may come from, he can read the pictures and enjoy them. They are one of the cheapest forms of amusement and the people do not have to go downtown to enjoy them. But how do we want this influence presented to our children? How may it be used in helping make them into the best type of American citizen? It is to answer this question that the censorship has been established.

"What has our present ordinance meant to us so far? In the days of Jerry O'Connor, before the censorship was put into the hands of the Second Deputy, whatever pleased Jerry O'Connor was passed. Jerry O'Connor was a sergeant of police. The pictures which were shown to the people of Chicago (nearly 200,000 of them visited the movies every day) were many of them unspeakable. The children in the streets were taught the newest brands of stealing, methods of breaking jail, etc., and imitated them in their play.

BEGINNINGS OF CENSORSHIP

"Under the police reorganization ordinance the censorship was put into the hands of the Second Deputy and the first person to hold this position was Major Funkhouser, chosen by civil service. He was impressed with the need of a real censorship and called into conference thirty or forty men and women from many representative groups in the city. For a time when there was any question about a picture this volunteer censorship board passed upon the pictures. The Mayor and the Chief of

(Continued on page 190.)

Some City Hall Pick-ups

EVENTS OF THE LAST FEW WEEKS have widened the split between Mayor Thompson and the City Council. On every vote affecting the Richberg-Ettelson controversy over the gas litigation, the Council has opposed him by a large majority. Last Monday his veto of the Nance resolution directing Mr. Richberg to continue in charge of the case was defeated by a vote of 53 to 15. The council also refused by a vote of 51 to 19 to ratify his appointment of E. S. Davis, Albert H. Severinghaus, and John A. Tortensen to the School Board. An interesting feature of the vote on these two questions was its political complexion. The Mayor's support came mainly from Democrats, only two of the twenty-two Republicans in the Council voting with him.

THE REFUSAL OF THE CITY COUNCIL last week to ratify the Mayor's appointments to the School Board will probably have the effect of retaining Mr. Davis and Mr. Severinghaus together with Charles S. Peterson, retiring members of the School Board, in office until after the municipal election in the spring of 1919. It was pointed out by those who proposed the Mayor's appointments that the ratification of these appointments would perpetuate the administration's control of the School Board for the next three years, although Mayor Thompson's term expires next spring.

DONALD RICHBERG seems to be winning all the trenches in his contest with Corporation Counsel Ettelson over the gas litigation. Last Monday the City Council adopted an ordinance definitely appointing him as special counsel in the gas litigation. On the previous Saturday, Judge Torrenson ruled that the City Council had the legal right to employ such counsel. The Corporation Counsel has stated that he will appeal against this ruling.

THE BOULEVARDING of a two-mile portion of Addison Street, a half section line street on the North Side, is being opposed by the City Club Committee on Highways, Bridges and Waste Disposal. The ordinance for boulevarding this street is now before the Streets and Alleys Committee of the City Council. It is advocated by property owners along Addison Street. The Club Committee takes the position that this is not a matter of merely local interest, that the city plan requires that section and half section line streets be reserved for general traffic. E. F. Hiller represented the committee last week before the Council subcommittee which has the subject in hand.

A New State Constitution?

ILLINOIS in one hundred years has had three constitutions—one adopted in 1818 upon the entrance of the state into the union, one in 1848 and one—the present constitution—in 1870. Many people in this state believe that fifty years (it would be 1920 before a new constitution could be adopted), is long enough, in these times of rapid political and social changes, to live under any one instrument of government. The constitution of 1870 is so inflexible that corrections of some of its evident mistakes, to say nothing of amendments to meet new conditions or to harmonize it with the spirit of the times have been very difficult to make.

THE COMING ELECTION

After many years of public agitation on this subject, the legislature of Illinois under the leadership of Governor Lowden, has given the voters a chance to decide whether a convention shall be called to revise the constitution. The resolution will be voted upon next November. It is the biggest political question before the people of Illinois for it may involve the form of our government for a generation or more.

"Constitutional Conventions in Illinois," prepared and just issued by the State Legislative Reference Bureau, is (or ought to be) the voters' handbook on this subject. It provides not only the historical background of constitution-making in Illinois and a careful analysis of the procedure to be followed in calling, organizing and conducting a convention, but an impartial presentation of the case for and against a convention and a statement of the problems likely to be considered.

WHY REVISE THE CONSTITUTION?

"Any argument in favor of a convention necessarily assumes the need for amending the constitution," says the report. Among the more important problems which would come before the convention, it lists and discusses the following:

1. Amendment of the taxation system to abolish the inequalities of the general property tax.

2. The initiative and referendum.

3. Reduction of the number of elective offices (the short ballot).

4. More complete suffrage for women.

5. Modification of the constitutional prohibition of legislative amendments by reference to title.

6. Limitation of Cook County representation in the legislature.

7. Increased measure of home rule for Chicago and Cook County.

8. Reorganization of the system of county and township government.

9. Needed changes in the judicial machinery.

10. Needed changes in the methods of levying special assessments and taxes and making appropriations. A number of specific proposals would be dealt with under this head.

11. Cumulative voting.

IN WARTIME

Should a constitutional convention be assembled in wartime? Would it interfere with our vigorous prosecution of the war? Would the delegates and the public be sufficiently interested in problems not bearing directly on the winning of the war to insure due consideration and a satisfactory result? The advocates of the convention reply that at the earliest, the convention could not complete its work before 1920 and that the legislature might even postpone the convention until 1921 or 1922. In any case, they say, the war is no excuse for shirking the problems of government. They do not believe that the war will interfere with careful work by the delegates or due consideration by the voters.

UPSETTING DECISIONS

Another objection to the convention plan is that a revision of the constitution would upset present judicial constructions. As the argument is stated in this report: "A new era of judicial construction would follow and confusion would ensue, not to be dispelled until the new provisions were explained and interpreted by the decisions of the Supreme Court." How do the advocates of constitutional revision meet this argument? They say:

1. The argument pushed to its logical conclusion would prevent any amendment to the Contsitution.

2. Many of the proposed changes are of a sort which would not need judicial interpretation. In many important cases, no definite constructions have been placed upon existing provisions.

3. The new constitution would undoubtedly be framed in the light of existing judicial constructions. Many of these constructions should be preserved, others should be overcome.

AN ALTERNATIVE METHOD

The "legislative proposal" method of amending the constitution is suggested as an alternative to the calling of a convention. Even its advocates admit that the method, as it is provided for in our present constitution, is seriously defective. Under it only seven amendments have been adopted in forty-seven years. Convention advocates reply that this plan has had its trial, that amendments to the amending clause have failed to win the approval of the voters on time past occasions. The work of the General Assembly in submitting amendments would not be as satisfactory as that of a convention. The revision should be more thoroughgoing than the General Assembly, faced with a mass of other legislation, would be able to make it.

"It should always be borne in mind," concludes the report, "that the convention is but a recommending body. It is a body elected by the people for one specific purpose, but its actions have no validity unless approved by the people. There is no danger of a convention's destroying any of the rights and liberties of the people, for it has no power independently of the people themselves. Even if all the changes here discussed were proposed by a convention and approved by the people, they would have the frame-work of the present government little altered, and the new constitution would be substantially the one of 1870, changed in the respects thought necessary to meet new needs. So far as provisions of the present constitution remained unchanged, nothing of judicial interpretation would be upset, and a little disturbance of legal continuity would result from changes carefully made, with a knowledge of problems presented by present judicial constructions of the constitution."

The Censorship of "Movies"
(*Continued from page* 188.)

Police stood behind the decisions of this board. The work, however, involved so much time that the board finally went to the City Council and asked for an appropriation for a paid board of censors. This was granted and the board was appointed under civil service. Thousands of pictures have been viewed by this board and only in a few cases have their decisions been reversed. But there has been so much publicity about these cases that the public has been led to believe that many decisions of the board have been reversed.

"In the first few months or two under Major Funkhouser many cases were taken into court. In every case the court sustained the decision of the board, so afterward there were very few appeals from the decision of the board.

BEST CENSORSHIP IN U. S.

"During two or three years our standards of censorship have been very definitely raised. Chicago is recognized all over the country as having the best standards in the United States. While the administration stood back of Major Funkhouser, we had the best censorship in the country, but when the Chief of Police began reversing his decisions (for the Chief under the ordinance has the final jurisdiction) vicious pictures, many of which had been prevented from coming to Chicago, began coming here—some under their old names, some under new.

"Now, when every warring country is reporting an increase in juvenile delinquency and when the Juvenile Court in Cook County reports an increase of 34 per cent in its cases during the last year, is no time to take away the protection which has been given to our children. The war is a challenge to protect our children better than we have done in the past. Why should we change our ordinance when under it we have developed the best standards in the country?

ATTACK ON FUNKHOUSER

"If Major Funkhouser is not the best man to conduct the censorship, let charges be brought against him to find out if he is or is not the proper person. Those who are opposed to Major Funkhouser should not hide behind an ordinance designed to protect the children of Chicago in order to get rid of him. If they want to fight Major Funkhouser, let them fight him openly not along paths which affect the welfare of our children. And if Major Funkhouser is separated from his position, let us hope that his successor will give us as good an administration as that which we have had under Major Funkhouser."

Replying to Miss Vittum, Mr. Darrow said that if Major Funkhouser has overruled but few decisions of the censorship board, that is in itself an admission that the board has in the main acted correctly. "I cannot see," he said, "why the city cannot trust a board of twelve men but must leave the decision to Major Funkhouser. Funkhouser is ready to overrule whatever *he* thinks ought to be overruled. I would as soon have Major Funkhouser as censor as any one man I know, but it is childish and absurd to say that any one man should have such power over us.

"The increase of juvenile delinquency can hardly be charged to moving pictures. It is due to the war. It has nothing to do as to whether or not the question of moral guardianship of the city should be left in the hands of one man.

BEST CENSORSHIP IS LEAST

"Miss Vittum says that we have the best censorship in the country. I think we have the worst censorship. We have the most but that does not mean the best. The strongest censorship is really the worst. There is nothing which can take the place of liberty even when it goes wrong. Are we children? Should we all be restricted in what we see and what we hear to what is good for the 12 or 14 year old child? If censorship had been applied throughout history we would have hardly a great book or a work of great art today.

"But if we must have a censorship it ought to be by a board representing different classes, different races, and different religions. If it cannot be left to such a board but must be lodged in the hands of a single man, then our whole system of government is wrong and democracy is a failure."

THE RESTAURANT which resorts to wheat mixtures as a subterfuge to evade its "No Wheat" pledge is not playing the game squarely.. The City Club obeys its pledge to the letter. Show that you appreciate this sacrifice by patronizing the dining-room.

GERMAN CHILDREN AND THE WAR

WHAT is happening to the child life and youth of Germany in this fourth year of war? An article by Dr. Paul Hildebrandt in the *Vossiche Zeitung,* Berlin, just made public by the U. S. Bureau of Education, tells of the early enthusiasm of German youth for the war and of their attitude today. "Dark shadows," according to the article, "are falling over the brilliant picture of 1914."

THE LOWERING OF STANDARDS

"Who can wonder," asks Dr. Hildebrandt, "that now in the fouth year of war our children exhibit signs of change? Too many of the restraints have been removed which should shape their development—the loosening of family ties, the father at the front, the mother employed away from home, and in the lower ranks of society doing the work of men; the omission of school discipline. Of the teachers of the Berlin public schools, for instance, two-thirds have gone into the army. The remainder are overworked.

POOR NOURISHMENT

"In addition, as time went on, especially in case of the students of higher institutions, and particularly in the towns, the hardship of inadequate nourishment appeared. It is the unanimous judgment of medical specialists that the children of the middle classes suffered most in this respect. General attention was attracted to the fact that the children were less sensitive to reproof, that they paid no more attention to threats, because the school authorities had directed that they should be treated with every leniency, and since promotions no longer represented any definite standard of accomplishment. . . .

"That spirit of voluntary service which at the beginning of the war revealed itself in its fairest aspect has now disappeared. Everywhere we hear lamentations over the increasing distaste shown for military service. Pupils collect articles now for the reward, not from patriotism, and the older pupils have their struggles. Shall they take advantage of the opportunity to leave school with a half-completed education, or shall they avoid placing themselves in a position where they will have to enlist for their country? . . .

"Furthermore, in these ranks of society which are less influenced by tradition, discipline, and education, we find increasing violations of the law. At the first this manifested itself merely in an increase of theft. More recently it has taken a decided turn toward personal assaults. It is true, the latter are still negligible in proportion to the total number of juvenile offences, but they are increasing every year. Already the number of violent crimes committed by youths in the city of Berlin is more than three times the number reported in 1914.

"Thus, dark shadows are falling over the brilliant picture of 1914. Every disciplinary influence, every effort of the still fundamentally sound German nation must be exerted to oppose this tendency, and to lead the children back to the path of rectitude."

COAL WEEK

THE week of June 3-8 has been designated "Coal Week" by the United States Fuel Administration, and there will be a special intensive drive throughout the United States during those days to urge the early ordering of coal. The State Council of Defense has issued a bulletin on this subject which says in part:

COAL SHORTAGE FEARED

"A very serious economic situation again faces us for the coming winter. There is every indication that unless strenuous measures are taken at once, there will be another and even worse coal shortage than existed during last winter. During the period from October 1st to March 31st the consumption of coal far exceeded production and while production is steadily increasing, it must be further augmented in order to obviate the danger of crippling our war industries, delaying the shipping of supplies and, what is still worse, actually impeding the progress of sending our soldiers to join our allies."

ORDER NOW

The State Council of Defense urges upon individual domestic consumers the immediate necessity of storing as much as possible of their winter's supply of coal, crowding and expanding their storage capacity to the utmost limit. It urges retail dealers to get ready to supply the domestic demand by placing their orders early and to expand their storage to the farthest limit, so as to carry as great a reserve as possible into the winter season with the hope of preserving it intact until January. It urges purchasers not to be over-fastidious in the kind or quality of coal they exact. They should be willing to use the coal that is available and, preferably, that which is nearest home. They are also admonished to make every effort to use screenings for current use. The enhanced demand for prepared sizes caused by the storage campaign will flood the market with screenings which cannot be disposed of unless a strenuous effort is made by every steam user to burn screenings for the current summer consumption.

TO GET MAXIMUM PRODUCTION

"Early buyers of coal should not get impatient if their orders are not filled promptly," says the State Council. "The intention of the early buying campaign is to flood the producers with orders so there will be no excuse for either mines or railroads to lose a single day's production. Delay in filling orders will mean that the campaign has been successful."

"IT WOULD BE DIFFICULT to overestimate the importance of bringing about the adoption at the November election of the proposal to hold a Constitutional Convention in Illinois. A thorough overhauling of the present Constitution is absolutely necessary to place the people of this great State in a position to deal properly with problems that confront them at this time and those that undoubtedly will arise out of this war. Unless our form of government is a failure the people can safely be trusted to act wisely and fairly upon the proposition submitted to them by a Constitutional Convention. I believe that if a Convention is called it will bring together as fine a body of men as ever sat in any similar body in any State, and that their work will prove vastly beneficial to the entire commonwealth. In my opinion no public service that can be performed by any one who cannot go to the war is more patriotic than to help to carry the Convention proposition at the coming election."— Governor Lowden.

CIAL! Arranged after going to press!
Wednesday, June 12, at luncheon
onditions in Sweden and
inland During the War"
Karl G. Dernby from Stockholm

The City Club Bulletin
A Journal of Active Citizenship

VOLUME XI   MONDAY, JUNE 10, 1918   NUMBER 23

TODAY!
Monday, June 10, at Luncheon
Rescuing the Children of the War Zone

"The Infantile Mortality Situation in France"

DR. PAUL F. ARMAND-DELILLE,
Public Health Service, France, and Major in the French Army.

"Child Welfare Work in France"

DR. WILLIAM P. LUCAS,
Chief Children's Bureau, American Red Cross, in France.

SPEAKING AT 1:00

America's Wasted Water-Power

Club's Utilities Committee Urges Measures to Protect Great National Asset

THE City Club Committee on Public Utilities last week in a letter to the House Committee on Water Power at Washington recommended a number of amendments to the water-power development bill, proposed by the administration.

Private corporations have for years been urging the greater development of the water-power resources of the country. Legislation to bring this about has been before Congress at many sessions. It has been charged by conservation advocates that this proposed legislation was selfishly inspired and did not sufficiently protect the rights of the public. The Shield's water-power bill, which has been a target for the conservationists, has twice passed the Senate —the second time last December.

There has now been introduced in the house, however, a bill which, according to Mr. Gifford Pinchot, meets the objections to former proposed legislation on this sub-

The City Club Bulletin
A Journal of Active Citizenship

Published Weekly Except July, August and September; bi-weekly during July, August and September

CITY CLUB OF CHICAGO

315 Plymouth Court   Telephone: Harrison 8278

DWIGHT L. AKERS, Editor

EDITORIAL BOARD
HERBERT H. SMITH, Chairman
FREDERICK D. BRAMHALL   S. R. WATKINS
PAUL R. WRIGHT

$1.00 per Year - - - - 10c per Copy

Entered as second class matter, December 3, 1917, at the postoffice at Chicago, Illinois, under the act of March 3, 1879.

ject and "opens the way to save for the people of the United States their most valuable national asset." It was formulated under the direction of the Secretaries of War, of Agriculture and of the Interior and has the backing of President Wilson. It proposes to create a federal power commission, consisting of the secretaries of these three departments, with an executive officer in charge. The commission would be authorized to issue licenses for periods of not to exceed fifty years for the construction and maintenance of hydro-electric power plants on the navigable waters of the United States or on streams upon the public lands. A condition of any grant is that the project must be "such as in the judgment of the commission, will be best adapted to a comprehensive scheme of improvement and utilization for the purpose of navigation, of water-power development and of other beneficial public uses." A minimum annual compensation to the government is provided for.

KEEPING THE WAY OPEN

The proposals of the City Club Committee on Public Utilities in reference to this new bill are for the purpose of further protecting the opportunity for a policy of public ownership and control. "Every reasonable encouragement and facility should be provided," says the committee, "for the expansion of government ownership and complete control of public utility service undertakings and natural resources. On that basis, water power or like resources should not be tied up in private hands without the right or power to recover for a long period."

The bill, as it stands, provides for the recapture of the rights and the properties by the government, upon an agreed valuation, at the expiration of the license term. The committee recommends that provision also be made whereby the United States, *a state or a municipality* after five years from the date on which the first part of the project is put into operation might acquire or recover on a year's notice the property and rights of the licensee. The committee recommends (in fairness to the investor who may have made large initial expenditures without a material return) that in case the project is taken over by the government before the expiration of twenty years from the time of the grant a bonus shall be granted to cover development cost. The maximum bonus, the committee suggests, should be 10 per cent, with ½ percent reduction for each year the plant has been operated.

FOR A JUST PURCHASE PRICE

The committee insists that ample depreciation, redemption, renewal and sinking-fund account provisions should be made, based on the cost value of the property, so that, in case of government acquisition, the property may be obtained at its true physical value at the time of purchase. Bond issues should also be limited in amount so that the property may not be unduly loaded when the government is ready to take it over. The committee recommends that in the valuations for purchase, no allowance be made for good will or for the "going concern" value of the enterprise.

Finally, the committee proposes that the government be empowered not only to regulate the rates for the sale of power but to charge a license fee for the use of power if it is employed in the production of staple articles of interstate commerce. The purpose of this recommendation is to prevent undue monopoly advantages in production resulting from the possession of cheap water power. The bill as drawn provides for regulation of rates, service and security issues by the regulatory bodies of the several states and in cases where such bodies do not exist or where interstate agreements cannot be reached, the exercise of such power is reserved to the federal commission. Interstate rates must be "reasonable, non-discriminatory and just to the consumer." The Public Utilities Committee accompanied its letter by a draft of the amendments needed to put its proposal into effect.

Housing War Workers in Chicago

City Club Institutes Inquiry
at Request of Government

THE City Club last week, at the request of the government, and with the co-operation of the Chicago School of Civics and Philanthropy, undertook an important piece of war work.

Thousands of new workers are coming to steel towns of northern Indiana to enlist in the great war industries which have grown up there like mushrooms. These towns do not have sufficient housing accommodations for the workers brought in by this rapid expansion of industry. As in other great war-work centers, the finding of decent living quarters for the army of industrial recruits is essential to the uninterrupted production of war supplies. So serious is this problem in many places throughout the country that Congress has provided an appropriation in excess of a hundred million dollars for the construction of new houses.

PROVIDING TRANSPORTATION

The government is also endeavoring, wherever possible, to supply the housing needs of the war industries by providing special transportation facilities by which workers may utilize housing accommodations at some distance from their places of work. In the case of the Indiana towns, it is attempting to ascertain the possibility of housing the workers at points in Chicago quickly accessible by train. It has been represented that there are many vacant houses, apartments, and rooms within a ten-minute car ride of the Englewood Station, from which express trains could be run to the war-work centers.

In order to ascertain the housing opportunities within this area, the Housing Bureau at Washington on May 31st wired the City Club to undertake a census of the vacancies to be found there. The call was urgent, the time allowed was short. A conference was called immediately, the work was planned and the investigation in the field started last Tuesday. It involved, besides a count of the vacancies an investigation of the character of the accommodations offered. The investigators were provided with cards on which they recorded the facts concerning the rentals, conditions as to heat, light, sanitation and other information which a prospective tenant would wish to know. Approximately 350 blocks were covered in the survey.

SCHOOL SUPPLIES WORKERS

The investigation was carried out mainly through the assistance of the Chicago School of Civics and Philanthropy, which provided thirty-six trained investigators for the work. Several volunteer workers from other sources were also enlisted. The survey was under the immediate supervision of Mr. Harry K. Herwitz, whose services were loaned by the Chicago Bureau of Public Efficiency, and of Miss Helen R. Wright, of the Department of Social Investigation, School of Civics. The City Health Department also aided by a special plumbing inspection.

The field work for the investigation covered a period of three days. The returns have been tabulated and a preliminary report forwarded to Washington.

To Help Win This War

This Club, at the request of the U. S. Food Administration, has disregarded its own interests by voluntarily agreeing to serve no Wheat in any form until the present wheat shortage is relieved.

NEW MEMBERS

Arden B. Lapham, Jr., Lapham Bros. & Company (hide brokers).

Bruce B. Paddock, Vice-Pres., Atlas Exchange National Bank.

Edmond W. Pottle, attorney.

Walter L. Read, Editor, Lyons & Carnahan.

Bowen W. Schumacher, Attorney.

Colin McK. Tennant, Robert G. Tennant & Son (insurance).

Boutelle J. Williams, C. M. & St. P. Magazine.

LUCIUS TETER last week was appointed regional director of the Chicago zone for the War Industries Board. This zone includes the northern part of Illinois and a portion of Indiana and of Iowa.

OSCAR E. HEWITT, formerly of the Chicago Herald, has left for England, France and Italy on special assignment to collect data for articles to be published by the Y. M. C. A.

WILLIAM L. CHENERY has accepted an appointment with the Committee on Public Information in Washington.

JOHN W. SCOTT of Carson, Pirie, Scott & Co. has accepted appointment as chief of the newly-created textile division of the War Industries Board. Mr. Scott will assist in such matters as arranging for co-operation with government bureaus in furnishing their supplies of textiles and textile products, in establishing and maintaining relations between the board and the industry and in determining with the industry the procedure to be followed in meeting civilian requirements.

WATCH FOR the Ham and Egg 40c special. The fry cook was swamped the last time it was on the bill.

CITY CLUB SIRLOIN a la minute is the steak that makes your mouth water.

OUR CHICKEN SALAD is the pride of the culinary department.

THE MAIL POUCH
Clean Bathing Beaches

Municipal bathing beaches will be open June 14th, according to an announcement of the Department of Public Works last week. Here is a letter from the Chairman of the Bathing Beach Committee of the Woman's City Club which contains a suggestion in this connection which ought to be remembered:

The Committee on Bathing Beaches of the Woman's City Club has endeavored from year to year to interest the public in keeping the bathing beaches free from refuse. Will you be willing to insert in the spring issues of your bulletin a notice to this effect? We feel that if our club women and men set the example and spread the publicity the public will probably follow suit.

There are on most of the beaches waste baskets where refuse can be deposited and at several beaches there are men employed in picking up refuse matter constantly. Perhaps by calling the attention of the public to these facts we will be able during the coming season to keep our beaches in better shape than the administrators have been able to do without the co-operation of the public.

(Signed) MRS. M. L. PURVIN.
Chairman, Bathing Beach Committee.

ON YOUR GUARD!

Please refrain, when in public places, or before strangers, from any remarks of a nature to weaken patriotic energy and confidence in our leaders and in our Allies, or from statements regarding the number or movement of our troops, the work in munition plants, etc. Information overheard may be reported where it can give aid or comfort to our enemies.

The above notice is being published throughout the country by the Fifth Avenue Association of New York under authority from the committee on Public Information, Washington, D. C. The Wartime Committee of the City Club recommends it to the attention of our members.

The City Club Bulletin
A Journal of Active Citizenship

VOLUME XI   MONDAY, JUNE 17, 1918   NUMBER 24

The Human Side of Tommy Atkins

Next Thursday, June 20, at Luncheon

ADA WARD of London

Official Entertainer to the British War Troops in France

"My Experience While Entertaining the Troops at the Front"

"The series of entertainments given by Miss Ada Ward and other concert artists have afforded the greatest pleasure to thousands of soldiers behind the firing line," says the *London Sketch*.

SPEAKING AT 1:00

Our Ambulance in France

THE City Club ambulance on the West Front has been serving on a quiet sector, according to our latest information. But even a quiet sector has its moments of interest. A recent letter from Rembert C. Anderson, the driver of our car, says in part:

"Was interrupted last night by the call of *'Americaine une voiture tout de suite.'* It was raining out, and what a ride I did have! Some places in among the trees it was so dark that I had to stop and wait for a star shell to light up the road for me. Of course I ran in low speed until I got out of these trees. On one side of the road is a mountain and on the other side a high fence of burlap camouflage, so that ahead, while it rained, was dense blackness. I could just make out the dim sky by looking up and guiding by that. One place I heard a wagon ahead and he heard me and both of us stopped. I pulled over to one side, hoping I wouldn't go into a ditch, and 'hollered' to him, 'allez,' and, by George, he nearly took something off the back of my car as he passed.

"When I reached the tirage it had stopped raining. The 'couche' in back, who had been wounded by machine gun fire, probably thought he was going to Paris from the length of time it took me to get him to the tirage. The poor old devil had another ride before him then, as one of the tirage cars took him immediately to a hospital further back."

Mr. Anderson also describes an air battle which he witnessed. In this fight, a French "75" brought down a German air-

The City Club Bulletin

A Journal of Active Citizenship

Published weekly Except July, August and September; bi-weekly during July, August and September

By the CITY CLUB OF CHICAGO

315 Plymouth Court   Telephone: Harrison 8278

DWIGHT L. AKERS, Editor

OFFICERS OF THE CLUB

GEORGE H. MEAD, President
CHARLES M. MODERWELL, Vice-President
ROY C. OSGOOD, Treasurer
CHARLES YEOMANS, Secretary
GEORGE E. HOOKER, Civic Secretary

EDITORIAL BOARD
HERBERT H. SMITH, Chairman
FREDERICK D. BRAMHALL   S. R. WATKINS
PAUL R. WRIGHT

$1.00 per Year - - - - 10c per Copy

Entered as second class matter, December 3, 1917, at the postoffice at Chicago, Illinois, under the act of March 3, 1879.

man. A piece of *"éclat"* struck within twenty feet of Mr. Anderson, after which, he says, he "ducked." "The Frenchmen think that Americans have no fear at all," he writes, "because we generally stand out and watch shells break, while a Frenchman will always break for an *abri*. The truth is that they have had three years and a half of it and know better than to take chances, while we are fascinated by the novelty."

Water Meters

NEXT Thursday, June 20th, is field day at the City Hall for those who have ideas on the subject of water meters. The Subcommittee on Water Meters, consisting of Aldermen Capitain, chairman, R. H. McCormick and Woodhull, reported to the Finance Committee last Friday a set of ordinances designed to bring about a general metering of Chicago within the next ten years. The Finance Committee has set next Thursday afternoon for a public hearing on these ordinances.

The ordinances provide that after August 1st all new premises must be metered. All existing service pipes are to be metered by districts and as rapidly as possible. All premises within a district are to be metered without discrimination. The city would own all meters and pay for their installation and maintenance out of the water fund. The present rate of 6¼

cents per thousand gallons would be retained, with a minimum charge of $4 per year for each household or other single occupancy. This minimum charge would be about 40 per cent. less than the present flat-rate minimum charge for similar premises.

If the proposed ordinances are passed it is expected that about a million dollars a year will be expended on water-metering during the next ten years, during which time the work of metering existing premises would be completed. It is expected, however, that the metering will make unnecessary expenditures for a large amount of new construction which would otherwise be require to make up for the water wastage.

The ordinances follow, generally speaking, the proposals of the Chicago Bureau of Public Efficiency in its report on water metering published last January. Harris S. Keeler, Director of the Bureau, discussing these ordinances last Saturday, said: "The adoption of these ordinances would make it possible to render better service to the consumers of water in Chicago. In the first place, the great reduction in water wastage would bring about better pressure conditions and allow water to be served regularly to the higher floors of buildings which at certain periods of the year, because of insufficient pressure, are only irregularly supplied. In the second place, the small consumer who is careful to avoid unnecessary waste and leakage would have his bills reduced from one-third to one-half. At the present time he is paying for the wastage by his neighbors. If water meters are not installed, an increase in water rates seems unavoidable for the expenditure for more pumps to make up for the wastage has depleted the water fund to such an extent that higher rates would have to be charged."

The proposal for universal metering has been endorsed by the City Club Committee on Water Supply. It also has the approval of the Woman's City Club, the Political Equality League, the Civic Federation, and the Citizens' Association. Other citizens' organizations are also considering the subject.

CITY CLUB COFFEE is the solution of the drink problem.

THE FORTY-CENT LUNCH is a popular feature in the dining-room.

The Future of Music Extension

By Victor S. Yarros, Chairman City
Club Committee on Music Extension

In the following article Mr. Yarros discusses the city's present opportunities for musical enjoyment and its need for more and better music and a wider audience. He invites suggestions on the subject for the consideration of the Music Extension Committee. They may be addressed to the Editor of the Bulletin.

WHAT more should be done in Chicago in the way of the peopleization of good music? Has not this city all the good music it can possibly assimilate? If there is a lack in any direction, just what is the lack, and what the particular direction?

Such questions as these have been asked of, and by, the members of the City Club committee on music extension. They are legitimate and interesting questions. Members of the Club who have ideas on the subject are cordially urged to give the committee their ideas. Meantime the writer, having pondered the matter for years, will set down a few suggestions of his own. They are not original, but they will bear repetition.

CHICAGO'S PRESENT OPPORTUNITIES

Remarkable progress has indeed been made in Chicago in the way of civic music extension. The Civic Music Association has done splendid work and would do even more and better work if it were more liberally supported. It has the right idea. It brings music to the people. It uses neighborhood centers, schools, small parks and school buildings in spreading the gospel of musical appreciation. It encourages community singing. It sends good musicians into sections remote from the loop and not likely to patronize the great musical organizations of the city. There is no limit to its activities; the only limit it is obliged to consider is financial.

The Chicago Symphony Orchestra gives each season a remarkable series of ten popular, low-priced concerts. No city in America offers any opportunity comparable to this to its humble lovers of music who aspire to full understanding and enjoyment of the regular symphony concerts

and the high-class recitals. The programs of the popular concerts are ideal. All we can ask is that the trustees of the orchestral association shall persevere and, if possible, slightly extend the series. It is doubtful whether sufficient patronage could be counted upon for more than twelve such popular concerts.

We have other good orchestras that give fairly interesting concerts at popular prices. One of these gives a few concerts each year in some of the city's schools. More concerts should be given in the schools, and this too is a question of funds.

OUR CHIEF PRESENT NEED

What we need more than anything else is an improvement of the scheme and methods of teaching music in the public schools. Here a radical overhauling is necessary. Music can be taught in a dull, uninspired, wearisome way, and it can be taught in a way that arouses love of and enthusiasm for all forms of good music. A feature of sound and vital musical instruction in the schools should be a series of young people's concerts and recitals. Special programs should be arranged and interpretative talks given for the benefit of the children. that are being introduced to the world of beautiful and significant music. The cultivation of love and enjoyment of good music should begin at school, and this implies competent teachers of music and sound, intelligent methods. In our schools the teaching of music is admittedly inadequate and perfunctory.

POPULAR CHAMBER MUSIC

What Chicago further needs is a systematic effort to popularize chamber music. The experiments made in this direction by the City Club committee were full of promise and encouragement. A series of chamber music recitals at popular prices —the programs being carefully arranged and all purely technical or academic or ultra-modern compositions being rigidly excluded—would gradually attract a sufficiently large group of patrons and amply justify itself as a means of elevating the musical standards of the community. Will some generous friend, or friends, of chamber music come to the rescue and support a chamber music organization? The committee has plans and ideas concerning chamber music, but it has no funds.

EDUCATION AND PLEASURE

The public demand for good music is great. Only, it must be intelligently met. Education should always go hand in hand with pleasure, and yet the public should be given not "what it wants," or thinks it wants, but what it can be taught to enjoy and admire. One or two compositions on each program should always be a little ahead of the average taste and standard. To give the same repertory year after year, especially if it be narrow and limited, is to alienate many potential music lovers from the popular art and produce the wrong impression on them. Hackneyed music is destructive of interest in and love of music. Variety is the spice of musical as of other vital activities. Professional musicians, and especially professional conductors and program makers, are as a rule not sufficiently in touch with the lay, amateur patrons of concerts and recitals. Much could be done for music extension if the musicians and lovers of good music had a club or other organization, or common meeting ground, where they might exchange notes and ideas regarding programs, new composers, tendencies and currents in musical life.

ALBERT A. HENRY is camp secretary for the Y. M. C. A. at Rockford.

ARTHUR M. BARRETT has left for France to engage in Y. M. C. A. work.

ALBERT B. DICK, JR., has entered the service of the United States Navy. He will be stationed at the Great Lakes Camp.

WE HAD A VISIT last week from Edward L. Burchard. Mr. Burchard is editing "The Community Center," official organ of the National Community Center Conference. His headquarters are at Washington.

RECENTLY WE REPORTED the appointment of Walter L. Fisher as the representative of the Ship-Building Labor Adjustment Board for the Great Lakes District. Mr. Fisher now has Irving K. Pond and Professor F. S. Deibler as associates in this work.

DR. JOHN R. WILLIAMS, of Rochester, N. Y., was the guest of the City Club Wartime Committee last Wednesday. Dr. Williams is the author of a report of milk distribution methods in Rochester, recognized as one of the most convincing demonstrations of the wastes and extravagances of competitive milk delivery systems.

ADDISON L. WINSHIP, civic secretary of the Boston City Club since 1907, is retiring from that position to engage in business.

SYDNEY STEIN, a member of the Club since 1914, died last week. He was a member of the law firm of Stein, Mayer and Stein.

CAPTAIN JAMES A. BRITTON visited the Club last week. He is division tuberculosis specialist at Camp Wheeler, Macon, Ga. Dr. Britton says that the United States Army is the "best ever."

PRESIDENT HARRY PRATT JUDSON of the University of Chicago has been made chairman of a commission which is to leave the United States for Persia within a month to make a survey of conditions there and to determine upon methods of relief. Persia is reported to be suffering both from lack of food and from disease.

A POSTCARD FROM LONDON received by Mr. Hooker last week from Major A. J. Carlson reads as follows: "The Gothas have been trying to make us step lively in these parts of late, but once here we feel sure that in the end the waltz is not going to be one of the Hun's liking." Before going overseas, Major Carlson, who is professor of physiology at the University of Chicago, was engaged in scientific work at Washington in the Food Division, Sanitary Corps, Surgeon-General's office. He was formerly chairman of the City Club Committee on Public Health.

Children of the War Zone

BECAUSE the children of a nation are its secondary defenses, because upon them depends the future of the nation, France today, with the co-operation of the American Red Cross, is undertaking a great program of child conservation. The child welfare work of the Red Cross there was described at the City Club luncheon last Monday by Dr. W. P. Lucas, chief of the Children's Bureau of the Red Cross in France. Dr. Paul F. Armand-Delille, of the Public Health Service and Major in the French Army, told of the work which his government is doing for children, particularly for the *repatriés* returning from the occupied portions of France through Switzerland.

IN THE TOUL SECTOR

The staff of the Children's Bureau of the American Red Cross has grown from eleven to about four hundred within a year, according to Dr. Lucas. There are about fifty or sixty doctors and the remainder are nurses and aides. The first work of the bureau, undertaken within a week of landing, was to take charge of a colony of evacuated children from the Toul sector. The order had gone out that children under seven (unable to wear gas masks) be removed at least twelve miles behind the lines. Over 2,000 children have thus been put in charge of the Bureau. It established a hospital, which now has two hundred beds, including fifty maternity beds. From this beginning, hospital and dispensaries have been placed at other points behind the lines. During the recent offensive the Bureau has been conducting emergency camps to care for refugee women and children. A similar service has been started for refugees in Paris.

But not all the work of the Children's Bureau is in the war zone. It has been aiding the French government in caring for *repatriés*. One of its most acute problems has to deal with the children of the congested refugee centers. Lyons, for instance—before the war a city of 450,000—has become a city of over 700,000 through accessions of war-workers and refugees. Building under war conditions was not possible, so temporary shacks were built to meet the congestion. To solve the special problems arising out of this condition, the Children's Bureau established a contagious diseases hospital, a hospital for acute cases and a convalescent home. Similar steps were taken in Bordeaux and other crowded centers.

EDUCATIONAL WORK

Educational work is an important part of the Bureau's program. Infant welfare exhibits giving information about prenatal care, nursing, children's foods, dental hygiene, etc., have aroused much interest. Seventy-two thousand people visited the exhibit at Lyons in the first nine days. Courses for "health visitors" have been established on a co-operative basis by the French government, the Rockefeller foundation and the Children's Bureau in connection with the tuberculosis and children's welfare work in a number of large cities.

Major Armand-Delille, who spoke particularly of the work among the *repatriés,* was for two years engaged in sanitation work at the Dardanelles and Saloniki. The *repatriés* are mostly women and children and very old people who are discharged from the occupied districts through Switzerland. Many of these people are in bad physical condition. They are given medical care and precautions are taken to prevent the importation of contagion.

Major Armand-Delille is studying American "infant welfare" methods.

A Farm for Prisoners

THE CITY OF CHICAGO is soon to establish a municipal Farm Colony for men prisoners of the House of Correction and a House of Shelter for women, if plans approved by the Finance Committee last Friday are ratified by the City Council. The creation of these two institutions was recommended by the Merriam Crime Committee in 1915 and a bond issue of $250,000 to provide the necessary funds was approved by the voters. There has been a long delay in putting the plans into effect owing to the need of obtaining additional enabling legislation and to the difficulty of finding an appropriate site. A site has now been found.

Both institutions are to be located, if the proposed plan is adopted, on a 372-acre tract near Willow Springs. The farm colony for men will contain 346 acres. It is expected that about 200 men from the House of Correction will be placed upon it during the summer months and about 40 men in winter. The work to be done by these men will consist of truck gardening, dairying and other farm work. The appropriation asked for the farm colony is $173,000, $100,000 of which is for land and the balance for live stock, farm implements, horses and trucks, equipment of buildings, water service and sewering, dairy buildings, greenhouses, heating plants, etc.

The farm colony plan is in accordance with modern ideas for the reformation of prisoners. The men during their service on the farm would be taught habits of industry and their environment would be more conducive to reform than the environment of the House of Correction. This reclamation work is the primary purpose behind the farm. At the same time, the men, with the produce raised on the farm, would contribute financially to their own support. It is estimated that this produce would amount to thirty or forty thousand dollars per year.

The appropriation asked for the House of Shelter for women is $48,400. The House of Shelter would be located on property adjacent to the farm colony.

Where Chicago Stands

A recent statistical study of thirty-six American cities, published by Reed College, Portland, Oregon, attempts to rank these cities in respect to eighteen different categories.

"Readers should be on guard against drawing conclusions from this study which surpass the evidence," says the report. In some cases the available data were not very recent and the ranking in such cases may be very different today. Nevertheless, however crude and tentative the figures may be, they are perhaps roughly indicative and Chicagoans will be interested in observing the ranking accorded "the Windy City." Chicago stands as follows:

1. Highest wage rates (average union wages in cents per hour in ten trades, 1914)   6th
2. Lowest cost of living (index numbers of the retail selling prices of seventeen food commodities, 1914)   11th
3. Lowest death rates (per thousand of population, 1911, corrected to a standard age and sex distribution)   16th
4. Lowest infant mortality rates (death rates of infants under one year per 1,000 born in 1915)   21st
5. Highest per cent of population married (25 years of age and over), 1910   8th
6. Largest church membership (per thousand population, 1916)   19th
7. Least child labor (per cent of children from 10 to 15 years of age, gainfully employed in industry, 1910)   17th
8. Largest park area per inhabitant, 1915   29th
9. Largest per cent of street area paved, 1915   13th
10. Least annual fire loss per inhabitant, 1910-14 .   18th
11. Largest amount of public property (in value) owned by city, 1913   25th
12. Largest circulation of library books for home use, per capita, 1910*   29th
13. Highest school attendance (children 6 to 20 years of age, 1910)   22nd
14. Largest amount (value) of school property per child in attendance, 1915   11th
15. Largest teachers' salaries, 1913-14   5th
16. Smallest number of pupils per teacher in public schools, 1913-14   35th
17. Least illiteracy (per cent of population 10 years and over unable to write, 1910)   18th
18. Fewest foreign born unable to speak English, 1910   30th

Safety First!

SAFETY FOR THE HOUSEHOLD. Circular No. 75, U. S. Bureau of Standards. January, 1918, 127 p.

"The hazards of the home have increased in modern times from the service of gas and electricity and the use of such dangerous articles as matches, volatile oils, poisons and the like," says this report. It treats comprehensively proper methods of installation and the personal precautions which are necessary to avoid accident. It is too voluminous and technical for general circulation, but it provides just the sort of information an Accident Prevention Committee should have in conducting safety propaganda for the home.

WATCH FOR the summer cold specials. Extra scouts are out looking for new ones. Send us your suggestion.

*These figures represent the conditions prevailing in the Chicago Public Library at the beginning of Mr. Legler's administration. Chicago now ranks high in this field.

One Thousand Dollars for Your Ideas

A HOUSING competition, with five prizes ranging from $100 to $1000, is announced in the Journal of the American Institute of Architects for May. The Journal describes the purpose of the competition, in part, as follows:

"While the indispensable contribution which architecture has to make to the world-wide problem of the house is of the highest importance, the experiences of the last half-century, in all the leading nations of the world, have demonstrated beyond further doubt that society must now and in some manner grapple with and correct those fundamental economic laws which have produced their cycles of congestion and slums in all our communities. . . . Land and building speculation continue to be the prime motives behind all housing undertakings, with the exception of those where there is sought a certain result which may be measured in terms of labor stability.

"As a result, we are continually piling up a more and more mountainous barrier between society and the democracy we profess to seek, while our communities, one and all, are given over to speculation, to congestion, and to all the evils of our unchecked policy of development, in which the individual is permitted to take his profit, no matter what loss or damage he may cause the community.

"With these bald facts now staring us in the face—with the known condition of landlordism to which the United States has descended as though inexorably doomed to the fate of other nations—with the knowledge of that huge loss in time and money in our war-making activities, due to bad housing and no housing—with the certainty that as a nation we must now boldly face this insistent social and economic problem with which the future of the United States is indisolubly bound up, the Journal of the American Institute of Architects believes that the time has come when we must cease the futile application of philanthropy and charity to the house problem, discontinue the hopeless attempt to solve the problem by restrictive legislation alone, and offer a positive and constructive program which may in some manner serve as a basis for future effort."

The competition is open to all citizens of the United States and Canada. It will close October 31, 1918 and the solutions will be reviewed by a jury of which Thomas R. Kimball, President of the American Institute of Architects, is chairman. The competition is under the general auspices of the American Institute of Architects and the Ladies' Home Journal. Full details can be obtained from the Journal of the American Institute of Architects, Octagon Building, Washington, D. C.

Should We Use Our Traction Fund for This?

THE CITY OF CHICAGO has incurred an indebtedness of about five million dollars to the Sanitary District, principally for the installation of the new street lighting system but partly also for current. The 1910 contract provided that the cost of the street lighting improvement should be met by the city in six annual installments, but the city because of its straitened financial condition has been unable to make these payments. Since 1916, judgments under this contract amounting to about three million dollars have been entered against the city in favor of the Sanitary District. Unless the city should find some extraordinary source of revenue for paying the other installments, judgments will presumably have to be confessed up to the full amount of the indebtedness—

which is now about five million dollars.

It is now being suggested that the city buy up these judgments with a part of the twenty-seven million dollars in the traction fund. The corporation counsel has given an opinion that such an investment from the traction fund would be legal. The plan was considered at the meeting of the Finance Committee last Friday. Objections to the plan were raised by some of the aldermen and the proposal was laid over for later consideration.

Harris S. Keeler, speaking for the Chicago Bureau of Public Efficiency, said that the trustees of the Bureau had given the proposal preliminary consideration and were unanimously of the opinion that it would be very bad public policy to use the fund for such a purpose.

Health Insurance

HEALTH INSURANCE as a subject for social legislation in this country is in the stage of intensive study by the states—apparently repeating the history of workmen's compensation legislation. Workmen's compensation, which, within a few years, has been almost universally adopted by the states as a method of dealing with industrial accidents, was preceded by a series of almost simultaneous investigations by official state commissions. In nine states at the present time—including Illinois—official commissions are studying the question of health insurance. Recently a joint conference of all these commissions was held at Cleveland for an exchange of experiences and methods.

It has often been said that organized labor is opposed to health insurance. Broadly speaking, this statement is inaccurate. The New York State Federation of Labor has approved the principle of health insurance and has drafted and introduced in the New York Legislature a bill for its adoption. The President of the California Federation of Labor in a recent letter said: "The American Federation of Labor is a democratic organization. We have taken no action as yet, as an organization, in the matter of health insurance. In eleven states, organized labor has gone on record for it, the New York Federation of Labor recently passing it without one dissenting vote. Organized Labor is on record here in California for health insurance, because we believe that it offers the same protection against the risks of illness that industrial accident insurance now gives against the hazards of industrial injury."

Remaking Men

THE American Association for Labor Legislation estimates that during the next three years if the war lasts, America must be prepared to care for 120,000 men disabled by the war. It calls attention, however, to the additional heavy toll which industry will take. There are now it says fully 100,000 disabled industrial workers in America.

"Social necessities," says the Association, "have developed wonderful possibilities of vocational re-education providing for the maimed and crippled the power of self-support, self-respect and economic usefulness. Clearly there is not a day to be lost if we are to do our duty by the boys who risk their future earning capacity for the ideals of democracy. And the industrial army likewise must be conserved!" The bulletin of the Association is sent in support of Senate Bill 4284 now pending in Congress for re-educating war cripples under the direction of the Federal Board of Vocational Education. The Association is also working for an amendment to this bill which would permit *industrial cripples* to regain their economic usefulness through the same system.

Club Committee Starts Work for New State Constitution

THE State Constitution Committee of the City Club, which is to work during the coming months for the adoption of the constitutional convention resolution at the polls next November, had its first meeting last Friday. Andrew R. Sheriff is chairman of the committee. An Executive Committee, consisting of Mr. Sheriff, chairman, George C. Sikes, vice chairman, Frederick D. Bramhall, William S. Hay, and Charles M. Thomson, was appointed to plan and direct the work.

The membership of the Committee is as follows:

Andrew R. Sheriff, chairman

Harry Brown	H. G. Spaulding
C. R. Holden	L. A. Stebbins
Harold F. White	W. F. Dodd
Frederick C. Woodward	James G. Skinner

A. A. Rolf	A. A. McCormick
Shelby M. Singleton	John P. McGoorty
Major E. B. Tolman	William D. McKenzie
John A. Fairlie	William R. Medaris
James J. Forstall	Walter Clyde Jones
Samuel B. King.	Everett L. Millard
John J. Arnold	Fayette S. Munro
Farlin H. Ball	Roy C. Osgood
Frederick D. Bramhall	Philip S. Post, Jr.
Randall W. Burns	Donald Richberg
J. Francis Dammann	Henry Schofield
Brode B. Davis	Charles H. Sergel
James A. Davis	John D. Shoop
Eugene H. Dupee	George C. Sikes
Stephen A. Foster	Douglas Sutherland
Clarence N. Goodwin	Charles M. Thomson
George I. Haight	J. Lyle Vette
William S. Hay	Victor S. Yarros
Henry Horner	Hubert E. Page

The Committee discussed plans of work for the coming months.

The City Club Bulletin
A Journal of Active Citizenship

VOLUME XI   MONDAY, JUNE 24, 1918   NUMBER 25

WEDNESDAY, JUNE 26, AT LUNCHEON

"Shall Chicago Have Universal Water Metering?"

A discussion of an ordinance pending before the City Council

HARRIS S. KEELER

Director, Chicago Bureau of Public Efficiency

FRIDAY, JUNE 28, AT LUNCHEON

"America's Labor Mission to the War Zone"

JOHN P. FREY

A Member of the Mission

The rise of the English and French labor groups to greater political power, their formulation of labor's war aims and their demand for social and political reconstruction after the war have been among the most significant tendencies of the year. The American labor mission to England and France brings important news of these great movements.

SPEAKING AT 1:00

Life on the Ocean Wave

"TO GO ALOFT in a howling breeze may tickle a landsman's taste," according to the Gilbert-Sullivan song of several decades ago. But before the war, steam transportation and our big "hotel" liners were making the sea rather uninteresting and unromantic. "Fritz," with his mines and U-boats, is making the sea interesting again for the adventurous landsman. Perhaps that has something to do with the enlistment of so many of our City Club members in the Navy of Uncle Sam. Some of them are already seeing service and more are in course of training. Some are doing important work in various branches of the service "behind the lines."

AYRES BOAL, who before the war was in the prosaic business of "real estate," is now ensign on a destroyer and presumably chas-

(*Continued on page* 210)

The City Club Bulletin

A Journal of Active Citizenship

Published Weekly Except July, August and September; bi-weekly during July, August and September

By the CITY CLUB OF CHICAGO

315 Plymouth Court   Telephone: Harrison 8278

DWIGHT L. AKERS, Editor

$1.00 per Year - - - - 10c per Copy

Entered as second class matter, December 3, 1917, at the postoffice at Chicago, Illinois, under the act of March 3, 1879.

THE LISTENING POST

JASPERSEN SMITH, of the law firm of Montgomery, Hart & Smith, died last Tuesday. Mr. Smith had been a member of the City Club since 1912. His death was a shock to his many friends in the Club.

PROF. P. ORMAN RAY, of the Department of Political Science, Northwestern University, is to teach at Columbia University during the summer session.

WE ARE GLAD to welcome into membership in the Club the following persons, who joined last week:

Henry M. Brooks, Secretary Wisconsin River Power Company.

J. Paul Clayton, Commercial Manager, Middlewest Utilities Company.

Albert E. Lucius, lawyer, Lucius & Lucius.

J. F. de la Motte, lawyer, Mayer, Meyer, Austrian & Platt.

L. E. Schoenfeld, Vice President Garibaldi Company, importers.

J. F. Strouse, Assistant Sales Manager, J. P. Black Company, printers.

RAYMOND ROBINS, head of the American Red Cross Mission to Russia, has returned to America. He arrived in Chicago yesterday (Sunday). Mr. Robins left Moscow on May 14th.

OF COURSE, CAPTAIN MERRIAM couldn't stay away from the fight! A dispatch from Italy concerning the present Austrian offensive says: "One phase of the battle, a secondary operation near Lake Garda, had as spectators Judge Ben Lindsay, and Capt. Charles E. Merriam of Chicago. During a luncheon with the colonel commanding they were able to note the progress of a successful counter-attack. The colonel left them temporarily, but returned before the dessert was over and announced that the operation had been entirely successful. Judge Lindsay spoke to a group of Italians from the United States and was able to realize how much of the heart of America is in the Italian and with what enthusiasm the Americans announce their intention of returning to the United States after the war. Lindsay and Merriam departed for Venice to meet Rizzo, the popular hero of the day."

EVERETT W. LOTHROP, formerly a member of the Club staff, is a lieutenant with the A. E. F. A letter received from him last week says that he is stationed at a large camp where newly arrived soldiers are "cleared" for the front.

E. S. BALLARD, formerly attorney for the City Club Milk Committee, has written from France to acknowledge a letter of appreciation from our directors. Mr. Ballard is in the service of the Director-General of Transportation, A.E.F. He says of his work for the Milk Committee:

"I felt honored in being selected for the work and the approval of the Committee is most gratifying. The preparation and trial of the case and the daily conferences at the Club were exceedingly interesting and enjoyable and your letter makes my recollection of those rather strenuous weeks even pleasanter than before. Please give my cordial remembrances to all of the Committee's members and accept my thanks for your kindness in writing.

"This piece of work over here looks rather long, but I am glad to be in it and have no doubt of the ultimate outcome."

The Finnish Revolution

Wealthy Classes, Backed by German Military Power, Make Finland Vassal State

"THE collapse of Russia and the subsequent events in Finland, which have ended in making that country virtually a German province, have entirely changed the Scandinavian situation," said Dr. Karl G. Dernby of Stockholm, speaking at the City Club luncheon, June 12. "Prior to the war there was an equilibrium between Russia and Germany in the domination of the Baltic. Swedes and even Norwegians regarded Russia as the most dangerous of their neighbors and, without any deeper love for Germany in other respects, looked upon her as a safe counter-balance to Russia. Denmark, however, ever since Germany robbed her of Schleswig, has been decidedly but silently anti-German. But when it became evident that the main issue of the Kaiser's game was not to save Europe from the Russian barbarian, as the German press liked to say, but to establish a world hegemony, most people in Scandinavian countries changed their views. And his ruthless warfare, especially the treatment of neutral vessels, also caused great losses in the number of his sympathizers.

PRO-GERMANS POWERFUL MINORITY

"The only country where the pro-Germans played any role was Sweden. Some persons in that country, few in number but rather powerful, have constantly tried to drag Sweden into the war as a vassal of German. As to their number, it may be said that the conservatives in the second chamber have only 58 out of 230 seats, and that the 'activists' constitute only a very small fraction of the conservative party. They are to be found among officials, army and navy officers, the clergy and university people. The most significant thing is that behind all the 'activist' movements can be traced German-Finnish conspiracy.

"A brief review of the events in Finland will explain this: The bulk of the population in Finland, about three and a half millions, consists of Finns, a rather pure Mongolian race. There are also in Finland about four hundred thousand descendants from Swedes, who many hundreds of years ago conquered the country. There have always been racial struggles between these two layers of population. The Swedes are as a rule the governing class. They are the wealthiest and the most cultivated. In many respects they are like the Prussian junkers. Therefore the social controversies in Finland have been most bitter.

TRAINS "WHITE GUARD" LEADERS

"In 1809 Sweden had to give up Finland to Russia. For many years Russia treated Finland liberally, but about 1890 the Czar tried to deprive her of all her rights and make her a Russian province. This united for a time both Finns and Swedes, socialists and conservatives, in a stubborn resistance to Russia. Germany soon understood how to profit out of the situation and years before the war planned to stir up anti-Russian movements in Finland. During the war, more than two thousand young Finlanders were taken over to Germany and given military education, in order eventually, with Swedish assistance, to go back and start a revolution. Those became later on the officers of the 'white guard.'

"The Russian revolution broke out and made Finland free. But the different population layers could not keep together. The socialists had a narrow majority in the diet of 1916. At the new election they lost it and that created a lot of discontent. Still more discontent was aroused by the formation of a bourgeoisie 'white guard.' This was followed by the establishment of a 'red guard' by the workingmen. Who really started the civil war it is impossible to say. But it was started. First the 'whites' were defeated, but after obtaining German assistance, they were able to claim the victory. Incredible atrocities were committed by both sides—the 'whites' especially seem to have slaughtered their prisoners en masse.

IN THE KAISER'S GRIP

"Who deserve our sympathy? It is impossible to judge easily, the situation is too complicated. But the 'reds'—poor, ignorant, cruel though they may be—fought for the freedom of their country and for their constitutional rights, whereas the educated, wealthy 'whites,' in order to save the culture and wealth of Finland and to keep down their political opponents, fought to make their country a German vassal state. Of course many 'white' Finlanders look on this regretfully, but it cannot now be helped. Finland is at present in the Kaiser's grip and he holds military control of both the Baltic and the ice coast. The Scandinavian countries now have only one power to fear. To resist Germany with military force would mean suicide. They have to remain neutral because they are between the devil and the deep sea."

The Mail Pouch

If you have a good idea, why not "pop" it in your own "vox pop"? The following letter was received last week:

Inefficient Marketing

"DEAR SIR: For a number of years it has been my custom to ride south on Western Avenue to the Beverly and Midlothian Country Clubs, and I have seen great numbers of wagons on this road coming north late in the afternoon, loaded with farm produce which, according to my understanding, is hauled to our South Water Street markets, the wagons getting in there early the next morning. It seems to me that this is a most inefficient method of bringing this produce to our markets. I realize the fact that it would be difficult to get the co-operation of the railroads in handling this, but it seems to me that arrangements could be made with the street car company to provide cars for the handling of this produce—the farmers to bring their wagons to the car line terminals, their produce to be packed into the street cars and hauled during the night downtown to the nearest point possible to our markets.

"It seems to me that our Club would do well to interest itself in this idea, and, if possible, lead to a more economical handling of this produce."

(Signed) L. H. CRAWFORD.

Wanted—Y.M.C.A.Workers

NATIONAL WAR WORK COUNCIL
Y. M. C. A.
347 Madison Ave., New York.
My Dear Sir:

At the suggestion of Dr. Orr of our Educational Department, I am writing to ask your co-operation in discovering secretaries for our Y. M. C. A. work in Italy. We need fully 200 before the middle of July who can qualify for this work in the Italian Army and I shall esteem it a great favor if you can bring to my attention any desirable candidates. We can send Italians who are forty-five years of age and Americans above draft age; no clergymen can be sent.

(Signed) CHARLES D. HURREY.

Legislation by Lawyers

"THE National Voters' League has just completed an investigation to discover the occupational character of Congress. The result is most interesting and significant.

"An overwhelming majority of voters throughout the country are farmers and laborers. Yet there are only 6 farmers and 4 representatives of labor among the 435 members of the House. The Senate has only 3 farmers and no laborers among its membership of 98.

"Lawyers predominate in both branches, with business men next in number. Of the 435 House members, 306 are lawyers and 90 are business men. This leaves 39, divided as follows: Newspaper men, 26; farmers, 6; laborers, 4; salesmen and clerks, 5; preachers, 2; educators, 3; physicians, 2, and social worker, 1. The latter is Jeanette Rankin, the only woman member.

"In the Senate 76 of the 98 are lawyers. Thirteen are business men, 2 newspaper publishers, 3 farmers, and 2 physicians."—From "The Searchlight on Congress."

THE DRIFT INTO WAR SERVICE continues among our members. All the more reason why you should loyally back the Club at this time.

WHY NOT INCREASE the number of your acquaintances at the Club? If you see a member sitting lonesomely by himself at lunch, introduce yourself.

C'MON, SKINNAY! Strawberry shortcake at the City Club every day!

Cleveland Meters a Success

Prove Practicability of
Chicago Meter Ordinance

THE proposal to meter Chicago's water supply was given a "boost" last Friday by E. W. Bemis, public utility expert for the city and formerly head of the Cleveland Water Department. Prof. Bemis spoke in favor of the proposal at a public hearing of the Finance Committee of the City Council. The entire City of Cleveland was metered under Prof. Bemis' direction and the results there, he claims, are a convincing argument for universal metering. Prof. Bemis is a member of the City Club Committee on Water Supply, which has endorsed the proposal for a general metering of Chicago.

WHOLE CITY METERED

"Scarcely 2 per cent of the premises in Cleveland are now unmetered," said Prof. Bemis. "That metering is popular there is shown by the fact that it has been continued and extended under different administrations and that the appropriations for meters have been passed by the City Council unanimously.

NO DISCRIMINATION

"The Cleveland plan was similar to that proposed for Chicago, namely, that the work should be done by districts and that all premises within a district should be metered without discrimination. The city protected the revenues of its Water Department and guarded against any tendency among consumers to use too little water by charging a minimum bill, as proposed in the ordinance under consideration here, though in a somewhat different form.

STOPS WASTE AND SAVES MONEY

"The effect of metering in Cleveland was to stop the waste. People found they could get all the water they wanted, if they would only cut out the leaks.

"What effect did the stoppage of water waste have on the need for new construction? When metering was adopted, Cleveland was just putting in a new pumping station, but this was to replace an old station and did not increase the pumping capacity of the city. From this time, 1904, to 1911, there was no new construction except in one district which would otherwise not have been served.

"My belief in the value of meters has been confirmed. At first there was popular prejudice against them, but the consumers have saved so much in their bills that they do not worry about meters any more. The fear that the health of the people might be impaired passed away in a few months when it became evident that there would be no such result."

CITY ENGINEER FAVORS METERING

The Chicago metering proposal was also advocated at this hearing by City Engineer Ericson. A survey of the Chicago water system has convinced Mr. Ericson that from 60 to 70 per cent of the water pumped in Chicago is wasted. Pumpage requirements, he said, have increased faster than the population. "Under existing conditions we cannot add tunnels and pumping stations rapidly enough to keep up with the growth of the city. After my investigation I came to the conclusion that the only solution is metering."

HEALTH CONDITIONS GOOD

Dr. Bundeson of the Health Department said that hundreds of communities which have been metered show a reduction in sickness and death rates rather than the contrary. It is often true, he said, that, where the faucets are left running, toilets are not properly flushed. He predicted that health conditions would be better rather than worse under a metering system.

The proposal was explained to the Committee by Harris S. Keeler, Director of the Chicago Bureau of Public Efficiency. Mr. Keeler is to address the City Club at luncheon on this subject next Wednesday, June 26.

At a subsequent meeting of the committee, last Saturday morning, the meter ordinance was approved for passage. It now goes to a vote of the City Council.

The metering of the city involves an expenditure of ten million dollars during the next ten years. It involves the water rates which you will pay for years to come. It is claimed that metering will save Chicago many millions of dollars. As a citizen and as a consumer of water you should hear Mr. Keeler's discussion of this important subject, next Wednesday.

Life on the Ocean Wave

(Continued from page 205)

ing Hun U-boats. He hints at some adventures worth telling about, but for the present those are deep, dark secrets. Before entering active service, Ensign Boal spent four months at Annapolis, learning the tricks for "strafing" Fritz.

LIEUTENANT HERBERT H. EVANS, formerly secretary of the City Council Committee on Local Transportation, is allowing others to settle Chicago's traction questions, while he "puts in his licks" for Uncle Sam at the Norfolk Navy Yard. Lieutenant Evans directed the overhauling of several of Germany's big boats, commandeered by the U. S. A., and their refitting for service in the cause of the allies. He is at home at this writing on a ten-day furlough. Lieutenant Evans is not a new recruit in Uncle Sam's Navy. He is a graduate of Annapolis and was on the Indiana when Sampson—or was it Schley?—sent Cervera's fleet to Davy Jones' locker in 1898.

ROBERT M. CURTIS, after a three months' intensive training course at Annapolis, was awarded his anchor as ensign and was put in command of a submarine chaser. Good-night Fritz! Ensign Curtis is only twenty-two years old, but it will be an unlucky U-boat that gets in his path. He is a son-in-law of Alfred L. Baker, formerly president of the City Club.

OGDEN T. McCLURG has the rank of lieutenant commander, with headquarters in the office of Capt. Moffett, Great Lakes Station. He has charge of the Ninth, Tenth and Eleventh Naval Districts.

ARTHUR H. BOETTCHER of Brown, Hanson & Boettcher, patent attorneys, is in the ordnance department of the naval aviation service. He is stationed at Washington. The reports of his effective work there, particularly along engineering lines, are confirmed by his recent promotion from the rank of ensign to that of lieutenant.

LIEUTENANT E. H. CLARK, of the firm of Otis & Clark, architects, has since May or June of last year been in charge of the public works office at the Great Lakes Naval Training Station. This office supervises all the construction work for the station.

Two of our members are helping to hold the money bags:

LIEUTENANT D. HIMMELBLAU, formerly of the accountancy staff of the North-western University School of Commerce, is assistant paymaster, stationed at Washington.

E. L. JOHNSON, of the Harris Trust and Savings Bank, is similarly employed, with the rank of ensign. He is at present at Harvard University taking a special course in cost accounting for naval construction.

JOHN A. JAMESON is a lieutenant in the naval reserves and is stationed at Great Lakes.

HENRY B. FREEMAN didn't have to leave Chicago to do his bit for Uncle Sam. He is a lieutenant in the naval ordnance department with headquarters in this city. His duties relate to the inspection of work on government contracts. Lieutenant Freeman was formerly a fire protection engineer with the Underwriters' Laboratories.

FRANK VAN INWAGEN, vice-president of the Illinois Engineering Company, is now Ensign U. S. N. R. F. and is in training at Annapolis before going into active service.

LIEUTENANT MALCOLM MACNEILL is executive officer of the naval auxiliary reserve school at the Municipal Pier. This is a school for the training of future officers of the navy.

ENSIGN JAMES CURTISS is instructor in navigation at this school.

DR. JOHN F. URIE is in charge of a naval hospital which is located just outside New Orleans.

A. B. DICK, JR, and H. F. OATES are the most recent recruits. Mr. Dick has just enlisted and, according to latest reports, is still "in detention" at the Great Lakes Station. Mr. Oates joined the naval auxiliary reserve school at the Municipal Pier last week.

Who's next?

THE ELIZABETH McCORMICK Memorial Fund which has been one of our sixth-floor tenants for several years is soon to move to larger offices in the Tower Building. The National Conference of Social Work will then move from its present office on the sixth floor into the rooms which are being vacated. Our sixth floor has so far been occupied only by civic or social agencies and it is hoped that in renting the space vacated by the National Conference another tenant of this sort will be found.

THE CLUB'S BAKER makes heavenly pies.

Should We Amend Our Constitution in Wartime?

"IF the proposal for a constitutional convention in this state is voted down next November," said Governor Lowden, addressing a meeting of the Midday Club recently, "you are going to meet the great problems growing out of the war with your hands tied by an iron-clad constitution, unresponsive to the changing conditions incapable of amendment. The situation will be serious." Governor Lowden in this address answered as follows the argument that no attempt should be made to alter the Constitution in wartime:

WAR MAKES CHANGES NECESSARY

"A good many people say, 'But the war is on.' In my humble opinion, that is the most persuasive reason in favor of a constitutional convention at this time. The war will bring new problems.

"We are not going to abandon the essentials of our old Constitution. Any new Constitution that we may adopt will take the old Constitution of 1870 as its groundwork and will build around that and modernize it in the way in which it would have been modernized if it had not been for the illiberal provisions against amendments which it now contains.

PREPARE FOR ACTION NOW

"If this resolution passes next fall the next General Assembly will be called upon to provide for the convention. If the war is still on and they in their wisdom so decide they can postpone the convention to 1920. Or, suppose they do not postpone it, the 102 men are elected; when they meet they have it absolutely within their power—there is no restraint upon such action by the convention—to adjourn from time to time just as has been done in Arkansas under similar circumstances, until in their judgment the time is propitious. If they wish to postpone actual forming of the Constitution and adoption until the war is over, that power is with them. *But when the war is over you are in a situation to act, you are in a situation to make our Constitution comply with our needs.*

"If on the other hand this resolution is voted down next autumn no one can tell when we will have a chance again to amend the Constitution. Because under the Constitution, with minority representation, there are enough of men in the General Assembly who probably are voting themselves out of office, to defeat the two-thirds vote required in order to submit the Constitution, and those of you who have been familiar with the efforts made in late years know how difficult it has been to secure such a resolution. . . .

HANDS TIED

"If it be voted down next fall you are going to meet the great problems growing out of the war with your hands tied by an iron-clad Constitution, unresponsive to the changing conditions, incapable of amendment. The situation will be serious because, let me tell you, any man who believes that a Constitution when it no longer meets the needs of the times is a safeguard against revolutionary action is relying upon a false philosophy. A constitution must develop to meet changed conditions. . . . If anyone thinks that a Constitution can permanently safeguard any right of the individual when that Constitution is permanently opposed by a majority of the people he does not understand the essence of democratic government. One of two things will be inevitable if we have to meet changed conditions without changes in the Constitution which will enable us to meet these changed conditions. Either the Constitution will be disregarded, and our Supreme Court, coerced by the absolute need of the time, will be driven possibly to a strained construction of many of its provisions, thus doing another and equally great injury to the cause of orderly government, or government will itself break down.

OPPORTUNITY OF DECADE

"My opinion is that we miss not only the opportunity of this decade, but we miss our most imperative duty if we refuse to vote for this resolution next fall. *My deliberate opinion is that we do untold injury to the orderly development of our State and its institutions if we fail to have the courage to face the representatives of our people in a constitutional convention and thrash out deliberately these great questions that are in the popular mind.*"

ARE YOU A GOOD SOLDIER? If so, you will not grumble because we are serving no wheat in the club dining-room. We are doing this at the request of Mr. Hoover.

The Human Side of Tommy

The human side of Tommy Atkins was pictured to our members last Thursday by Ada Ward of London. She has seen Tommy in France under all sorts of conditions except those at the firing line—on his way to the front, during his rest period, behind the lines, in the hospital to which he has returned, perhaps shattered in body and mind.

A "Comic Stunt"

Miss Ward was in France as an entertainer for the British soldiers. Her dreams of going to France as a new Joan of Arc vanished, she said, when the opportunity to go came as an invitation to furnish a ten-minute "comic stunt" with a British concert party. She went, she took her blackboard and did her "stunt" and she has returned to tell us what she thinks of "Tommy" Atkins.

Among the pictures which she drew for us last Thursday was one of the hospital where her first appearance was made and of the wounded—some carried in, some limping in, some groping in, eager for the amusement which was to be provided for them. She found them a cheery lot after all. "One boy, so battered and bandaged that only one eye was visible, still managed," Miss Ward said, "to wink at me with that eye." Another picture was that of a great audience at a military camp, packed together, perspiring, suffocating and smoking till it was almost impossible to see across the room. "I was thoroughly smoke-cured before I left France," said Miss Ward.

A Case of Nerves

Miss Ward told many stories of the boys —not the least pathetic and amusing being that of the Tommy who, after eight days in the trenches, lost his nerve at the sight of clean sheets and wept for an hour and a half.

Miss Ward thinks that Tommy is "splendid." He is not the ungodly, uncouth person that he is sometimes pictured. He is after all, only a big child, with a naive sense of humor and an infinite capacity for fun.

Summer Reading

The Public Library has just placed the following books on deposit in the City Club Reading Room. They will remain there for three months:

Balzac—Old Goriot.
Barclay—White Ladies of Worcester.
Beach—The Ne'er Do Well.
Beach—The Net.
Bottome—The Second Fiddle.
Brown—The Prisoner.
Burnett—T. Tembaron.
Campbell—A Soldier of the Sky.
Dilnot—Lloyd George.
DuMaurier—Peter Ibbetson.
France—Crainquebille.
Harrison—Angela's Business.
Howells—The Rise of Silas Lapham.
Kelley—Over Here.
Kester, P.—His Own Country.
Knyvett—"Over There" with the Australians.
Kyne—Webster—Man's Man.
Lagerlöf—The Emperor of Portugallia.
Leacock—Further Foolishness.
Leblanc—Golden Triangle.
Lowndes—The Red Cross Barge.
Mason—The Four Feathers.
Munday—Eyes of the Army and Navy.
Nepean—My Two Kings.
O'Brien—Best Short Stories.
Oppenheim—The Pawns Count.

Poe—Tales.
Poole—The Harbor.
Poole—His Family.
Porter—Oh, Money! Money!
Rocheleau—Transportation.
Shaw—Plays Pleasant and Unpleasant.
Sparks—Men Who Made the Nation.
Spring—Non-Technical Chats on Iron and Steel.
Stevenson—A King in Babylon.
Strindberg—Plays.
Talbot—Submarines—Their Mechanism and Operation.
Train—The Earthquake.
Trolloppe—Barchester Towers.
Turgenieff—Fathers and Children.
Turgenev—Smoke.
Walker—Portmanteau Plays.
Webster—Just Patty.
Wells—Bealy.
Wells—Vicky Van.
Wharton—Custom of the Country.
White—The Leopard Woman.
Wright—The Winning of Barbara Worth.
Zangwill—The Master.

THE KITCHEN STAFF wants to put on the bill of fare your favorite summer dishes. Write your suggestions to the chairman of the House Committee, City Club.

The City Club Bulletin
A Journal of Active Citizenship

VOLUME XI   MONDAY, JULY 1, 1918   NUMBER 26

ANNOUNCEMENTS

There will be no luncheon meetings this week or next, unless announced by a special postcard.

Beginning with this issue and for the rest of the summer, the Bulletin is issued every two weeks in homeopathic doses of four pages.

To afford members an opportunity for shooting firecrackers and re-reading the Declaration of Independence, the Club House will be closed all day next Thursday, the Fourth of July.

The address by John P. Frey on the labor situation in Great Britain and France was crowded out of this week's issue. We will print it in our next number.

One of Our Flyers

WHEN the City Club purchased an ambulance for service on the West Front, it was planned that Mr. Gale Willard, a member of the Club, then in France, should be its driver. At the last minute, Mr. Willard changed his plans and joined the aviation corps. A cablegram from France last week announced that Mr. Willard—now a lieutenant—had been mentioned for bravery in action.

LEARNING TO FLY

Lieutenant Willard's training with the LaFayette Escadrille began in June, 1917, and he was breveted in October. Then he was sent to Pau for acrobatics, and afterward was with the French at Belfort. Last February he was ordered to report in Paris for transfer to the American Army,

and, while waiting, was sent by the French to a school for shooting in the forest of Chantilly. Some of his experiences at this school, as related in a letter to his mother, are printed below. In March he was given his commission in the American army and ordered to the front.

A Chicago newspaper last week, in referring to Mr. Willard, said:

"Gale Willard, one of the American youths mentioned in the dispatches, was called before his fellow soldier comrades and given the insignia that tells to the world that the wearer is worthy of special mention for his brave acts. He is the son of Mr. and Mrs. Charles E. Willard, 6018 Stony Island Avenue, and although only 23 years old has won the certificate of appreciation awarded to him by the French

The City Club Bulletin

A Journal of Active Citizenship

Published Weekly Except July, August and September; bi-weekly during July, August and September

By the CITY CLUB OF CHICAGO

315 Plymouth Court   Telephone: Harrison 8278

DWIGHT L. AKERS, Editor

$1.00 per Year - - - - 10c per Copy

Entered as second class matter, December 8, 1917, at the postoffice at Chicago, Illinois, under the act of March 8, 1879.

government for his services in the French aviation branch of the service. This certificate was forwarded by him to his parents and was only received by them a few days ago. And the message coming to them today telling of his services with the American flyers completed the joy in their home, where he is the only son."

SOME LETTERS

Two letters, long delayed in transit and just received, have been sent us by Lieutenant Willard's mother and are printed below, in part:

March 14, 1918.

I am at a shooting school in the heart of one of the oldest forests in France. The forest is very beautiful, no undergrowth. It is just such a spot as we fancy Robin Hood and his merrie men gamboled in.

I had quite an interesting time today. I shot from a plane at a target on the ground. We have a Vickers machine mounted on the plane so that when you fire the plane has to be turned in the same direction, in other words to aim the gun you aim the machine. The French—all of them—glided at the target so that they had to get the up and down as well as the sidewards (this is a bit obscure but I hope you understand it). I dived perpendicularly at the target with the result that I put ten balls in it. The target is a huge white object built in the shape of an airplane. Of course when I came down I was most severely reprimanded for having dived so steeply. I said one had to do that way at the front. To which the lieutenant merely shrugged his shoulders and said, "But this is not the front." There was nothing to say to that kind of reasoning and so I retired as gracefully as possible. The lieutenant then put out his hands and congratulated me heartily as having broken the record.

The Boches come every night on their way to Paris. The lights have to go out at the first alarm. The French are furious. They say two or three times a week is all right but that every night is disgusting. The other night a bomb struck the corner of a hangar

destroying that part of the building, threw dirt all over the place but injured "nary a one." The Huns then slipped along to Paris and "tossed a few eggs."

April 3, 1918.

I received my own machine yesterday and it was camouflaged to the Nth degree, but is almost new as it has had but a few hours in the air.

PATROLLING IN THE CLOUDS

I had a patrol yesterday and took my new machine. It went off the ground well enough. I climbed steadily until I had thirty-five hundred metres when the clouds closed in under me. In coming down thru the clouds I shut off the motor. It's an eerie feeling. You are all enclosed in a white fog with not even the tips of the wings visible. There you are sliding down thru the enveloping wet white cloud with just your feet, hands and instruments visible, and, always when you come out, the machine is lopsided, nose high or something off.

Today I took out the machine to try out the machine gun. There is a large field near us with a white cross on the ground which constitutes the target. I got off all right, and went up to five hundred metres, nosed the plane over, threw the gun in gear and fired. One of the great inventions of the war has been the synchronizing of the gun with the propellor, a statement which means so timing the gun that it will only shoot when the blade of the propellor is not in front of it. In the early days of the war the aviators used to touch their hats to each other and sail on by. Then it was the French pilots, we must confess, who started taking up shot guns. After that Garros, who so recently escaped from Germany, conceived a plan of putting short slabs of steel on each blade of the propellor so that, altho some of the machine gun bullets would be deflected by the metal, the vast majority would go through. Then came this last invention which is really a remarkable though rather complicated one.

AN AIR "CIRCUS"

The group flying of the airplanes is really a most beautiful sight. There is a bombing squadron here which has all the machines ready to start from the ground at once when going out to make a raid. The planes, at a given signal, leave the ground at intervals of about thirty seconds. Then place themselves in goose formation above the field and fly away. You know each escadrille has a distinctive mark painted on the fuselage and so when a number of planes all of the same type and all with the same insignia leave in a formation it is really a very interesting sight.

To Avoid a Water Shortage

And to Keep Rates Down, Our Water
Supply Should be Metered, Says Keeler

THE only sure and satisfactory method of improving our water service and of avoiding higher rates is to meter our water supply, according to Harris S. Keeler, Director of the Chicago Bureau of Public Efficiency, who addressed the City Club at luncheon last Wednesday. Mr. Keeler spoke in support of the water meter ordinance recommended by the Finance Committee and now pending in the City Council.

WATERLOGGED

"The Chicago water works," said Mr. Keeler, "is pumping 260 gallons of water per capita per day—more than is pumped by any other American city except Buffalo and about twice as much as can possibly be consumed for any useful purpose. Of this we know that the amount used for industrial purposes, which is now metered, is equivalent to about 50 gallons. Statistics from places like Cleveland, Milwaukee, and Oak Park, where metering is universal, show that an average of about 40 gallons per person per day is all that can be made any real use of for domestic purposes. If to these two items is added that which is used for public purposes—fires, parks, etc. —and that which is lost through leakage in distribution, it will be found that a daily per capita pumpage of about 125 gallons would provide an abundant supply for Chicago. Thus more than half of the present pumpage is lost through waste and leakage which can be prevented. This preventable loss is equal to the load of 700 sixty car freight trains daily. It exceeds the combined pumpage of Milwaukee, Cleveland, Boston, and St. Louis. To pump this wastage requires the consumption of more than 100,000 tons of coal annually.

WE PAY FOR SERVICE

"Because we have Lake Michigan at our doors, many persons seem to think that the water is free and that we do not need to bother about water that is wasted. But Chicago's water problem is essentially a problem of transportation. Of course, the water in the lake is free. But to be of use to us it must be delivered to our homes and places of business. What we pay for is not the water itself but the service of transporting and delivering it.

"In certain parts of the city it is often impossible to get water upon upper floors. The reason is that because of excessive waste and leakage we have to overload our transportation facilities, pumping water which serves no one. The pumping and transporting of this waste and leakage means an increase in the velocity of water through the mains; this in turn increases the friction loss and brings about a reduction of pressure at the point of consumption, which sometimes prevents the supply of water from reaching the second or third floors of apartment houses. Efforts in the past to overcome this difficulty by installing more pumps and larger mains have failed to keep pace with the growing wastage and to remedy satisfactorily pressure conditions. Similar efforts in the future are not likely to meet with any greater success. If, however, unnecessary waste and leakage were eliminated the problem of pressure would be solved.

LEAKS COST US MILLIONS

"This improvement in service is the primary object of eliminating waste and leakage, but reduction in the amount of water pumped would also mean a great financial saving. We are spending millions of dollars for new tunnels, pumps, and mains to pump and transport this water which is afterward lost through waste and leakage. Expenditures for this purpose have already exhausted the water fund and have made it necessary to resort to borrowing on water certificates. If similar expenditures are to continue year after year a raise in water rates will be unavoidable. On the other hand, if we will only eliminate the wastage, not only will such an increase be unnecessary but ultimately it may be possible to make a reduction in present rates. If a policy of universal metering is adopted now the total saving in water works costs during the next thirty-five years will probably be not less than $135,000,000.   (Continued on next page)

"But how are we going to eliminate water waste? The method of house to house inspection of plumbing facilities has never been successful. It is expensive, annoying to the consumer, and ineffective. It penalizes both the careful and the wasteful consumer. Metering of the water supply, on the other hand, wherever tried, has been very effective. *In communities where it has not been tried* metering is often violently objected to, but I know of no city that has adopted meters and has later gone back to the flat rate system." Mr. Keeler cited the successful metering experience of Cleveland, which was described in last week's Bulletin.

WATER IN ABUNDANCE

"The objection to metering," Mr. Keeler continued, "comes from a lack of understanding, particularly from a belief that metering would restrict the normal and desirable use of water and that the public health might suffer. This has not been the experience of communities where metering has been adopted. The Health Commissioner of Milwaukee, where metering has been in effect for a long time, told me the other day that he was convinced, after investigation, that there is no connection between metering and health conditions. And Milwaukee has no provision for a minimum bill such as that provided for in the Chicago ordinance, which encourages the use of water up to a minimum amount. In Cleveland consumers must pay for a minimum allowance of water whether they use it or not, but two-thirds of them find that less than this minimum allowance, which they must pay for, satisfies their requirements. With unnecessary waste and leakage eliminated in Chicago everyone, including those who live on upper floors, could obtain promptly and at all times an abundant supply of water. Such a condition has never existed in this city, and it is safe to predict that it never will exist until meters are universally installed. When this is done water in abundance can be furnished so cheaply that no one need think of restricting his use of it.

THE NEW ORDINANCE

A small percentage of the premises in Chicago are already metered, according to Mr. Keeler, but over ninety per cent are still paying a flat rate. The meter ordinance before the City Council provides for a complete change to a meter basis. After August 1st, all new service pipe installations would have to be metered and old pipes would be metered within the next ten years. This metering would be done by districts, and all consumers within the district would be metered without discrimination. The cost of installing and maintaining the meters would be borne by the City out of the water fund.

Referring to this minimum charge, Mr. Keeler said: "The average consumption per household in Oak Park, where metering is universal and where water is used lavishly, could be purchased at the rates charged in Chicago for $4 per year, which is the amount of the minimum bill fixed by the pending ordinance. Consumers could use up to this amount without any extra charge. This is considerably less than is now paid by thousands of small consumers who at present are paying too much for the water which they use and who under the new ordinance would have their bills substantially reduced. The establishment of a minimum charge will also prevent any crippling of the water fund while the meters are being installed.

DEPARTMENT FAVORS METERS

"The officials of the water department," Mr. Keeler said in conclusion, "have been urging metering for many years, and considered from every angle it seems to be the only sure and satisfactory method of eliminating waste and leakage and of making it possible to furnish satisfactory and economical water service in Chicago. The Council should adopt the meter ordinance now before it."

At the conclusion of Mr. Keeler's address, there were numerous questions from the floor. Two of his hearers stated that meters had been installed on premises owned by them—consisting of six-flat apartment buildings, with three baths for each apartment—and that their water bills had since materially increased. In reply Mr. Keeler said that premises of this sort on a frontage basis are probably getting more water than they actually pay for and that the metering of such premises will increase the cost of water. On the whole, however, general metering of all consumers would mean, not only economies to the City, but substantial reductions in the water rates paid by the average consumer.

THIS IS A CLUB! Be clubby!

9   *Commerce.*

Prof.David Kinley,

Urbana,

Ill.

The City Club Bulletin

A Journal of Active Citizenship

VOLUME XI.	MONDAY, JULY 15, 1918.	NUMBER 27

TWO "TALK DAYS" THIS WEEK

Tuesday, July 16, at Luncheon

"Recruiting the Second Line"

Nicholas Van der Pyl

U. S. Employment Service

To insure the speedy production of the huge quantities of ships and munitions needed for the prosecution of the war, Uncle Sam has put into operation some radical measures for obtaining the necessary labor supply and distributing it among the various war industries. Under regulations recently adopted, no manufacturer of war products, employing one hundred or more men, may hire workers except through the U. S. Employment Service.

Mr. Van der Pyl will speak of this and other measures designed to change the American labor market from a peace to a war footing.

Thursday, July 18, at Luncheon

"Life in London in Wartime"

Andrew Home-Morton OF LONDON

President British Association of Rotary Clubs

What the air raids and other wartime factors have done to the home and business life of London will be the subject of Mr. Home-Morton's talk.

SPEAKING PROMPTLY AT ONE

Uncle Sam's Labor Market

One of the big tasks involved in getting our industries upon a war footing is that of obtaining quickly a sufficient supply of labor for essential war industries and of distributing it among the various branches of government work in such a manner that the war industry program will move forward to a co-ordinated result. The government's measures to meet this emergency are radical and far-reaching. While they

Ghe City Club Bulletin

A Journal of Active Citizenship

Published Weekly Except July, August and September; bi-weekly during July, August and September

By the CITY CLUB OF CHICAGO

315 Plymouth Court   Telephone: Harrison 8278

DWIGHT L. AKERS, Editor

$1.00 per Year - - - - 10c per Copy

Entered as second class matter, December 8, 1917, at the postoffice at Chicago, Illinois, under the act of March 8, 1879.

primarily affect the war industries, they also indirectly affect those industries which are classed as less essential.

We are to have the opportunity of hearing the new methods explained at the "talk day" luncheon next Tuesday. The speaker will be Mr. Nicholas Van der Pyl, representing the U. S. Employment Service. The opportunity to hear this subject discussed by a man in close touch with conditions should not be missed by our members.

The Mail Pouch

Here's Your Chance

Editor, City Club Bulletin: The War Recreation Board is anxious to get in touch with a few good men of organizing ability, who will be able to give a few hours volunteer service each week, particularly on Saturday and Sunday afternoons. The work to be done is the organization of small automobile parties, securing the machines and arranging the tours, so that visiting soldiers and sailors in Chicago may have an opportunity to see the parks and other points of interest. Such work is being done in other cities, and there is great demand for it here.

Any member of the City Club who could assist in this way should kindly report to the War Recreation Board, 120 West Adams Street.

Very truly yours,
FRANK D. LOOMIS, Secretary.

City Club of Chicago: The Bulletin has been reaching me quite regularly and I have been glad to get it and its news of Chicago and City Club doings.

My address is changed to that given below, as I am now with an Artillery regiment and hope it won't be long before we will be where we can make good use of the strenuous training period we've been going thru here.

With best wishes for the City Club.
(Signed) H. S. Marsh.
2nd Lt., 18th F. A., A. E. F.

Recruits

ROY GRIFFITH, editorial writer for the Chicago American, has enlisted in the Tank Corps. He has promised us a story.

DR. RICHARD S. AUSTIN has been commissioned Lieutenant in the Medical Reserve Corps.

THOMAS G. GAGE is serving in the Quartermaster's Corps.

JOHN E. GAVIN has joined the colors and is stationed at Camp Jackson, South Carolina.

I. M. BREGOWSKY, chemist for Crane Company, has accepted an appointment as expert metallurgist and chemist with the Ordnance Department, Production Division, for the Chicago District.

GILBERT L. CAMPBELL has gone to Philadelphia to take a position with the U. S. Shipping Board, Emergency Fleet Corporation. He has written us of a very pleasant visit to the City Club of Philadelphia.

DR. M. L. BLATT has been appointed captain and is in the army medical service at Camp Hancock, Augusta, Ga.

When You Go Fishing

Up in the big north woods, pull your boat into a convenient spot, drop your hook in the water and and light a City Club cigar. In a minute the "muskies" flock about your boat, scenting the delightful aroma. Our cigar salesman says so. It may be a fish story, but more wonderful stories than that have come out of the North woods.

Our members take City Club cigars on their vacations because they are the best vacation smoke and because they can be bought by members at a saving of about 15 per cent. "Mac" will send you the cigars by mail or express—or a telephone call will do the trick.

A Menace to Morale

Inter-Belligerent Conference Would Aid Germany, Says Member of American Labor Mission

"THE proposal for an inter-belligerent conference, which threatened to drive a wedge between the workers of Great Britain and France and their governments," though in part actuated by sincere motives, was also in part inspired by German money and German propaganda, in part by political and personal motives, according to John P. Frey, editor of the Iron Moulders Journal. Mr. Frey was a member of the American labor mission, which returned several weeks ago from England and France. He spoke at the City Club Friday, June 25, on the labor situation in Great Britain and France, particularly in its bearing on international politics.

FOR WILSON'S WAR AIMS

"There is one point on which labor in England and France, whether trade unionist or socialist, is agreed," said Mr. Frey. "It is unanimously for the war aims announced by President Wilson. There has, however, developed in France and Great Britain a sentiment not altogether unlike that behind Lenine and Trotzky, a feeling that if the workers of all belligerent countries would get together in a conference, the war might be brought more speedily to an end.

"German propaganda has undoubtedly been among the influences at work to arouse this sentiment in Great Britain and France. I do not believe that German gold has had any influence in Great Britain, but in France there is good ground for the belief that German money has influenced some of the leaders. We need not be surprised later to hear the arrest of some of the men who have been advocating the international labor conference.

PERSONAL AND PARTY POLITICS

"Political and personal motives have also played a part in creating the demand for such a conference. Political leaders have been governed by considerations affecting party strength. Albert Thomas, in France, socialist and former member of the Cabinet, would like to succeed Clemenceau, and it is no secret that, in Great Britain, Arthur

Henderson wishes to succeed Lloyd George. Henderson's position, which brought about his resignation from the War Cabinet was tied up with the demand by the Russians for an international labor conference at Stockholm, and he has since felt it necessary both to defend this position and to strengthen the influences which would help later to put him in Lloyd George's place.

"The Labor Party in Great Britain is not united. It is made up of several distinct groups, including about three and a half million trade unionists, about thirty thousand members of the Independent Labor Party, represented by such men as Ramsay MacDonald, Snowden, Jowett, and other out-and-out pacifists, the British Socialist Party, the National Socialist Party, and the Fabian Society. The trade union element furnishes the main financial support for the party, but the Independent Labor Party wants to 'run things,' to be the tail that wags the dog.

LACK OF UNITY

"The demand for the revival of the 'international' was embodied in a clause of the program adopted by the Inter-Allied Labor Conference which met last February. But the members of the conference were anything but united on the meaning of this clause. Henderson was of the opinion that the proposed conference should not go beyond conversations. There were others who held that the language of the clause meant just the opposite and that to hold conversations only would be worse than to have no conference at all. Some of them said that it was doubtful whether Germany would allow delegates to attend this conference, or whether, if they were permitted to attend, they would be able to discuss freely the proposals of the allies. Others believed that if German delegates did attend and a program could be worked out, the German delegates might go back and force their Government to adopt the terms approved by the conference.

"The agitation for a conference was a serious menace to the cause of the Allies, because it was driving a wedge between the workers and their governments, and there was danger that it might interfere with the steady flow of munitions and food to the front. Such a conference might also have aroused in the minds of millions of people a hope that the fighting could be stopped by this means and this hope would have been used by Germany to slacken the efforts of the Allies. In the end the international would have proved merely a piece of that wonderful system of propaganda by which Germany has been carrying out her program. There is proof—I could pile this table high with documentary evidence—that the idea of an International, developed by the socialists in Germany, sincerely no doubt, was seized upon by the German government as one of its weapons and preached, with the aid of German money, in every country outside of Germany, including the United States.

"The American Labor Mission went to England and France with the purpose of killing that idea. In England we found strong support for our position from leaders of the trade union element in the labor party, from such influential trade and union leaders as Havelock Wilson, Ben Tillett and Davis of the metal workers. In France, however, nearly every one whom we met at the beginning favored the International.

AMERICAN LABOR HOLDS KEY

"Now there can be no International unless American labor co-operates, for the American government holds the key to the international situation, and by the same sign, American labor holds the key to the international labor situation. And we told English and French labor that so long as the German armies were on French or Belgian soil we would never meet with the Germans in conference. We said that American labor was united upon the war aims of our Government and united with the Government in the prosecution of the war.

"As a result of our work, I believe that the idea of an International is waning. Recent dispatches from France indicate that Albert Thomas has now come out against it. Henderson has greatly modified his position. The only group in Great Britain which has made no change in its position is the independent labor party."

THE HOUSE COMMITTEE is much pleased by the attendance in the restaurant this summer. Summer is always the hollow of the wave in the dining room attendance, but this year conditions are better. Last month nearly a thousand more meals were served than during the corresponding month of 1917. The House Committee is planning a special bill of fare that will make this the best summer eating-place in the loop.

PROFESSOR HOWARD WOODHEAD, a member of the City Club prior to 1916, when he moved to Pittsburgh, is now in Y. M. C. A. service in France. He was mentioned in a cable message recently as having refused to leave his Y. M. C. A. hut when it was under fire "until a French officer ordered him shot if he persisted in remaining under fire."

NEXT THURSDAY'S LUNCHEON TALK will be about wartime conditions in London. Mr. Home-Morton's address before the convention of Rotary Clubs at Kansas City—which he attended as president of the British Association of Rotary Clubs—contained a very interesting account of the air-raids and their effect upon the home and upon business life. Mr. Home-Morton is a consulting engineer and industrial works designer. Don't miss this talk!

ADDITIONS TO THE CLUB since our last issue:

Louis J. Lawrence, Williams & Peters (coal).

C. A. McCulloch, General Manager Frank Parmalee Company.

Joseph L. Moss, Chief Probation Officer, Juvenile Court.

Fred A. Sager, Consulting Engineer, Arnold Company.

Joseph L. Strauss, Treasurer Columbia Colortype Company.

FOR THE CONVENIENCE OF MEMBERS who need notarial service, Miss Faith Neuman of the Club office, fourth floor, will be at her desk daily, except between one and two o'clock—on Saturdays until one.

The City Club Bulletin
A Journal of Active Citizenship

VOLUME XI   MONDAY, JULY 29, 1918   NUMBER 28

Over Sunday—Don't Forget These "Talk Days"!

MONDAY, JULY 29, AT LUNCHEON
"The Present and the Future of Lithuania"

Dr. John Szlupas
Recently returned from Russia

Lithuania, on the border between Russia and Germany, is a victim of the "German peace" imposed upon the conquered eastern provinces. Lithuania is under German domination and a German prince has been selected as her king.

Dr. John Szlupas, the speaker at Monday's luncheon, returned but a few weeks ago from a several months' visit to Russia and Sweden where he was in touch with the movement for the Lithuanian independence. He brings back important and reliable information about the conditions in that unfortunate country.

WEDNESDAY, JULY 31, AT LUNCHEON
"The Y. M. C. A. with the American Army at the Front"

Francis W. Parker
Formerly Divisional Secretary Y. M. C. A., France

Members of the City Club will be glad of this opportunity to hear of the "real thing" from one of their fellow-members who was "over there."

Speaking at 1:00

OUR MEMBERSHIP has been "swelled" by three since our last issue. We are glad to welcome into the Club the following new members:

William A. Kroeplin, Secretary-Treasurer, Sheet Metal & Conveyor Co.

John G. Martin, Titus Blatter & Co.

Longley Taylor, Christian Science practitioner.

MAJOR JOHN A. ROBISON has been called to the colors and is stationed at Cincinnati. He is surgeon to the training detachment of the University of Cincinnati.

The City Club Bulletin

A Journal of Active Citizenship

Published Weekly Except July, August and September; bi-weekly during July, August and September

By the CITY CLUB OF CHICAGO

315 Plymouth Court   Telephone: Harrison 8278

DWIGHT L. AKERS, Editor

$1.00 per Year   -   -   -   10c per Copy

Entered as second class matter, December 3, 1917, at the postoffice at Chicago, Illinois, under the act of March 3, 1879.

WAR MAKES CHANGE IN LONDON LIFE

Raids by German Aircraft Described by Andrew Home-Morton of London

FOUR years of war have done many things to the famous old town, London, England. In the daytime, according to Andrew Home-Morton, President of the British Association of Rotary Clubs, who addressed the City Club at luncheon July 18, there is little change in its outward aspect, except for the prevalence of the men in uniform, women in nurses' garb, and wounded soldiers. But London at night is a strange and a different city.

Lights Out

"The old London," said Mr. Home-Morton, "was gay and bright, but now the lamps are dimmer or put out, the shutters of the houses are closed and London gets ready for a possible air raid. Sometimes at nights, if the wind is right, I can hear the pounding of the guns in Flanders.

"About three times a month we have a night visitation from 'Fritz.' He picks out a moonlight night when the reflection upon our little river shows a silver streak which guides him from the coast right into the heart of the city. When the raiders are sighted, warning signals are given and everybody makes for shelter.

The Barrage

"The anti-aircraft guns, stationed in open spaces, where they will not damage surrounding property, put up a barrage when Fritz arrives—not for the purpose of making a direct hit but in order to churn up a gale which will so interfere with navigation as to prevent much attention to the bombing."

Mr. Home-Morton described the noises of the bombardment—the gunfire becoming more intense as the machines approach, the rising and falling sound of the Gothas, the shrapnel falling on the roofs, perhaps a dull, sickening thud which signifies a direct hit near by. This sort of thing may go on for several hours. Finally it becomes quieter and the signal that all is clear is given on the bugle by Boy Scouts. Four hundred of these boys for a period of about half an hour make London the most musical city in the world.

The air raids, Mr. Home-Morton said, began with the Zeppelins. These were followed by night raids by aeroplanes, and then came the great daylight raid in force. The defenses have now become so efficient, however, that such raids are no longer possible in daytime.

The Eastern Provinces

It is rumored that the enemy's next peace offensive will consist of an attempt to gain a free hand in the east by large concessions to the western allies. In meeting such a proposal the allies will naturally consider what may happen within another generation if Germany is allowed to exploit her eastern successes to the full. A "German peace" in the east, through German domination of the conquered provinces, is a peril which we cannot ignore. It is therefore particularly fortunate that we are to have on Monday, July 29th, at luncheon, an authoritative account of the present conditions and the future of one of the provinces now under German control—Lithuania.

Germany's attitude toward Lithuania is reflected in a recent comment from the *Vossiche Zeitung*: "Germany did not occupy Lithuania and the frontier provinces in order to free the people living there, but to gain a zone of protection against the fatherland's enemies. The fate of the frontier nationalities must be wholly one with the future interests of Germany."

Dr. Szlupas, the speaker at the Monday luncheon, has just returned from a visit of several months in Russia and Sweden, where he obtained very reliable information about conditions in Lithuania.

"WHO FOR SUCH DAINTIES would not stoop? Soup of the City Club, beautiful Soup!" cried Alice, sampling the "cream of asparagus."

U. S. TO CONTROL LABOR RECRUITING

Government Restrictions on Private Employment Will Reduce Labor Turnover, Says Nicholas Van der Pyl

AFTER August 1st, private recruiting of common labor for war industries is prohibited by proclamation of the President. The employment of such labor will be in charge of the Employment Service of the U. S. Department of Labor. Nicholas Van der Pyl of Washington, representing the Employment Service, in an address at the City Club on July 16, described the plans of the government for recruiting and stabilizing the labor supply for the war industries. Charles J. Boyd, Superintendent of the Illinois Free Employment Offices, which are co-operating with the U. S. Employment,Service, presided.

WORK OR FIGHT

"If this war is to be won," he said, "it is to be won by the workingmen at home as well as by the boys at the front. Jumping jobs and idling must stop. 'Work or fight' is the order given by Provost General Crowder. The day is over for private recruiting of labor. The private employment agency, with its graft, its encouragement of labor turnover, its specialization of 'bum' and 'hobo' labor, is at the end of its career. The U. S. Employment Service, under the direction of Hon. J. B. Densmore of Montana, is destined to revolutionize the employment situation of this country.

LABOR TURNOVER COSTLY

"It has been found that of the 8,000,000 industrial workers there is an annual turnover of about 32,000,000. That is, every man in industry on an average changed his job every three months. The loss in wages and the cost of changing involves an annual loss to the workers of close to $400,-000,000 a year. The economic loss is more serious. It affects the Nation's efficiency in the prosecution of the war.

"Production, not profit, is every man's duty today. Whether employer or worker, that is the only patriotism that counts, that is the only service that will win the war. The employer needs to remember that indiscriminate advertising for help and indiscriminate recruiting is simply retarding production, and tying the hands of the Government in the successful prosecution of the war. The worker needs to learn that jumping his job, taking a day off 'just for fun,' or working at non-productive labor is tying the hands of the Government.

"After August 1st, private recruiting of common labor for war industries is prohibited by proclamation of the President. This order will undoubtedly be extended to skilled labor in the near future. By this order, the U. S. Employment Service becomes necessary to the employer and the worker.

HOW THE SYSTEM WORKS

"The far reaching influence of the U. S. Employment Service is readily seen in the character of its organization. The country is divided into 13 districts, each with its chief, corresponding to the divisions of the Federal Reserve Banking System. Each state has a Federal Director, working in co-operation with established state and municipal employment agencies. The Employment Service is represented by agencies in 29 cities of over 200,000 population, in 238 cities of between 25,000 to 200,000, in 512 towns and cities from 8,000 to 25,000 and in all other towns by postmasters and rural delivery mail carriers.

"Practically the whole country is now covered. Daily reports are sent in to the Agency just above, noting the surplus or the deficiency of labor in the particular locality covered by the Agency. So far as possible, clearance is made with the point geographically nearest. And so far as that is impossible, clearance is made through the general division superintendents, and finally in the main office in Washington.

"The U. S. Employment Service is thus able to bring the man and the job together and to arrest the disastrous waste incident to the turnover of labor."

HARRIS C. LUTKIN has gone to Philadelphia to join the legal staff of the Emergency Fleet Corporation.

Looking at a Librarian's Shoes

"The persistence of politicians and their friends in the pursuit of jobs, despite the hurdle placed in their path by the civil service law, is worthy of a better cause. A recent illustration is found in the case of Alexander J. Johnson, an active leader in the political organization which landed William Hale Thompson in the chair of mayor of Chicago and is now out to boost him into a nomination for United States senator.

"Mr. Johnson, not content with having a mere civil service commissionership, as a patronage appointment, has wanted, and apparently still wants, to be librarian in active charge of the public library system of Chicago. This is indicated by the reported action of the Library Board in making requisition for an assistant librarian. Such a certification, according to precedent, could be made from the names remaining on the list for librarian. This is under the theory that one who can pass an examination for a superior position in a given line is qualified for an inferior position in the same line. When Mr. Johnson resigned temporarily from the civil service commissionership to take the examination for librarian, apparently Mr. Putnam, the librarian of congress, who was one of the examiners, would not lend his good name to the project of letting Mr. Johnson ride over the heads of competitors trained in the profession of librarians to the top place on the list. But Mr. Johnson did get fourth place.

"Today Mr. Johnson is probably being called on for trojan work in the interests of the mayor's senatorial aspirations, and simultaneously the Civil Service Commission is being called on for an assistant librarian. The two experienced librarians ahead of Mr. Johnson on the librarian list live at Los Angeles and Denver, and are said to prefer staying at those distant cities to moving to Chicago under all the circumstances. So there's Mr. Johnson's chance.

"We don't know whether Mr. Roden, the librarian who defeated Mr. Johnson and all comers in the test last spring, has asked for an assistant librarian or not. We'd guess he has not. His probation period as librarian has some two months yet to run. We imagine it wouldn't make for the librarian's peace of mind and efficiency to have Mr. Johnson, in the role of assistant librarian from the list for librarian, standing at his elbow and looking at his shoes. As to Mr. Johnson's possible state of mind in such a situation, we are reminded of what Mr. Dooley used to intimate was the favorite occupation of vice-presidents at Washington—wishing they could put poison in the president's tea. But the situation is no joke."—*Civil Service News, July 25, 1918.*

An Inquiry and a Request

Has the Library Committee, in making up its list of magazines for the reading room, omitted any periodical essential to your happiness or which would contribute to your enjoyment of the half-hour after dinner spent in the reading room?

The Committee desires your co-operation in making up its new subscription list. It wants you to suggest the addition of any periodical which you believe would be read and enjoyed by any considerable group of members. Don't hesitate but send your suggestion at once to the Library Committee, Frederick Rex, Chairman.

FREDERICK A. DELANO has resigned his position at Washington on the Federal Reserve Board and will go to France as a member of the Engineering Corps with the rank of Major.

SATURDAY AFTERNOON CLOSING!

Beginning Saturday, July 27th, and for the month of August, the Clubhouse will be closed every Saturday after 3:30 p.m.

Commerce

umber
:he ad-
·anged
ular is-

Prof.David Kinley,

Urbana,

Ill.

City Club Bulletin

A Journal of Active Citizenship

MONDAY, AUGUST 19, 1918   NUMBER 29a

(, AUGUST 20, AT LUNCHEON

AUGUSTUS NASH

Cleveland, Ohio

Representing Provost-Marshal General Crowder

ining Our Selective Service Men"

rshal General wishes to put before the citizens of Chicago through
r the instruction of selective service men before they are called to

cted modification of the draft ages, upward and downward, this
ncreasing number of men. It is, however, a matter of special im-
ns interested in the mobilization and effective training of our army.

Speaking at 1:00

The Listening Post

. J. Smergalski and ave just joined the s Assistant Depart-Travelers' Insurance alski is Superintend-iters, West Chicago Mr. Wolverton is e Insurance Depart-s & Company.

z, one of our house he fighting forces in

I returned from my t thanks to the Lord eing hurt a bit. I ers published about : Australians in con-junction with an American detachment on the morning of the Fourth of July on the front, in which we came out victorious. Well, certainly it is a horrible thing that a man can see and go through, but every one of us have to stand it as there is no other way to do it. If I ever return safe to the U. S. A., as I hope that God will help me, I will be glad to tell and picture you all about the fighting."

ORNO B. ROBERTS has received his lieutenant's commission in the aviation corps.

MATTHEW BEATON, JR., who was first lieutenant, has been promoted to Captain and is personnel officer of the 343d Infantry at Camp Grant.

Looking at a Librarian's Shoes

"The persistence of politicians and their friends in the pursuit of jobs, despite the hurdle placed in their path by the civil service law, is worthy of a better cause. A recent illustration is found in the case of Alexander J. Johnson, an active leader in the political organization which landed William Hale Thompson in the chair of mayor of Chicago and is now out to boost him into a nomination for United States senator.

"Mr. Johnson, not content with having a mere civil service commissionership, as a patronage appointment, has wanted, and apparently still wants, to be librarian in active charge of the public library system of Chicago. This is indicated by the reported action of the Library Board in making requisition for an assistant librarian. Such a certification, according to precedent, could be made from the names remaining on the list for librarian. This is under the theory that one who can pass an examination for a superior position in a given line is qualified for an inferior position in the same line. When Mr. Johnson resigned temporarily from the civil service commissionership to take the examination for librarian, apparently Mr. Putnam, the librarian of congress, who was one of the examiners, would not lend his good name to the project of letting Mr. Johnson ride over the heads of competitors trained in the profession of librarians to the top place on the list. But Mr. Johnson did get fourth place.

"Today Mr. Johnson is probably being called on for trojan work in the interests of the mayor's senatorial aspirations, and simultaneously the Civil Service Commission is being called on for an assistant librarian. The two experienced librarians ahead of Mr. Johnson on the librarian list live at

Los Angeles and D prefer staying at thos ing to Chicago unde: So there's Mr. John

"We don't know the librarian who and all comers in th asked for an assist We'd guess he has r riod as librarian has to run. We imagin the librarian's peace to have Mr. Johnso ant librarian from standing at his elbo shoes. As to Mr. J of mind in such a minded of what M mate was the favor presidents at Wasl could put poison in t the situation is no *News, July 25, 191*

An Inquiry

Has the Library up its list of mag room, omitted any your happiness or w to your enjoyment dinner spent in the

The Committee tion in making up it It wants you to sugg periodical which you and enjoyed by any members. Don't h suggestion at once t tee, Frederick Rex,

FREDERICK A. D position at Washing serve Board and w member of the Engi rank of Major.

SATURDAY AFTERNOON C

Beginning Saturday, July 27th, and for 1 August, the Clubhouse will be closed ev after 3:30 p.m.

Prof.David Kinley,

Urbana,

Ill.

The City Club Bulletin

A Journal of Active Citizenship

VOLUME XI   MONDAY, AUGUST 19, 1918   NUMBER 29a

TUESDAY, AUGUST 20, AT LUNCHEON

AUGUSTUS NASH

Cleveland, Ohio

Representing Provost-Marshal General Crowder

"Training Our Selective Service Men"

The Provost-Marshal General wishes to put before the citizens of Chicago through Mr. Nash, a plan for the instruction of selective service men before they are called to the colors.

Under the expected modification of the draft ages, upward and downward, this plan will affect an increasing number of men. It is, however, a matter of special importance to all citizens interested in the mobilization and effective training of our army.

Speaking at 1:00

The Listening Post

JOHN J. FALVEY, T. J. Smergalski and W. B. Wolverton have just joined the Club. Mr. Falvey is Assistant Department Manager of the Travelers' Insurance Company, Mr. Smergalski is Superintendent of Recreation Centers, West Chicago Park Commissioners. Mr. Wolverton is manager of the Marine Insurance Department of Fred S. James & Company.

LORENZO MARTINEZ, one of our house employes, now with the fighting forces in France, writes:

"Just two days ago I returned from my first Over the Top, but thanks to the Lord I came out without being hurt a bit. I am sure that the papers published about the drive made by the Australians in con-junction with an American detachment on the morning of the Fourth of July on the front, in which we came out victorious. Well, certainly it is a horrible thing that a man can see and go through, but every one of us have to stand it as there is no other way to do it. If I ever return safe to the U. S. A., as I hope that God will help me, I will be glad to tell and picture you all about the fighting."

ORNO B. ROBERTS has received his lieutenant's commission in the aviation corps.

MATTHEW BEATON, JR., who was first lieutenant, has been promoted to Captain and is personnel officer of the 343d Infantry at Camp Grant.

The City Club Bulletin

A Journal of Active Citizenship

Published Weekly Except July, August and September; bi-weekly during July, August and September

by the CITY CLUB OF CHICAGO

315 Plymouth Court   Telephone: Harrison 8278

DWIGHT L. AKERS, Editor

OFFICERS OF THE CLUB

GEORGE H. MEAD, President
CHARLES M. MODERWELL, Vice-President
ROY C. OSGOOD, Treasurer
CHARLES YEOMANS, Secretary
GEORGE E. HOOKER, Civic Secretary

EDITORIAL BOARD

HERBERT H. SMITH, Chairman
FREDERICK D. BRAMHALL   S. R. WATKINS
CHARLES M. WILLIAMS   PAUL R. WRIGHT

$1.00 per Year - - - - 10c per Copy

Entered as second class matter, December 3, 1917, at the postoffice at Chicago, Illinois, under the act of March 3, 1879.

Vol. XI   Monday, August 19, 1918   No. 29a

"The punishment suffered by the wise who refuse to take part in the government is to live under the government of bad men."—Plato.

Mr. Johnson Again

THE librarian of the Denver Public Library, to whom was offered the position of assistant librarian for the Chicago Public Library, has, it is reported, definitely declined the position. Predictions are now being made that the Civil Service Commission will proceed to certify Mr. Alexander Johnson, one of its own members, to the position. A protest which was made by the City Club Committee on Public Library against this prospective appointment was published in last week's City Club Bulletin. The Committee held that the librarian's eligible list was not a proper eligible list from which to certify an assistant librarian.

The Civil Service News in an editorial in its issue of August 15th, referring to this situation and commenting upon the theory advanced to justify this appointment, namely, that a competitor who showed qualifications requisite for a higher position would be qualified for a lower, said:

"This has overlooked the fact that this practice amounts to limiting and shutting off competition for a lower position, and that it may operate in the interests of a favorite of the powers that be who has his eye on the higher position. That is the case in reference to the position of assistant librarian at Chicago, to which post the civil service commissioners are apparently bent on certifying one of their own number who took the recent examination for librarian and got marks giving him fourth place on the list, below the professional librarians with whom he competed. We are told by representatives of the younger generation of trained library workers in the various libraries of Chicago that some of their number who did not feel qualified to compete for the librarianship would like to have a chance at competing for the position of assistant librarian for which they are qualified by training and experience.

"It is true no doubt that Mr. Johnson, the civil-service-commissioner-librarian-eligible-prospective-appointee-as-assistant-librarian, has had some experience in keeping political books. And no doubt as editor and publisher of the *Swedish Courier* for about thirty years he has probably had some sort of a library in his office. But public library administration is a profession, in which there are experts. The Chicago public is entitled to a competition for the position of assistant librarian that will secure a competition of experts for this position. The service is entitled to an examination that will inspire the younger generation of workers in the Chicago library system with confidence that they will have the opportunity to rise on their merits and that no political favorite can get in ahead of them.

"The graceful thing for Mr. Johnson to do would be to announce that he would not under any circumstances accept a certification as assistant librarian from the list for librarian. In fact he is in position to move that the civil service commission rescind its action, taken by his two colleagues, ordering certification from the librarian list."

DONALD J. BEATON, who was second lieutenant in the Army Transport Service, has been promoted to a first lieutenancy, and is stationed at New York.

HAMILTON DAUGHADAY has entered Y. M. C. A. service. He is at present at the Great Lakes Station but expects to leave soon for overseas.

"Over the Top" with Major Atkins

A LITTLE, gray-haired man in a khaki suit, his features burned by the sun, walked into the Clubhouse last Thursday, just before the lunch-hour. On his head was a bronze helmet camouflaged with gunny-sacking. In one hand he carried a Mauser rifle, capped with a wicked-looking bayonet. In his other hand was a German helmet carried like a pail and filled with sundry trinkets from the battlefields of France. From his shoulders hung a gas-mask. A satchel filled with bits of shells, with small-arms of various kinds, including a combination revolver and stiletto and a "potato masher" grenade, with aeroplane parts, gas masks of various types and other souvenirs completed the equipment. Shoulder-straps of red identified the Army in whose ranks he served. He had come, not to bring terror with those ugly engines of death but to bring from France the story of what our American boys are "up against," how they are fighting and what the Salvation Army is doing to aid them and to sustain their morale. The "properties" had for the most part been obtained by Major Atkins near Luneville and at Cantigny when he went "over the top" with the boys of Major Roosevelt's battalion to which he was attached.

AMERICAN TROOPS HAVE DASH

Major Atkins, at the luncheon, spoke glowingly of the American troops. He praised their sobriety, their dash and courage and their general morale. Major Atkins went with Major Roosevelt's battalion from their training right up into the front lines and shared with them the hardships of the long marches, the weary days in the mud and filth of the trench, the baptisms of fire and gas, the dashes "over the top." On one occasion, when the Germans laid down a barrage, which prevented the medical corps from reaching the front line, he was in charge of the wounded.

Major Atkins' work typifies the service which the Salvation Army renders at the front. Sharing the hardships and dangers of the men, they have furnished them not merely "coffee and doughnuts" but inspiration and good cheer. Their personal relationship with the boys is on a plane of genuine comradeship. "I was one of the boys," said Major Atkins, describing his footsore condition on the march to the Montdidier front, "and of course I had to put up with the things which the boys were suffering."

Major Atkins will return to France in about four weeks to rejoin Major Roosevelt's battalion. Major Roosevelt has asked that he be appointed chaplain for the battalion and it is probable that he will return in that capacity. We hope that he will soon return to this country with a new and larger arsenal of deadly weapons captured from the enemy.

After the meeting, a large number of new Salvation Army pledge cards were turned in. It is not too late to make your subscription through the Club. It need not be paid now. The Club will collect with your next bill for quarterly dues.

"Fighting McKie"

A SEATTLE boy, in the early days of the war, enlisted with the Canadians, saw service on the battlefronts at Ypres, at the Somme, at Vimy Ridge and at Lens and, incapacitated by gas and suffering from shell-shock, returned to this country to recuperate. This was Sergeant McKie ("Fighting McKie"), who spoke at the City Club last Tuesday. Sergeant McKie, prevented by his physical condition from enlisting here, left immediately after his address for England, hoping that he would be permitted to re-enlist in some branch of the service there.

Sergeant McKie's story was one of those narratives of "blood and iron," of personal fortitude under hardships and nerve-racking dangers—stories with which we will become more and more familiar as our own boys drift back from the front. Those who failed to attend the meeting missed a story of unusual interest.

The care of the returned, disabled soldier was a subject upon which Sergt. McKie spoke most emphatically. Many of them with physical capacities impaired or suffering from "nerves" will seek employment. Employers will find that, for a time, the hiring of a few disabled soldiers will be a good business advertisement as well as a patriotic act. But when they find that the physical disabilities of the soldier interfere with his efficiency the story may be different. "In such a case," urged Sergeant McKie, "don't discharge him and say that the soldiers are no good as workmen and that you won't employ them any more. Find out what that soldier is capable of doing and try to fit him into a place where he can make good."

Sergeant McKie visited the Club fre-. querl., during h.s brief stay in Chicago.

The Mail Pouch

A Letter from Mr. Perkins

THE CIVIC SECRETARY has received the following letter from Dwight H. Perkins. It is an appeal for help and suggestions on a very important problem. We are sure that Mr. Perkins would appreciate any suggestions from members of the City Club:

You will be interested I know to learn that I am temporarily a resident of Philadelphia and that I am in the employ of the Emergency Fleet Corporation in the Housing Division. We are building towns or parts of towns for shipyard workers, and my assignment is to organize, push and develop the construction of schools and communal buildings. My district extends from Maine to Florida.

I am expected to study the needs, discover existing facilities if there are any, and make recommendations and state problems in detail so that a structural campaign may be inaugurated. In short the government realizes that houses alone do not constitute residence areas —and for every reason it proposes to do the scientific thing.

How I wish Hudnut's report of our work on town planning and community centers had been printed. I could make good use of it now.

Don't you want to write to me and express your ideas on how clubs, forums, libraries, gyms, clinics, markets, playgrounds, pageants, etc., etc., can be conducted without mistake or waste?

It is a large order and a great responsibility if they do anything more than schools, and I want the help and thought of my friends.

If you should accidentally happen to notice that I am not attending the City Club, you will know the reason why.

Sincerely,
6432 Drexel Road,　DWIGHT H. PERKINS.
Overbrook, Philadelphia, Pa.

PROF. HENRY SCHOFIELD of the Law Department of Northwestern University, whose death was recorded last week, was a member of long standing in this Club. He joined us in 1905 and has at various times been associated with our civic activities.

The City Club in Summer

From the baking street, you step into the cool corridors of the Club House. You shed your hat and coat.

"Boy, a towel!"

In five minutes you are shivering deli- 'ciously under the coldest shower in Chicago.

An interval of ten minutes and then—

Washed and scrubbed and brushed, feeling pink all over, you sit at a table in the big dining room with your favorite summer dish before you and drink iced tea through a straw.

At the next table, observe the big fat man keeping cool with a big red apple and a glass of cider.

All this time, out in the Sahara desert of the loop men are going about the streets with wilted collars and with beads of perspiration streaming into their eyes. Lucky dog to be refrigerating here, out of it all!

Now, because you are engaged in a necessary industry, you ought to have a little more relaxation before returning to the afternoon task.

SO!

You retire to the lounge, light a City Club cigar and pick up a magazine. The chairs are soft and cosy.

—Or, you submerge to the basement with some of the boys and shoot a friendly game of pool.

—Or you spread yourself luxuriously on one of the davenports in the lounge and for a half hour add your sonorous breathing to that of the chorus of sleepers. Many of our best citizens do that!

Now you are ready to venture again into the heat-laden canons of the loop. You feel "peppy" again—ready for the battle of life.

"Boy, my coat and lid!"

And leaving a little small change for your dinner, you buy another cigar, tip your hat to the doorman and are gone.

Tomorrow you will return towing a friend. And before he goes he will sign an application for membership, for he will know that here is an oasis of coolness and comfort in the midst of the hot and dusty city.

A SENSITIVE PALATE will find food to its taste in the club dining-room.

The City Club Bulletin
A Journal of Active Citizenship

VOLUME XI   MONDAY, AUGUST 26, 1918   NUMBER 30

MONDAY, AUGUST 26, AT LUNCHEON
"The War Labor Policies of the Government"
HUGH REID
U. S. Department of Labor, Washington, D. C.

It is hardly an exaggeration to say that the readjustment, which is under way, of the labor supply of the nation to the task of making war, the shifting of labor from non-essential to essential industries, the provision of housing and other accommodations for workers in the munition centers, the steps taken for the preservation of good working relations between employers and employes, the solution of the many other labor problems with which the government is faced in bringing the country to a war basis, constitute almost an industrial revolution.

Hugh Reid, who is secretary to Louis F. Post, Assistant Secretary of Labor, has been helping to work out the policies of the government toward labor. Members of the City Club should hear his analysis of this important problem.

Speaking at 1:00

The War and Our Schools
Educational System Being Crippled—Club
Committees Submit Program for Betterment

Our American public schools, which should be marching ahead to constantly higher standards of efficiency and usefulness, are being crippled under prevailing war conditions, according to the City Club Committee on Education and the Wartime Committee of the Club. These two committees have sent to the National Council of Defense a memorial urging the adoption of a national policy for educational betterment as a war emergency measure.

The communication is signed by William J. Bogan, Acting Chairman for the Committee on Education, and Mr. William B. Moulton, Chairman of the Wartime Committee. It is as follows:

"WE believe that the educational situation in our country today is sufficiently disquieting to call for a warning and an appeal from your body to the school officials, school boards, and citizens of the nation as a war emergency measure. Even

The City Club Bulletin

A Journal of Active Citizenship

Published Weekly Except July, August and September; bi-weekly during July, August and September

By the CITY CLUB OF CHICAGO

315 Plymouth Court   Telephone: Harrison 8278

DWIGHT L. AKERS, Editor

OFFICERS OF THE CLUB

GEORGE H. MEAD, President
CHARLES M. MODERWELL, Vice-President
ROY C. OSGOOD, Treasurer
CHARLES YEOMANS, Secretary
GEORGE E. HOOKER, Civic Secretary

EDITORIAL BOARD

HERBERT H. SMITH, Chairman
FREDERICK D. BRAMHALL   S. R. WATKINS
CHARLES M. WILLIAMS   PAUL R. WRIGHT

$1.00 per Year - - - - 10c per Copy

Entered as second class matter, December 3, 1917, at the postoffice at Chicago, Illinois, under the act of March 3, 1879.

Vol. XI   Monday, August 26, 1918   No. 30

if pre-war efficiency were being maintained, the failure of the schools to meet the increased war-time obligations and opportunities would be alarming. But, as a matter of fact, judging only by former standards, which should now be considered outworn, the schools of the country are being progressively crippled. Proper equipment is not being maintained, and thousands of teachers are being forced by pitifully inadequate salaries to leave their profession, their positions frequently remaining vacant, and being filled, when at all, by untrained and inexperienced recruits—and this in the face of a situation where the calling of fathers to war service, and mothers to industry, makes it increasingly necessary for the schools to act in loco parentis, and where the ultimate national need is for educated manhood and womanhood, a need which will not be found any less urgent in the reconstruction to come.

"We believe that among other things the following points should be stressed in any action that your body may take, and respectfully submit them for your consideration.

"1. The expansion and diversification of both elementary and secondary education so that a democratic equality of opportunity for preparation for the callings of their choice may be offered the children of our people.

"2. The provision of adequate part-time and continuation schools, which shall train for citizenship as well as for vocations.

"3. The development of vocational guidance and industrial education in both urban and rural communities, in proper relation to each other and to the needs of our democracy.

"4. The encouragement of the general development of community centers as a most effective means of Americanization.

"5. The provision of adequate facilities for the teaching of English to non-English speaking people.

"6. The requirement that all our children shall be taught in the English language, in both public and private schools, a foreign language to be taught only as a subject in the curriculum.

"7. The provision of ample playground facilities, as a part of the public school system.

"8. Continuous medical and dental inspection throughout the schools.

"9. The organization and equipment of special classes for children who are sub-normal either mentally or physically; and also special classes for children who are found capable of making more rapid progress than is possible in the standard school.

"10. Properly organized school lunches for under-nourished and badly nourished children.

"11. Better enforcement of Compulsory Education laws, and the universal establishment of a minimum school-leaving age of sixteen years.

"12. The establishment of complete systems of modern physical education.

"13. The establishment of a Federal Department of Education, headed by a cabinet officer.

"14. The wider use of the school plant, securing increased returns to the community through additional civic, social, and educational services to both adults and children.

"15. The establishment of self-governing school and district councils of teachers for the purpose of utilizing the experience and initiative of the teaching body in the conduct of the schools, the recommendations of such councils to be made a matter of official public record.

"16. A thorough-going revision upward of teachers' salary schedules, to meet the increased cost of living, and the growing appreciation of the value to the community and the nation of the teachers' services.

"17. The liberal, ungrudging reorganization and increase of school revenues on a war-emergency scale, as the only basis upon which to secure the expansion of our schools along these lines.

"England and France, with their resources strained by the past four years, and facing unprecedented immediate demands, are making huge increases in the appropriations for their schools. Surely the people who gave the world the conception of free, democratic education must not longer loiter behind."

England's Political Revolution

GREAT BRITAIN has just completed a great political revolution. Under the "Representation of the People Act," adopted by Parliament last winter, after a prolonged deadlock between the Commons and the Lords, the electorate has been increased from eight to sixteen million and a thorough-going revision of the election machinery has been brought about. Woman's suffrage, proportional representation, absent voting and many other radical innovations were made. The new law "erects an electoral system which is almost entirely new," writes Frederic A. Ogg in the *American Political Science Review* for August; "and the measure itself is to be thought of as a general electoral law, more comprehensive and far-reaching than any kindred act in English history."

AN OUTGROWTH OF WAR

Why did Great Britain, her energies bent upon the prosecution of the world's greatest war, undertake at this time the working out of a great democratic, political revolution? The war itself supplies the answer. "It was seen," says the London *Nation,* "that no future Parliament, charged as it must be with the reconstruction of the social order, could spring from a register that shut out the soldiers and sailors who were deciding the point whether there should be an Empire or a Parliament at all; or if it included them, excluded the munition workers, who kept the soldiers and the sailors fighting; or if it opened the door on the men munitioners, shut it on the women; or again in taking all these classes in, omitted their substitutes and helpers. And the moment this new constituency came into scale, its weight broke down the old machinery of registration and classification."

The extensions of the suffrage to hitherto disfranchised classes were made, broadly speaking, upon the principle that the right to vote is a personal right inherent in the individual. Residence is the chief qualification. "The act," says Prof. Ogg, "swept away the entire mass of existing intricate parliamentary franchises and extended the suffrage to all male subjects of the British crown, twenty-one years of age or over and resident for six months in a constituency." It establishes practically complete manhood suffrage, adding thereby about 2,000,000 men voters to the electorate.

THE FRANCHISE FOR WOMEN

Six million voters are added by the granting of a limited suffrage to women. The act confers the parliamentary franchise upon every woman over thirty years of age who occupies a home (without regard to value) or any landed property of the annual value of £5, of which either she or her husband is the tenant. In local elections women twenty-one years of age or over, occupying premises in their own right, were already entitled to vote; under the new act, the wife of a man who so occupies premises is also entitled to vote, if she is thirty years of age or over. The degree of suffrage granted to women is not so large as its most ardent friends had hoped, but it reaches farther than any similar grant made to men in previous extensions of the franchise.

The demand that the soldiers and sailors be allowed to vote was one of the most conspicuous reasons for the enactment of the new reform bill. Many of the men in service had lost their residence and other qualifications as voters; they were also, in most cases, too far from home to vote. The new bill provides the machinery for absent voting or voting by proxy in the case of soldiers and sailors. It also provides for absent voting by the civilian electorate, thereby extending the suffrage to thousands of men who had been disfranchised because their occupation had kept them from home at election time.

A Compromise on "P. R."

The deadlock between the House of Lords and the Commons, which almost defeated the bill, was caused by a division of opinion on the subject of proportional representation. Three times the Lords put in amendments providing for this innovation, and each time the Commons refused to concur. The backing of this radical measure by so conservative a body as the House of Lords has occasioned much surprise. The explanation is made that the Lords feared the consequences of the extension of the franchise and desired to assure the election of at least a conservative minority. A compromise was finally reached under which Commissioners are to work out a plan for the election of about one hundred members by "proportional representation," from constituencies electing from three to seven members each.

Plural Voting Limited

There has been a long agitation in England for the adoption in elections of the principle of "one-man-one-vote." "Plural voting," the system by which some persons may vote in more than one constituency, has been much modified but not entirely elminated by the new act. No elector may now vote in more than two constituencies; formerly it was not uncommon for one person to vote in six or seven. Plural voting was made convenient by the custom of holding elections in different constituencies on different days. Under the new act, parliamentary elections will be held on the same day in all constituencies.

The act also provides for a redistribution of seats so as to equalize more nearly the electoral strength of the constituencies, for changes in the methods of registration, for the further limitation of campaign expenses and for various other important changes in political methods. One very novel provision of the act is that requiring a deposit of £150 by every candidate, to be forfeited if he receives less than one-eighth the votes cast. The purpose of this is to prevent a multiplicity of candidates.

The new reform act is looked upon by the democratic forces of Great Britain as an instrument of great potentialities for the future. "A new political order begins," says the *Nation,* "inspired by fresh ideas and springing from an almost unused taproot of experience, and if it does not at once make all things new, it illumines the hope of social justice and throws out a signal of defeat to the now prevailing kingdom of violence."

The clubhouse is now open at all hours to enlisted men in the United States Army and Navy. For a long time the club's facilities have been utilized on Saturday afternoons and evenings by men in uniform, but many of the boys have inquired if the club's privileges might not also be available at other times. The Soldiers and Sailors Entertainment Committee of the Club believes that this further extension of the courtesies of the Club will not in any way interfere with the use of the club by the members and are glad to add in this way to the comforts of the enlisted men when on leave.

John D. Shoop, Superintendent of Schools, who died suddenly August 9th, had been a member of the City Club since 1914. He was a member of the Club's Committee on Immigration and of its Committee on State Constitution.

Last Monday, at luncheon, Augustus Nash of Cleveland, representing the Provost-Marshal General, explained to the members of the City Club a new plan for the preliminary instruction of selective service men. Sixteen members of the City Club, following the address, volunteered their services in the working out of this plan in Chicago. Other members who care to enlist in this service should get in touch with Herbert J. Friedman, 6 S. Clark St., Franklin 3230.

The recent appeal to Club members for contributions for the Salvation Army brought in pledges in excess of eight hundred dollars. Some cash contributions also were made following the address of Major Atkins. The opportunity is still open for Club members to subscribe. Just send us word and the amount pledged will be collected with your quarterly dues, October 1st.

The City Club Bulletin
A Journal of Active Citizenship

VOLUME XI   MONDAY, SEPTEMBER 9, 1918   NUMBER 31

THE LISTENING POST

URBAN A. LAVERY sailed for France the last week in August.

CHARLES E. REED entered Great Lakes August 5 in the disbursing office.

JOHN M. McVOY left September 4 for Camp Forest, Ga., in infantry service.

SCHUYLER C. BRANDT, manufacturer's agent (wholesale furniture), has joined the Club.

ALBERT W. CHASE, copy reader on *The Chicago Tribune,* enlisted in the navy August 6.

DR. HENRY B. THOMAS has been called to the service as surgeon with the title of captain.

PROF. RALPH E. HEILMAN is in New York city with the ship building adjustment board.

DR. JESSE R. GERSTLEY left last week for the medical training camp at Camp Greenleaf, Ga.

MALCOLM D. VAIL has been enrolled in the Quartermaster's Corps of the Navy, Ground Force Aviation.

DR. FRANK BILLINGS is in active service overseas and it is understood he is to remain for the period of the war.

W. J. Morden has entered the active service of the United States Army as first lieutenant, Engineers' Reserve Corps.

THE CLUB HOUSE will hereafter be open on Saturday afternoons and evenings. During August it was closed after 3 p. m.

LAWRENCE G. LEOPOLD has enlisted in the U. S. Naval Reserve as first-class yeoman and is stationed at Pelham Park, New York.

TEMPLE WILLIAMS of the law firm of Zane, Morse & McKinney has joined the legal staff of the Fuel Administration at Washington.

EARL D. HOSTETTER is in the field artillery, Central Officers' Training School, at Camp Taylor, Ky., and has enlisted for the period of the war.

ROY F. PERKINS, cashier for the Peter Schuettler Company, has accepted a position as an accountant with the Income Tax Division at Washington.

GEORGE E. TRAUB has entered the motor car service in the Army and will undergo a two months' course of training at the Harrison Technical High School.

Harry McClure Johnson has received a commission as first lieutenant and is at present assigned to the quartermaster general's office, Methods Control Division, at Washington.

E. J. FOWLER, of the Commonwealth Edison Company, is a Major in the Quartermaster Corps at Washington. He is with the Information and Statistics Branch of the Methods Control Division.

NORTHWESTERN UNIVERSITY, through the Lindgren Foundation, is sending Dr. Lynn Harold Hough, professor of historical theology in Garrett Biblical Institute, abroad to lecture on the churches and the moral and spiritual aims of the war. Professor Hough's speaking mission has received the favor of the British Ministry of Information, under whose auspices his work will be done. He expects to be in

The City Club Bulletin

A Journal of Active Citizenship

Published Weekly Except July, August and September; bi-weekly during July, August and September

By the CITY CLUB OF CHICAGO
315 Plymouth Court   Telephone: Harrison 8278

DWIGHT L. AKERS, Editor

OFFICERS OF THE CLUB

GEORGE H. MEAD, President
CHARLES M. MODERWELL, Vice-President
ROY C. OSGOOD, Treasurer
CHARLES YEOMANS, Secretary
GEORGE E. HOOKER, Civic Secretary

EDITORIAL BOARD

HERBERT H. SMITH, Chairman
FREDERICK D. BRAMHALL   S. R. WATKINS
CHARLES M. WILLIAMS   PAUL R. WRIGHT

$1.00 per Year   -   -   -   -   10c per Copy

Entered as second class matter, December 3, 1917, at the postoffice at Chicago, Illinois, under the act of March 3, 1879.

Vol. XI   Monday, September 9, 1918   No. 31

America in time to offer courses in the winter quarter at Garrett. Professor Hough has sailed for England.

SEVERAL OF OUR MEMBERS have entered the chemical warfare service of the army. Bruce D. Smith, vice-president of the Northern Trust Co., and Urban A. Lavery, formerly on the staff of the American Protective League at Washington, have received commissions as Captain. Ridsdale Ellis is also assigned to this branch of service. He is stationed at present in Chicago.

Labor to Gain From War

HUGH REID of the U. S. Department of Labor spoke on August 26 of the chaotic condition in the labor field resulting from employers bidding against each other. This resulted in an enormous turn-over with unsatisfactory results to the employer and employe. To remedy this and other unsatisfactory conditions of labor for war production it became apparent that some adequate means of control would have to be worked out. The final result was the creation of the War Labor Board made up of six representatives chosen by labor organizations and six representatives chosen by the employers. Each group was then requested to choose a chairman for its group, the chairman of each group to alternate every other day to preside over the whole board. Frank P. Walsh was chosen to represent labor and ex-President William H. Taft to represent the employers. Each group has pledged itself after due consideration to abide by the findings of the War Labor Board, whatever they may be, for the period of the war.

One important requirement or ruling that the board has established is that no employer having more than 100 men in his employ can hire men without making his request through the United States Employment Service. A ruling has also been put into effect that labor must not be taken away from its own field into another territory if it can be employed there.

One of the fundamental principles agreed on by the employers and employes was the eight-hour day as being the most efficient for production. Mr. Reid predicted that the methods of adjustment and the principles established for the working out of the labor problems by the War Labor Board would probably be maintained after the close of the war and that the gain to labor in recognition of these principles would be of inestimable value for its future welfare.

City Club Publishes Map

The City Club today, September 9, is publishing a large-scale base map of Chicago. This map, originally prepared by the Playground Association of Chicago, was presented to the City Club when that organization was discontinued. It has now been corrected to date and application is being made for copyright. The proceeds of the sale will be placed in the Publication Fund of the Club.

The map is printed in 24 sections and when mounted measures about eleven by eighteen feet. Its scale is eight inches to the mile. It is the largest base map of Chicago which has been published.

The price for a complete set of blue line prints of the map unmounted will be $35— the price for a set of brown line prints, $50. The price for single sections will be $1.50 for blue line prints and $2 for brown line prints. A reduction in price will be made to educational institutions, civic organizations and to others using the map for public or educational purposes.

England Plans Big Educational Reform

IN the last issue of the Bulletin there was printed a memorial sent by two City Club committees to the National Council of Defense. It called attention to the impairment of our school system under war conditions and urged—as an emergency war measure—the promotion of a program for educational betterment.

A PRODUCT OF THE WAR

England has already been stirred by the war to a consciousness of the need for more and better education. It has come home to her that the generation which is growing up must "carry on" for the hundreds of thousands who have given their lives or their health and strength for their country. The House of Commons a few weeks ago gave its assent to a great educational reform bill and the approval of the House of Lords, if not already given, is assured. The bill has the support of practically all classes. The British Labor Party has made the improvement of the educational system the cornerstone of its program for social reconstruction after the war.

The purpose of the new education bill, according to Mr. Herbert Fisher, Minister of Education, its author, is to obtain as great an extension of public education as possible consistent with preservation of the present administrative system.

PUTS MILLIONS TO SCHOOL

First, it does away with the "half time" system and provides compulsory full-time education for children up to fourteen years of age. As originally introduced, the bill forbade the labor of children under that age, but before it passed the House of Commons it was amended so as to allow parents to put children to work for an hour before and an hour after school.

There are in England nearly three million young people between the ages of fourteen and eighteen, two-thirds of whom have received no systematic schooling since the age of fourteen. The new bill, as it was presented by Mr. Fisher, extended educational opportunities to these young people through a system of compulsory attendance at continuation schools for at least eight hours per week. This encountered opposition from some employers, and before the bill passed the Commons a compromise was arranged. As the bill is now drawn, compulsory attendance at continuation schools, in so far as it affects young people of over sixteen, is suspended for a period of years. This compromise, in fact, is formal only, for it would be practically impossible for several years to obtain a sufficient number of competent teachers for the millions who would be added to the school rolls.

The bill works many other important changes in England's educational system. It provides liberal state aid to local authorities in support of educational plans which have received the approval of the national board. It provides for the training of mothers in prenatal and infant care. Nursery schools are to be established for children under six whose mothers are at work. The system of medical attention and school nursing is to be extended and improved. Better facilities for recreation and physical education are to be provided.

The British Labor Party, while commending the bill as far as it goes, considers it only a first step and has formulated a program which looks beyond it to a more complete and more ideal system. That ideal, perhaps the most forward-looking of any which has been expressed in England, is the corner-stone of the social reconstruction program of the party. It is embodied in the following resolution adopted early in July:

That the Conference holds that the most important of all the measures of social reconstruction must be a genuine nationalization of education, which shall get rid of all class distinction and privileges and bring effectively within the reach, not only of every boy and girl, but also of every adult citizen, all the training, physical, mental and moral, literary, technical, and artistic, of which he is capable. That the Conference, whilst appreciating the advances indicated by the proposals of the present Minister of Education, declares that the Labor Party cannot be satisfied with a system which condemns the great bulk of the children to merely elementary schooling with accommodation and equipment inferior to that of the secondary schools, in classes too large for efficient instruction, under teachers of whom at least one-third are insufficiently trained; which denies to the great majority of the teachers in the kingdom, whether in elementary or in secondary schools (and notably to most of the women), alike any opportunity for all-round culture as well as for training in their art, an adequate wage, reasonable prospects of advancement, and suitable superannuation allowances; and which, notwithstanding what is yet done by way of scholarships for exceptional geniuses, still reserves the endowed secondary schools, and even more the universities, for the most part, to the sons and daughters of a small privileged class, whilst contemplating nothing better than eight weeks a year continuation schooling up to eighteen for 90 per cent of the youth of the nation.

The Conference accordingly asks for a systematic reorganization of the whole educational system, from the nursery school to the university, on the basis of (a) social equality, (b) the provision for each age, for child, youth, and adult, of the best and most varied education of which it is capable, (c) the educational institutions, irrespective of social class or wealth, to be planned, equipped and staffed according to their several functions, up to the same high level for elementary, secondary or university teaching, with regard solely to the greatest possible educational efficiency; and (d) the recognition of the teaching profession, without distinction of grade, as one of the most valuable to the community.

 At the Sign of the Book

THE MEANING OF ARCHITECTURE. An Essay in Constructive Criticism by Irving K. Pond. Marshall Jones Co. 1918. 226 pp. $2.00 net.

AS an expression of the idealism dominating the work of an architect who is a philosopher as well as a craftsman, this book will appeal to many readers outside the architectural brotherhood. Members of the City Club will find many reasons for being interested in it besides the initial—and very good—reason that they know Mr. Pond as a member of the Club and his firm as the architects of our building. Perhaps to our members Mr. Pond's book will have two main lines of appeal:

1. It embodies, as a detail of the author's general philosophy, a criticism of much of our present-day "civic architecture." Architecture, Mr. Pond holds, should be an expression of its own time and place. So, while he goes to the Greeks for inspiration and for those ideals of honesty, proportion and restraint in art, 'which are the heritage of all sincere artists, he appeals strongly for expression in terms of our own modern democratic "time-spirit." Much of our "civic architecture," hiding its steel framework behind "Greek columns," mere shells serving no structural purpose, Mr. Pond regards as dishonest and a confession of architectural barrenness.

2. Members of the City Club will be more than ordinarily interested in Mr. Pond's general ideas of architecture because they are the key to the structure of our own clubhouse. "To him who conceives of life as a struggle—a battle royal—and to him especially whose philosophy holds that the struggle is not to be ignored, but that it is to be made a means to the final achievement of the ideal," Mr. Pond's book is chiefly directed, for that conception of life dominates his book and is embodied in his architecture. That struggle toward better things in the civic field—the fundamental purpose of the City Club—Mr. Pond wrought symbolically into the architecture of our club building.

This conception Mr. Pond develops in his architecture by a revelation of the conflicting strains and stresses in the structure. To him, a building is not simply an arrangement of dead masses in forms which are pleasing to the eye; it is a living thing, the embodiment of elemental forces. In it there is an interplay of strains and stresses which the sincere architect, far from concealing, will strive to render poetically in the lines of his structure. For instance:

Soaring vertical lines, revealing the rising, supporting forces of a structure, stir in us emotions of aspiration and faith—horizontal lines, on the other hand, with their effect of heaviness and restraint, appeal chiefly to our intellectual nature.

Members of the Club, who are interested in the working out of this idea, will find it illustrated in our clubhouse—not only in the fundamental lines of the structure, but in those puzzling little designs or motifs in the wall decorations, in the wood-carving and elsewhere in the Club. Those designs, with their vertical or "aspiring" lines, meeting the horizontal lines or the cube-like obstructions, bending but not breaking under the pressure, symbolized in the mind of the architect the civic endeavor for which this Club stands—struggling upward against obstacles, bending but not breaking under them and yielding gracefully to the dominating influence of the intellectual and logical forces.

The book contains much else that is stimulating and instructive. It has been placed in our reading room.

CHEERFUL talk is better than silence. Your table neighbor is probably inclined to be chatty if you give him the opening.

The City Club Bulletin

A Journal of Active Citizenship

VOLUME XI.   THURSDAY, SEPTEMBER 19, 1918   NUMBER 31a

Yesterday—

Alderman Capitain spoke at the City Club in favor of the proposed traction ordinance.

TODAY—

Ald. Ulysses S. Schwartz and Ald. Walter P. Steffen will tell why they are opposed to it.

Speaking promptly at 1:00

Tomorrow—

George C. Sikes will continue the discussion in the negative.

Monday—

Walter L. Fisher will close the discussion.

These discussions are intended to aid you in deciding how to vote on the traction issue next November. DON'T MISS THEM!

Traction Ordinance Urged

Ald. Capitain Explains Provisions
at First Meeting of Traction Series

VOTERS of Chicago were urged yesterday to support the proposed traction ordinance by Ald. Henry D. Capitain, Chairman of the Local Transportation Committee of the City Council. He spoke at luncheon at the first of the City Club's series of traction meetings.

"The consolidation of surface and elevated railway lines, in conjunction with necessary subway construction, has come to be considered the ideal solution of the traction problem," he said. "It is this solution which the present ordinance is trying to accomplish.

"What we are to bring about," continued Ald. Capitain, "is the improvement of our transportation system. Our people are scattered over an area of nearly 200 square miles, the average ride is longer than in any other city and yet 80 per cent of those who ride in our cars have to rely upon the slowest means of transportation-surface lines. By this ordinance we are planning to extend primarily our rapid transit sys-

The City Club Bulletin

A Journal of Active Citizenship

Published Weekly Except July, August and September; bi-weekly during July, August and September

By the CITY CLUB OF CHICAGO

315 Plymouth Court   Telephone: Harrison 8278

DWIGHT L. AKERS, Editor

OFFICERS OF THE CLUB

GEORGE H. MEAD, President
CHARLES M. MODERWELL, Vice-President
ROY C. OSGOOD, Treasurer
CHARLES YEOMANS, Secretary
GEORGE E. HOOKER, Civic Secretary

EDITORIAL BOARD

HERBERT H. SMITH, Chairman
FREDERICK D. BRAMHALL   S. R. WATKINS
CHARLES M. WILLIAMS   PAUL R. WRIGHT

$1.00 per Year - - - - 10c per Copy

Entered as second class matter, December 3, 1917, at the postoffice at Chicago, Illinois, under the act of March 8, 1879.

Vol. XI   Thursday, September 19, 1918   No. 31a

tem, so that by the end of six years, from 60 per cent to 70 per cent of our people (instead of 20 per cent) may have fast transportation. Estimates of savings of time on single trips range from fourteen to thirty-nine minutes per trip. These savings in time will enable many of our people, particularly our working people, to move into the outskirts of the city where they can own their homes."

Ald. Capitain outlined the elaborate construction program contained in the ordinance, comprising elevated and surface line extensions, rapid transit and surface line subways, additional trackage for express service, extensions of platforms to allow the operation of longer trains, additional rolling stock, etc. Congestion downtown will be much relieved, he asserted, by the construction of the surface line subways, which he estimated would remove at least 200 cars per hour from the streets, and by the increase in rapid transit facilities, which will reduce the load on the surface cars. Estimates have been made that from 40 per cent to 50 per cent of the cars can be kept from the downtown district.

The "trustee plan" is one of the most discussed features of the ordinance. Referring to this, Ald. Capitain said: "Many people in Chicago believe in municipal ownership and operation; others in municipal ownership but private operation. The Committee decided upon a modified form of the so-called Boston plan. When the trustees were first approached with the plan of turning the traction properties over to trustees, to be operated without profit, they strenuously objected but finally agreed to a modified plan for furnishing transportation at cost. Under this plan there will be no division of net profits but all surplus receipts will go to an amortization fund. The companies also agreed that after 1929 they would forego all control over the lines and allow the city to name the trustees. Until that time, however, the properties are to be controlled by a board which has been selected by agreement between the companies and the city. Most of those who comprise that first board were selected, not by the companies, but by Mr. Fisher and myself.

"After 1930 the city will name all the trustees. After that date, therefore, the city will to all intents and purposes own and control the properties. Some people contend that it is preferable to get the properties by purchase but they haven't shown us yet how it can be done. In any case, the right is reserved for the city to purchase on six months' notice. This ordinance gives the city the prospect of municipal ownership in 1930 without having to pay for it.

"It has been said that we should have had more members on the initial board who are in favor of municipal ownership or closer in touch with the car riders. But would not the desire to discredit municipal ownership be an incentive in itself, for the members of the board to give the best service possible, prior to the date when the city itself will determine the method of selection. In any case, we ought to have men accustomed to handling big properties."

The rate of return to investors, Ald. Capitain said, would be about 6.2 per cent up to 1932 and after that date about 5.7 per cent. "The reason," he said, "why we have been able to hold the return down to this figure is that the fares and transfer charges will be regulated to meet the fixed charges. . . Some people are afraid that we are taking away the transfer privilege. That is not true. Between surface lines or between elevated lines transfers will be

(Continued on page 248)

A. B. C. of the Traction Ordinance

THE proposed traction ordinance, submitted to the citizens of Chicago by the City Council to be voted on at the November election, is the most comprehensive traction legislation proposed since the 1907 ordinances. It has aroused much controversy. The City Council approved it by a vote of 48 to 20. The Mayor vetoed it and the Council passed it over his veto by an increased majority. The ordinance was attacked before the grand jury and two cases are now pending in courts to keep the proposition off the ballot at the November election.

The ordinance was prepared by the Local Transportation Committee of the City Council through its special Traction Counsel, Walter L. Fisher, in negotiation with representatives of the traction companies. Its "high spots" are as follows:

1. *Construction Program.* It provides for a comprehensive program of extensions and additions to the surface and elevated lines and the building of new subway lines, substantially according to the plans recommended by the Chicago Traction and Subway Commission of 1916.

The new subways are to be provided from funds furnished by the city (including its traction fund) and shall be owned by the city but privately operated. The operating company is to pay a rental of 6 per cent upon the investment for the use of these subways.

2. *Unification.* The ordinance provides for the unified operation and control of all the traction properties—including the subways when built—by a single company, which shall, according to the ordinance, be "a corporation not for profit."

3. *The Trustee Plan.* Control of the company and its affairs is lodged in a board of nine trustees, with no financial interest in the property and declared by the City Council to be, in its judgment, "men of business ability and public spirit and qualified to direct and manage the local transportation system." Trustees may appoint an executive committee of three of its members to have immediate charge of the management and operation of the properties.

The Board of Trustees for the period up to 1930 (approximately) has been named and the selections approved by the City Council. It consists of E. D. Hulburt, Harrison B. Riley, George G. Tunnell, John F. Smulski, Joseph E. Otis, John W. O'Leary, Henry A. Blair, Leonard A. Busby, and Britton I. Budd. After 1930 the city may, in a manner to be provided by ordinance, designate the trustees who are to be elected by the company.

4. *Returns on Capital Account.* The new company is to take over the properties subject to outstanding liens, which shall not exceed 65 per cent of the capital account, and which shall be entitled to a return of not to exceed 5 per cent. The remainder of the capitalization is to consist of obligations having no rights of foreclosure or bearing any date of redemption. These obligations are to be entitled to an annual return of 8 per cent until July 1, 1932, and of 7 per cent thereafter. Together, it is estimated, the return on all outstanding obligations at the effective date of the ordinance will average a return of 5.96 per cent over a period of 30 years.

5. *Capital Account.* The capital of the company is fixed at $220,114,428.46 plus additions or minus deductions since June 30, 1916. This capitalization is based upon the capital accounts of the surface lines as certified by the Board of Supervising Engineers and upon the valuation of the elevated lines by the Traction and Subway Commission in 1916.

6. *Amortization.* An amortization fund is established into which shall be paid annually after the first five years one-fourth of one per cent of the then outstanding capital—this amount increasing in five year intervals to one-half per cent, three-quarters per cent, and finally one per cent. Into this fund shall also be paid all "surplus receipts" remaining after all prior payments required by the ordinance have been made. This fund is to be used for the reduction of the capital account. From it expenditures may be made for betterments or extensions which would otherwise be added to capital, and for the retirement of outstanding obligations.

7. *City Purchase.* The properties may be purchased by the city upon six months' notice, subject to outstanding liens. The purchase price is fixed at an amount equal

to the capital account less the outstanding liens.

8. *Fares and Transfers.* The ordinance retains the present five-cent fare for a continuous trip in one general direction within the city limits, but the company may impose a charge of not to exceed two cents for a transfer between rapid transit and surface lines. Rates of fare or transfer charges or both are to be increased to meet any deficit caused by expenditures (other than capital expenditures) required under the ordinance. These expenditures consist—in order of priority—of (1) operating expenses, including payments into certain special funds and taxes, (2) interest charges, (3) subway rentals, (4) payments into amortization fund, and (5) payments on obligations not secured by liens. (See item 4 above.) Deficits occasioned by these expenditures are cumulative and are to be paid out of the gross receipts of subsequent years.

9. *Service.* The Company agrees to comply with all lawful regulations of service which may be prescribed by the city and the city reserves the right to make and enforce service regulations "which may be necessary or appropriate to secure in the most ample manner the comfort, health, safety, and accommodation of the public."

10. *Maintenance and Renewals.* The company is required to set aside for maintenance and repairs at least 6 per cent of the gross receipts and to pay into a renewal and depreciation fund 8 per cent of the gross receipts.

11. *Franchise Period.* The franchise grant to the company is for an indeterminate period, subject to the right of the city to purchase the properties.

The City of Chicago does not at this time have the powers necessary to make this ordinance effective. If it receives the approval of the voters at the November election the necessary additional powers will be sought at the next session of the legislature.

Those who wish to study the provisions of the ordinance in greater detail than as outlined above will find it in the Council proceedings of August 22d, pages 1021-59.

GOOD FOOD, tastefully served, at moderate prices! Where? At the City Club.

SUGGESTIONS FOR NEW DISHES are always welcomed by the management.

Traction Ordinance Urged
(*Continued from page 246*)

issued as at present, but a two-cent charge may be made from one system to another."

The amortization feature, said Ald. Capitain, puts the city in a position to acquire the property later on very good terms. "The city will probably invest about $150,000,000 in subways and in thirty years about $75,000,000 to $80,000,000 of the value of the other properties will be amortized. I believe that at the end of thirty years, the property can be acquired for approximately $250,000,000. If any mistake was made in the framing of the 1907 ordinances it was that the net receipts were placed in a traction fund where they have lain idle instead of being used to amortize the capital. The capital account of the surface lines would be about $110,000,000 rather than $150,000,000 if that had been done."

Ald. Capitain was not able in the time allotted to complete his discussion of the ordinance. Other features will be brought out at the ensuing discussions.

Among the questions asked Ald. Capitain from the floor at the end of the discussion was that of the valuations allowed in the ordinance. He said in reply that it is true that the valuations under the 1907 ordinance, upon which these are based, contain many intangible values. He quoted Governor Dunne, however, as having said that in 1907 the city had made a bargain with the companies and that since that time all changes in capital account had been carefully checked by the board of supervising engineers. In the new ordinance, Ald. Capitain said, no allowance is made for construction profits and these intangibles will not be included in the charges to capital account for new construction. The question of the relation of the agreed valuations to the actual physical properties of the companies was also raised, but on account of the lateness of the hour not fully discussed.

"It is passé for public officials to resent the queries and criticisms of plain citizens. The modern way is to turn attack into cooperation, to clear away doubt and uncertainties, and to carry out the will of the leaders of public opinion or fearlessly to show why not."—Philadelphia Bureau of Municipal Research.

'ot. Sei,

y ye
.. EXTRA ISSUE
SPECIAL TRACTION
NUMBER—B

niversity of Illinois, Library,
Urbana,
Ill.

The City Club Bulletin
A Journal of Active Citizenship

VOLUME XI.   FRIDAY, SEPTEMBER 20, 1918   NUMBER 31b

TWO MORE TRACTION DISCUSSIONS

TODAY—Friday, September 20

George C. Sikes will continue the discussion in opposition to the ordinance.   *Speaking promptly at 1:00*

Monday—September 23

Walter L. Fisher will give the closing affirmative argument.

These discussions are intended to aid you in deciding how to vote on the traction issue next November. DON'T MISS THEM!

Assails Traction Agreement

ALD. ULYSSES S. SCHWARTZ yesterday, at the second meeting in the City Club's traction series, replied to Ald. Capitain's argument for the traction ordinance as reported in yesterday's issue of the Bulletin. He attacked the provisions of the ordinance and urged its defeat by the voters next November.

"The plan of physical improvement outlined by Ald. Capitain," he said, "I, in the main, accept. Nor does my opposition arise because this is a trustee plan. I was for the plan as it was first presented, at a time when the committee was against it and the chairman of the committee called it 'camouflage.' But when I saw the trustee plan maimed and mutilated, I thought it my duty to oppose the ordinance.

"The City Council, in this ordinance, has accepted the valuation of the surface lines as arrived at under the 1907 settlement—a valuation of approximately $150,000,000.

This was made up of the $50,000,000 valuation of the old properties agreed upon in 1907 ($8,000,000 in excess of actual value) and the additions to capital since that time, which—with the 15 per cent allowed for contractor's profits and brokerage—amounted to $1.15 for every dollar invested. Efforts in the City Council to obtain a new valuation of the surface lines were defeated.

"The proposed ordinance makes it the duty of the board of trustees to raise the fares or the transfer charge when the revenues fall below the amount necessary to bring the agreed return upon this valuation. According to the report of Barrow, Wade, and Guthrie, the surface lines prior to 1916 earned 7.55% on this valuation. Taking into account the 15% which represented no investment, they earned over 8½%. But the companies felt that under prevailing conditions, the 5-cent fare would not continue

The City Club Bulletin

A Journal of Active Citizenship

Published Weekly Except July, August and September; bi-weekly during July, August and September

By the CITY CLUB OF CHICAGO

315 Plymouth Court   Telephone: Harrison 8278

DWIGHT L. AKERS, Editor

$1.00 per Year - - - - 10c per Copy

Entered as second class matter, December 3, 1917, at the postoffice at Chicago, Illinois, under the act of March 3, 1879.

Voy. XI   Friday, Sept. 20, 1918   No. 31b

to provide the earnings to which they had been accustomed.

"The rate of return to the surface lines provided for in this ordinance has been estimated at 6.2% prior to 1932 and at 5.8% thereafter. But there is no assurance that this is the rate that will have to be paid, for the securities of the companies are to be refunded during the term of these trustees. There is no guarantee that they will not be refunded at a higher rate.

"Assuming the estimated return of 6.2% to the surface lines—that return will be, not on every dollar of investment, but on $1.15 for every dollar of actual value. That means an actual return of 7.1%. And it will be the duty of the trustees to raise the fares when this return is not provided.

"In the case of the elevated lines, the valuation agreed upon is about $72,000,000. On this valuation the annual return under the ordinance will be about $4,300,000. As the past revenues of the elevated companies have not exceeded $3,200,000, we are giving them an increase of $1,100,000 in their annual earnings.

"Another feature of the ordinance: The companies under the 1907 agreement were required to pay $5,000,000 toward the new subway. Under this ordinance they are released from this obligation.

"That is the price we pay. What are we getting? We are getting what is called a trustee plan. I was for the trustee plan at a time when the members of the committee were against it. But when the trustees were announced I was amazed to find among them Mr. Busby, Mr. Budd, and Mr. Blair. The others also had large business interests. The board, in fact, differs very little from the board of directors of any large corporation. With Busby, Budd and

Blair at the very fountain-head of control— for the other men cannot give the time to the affairs of the company—the transportation system will be run very much as it has been run in the past.

"It has been urged in justification of this plan, that during the period for refunding the securities, the investors should retain control of the properties. But the bond-holders have no voice now in the management of the properties. The men who are in control are not the men who have put money in the property. Before the term of this board expires large sums of money are to be raised and the securities are to be refunded. My belief is that in this the controlling influence on the board will serve its Wall Street masters as it has in the past.

"It had been my hope that through this board of trustees we could get honest financing. I insisted that the city should have representatives on the board, for the city, if it ever buys the property, must ultimately pay for every dollar added to capital and the board will determine what charges shall be made to capital. The city's traction fund is to be invested in subways under the direction of this board but the city has no representative on the board. Only a representative of the city can be trusted to look at questions primarily from the service point of view. The board will be responsible to no one during the most important decade of traction history. But my amendment to place representatives of the city on the board received no consideration.

"We can lose nothing by waiting. Construction of new lines cannot possibly be started for two years, longer if the war lasts. If we wait, the time for the expiration of franchises will be nearer at hand. Perhaps, if a constitutional convention is held, we may be able to get financial powers which will enable us to obtain a much better ordinance than we can get today. If the ordinance is defeated next November, the companies within a few months will be asking for a new ordinance or better terms than this, as they have done in the past each time they have been prevented from getting what they asked."

Ald. Schwartz stated that he was also influenced in his opposition to the ordinance by the rumors of dishonest methods used in obtaining its passage. He quoted the findings of the grand jury upon evidence of corruption and undue influence used in its passage.

The City Club Bulletin

A Journal of Active Citizenship

VOLUME XI.   MONDAY, SEPTEMBER 23, 1918   NUMBER 32

CALENDAR OF COMING MEETINGS

TODAY—Monday, September 23, at Luncheon
"THE TRACTION ORDINANCE"
Final Meeting in the series.
WALTER L. FISHER

THURSDAY, September 26, at Luncheon
"WAR TIME EUROPE"
England, France and Italy
E. N. NEWMAN

Mr. Newman, the well known travel lecturer, has just returned from a tour through some of the allied countries. He was accorded exceptional privileges by the governments of these countries, which enabled him to gather unusual material.

Sikes Attacks Traction Program

THE traction program now before the community is the culmination of a sinister frame-up on the part of the traction interests, and these interests, under cover of war conditions when the people are not alert to local issues, are trying to obtain terms which they could not hope to obtain in peace times, according to George C. Sikes, who spoke at the third City Club traction meeting last Friday at luncheon. He charged that the ordinance had been jammed through and that the ordinary citizen had been given little opportunity to form a judgment based on understanding, but had been compelled to base his opinion upon confidence in or prejudice against the personalities of leaders.

"I insist," he said, "that most of the public-spirited supporters of the ordinance are not acting upon independent judgment, but are blindly following the leadership of Walter Fisher and Ald. Capitain—whose honesty of purpose I concede—but whose judgments, I believe, have become distorted and lack proper perspective because of long-continued, close and nerve-wearing contact with the exasperatingly difficult Chicago traction problem. . . . I believe that Mr. Fisher, after years of honest and clever effort on this traction question, has been out-

The City Club Bulletin

A Journal of Active Citizenship

Published Weekly Except July, August and September; bi-weekly during July, August and September

By the CITY CLUB OF CHICAGO

315 Plymouth Court   Telephone: Harrison 8278

DWIGHT L. AKERS, Editor

$1.00 per Year - - - - 10c per Copy

Entered as second class matter, December 3, 1917, at the postoffice at Chicago, Illinois, under the act of March 3, 1879.

Vol. XI.   Monday, September 23, 1918   No. 32

manœuvered at the finish, and has been jockeyed out of his position on nearing what he expected to be the victorious home-stretch."

The ordinance has not been properly presented to the people, said Mr. Sikes. Few copies are available and no non-technical analysis has as yet been prepared for the benefit of the voter. The champions of the ordinance are trying to drive it through by "the force of business, political and newspaper power."

Only Part of Program

Neither has the program been given to the people in full. Additional legislation will be necessary before the ordinance can become effective. "But what kind of legislation? Who is authorized to say what the form of the bill shall be? Suppose Walter Fisher should die before the legislature meets. A person might favor this ordinance and yet be very much dissatisfied with a legislative act framed to give it effect."

Mr. Fisher, said Mr. Sikes, should make public before election day the precise draft of the bill he has in mind, and the trustees and the City Council should go on record publicly as saying that they will favor the passage of that bill and no other.

"Why the haste anyway?" asked Mr. Sikes. "Construction work cannot begin until after the war is over and little can be accomplished now except to give added value to traction securities."

Coming to the ordinance itself, Mr. Sikes criticized it on these grounds:

"It sanctifies and gives full legal effect for all time to excessively high valuations.

"It provides high rates of return, not upon new capital to be raised in war times under difficult conditions of the money market, but on old capital already invested in the plant, upon which the owners have been making liberal profits in the past. Much of the actual new money first to be spent in construction work is to be furnished by the city, out of its traction fund, at a lower rate of return than that allowed by the ordinance to the stockholders on old capital.

The Right to Raise Fares

"The ordinance gives to a board of trustees, representing primarily the investors, composed almost entirely of traction men and bankers, the absolute power to raise fares to any figure they may deem necessary to insure the payment, not of reasonable returns upon a fair valuation, but of excessively liberal returns upon a high valuation.

"The grant is far more liberal in nature than would be given to a corporation of the ordinary type, yet the men who are to exercise the dominant control under it are the same old crowd. The City Council virtually has offered to abdicate its powers of control over local transportation matters in Chicago for the next twelve years, and has vested its authority in such matters in a self-perpetuating board of nine trustes, responsible in no wise to the public, and not removable in any way or for any cause. The board as now constituted has the power to fill vacancies in its own membership without asking the approval of the City Council or any other agency.

"I am informed that refunding provisions are likely to operate to benefit existing bondholders, at the expense of the public, through the early refunding at higher rates of interest of low-interest bearing bonds now selling considerably below par that do not mature for a decade yet. I ask the champions of this ordinance for light on this point.

Return Is Excessive

"Public utility commissions, in ascertaining a reasonable rate, are presumed to do so in relation to a valuation that disregards all fictitious elements, or water. Rates fixed by utility commissions, too, are for undertakings in which the element of risk is prominently involved, while under this proposed trustee plan risk is practically eliminated. Under various provisions of the ordinance, too complicated to explain in brief space, the profits to be allowed to investors are somewhat higher, even than the figure of 8 per cent on stock given above and the prescribed rate of return on bonds. Nowhere else, so far as I know, are rates allowed stockholders under the service-at-cost plan, with our without trustee management, so high as in this ordinance proposed for Chicago.

THE SAME OLD CROWD

"I know of no other instance of trustee management in which utility men have been placed in control, as they have been in Chicago. Of the nine trustees, five, or a controlling majority, may be classed as traction men. Mr. Busby and Mr. Blair are important officials of the surface line system. Mr. Budd, of the elevated system, is assumed to be the representative of Mr. Insull on the board. Mr. Riley is a director of one of the surface line companies. Mr. Smulski has shown that he is in sympathy with the point of view of the traction interests. Of the other four trustees, Mr. Tunell is a man of progressive views as well as ability. He is probably the only one of the nine trustees who is in sympathy with the public ownership point of view. Mr. O'Leary, Mr. Hulbert, and Mr. Otis are said to be high class men—of the type that might properly constitute part of the membership of such a board. They are conservative, however, and might naturally be expected to defer much to the men of actual street railway experience on the board. The board as constituted doubtless will be dominated by Busby, Blair and Budd, the last named acting as Sam Insull's dummy."

CLEARING UP SOME POINTS

Taking up various "talking points" for the ordinance, Mr. Sikes said:

"Complete unification is highly desirable. It will be of benefit to the traction interests as well as the public, however, and the city should not be required to pay a hold-up price in order to secure unification.

"The amortization feature is of value as a recognition of the correct principle, but the payments into the amortization fund for which provision is made are absurdly inadequate.

"The program of physical construction as outlined looks attractive. However, this building program, which is to extend over at least nine years, is outlined in detail in advance, so far as the City Council is concerned, and the power of the Council to modify the program is surrendered abso-

lutely. Whatever discretion is left regarding improvements rests with the trustees.

"It is said that the program represented by this ordinance should be adopted because the effect will be to take the traction question out of politics. That, to my mind, is the most damnable feature of it. To take a question out of politics is to take it out of popular control—to prevent the people from having any real voice in dealing with it. In Germany questions of war and peace are not in politics. The kaiser decides those matters without interference from the representatives of the people. We do not want transportation questions, either of the nation or of local communities, taken out of politics. We want them kept right in politics all the time—that is, continuously subject to complete public control.

PLAYING POLITICS WITH TRACTION

"Taking the traction question out of politics is quite a different thing from 'playing politics' in a trifling way with important public issues or from requiring the men given by this ordinance control of the Chicago traction system to refrain from using their power to dominate politics. I believe this traction program as partially set before the public by the City Council has within it serious possibilities of political manipulation of the most dangerous sort. The tendency of all self-perpetuating bodies is to deteriorate. As I have stated, the board itself fills any vacancies that may occur in its membership. It is not a violent assumption to suppose that Sam Insull and Roger Sullivan might be made trustees. With Insull and Sullivan to furnish the leadership, and with Busby, Blair, and Budd as followers, the five constituting a controlling majority of the board, there is no limit to what might be expected in the way of political activity of a dangerous nature. With large contracts and enormous patronage possibilities at their disposal, the trustees might become the dominating factor in the politics of city and state. This picture may be characterized as fanciful. But its realization is a possibility."

Mr. Sikes concluded his address by propounding ten questions to Mr. Fisher, which were as follows:

1. Don't you think the draft of the bill to be presented to the legislature, as a necessary part of the traction program, should be made public before the referendum vote is taken on the traction ordinance as passed by the City Council?

2. Please explain what may happen, and

what is likely to happen, under the refunding provisions of the ordinance.

3. Please state in precise figures how much, if anything, various financial provisions of the ordinance will add to the rates of return as stipulated—that is to the 8 per cent on stock or debentures and the interest rates bond money will draw.

4. Do you agree with the assertion of some champions of the ordinance that the traction question should be taken out of politics?

5. What was supposed to be the effect of the stipulation in the ordinance that no trustee should be financially interested in the undertaking, if Messrs. Busby, Blair, and Budd can qualify as trustees?

6. Do you know of any instance of service-at-cost or trustee management of a public utility in which such a large return as 8 per cent or even 7 per cent on the stock is allowed?

7. When this ordinance was drafted, vesting large discretionary powers in the board of trustees, without the safeguards, checks and forfeiture and penalty clauses that usually attach to a franchise grant, was it ever supposed for a moment that Busby, Blair, and Budd would be trustees?

8. If the usual safeguards and forfeiture and penalty clauses of an ordinary franchise ordinance are dispensed with, on the theory that the trustees are virtually public servants, then ought not the trustees, following further the analogy with public officials, to hold for shorter terms, or as least be subject to removal?

9. Why does this traction question have to be settled so quickly in war time, when construction work cannot begin until the war shall be over?

10. Don't you agree that driving this question to a settlement now—in view of the differences of opinion about it and the certainty of the development of animosities over it—tends to impair that spirit of unity and mutual confidence among the people that is essential to the most effective prosecution of the war? If the proposed traction program be not received with a fair degree of popular unanimity, is it not the part of patriotism to postpone the settlement for a time?

Mr. Fisher speaks to the Club on the traction question Monday, September 23, at luncheon. This will conclude the series of traction talks.

STEPHEN T. MATHER, formerly Vice-President of the Club and now director of National Parks, Washington, D. C., paid us a visit the other day. He was returning to Washington from a trip to California. He spent some time in the High Sierra country.

ARTHUR W. BURNHAM now holds a commission as Captain in the Infantry, and is at present instructor in the Central Officers' Training School, Camp Lee, Virginia.

BUCKINGHAM CHANDLER has accepted an appointment for service overseas with the Red Cross.

HAROLD H. SWIFT has received a commission as 2nd Lieutenant in the Sanitary Corps.

DR. DANIEL N. EISENDRATH has been called into service of the U. S. Army under the Surgeon General.

JOHN S. VANBERGEN has been promoted to the rank of Captain in the Quartermaster's Corps, Washington, D. C.

ALFRED T. CARTON has been enrolled as a Lieutenant in the U. S. Naval Reserve. He is on active duty at Great Lakes Naval Training Station.

The following persons have been received into Club membership:

Dr. Frank O. Beck, Wabash Parish and Boys' Court.

I. T. Kahn, Christian Science Practitioner.

Oliver E. McCormick, Middle West Utilities Company.

James F. Sanborn, O'Bannon Corporation.

THE DEATH OF REV. JENKIN LLOYD JONES on September 12th removes from the roll of the Club one of our charter members. Mr. Jones was born in South Wales in 1843 and came to this country while a child. Completing his education after three years of army service during the Civil War, he entered the ministry. In 1882 he founded All Souls Church in Chicago and was its pastor from that time on. He was also the founder and director of the Abraham Lincoln Centre. He was instrumental in founding the Congress of Religions and was its secretary until 1905. Mr. Jones' activities outside his church were varied. He was an editor, an author and a teacher, and he engaged in many philanthropic and civic enterprises. He was a prominent peace advocate and gave much of his energies in his later years to promoting the peace movement.

⸝ City Club Bulletin

A Journal of Active Citizenship

MONDAY, OCTOBER 7, 1918   NUMBER 33

ARENCE DARROW

will address the Club

)NESDAY, OCTOBER 9, at Luncheon

His subject will be

Experiences in the War Zone"

ıg his ten weeks' trip, visited all parts of the French front

Speaking promptly at 1:00

ıing Post

this issue resumes

ı in Washington where
: War Labor Policies
ankfurter is chairman.

embership in the City
ıduction to any other

ıs left for Washington
and Dock Industrial
U. S. Shipping Board.

ı to Europe, how would
: of having two sub-
'' in the midst of your
ıappened when Ernest
essed the City Club,
, crossed the Atlantic
ighting fronts. There
ty-two destroyers and

eighteen transports carrying 47,000 men. The first shot from one destroyer sounded the knell of one U-boat, the other submarine was sunk after it had torpedoed a tanker. Mr. Newman described this experience in his City Club address.

LT. HENRY C. A. MEAD, a member of the City Club and son of the President of the Club, Prof. George H. Mead, was reported in last week's casualty list as having been severely wounded. Prof. Mead, however, has had word that the would is not serious.

SIGNALER TOM SKEYHILL of the First Australian Army Corps, a veteran of five fronts, spoke at the City Club Saturday, September 21. He made an eloquent appeal for civilian support of the armies. The efforts of the allied armies had failed more than once on the point of complete success, he said, and the heroism and sacrifice of the men rendered vain, because of the inadequacy of the supplies needed to drive the results home. This reminds us ⸝ that *You Can Still Buy Liberty Bonds.*

what is likely to happen, under the refunding provisions of the ordinance.

3. Please state in precise figures how much, if anything, various financial provisions of the ordinance will add to the rates of return as stipulated—that is to the 8 per cent on stock or debentures and the interest rates bond money will draw.

4. Do you agree with the assertion of some champions of the ordinance that the traction question should be taken out of politics?

5. What was supposed to be the effect of the stipulation in the ordinance that no trustee should be financially interested in the under-taking, if Messrs. Busby, Blair, and Budd can qualify as trustees?

6. Do you know of any instance of service-at-cost or trustee management of a public utility in which such a large return as 8 per cent or even 7 per cent on the stock is allowed?

7. When this ordinance was drafted, vesting large discretionary powers in the board of trustees, without the safeguards, checks and forfeiture and penalty clauses that usually attach to a franchise grant, was it ever supposed for a moment that Busby, Blair, and Budd would be trustees?

8. If the usual safeguards and forfeiture and penalty clauses of an ordinary franchise ordinance are dispensed with, on the theory that the trustees are virtually public servants, then ought not the trustees, following further the analogy with public officials, to hold for shorter terms, or as least be subject to removal?

9. Why does this traction question have to be settled so quickly in war time, when construction work cannot begin until the war shall be over?

10. Don't you agree that driving this question to a settlement now—in view of the differences of opinion about it and the certainty of the development of animosities over it—tends to impair that spirit of unity and mutual confidence among the people that is essential to the most effective prosecution of the war? If the proposed traction program be not received with a fair degree of popular unanimity, is it not the part of patriotism to postpone the settlement for a time?

Mr. Fisher speaks to the Club on the traction question Monday, September 23, at luncheon. This will conclude the series of traction talks.

STEPHEN T. MATHER, formerly Vice-President of the Club and now director of National Parks, Washington, D. C., paid us a visit the other day. He was returning to Washington from a trip to California. He spent some time in the High Sierra country.

ARTHUR W. BURNHAM now holds a commission as Captain in the Infantry, and is at present instructor in the Central Officers' Training School, Camp Lee, Virginia.

BUCKINGHAM C[an appointment for s[Red Cross.

HAROLD H. SWIF[mission as 2nd Lieut[Corps.

DR. DANIEL N. [called into service of [the Surgeon General

JOHN S. VANBER[to the rank of Capta[ter's Corps, Washing

ALFRED T. CARTO a Lieutenant in the He is on active duty Training Station.

The following p[ceived into Club men

Dr. Frank O. Bee[Boys' Court.

I. T. Kahn, Chr tioner.

Oliver E. McCo Utilities Company.

James F. Sanborn tion.

THE DEATH OF JONES on September roll of the Club one bers. Mr. Jones wa[in 1843 and came to child. Completing hi years of army service he entered the ministr All Souls Church in pastor from that tin the founder and dir[Lincoln Centre. H[founding the Congre[its secretary until 19[ties outside his chur was an editor, an au[he engaged in many [enterprises. He was vocate and gave muc[later years to prom[ment.

The City Club Bulletin
A Journal of Active Citizenship

VOLUME XI.   MONDAY, OCTOBER 7, 1918   NUMBER 33

CLARENCE DARROW

will address the Club

NEXT WEDNESDAY, OCTOBER 9, at Luncheon

His subject will be

"My Experiences in the War Zone"

Mr. Darrow, during his ten weeks' trip, visited all parts of the French front

Speaking promptly at 1:00

The Listening Post

THE BULLETIN' with this issue resumes weekly publication.

HERBERT F. PERKINS is in Washington where he is associated with the War Labor Policies Board, of which Felix Frankfurter is chairman.

HOUSE RULE 23: "Membership in the City Club constitutes an introduction to any other member."

ARTHUR S. FIELDING has left for Washington to serve in the Marine and Dock Industrial Relations Division of the U. S. Shipping Board.

IF YOU WERE TRAVELING to Europe, how would you enjoy the experience of having two submarines suddenly "bob up" in the midst of your convoy? That is what happened when Ernest N. Newman, who addressed the City Club, Thursday, September 26, crossed the Atlantic in his recent trip to the fighting fronts. There were in the convoy thirty-two destroyers and eighteen transports carrying 47,000 men. The first shot from one destroyer sounded the knell of one U-boat, the other submarine was sunk after it had torpedoed a tanker. Mr. Newman described this experience in his City Club address.

LT. HENRY C. A. MEAD, a member of the City Club and son of the President of the Club, Prof. George H. Mead, was reported in last week's casualty list as having been severely wounded. Prof. Mead, however, has had word that the would is not serious.

SIGNALER TOM SKEYHILL of the First Australian Army Corps, a veteran of five fronts, spoke at the City Club Saturday, September 21. He made an eloquent appeal for civilian support of the armies. The efforts of the allied armies had failed more than once on the point of complete success, he said, and the heroism and sacrifice of the men rendered vain, because of the inadequacy of the supplies needed to drive the results home. This reminds us that *You Can Still Buy Liberty Bonds.*

The City Club Bulletin

A Journal of Active Citizenship

Published Weekly Except July, August and September; bi-weekly during July, August and September

By the CITY CLUB OF CHICAGO

315 Plymouth Court   Telephone: Harrison 8278

DWIGHT L. AKERS, Editor

$1.00 per Year - - - - 10c per Copy

Entered as second class matter, December 3, 1917, at the postoffice at Chicago, Illinois, under the act of March 3, 1879.

Vol. XI.   Monday, October 7, 1918   No. 33

The Assistant Librarianship

"A noticeable calm has succeeded the feverish haste with which the Chicago Public Library Board sought to fill the position of assistant librarian. Can it have any relation to the fact that Civil Service Commissioner Alexander J. Johnson was nominated for Cook County Commissioner in the recent primary?

"Last summer the board was in such a hurry to secure an assistant librarian that it could not wait to call an examination. It asked the civil service commission to certify an appointee from the list for librarian. Mr. Johnson was third from the top of this list. Uncharitable persons charged that the library board was actuated by a desire to provide a comfortable berth for Mr. Johnson, having a strong intimation that the two out of town men ahead of him would waive appointment rather than leave better paying positions for a subordinate post in Chicago.

"The first two waived as expected, but the board calmed down in its enthusiasm after Mr. Johnson was put forward as the city administration candidate for county commissioner. It lost interest altogether when he was nominated, and a few days after asked the civil service commission to set aside for the present its request for a certification.

"The chain of circumstances is unpleasantly suggestive. If the need for an assistant librarian is so great that the librarian list must be called upon to fill it, the board should go through the list of eligibles until one is found in a position to accept it. If there is more time in which to fill the place an examination for the position should be called. If the place is not actually needed for the proper management of the library it most assuredly should not be held open as a haven of refuge for any political lame duck, whoever he may be. The board should act now, not after the November election, if it would keep its motives free from suspicion."—*Civil Service News, September 26.*

Road Bonds Urged

NEXT November, Illinois voters are to decide whether the $60,000,000 road program, provided for by the state legislature in 1917, shall be approved. Construction will, of course, not begin until after the war, but it is planned that all the preliminaries shall be cared for now in order that work may begin as soon as materials and labor are released from war uses.

Last Thursday at luncheon, Robert W. Dunn, general counsel of the Illinois Highway Improvement Association, explained the road-building program to members of the City Club. The motion picture exhibition announced for that meeting was not given owing to a delay in the shipment of the film.

"The backward condition of Illinois roads is well known," said Mr. Dunn. "The question is how are we to improve them and do it quickly.

STATE AID PLAN TOO SLOW

"Formerly road improvements and repairs in Illinois were under the control of three road commissioners in each road district or township. You can imagine the result of leaving this work in the hands of petty politicians. The Illinois Highway Improvement Association was formed to secure legislation for a more systematic and centralized control of road-building throughout the state. The Tice bill was passed providing for the apportionment of automobile license fees among the counties of the state for road improvement on the condition of equal contributions from the counties themselves. The control of the expenditures, however, was left with the state. In many counties, the state ran up against the jealousies of local road commissioners and others and by the end of four years only four hundred miles had been built. Sixteen thousand miles of improved road are needed in Illinois. You can judge for yourself how far we could get on this program at the rate at which we were going.

A BIG PROGRAM

"Some new plan was necessary, so the $60,000,000 bond issue proposal upon which we are to vote in November, was presented to the legislature. This provides that, subject to a referendum, the state may issue, for road improvements four per cent bonds, aggregating $60,000,000. The bill adopted by the legislature embodies a construction program covering 4,800 miles of hard road, extending in every direction throughout the state and touching practically every important point.

"The bonds are to be issued only as required and the proceeds are to be spent under the direction of the Highway Department of the State. Construction will not start until after the war and will then proceed simultaneously

STATE OF ILLINOIS

STATE BOND ISSUE
ROAD SYSTEM

REMEMBER, That this proposition must receive a majority of the votes cast at the November, 1918, election, in order that the proposed system may be built.
REMEMBER, Principal and interest of bonds to be paid entirely from motor fees.

Map of the System of Improved Roads provided for in the $60,000,000 road-building program to be voted upon November 5.

in all parts of the state. The entire system can be completed within five years.

"Governor Lowden has promised that he will not permit the bonds to be issued until after the war. The Governor in a recent statement called attention to the fact that this construction program at the close of the war would help to take up the expected slack in labor at that time. He estimates that half of the total expenditure will be in the nature of payments to labor.

"Another bill passed by the legislature at the same session provides that automobile license fees, the amount of which have been fixed by law, shall be placed in a fund to pay the interest on these bonds and eventually to retire them. The fees, it is estimated, will yield about $3,-400,000 per year, more than enough to pay the entire cost within the twenty-five-year term of the bonds. Not one cent of additional taxation will be required."

The approval of this measure, Mr. Dunn said, requires an affirmative vote by a majority of those voting at the election. A failure to vote on the proposition is, therefore, equivalent to a vote against it.

The Control of Traction
Sikes Replies to Fisher

GEORGE C. SIKES, who spoke before the City Club, Friday, September 20, in opposition to the traction ordinance, has asked permission to reply to assertions made by Mr. Fisher, who followed him in the traction debate. Mr. Fisher has been invited to reply to Mr. Sikes through the columns of the Bulletin. The letter from Mr. Sikes follows:

To the Editor:—Inasmuch as Mr. Fisher had the last say in the traction debate before the City Club, I ask the privilege of a few words in rebuttal through the Bulletin.

Critics of this ordinance make certain assertions concerning it, which are met by counter assertions from its champions. I believe that a group of fair minded men should be asked to pass judgment on disputed points, after listening to arguments, and render for the information of the public a responsible statement in writing as to the merits of rival contentions.

I wish in this communication to deal especially with the subject of control.

In my talk before the City Club, I asserted that the City Council, by this ordinance, "virtually has offered to abdicate its powers of control over local transportation matters in Chicago for the next 12 years, and has vested its authority in such matters in a self perpetuating board of nine trustees, responsible in no wise to the public, and not removable in any way or for any cause." Mr. Fisher countered with the assertion that my position was grossly incorrect, and read the ordinance provision on the subject of regulation. I used the word "control," which is broader than the word "regulation."

The language of the ordinance on the subject of regulation sounds well, but Mr. Fisher must understand better than I do that it is of little value without other legislation from Springfield than that which we are certain of obtaining as a part of this traction program. An act of the Legislature merely ratifying this ordinance, without repeal of the portion of the utilities law depriving Chicago of home rule, would leave of small worth the section of the ordinance purporting to reserve to Chicago powers of regulation. While Mr. Fisher and some of the other champions of this ordinance personally favor the policy of home rule, they have never indicated that the restoration of home rule was an essential part of this traction program. Other champions of the ordinance, including the politically powerful utility interests, have no intention. if they can help it, of permitting the repeal of the provision of the existing public utility law under which regulation of public utilities is transferred from the city to the state. It was the purpose of the 1907 ordinances to reserve to the city by contract larger powers of regulation than were given by statute, which could be done under the law of that time, though not under the law as it now stands, because by the existing statute the Council's powers are subordinate to those of the state commission. By the 1907 ordinances, the companies were obligated "to comply with all *reasonable* regulations of the service" prescribed by the City Council. It was further stipulated that the companies should be bound by the opinion of the board of supervising engineers as to what regulations might be reasonable. The pending ordinance obligates the company "to comply with all *lawful* regulations" prescribed by the city. Under the existing utilities statute, few city regulations of importance would be lawful; or at least council regulations could be overridden by the utilities commission. Nor would they be made effective by a legislative act validating this ordinance, unless accompanied by other legislation affirmatively conferring the powers upon the city, as against the state commission. And, as I say, we have no assurance that the champions of this ordinance who believe in home rule intend to insist upon legislation restoring home rule. If they were following the spirit that actuated the community in insisting upon the repeal of the Allen law, as a preliminary to the settlement of 1907, they would make it a vital and indispensable part of the present traction program that the provision of the utilities law taking home rule away from Chicago be repealed. If the policy of state regulation is allowed to remain in effect, the Legislature might interfere again in 1928, and prescribe some other method of selecting the trustees at that time than the method provided in the ordinance.

Passing from regulation to control, which is the term I used. While the City Council now has little, if any, regulating power over public utilities that cannot be overridden by the commission—nor can it acquire such power by a contract ordinance without affirmative legislative sanction—it does possess a large measure of control in the broader sense, which I contend it is surrendering by this ordinance to the board of trustees. The ordinance outlines in detail an elaborate and costly construction program, which it is expected to take a decade to carry out. The Council will have nothing further to say about that program; it will have no power to modify it. The ordinance reads: "The foregoing improvements, extensions and additions to the local transportation facilities in the City of Chicago shall be made under the provisions of this ordinance, *as and when directed* by the trustees," except that certain things shall be done within the first three-year period and certain things in the second three-year period. However, there are no penalties for failure on the part of the trustees to carry out the specific directions of the ordinance.

Under the 1907 ordinances, supervision of construction and control of accounting rests with the board of supervising engineers, of which B. J. Arnold is chairman, one of the other two members of which is an appointee of the mayor, subject to council confirmation. Under the pending ordinance, the board of supervising engineers is abolished, and its powers conferred upon the board of trustees.

Another matter as an illustration of my point. A full and complete grant of authority, unlimited as to time, is given by the ordinance to "carry and handle express matter, baggage, mail, milk, parcels, and such other package freight as may be designated by the trustees, and at rates to be fixed and regulated by the trustees." I believe in the policy of using street cars as carriers of express matter and parcels. But the development is still experimental, and the Council should retain the power to modify the grant as well as to regulate use under the grant. Instead, it has turned its powers of control in this respect over to the board of trustees. It has abdicated.

Limitations of space forbid further comment along this line. Just a word, however, about an alternative program.

Mr. Fisher says critics of this ordinance have no constructive program to propose. The local transportation committee refused to consider suggestions, which were offered, to work out a solution along other lines. The program of direct municipal ownership can be put into effect within three years, if the constitutional convention be authorized at the November election, and if the defeat of this ordinance be so decisive as to make it evident that the people desire no settlement of the traction question except upon the basis of actual direct municipal ownership and operation.

GEORGE C. SIKES.

Registration

Remember—

Your last chance to register for the November election will be Tuesday, October 15. Every person who failed to register October 5, must register on this date if he is to vote November 5. All previous registrations are cancelled.

Not only are important state and county offices to be filled at this election but vital questions of public policy are to be settled. These questions involve the approval or disapproval of:

The resolution for a state constitutional convention;

The proposed traction settlement ordinance;

The sixty-million dollar bond issue for good roads;

The three million dollar bond issue for the Michigan Ave. extension;

The private banking act adopted by the legislature at its last session.

Remember! October 15 is the last day on which you can qualify for voting on these important issues.

9 **NOTICE**

going to press, the seriousness of the
mic situation has made it seem desirable
o public meetings should be held unless
utely essential. The meeting announced
has, therefore, been cancelled.

The City Club Bulletin

A Journal of Active Citizenship

VOLUME XI. | MONDAY, OCTOBER 14, 1918 | NUMBER 34

World Relies on Wilson, Says Darrow

"ASIDE from the military geniuses of the war, the one man upon whom the eyes of Europe rest is President Wilson," said Clarence Darrow in his talk at the City Club last Wednesday. "The working people believe in him, more even than in themselves. They believe in his democracy, his sense of justice. His words are never misunderstood. They feel that victory is certain and that there will be a just settlement—just to the allies and just also to our enemies. For such a peace, every man in Europe relies first of all upon President Wilson."

Mr. Darrow made a ten weeks' trip this summer to England and France. In his talk he sketched those countries as he saw them at war

—from the time when he left New York with a troop convoy of fourteen ships protected by aeroplanes, destroyers, a cruiser, and other means of fighting the U-boats, to the time when he stood upon Vimy Ridge and watched the allied armies hurling thousands of projectiles upon the German lines in one of the great battles of the war.

That England was at war, Mr. Darrow said, was evident from the moment he set foot in Liverpool. Soldiers were everywhere—soldiers from every country, "including Germany." The great parks and estates along the railway to London, formerly used only for their scenery, had been cut up into farms. These farms were worked

The City Club Bulletin

A Journal of Active Citizenship

Published Weekly Except July, August and September; bi-weekly during July, August and September

By the CITY CLUB OF CHICAGO
315 Plymouth Court   Telephone: Harrison 8278

DWIGHT L. AKERS, Editor

$1.00 per Year   -   -   -   -   10c per Copy

Entered as second class matter, December 3, 1917, at the postoffice at Chicago, Illinois, under the act of March 3, 1879.

Vol. XI.   Monday, October 14, 1918   No. 34

mostly by women. "England before the war," said Mr. Darrow, "produced for herself about twelve weeks' food. She now produces thirty weeks' food. England is learning by experience that however important land may be for scenery it is more important for the support of human life. She will remember this after the war."

In London, as at Liverpool, soldiers were everywhere. Everywhere women were doing the work of men. At the depots soldiers were going to the front; day after day also the long trains of wounded came in, the daily grist of maimed and crippled soldiers.

IN FRANCE

The English Channel when Mr. Darrow crossed was filled with ships. There were seaplanes overhead and destroyers everywhere watching for submarines which might evade the nets. Submarines, he said, sometimes get inside the nets but they almost never get out. Boulogne was dark when he arrived but in the morning the fact of the war was revealed by the buildings which had been gashed by bombs from the aeroplanes. The channel cities have been subjected to constant raids. "One wonders," Mr. Darrow said, "that the people of those cities can sleep at night. But they have got used to the war. They have simply learned a new way of facing death and they have accepted it as one of the many ways in which it comes. The war is apparently a commonplace today."

THE DESTRUCTION OF WAR

Progress toward the battle line was marked by constantly new evidences of the war—the destroyed buildings and towns, the huge ammunition dumps —stacked like cord-wood and stretching for mile after mile—the great training camps, the streams of motor trucks, of cannon, of soldiers—all going east. "As we neared the front, we saw no trees—only men who could fight or those who look after the fighting men. All through Northern France the towns are destroyed, often so completely that the land-

marks are entirely gone and even the location of houses cannot be determined. All life is gone except that of the soldiers. The fields are marked so thickly with shell-holes that it seems impossible that men could have lived there—yet men have lived there, men have died there, and men have gone again back to risk their lives."

Mr. Darrow visited Amiens, soon after it had been freed from the menace of the enemy's guns. It was a deserted city—a city whose population of 125,000 had melted away to escape the German cannon, leaving everything behind. One of every dozen houses had been destroyed—the city was as if it had been stricken by a plague.

AT VIMY RIDGE

Vimy Ridge, formerly a peaceful vineyard region but now the graveyard of probably a hundred thousand soldiers and strewn with the debris of battle, was the viewpoint from which Mr. Darrow saw the two armies, burrowed into the earth, locked in in their struggle. Mr. Darrow spent a part of that day with some officers in a dugout on Vimy Ridge. "When we left," he said, "nobody seemed to care to go away with us. They had been in the presence of death for months and were used to it.

FATALISM OF SOLDIERS

"I have tried to analyze their psychology. When the war broke out, it is said, there was a great religious revival. The cathedrals and churches were filled with people. Men were stunned and, faced with something beyond their comprehension, turned to religion for consolation. Mediums drove a thriving business. Many people, finding consolation nowhere else, turned to drink. But all this is changed. The churches are filled no more and no less than before the war. I have talked with many French, English and American soldiers and find that they have become fatalists. 'If a bullet is meant for me,' they say, 'it will get me. If not, it won't touch me.' They are used to death. There are no doors, they feel, strong enough to bar it. So they go on about their business. Going up to the battlefield, their faces show no signs of hesitation or fear. They go as they would go to their day's work in a rolling mill and they come back as they would come when their day's work is finished."

AMERICA'S CONTRIBUTION

"American is a word to conjure with in England and France," said Mr. Darrow, discussing our relations with those countries. "There is no complaint that America delayed so long but only gratitude that we are there. England and France feel that there is now no possibility of losing the war. The American army has not only added its own strength to the forces of the allies but has doubled the strength of every British or French soldier who had grown weary of the fighting."

Japan in the World War

MORE sympathetic attitude on the part of the American people toward Japan was ged by Dr. Sidney L. Gulick at the City ub Tuesday, October 1. Dr. Gulick was for any years a resident of Japan and is the thor of many books and articles on American d Japanese relations. He is the proponent the much discussed plan for a general limita- n of the annual immigration from any na- nality to 5 per cent of the naturalized citi- ns from that nationality and their American- rn children. By such a plan, having universal plication, Dr. Gulick believes that a limitation oriental immigration can be effected without iction. Dr. Gulick at present represents the deral Council of Churches of Christ in Am- ica.

The subject of Dr. Gulick's address was apan and the World War": "In spite of e great service rendered by Japan in the ar," said Dr. Gulick, "there has been in this untry a widespread agitation against the panese and suspicion against the sincerity of eir motives in the war. Americans have ac- pted uncritically charges against Japan, many which are absurd on their face. They have spected Japan of a desire to set up a great ilitaristic empire by the over-throw of other siatic nations.

"One of the charges against the Japanese has en that she failed to send armies to the as- stance of Russia and France because she was tting ready to strike for herself at the ap- ropriate moment (possibly in alliance with iermany) to establish control over Siberia and her Asiatic countries. If this had been her m the time to strike would have been a year ;o. It is true that some of the professors : the Imperial University at Tokyo, believing iat Germany would win the war, were urging iat the Anglo-Japanese alliance be given up. he Japanese government, however, did not illow this imperialistic element and even placed representative of Great Britain in the for- gn office as advisor to Japan on international iestions. If there had been any idea of throw- g over the alliance, certainly no such action ould have been taken.

EASY TO EXPLAIN

"The failure of Japan to send military as- stance to Russia and France is easy to explain. either Russia or France sent any request to apan for assistance. To have participated in ussia, Japan would have had to send her army x or seven thousand miles over the single ack Siberian Railway, a line of communication ver which the Japanese government has no ntrol. Russia did not want a Japanese army; ie wanted munitions and Japan shipped her

large quantities of war supplies. To have sent troops to France, Japan would have had to transport them for a distance of twelve to four- teen thousand miles. Who's ships would she have used? It is estimated that it would have taken Japan six years to transport a million men to France in her own ships.

"The failure of Japan to return Tsingtao to China after she had conquered it from the Germans is another ground of criticism against Japan. The reason for withholding it was the existence of a treaty between China and Ger- many in which China was required to pay Ger- many for its return. Until China declared war this treaty held and China would probably have been compelled to return Tsingtao to the Ger- mans.

THE ULTIMATUM TO CHINA

"Japan's twenty-one demands upon China have been much misunderstood. Japan's ulti- matum to China included substantially only those points to which China had previously agreed by negotiation. In considering Japan's demands upon China, this must be taken into account: China and Japan are an economic unit. For every acre of land in Japan capable of cul- tivation there are 4.2 persons. From this land, the Japanese people cannot possibly get food and clothing and produce the other necessities of life. Japan, for that reason, has entered into treaty relations with China. She is dependent on China for her very life. The Japanese feared that when the war was over the plundering, militaristic nations of Europe would try to get their hands on China. The attitude of Euro- pean nations towards China has, I am sorry to say, been far from fair. Even Great Britain forced the opium trade on China and estab- lished a British sphere of influence. Japan is so dependent upon China that she could allow no nation, not even China herself, to keep her from the necessities of life. I grant that her policy is militaristic, but it is a policy which has been adopted in view of the militaristic attitude of the Occidental nations.

"Many Americans believe that Japan was anxious to intervene in Siberia, but the evidence for this is very faulty. Japan hesitated to fol- low the request of France and Great Britain that she intervene. The military and naval party was, of course, strongly interventionist but the political powers felt that Japan would be taking a dangerous step.

AMERICA'S POLICY

"My mind is clear as to the policy which America should adopt toward Japan and China. I am a friend of China as well as of Japan and have been anxious that Japan's policy should not work injury to China. It is important that

Japan should not overrun China. But we should on the other hand, be fair to Japan and give her the assurance that the Western nations will not interfere in China. That can be accomplished, I believe, only by the acceptance of President Wilson's policy for the creation of a League of Nations. Such a league would give Japan ready access to her raw materials in China but would refuse to permit the exercise of military control. China, too, must be prevented from shutting Japan away from her raw materials and the military spirit which is already developing in China must be checked. Finally America must treat the Japanese people fairly in this country."

Dr. Gulick described his immigration restriction plan, mentioned above. "We can't open our doors wide," he said. "We should admit the number from each nation that we can readily assimilate and that depends upon the number who are already in this country, and who have been Americanized."

OUR EDITORIAL BOARD has lost two of its five members. Charles M. Williams has entered Y. M. C. A. service, "Somewhere Down South." Paul R. Wright has gone to Siberia as a war correspondent for the Daily News. Chairman Smith, Professor Barmhall and "Si" Watkins remain to us and we have hopes of retaining them. Mr. Smith is on the staff of a Congregational weekly, which we believe is an essential industry. Professor Bramhall served Uncle Sam at Washington this summer but has now been restored to us. Si's military genius, we fear, is born to blush unseen at the chessboard. Napoleon, it is said, could not have passed our army examination and Si is just about his size.

JOEL D. HUNTER, assistant superintendent of the United Charities, is again a member of the City Club. Mr. Hunter was formerly chief probation officer of the Juvenile Court. He resigned last winter and left Chicago to become secretary of the California State Board of Charities and Corrections. He returned to Chicago, September 1, to accept his present position with the United Charities. We are glad to welcome him back to Chicago and into the Club.

ANDREW R. SHERIFF, chairman of the City Club committee on state constitution, has been appointed chairman of the speakers' committee for the constitutional convention campaign in Cook county.

ORVILLE J. TAYLOR, JR., is major judge advocate with the 86th Division of the army in France.

If you have not returned your committee card, with first, second and third choices indicated, please send it in at once.

CAPT. A. A. SERCOMB
Killed in Action

★ Two Gold Stars ★

Last week, word came of the death of two of our members in service. Capt. Albert A. Sercomb, in command of Battery F. of the 124th Field Artillery, was killed in action. He was wounded by shell fire and died in the hospital. Capt. Charles D. Waterbury died in Washington, October 9th, of pneumonia.

ALBERT A. SERCOMB enlisted in the First Illinois Field Artillery, now the 149th, in 1915. He served on the border as mess sergeant, Battery C ("the Millionaires"); later he was promoted to the rank of first sergeant and was transferred to the 3rd Illinois Field Artillery, now the 124th. He was made regimental sergeant major, then promoted to a lieutenancy and received his captain's commission January 8, 1918.

Capt. Sercomb was born in Chicago and was 38 years of age. He was the son of the late A. L. Sercomb, manager of the International Silver Company, Chicago, and was himself identified with that firm as manager of one of its departments. He was an alumnus of Williams College. He leaves a widow and a brother, Henry H. Sercomb.

CHARLES D. WATERBURY was in charge of the drafting room of the cantonment division, Quartermaster's Department at Washington. Here he had the supervision of over one hundred draftsmen engaged in this most important government

vork. He had been in Washington since last
anuary.
Capt. Waterbury was born in 1868, at San-
usky, Ohio. He graduated from the Mass-
chusetts Institute of Technology in 1895. Since
901 he has been associated with the firm of
ond & Pond. He joined the City Club in 1904

and was active in its committee work. His chief
civic interest was in the field of housing and he
served faithfully and capably as a member of the
City Club Committee on Housing Conditions
and of the Housing Committee of the Association of Commerce. Capt. Waterbury was a
resident of LaGrange. He leaves a widow.

The Control of Traction
A Letter from Mr. Fisher

To the Editor:

On my return to Chicago I find your lettter
nviting me to reply to the letter of Mr. George
. Sikes, published in your issue of October 7th.
Ir. Sikes calls his letter a rebuttal, but inas-
uch as the advocates of the traction ordinance
iave the affirmative of the issue, they are cer-
ainly entitled to what Mr. Sikes calls "the last
say in the traction debate." Otherwise objections might seem to be without an effective answer. The people of Chicago are to have the
last say on the ordinance after the debating is
finished and no "group of fair-minded men" such
as Mr. Sikes suggests can be substituted for the
people or for the contending parties in the debate. Personally, all that I ask is that those
who decide this question shall be "fair-minded."
I am not without hope that among even the
present objectors there may be men "fair-
minded" enough to admit that their objections
have been shown to be unfounded.

Mr. Sikes states that his communication deals
"especially with the subject of control," which
he evidently regards as the most important question. I shall, therefore, devote what I have to
say especially to the question—what, if anything,
does the City lose, and what, if anything, will
it gain by this ordinance *in the matter of control?*

If we are to decide intelligently whether the
City's control will be increased or diminished
by the ordinance we must compare the control
which the City now has with the control it will
obtain under the ordinance. Mr. Sikes expressly
concedes that under the present statutes of Illinois the "City Council now has little, if any, regulating power over public utilities," "because by
the existing statute the Council's powers are
subordinate to those of the State (Public Utilities) Commission," but he attempts to draw a
distinction between "regulation" and "control"
and claims that now the City Council "does possess a large measure of control in the broader
sense," which he contends "it is surrendering by
this ordinance to the Board of Trustees."

I am unable to find any justification whatever
for this assertion and I invite the attention of
all "fair-minded men" to the indisputable facts.
"Regulation" certainly embraces everything that
"control" can cover with respect to service and

rates of a public utility after it is constructed.
It probably includes all extensions and improvements that are essential to adequate service.
The only possible question that could arise is
whether the power to "regulate" gives "control"
over construction of new lines or additions not
authorized by ordinance. This seems to be Mr.
Sikes' idea, because the particular matter to
which he refers in support of his assertion that
the City is *"surrendering"* by this ordinance some
measure of "control in the broader sense" is that
the ordinance provides a definite construction
program to be made *"under the provisions of
this ordinance* as and when directed by the Trustees" with the definite requirement that certain
extensions and improvements *must* be made
within the first three-year period after the ordinance takes effect, and that certain others *must*
be made in the second three-year period. As to
these first six years, his claim can only be that
because the City Council absolutely requires the
Trustees to carry out the construction and improvement program provided for this period, the
City Council has in some way lost "control" over
construction. By this argument, the more the
City requires the Company to do and the more
definitely it requires it to be done, the less "control" the City has over the matter. By this
argument the City loses control by exercising
control, and in a certain sense this is true, but
it is no objection to the exercise of control. If
we are to have what we so desperately need
—a comprehensive local transportation system—
we must adopt a definite construction program,
even though it be "elaborate and costly," and
when we require this program to be carried out
within a definite period of time we voluntarily
limit our control by its very exercise to this extent. I assume, however, that this sort of limitation is precisely what the people of Chicago
wish. We cannot eat our cake and still have
it uneaten. Having decided, after the most ex-
haustive investigation, upon the extensions and
improvements that should be made during the
next six years, we wish to provide that these
improvements and not something else shall be
carried out.

So far as the extensions and improvements
outlined in the ordinance to be made after the

first six years, what the ordinance does is to obligate the Company to carry them out "as and when directed by the Trustees" but "*under the provisions of this ordinance,*" and this ordinance expressly provides not only what Mr. Sikes quotes with respect to compliance "with all *lawful* regulations of the service" prescribed from time to time by the City but expressly reserves to the City "the right to make and enforce all such orders and regulations as shall be necessary or appropriate to secure adequate local transportation accommodations for the people and to insure their comfort and convenience" (Section 9), and further that "the Company shall at all times construct such additions to and extensions of both the rapid transit and service lines as may be required for furnishing adequate local transportation facilities and service under the principles and provisions in this ordinance and in Exhibit B set forth" (Section 5). Mr. Sikes does not refer to these provisions. They destroy every possible objection to the substitution of the word "lawful" for the word "reasonable," which I made because I thought it better to have the Company agree to comply with any regulation which the City could hereafter acquire the lawful right to make.

The ordinance further expressly provides that "the City shall have the right to proceed by injunction, mandamus or other appropriate legal proceeding to compel the performance by the Company and by the Trustees of their respective duties and obligations under this ordinance." (Section 29.) It does not provide for fines or other penalties, for the conclusive reason that under the principle of "service at cost" the strap hangers would be the ones who would pay the fines. It does not provide for a forfeiture because forfeiture provisions are practically never enforceable, and because the City would be forfeiting this ordinance because of the action or inaction of its own trustees. The security holders would have to be given a permanent and controlling voice in the selection of the trustees if there was a forfeiture provision.

The principal objection of Mr. Sikes has been that the City has not had sufficient "control" over the selection of the first Board of Trustees, although he admits that at least four of its members are proper selections. Surely the City makes a distinct gain in selecting the Trustees of whom Mr. Sikes approves. If this ordinance does not become effective, the City will have absolutely no voice whatever in the selection of any of the Directors who will manage the street railways until 1927 and the elevated railways for many years thereafter. Surely Mr. Sikes would not—because the City does not now "control" the selection of all of the Trustees or Directors—have the City refuse to permit extensions and improvements which, on the best information and advice we now have, would clearly be proper parts of a comprehensive local transportation system. Regarding control of expenditures and

accounting the new ordinance contains all of the safeguards we now have and some new ones, such as the drastic provisions for competitive bids on all contracts over $5,000.00. (Section 6.)

Just what is it, the "control" of which the City will lose by this ordinance? Control consists of the power to compel and the power to prevent. The City certainly loses no power to compel which it now has; on the contrary it gains greatly here. It certainly loses none of its power to prevent. Not one of the extensions provided by this ordinance can be made without the consent of the City by another ordinance hereafter passed and based on frontage consents then on file. All subway contracts and payments are to be made by the City itself. The Trustees merely supervise construction and submit plans and estimates to the City for approval. It is true that the powers of the Board of Supervising Engineers under the 1907 ordinances are transferred to the Board of Trustees under the new ordinance, but it is also true that the City

STATEMENT OF THE OWNERSHIP, MANAGEMENT, ETC., REQUIRED BY THE ACT OF CONGRESS OF AUGUST 24, 1912,

Of THE CITY CLUB BULLETIN published weekly, except July, August and September; bi-weekly during July, August and September, at Chicago, Illinois, for October 1, 1918.

State of Illinois, County of Cook, ss.

Before me, a notary public in and for the State and county aforesaid, personally appeared Dwight L. Akers, who, having been duly sworn according to law, deposes and says that he is the editor of THE CITY CLUB BULLETIN and that the following is, to the best of his knowledge and belief, a true statement of the ownership, management, etc., of the aforesaid publication for the date shown in the above caption, required by the Act of August 24, 1912, embodied in section 443, Postal Laws and Regulations, to-wit:

1. That the names and addresses of the publisher, editor, managing editor, and business managers are: Publisher, City Club of Chicago, 315 Plymouth Court, Chicago. Editor, Dwight L. Akers, 315 Plymouth Court, Chicago. Managing Editor, None. Business Managers, None.

2. That the owners are: The City Club of Chicago, a corporation organized under the laws of Illinois. No stock. George H. Mead, president, 1537 E. 60th St.; Charles M. Moderwell, vice-president. 3325 Michigan Ave.; Roy C. Osgood, treasurer, First Trust and Savings Bank; Charles Yeomans, secretary, 231 Institute Place.

3. That the known bondholders, mortgagees, and other security holders owning or holding 1 per cent or more of total amount of bonds, mortgages, or other securities are: None.

4. That the two paragraphs next above, giving the names of the owners, stockholders, and security holders, if any, contain not only the list of stockholders and security holders as they appear upon the books of the company but also, in cases where the stockholder or security holder appears upon the books of the company as trustee or in any other fiduciary relation, the name of the person or corporation for whom such trustee is acting, is given; also that the said two paragraphs contain statements embracing affiant's full knowledge and belief as to the circumstances and conditions under which stockholders and security holders who do not appear upon the books of the company as trustees, hold stock and securities in a capacity other than that of a bona fide owner; and this affiant has no reason to believe that any other person, association, or corporation has any interest direct or indirect in the said stock, bonds, or other securities than as so stated by him.

DWIGHT L. AKERS,

Sworn to and subscribed before me this 23rd day of September, 1918.

FAITH NEUMAN,

(SEAL)　　(My commission expires June 20, 1922.)

ıs selected the majority of the First Board of rustees and will select all of its successors.

The ordinance provides that "the Company ıall be a corporation not for pecuniary profit ıd the entire control and management of the ompany and of its affairs, property and funds hall be vested in a Board of Trustees or Direcors. The said Trustees or Directors shall be ine in number and *shall be selected* and hold ffice *in the following manner and subject to the ollowing limitations and conditions."* Among he conditions specifically provided is that begining in 1928 the City shall designate the persons ʋho are to be elected as trustees. The ordinance urther provides that it shall not take effect or e in force unless or until * * *

"2. The legislature of Illinois shall have passed, and ıere shall be in effect, such statute or statutes of the tate of Illinois as may be necessary or appropriate to uthorize or validate an ordinance containing such pro`sions as are incorporated in this ordinance, and to enale the same to be carried into effect, *including the rganization of a corporation of the character and having he authority and powers in this ordinance provided to be xercised by the Company;* and

"3. The Company shall have been organized in conormity with the provisions of this ordinance, and the ntire control and management of the Company and of its ffairs, property and funds shall have been vested in a oard of Trustees or Directors *of the character described ι this ordinance and subject to the provisions hereof."* Section 34.)

The ordinance further provides that "by its cceptance of this ordinance the Company agrees hat after the effective date hereof the Company hall not without the consent (by ordinance) of he City change its charter *or method of selecting its Trustees or Directors."* (Section 1.)

With respect to the carriage of express matter and parcels, the powers of regulation and control already quoted amply protect the public, and the very section which relates to this matter provides that "express matter and package freight shall be transported at such times and in such manner as shall not interfere with passenger service."

Today, as Mr. Sikes expressly admits, the City of Chicago can control neither the service nor the rates of fare. Under the administration of Governor Dunne and with his sanction, home rule over public utilities was taken from Chicago and vested in the State Public Utilities Commission. If the statutes remain as they are, the City has certainly lost no right of regulation or control which it now has. If appropriate legislation is passed validating the provisions of this ordinance, the City will regain its powers of regulation and control to whatever extent the new legislation goes. I have advocated and still advocate the complete restoration of home rule over public utilities in this City. This ordinance cannot go into effect unless enabling legislation is enacted, and further, unless it is approved by the City Council as being appropriate for the purpose. I can give the assurance which Mr. Sikes asks that so far as I am concerned I "intend to insist upon legislation restoring home rule." I may be permitted, however, to add that even if the legislature should insist that the State

Public Utilities Commission should retain some supervisory jurisdiction the "control" of the City will necessarily be increased under this ordinance before it can possibly become effective. The legislation must validate trustee management and service at cost or the ordinance cannot take effect. Under trustee management and service at cost neither the trustees nor the security holders can have any incentive to furnish poorer service than the public is willing to pay for, and it is difficult to conceive how the State Commission would ever be called upon to exercise supervision over either service or rates even if it retained the authority to do so.

Mr. Sikes says, "If the policy of state regulation is allowed to remain in effect the legislature might interfere again in 1928 and prescribe some other method of selecting the trustees at that time than the method provided in the ordinance." This is an illuminating objection. May I ask why the legislature would wish to change the method of selecting the trustees in 1928, "if the policy of state regulation is allowed to remain in effect?" The rights and the rate of return of the security holders will have been definitely fixed by 1928 and there will be no interest involved but the public interest. If it be granted, however, that the legislature can always pass new legislation surely Mr. Sikes would not propose that we refuse to go forward because of this possibility. He does not oppose municipal ownership of public utilities notwithstanding the fact that the legislature at any time by merely passing a new statute could put even a city owned water system under the jurisdiction of the State Commission or change the method of selecting the managers of such utilities.

On the contrary, Mr. Sikes' "constructive program" is "actual, direct municipal ownership and operation," which he says can be brought about by constitutional revision within three years;— assuming that we get constitutional revision that will make municipal ownership possible, and ignoring the altogether probable necessity of obtaining new statutes before we can make it practicable. This ordinance in no way prevents municipal ownership whenever the constitution permits it and the people desire it. On the contrary, it expressly reserves the right to take over the properties on six months' notice without the expense, delay and uncertainty of eminent domain proceedings, which is the only method (except agreement) by which we could acquire the elevated railroads. We have the right to take over the surface lines on payment of their capital account under the ordinances of 1907. We have allowed them only that valuation in the pending ordinance. In my judgment we cannot legally take them over for less and it would be a breach of faith to undertake to do it. Nothing could so discredit municipal ownership and prevent the sale of municipal securities on fair terms as an attempt to repudiate the securities issued under the assurances of the ordinances of

1907. The Surface Lines have not repudiated their agreement of a five cent fare. They have simply asked the City Council for an increase to meet the increase in wages which they have been ordered to pay as a war measure. So far as valuations are concerned, the valuation of the elevated railroads alone is subject to question by "fair-minded men." That valuation is based on the appraisal by three engineers of the highest standing of the reproduction cost of the physical property less depreciation, using as the cost of labor and material the average costs of the ten years preceding June 30, 1916. I think it is a fair adjustment of the conflicting interests. It certainly cannot be excessive to an extent that should be allowed to stand for one moment in the way of the immediate improvement which a comprehensive local transportation system alone can provide for this community.

WALTER L. FISHER.

The Listening Post

SUMNER S. WEIL is in a machine gun battalion at Camp Hancock, Ga.

SPENCER GORDON is a cadet in the Balloon School, Arcadia, Cal.

LOUIS BERNSTEIN, a member of the City Club since 1915, died Sunday, October 6.

ARTHUR L. HAMILTON, a member of the Board of Directors of the Club, is in France in Red Cross work.

E. M. HIBBERD has enlisted in the U. S. Marine Corps and expects to be called for service within a few days.

LAWRENCE THOMAS is now a member of Sanitary Train No. 343, which forms a part of the Black Hawk Division, now on the firing line in France.

J. KENNICOTT BRENTON, assistant county agent, has left Chicago to become director of the Home Service section of the Red Cross. Mr. Brenton was secretary of the City Club Committee on State and Local Charities.

ASKEL G. S. JOSEPHSON, chairman of the Swedish Study League, has sent us a very interesting program of that organization for the coming year. The program deals particularly with "Reconstruction After the War." City Club members who are contributing to this program are Prof. Frederick D. Bramhall, Prof. Harold G. Moulton and Jens Jensen.

Some of the members who returned committee choice cards forgot to sign them. Any member who suspects himself of such an omission should notify the office.

Committee Reorganization Under Way

A LL members of the Club have been invited to join in its committee activities during the coming year. The committee scheme has been completely revised. A number of modifications have been made in the list of committees and a reorganization of personnel is under way.·

The committees, during the coming year, will be associated in certain groups for co-operative action. Each of these groups will be represented in the Public Affairs Committee, so that a more immediate relationship may be maintained between the civic committees and the body which, under the by-laws has charge of "the investigation and discussion of public affairs by the Club." The committee groups with their representatives in the Public Affairs Committee are:

Public Safety Group.
Represented by Carl Miner.

PUBLIC HEALTH COMMITTEE (with which are merged the committees on Accident Prevention and on Vice Conditions).

PUBLIC ORDER AND SAFETY COMMITTEE (with which is merged the Committee on Fire Protection).

Public Works Group
Represented by Elmer C. Jensen.

CITY PLANNING COMMITTEE (which will deal also with "housing").

PUBLIC UTILITIES COMMITTEE.

COMMITTEE ON HIGHWAYS, HARBORS AND WHARVES (a merger of two of the civic committees).

WATER SUPPLY COMMITTEE (with which is merged the Committee on Drainage and Sewerage).

Government and Finance Group
Represented by George C. Sikes.

COMMITTEE ON POLITICAL NOMINATIONS AND ELECTIONS.

CIVIL SERVICE COMMITTEE.

COMMITTEE ON TAXATION AND PUBLIC EXPENDITURES (a consolidation of two committees).

STATE CONSTITUTION COMMITTEE.

LEGISLATIVE PROGRAM COMMITTEE (new).

Public Welfare and Education Group
Represented by Frederick S. Deibler.

PUBLIC EDUCATION COMMITTEE.

MUSIC EXTENSION COMMITTEE.

COMMITTEE ON PARKS, PLAYGROUNDS AND BEACHES.

COMMITTEE ON IMMIGRATION AND CITIZENSHIP.

COMMITTEE ON LOCAL AND STATE CHARITIES.

LABOR CONDITIONS COMMITTEE.

Commerce

Prof.David Kinley,

UNIVERSITY OF ILLIN

Urbana, DEC 21 1

Ill.

PRE-ELECTION ISSUE

The City Club Bulletin

A Journal of Active Citizenship

VOLUME XI.	MONDAY, OCTOBER 28, 1918	NUMBER 35

The Big and "Little" Ballots

THE paper shortage will not be evident at the election November 5. Every voter will be presented with three ballots on which to designate his choice of candidates and his decision upon the referendum issues.

THE CANDIDATES' BALLOTS—besides the regular ballot there will be a special ballot for municipal judges—will in most districts call for the filling of nearly sixty offices. The voter who wishes to devote a part of his time between now and election day to a study of the personalities and records of the 200 different candidates who· are appealing for his support will find the check list printed elsewhere in this Bulletin a valuable aid. Members of the City Club should give the closest possible study to this list so as to vote intelligently and upon as many offices as possible. *They should also take the first step toward eliminating. such absurdly long ballots by voting for the constitutional convention. Without amendment of the constitution no reasonable shortening of the ballot can be accomplished.*

THE PROPOSITION BALLOT will present five questions to the voters:

1. *The constitutional convention.* The recasting of the fundamental law of the state is everywhere recognized as a necessity. Our present constitution dates from 1870. It fails in many respects to meet the needs of a community which has moved far in advance of the industrial and political conditions of that day. During the forty-eight years since its adoption, the limitation upon amendments has resulted in the accumulation of a large number of important problems which cannot be solved except by a change of the constitution.

All political parties are pledges to the support of the resolution for a constitutional convention.

The Governor is for it. The last General Assembly endorsed it. Citizens' organizations throughout the state, including the City Club Committee on State Constitution, are solidly behind it. *But there is this danger:*

The present constitution provides that any call for a constitutional convention must receive, for approval, *a majority of all votes cast at the election* at which the proposition is submitted. Failure to mark your ballot on the constitutional convention proposal will count as though you had voted "No." *For this reason it is imperative that every citizen should vote upon it. Be sure that you remember this and that your friends also understand it.*

2. *The traction issue.* The referendum on the proposed traction settlement ordinance has aroused "no end" of controversy in the community. The City Club, through the series of traction meetings reported in previous issues, has endeavored to place before its members a full and fair discussion of the ordinance by representative leaders on both sides. An outline of its main provisions will be found in the Bulletin of September 19.

3. *The good roads bond issue.* The City Club Committee on Highways, Bridges and Waste Disposal last week endorsed this measure and urged members of the club to vote for it. It calls for the construction of a state-wide system of hard roads, to. cost ultimately about $60,000,-000. This cost is to be paid, in the first instance, by the issuance of bonds, but interest on these bonds is to be paid and the bonds are to be retired out of funds derived wholly from automobile fees. No taxation will be necessary.*

The measure is non-controversial. As in the

*A fuller discussion of the good roads bond issue will be found in the City Club Bulletin of October 7.

The City Club Bulletin

A Journal of Active Citizenship

Published Weekly Except July, August and September; bi-weekly during July, August and September

By the CITY CLUB OF CHICAGO

315 Plymouth Court   Telephone: Harrison 8278

DWIGHT L. AKERS, Editor

$1.00 per Year   -   -   -   10c per Copy

Entered as second class matter, December 3, 1917, at the postoffice at Chicago, Illinois, under the act of March 3, 1879.

Vol. XI.   Monday, October 28, 1918   No. 35

case of the constitutional convention resolution, the chief danger of defeat lies in a possible neglect by the voters. It must receive a majority of all votes cast at the election.

4. *The private banks bill.* This bill was one of the chief measures enacted by the last legislature. It was passed in response to a public demand that "fly-by-night" private banks, now subject to neither national nor state control, should be brought under supervision. Public interest in this legislation was aroused by the continued failures of banks of this character in which the savings of many poor people had been invested.

The bill provides that after January 1, 1921, no person, partnership or association in Illinois, except banks incorporated under the state or federal laws, shall transact a banking business or use the word "bank." All such businesses will thus be brought under the direct supervision and control of the state, will be subject to inspection and must conform to the banking practices and limitations laid down in the act.

5. *The $3,000,000 bond issue for the Michigan avenue improvement.* The voters of Chicago in 1914 approved a bond issue of $3,800,000 for the widening and extension of Michigan avenue according to the plans of the Chicago Plan Commission. An additional issue of $3,000,000 is now asked for. The reason assigned for this request for additional funds is the heavily increased cost of labor and materials.

Voters should not allow questions of great public importance, such as the above, to be decided by minorities. It is particularly important that such proposals as those for a constitutional convention and for the good roads program, which require a majority of those voting at the election, should not be decided in the negative by mere apathy.

REMEMBER THE PROPOSITION BALLOT AND VOTE ON EVERY QUESTION!

Chicago's Special Need for a Constitutional Convention

UNIFICATION OF LOCAL GOVERNMENTS.
SHORT BALLOT.   REVENUE REFORM.
COURT REORGANIZATION.

The following statement has been issued by the Chicago Bureau of Public Efficiency:

During the past half century there has been enormous improvement in all kinds of machinery —except the machinery of government. In fact, since the adoption of the Illinois Constitution of 1870, the mechanism of local government in Chicago and Cook County has grown more complex and unwieldy. There are overlapping governments, many elective officials striving to function independently of one another, and lack of centralized responsibility.

The greatest needs of Chicago are unification of local governments, the short ballot, and court reorganization. Unity and simplicity should be substituted for multiplicity and complexity. This is impossible without extensive changes in the State Constitution.

Since its organization in 1910, the Chicago Bureau of Public Efficiency has been engaged continuously in the study of problems of government in this community, especially those of administration. While the published reports of the Bureau have indicated ways in which savings might be effected and efficiency promoted by action of those in control of the various governmental offices, these reports also have pointed out that many improvements of far-reaching importance can be brought about only through changes in the Constitution of the State. For this purpose a constitutional convention will provide the only adequate procedure. The process of submitting amendments one at a time will not meet the needs of the situation.

The Legislature may submit amendments to but a single article of the Constitution at any one session. The program for the unification of local governments, the short ballot, and court reorganization would call for the modification of at least four articles of the present Constitution— Article IV, relative to powers of the legislature; Article VI, which prescribes the present judicial organization; Article VIII, dealing with education, which requires the county superintendent of schools to be an elective official; and Article X, relating to counties, which contains rigid specifications applicable to Cook County that ought to be eliminated.

In addition to the program of special concern to the people of Chicago and Cook County, there is, by common consent, need for changing Article IX, relating to revenue. Modification of the revenue provisions of the Constitution is necessary for Chicago as well as for the State at large. Other basic changes urged with influential backing call for the consideration of amendments of at least nine articles altogether. Obviously,

CAPT. CHARLES D. WATERBURY

Capt. Charles D. Waterbury, whose death at Washington was announced in our last issue, was identified with the City Club in many of its activities. As an architect, associated with Pond & Pond, he had a very important part in the planning and construction of our clubhouse. He was a member of our Committee on Housing Conditions and the Club on many occasions profited by his advice and assistance in dealing with this subject. His death has caused deep sorrow among his many friends in the Club.

the process of changing the Constitution by amending one article at a time would take many years.

Opinions will differ with respect to specific plans for city and county consolidation, the short ballot, and court reorganization, but the need for thorough and reasonably prompt action of some sort on these and other matters calling for consideration is plain, and virtually no progress can be made with any plan until existing constitutional limitations shall be modified. Therefore, the Chicago Bureau of Public Efficiency joins with other civic organizations in urging a favorable vote at the November election on the proposition to call a convention to revise the Constitution of Illinois.

What Chicago desires is not special privilege as compared with other cities in the state, but enlarged powers and the removal of restrictions, so that its affairs may be carried on in a manner creditable to the commonwealth and to itself.

October 21, 1918.

SIDNEY G. WILLIAMS, manager of the Accident Prevention Division, National Safety Council, R. R. Baldwin, lawyer, and Rev. Frank Fitt, are new members of the City Club.

Why You Should Vote for a New State Constitution

A MERICA would not think of fighting a twentieth century war with the ammunition and weapons of 1863. Neither can Illinois successfully meet her present-day problems with a constitution adopted soon after the civil war and framed to meet conditions prevailing at that time.

OLD CONSTITUTION BARS PROGRESS.

So far is our present constitution behind the times, so many limitations does it put upon our progress, that a demand has arisen throughout the state for a thorough-going revision. Illinois needs and wants an up-to-date, efficient system of government. She needs a taxation system that will bear equitably upon all citizens of the state. She needs many other changes in the laws which cannot be made under the present constitution because the convention of 1870 could not forsee the needs and problems of this generation.

DEMAND FOR NEW CONSTITUTION IS UNIVERSAL

The demand for a new constitution has the backing of all political parties and of citizens in all parts of the state. The Governor of the state is a strong supporter of the proposal for revision.

The State Legislature at its last session adopted a resolution for the calling of a constitutional convention. This resolution becomes effective only if the voters of the state approve it. They will have the chance to do this at the election on November 5, 1918.

Every citizen should vote upon this proposition, for it must have the approval of a majority of *all citizens voting* in the election. For this reason *failure to vote on the proposition is equivalent to a vote against it.*

THE NEED IS IMMEDIATE

The resolution for a constitutional convention should be adopted *now*, for the preliminaries of calling the convention, the election of delegates, the framing of the new constitution and its approval by the voters at an election will require several years of time. Failure to adopt the resolution will make a new constitution impossible for years to come.

PREPARING FOR AFTER THE WAR

Illinois should be ready, as early after the war as possible, to meet the new problems arising out of the war, but she cannot meet them with her hands tied by the constitution of 1870.

(*The above statement is from a folder prepared by the State Constitution Committee of the City Club and printed for state-wide distribution by the Constitution Convention Campaign Committee.*)

A Check List of Candidates

ELECTION OF NOVEMBER 5, 1918

Your Vote for a Constitutional Convention Will Help
Toward the Ultimate Elimination of the "Long Ballot"

OFFICE	REPUBLICAN	DEMOCRATIC	SOCIALIST
U. S. Senator	Medill McCormick	James Hamilton Lewis	William Bross Lloyd
State Treasurer	Fred E. Sterling	James J. Brady	Robert L. Harvey.
Supt. Public Instruction	Francis G. Blair	Edwin Strauss	Emma Pischel
Congressman at Large	Richard Yates	William E. Williams	C. C. Brooks
(2 to be elected)	William E. Mason	Michael H. Cleary	Frank Watts
Trustees University of	Cairo A. Trimble	John M. Crebs	Ellen Persons
Illinois	John M. Herbert	S. B. Montgomery	Mary O'Reilly
(3 to be elected)	Margaret D. Blake	Mrs. Mary O. Gallery	Antoinette R. Young
President Sanitary District	Alexander N. Todd	James M. Dailey	Clarence W. Shaw
Trustees Sanitary District	William J. Healy	James M. Dailey	Clarence W. Shaw
	Harry E. Littler	Fred D. Breit	Marion Wiley
(3 to be elected)	Willis O. Nance	Charles E. Reading	Robert C. Desmore
Sheriff	Charles W. Peters	Anton J. Cermak	Adolph Dreifuss
County Treasurer	Bernard W. Snow	Harry R. Gibbons	Karl F. M. Sandberg
County Clerk	Charles G. Blake	Robert M. Sweitzer	John M. Collins
County Judge	Edwin A. Olson	Thomas F. Scully	William A. Cunnea
Judge Probate Court	Frederic R. De Young	Henry Horner	Carl Strover
Clerk Probate Court	John F. Devine	Frank J. Walsh	Bernard Kortas
Clerk Criminal Court	William R. Parker	James M. Whalen	Charles Hallbeck
Bailiff Municipal Court	William J. Umbach	Dennis J. Egan	John S. Peterson
Clerk Municipal Court	James J. Kearns	Frank X. Rydzewski	Andrew Lafin
County Superintendent of Schools	A. O. Coddington	Edward J. Tobin	Sophia V. L. Rodriguez
Board of Assessors	Charles Krutckoff	Michael K. Sheridan	George Koop
(2 to be elected)	Charles Ringer	John Cervenka	Frederick G. Wellman
Board of Review (full term)	William H Reid	P. A. Nash	Adolf Bayer
Board of Review (vacancy)	Charles V. Barrett	William P. Feeney	
President County Board	Charles N. Goodnow	Peter Reinberg	John G. Flora
County Commissioners	Charles N. Goodnow	Peter Reinberg	John G. Flora
(from the city—10 to	William McLaren	John Budinger	Joseph M. Mason
be elected)	James H. Johnson	Joseph M. Fitzgerald	Joseph H. Greer
	Louis H. Mack	Thomas Kasperski	C. M. Strom
	Alexander J. Johnson	Daniel Ryan	Abe Basofin
	George Seebacher	Bartley Burg	M. Silverman
	Charles A. Griffin	Robert W. McKinlay	J. H. Rappaport
	Patrick H. Moynihan	Emmett Whealan	H. Sroenier
	Ernest M. Cross	Frank J. Wilson	John M. Feigh
	Tom Murray	Albert Nowak	A. C. Harms
County Commissioners	William Busse	James G. Wolcott	Charles Zweilly
(from country towns	Joseph Carolan	Anton Maciejewski	H. G. Moeller
—5 to be elected)	William H. Maclean	Paul Kamradt	Peter Van Bodegraven
	George A. Miller	James H. Wells	Otto Wolf
	Dudley D. Pierson	James M. Lynch	H. Loensman

Remember the little ballot and vote on every proposition!

Your first chance to take a crack at the "long ballot"! Vote for a constitutional convention.

REPUBLICAN	DEMOCRATIC	SOCIALIST
Martin B. Madden	George Mayer	G. J. Carlisle
James R. Mann	Leo S. LeBosky	Robert H. Howe
William W. Wilson	Fred J. Crowley	Joseph A. Ambros
R. S. Zalewski	John W. Rainey	Carl G. Hoffmann
Lewis C. Mau	A. J. Sabbath	Emil Jaeger
Hervey C. Foster	James McAndrews	William F. Kruse
Niels Juul	Frank M. Padden	J. Louis Engdahl
Dan Parillo	Thomas Gallagher	
Fred A. Britten	James H. Poage	Charles Kissling
Carl R. Chindblom	P. J. Finnegan	Irving S. Tucker

REPUBLICAN	DEMOCRATIC	SOCIALIST
Francis P. Brady		P. H. Geluck
Samuel A. Ettelson	William J. Hennesey	W. L. Berteau
Morton D. Hull	Andy Coleman	Leo B. Shire
Frederick B. Roos	Thomas C. Stobbs	W. Van Bodegraven
Frank Trefil	Patrick J. Carroll	Charles Toepper
Frank P. Sadler	W. J. McInerney	J. W. Deal
Albert C. Clark	J. J. Mulcahey	Zephiere Pepin
Adolph Blazek	John J. Boehm	Joseph Mark
Andrew Wright	Edward J. Glackin	
J. Frank Hemmons	John T. Denvir	Daniel A. Uretz
Edwin Farrar	Edward J. Hughes	Thomas L. Slater
Henry W. Austin	George R. Bruce	T. F. Lippold
C. G. Hutchinson	Daniel Herlihy	Carl A. Juberg
A. Rostenkowski	John Broderick	
William F. Peters	Patrick J. Sullivan	George Schmidt
Willett H. Cornwell	Edward J. Flynn	Robert Norberg

TIVES (Three to Be Elected From Each District)

REPUBLICAN	DEMOCRATIC	SOCIALIST
William M. Brinkman	John Griffin	C. W. Howorth
Sheadrick B. Turner		
Roger J. Marcy	S. E. Weinshenker	Arthur E. Smith
	Frank Ryan	

Randall E. Marshall (Independent)

REPUBLICAN	DEMOCRATIC	SOCIALIST
Adelbert H. Roberts	George G. Noonan	H. S. Smith
Warren B. Douglas		

William G. Anderson (Independent)

REPUBLICAN	DEMOCRATIC	SOCIALIST
Emil O. Kowalski	James P. Boyle	
	Frank McDermott	
Theodore K. Long	Michael L. Igoe	Orren W. Horton
Sidney Lyon	John F. Healy	
E. A. W. Johnson	Robert E. Wilson	A. W. Harrack
Ralph E. Church		
Albert F. Volz	John W. McCarthy	Clarence H. Owen
Howard P. Castle		
David E. Shanahan	Joseph Placek	A. F. Pasecky
	Thomas A. Doyle	
Edward B. Lucius	Frank J. Ryan	Kellam Foster
William H. Cruden	William S. Callahan	
C. A. Young	James W. Ryan	J. A. Gajeski
G. A. Dahlberg		
Thomas Curran	Peter F. Smith	E. J. Maruska
	Joseph Perina	
Edward W. Smejkal	Jacob W. Epstein	
	Charles Coia	
S. P. Roderick	James P. O'Brien	Frank J. Blaha
James M. Kittleman	J. T. Prendergast	
F. J. Bippus	Michael F. Maher	H. W. Harris
Thomas P. Devereux	Benjamin M. Mitchell	
Edward M. Overland	Thomas P. Keane	William Mack
William G. Thon		

(Continued on next page)

STATE REPRESENTATIVES	REPUBLICAN	DEMOCRATIC	SOCIALIST
25th District	C. L. Fieldstack	John G. Jacobson	Adolph Germer
	Theodore Steinert		
27th District	Edward Walz	Joseph Petlak	
		James M. Donlan	
29th District	B. F. Clettenberg	Bernard J. Conlon	Evar Anderson
		L. C. O'Brien	
31st District	Carl Mueller	John J. Kelly	A. F. Almgreen
	James A. Steven	Frank J. Seif, Jr.	

SOCIALIST LABOR CANDIDATES
U. S. Senator—John M. Francis.
State Treasurer—Samuel J. French.
Superintendent Public Instruction—Edward Horr.
Trustees University of Illinois—Mrs. Emma B. Denny, Gustave Jenning, Mrs. Gertrude Carm.
Congressman at Large—William Hartness, Joseph Hamrle.

PROHIBITION CANDIDATES
U. S. Senator—Frank B. Vennum.
State Treasurer—Orrin L. Dayton.
Superintendent Public Instruction—Eldon G. Burritt.
Trustees University of Illinois—Mary Whittemore, William M. Hamilton, Carrie V. Hoff.
Congressman at Large—Charles P. Corson, Edward E. Blake.

THE JUDGES' BALLOT
Municipal Court of Chicago

Chief Justice	Harry Olson	Michael F. Sullivan	Samuel Block
Associate Judge			
(vacancy)	Irwin Hazen	Daniel J. McMahon	
Associate Judges	Earl C. Hales	Charles A. Williams	John LaDuca
(10 to elect)	Daniel P. Trude	John K. Prindiville	Nils Juul Christensen
	Bernard P. Barasa	Joseph P. Rafferty	Bernard Berlyn
	Arnold Heap	Rocco De Stefano	Benjamin Cossman
	William N. Gemmill	John Mahoney	Joseph Morris
	William K. Steele	Harry M. Fisher	James W. Lafferty
	Charles F. McKinley	Joseph LaBuy	H. O. Forsberg
	Thomas J. Graydon	Stanley Walkowiak	James G. Fay
	James F. Burns	John F. Bolton	C. Freiman
	Clarence S. Piggott	John J. Rooney	Victor Koehler

The City Club Committee on State Constitution favors the calling of a convention to revise the fundamental law of the state. Vote "Yes" on this proposition November 5.

You cannot escape the responsibility of a vote upon the "little ballot" issues. On some of these measures your failure to vote is equivalent to a vote in the negative.

A Lesson From Experience

"CERTAIN unfortunate aspects of the Twelfth Street and Michigan Avenue widening projects and the proposed Ogden Avenue extension," supply the text for a report issued by the Chicago Bureau of Public Efficiency urging that the city be given power, in making public improvements, to take property in excess of actual requirements. This power, says the Bureau, can be acquired only through constitutional amendment, and the report is issued in the hope that it may help the movement for a constitutional convention, upon which the people are to vote at the coming November election. The summary and conclusions of the report, copies of which may be obtained from the office of the Bureau, at 315 Plymouth Court, are as follows:

"A study of the manner in which the Twelfth Street and Michigan Avenue improvements have been carried through discloses certain startling conditions that should challenge the attention of the community and lead it to prevent their recurrence in the future.

"In taking by condemnation property for these street-widening projects, small and odd-shaped remnants that are unsuitable for building purposes have been left in the hands of private owners.

A FLAGRANT EXAMPLE

"The most flagrant example is furnished by a corner lot known as the Price property which had a frontage of 166 feet on Twelfth Street and 71 feet on Wabash Avenue. In widening Twelfth Street at that point, the city took 68

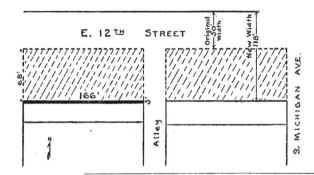

"THE PRICE PROPERTY"

Lot remnant with a frontage of 166 feet on 12th St., as widened and a depth of only 3 ft. Originally the lot extended back 71 ft. from 12th St.

the 71 feet. This left in the possession of the ivate owner a lot remnant with a frontage of 6 feet on Twelfth Street and a depth of only ree feet. The city was required by the courts pay the full value of the entire 71 feet though secured title and control to but 68 feet thereof. "A lot three feet deep with a frontage of 166 et on an improved street might be used for llboards but not for much else. So long as remains under separate ownership it must con- itute a nuisance and may be an eyesore.

"Experience in other cities shows that lot rem- ants unsuitable for building purposes, instead f being sold speedily to owners of adjoining roperty, do in fact remain under separate own- rship for long periods of time.

"The widening of Twelfth Street and Michi- an Avenue left many other lot remnants as hown on the diagrams accompanying this re- ort.

ON MICHIGAN AVENUE

"On Michigan Avenue the city took all of, r parts of, lots having a total frontage of ap- roximately 3,000 feet. This does not include roperty taken for plazas. When the improve- nent is actually completed, along this 3,000 feet here will be lot areas with a frontage of 617 eet, having depths varying from five feet to 14 eet. Thus, so long as these remnants remain nder ownership separate from that of adjoin- ng property—and this may be for many years— pproximately one-fifth of the entire frontage nvolved in the widening process will remain acant or will be used only for billboards, small ne-story shops, or other makeshift structures.

DIAGONAL STREETS WORSE

"When it comes to diagonal streets, the situ- tion is likely to be even worse. The proposed)gden Avenue extension, which is to be cut hrough as a new diagonal street, if carried out n accordance with the present survey, will leave 3 remnants (with a frontage of approximately ,300 feet on the proposed new street) that will e too small or too irregular in shape to be vailable for building purposes.

"Small and odd-shaped lot remnants not only result in public nuisances, but their existence de- feats one of the main purposes of street widen- ing—that of securing an imposing thoroughfare.

"Another consequence of such situations is that the city or other property owners, or both, suffer financial loss through inability of the authorities to collect as much in special assessment benefits and in taxes as otherwise might be secured.

THE SOLUTION

"The way to prevent these abuses is to confer upon the City the power of excess condemnation. Under this power the City, in making a public improvement, could acquire by condemnation more property than is necessary for the precise, narrow purpose of the improvement, using the excess property so taken in any way that might be in the public interest, or selling it for private use subject to restrictions calculated to promote the larger purpose of the improvement.

"In the case of a street widening or opening, the possession of such power would enable the City to take by eminent domain, in addition to land that is to form a part of the street, such areas along the improved thoroughfare as may be needed for the formation of suitable building lots, and to sell them subject to restrictions as to use.

"The original Chicago Plan report, prepared under the direction of Mr. Daniel H. Burnham, published in 1909, laid emphasis upon the need for the power of excess condemnation. Since that time several states—Ohio, New York, Massachusetts, Wisconsin, and Rhode Island— have amended their constitutions so as to auth- orize excess condemnation. Illinois has done nothing in connection with this subject. If the recommendations of the report of 1909 with re- spect to excess condemnation had been put into effect, the abuses in connection with the Twelfth Street and Michigan Avenue widening projects and the proposed Ogden Avenue extension, to which this report directs attention, could have been, or could be, avoided.

"Constitutional and statutory changes needed

Club Committee Endorses Road Bonds

The City Club Committee on Highways, Bridges and Waste Disposal has considered carefully the proposed Sixty Million Dollar State Hard-Road bond issue which is to be voted upon at the election November 5, 1918. As a result the Committee unanimously and unreservedly endorses this bond issue. It urges all members of the City Club to vote "Yes" on this proposition on the little ballot and to impress upon their friends and acquaintances the importance of doing the same. It likewise urges the public to vote in the affirmative on this proposition.

The Committee has been unable upon inquiry to discover any opposition to this measure, but it requires for adoption a majority of all votes cast at the election. A failure to vote will therefore be in effect a vote in the negative.

CITY CLUB COMMITTEE ON HIGHWAYS, BRIDGES AND WASTE DISPOSAL.

    F. G. HEUCHLING, *Chairman.*
    CARLTON R. DART, *Secretary.*

The Listening Post

Remember the little ballot and vote on every proposition!

OWING TO THE 'flu," no meetings are being held at the City Club at present. The address which was to have been made to members of the Club by Governor Lowden, Saturday, October 19, had to be cancelled on this account. We had relied upon our report of this address to fill up the columns of the Bulletin and its cancellation late in the week left us without our leading article. Our last week's number was, therefore, omitted.

REDMOND D. STEPHENS is captain in the quartermaster's department at Washington.

JOHN R. RICHARDS, director of recreation and playgrounds of the South Park System, has been appointed one of a committee of five in Washington which is to undertake the enforcement of proper living conditions among war workers. This committee was named last week by the Department of Labor.

WORD HAS BEEN RECEIVED that Lieutenant Robert M. Curtis, a member of the City Club, who was on the U. S. submarine chaser 219 when it was sunk two weeks ago, is now recovering in a hospital in Naples. The sinking of the boat was the result of an explosion which occurred while the boat was taking on coal. Two men were killed and several, including Lieutenant Curtis, were wounded. Lieutenant Curtis has cabled that he expects to return to duty within about two weeks. Lieutenant Curtis is a son-in-law of Alfred L. Baker, formerly president of the City Club.

The City Club Committee on Highways believes that a vote for hard roads is hard sense.

---

to give the City the power of excess condemnation should be made speedily so that the municipality may obtain more satisfactory results in carrying out other features of its city planning program. In urging action to secure the needed enlargement of powers, the Bureau does not mean to intimate that projects already under way should not have been started, or that new projects should be delayed. It will take several years to bring about the desired constitutional changes. Important public improvements cannot be held back to await the outcome of a constitutional convention. The purpose of this report is to emphasize the need for securing the power of excess condemnation as soon as possible; not to interpose new obstacles to projects which it is hoped to carry out in the near future.

CITY SHOULD GET FULL TITLE

"In amending the Constitution to authorize the exercise by governmental agencies of the power of excess condemnation, provision should be made for the passing of full title when property is taken under the law of eminent domain. At present, the agency taking property in Illinois by condemnation secures only the right of use for a specific purpose. If the City condemns land for a school site, for example, and later abandons the use for that purpose, the property reverts to the original owner or his heirs. Where property has been acquired in good faith for a public purpose and full value has been paid therefor, and it is later found that such property is no longer needed for the particular purpose for which it was acquired, the City should have the right to treat it as a public asset, and to change its use or sell it.

"In the interest of the city planning movement railroads also should be permitted to sell property which they may take under condemnation proceedings for railroad use but which later may not be needed for railroad purposes. Under a plan of wise rearrangement of terminals in Chicago, much property now in the possession of the railroads should be freed for other uses. It should be possible to carry out such a plan without reckoning with the heirs of original owners of property taken by condemnation, who received full value for the lands at the time of acquisition."

DEC 2 1 191b

The City Club Bulletin

A Journal of Active Citizenship

FRIDAY, NOVEMBER 8, AT LUNCHEON

ARTHUR GLEASON

Author and Editor, New York

"British Labor and the War"

Mr. Gleason is with the Committee on Public Information. He was formerly associate editor of Colliers Weekly and has served on the editorial staff of the Survey, Harper's Weekly and other well known magazines. He was in England at the outbreak of the war and has been there and in France almost continuously since that time. He has just published (jointly with Mr. Paul U. Kellogg of the Survey) a book on the subject above announced for his City Club address.

SATURDAY, NOVEMBER 9, AT LUNCHEON

SAMUEL GOMPERS

President of the American Federation of Labor

Mr. Gompers will speak about the recent visit of the American Labor Mission to the allied countries.

On Friday evening, November 8, Mr. Gompers is to address a mass-meeting at the Auditorium under the auspices of the American Alliance of Labor and Democracy. Among those who will attend this meeting are members of the cabinet, the governors of twelve states, and members of the councils of defense of several neighboring states. It is expected that a number of these distinguished guests will attend the luncheon at the City Club.

MONDAY, NOVEMBER 11, AT LUNCHEON

FREDERICK C. HOWE

Commissioner of Immigration, Port of New York

"Reconstruction"

Mr. Howe's activities in American public life have been of a varied character. He was formerly a member of the Cleveland City Council and of the Ohio State Senate. He was on one occasion sent to Great Britain by the United States government to study the subject of municipal ownership there. He is at present U. S. Commissioner of Immigration at the Port of New York.

Mr. Howe is the author of many well known books on public affairs, including "The City— the Hope of Democracy" and "The British City."

The City Club Bulletin

A Journal of Active Citizenship

Published Weekly Except July, August and September; bi-weekly during July, August and September

By the CITY CLUB OF CHICAGO

315 Plymouth Court   Telephone: Harrison 8278

DWIGHT L. AKERS, Editor

$1.00 per Year   -   -   -   -   10c per Copy

Entered as second class matter, December 3, 1917, at the postoffice at Chicago, Illinois, under the act of March 3, 1879.

Vol. XI.   Monday, November 4, 1918   No. 36

United to Serve

One patriotic drive for funds on the part of all seven officially recognized agencies engaged in welfare work among our land and naval forces is planned in the United War Work Campaign, from November 11-18. In a nation-wide effort for service and sacrifice, it will sweep aside all creeds and all races in its general appeal. The organizations combining their individual demands are the Young Men's Christian Association, the Young Women's Christian Association, the National Catholic War Council, the Jewish Welfare Board, the War Camp Community Service, the American Library Association and the Salvation Army. Every man in uniform has personally benefited by the care with which these agencies have attended him, at his training camp, on the transports and on the other side. To continue these activities for another year the united organizations ask for $170,500,000, a sum of money immense in the aggregate but representing only $1 a week for each man in the army and navy.

THE GOAL

Young Men's Christian Association.	$100,000,000
Young Women's Christian Assn....	15,000,000
National Catholic War Council....	30,000,000
Jewish Welfare Board...........	3,500,000
War Camp Community Service....	15,000,000
American Library Association.....	3,500,000
Salvation Army.................	3,500,000

Illinois' quota is $12,740,000.

"I SURE MISS the City Club luncheons, talks, and comforts," writes one of our members, who is in government service at Washington.

JOHN S. MILLER, JR., is in service in France with the rank of major, 333rd Field Artillery.

Remember the little ballot and vote on every proposition!

The City Club and the Traction Question

PRESIDENT GEORGE H. MEAD, last Thursday, with the approval of the directors, issued the following statement defining the position of the City Club toward the pending traction issue:

"In dealing with controversial issues that arise in Chicago, the City Club has uniformly pursued the policy of shedding light by public discussion, but has not adopted one side or the other. In this manner the Club has provided a forum for discussion while it could keep in its membership all those who are honestly interested in the solution of Chicago's problems, however they have differed as to the form which the solution should take. In controversial matters there is no one and no board nor committee that can speak for the Club as a whole. The committees of the Club present from time to time reports on matters of public interest and concern, but these committee reports represent only the judgment and decision of the committee itself. Furthermore, in case of sharp controversy it is the rule of the Club that only those reports should be published which present adequate reasoned grounds for the opinions of the committees. The Club does not undertake to add weight but to shed light.

"Thus, in the traction issue now before the public, the City Club has presented the most competent discussion from both sides that has been offered in the city. Its committee on Public Utilities has sent in to the Public Affairs Committee a majority and a minority report. The majority report favors the passage of the ordinance. The minority report advises its defeat. Neither report has undertaken to give an adequate statement of the reasons for and against, and following its tradition in such situations the Club does not publish the reports.

"The Civic Secretary of the Club, Mr. George E. Hooker, and another member of the office staff, have been active as individuals in the campaign against the ordinance, in the exercise of their undoubted rights as citizens of Chicago. They in no way represent the Club in their activities. The President and Vice-President and many members of the Board of Directors as individuals are in favor of and working for the passage of the ordinance, and in their opinions and activities they do not represent the City Club.

"The City Club is jealous of its position, won through years of activity in civic struggles, as a field within which all those honestly interested in solving Chicago's problems, may join in investigation and debate. It is almost universally true that what is most needed for the solution of these problems is more light."

Remember the little ballot and vote on every proposition!

City Council Favors Convention

THE City Council of Chicago is on record in favor of the calling of a constitutional convention. A special committee of the Council on the constitutional convention has issued an appeal to voters to support the resolution for such a convention when it is before them for adoption at the election, November 5.

The committee says, in part:

"You are undoubtedly aware of the complicated form of our local governments, and of the inequalities and deficiencies of our obsolete system of levying and assessing taxes. *A revision of the Constitution would make it possible to bring about a simplification.*

"The number of elective officers specified in the Constitution, in addition to those serving the various local governments, is such that the voter, confronted on election day with a ballot of confusing length, finds it impossible to make a discriminating choice, and is reduced to the necessity of either not voting for some offices or of making a haphazard guess. As the duties performed by many of these officers are of a routine nature, their elimination from the ballot would enable the voter to center his attention on the important offices. *Revision of the Constitution is necessary to secure the Short Ballot.*

"To provide for its local governmental needs, Chicago has been compelled to go to every legislature in session since 1870 to plead for the passage of some law that would permit it to keep step with its progress. How badly these laws were needed may be seen from the fact that the original Cities and Villages Act, under which Chicago is governed, adopted by the legislature in 1872, contains only 193 paragraphs, while the additions thereto, through various amendments and new laws passed since that time, number 1,200 paragraphs. *Revision of the Constitution is necessary to give Chicago greater control over its local affairs.*

"A number of other constitutional changes have been suggested as necessary to make our state and local governments more efficient and economical. Most of these subjects have been widely discussed during recent years. The value of some may be controversial. Changes in the Constitution would undoubtedly be submitted to the voters for their approval or disapproval as separate articles. In any event, the voter would have the final word on any subject.

"To those who fear that the convention method would open the way for faddists or special interests to secure an incorporation of ill-considered or harmful matters, we urge our supreme confidence that the people of Illinois have not lost their power and ability for self-government, and that they can be trusted to give intelligent, discriminating and honest expression to ·their

wishes in respect to those matters which make for the common good. In this connection, attention is called to the fact that the conditions for popular control are practically ideal, viz.:

1. Popular vote for calling the convention.

2. Popular vote on delegates to the convention.

3. Popular vote to ratify or reject the work of the convention.

"The opportunity is before us to secure a constitution that will permit our State to keep pace with modern progress in legislation and enable it to deal effectively with the new problems that will arise from this world war."

The report is signed by Alderman John A. Richert, chairman of the committee. Other members of the committee are:

U. S. Schwartz	Henry D. Capitain
A. A. McCormick	William F. Lipps
Ross A. Woodhull	Harry E. Littler
Otto Kerner	Joseph O. Kostner

English a la Cincinnati

The following gems have been compiled from letters received by the Cincinnati Red Cross from wives and mothers of men in service:

"My husband got a few days furle and has been away on the mind sweepers."

"You have changed my little boy to a little girl. Will it make any difference."

"Will you please send my money as soon as possible, as I am walking about Boston like a bloddy pauper."

"I do not receive my husband's pay. I will be compelled to live an immortal life."

"My Bill has been put in charge of a spittoon (platoon). Will I get more pay?"

"I am writing to you to ask you why I have never received my elopment. His money was kept from him for the elopement for me which I never received."

"Please send me my allotment. I have a little baby and knead it every day."

SINCE THE CITY CLUB, at the suggestion of its Soldiers' and Sailors' Entertainment Committee, extended its privileges to enlisted men, the clubhouse has been used for many different purposes. Last week we had our first military wedding. Sergt. Karl Buck of the Motor Truck Division and Mrs. Mary M. Snyder were married last week at the City Club by Rev. O. F. Jordan, one of our members. Sergeant and Mrs. Buck left for the South immediately after the ceremony.

An Argument for Excess Condemnation

LAST week the Bulletin contained an article summarizing the conclusions of the Chicago Bureau of Public Efficiency from its study of "excess condemnation." The Bureau showed, by illustrations from Chicago experience, the evil resulting from the present constitutional restriction upon the city's buying power in acquiring real estate for public improvements. As the city may purchase only the real estate actually needed for the improvement, many odd-shaped and useless remnants are left, which cannot conveniently be joined up with adjacent property and which often—as billboard sites or as uncared-for vacant premises—become eyesores to the neighborhood.

The illustration below is a case in point. The black areas indicate some of the remnants which will result under our present policy from the cutting of the proposed Ogden Ave. diagonal extension.

The need for conferring "excess condemnation" powers on cities is a subject which, the Bureau believes, should be considered by a constitutional convention.

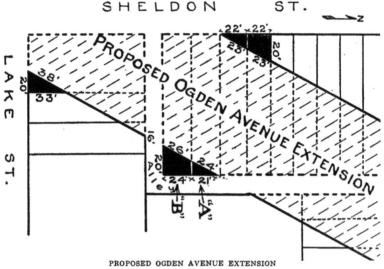

PROPOSED OGDEN AVENUE EXTENSION

Lot remnants "A" and "B", with frontage of 24 feet and 26 feet, respectively, on the proposed Ogden avenue extension, will be separated from the rest of the block by a 16-foot alley, which will bound the property on two sides. Special difficulty is encountered, when a diagonal street is cut through, in making the alley arrangement conform to a new street and lot layout.

ALBERT L. HOPKINS, who has been in the office of Chief Counsel of the Interstate Commerce Commission at Washington, D. C., has entered military service.

CAPT. ALBERT A. HENRY is stationed at Washington in the office of the Third Assistant Secretary of War.

DR. H. I. DAVIS has accepted from the American Red Cross a commission for service in France. Dr. Davis is head of the Psychopathic Hospital of Cook County.

"It is a comfort to know when you buy a liberty bond, that if, later, you get in a tight place, you can sell the bond and get full value for it immediately. Nevertheless, when you encourage the sale of bonds you are fighting the idea of thrift, which is the basic idea of finance. What good does it do the government if I lend it a thousand dollars today and get a liberty bond and then tomorrow sell that bond to someone else for a thousand dollars? I simply carried it for one day and the other person who bought it of me might just as well have subscribed for it in the beginning! He is the one carrying the burden and not I. If we do our full duty we must not only subscribe and not only save in order to make good our subscription, but we must hold the bond to the end of the war."—*Irving Fisher.*

The City Club Bulletin

A Journal of Active Citizenship

Captain Charles E. Merriam

will address the City Club

THURSDAY, NOVEMBER 14, at Luncheon

SUBJECT: *"Italy and the War"*

Captain Merriam returned only a few weeks ago from Italy where he was in charge of American propaganda work for the Bureau of Public Information. His official position gave him unusual opportunities for observing Italy, both on the fighting line and on her "home front."

British Labor and the War

BRITISH labor is behind the Wilson program, according to Arthur Gleason, who spoke at the City Club luncheon last Friday. Mr. Gleason recently returned from England where—except for one year during which he was with an ambulance corps attached to the Belgian army—he has been almost continuously since the outbreak of the war. During his stay there, he studied particularly the political and labor movements of Great Britain. Mr. Gleason was formerly associate editor of Collier's Weekly and has also served on the editorial or contributing staffs of the Survey, Harper's Weekly, and other American journals. He said in part:

"Mr. Wilson's policy on international questions is the policy of British labor. Both Mr. Wilson and the British Labor Party believe in making a clean cut discrimination between the German government and the German people. British labor knows that seventy million people cannot be exterminated, that they must be lived with, but that the German government must be rendered powerless to disturb the peace. The main plank in the platform of the British labor party, therefore, is the League of Nations. When President Wilson announced this as a part of his program, British labor signed in at once and practically forced the adherence of other nations.

"Certain discoveries of the war have been brought home to the common people of England. One is that when unemployment disappears, as it has done during the war, the wage scale *does* go up. Labor is therefore planning to do away with unemployment after the war, through an extensive program of public works, reforestation, housing, etc.

"Another discovery is that where life can be conscripted, wealth, which is not so sacred as life, can also be conscripted. When a nation has once made a universal conscription of its

The City Club Bulletin

A Journal of Active Citizenship

Published Weekly Except July, August and September; bi-weekly during July, August and September

By the CITY CLUB OF CHICAGO

315 Plymouth Court   Telephone: Harrison 8278

DWIGHT L. AKERS, Editor

$1.00 per Year   -   -   -   -   10c per Copy

Entered as second class matter, December 3, 1917, at the postoffice at Chicago, Illinois, under the act of March 3, 1879.

Vol. XI   Monday, November 11, 1918   No. 37

people, they will be content not to go back to their former condition. Unless some sort of program of change is put through, we may be facing a condition of anarchy.

"In fact, the returned soldiers are the most radical element in the community. Mr. Balfour, in a recent study, found that the most radical industrialists are the returned soldiers. Having gone to the front to fight Prussianism they are not disposed to submit to industrial Prussianism at home. I don't believe that our boys, either, when they come home from France, will be willing to go back into industry under conditions which expose them to the risks of unemployment or to pay the cost of the war in taxes.

SELF-GOVERNMENT IN INDUSTRY

"The British workingman sees, probably for the first time, that if he is to share more fully in the product of labor, total production must be increased. In order to get this increased production, the British employer during the war has made concessions. Labor has been given a share in the management of industry. This policy has been urged by the government through the 'Whitley reports.' Employers are putting it into effect voluntarily. These reports call for the formation of shop, district and national committees within an industry to participate with the employer in the fixing of work shop conditions and the terms of production. The Rolls-Royce company, for instance, asks its workers to come into the time-room and to assist in determining the amount of speeding up that will be necessary. Ultimately these committees may have something to say about the control of credit, markets, etc. This is self-government in industry. We in America ought to study this tendency for sooner or later the impact of this movement will be felt here.

"British labor has both an industrial expression, in the trades unions, and a political expression, in the British Labor party. It has learned that the industrial movement in itself is insufficient.

"The head of the Labor party, Mr. Arthur Henderson, is one of the men chiefly responsible for the winning of this war. His task has been to keep the extreme right and the extreme left of the British labor movement together. To call Mr. Henderson a pacifist and defeatist is bitter untruth. One son is dead on French soil, another is incapacitated for life through the war and a third is at the front. Mr. Henderson is the leader of labor now and is likely some time to be the leader of his country for labor is marching on to a control of the government. The coming election, if called, will probably continue the present executive. Lloyd-George will remain in office but after the war British labor will gain seat after seat and, I believe, within ten years will control the country.

A NEW ORDER

"We are facing today a situation as great as that during the French revolution. There is a new spirit abroad in the land and that new spirit and the new machinery which is being devised to give it expression, are bringing in a new social order."

At the close of Mr. Gleason's address he answered many questions from the floor. Some of his points were as follows:

"The British labor movement is not Bolshevik in character, nor does it sympathize with anarchy. It is essentially conservative and moves slowly, along evolutionary lines, in accomplishing its purposes."

"Lloyd-George felt that in order to win the war it was necessary to form a coalition with certain reactionary leaders. In so doing, however, he lost the confidence of the British labor movement."

THE INTERNATIONAL CONFERENCE

"The Labor party believes that, had the government permitted a meeting with the minority socialists of Germany, such a conference might have permitted an explanation of the purposes of the Allies, which would have hastened the disintegration now taking place in Germany. It believes thoroughly in the International."

"A new equalitarian basis of wages is being arrived at. This is due to the fact of the war. There is no wage system in the army—and it works. There is in the army, on the whole, an equality of sacrifice between officers and men. But in industry at present there is no equality of sacrifice. What the Labor party aims at is a national minimum of the necessities and amenities of life."

WOMEN AFTER THE WAR

"Women workers in England will probably have a hard time immediately after the war. They will be underpaid and will be looked upon as 'scabs' in the labor market. The trades unions, none too swiftly, are admitting women into their ranks and the women gradually are being organized."

ext Step Toward the Convention

HE approval by the Illinois voters last Tuesday of the resolution for a constituional convention paves the way for a thoroughoing reconstruction of the framework of our tate government.

Under the provisions of the present constituion, it becomes the duty of the General Assemly at its next session to provide for a convenion to consist of double the number of members f the Senate. As there are fifty-one members f the Senate, the convention will be a body of 02 members.

Qualifications for delegates to the convention re the same as those for state senator. The elegates must also be "elected in the same anner, at the same places and in the same disricts" as members of the Senate. Differences f interpretation of this last requirement may ave an important bearing on the character and ersonnel of the convention. A non-partisan lection of delegates with nomination by petition s generally conceded to be desirable as a means f eliminating party bias from the deliberations f the convention. If only *constitutional* proisions for the election of members of the enate must be observed in the election of deleate there is no legal obstacle to the adoption of such a scheme. If on the other hand all *statutory* provisions must be observed, the election will have to be on present party lines and possibly even nominations will have to be made in party primaries. Precedent in the framing of the present and former constitutions of Illinois supports the view that statutory provisions must be taken into account. On the other hand arguments based on decisions of the courts and the precedent set by Ohio in holding a non-partisan election for delegates to its constitutional convention are presented to sustain the former interpretation. This is one of the difficulties which the legislature will have to iron out in preparing its call for the election.

There is no provision in the constitution which determines the date for the election of delegates, unless the clause previously quoted be interpreted to mean that delegates must be chosen at the same *time,* as members of the senate. Neither logic nor precedent, however, seems to justify this interpretation and it is believed that there is no constitutional objection to a special election for delegates, if the legislature should see fit to provide such an election. There will be no general state-wide election until November, 1920.

Besides fixing the call for the election, the General Assembly is required by the constitution to designate the time and meeting place for the convention, fix the pay of delegates and provide for the expenses of the convention.

The convention must meet within three months of its election and the alterations or amendments which it proposes must be submitted to the voters of the state for ratification or rejection within two to six months of adjournment. The passage of the necessary legislation by the General Assembly, the election of delegates, the deliberations of the convention, and the ratification of amendments will consume, it is estimated, at least two years of time.

The revision of the underlying law of the state may be looked upon as a necessary part of the general program of reconstruction following the war. In the state, as in the nation, the next few years will probably see a searching examination of the foundations of our economic and political life and an effort to adapt our institutions of government to the needs of our rapidly changing society. In this process, the writing of a new and modern constitution for the state is fundamental.

An Invitation

THE Municipal Art Committee was not included in the list of civic committees recently submitted to members in connection with the pending committee reorganization. It has been decided, however, that in view of the important work done by this committee in the past and the important field of work which still exists, it shall be continued during the coming year. The Civic Secretary has, therefore, been asked to afford members, who so desire, opportunity to join this committee. *Any member of the Club who desires to join will kindly send his name at once to the civic secretary.*

AMONG the successful candidates at last Tuesday's election are the following members of the City Club:

Medill McCormick, U. S. Senator.
Henry Horner, Judge of the Probate Court.
Daniel Trude and Harry M. Fisher, Associate Justices, Municipal Court.

DR. ROBERT ELLIOTT GRAVES has been commissioned captain in the Medical Corps. He has left Chicago to take up his war duties.

DEMAREST LLOYD, E. H. Cassels, and H. R. Kern have entered the Central Officers' Training School at Camp Zachary Taylor, Ky.

DR. MILTON M. PORTIS has accepted a commission as Captain in the Medical Corps.

C. S. HOLCOMB has a lieutenant's commission in the army and is stationed at Camp Humphrey, Va.

Should Our Suburbs Be Annexed?

THE question of annexing suburban communities comes up perennially at Chicago elections. The voters within the city have generally by large majorities favored such annexations but the residents of the communities affected have generally been opposed to them.

WHY ANNEX OUR SUBURBS?

Annexation advocates have often asserted that as a matter of duty suburbanites should be willing to assume a part of the responsibilities of government of the city from which they draw so much of personal advantage. But does a suburban community have anything to gain for itself by annexation? A committee of the Cleveland Chamber of Commerce, which has been investigating the desirability of annexing suburban communities around Cleveland, answers the question in the affirmative in a report, which was published recently. The committee concludes that "the best interests of Cleveland include the best interests of the suburb," and that "in general the communities included in the territory under consideration are actually, if not legally, a part of Cleveland, and those considerations which are vital to Cleveland's welfare are of far greater importance to the suburb than are those which pertain to these suburban communities alone."

The advantages to be derived from annexation, according to the committee's report, may be summarized as follows:

"Elimination of wasteful duplication of governmental functions.

"Permission of a more scientific planning of future improvements.

"Maintenance of the prestige of Cleveland in the matter of its rank in size.

"A more equitable distribution of responsibilities and advantages incident to urban life."

SCHOOLS IN OUR SUBURBS

Do the suburbs offer better school advantages than the city? That is the question which has influenced many residents of suburbs to oppose annexation. The Cleveland Committee, while admitting that in some of the adjacent suburbs school instruction is as good as that furnished in the city schools, says that Cleveland is offering many educational advantages that are not to be obtained in the suburbs—"among these are specialized technical and commercial, normal, night, special schools, etc., none of which is available to suburban residents without the payment of a considerable fee."

EVERYBODY IN IT

"A valuable advantage to be gained by citizens of the suburbs through annexation," says the Committee, "is the right to participate in the government of which all are primarily interested. Practically all of the residents of the suburbs have their commercial and industrial interest within the city limits of Cleveland. Although millions of dollars are so invested, yet the owners of this wealth have no voice in making the rules which govern this property, and the suburban residents who are employed in Cleveland are unable to vote on any question involving the betterment of working conditions."

Another advantage claimed by the Committee on annexation, is that an improved government might be obtained by a consolidation. "The point that impresses itself most forcibly upon your investigators was that the advantages enjoyed under a large governmental unit outweigh the advantages of a small governmental unit. The greater organization, through its specialized departments and because of its size, is enabled to bring about results that are impossible of attainment by the smaller units. We need not here enumerate the various departments and activities which Cleveland can economically support, and which are prohibited in the suburbs through the higher per capita cost."

Our Third Gold Star

LIEUTENANT GORDON R. HALL died September 18th of wounds received in action, according to a telegram received last week by his father Lewis T. Hall, 11 W. Walton Place. Lieutenant Hall had been a member of the Club since 1911. He was director of publicity for the W. D. Allen Company. This is the third death within a few weeks among our members in service. The deaths of Captain Albert A. Sercomb and Captain Charles D. Waterbury were reported in previous issues of the Bulletin.

Lieutenant Hall was born in Chicago February 28, 1887. He attended the second officers training camp at Fort Sheridan and after his graduation was commissioned a second lieutenant. He was ordered home to await assignment and on December 13 he sailed for France. He attended the artillery school at Saumur, France, for three months upon arrival, spent two months behind the front lines and then was sent back to the school as an instructor. Later he was attached to the 320th field artillery, and after having served with that regiment for a short time, was transferred to the 308th artillery. He served on the front lines with both regiments.

Lieutenant Hall was graduated from Amherst in 1909. He is survived by his parents and a sister, Mrs. E. J. Walker. The father is connected with the interior decorating department of Marshall Field & Co.

LAST WEEK, the Club welcomed into its membership Mr. A. M. VanAuken, Cost Engineer, C. B. & Q. R. R., and Mr. Charles I. Brayton, Manager Block, Maloney & Company (brokers).

The City Club Bulletin

A Journal of Active Citizenship

VOLUME XI.   MONDAY, NOVEMBER 18, 1918   NUMBER 38

THURSDAY, NOVEMBER 21, AT LUNCHEON
Rt. Rev. HENRY R. WAKEFIELD
Bishop of Birmingham, Chaplain in the British Army
"Reflections on the World War"

In addition to his activities in the church, Bishop Wakefield has had an active public career as member of the London School Board, Mayor of Marylebone, Chairman of the Central Committee of the Unemployed and member of the Royal Commission on the Poor Law.

TUESDAY, NOVEMBER 26, AT LUNCHEON
MARY VAN KLEECK
Director Woman in Industry Service, U. S. Department of Labor
"Women in Industry in the War"

FRIDAY, NOVEMBER 29, AT LUNCHEON
E. T. GUNDLACH
U. S. Department of Labor
"The Government's Labor Policies"

The Coming Reconstruction

ON Victory day, a large audience, forsaking for a while its horns and rattles, gathered at the City Club to hear a discussion of the great new problems of reconstruction which peace has brought to the nation. The speaker was Frederick C. Howe, whose writings on the political and social problems of the day are, we believe, known to all members of the City Club. Mr. Howe is commissioner of immigration at the port of New York.

"A reconstruction period," said Mr. Howe, "is always the most critical period in a nation's history. It is easy at such a time for private interests to become ascendant. The Civil War gave us our present system of the protective tariff. The railroads, during the reconstruction period which followed that war, laid hands on the public domain with the result that millions of acres of land are now owned by a comparatively few people. Wall Street had been invited into the government to help finance the war, and it stayed.

"One of the great issues before the American people, now that the world war is ended, will

The City Club Bulletin

A Journal of Active Citizenship

Published Weekly Except July, August and September; bi-weekly during July, August and September

By the CITY CLUB OF CHICAGO
315 Plymouth Court   Telephone: Harrison 8278

DWIGHT L. AKERS, Editor

$1.00 per Year   -   -   -   -   10c per Copy

Entered as second class matter, December 3, 1917, at the postoffice at Chicago, Illinois, under the act of March 3, 1879.

Vol. XI   Monday, November 18, 1918   No. 38

be a struggle for the control of taxation. The question of who is to pay the cost of the war will be the greatest issue of the reconstruction period. The future control of the railroads also comes up for consideration. Another great special interest is involved here. Finally, there is the question: How is America to use her surplus wealth? We are the richest nation of the world. We are about the only great credit nation. Undeveloped countries will come to us instead of to the European financial centers for credit, for their leadership has been lost through the war. There is no question more important to America than that of dollar diplomacy or financial imperialism. Never have such great economic stakes been played for in the history of the world."

AGRICULTURE AFTER THE WAR

One of the consequences of all great wars, according to Mr. Howe, has been the destruction of agriculture. "This war," he said, "has stripped the land of continental Europe of its labor. To revive agriculture a new kind of credit will have to be established. The future of the world depends upon the kind of credit agencies to be developed after the war, for without this the world may not be able to rebuild itself. Famine is likely to be abroad in those lands where credit is not sent down in small amounts to the people but concentrated for the benefit of large financiers.

"This war marks a definite break in the life of America, ends the long period of individualism, the period when the things which should be public were confused with the things which should be private. It ends the period of laissez faire and brings us to something akin to the state of socialism of Europe.

"The government will, for instance, have to keep the railroads, as a means of maintaining our trade position. The nation cannot afford to leave its agencies of communication in the hands of speculators and profiteers. Germany

built herself up largely through her control of the railroads. We ought to inaugurate a great policy of railroad extension at the end of the war. Hundreds of millions of dollars could be profitably spent and thousands of our soldiers employed in the improvement of the railroads.

"There is no reason why waterways should not be developed as in Europe. I remember the shipping on Lake Erie when I was a boy, but today almost every port on the lake is owned by a railway or by some corporation like the United States Steel Company. The control of the greatest inland waterway in the world has thus slipped into private hands. Europe carries her bulk freight largely by water, we carry ours largely by railway. Millions of dollars ought to be expended in developing an integrated system of rail and water ways."

EDUCATION OF THE FUTURE

The promotion of education has been recognized in Great Britain as one of the great problems of the reconstruction period. Mr. Howe discussed the report of one of the important committees of the British government on this subject. It is, he said, not primarily a report on education at all. It holds that there is no use in talking about education when people need food, need decent homes, and shorter hours of work—that England must change the foundations of her society if she is to have a decent educational system.

Mr. Howe urged that the reconstruction period be utilized for a revision of our educational system. "All our educational resources," he said, "ought to be mobilized at the end of the war so that every soldier who wants to can go to school." He cited Denmark's system of adult education as the nearest approach to his conception of the opportunities which we should afford our soldiers. Denmark provides in the people's high schools a six months education, similar in many respects to our Gary plan, for people from 18 to 50 years of age. The period is short but is so intensive that the students gather a good education both of a cultural and a serviceable character. Denmark has by this means raised her standard of literacy above that of almost any other European nation. A modification of our educational system along these lines, Mr. Howe believes, would have beneficial effects upon the general school curriculum.

LAND SETTLEMENT

The Committee on Agriculture and Fisheries in England is the author of a report on "The Agriculture of Tomorrow." It advocates a land settlement policy similar to that of Ireland and Australia and outlines a new kind of farm colony for the returned soldier.

Mr. Howe does not favor the plan of utilizing the returned soldiers in the reclamation of waste land. The reclamation of these lands, he said,

(Continued on page 294)

Italy Today and Tomorrow

TALY'S sacrifices to the cause of the Allies have been greater than those of any other >untry except Belgium, according to Captain harles E. Merriam who spoke at the City Club st Thursday. Captain Merriam from last arch until his return to this country a few eeks ago was commissioner to Italy from the ommittee on Public Information, in charge of .e American "propaganda" bureau.

Capt. Merriam went to Italy at probably the ost disheartening period of the war for the llies. The British and French armies had just istained the serious defeat of the first great erman offensive and Italian morale was still iffering from the terrible losses sustained at aporetto the preceding October and from the ong cold winter and the critical food situation vhich she had been passing through.

GERMAN PENETRATION

"Italy has prosecuted the war under peculiar ifficulties," said Captain Merriam. "For a eneration prior to the war Italy had been a eld of economic penetration by Germany. Ger- an capital had organized banks and great in- istrial corporations in Italy and German money as influential in many directions. There were lso important social and intellectual connec- ions between Italy and Germany. The German ambassador had been clever and popular and had established many social relationships in Italy. All these things were soil in which the Germans were able to plant and grow their propaganda.

ITALY'S SACRIFICES

"Italy's position was also difficult because of the great sacrifices which she had made in the war. Without disparaging the sacrifices of the other allied powers, it may be truly said that ex- cept for Belgium, Italy has made greater sacri- fices for the allied cause than any other nation for the extent of her sacrifice must be measured by the margin which she had to give. Italy is not a rich country. Before the war she had many difficulties with her national finance and the idea that she could carry the load of a three years' war with an almost complete mobilization of her man-power would have seemed ridiculous. That she has done this has meant that the Italian people have had to sacrifice to a point actually below the margin of existence.

MARKETS BREAK DOWN

"Italy does not produce coal, iron or oil. She does not raise enough grain to feed herself. When the war broke out all these necessities of life went sky-rocketing in price because Italy had no large amount of shipping and was unable to get it from the Allies. On the other hand the market for Italy's chief products, wines, silks, art works and other luxuries, was cut off by the lack of shipping and the reduced buying power of the Allies. Italy was left in almost a hopeless economic condition.

"Italy's contribution to the success of the war has been vital. If she had not been in the war, Austria could have mobilized against Russia in the east or against France and England on the west. Contrary to general belief, the mobiliza- tion of man-power in Italy has been as complete as that in any other allied country.

SOCIALIST OPPOSITION

"Another difficulty which Italy encountered in prosecuting the war was the opposition of a considerable element of the population. The Italian socialists, who possessed from a quarter to a third of the voting power of Italy, were opposed to the war from the start and fought openly against every phase of the military ac- tivity. Some of its most brilliant leaders favored the war and broke away from the party but the mass remained against the war and maintained through their newspapers a most bitter opposi- tion. In this they were aided by all the pro- German elements. Italian socialists of the most radical type are Bolshevist and have openly ex- pressed sympathy with the Bolshevik party of Russia. Only last September the socialists pro- posed to call an international labor conference at Rome to be followed by a series of general strikes. So not only at the front but behind the lines a great battle has been raging in Italy.

"I mention these things merely to indicate how great was the determination and resolution of the government and of the people as a whole in carrying on the war.

EXPLAINING AMERICA

"The task of our bureau in Italy was to ex- plain America's war aims and preparations. It was necessary to counter-act the feeling not only in Italy but in other allied countries that America could not contribute largely to the suc- cess of the war. German propagandists were trying to make the people believe that America's participation in the war was the greatest Yankee bluff ever. America might send food and am- munition but she was doing this already to the extent of her ability. She might send two or three divisions to parade around Europe but she could not raise a large army or transport it to Europe. It was our task to hearten the people of Italy by explaining to her why America came into the war and what she was planning to do to contribute to its success.

"Our bureau had a staff of about forty people. We had sections in charge of speakers, moving picture propaganda and the air propaganda into Austria. We also organized a news service in Italy. The Committee on Public Information, through Walter Rogers, organized an American

A WAR POSTER EXHIBITION

will be held at the City Club
NOVEMBER 25 TO DECEMBER 9

The display will include a representative collection of posters, made for the government and for the allied war services by the best poster artists of America. It will also include some of the best designs by English, French, Canadian, Russian and Italian artists.

This is the official exhibit of the U. S. Committee on Public Information. It is being shown in various American cities under the direction of the Newark Public Library.

BRING YOUR FRIENDS TO SEE IT!

news service all over the world and we received from this news service from 500 to 1000 words a day which were translated and sent to the Italian newspapers. We arranged for six or eight Italian journalists to visit America as guests of the government so that they might with their own eyes see America's preparations.

"Our propaganda was no more than a straight presentation of the facts. We found that plan after all to be the best, for in the end we found that the truth went farther than the lies which were being circulated through German influence."

POLITICAL LEADERS

Captain Merriam dicussed some of the leading personalities in Italian politics: Prime Minister Orlando, he said, is a professor of political science and a well-known figure in Italian politics. Sonnino, secretary for Foreign Affairs, has been a prominent figure ever since the new Italy was born. He is a man of forceful character, partly Jewish and partly English, but the most Italian of Italians so far as national sentiment is concerned. He is conservative and praetical. Bisolotti, one of the most powerful cabinet leaders, represents the radical element. He is a socialist who left his party to enter the army as a private, was wounded and later entered the cabinet. He is a radical and idealist, though nationalistic in feeling. In the background is the figure of Giolitti, who for twenty years has been the national boss of Italy. His powerful influence in parliament was used in opposition to the declaration of war but he was swept aside. He has remained a powerful figure against the war and has probably given assistance to the socialists in their opposition.

OUR RELATIONS WITH ITALY

"The relations between the United States and Italy are probably closer than those of any other two countries. There are probably four or five million people in America of Italian blood.

About 70,000 Italians went back to Italy at the beginning of the war to enlist in the army and about 200,000 men of Italian origin are in our own army. Italy has been greatly impressed by America's contribution to the war and the fighting quality shown by the American troops. Our greatest contribution to her morale, however, has been the disinterested character of the motives with which we entered the war. That has made a colossal impression in Italy. To people who urged that Italy should have kept out of the war, the reply is now made that America, who had no material interests at stake, who had no Alsace-Lorraine or Italian Irredenta, who had millions of Germans and Austrians in her population and for three years had listened to arguments pro and con, had finally concluded that in the interest of humanity she could not stay out of the war and had given her impartial decision in favor of the Allies.

"This is the most solemn hour in the history of the world. The militarism which has been destroyed is a medieval survival. The barnacles have been cleared away. The world stands at a perilous point facing the future and not knowing which way to turn. We are faced by great problems of internal and international reconstruction, problems of the relation of class to class, of civilized peoples to the semi-civilized people of the world and of one civilized nation to another. We must look to Italy for aid in the solution of these great problems."

Step Lively

A new Membership Extension Committee is being organized. S. Bowles King is its chairman. At a preliminary meeting last week a lively campaign was planned to remind members to remind their friends of the privileges of the Club.

But why wait for the committee? If the man at your elbow in the office is good club timber, slip him an application card.

Self-Government in Industry

"The Whitley Reports"

NGLISH industry, according to Arthur Gleason, whose recent address at the City lub was reported in our last issue, is making .pid strides in the direction of self-government rough the voluntary adoption by many indusies of the plan for national, district, and orkshop "industrial councils" proposed in the -called "Whitley Reports" to the British Renstruction Committee. The proposals of the hitley committee, have, with modifications, een adopted by the British government as a art of its reconstruction policy. They have een referred to as "one of the most significant nd far-reaching developments of the war so far s labor is concerned."

MUST ORGANIZE BOTH SIDES

The formation of industrial councils is being romoted by the Industrial Reconstruction ouncil, an unofficial body, working however in ose relation with various government departents. The purpose of this organization is "to reach the doctrine of self-government for inustry and the reconstruction of industry by the ndustry itself; the complete organization of very trade, with every man in his union and .very employer in his association, and from the wo an elected trade parliament in every trade, vith proper status and adequate powers."

The first Whitley report issued March, 1917, :tated, as the considered opinion of the comnittee, "that an essential condition of securing permanent improvement in the relations beween employers and employed is that there :hould be an adequate organization on the part)f both employers and work people. The pro)osals outlined for joint co-operation throughout :everal industries depend for their ultimate suc:ess upon their being such organization on both :ides; such organization is necessary also to pro'ide means whereby the arrangements and agreenents made for industry may be effectively car'ied out."

WHY COUNCILS ARE FORMED

"The primary object of industrial councils," :ays a statement issued by the Ministry of _abor, "is to regularize the relations between :mployers and employed. But they will serve nother urgent need, and in so doing will give o work people a status in their respective inlustries that they have not had hitherto.

"There is a large body of problems which beong to industry and to politics. They belong o politics because the community is responsible or their solution and the State must act if no)ther provision is made; they belong to industry)ecause they can be solved only by the knowl'dge and experience of the people actually engaged in industry. Such problems are the regularization of employment, industrial training, utilization of inventions, industrial research, the improvements of design and quality, legislation affecting workshop conditions—all of them questions which have hitherto been left in the main to employers, but which in reality constitute an important common interest on the basis of which all engaged in an industry can meet.

THE RECONSTRUCTION PERIOD

"The termination of the war will bring with it a mass of new problems of this nature; for example, demobilization, the training of apprentices when apprenticeship was interrupted by military service, the settlement in industry of partially disabled men, and, in general, the reconversion of industry to the purposes of peace. It is urgently necessary that the Government should be able to obtain without delay the experience and views of the people actually in industry on all these questions. It proposes, therefore, to treat industrial councils as standing consultative committees to the Government and the normal channel through which it will seek the experience and advice of industries.

SELF-GOVERNMENT

"Further, many of these problems can be handled by each industry for itself, provided that it has an organization representative of all sections and interests within it. The establishment of industrial councils will therefore make unnecessary a large amount of 'government interference,' which is at present unavoidable, and substitute for it a real measure of 'self-government' in industry."

Industrial councils are described as follows in a joint memorandum issued last June by the British Ministers of Reconstruction and of Labor: "A joint industrial council is voluntary in character and can only be brought into existence with the agreement of the organizations of employers and workpeople in the particular industry, and the council itself is composed inclusively of persons nominated by the employers' associations and trade unions concerned. The industrial council is moreover within very wide limits able to determine its own functions, machinery and methods of working."

The enforcement of the agreements of the industrial councils is entirely a matter for the industry itself, although it is the conclusion of the Whitley Committee that "it may be desirable at some later stage for the state to give sanction of law to agreements made by the councils but the initiative in this direction should come from the councils themselves."

The first great industry to be organized na-

Good Timber?

That friend you took to the Club to lunch last Wednesday — Would he make a good member of the City Club? Think it over. Henry P. Chandler is chairman of the Admissions Committee.

---

tionally along the lines of the Whitley report is the pottery industry. The industrial council for that industry consists of 30 representatives of employers and an equal number of operatives. The number of employers in this industry is between 400 and 500 and the number of workers about 50,000. The object of the council as given in the *Labor Gazette* last February, indicates the kind of practical subjects which will be dealt with by such bodies. This is stated to be:

"The advancement of the pottery industry and of all connected with it by the association in its government of all engaged in the industry. It will be open to the council to take any action that falls within the scope of its general object. Its chief work will, however, fall under the following heads:

(a) The consideration of means whereby all manufacturers and operatives shall be brought within their respective associations.

(b) Regular consideration of wages, piecework prices, and conditions, with a view to establishing and maintaining equitable conditions throughout the industry.

(c) To assist the respective associations in the maintenance of such selling prices as will afford a reasonable remuneration to both employers and employed.

(d) The consideration and settlement of all disputes between different parties in the industry which it may not have been possible to settle by the existing machinery, and the establishment of machinery for dealing with disputes where adequate machinery does not exist.

(e) The regularization of production and employment as a means of insuring to the workpeople the greatest possible security of earnings.

(f) Improvement in conditions with a view to removing all danger to health in the industry.

(g) The study of processes, the encouragement of research, and the full utilization of their results.

(h) The provision of facilities for the full consideration and utilization of inventions and improvements designed by workpeople and for the adequate safeguarding of the rights of the designers of such improvements.

(i) Education in all its branches for the industry.

(j) The collection of full statistics on wages, making and selling prices, and average percentages of profits on turnover, and on materials, markets, costs, etc., and the study and promotion of scientific and practical systems of costing to this end. All statistics shall, where necessary, be verified by chartered accountants, who shall

make a statutory declaration as to secrecy prior to any investigation, and no particulars of individual firms or operatives shall be disclosed to any one.

(k) Inquiries into problems of the industry, and where desirable, the publication of reports.

(l) Representation of the needs and opinions of the industry to Government authorities, central and local, and to the community generally."

CO-OPERATION IN INDUSTRY

The formation of industrial councils, according to Mr. Gleason, is proceeding rapidly in Great Britain by the voluntary adoption of the Whitley plan by employers and employees. A statement issued October 1917 by a large number of officers of trade associations, editors of trade papers and others states: "The opposition to our proposal will probably come chiefly from employers who have not grasped the full significance of the new spirit in industry. As a matter of fact, employers no less than employed have a great deal to gain from such an arrangement. Their position in relation to the Government would be immensely strengthened by the co-operation of labor in matters which many of them have hitherto regarded as outside the scope of joint action."

New Reading Matter

THE PUBLIC LIBRARY has placed the following books on deposit, for three months, in the City Club Reading Room:

Allen—Mettle of the Pasture.
Atkinson—Hearts Undaunted
Barclay—The Rosary
Bartlett—The Wall Street Girl
Benson—Michael
Biggers—Seven Keys to Baldpate
Bindloss—The Girl from Keller's
Bindloss—Harding of Allenwood
Bindloss—The Lure of the North
Bosher—Kitty Canary
Brown—How Phoebe Found Herself
Cameron—The Involuntary Chaperon
Chambers—The Dark Star
Chapin—Mountain Madness
Daviess—The Golden Bird
DeMorgan—When Ghost Meets Ghost
Diver—Desmond's Daughter
Dostoevsky—The Brothers Karamazov
Doubleday—The Green Tree Mystery
Dowd—Polly and the Princess
Dubois—The Lass of the Silver Sword
Ferber—Cheerful by Request
Greene—The Devil to Pay
Hagedorn—Barabara Picks a Husband
Hopkins—Our Army, How to Know It
Hopkins—Our Navy, How to Know It
King—The Side of the Angels
Lardner—Treat 'Em Rough
Lynde—After the Manner of Men
McClung—The Next of Kin
McCutcheon—The City of Masks
McIntyre—Ashton-Kirk Criminologist
Oemler—Slippy McGee
Ogden—The Rustler of Wind River
Oppenheim—The Kingdom of the Blind
Oppenheim—The Zeppelin's Passenger
Orczy—A Sheaf of Bluebells
Ridge—Madame Prince
Ruck—The Years for Rachel
Seltzer—Firebrand Trevison
Sinclair—The Belfry
Stacpoole—Sea Plunderers
Tompkins—The Seed for the Righteous
Troubetzkoy—The Ghost Garden
Warman—Snow on the Headlight
Webster—The Real Adventure
Wells—Joan and Peter
Whitehead—Dawson Black, Retail Merchant
Widdemer—You're Only Young Once
Willsie—Still Jim

Labor Unions in the Public Service

HOULD employes of the government be allowed to form labor unions? Is a strike by mployes in the civil service an act of rebellion gainst the government and to be suppressed as uch? Probably the most conspicuous civil serve strike on record is the two-day "walk-out" f the London police last September. "Regarded s a labor conflict," says the London *Nation* writg of this strike, "this issue is the most rapid, he most complete and the most ignominious ollapse of the employer on record. And not he least significant circumstance is that here the mployer is the State." The policeman's strike pparently won a large measure of public support. The wage scale was raised, other conessions were made, and, while formal recognrion of the union was not granted, the principle f "collective bargaining" was agreed to.

The large measure of government ownership nd operation of industry adopted in this and ther countries since the beginning of the war nd likely to be retained for at least a considrable period after the cessation of hostilities ives these questions special point at this time. any existing labor unions, by the nationalizing f industries, have been brought into direct baraining relations with the government. Emloyes of government departments, particularly f various branches of the postal service, also ave organizations with a membership of many :housands.

The case against unions of government employes is stated by William Dudley Foulke in a recent issue of "Good Government," the monthly ɔrgan of the National Civil Service Reform Association. Mr. Foulke's article excited a lively discussion in subsequent issues.

Mr. Foulke at the outset concedes "the right ɔf all persons, whether in the service or not to organize for their mutual advantage provided such unions do not engage in any political activity, or contemplate any resistance to the government." He expresses a strong friendliness for labor unions as agencies which have helped to maintain standards of living and to resist the tyranny of accumulated wealth.

"But," he continues, "those in the civil service are not in the same position; they are not employes of private capitalists; they are the servants of the state; they have not the right to resist the government; they have no right to strike or to combine for the purpose of striking or to exert pressure of any kind upon their employers by means of their organizations. The men in the military service cannot combine for the purpose of securing an advance in pay or pensions or other things they desire. The terrible example of the dissolution of the Russian army under organizations which took control of it on behalf of the particular interests of the private soldiers is a warning we cannot fail to see. In-

deed any resistance to the government by such an organization is not a strike at all, it is a mutiny, and by military law it may be punished with death."

Mr. Foulke cites, as illustrations of his argument, the strike of the French postal and telegraph employes in 1909 and the political activities of civil service unions in England. He refers to a threat of the editor of the Civil Service Chronicle in New York in 1913 that he would, hand over the votes of 100,000 civil service employes to Tammany Hall, in case Mr. Mitchell would not promise to raise the salaries and oppose reductions in the city's forces.

"It may be true," continues Mr. Foulke, "that our civil service organizations have not yet ordered a strike, but this has been done in France and in England, and it is inevitable that the time will come when that will be done in America. What the effect of such a strike would be in a war like the present cannot be contemplated without consternation. It is indeed to be hoped that post office and other employes will be too patriotic thus to obstruct the work of the government during this life and death struggle, but in other places, in the shipping industry for instance, patriotism has not always restrained the labor unions."

William Scarlett of Federal Employes Union No. 4 in a reply to Mr. Foulke upholds the right of employes to organize and to exert political influence in so far as it is not of a "pernicious" character. He concedes the case against strikes. The majority of Federal employes, he says, share the view that a strike among government employes is well-nigh inconceivable. The Constitution of the National Federation of Federal Employes provides that "under no circumstances shall this Federation engage in or support strikes against the United States Government."

Alfred Bishop Mason in the November number of "Good Government," just issued, claims that unionization tends to prevent strikes, that "it is so written in the bond of the National Federation of Federal Employes." "The more self-respect Labor has, the more it will unionize itself and the less it will sell its votes for the sake of employment. The specific prohibitions of political activity in Director General McAdoo's circular order to railroad employes all have a basis of reason (provided 'political purposes' and 'political fund' are construed to mean partisan purpose and partisan fund), but outside of these there is nothing worth while to democracy to be gained and much to be lost by making federal employes political eunuchs."

(*To be concluded*)

"TALK DAYS" enable members to see some of the interesting and famous personalities of the day.

HELP OTHERS

Don't keep to yourself the advantages of the City Club. Perhaps your office neighbor has qualities which would help the City if linked with the effort of others through the City Club.

THINK IT OVER

The Listening Post

CAPT. HAROLD H. SWIFT is in the Personnel Section of the Adjutant General's Department.

TENNEY S. FORD is with the engineering department of the Pratt Engineering and Machine Company at Little Rock, Ark.

RALPH H. HOBERT has been commissioned as second lieutenant in the army.

W. F. DUMMER has presented to the library a copy of Arthur Henderson's "War Aims of Labor," and a copy of the Reconstruction Program of the British Labor Party. They have been placed in the reading room.

CHARLES H. SWIFT has entered the service of the U. S. army with a commission as Lieutenant-Colonel in the Ordnance Department. He is with the American Expeditionary Force in France.

WORD HAS BEEN RECEIVED that O. H. Breidert, one of our members, has arrived in France. Mr. Breidert is a member of the Engineering Corps. He was chief draughtsman for Childs & Smith, Architects.

CAPT. GUY L. JONES, 31st Field Artillery, is at Camp Meade, Maryland.

THE CITY CLUB extends sincere sympathy to Professor Andrew C. McLaughlin, whose son, Capt. R. H. McLaughlin, according to reports received last week, has been killed in action.

PROF. J. PAUL GOODE expects to leave soon for France for the Y. M. C. A.

The Coming Reconstruction

(*Continued from page* 288)

is likely to cost more than their real value and would be more likely to put dollars in the pockets of speculators than to help the men.

THE DECLINE IN AGRICULTURE

"America," said Mr. Howe, "must check the decline in agriculture which has accompanied the growth of tenancy and the drift to the cities. The war has stripped the land of a million and a half men. Food production is diminished. More and more people are living in towns and fewer are living in the country. There are millions of 'slacker acres.' One-fourth of the land is owned by a comparatively few people.

"I am not interested in the peasant type of agriculture. You can't build a democracy on a tenant population. A free state is no place for the economic serf. America is not democratic through her bills of right but because our fathers went out and built homes on the land. But when our immigrants come the land is gone and we send them to the mines and slums."

FARM COLONIES FOR SOLDIERS

Mr. Howe advocated, to aid in the restoration of agriculture, a policy of land settlement similar to that recommended by the British Committee above referred to. Farm colonies, he said, should be established for the returned soldiers. There should be villages with small holdings attached to the houses and with pastures and fields in the encircling areas. "Our system of scattered living on the farms is unnatural," he said. The men should be given a chance under experts to see if they like this sort of life. These villages would afford opportunity for the development of co-operative schemes. There are differences of opinion about the question of tenure: One group favors selling the holdings outright; another favors sale but believes that the government should retain control of the resale of the land and should reserve the right to require certain kinds of cultivation; a third group is working out a modified single tax scheme. "Whatever plan is agreed upon," said Mr. Howe, "I feel that these be freeholds and not mere tenant holdings." He said also that he favored these communities not only for soldiers but for anybody. "But we can make a beginning with the soldiers."

CAREFULLY SELECTED FOOD, prepared by experts in a spotless kitchen, is one of the secret of our successful menus.

The following books from the last collection placed on deposit in the City Club by the Chicago Public Library are missing:

O'Brien—Best Short Stories
White—The Leopard Woman

The City Club Bulletin

A Journal of Active Citizenship

VOLUME XI.   MONDAY, NOVEMBER 25, 1918   NUMBER 39

THANKSGIVING WEEK

TUESDAY, NOVEMBER 26, AT LUNCHEON
MARY VAN KLEECK
**Director Woman in Industry Service, U. S. Department of Labor
Member National War Labor Policies Board**

"Women in Industrial Reconstruction"

Miss VanKleeck's appointment as a member of the War Labor Policies Board has been hailed as a recognition by the government of the new industrial status of women. Miss VanKleeck was formerly director of the Women's Division of the Ordnance Department.

WEDNESDAY NOON, NOVEMBER 27

THANKSGIVING DINNER
Vermont Turkey with All the Trimmings

THURSDAY, NOVEMBER 28—THANKSGIVING
Club Closed All Day

FRIDAY, NOVEMBER 29, AT LUNCHEON
E. T. GUNDLACH
U. S. Department of Labor

"The Labor Policies of the Government"

The new instruments devised by the government for the adjustment of the labor market during the war are likely to have far-reaching effects on the industrial relations of the future. Mr. Gundlach has been officially identified in a responsible capacity with the task of carrying out of the government's labor program.

MONDAY, DECEMBER 2, AT LUNCHEON
PIERRE BLOMMAERT
Representing the Belgian Government

"Belgium at the War's End"

Rev. Blommaert served as a stretcher-bearer in the Belgian army and later became a chaplain. He was awarded the Croix de Guerre for his devotion and his "courage and self-denial in the field of combat." He is speaking in this country as the accredited representative of his government.

Ghe City Club Bulletin

A Journal of Active Citizenship

Published Weekly Except July, August and September; bi-weekly during July, August and September

By the CITY CLUB OF CHICAGO
315 Plymouth Court　　　Telephone: Harrison 8278

DWIGHT L. AKERS, Editor

$1.00 per Year　-　-　-　-　10c per Copy

Entered as second class matter, December 3, 1917, at the postoffice at Chicago, Illinois, under the act of March 3, 1879.

Bring your wife or sweetheart

Your cousins, your sisters

Your wife's cousins and their sisters

To see the War Posters

At the City Club　　　　　Nov. 25-Dec. 9

Vol. XI　Monday, November 25, 1918　No. 39

Labor Unions in Public Service

(*The first installment of this article was devoted mainly to the objections to unionism in public service, as presented by William Dudley Foulke in the columns of "Good Government." This installment contains the other side of the case as stated by Ordway Tead and by an editorial in the London Daily News.*)

ORDWAY TEAD of the Bureau of Industrial Research, replying to Mr. Foulke, asserts the right of public employes to strike as well as organize. Mr. Foulke's arguments stand, he says, only if it is assumed "that the State is sufficiently wise to know what its employes need and sufficiently generous to provide it when it is known; or that the State, as State, is an all-powerful agent whose dictates are not to be questioned and whose power is not to be lessened by any show of resistance by its subjects." . . . . "Government bodies almost never voluntarily and of their own initiative make changes in the terms and conditions of employment of their employes." . . . There is but one way for the rights of public employes "to be fully and fairly considered in relation to the rights of the department heads and of the taxpayers: and that way is by representation of the workers in the conduct of the department's affairs in the determination of its policies."

Mr. Tead regards the right to strike to be as fundamental in a democracy as the right of revolution. "It gets us nowhere to exact promises from labor organizations that they will not strike. There is but one preventive of strikes, alike in public and private employment. It is the same preventive we adopt to prevent revolution. Create conditions of constitutional, representative assembly and procedure which assure fair treatment to all represented. This the unions help to do. They exert a pressure which requires common deliberation over problems which affect them. Collective dealings in the public service bring this result. But they will work toward an end which is far more fundamental. The operation of government departments and agencies on a basis of participation in management by the workers will result in a fostering and cultivation of the sources of interest, initiative and worthwhile personality."

ARE STRIKERS REBELS?

The editor of "Good Government," in replying to Mr. Tead, asks some questions. "There is no such thing as a right to rebellion," he says. "Only when rebellion is *successful* does it become right. Are strikers against the government to be treated like rebels, or how? Is an unsuccessful strike to be regarded as right, or only a successful one?"

"The public," he continues, "is also made up of human individuals with rights and interests exactly like those which Mr. Tead so ably claims for the civil servants. And if civil servants may strike, why not military servants? And if not military servants, how can a line be drawn between men in khaki uniform and men in the blue uniform of essential railways, or the blue uniform of the essential workshop?"

THE LONDON POLICE STRIKE

The strike of the London police apparently had, on the whole, popular acquiescence and sympathy. Even the conservative London Times wrote: "Of course, it is a serious thing for state servants to strike, but the real questions are whether they had a just grievance and whether the State had left open to them any other way than a strike of getting their grievance heard."

The London Daily News put the case for the men thus: "It is, therefore, of the utmost importance that an organization shall exist to enable the employes to press their reasonable claims and grievances without delay by some orderly machinery of representation. Many who will admit that postmen, policemen, and other public servants ought to have this right, still boggle against allowing them in the last resort the right to strike. But this, if we may say so, is mere feeble-mindedness. If organization of the employes and a regular machinery for communication with the public authority exists, the chance and the justification of a strike are re-

(*Continued on page 298*)

"LOW-BROW NIGHT"

FRIDAY, DECEMBER 6

One of those famous, get-together fellowship dinners.

All members, *even high-brows*, expected.

The committee maintains a mysterious attitude about what is to happen but a private wire to the editor indicates that there will be " some doings."

KEEP THIS EVENING FREE

Peace and Reconstruction

'I AM GLAD that your president is going to the peace conference," said Bishop Henry . Wakefield of Birmingham, England, in his ddress at the City Club last Thursday. "I am lad that he is going over not only because of he influence of his great personality in the settle- ent but because the United States may come to now, through the reception accorded your presi- ent, the feeling toward America which inspires ll countries. President Wilson will not be ble, if the conference lasts for a year, as we may xpect, to be with it to the end, but he will give a lasting stamp to the proceedings—the stamp not only of his own personality but also that of America.

"It is easier to make war unitedly, than to make peace unitedly. It is easier to go into battle with a common front than it is to gather around the peace table and draw up the terms of settlement. We must be careful, therefore, not to hamper in any way those who are charged with this task."

Great Britain is facing a great social problem through the loss of so much of her manhood, ac- cording to Bishop Wakefield. "We have lost about 750,000 men, and we have lost them at an age when they are most needed. They include our most distinguished young fellows, men whom we expected to become our greatest parlia- mentarians, our leading professional and business men, our best social workers. The younger men, men who do not have the training and experience of those whom we have lost, will have to take their places.

"The training of our young men has of course been inadequate during the war. With the father, perhaps, at the front and the mother in a munition factory discipline was relaxed. The supervision of the schools was inadequate be- cause of the lack of teachers, many of whom were, of course, in the army. Boys of 16 re- ceived wages larger than their fathers had ob- tained and acquired expensive tastes, without at the same time receiving the proper discipline."

The problem of reconstruction, Bishop Wake- field said, will be much more difficult in Great Britain than in this country. "As I travel over your country," he said, "you seem to me the most perfectly prosperous people that my eyes have ever looked upon. You have not suffered dis- location to the extent that we have, but you must see to your problems of social reconstruction."

Many British soldiers, according to Bishop Wakefield, having served for four and a half years in the trenches feel that they have done enough work for their country and that it is their turn for a bit of a rest. We must see to it, he urged, that when they come back they are given work that appeals to their interest. The mass of soldiers will probably not care to go to the land, but many of the best educated men who served in offices before the war, will not wish to go back to office life and will seek enlarged opportunities in the States and in Canada.

Demobilization in England will not be so difficult as expected, said Bishop Wakefield. The Ministry of Reconstruction, with the advice of the best employers and the best leaders of labor in the country, has been devising plans for a long time. Many of the soldiers have places waiting for them. These men can be demobilized first. Then the very skilled men who can always find employment can be demobilized. The remainder, those who constitute the great mass, will have work for at least several years. No roads have been mended during the period of the war. No building has taken place. Rolling stock on the railroads is in bad condition. Great housing schemes are being considered. "The real test will come several years hence. Then we will be able to see whether capital and labor can get on together."

What should be the ideal determining the course of social reconstruction? Everybody who comes on this earth, said Bishop Wakefield, should be insured the possibility of fulfilling his individuality for the benefit of all mankind. How can you expect a child who comes into the world under conditions in which he cannot thrive, whose father earns wages so low that the mother perhaps must leave her home to work, who grows up and takes his place in the world with inadequate training—how can such a person grow up into a patriotic and civic-minded citizen? In every country we must see that *citizens* are brought up and then we can demand from them an understanding of the responsibilities of citizenship.

The New Committees

The Public Affairs Committee held two long sessions last week to perfect the civic committee organization. Over three hundred requests for committee appointments have been received from members. The task of classifying these requests and other preliminary work has occupied more time than was expected but it is hoped that the appointments will be completed in time for announcement in our next issue.

Any member who forgot to submit his committee choices should send them in at once to the Civic Secretary.

In Memoriam

Two of our members died last week, Glenn B. Roberts and Henry Hassel. Mr. Roberts, a member since 1912, was in the advertising business. He was vice-president of the Roberts-Bailey Company. Mr. Hassel retired from business several years ago. He joined the City Club in 1915. His son, Otto Hassel, is a member of the Club.

The City Club friends of Mr. Roberts and Mr. Hassel will be deeply grieved to learn of this loss.

Mary VanKleeck

"FOR many months," says a recent editorial in the *New Republic* commenting upon the appointment of Miss Mary VanKleeck (our speaker at the City Club next Tuesday) as a member of the War Labor Policies Board, "Miss VanKleeck has been director of the Women's Branch of the Industrial Service Section of the Army Ordnance Bureau. She has been required to co-operate with the commanding officers of government arsenals in the practical solution of problems arising out of the introduction of women into these vast government factories. She and her assistants have been called into similar co-operation by private concerns engaged upon munitions contracts. In these plants, they have succeeded in averting many of the difficulties that have retarded production in shops where women were indiscriminately hired and employed without expert supervision.

"That they have proved their value to the government seems conclusively demonstrated not only by Miss VanKleeck's appointment to the War Labor Policies Board, but especially by the Board's recognition of her not merely as the representative of women as women but of women as industrial citizens with rights and responsibilities co-equal with the responsibilities and rights of men."

Labor Unions in Public Service

(*Continued from page 296*)

duced to a minimum. No extravagant or unjust demands of the employes could have any real chance of enforcement through a strike. For what might seem to be the technical power of a strong union to enforce its will—viz., the grave inconvenience to the public of a stoppage of its service—must in almost all cases tell decisively and speedily against the unreasonable strike. For such a strike, following deliberate negotiations between the organized workers and the authority, conducted in the public eye, could not fail to arouse a resentment among the general body of the public that would preclude the possibility of success. It is not true that a strong union, even in the most fundamental trades, such as mining, transport, postal service, banking, could seriously blackmail employers, the consumer, or the taxpayer, if adequate provisions existed for regular orderly conference between the parties, accompanied by full publicity for all essential facts. But unless the formal and real right to strike as a last resort is fully admitted, there will always remain a disposition among obstinate employers or obtuse and dilatory authorities to bluff, evade, cut down, or procrastinate, leaving genuine grievances to fester and inflame until human nature finds a violent vent."

Eat no breakfast Wednesday and come to the City Club for lunch.

The City Club Bulletin
A Journal of Active Citizenship

VOLUME XI.   MONDAY, DECEMBER 2, 1918   NUMBER 40

MONDAY, DECEMBER 2, AT LUNCHEON
REV. MAJOR PIERRE BLOMMAERT
Representing the Belgian Government
"Belgium at the War's End"

Rev. Blommaert served as a stretcher-bearer in the Belgian army and later became a chaplain. He was awarded the Croix de Guerre for his devotion and his "courage and self-denial in the field of combat." He is speaking in this country as the accredited representative of his government.

FRIDAY, DECEMBER 6, AT DINNER
"LOW-BROW NIGHT"

If you are a low-brow you *belong* in the crowd. If a high-brow, come and see what a low-brow looks like and how he acts.

Reservations will be made in the order of receipt. Dinner at 6:30.

Women in Industrial Reconstruction

WOMEN in industry as well as men will have to make sacrifices during the reconstruction period, but any displacement of labor for the benefit of men now in service ought not to be at the expense of women as a class. The problems of women in industry should be dealt with as a part of the industrial reconstruction as a whole, not as mere sex or class questions. These views were expressed by Miss Mary Van-Kleeck of the War Labor Policies Board of the government in her address at the City Club last Thursday. Miss VanKleeck said in brief:

America, unlike Europe, did not get deeply enough into the war to suffer over a long period a general break-up of her established forms. Our "reconstruction" work will therefore be for the most part a product of our wisdom and choice, rather than of necessity. It will seem easier for us, than for Europe, to go back to the starting point. Our problem, strictly speaking, will be one of industrial "readjustment" rather than of "reconstruction."

The immediate, pressing problem is the transfer of industry from a war to a peace footing with a minimum of unemployment. It is the same problem on a larger scale that we have encountered—and solved so badly—in our seasonal industries. But the problem of unemployment that we are facing is even more difficult. If there are more men than jobs, the way is open for a change of relations between employes and employer, for a lowering of the standards of employment—smaller wages and longer hours. Already there are signs that the leaders on both sides are lining up for a struggle on this issue.

If this goes on we will reap a harvest of discontent in America. Some effective means

The City Club Bulletin

A Journal of Active Citizenship

Published Weekly Except July, August and September; bi-weekly during July, August and September

By the CITY CLUB OF CHICAGO
315 Plymouth Court   Telephone: Harrison 8278

DWIGHT L. AKERS, Editor

$1.00 per Year   -   -   -   -   10c per Copy

Entered as second class matter, December 3, 1917, at the postoffice at Chicago, Illinois, under the act of March 3, 1879.

Vol. XI.   Monday, December 2, 1918   No. 40

of negotiation between employers and workers must be worked out—procedure which will leave no suspicion of unfair dealing on either side.

The replacement of the returned soldier in industry ought not to affect women differently from men. It would not be fair to ask one class to surrender its place in industry for the benefit of another class. Fewer women than we have supposed went into industry solely for patriotic reasons and can therefore give up their occupations without a sacrifice.

Before and during the war, probably because the man has been considered the bread winner, the wage scales for women have on the whole been lower than those for men in the same occupation. This has caused a lowering of family standards, for the typical wage earning woman has dependents. Probably a large amount of child labor is due to the low wages paid to women. The effect of the lower wages paid to women upon the wages of men—and so upon the standard of living of families—must also be considered.

EQUAL WORK—EQUAL WAGES

During the war it has been demonstrated that women can do many kinds of work to which it was formerly believed they were not adapted. Employers have also acquired the habit of looking over their plants to ascertain the positions in which women might replace men. Given this demonstration of woman's ability to do new kinds of work and the open-minded attitude of employers, there is danger that women will be substituted for men—not because the men are going to war—but in order to force general wages down. That must be faced as a problem which may affect seriously the standard of living. Whatever the plan of wage determination is to be in the future, it ought to provide for a standard of wages based, not upon the sex, but upon the occupation of the worker.

During the reconstruction period a large extension of legislation for the protection of working conditions will be needed. The Illinois standard of a ten-hour working day for women is not one that the State may be proud of. An enormously increased production of commodities will be demanded of America. If we do not conserve our labor power we will not be able to reach our maximum production. England during the war learned the lesson that good wages, short hours, fair working conditions and a sense of justice on the part of the worker are essential to maximum production. The shell shortage early in the war was traced in part to the reckless overworking of the employes, with its results in increasing the labor turn-over, absenteeism and inefficiency.

INDUSTRIAL DEMOCRACY

Justice and peace in industry will depend on the working out of effective instruments of negotiation between employers and employed. If employers adhere to the exercise of autocratic government in industry, without consulting the wishes of employes, they are likely to get a jolt. There are new ideas abroad in the world, ideas which will not be prevented from crossing the ocean by any shortage of ships. There is a feeling that industry must be managed more democratically.

DECENTRALIZING CONTROL

The control of the federal government over working conditions is likely to be weaker from now on. During the war the government was the great purchaser of goods and the great employer. Now that the government is no longer an employer and buyer on so large a scale, we will have to meet our industrial problems again to a large extent through state and municipal action or through the industries themselves. We are splitting up. The dollar-a-year men are coming back from Washington to resume their private pursuits. The settlement of our problems depends, to a considerable extent, on how far we have a national goal. The less we have such goal and the more individual interest plays a part, the less likely are we to develop a worth while social program.

A PROGRAM OF LEGISLATION

At the close of her address, Miss VanKleeck was asked to outline her program of social legislation for women. She mentioned the following as among the most necessary measures: A further restriction of the working hours for women; prohibition of night work; the strengthening of administrative machinery; the extension of vocational training; the withdrawal of children under 16 years of age from industry; a strengthening of the employment exchanges; better provision for the health of the workers; an extension of Workmen's Compensation; a better handling of public works appropriations.

AN ARCTIC ATMOSPHERE at luncheon is bad for the digestion. Thaw out, for Heaven's sake!

Wanted—161 Men

Who joined the Club in the past year to attend the
LOW-BROW DINNER, Friday evening, Dec. 6 at 6:30.

If you haven't accepted, call up the Club *Now*.

Continue the Fight

THE American army and navy have accomplished a revolution in the control and elimination of venereal diseases. To reduce the number of men incapacitated for service by these diseases, to insure the return of the men to civil life uncomtaminated by disease, as well as to protect the moral standards of the army and navy, measures were adopted through which, according to Secretary McAdoo, "four million soldiers and sailors have received greater protection against venereal diseases than they received, before the war, in civil life."

Will demobilization mean the return of these men to communities in which vice with its hideous product of disease, poverty and mental and moral degeneration is still rampant? Warnings against a slump into such conditions were sounded by the heads of the army and navy soon after the armistice was signed. "The campaign begun in war to insure the military fitness of men for fighting," said Secretary Daniels, "is quite as necessary to save men for civil efficiency." Secretary, Baker wired the Governors of the states urging that the control over venereal diseases established during the war be not relaxed.

A campaign against venereal disease as an after-the-war problem is being vigorously waged on behalf of the government by the United States Public Health Service. The program which it urges communities everywhere to adopt, embodies four points:

1. The suppression of "red-light districts" and of every form of commercialized vice.

2. The provision of facilities for the prompt treatment of venereal diseases. The Public Health Service in elaboration of this point urges the quarantine of diseased prostitutes, permanent segregation of those who are feeble-minded and medical treatment and industrial education for the others; the creation of clinics for venereal cases and the admission of such cases to hospitals; the suppression of quacks and quack remedies; the reporting of venereal diseases to state boards of health and the quarantining of patients who refuse to follow prescribed regulations to prevent the spread of disease.

3. The spread of education with regard to venereal diseases and sex matters.

4. The provision of opportunities for wholesome companionship and recreation as a substitute for the saloon and the brothel.

The Public Health Service appeals for the support of citizens everywhere in this campaign to protect the physical and mental efficiency of the nation. "With war's final end," it says in a circular just issued, "many war buildings, war jobs and institutions will go to the scrap heap. But every item in the program of venereal disease control is as necessary to successful peace as to successful war. There should be no peace with prostitution, no truce with the red-light district, no armistice with venereal diseases."

Major Blommaert

CHAPLAIN PIERRE BLOMMAERT, who speaks before the City Club, Monday, December 2, at luncheon as the representative of the Belgian government, is one of the most forceful and picturesque of the Belgian clergymen who have been made prominent by the Great War. He was educated for military life as a civil engineer and was entered in the Second Infantry Regiment in 1901. Later he studied theology and entered the ministry.

At the outbreak of the war he laid aside ecclesiastical robes and titles and was assigned to the delicate and dangerous duty of stretcher-bearer. He later became a chaplain and it was chiefly through his reports and efforts that the Belgian Protestant Chaplain's Corps, of which he became chief, was organized.

Owing to distinguished services he was made in July, 1914, "Officer of the Academy"; also "Chevalier of the order of Leopold." He has also been awarded the Croix de Guerre "in recognition of the great devotion he has shown in his work both at the front and in the rear, and of his courage and self-denial on the field of combat."

TAKE PITY on your lonesome neighbor at the table. Maybe he is a new member. Don't let him think this Club's an icebox.

A BLOW-OUT
For City Club Members Only

Fifteen years ago the CITY CLUB came into the world.

On Friday night, Dec. 6, we will celebrate the anniversary.

LOW-BROW DINNER— for low-brows and high-brows— 6:30.

Phone the office or leave word at the desk.

We Want YOU

Dude Clothes or Duds?

November 29, 1918.

City Club of Chicago:—I enclose the card for a "Low-Brow" night, as per your request. When I noticed the notation "Do not be a Dud" I took it to mean it meant wear your dress suit.

I notice on the card, however, that we are strictly admonished to wear our working clothes, so I am at a loss to know how to prevent being a dud.

In searching the latest lexicons I find that a Dud is a man with shabby clothes. Dud-man is even designated as a scarecrow, and the author also refers to Dod-man and I find upon looking up the latest on this word that there is an English version making the Dod-man correspond to the common snail, so I take this interpretation to be the correct one, and congratulate the program committee.

UNCLE DUDLEY.

Note.—Dude Clothes are Barred.

WHEN THE DINNER BELL RINGS, make a bee-line for 315 Plymouth Court.

Posters

WHAT should a poster be? City Club members are invited to express their preference among the American war posters which have been placed on display in the corridors and lounge of the City Club. Voting blanks are to be provided in which weights of 50 are given for excellence in carrying the message, 20 for design, 20 for lettering and 10 for skillful use of color.

"What should a poster be? Hamilton King says it should 'seize a moment—exploit a situation.' It should catch the attention, hold the interest, pierce the understanding, stir the feelings, and impel the will.

"To do this it should not be a phrase with an illustration, nor a picture with an explanation. It should resemble one dramatic moment on the stage when, through eye and ear at once, we are moved to live the scene. 'Out, damned spot,' says Lady Macbeth, and washes her hands. So the spectator-audience shivers. Neither the words nor the action would produce the shiver alone. So, 'I want you,' says Uncle Sam, and fixes you with finger and eye. Both figure and words should unite and that simultaneously, to produce the thrill that has responded to the message in so many boyish breasts, even as Kitchener's poster shook the Yankee's heart in 'Over the Top.'"

"Artists," says Louise Connolly, "make demands about the technique of posters. They speak of a picture as being done in 'poster style,' when it has little or no shading to make it look natural or 'photographic,' when the outline is like a scheme or pattern, and the color is flat and in splotches. They use few colors; they make a design of the lettering and the picture together; they sometimes make a bilateral design, balancing on the two sides, but often they prefer the picture markedly out of balance, and balance up with the lettering. They make one point catch the eye chiefly, and have the rest subordinate to but harmonious with that chief feature. Clever designs for posters are common, but strangely enough, clear and pleasing lettering is not. Really the Germans follow these artistic poster rules more strictly than most Americans, but the French are quite daring in violating them, freely using for war posters pictures that tell a story."

The above paragraphs are taken from a pamphlet prepared for the war poster exhibition by the Newark Public Library and on sale at the City Club.

The exhibition will continue until December 9. Bring your family and your friends to see it.

THREE NEW MEMBERS enlisted last week, just under the wire for the "low-brow" night. They are: William A. Alexander, Vice-President Earnshaw Knitting Co.; E. L. Kennedy, Manager Holden Shoe Company; R. L. McLellan, Sales Engineer Westinghouse Electric and Manfacturing Co.

The City Club Bulletin
A Journal of Active Citizenship

VOLUME XI.　　　　MONDAY, DECEMBER 9, 1918　　　　NUMBER 41

NEXT WEDNESDAY, DECEMBER 11, AT LUNCHEON
DR. WOODS HUTCHINSON, New York

Dr. Hutchinson was engaged in work with refugees on the western front for about a year. He has been on every battle front from Flanders to Italy. Dr. Hutchinson's writings on health questions are well known to the American people.

Members who heard Dr. Hutchinson's address before the Club several years ago will remember that he is a good story teller.

NEXT SATURDAY, DECEMBER 14, AT LUNCHEON
"The American Negro and Reconstruction"
JOHN R. SHILLADY, New York

Mr. Shillady is secretary of the National Association for the Advancement of Colored People, an organization representing both the white and black races. His address before the City Club two years ago, when he was secretary of the Mayor's Unemployment Commission in New York will be recalled by those who heard him as one of unusual interest.

Remember: Saturday is Ladies' Day
Speaking at 1:00.

High Jinks at the City Club

I care not for Yacht clubs and brine,
Nor for Athletic clubs and wine,
Give me pure high-brow uplift!
"Dry" old City Club for mine!

THE City Club climbed down from its high horse last Friday and celebrated its fifteenth birthday with songs and irreverent jests. Fifteen years of sustained high-brow endeavor were forgotten and repressed "low brow" instincts given free rein. The veneer of dignity cracked, the lid was off and our best citizens said and did the most surprisingly "low-brow" things.

Fifteen candles were on the cakes and the tables were brilliant and inviting when the boys filed in to dinner. An orchestra led by "Al"

Yeomans dispensed sweet music for the occasion. Charles Yeomans led the singing of the City Club anthem and after the "Amen" Joe Palise sent on one of his famous turkey dinners.

Frank Moulton swung the gavel. First, Horace Bridges was announced as the orator of the evening. Horace (we can call him "Horace" now) was most felicitous in his remarks. He scintillated for fifteen minutes on the remarkable civic regeneration which the City Club had accomplished for Chicago during the last fifteen years.

After Horace had concluded, a burley cop entered the room, evidently under the influence,

Ghe City Club Bulletin

A Journal of Active Citizenship

Published Weekly Except July, August and September; bi-weekly during July, August and September

By the CITY CLUB OF CHICAGO

315 Plymouth Court　　Telephone: Harrison 8278

DWIGHT L. AKERS, Editor

$1.00 per Year　-　-　-　-　10c per Copy

Entered as second class matter, December 3, 1917, at the postoffice at Chicago, Illinois, under the act of March 3, 1879.

Vol. XI.　　Monday, December 9, 1918　　No. 41

for he was afflicted with the blind staggers. Every member who lived in Chicago fourteen years ago recognized at once the Chicago police force of that day, before the heavy hands of Capt. Piper and the City Club had brought about the well-known regeneration of the force. As the copper tried to find a steady spot on which to lean, a choir consisting of Charles Yeomans, F. W. Burlingham and Charles Hull Ewing struck up this little ditty:

When the enterprising burglar's not a-burgling—not
 a-burgling,
When the cutthroat isn't occupied in crime—pied in
 crime,
He loves to hear the little brook a-gurgling—brook
 a-gurgling,
 And listen to the merry village chime.

When reformers are not causing him annoyment—
 him annoyment,
By placing him without the social bans—social bans,
His capacity for innocent enjoyment—cent enjoyment,·
 Is just as great as any honest man's.

At this moment, a smart looking officer entered the room. Capt. Piper—for it was indeed he—chimed in the singing and these were his words:

My name it's Captain Alexander Piper—ander Piper,
 At investigating coppers I'm a scream—I'm a scream,
By your club's request I'm trying to decipher—to de-
 cipher,
 What your patrolmen take to make 'em dream.

He searched that copper, took his flask away, made him stand up straight and toe out. When the copper marched from the room in the footsteps of Capt. Piper, he looked like an ·honest-to-goodness police officer. This was the verse the copper sang:

When investigating duty's to be done—to be done—
 When reformers organize for checking crime—check-
 ing crime,
When the City Club sends Piper and his gun—and
 his gun,
 A policeman has a most unhappy time.

The reporter learned later that Capt. Piper was only Barrett Conway and the copper only E. G. Fassett in disguise.

The Piper stunt drew many laughs. We did feel, however, that the program committee stepped over the line a little in trying to em-

barrass Everett Millard. Millard, as everybody knows, is chairman of our Municipal Art Committee and as such is the man who put the billboards out of business in Chicago. Four or five villains stalked into the rooms carrying advertising signs on sticks and surrounded Millard so he couldn't get away. Then the choir sang this song at him:

· Air: "Got style all the while."

Billboard, Oh! Billboard,
 Come down off your perch,
No more shall your bunk
 Our fair city besmirch.

Our bachelors chaste
 Are now safe from the stare
Of the corset ad lady
 With smile debonnair.

No more shall old maidens
 Be shocked till they sneeze
By underwear athletes
 And garter-clad knees.

Hair tonic Godiva's
 A dream of the past
And Kirk's soapless Hobo's
 Been lashed to the mast.

The City Club high brows
 Have made a fine start
Toward junking the signs
 For Municipal Art.

Millard was pink about it but what could he do. His remarks when he was called upon by the chairman, were graceful and to the point considering the occasion.

Irving K. Pond gave a lecture on the Bureau of Public Efficiency which was standing in one corner of the room. It was an antiquated old piece and shone only by the reflected light of its mirror (which we presume was the City Club, although Mr. Pond didn't say so). Mr. Pond's address was in his usual dignified vein and was received with the respectful but hearty applause that was its due.

It may be a surprise to some members that the "pop symphony concerts" which we listen to on Thursday evenings at Orchestra Hall were the idea of Victor Yarros and his band of community music enthusiasts on the Music Extension Committee. In honor of this service a male quartette playing tin whistles and horns rendered some of the good popular music of the day, including "Over There." The choir gave a vocal selection, as follows:

Air: "Son of a Gambolier."

We are, we are, we are, we are,
 A popular orchestray
We offer popular concerts
At a popular price to play,
The City Club's our foster ma,
 Vic Yarros is our pa, for
We are, we are, we are, we are,
 A popular orchestra.

The applause of the audience showed their appreciation of good, native-American music. At least, they knew what they liked. The pop orchestra was composed of Messrs. Goettsch Hickock, Kennicott and Frantz.

One of the most successful events of this

(Continued on page 309)

America's Bulgarian Diplomacy

HY did Bulgaria enter the war on the side of the Central Powers? With our eyes irned to the future and our thoughts centered pon the peace table, this question may seem to ave only historical interest, but according to Dr. lmer E. Count and Dr. Edward B. Haskell, ho spoke at the City Club last Thursday, the iture peace of the Balkan states and of Europe dependent upon our answer to this question. oth Dr. Count and Dr. Haskell lived for many ears as missionaries in Bulgaria and were there uring the early period of the war. They speak, herefore, with authority on the political prob-ms of that and the other Balkan states. They rere in Chicago last week as delegates to a con-ention of Bulgarians from Macedonia which et to formulate a statement of principles for resentation at the peace conference.

AMERICAN POLICY ENLIGHTENED

Dr. Count and Dr. Haskell gave high praise o American diplomacy toward Bulgaria during he war. American diplomacy, they said, was irected toward the detachment of Bulgaria rom her alliance with the Central Powers. The isastrous mistakes of the entente powers in ealing with Bulgaria were not repeated by ashington. Events in the Balkans have justi-fied American diplomacy.

Dr. Count was the first speaker. He said in brief: The Balkan peninsula may be said to have been the storm center of the war. One of the weaknesses of the entente policy was its fail-ure to grasp the importance of the Balkan states, particularly of Bulgaria, in the conduct of the war.

In 1914, at least three-fourths of the people of Bulgaria favored the allied powers. Why then did Bulgaria enter the war on the other side?

THE TINDER OF WAR

At the end of the Balkan wars, Bulgaria had been conquered and compelled to surrender. Following the defeat of Turkey, the territory of Serbia and Greece had been doubled and that of Bulgaria increased a little. The increase of Serbian territory had aroused the jealousy of the Central Powers. Turkey, which was an ally of the Central Powers, had been defeated and greater Serbia, backed by Russian influence, was a threat to the whole great design for the Bag-dad Railway and for German control of Meso-potamia. The Central Powers, if they were to re-create their prestige in the Balkans, had to break down Serbia. The first pretext to make war upon Serbia was seized and the great war followed. The Balkan question was the match which set the whole world on fire. That in itself is a reason why statemen should concern them-selves in working out a permanent solution for the Balkan problem.

During the Balkan wars a treaty was signed by Serbia and Bulgaria, by the terms of which the settlement of the dispute between these na-tions over Macedonia was to be left to the Czar of Russia. But Serbia was inspired by Greece to make a secret treaty affecting Macedonia and after the war Serbia tore up her agreement with Bulgaria and treated it as a scrap of paper. Bul-garia was defeated and had to submit to the loss of Macedonia, which is chiefly Bulgarian in lan-guage and in national sentiment.

After war was declared between the Allies and the Central Powers Bulgaria endeavored to ob-tain a recognition of her claims from the entente. Bulgaria literally besieged the British Foreign Office to obtain such recognition. She was postponed and temporized with for three months and was finally turned down. In the meantime Germany was busy. She told Bulgaria that she could not get justice from the entente, that the entente, angry as it had been about the violation of the Belgian treaty, had winked at the tear-ing up of the treaty with Serbia. They urged Bulgaria to seize this opportunity to take Mace-donia for herself.

BULGARIA FRIENDLY TO ALLIES

The Bulgarian people were friendly to the entente. Ten days before Bulgaria was mobil-ized on the side of Germany, five of the oppo-sition leaders in a conference with the King told him that this policy meant the destruction of Bulgaria and probably the loss of his own dy-nasty. One of these leaders even went so far as to warn the King that he might lose not only his dynasty but his head, and was put in prison for his boldness. That is merely one incident showing the general favoritism of Bulgaria for the cause of the allies. The Bulgarians had no love for Germany and have been great admir-ers of the Anglo-Saxon peoples. Many of the streets of Sofia are named after English states-men—none for Germans. Bulgaria supported Germany in the war in order to carry out her national ideal of union with Bulgarian Mace-donia.

THE KEY TO THE ARCH

Had the allies understood the vital relation of Bulgaria to the war and acted upon this knowledge the war would have been over years ago. America would not have had to enter the war. Bulgaria was the key to the situation. Had she allied herself with the entente, Greece would have followed suit and Roumania would have entered the war over a year earlier than she did and under different conditions. Serbia had so far succeeded in keeping Austria back, and if she had been supported by Bulgaria, Greece and

Roumania, would have probably continued to do so. Turkey would have been isolated, the Allies would have gained control of the Dardanelles and would have been able to send supplies to Russia. If Russia had received supplies her defeat might have been prevented.

"When I went through Budapest before America entered the war," said Dr. Count, "Germans told me that they could not understand why the entente had failed to seize its opportunity in Bulgaria. 'We lost little when we lost Italy,' they said, 'but we gained greatly when Bulgaria entered the war on our side.'

AMERICA'S WISE DECISION

"I am proud that America showed more wisdom than the entente in her diplomacy toward Bulgaria. It has been the policy of President Wilson in spite of the opposition of some 'statesmen,' to win Bulgaria from the arms of the Central Powers. He saw that it was not a wise course to weld Bulgaria more tightly to her alliance with the Central Powers. Germany saw the effect of President Wilson's policy in Bulgaria, and the Kaiser made a special trip into the Balkans to persuade Bulgaria to declare war on America. Other influences were brought to bear and Serbs and the Greeks in this country were trying to accomplish the same thing but they did not succeed."

American diplomacy in the Balkans succeeded in saving the situation for the allies. When Bulgaria forsook her alliance, the Central Powers realized immediately that they would not be able to hold out. Bulgaria's change of attitude was due to the fact that diplomats in Sofia understood the American viewpoint and believed that America would stand for justice for Bulgaria. With America's help, Bulgaria believes that she will be able to get justice at the peace table at Paris.

TERRITORIAL DISPUTES

Dr. Haskell discussed the disputes between Bulgaria and her neighbors over the Dobrudja and Macedonia. The Dobrudja had been given to Roumania in return for the surrender of Bessarabia to Russia, and Roumania had extended her boundaries on several occasions at the expense of Bulgaria. If the Danube, which is a natural boundary, were fixed as the line between Bulgaria and Roumania, peaceful relations between those countries would probably be the result. Roumania ought to be satisfied, as she would still have access to the sea and would probably have brought within her boundaries the Roumania population of Transylvania.

There also remains, as a point of dispute, the Macedonian region covered in the secret treaty of 1912 between Greece and Serbia. In a plebiscite in 1872 over three-fourths of the people in this region declared themselves to be Bulgarians. If Serbia is given access to the Adriatic sea and Bosnia and Herzegovina are united with her as they ought to be, she should be satisfied. If the Bulgarian speaking people of Macedonia were united to Bulgaria, the territorial dispute could probably be smoothed out and in five or ten years Serbia and Bulgaria would be the best of friends.

ATROCITY CHARGES

Dr. Haskell also discussed the atrocity charges which have been lodged against the Bulgarians. There have been atrocities, he said. He mentioned one instance of brutal treatment of a civilian population by Bulgarian troops. When these troops entered a certain province which had formerly been Bulgarian, they believed that they were entering as liberators, but they were not welcomed as such, for the people during their long association with Serbia had become Serbian in feeling. Bulgaria made the mistake of drafting boys from this region into the army on the theory that they were Bulgarians. The people, however, were intensely angry at this and had a right to be, for they considered themselves Serbs and refused to fight against their kinsmen. They planned an insurrection, and in the absence of Bulgarian troops seized quantities of arms and munition, fell upon the Bulgarian civil authorities and murdered them to a man. When the Bulgarian troops returned the insurrection was put down with brutal hands. Villages were burned and many people, including women (many of whom were involved in the insurrection), were killed.

"We must remember," said Dr. Haskell, "that the Balkan peoples feel toward each other about as we feel toward Germany today." However, where he had been able to test out the stories of atrocities, he had usually found them to be greatly exaggerated or false. The famous Bulgarian "Hymn of Hate," he said, he had discovered upon inquiry to have been written *before the war* by a minor Bulgarian poet. In a wide acquaintance with Bulgarian papers he had never seen it quoted. He was convinced after inquiry at the American embassy in Constantinople, that the charge that thousands of Serbian girls had been sent into Turkish harems had no foundation.

Demobilizing Our Service List

When Johnny comes marching home again
　　Hooray, hooray.
We'll give him a hearty welcome then
　　Hooray, hooray.
We'll shake his hand and drink a toast
We'll print his name in the Listening Post
And we'll all be gay
　　When Johnny comes home.

When Johnny comes marching home or the dollar-a-year man returns to his desk we want to know it. We want to hear his story. We know that some of our members in the army and navy have had some thrilling experiences. We hope they will let us tell them, through the columns of the Bulletin, to their friends in the Club.

Any member in service should at least notify the secretary of the Club when he is "demobilized" and give us his new address for mail.

Notes on Some Books About

Peace and the New Society

By Aksel G. S. Josephson

"The men in the trenches, who have been freed from the economic serfdom to which some of hem have been accustomed, will, it is likely, return to their homes with a new view and a new imatience of all mere political phrases, and will demand real thinking and sincere action."

WOODROW WILSON.

HE, purpose of these notes is to call attention to a number of books and pamphlets it have appeared since the outbreak of the ar and that discuss the problems of the comιg peace and point forward to the new era that ; to come after peace has been made, an era, we ope and expect, full of promises of greater iberty for the individual, better order in the elations between individuals and nations.

In these books leading personalities and young ournalists vie with each other to place before he public their views of what form this new ociety *ought* to take, all filled with a desire to ive words to their thoughts, to assist in the olution of this the most important and the most ifficult problem that has arisen for centuries.

It was only natural that the books published uring the first months of the world war looked ackward rather than forward. For instance he collection of studies of the causes of the war, ssued by a number of Oxford professors under :he title *Why We Are at War*. Another book of this kind is, as the title indicates, *The His'orical Backgrounds of the War* by F. C. Adκins (N. Y.: R. M. McBride). It is a study of the antecedents of the belligerent nations in order to find therein an explanation of the present situation. The author, who is a teacher of ιistory, says, however, in his preface that his object is not so much to impart exact information as to provoke thought. In this lies the real value of the book: real thoughts, clear, sharp, consistent thinking is just what we need at the present time. We meet with so much loose :alk, the result of muddled thinking.

How Diplomats Make War, by Francis Neilson (N. Y.: B. W. Huebsch) is also a book that looks backward, but in order to point to a brighter future. It closes with the following words: "Each people now the war is in progress is actuated subconsciously by the notion that the end of the war will bring the freedom that will raise them up out of the slough of the past. The vision of the men in the trenches is one of peace and disarmament; but whether the close of the strife will open an era of an unarmed enduring peace is a question which will depend entirely on the people themselves. Governments ηave made the war; only the peoples can make an unarmed peace." Neilson is the radical politician, Charles Seymour, on the other hand— *The Diplomatic Background of the War* (New Haven: Yale Univ. Press)—is the scientific in

vestigator and George Adams Gibbons the wideawake, cleareyed journalist with many opportunities to look behind the scenes—*The New Map of Europe* and *The Reconstruction of Poland and the Near East* (N.Y.: Century Co.).

Peace propositions appeared at an early date, made both by individuals and organized bodies of men: peace societies and political groups. These proposals were collected by the American Association for International conciliation in New York and published under the title *Towards an Enduring Peace*.

Recently another collection of similar documents has appeared, edited by Emily Greene Balch, under the title *Approaches to the Great Settlement* (N. Y.: B. W. Huebsch). Only those proposals that have come from labor and socialist groups are here printed in extenso, as the others are easily available in public documents and other official publications. Besides printing the texts the author reviews the various proposals. The volume covers the period from the issuing of the President's peace note in December, 1916, to the various replies to the Pope's note of August, 1917.

Theoretical problems of many kinds have been raised in connection with the war and the altered relations between men which it has created. Some of these were discussed in a few lectures at Bedford College for Women in February and March, 1915, and afterwards published under the title *The International Crisis in its Ethical and Psychological Aspects* (N. Y.: Oxford Univ. Press). The various lectures dealt with the following subjects: "The morality of strife in relation to the war"; "Herd instinct and the war"; "International morality: The United States of Europe"; "The changing mind of a nation at war"; "War and hatred"; "Patriotism and the perfect state." The author of the last study, Bernard Bosanquet, points out that the value of our patriotism depends on what we desire for our country and closes with the following words: "The patriotism we have tried to portray implies and demands that we should desire for our country, not a triumph of vanity and selfinterest, but a share in such a solid work of organization as shall be most favorable to the performance of a true state's function in *every* community of Europe. Thus alone can we deserve well of our country, and our country of the world."

William E. Ritter takes the standpoint of the

scientist, especially the biologist, in his book *War, Science and Civilization* (Boston: R. G. Badger). His thesis is that "if man would make earth yield the most possible for his wants, he must find a more rational and effective way of distributing it than by means of war." As the author remarks in the introduction to the book, it treats of civilization rather than war. It might be worth while, in connection with this book, to call attention to another which, however, has nothing to do either with war, peace or reconstruction, but deals with a science that has been called "essentially a reformer's science": *Culture and Ethnology* by Robert H. Lowie (N. Y.: D. C. McMurtrie). "As the engineer calls on the physicist," he says, "for a knowledge of mechanical laws, so the social builder of the future who should seek to refashion the culture of his time and add to its cultural values will seek guidance from ethnology."

How humanity shall be dragged out of the mire into which the war has thrown it is a question that was raised very early. Six American university professors and one retired admiral make up *one* group that has tried to solve the riddle, some English liberal and radical politicians and writers, another. The speculations of the former were published under the title *Problems of Readjustment After the War* (N. Y.: D. Appleton & Co.). Here we find discussed such topics as "War and democracy," "The crisis in social evolution," "The war and international law," "The conduct of military and naval warfare," etc. "Is this the end of European democracy?" asks the author of the first, Albert Bushnell Hart. "Will example and military pressure cause the end of American democracy?" And he points out that "popular government in America depends upon the power of democracy to repel the shock of militarism." In the English volume, *Towards a Lasting Settlement*, edited by Charles R. Buxton (N. Y.: Macmillan Co.), other subjects are discussed: "The basis of permanent peace," "Nationality," "War and the woman's movement," "The democratic principle and international relations" are the titles of some of these studies. G. Lowes Dickinson, author of the opening essay, asks: "What makes for peace?" and he answers his own question thus: "Not religion, not science, not learning, not education. All these serve war as much as they serve peace. There is one only that works for peace, that human reason that is also human charity."

The annual meeting of the American Academy of Political and Social Sciences was held shortly after the entry of the United States into the war against Germany. The subject under discussion was *America's Relation to the World Conflict* and the papers that were read on the occasion were printed in the number for July, 1917, of its *Annals*. Walter Lippman, in his address on "The World Conflict in its Relation to American Democracy," says: "We who have entered the war to insure democracy in the world will have raised an aspiration that will not end with the overthrow of Prussian autocracy. We shall turn with fresh interests to our own tyrannies—to our Colorado mines, our steel industries, our sweatshops and our slums. We shall call that man un-American and no patriot who prates of liberty in Europe and resists it at home." And Emily Green Balch, in speaking of "The War in its relation to Democracy and World Order" affirms that "the time is to come somehow, sometime, when the ruling type of our civilization will be a co-operative world order in which the element of coercions will be shrinking more and more and in which the element of free, spontaneous, joyful fellowship will be ever greater and greater." Two other numbers of the *Annals,* for July and September, 1915, deal with *America's Interests as Affected by the European War* and *America's Interests After the War.*

The University of Chicago has made a substantial contribution to the discussion of the subject of these notes by publishing a volume of *Readings in the Economics of War,* compiled by Professors J. Maurice Clark and Harold G. Moulton of its own faculty and Walton H. Hamilton of Amherst College. While two of its three main divisions, those dealing with the economic background of war in general and with the proper organization of the industrial system for war, treat of what now is past, the third is concerned with questions of the future, with "the changes which have come in the wake of the war and with the problems of reorganization and group welfare which will have to be met." This last division, however, occupies only 50 of the book's 676 pages, while the second fills over 550. The explanation is, of course, that the work was planned and executed in the midst of the struggle, though it so happened that when it was ready for publication the struggle was nearly over and the smallest part of the book might seem to be just now the most significant. But only seemingly. The statements collected about the mobilization of the country's resources for war will have their significance in considering afterwar problems. I quote the opening sentences in the Introduction to the last division of the book: "The war is but a stage in a continuous process of economic and social development. With its termination will come no end of change and no cessation in the need of controlling development. On the contrary, there will gradually emerge a new situation, new problems, and the need of many new adjustments. The resources of the country, the organization of industry, and the services of the people which have been used for a single military end will have to be made to serve other purposes."

It is necessary to come to a clear understanding of the aims of the war, says George G. Armstrong in *Our Ultimate Aim in the War* (London: G. Allen & Unwin). And he considers that England, having taken the lead in so many iberal movements, ought to lead the way in the straightening out of the present tangle. "The ime has come to consider whether the war may ot shortly be ended by international agreement 1 which the United States shall participate." hus wrote about the end of 1916 in the New ork *Times* a mysterious author who called him- If "Cosmos" and it is said in the introduction , the letters, as collected in bookform: *The asis of Durable Peace* (N. Y.: Scribner's) hat his competence and authority would be recognized in both hemispheres, were his name nown! The peace, he finds "depends on a witholding of all acts of vengeance and reprisal" and the upholding of the principle of democracy.

"The propitious future of mankind is in the hands of the armies of the democracies and the radical and labor organizations of the world," says Horace M. Kallen. His contribution to the solution of the world problem bears the title *The Structure of Lasting Peace* (Boston: Marshal Jones Co.) The cause of the present situation is nationalism with its military system, its economic competition and its industrial slavery. The straightening out of the tangle must be done in the sign of internationalism.

Nothing short of the abolition of the competitive system and of private ownership can create a lasting peace in the opinion of Thorstein Veblen, the author of a trenchant *Inquiry into the Nature of Peace and the Terms of Its Perpetuation* (N. Y.: Macmillan). As yet, however, strife is regarded as a necessary part of the order of nature.

The moral issue in the world war is the subject of Morris Jastrow's reflexions in *The War and the Coming Peace* (Philadelphia: J. B. Lippincott Co.). "The triumph of the moral issue involved in the world war is the victory of Ahuramazda over Ahriman, the overcoming of evil by the overthrow of power—the enthronement of right as against might; and this will be followed, as surely as the day follows the night, by the dawn of a new era of light and peace for the entire world." In a previous book, *The War and the Bagdad Railway* (Lippincott) the same author narrates the history of Asia Minor and points out its importance in the present conflict; the Eastern question must, on this point is he emphatic, be solved in the spirit of co-operation, not of competition.

(*To be continued*)

High Jinks at the City Club

(*Continued from page* 304)

eventful evening was Charles Yeomans' sympathetic rendering of a song written by Donald Richberg in honor of the tenth birthday of the Club. Even the singing of "The Long, Long Trail" did not reach the depth of sentiment that Mr. Yeomans put into the song. The air was that of the famous heart-song "Love me and the World is Mine." For the sake of the coming generations of City Club members, the words are here reproduced:

    I sought afar as in a dream
    A club that paradise must be
    With angel members—so 'twould seem—
    Lo! City Club! We founded thee!
    Gambling games may not be played here
    Cocktails not be made here
    Man may not a maiden woo
    We'll be pure, though we be lonely
    With the righteous only
    It's too good to be quite true!

    Refrain
    I care not for Yacht clubs and brine,
    Nor for Athletic clubs and wine,
    Give me pure high-brow uplift!
    "Dry" old City Club for mine!

    The club soars on to realms above,
    Still "higher-up" it seems to go.
    Yet finding graft, though seeking love,
    The love that only angels know!
    Bright accountants seek to guide us,
    Politicians chide us,
    Or betray us with a kiss;
    All the joys of bridge or polo,
    Operatic solo,
    Are as naught compared to this!

Henry P. Chandler made a straight from the shoulder four-minute talk, urging every member present to get new members for the Club. You'll hear more about that later, but you might as well get started now. S. Bowles King, who, by

the way, was top-sergeant of the program committee, told of the plans of the Membership Extension Committee.

The chairman called on several members for impromptu remarks. T. K. Webster, second president of the City Club, got off this little verse:

    The Frenchman faces shot and shell
    With pants as red as flame.
    The Scotchman wears no pants at all
    But he gets there just the same!

At this moment the reporter fainted and was carried out. He learned later that the program was concluded by remarks from Walter L. Fisher and George E. Hooker.

The instrumental music for the evening was rendered by an orchestra consisting of Alfred Yeomans, conductor, Messrs. Korten, Moss, C. Yeomans and Burlingham, assisted by some friends not members of the Club. Piano accompaniments were played by Thomas Tamlyn. Most of the lyrics were written by S. Bowles King.

You are invited to the sixteenth birthday party one year hence.

Good Reading

THE Chicago Public Library will loan to the City Club each week a few volumes, in addition to its regular book deposit, of the latest fiction, biography, essays, etc. These books will be placed in the reading room each Monday and an equal number of books which have been read by members of the Club will be returned.

HE MAY BE A DENTIST

There may be a man on your block out home who could add much to the City Club. You may meet him on the train going out at night. His ideas make him available or otherwise for City Club membership. Propose his name to the Committee on Admissions, Henry P. Chandler, Chairman.

Belgium's Story

THE City Club has several times welcomed representatives of Belgium at its noon meetings and each time has gathered new inspiration from their stories of the splendid resistance of the Belgian people to the German armies and their long-suffering during the German occupation. Last Monday Major Pierre Blommaert of the Protestant Chaplains Corps, representing the Belgian government, brought to our members King Albert's message of gratitude to America for her aid to Belgium and an appreciation by the King of the great moral and spiritual influence which America contributed to the war.

The Germans, said Major Blommaert, underestimated the Belgian people, as they under-estimated practically every people against whom they fought. They tried unsuccessfully to divide the nation by stirring up old prejudices between the Flemings and Walloons. They tried to break the spirit of the people. The Belgians are naturally a jovial people. They did not lose their sense of humor even in the face of the national tragedy. Many practical jokes were played by the Belgians upon the serious and uncomprehending German soldiers, as in that instance when, forbidden to show enthusiasm for the successes of the allied armies, the Belgians celebrated a great Italian victory by wearing macaroni in their buttonholes.

"Belgium is not exhausted," said Major Blommaert. "We have come out of the war a greater people than we were before. Through suffering we have gained character and national feeling. In five or ten years Belgium will be a greater and a wealthier nation than before the war.

"But we will need help. We will need, first of all, the help of Germany. We have no hatred of Germany but we must have justice from her. One of the tasks at the peace table will be to insure the assistance of Germany in the restoration of Belgium. We will need your help also. Belgium needs not only a physical but a moral reconstruction, and America can help not only in a material way but by the example of her free spirit."

Hero Sons

Three of our members have lost sons in action. Word came recently of the death of Lieut. George A. McKinlock, Jr., of Winnetka. The death of Capt. R. H. McLaughlin, son of Professor Andrew C. McLaughlin, was recorded in an earlier issue. Several weeks ago news was received of the death of A. A. McCormick, Jr., of the aviation service.

The following lines dedicated to Mr. McCormick were printed in the Chicago Tribune:

He fell a bright young star
From the September sky of France.
Too soon?
But he had led an airy swarm
Along our Southern gulf's fair winter shores;
And he had reached, above the new-made Alps,
The spires of Milan, the Italian plain,—
That beatific vision
Freshened for his young eyes
And for our older day.
And he lived on to glimpse
A vision greater still;
The triumph of the cause for which he wrought—
And died.   H. B. F.

The City Club extends its deepest sympathy to the fathers of these young men who have made the great sacrifice.

CABLEGRAMS FROM PAUL R. WRIGHT, a member of our editorial board, arrive from Vladivostok at frequent intervals. Mr. Wright is special correspondent there for the Daily News. The "Hit and Miss" editor of this paper wrote recently: "Paul Wright, the well known microscopist and correspondent, is making a microscopic investigation of Asia for the Daily News, and, as Asia is quite a large place, Paul is likely to be away some time."

ONE OF THE WAR POSTERS recently on display at the City Club was the work of Miss Carrie Evelyn Lyon, daughter of F. Emory Lyon, a member of this Club.

The City Club Bulletin
A Journal of Active Citizenship

VOLUME XI.	MONDAY, DECEMBER 16, 1918	NUMBER 42

A BETTER CITY

You want a better Chicago. Your cancelled check for membership dues in the City Club proves that. You can help the city by getting more men behind the ideas of progress for which you stand. Haven't you in mind now a man who would be looked on with favor by the Committee on Admissions?

Next Wednesday, December 18, at Luncheon

" Russia and the Bolsheviki "
PROF. RALPH B. DENNIS
Northwestern University

Prof. Dennis is one of the most recent American observers of Russian conditions. He left Russia last September after a stay of many months during which he had exceptional opportunities for learning conditions. His analysis of the Russian situation is said to throw new light upon the perplexing problems of Europe's "dark continent."

Now that the Armistice is Signed—

AND the period of reconstruction is upon us, a big drive has been started to restore the membership of the Club to at least its pre-war dimensions. Our membership losses on account of the war conditions were probably no greater in proportion than those of similar organizations in Chicago, but the maintenance and improvement of the Club facilities and the effectiveness of its civic work depend to considerable extent upon the size and character of the membership list.

WATCH US CLIMB!

Now then! A committee has been formed to steer the campaign, but every member is expected to get out of the car and push like Sam Hill.

A membership of 2,500 by January 1! That's the target. It's no small task to add 700 new members to our list, but with every member shooting 100 per cent it can be done.

The committee that is in charge of the drive went into "high" last week with an appeal to members for help in its work. Each member was asked to pledge one new member and to furnish to the committee the names of five "prospects." A loyal response is expected.

SOME TIPS

One or two pointers from the membership extension committee:

One of the surest ways of clinching a "prospect" is to please his stomach. Not that any man joins the City Club for its creature comforts alone, but oftentimes a good lunch is the final touch in persuasion. Why not invite him to dinner?

Many organizations, not connected with the Club, hold meetings here. Those who attend these meetings, who have seen the Club and sampled its kitchen, may want to join. If you know any man in any such organization who is good timber, give him an opportunity to join.

Not every man is a City Club man. You know the purposes of the Club and the type of man who belongs here. The quality of the Club membership is more important even than its size.

The membership extension committee has been reorganized and enlarged for the drive.

The City Club Bulletin

A Journal of Active Citizenship

Published Weekly Except July, August and September; bi-weekly during July, August and September

By the CITY CLUB OF CHICAGO
315 Plymouth Court   Telephone: Harrison 8278

DWIGHT L. AKERS, Editor

$1.00 per Year - - - - 10c per Copy

Entered as second class matter, December 3, 1917, at the postoffice at Chicago, Illinois, under the act of March 3, 1879.

Vol. XI.   Monday, December 16, 1918   No. 42

It is as follows: S. Bowles King, Chairman; Frederick D. Bramhall, Barrett Conway, Frederick Dickinson, Eugene G. Fassett, Julius Goettsch, Dr. C. S. Bacon, F. S. Hickok, D. R. Kennicott, James Mullenbach, Everett L. Millard, Herbert H. Smith, F. D. Porter, C. H. Perrine, F. C. W. Parker, Wiley W. Mills, Haven ReQua, Frederick Rex, W. S. Reynolds, Paul Steinbrecher, James R. Ozanne, Claude K. Brown, I. K. Pond, N. Tracy Yeomans, Eddy S. Brandt.

Extra ammunition in the form of literature and application blanks can be had on request.

Christmas Is Coming And—

It will probably be for America the merriest Christmas in years. The reaction against the stringent economies of war time will probably arouse a greater spirit of liberality and result in even more generous giving than before the war.

But this is not an ad. We are not suggesting that you ought to buy from us a green and yellow necktie for father or a mechanical top for little Willie. We do wish to remind you of the invitation extended to you last week by the House Committee to chip in on a Christmas fund for the fifty-one employes of the Club.

Length of service is a determining factor in the distribution of the Christmas money to Club employes. Twenty of our employes have been in the service of the Club for five years or more—one of them for thirteen years, another for twelve, a third for ten years. With some of these employes, members are acquainted; others have served unseen but have nevertheless contributed in large measure to the comfort of the members.

The House Committee is expecting a generous response to its invitation.

Politics and the Convention

HOW is the constitutional convention to be elected? That will undoubtedly be one of the big questions at Springfield when the legislature meets next January. "It is generally conceded," says the Citizens Association of Chicago, in a report just issued, "that constitutional revision should be worked out on a plane entirely above partisanship. It is evident that a Convention made up of delegates elected on a party basis rather than on account of special fitness would neither be likely to do its work well nor to inspire public confidence. Therefore most persons who have given thought to the matter are strongly of the opinion that it is highly desirable, from the standpoint of the public, that the delegates to the Constitutional Convention be chosen, if possible, on a non-partisan basis."

A strict construction of the language of the constitution raises doubt as to the power of the legislature to provide for the non-partisan election of delegates to the convention without changing the general election law. The differences of interpretation on this point were discussed in a previous issue of the City Club Bulletin. The Citizens Association in its report cites an opinion of the Attorney-General of Ohio interpreting similar language in the Ohio constitution prior to its revision and upholding the right of the legislature to fix the manner of election, except so far as limited by the constitution itself. The non-partisan election plan was used in Ohio.

A Lawyers Committee, composed of Charles R. Holden, John P. Wilson, John S. Miller, S. S. Gregory, Levy Mayer, Silas H. Strawn, Frederick Bruce Johnstone and Clarence S. Darrow, has been appointed by the Citizens Association to prepare an opinion as to whether, "first, an act providing for the nomination of candidates for delegates to the constitutional convention by petition only would be constitutional and, second, whether an act providing for the election of delegates on a separate ballot without any party designation, would be constitutional." Governor Lowden, referring to this committee in a letter to the President of the Citizens Association, said: "I hope they will find some way by which partisan nominations may be avoided."

New Members

T. A. Buenger, Assistant Manager, William F. Tempel & Co., Brokers.

Thomas St. Clair Evans, Industrial Secretary, International Committee, Y. M. C. A.

BE A RECEPTION COMMITTEE of one whenever you sit at table with a stranger.

America in the Remaking

F America is to avoid revolutionary upheavals like those occurring in Europe, it will be not rough our intelligence but through our pros- :rity, according to Charles Zueblin, who spoke : the City Club last Monday. Mr. Zueblin pre- cted for America the greatest era of prosperity its history. Our men will not return from urope with revolutionary ideas, he said. They iven't been there long enough to acquire them. hen they return they will find prosperity and iat does not make for revolution. They will,)wever, come back with a feeling that America ust not be behind other countries. If the Brit- h labor party succeeds in establishing an eight-)ur day in England and in bettering conditions other ways, our men will insist upon equally ood conditions here.

No Place for Standpatters

Mr. Zueblin appealed for a progressive atti- ude of mind toward the problems of reconstrue- ion. This war, he said, was fought by the 'oung men and we have no right to show any ign of age in the manner in which we face these roblems.

Some changes we adopted for the period of the war, he continued. Others ought to be made)ermanent. The railroads were in absolute :haos a year ago. Six of the best railroad men n the country had tried to untangle the difficul- :ies in which our transportation system was en- neshed. They failed. Finally we did the only)ossible thing and put the railroads under one lead. The roads ought not now to be turned)ack to private control.

Keep Up the Standards

Industrial standards ought not to be lowered. Three things we ought to insist upon in the read- ustment of industry: Short hours, high wages ind increasing productivity. The fancy wages)aid in war industries will not continue, of :ourse, but the minimum standard will not go lown. We must stand for progress in the short- :ning of hours and in the increase of production.

The heavy labor turn over in some industries s a burden upon production, Mr. Zueblin said. Many industries have an annual turn-over of {00 or 400 per cent and the average annual turn-)ver for the country is about 100 per cent. The :ause of this turn-over lies not only in condi- ions in the shop but in the home environment of he workers. The fellows over there have been well cared for and they will not be willing to :ome back to slum conditions here.

Mr. Zueblin spoke of the tremendous and im- portant task before the employment service of the United States in securing the re-employment of soldiers and war workers and urged the main- tenance of employment exchanges through which the conditions of the labor market might be accurately ascertained and made known. We are confronted by a greater and speedier up- heaval of labor than before the war, he said. The elimination of the private employment agen- cies, of which there were about ten thousand before the war, marks a big step forward, for the purpose of these agencies was to disrupt in- dustry and increase the labor turn-over.

Our Leadership

Pessimists and malcontents were taken to task by Mr. Zueblin. One of the tragedies of the war, he said, has been the campaign of vituper- ation and fault-finding that followed the signing of the armistice. It would hardly seem, he said, that we had won a victory or had any leader- ship at all from the amount of grumbling and criticism that we have had. We must be on our guard against the pessimists and malcontents. They are undoing the work which we entered the war to accomplish.

The Government and Labor

IS there among employers a misconception of the aims and purposes of the government towards labor? E. T. Gundlach of the Depart- ment of Labor, speaking at the City Club No- vember 29th, said that he had been surprised at the misunderstanding of the government's atti- tude among many employers in the Middle West. Mr. Gundlach's address was an inter- pretation of the policies of the government toward labor.

In the exercise of executive power, Mr. Gund- lach said, all labor questions during the war were placed under the supervision of the Labor Department. The Secretary of Labor, it is true, is a union man and there are representatives of organized labor in the department, but the staff of the department also contains representative employers and others having no connection with "labor." There has been no attempt, as charged, to unionize labor. Mr. Gundlach described the machinery of the department for the arbitration and conciliation of labor disputes. The deci- sions of the bodies formed for this purpose, while not binding for the future, will, he said, probably be accepted hereafter as precedents in dealing with labor problems.

In the government's policy toward labor two points have had special prominence, according to Mr. Gundlach. The government has urged employers to take an attitude of conciliation toward labor, to demonstrate a willingness to talk things over and to recognize the point of view of the employe. That does not mean at all that the employer must give in to the worker on every point. Neither is it simply a question of wages and hours. There are ideas and sentiments of democracy which are common to all people— working people no less than the employers—and working people feel that there should be more democracy in industry. They demand that working people should not be treated as mere machines. The policy of the government has been to get employers and working people together and to encourage them to talk things over and to deal fairly with each other.

The second point in the government's labor policy, Mr. Gundlach said, is a recognition of the right of the laborer to bargain with the employer. Labor does not want benevolence, it wants what it believes to be its rights. The laboring man has something to sell and he wants to bargain for it on equal terms with the employer. If we recognize the laboring man's right to bargain, we must also recognize his right to bargain collectively. Collective bargaining does not necessarily mean bargaining with unions—it may mean bargaining with a shop committee. The government, of course, cannot undertake to enforce collective bargaining. It cannot force a conciliatory attitude on the part of the employers. But it believes the way to hold off Bolshevikism is by working through and co-operating with labor leaders of the right type.

Reconstruction, Mr. Gundlach concluded, does not mean simply a return by the employer to the era of easy picking. Labor will get its share of the product and the employer will get the margin which is necessary to stimulate men to management. Only those men who feel the spirit of the new day, who show a spirit less narrowly patriotic and more international will be able to lead.

CHIEF JUSTICE BARRETT last week appointed Masters in Chancery in the Circuit Court, among whom are the following members of the City Club: Sigmund Zeisler, Louis J. Behan, Farlin H. Ball and James P. Harrold.

CHRISTMAS CIGARS—all kinds, all prices—are on sale to members at the City Club at very low rates by the box.

Medical Science and War

"THE hypodermic has beaten the howitzer," according to Dr. Woods Hutchinson, who spoke at the City Club last Wednesday. Dr. Hutchinson spent eleven months on the battle lines in France and Italy. Through the advance in medical treatment and nursing care, he said, the death rate from all causes was held at about 2 per cent per annum. Fifty years ago this was about the normal death rate in times of peace.

DOCTORS A TARGET

If a wounded man lived for three or four hours until he could get under the doctor's care, he could be saved in about ninety-five per cent of the cases, Dr. Hutchinson said. About eighty per cent were returned to the firing line within forty days. It was because the doctor was not merely an angel of mercy but a maker of new soldiers that the Germans no longer observed the traditional immunity of the doctor but shot him down as mercilessly as a private soldier. One doctor was rated as equivalent to 800 private soldiers.

The way in which the wounded were handled was nothing short of marvelous, according to Dr. Hutchinson. He had never supposed that it would be possible for machinery to operate so smoothly. He described the organization and equipment which made this possible and spoke of the remarkable achievements of medical science in the war.

A MIRACLE IN MEDICINE

The Dakin solution, as used in connection with the Carrel treatment, he described as one of the most wonderful of these accomplishments. This solution, he said, contains chlorine gas, strong enough to kill all the germs, but it is so evenly and perfectly balanced that it will be neutralized by the soda in the system before it has had a chance to injure the tissues. Chlorine has saved more lives in this way than it has destroyed through its use as poison gas. The treatment of tetanus marks another great advance in medical science in this war.

The measures taken to protect the health of the army were most effective, Dr. Hutchinson said. They show the results which can be accomplished when the doctor and the nurse are given a chance. The boys were well fed and well cared for, their water supply was protected, the fly nuisance was practically eliminated. The incineration of garbage and nightsoil proved effective in getting rid of germs, keeping the drinking water pure and eliminating breeding places for flies. Dr. Hutchinson suggested the practicability of applying similar methods in civil life. He expressed the belief that the men who were in France, having observed the good results the public health work in the army, would be glad to support such measures in a greater degree when they returned.

Dr. Hutchinson discussed also the spread of influenza in this country and the precautions which should be taken against it. The epidemic, he said, did not start in Spain and was not even very widespread there. It started in Central Asia and spread over Europe as it has done about every thirty years for the last century and a half. Not until it reached this country did it assume its present virulent form, resulting in the death of about 350,000 people.

The use of masks to check the epidemic was advocated by Dr. Hutchinson. If universally adopted, masks would stop the spread of the disease, he asserted, within ten days. In San Francisco through the labor unions, the stores and other means the people were induced to use the mask and the epidemic was checked in about ten days. It has been contended that this was mere coincidence, but Dr. Hutchinson is convinced that the mask proved its effectiveness in this instance. The disease, he said, is transmitted from nose to nose or mouth to mouth by sneezing, coughing, etc. The germ may get through one mask but it can hardly get through two. It is spread particularly by people in the early stages who do not know that they are infected.

A Message to Wilson

Prior to President Wilson's departure for Europe, the Wartime Committee of the City Club wired him the following expression of goodwill:

"Believing that the American people is wholeheartedly devoted to the great purposes of establishing 'the reign of law based upon the consent of the governed and sustained by the organized opinion of mankind,' we wish you Godspeed upon your departure for the peace congress and success in the task of securing, by the co-operation of the peoples of the world, a firm league of free nations."

Can We Consolidate Our War Gains?

THE Rochester conference on American reconstruction problems, called by the National Municipal League, adopted the following platform "for consideration and support by all citizens who desire to see the United States in a more advanced position at the end of the war than at its beginning." The platform calls for the maintenance of many of the great powers which have accrued to the government during the period of the war. It reads as follows:

During the war, as measures of necessary national efficiency, numerous matters formerly within private control, passed to the control of the people. Some of these things should undoubtedly be returned promptly to private enterprise, but the American people will miss a great opportunity if they allow certain of these temporary powers to slip through their fingers in the next few months, viz.:

EMPLOYMENT

1. During the war the long-desired Federal Employment Service has been created and the national government has assumed responsibility for connecting employers and workers in the only right and efficient way. This Service should be continued, generously financed by Congress and should be encouraged to extend its sphere to include the education of employers in modern principles of employment.

CONTROL OF CORPORATIONS

2. Corporations, particularly those doing an inter-state business, have become a great source of Federal revenue and may reasonably be expected to continue to be such. Federal control and supervision of their practices should be continued and extended, for they are national, not merely state-wide, in the problems they create. Effort should be made to free them from conflicting and ineffectual state regulation by a Federal incorporation procedure.

PUBLIC OWNERSHIP AND CONTROL

3. The government has assumed control of railroads, telegraphs and telephones, opening the opportunity for either federal ownership with public or private operation or a reorganization by economical regional systems under a method of control that will protect the private capital by ensuring a reasonable return yet removing speculative and anti-social features of the private ownership of the past with its relatively feeble and negative scheme of regulation. Whichever principle is adopted is a smaller matter than that the essential features of our present control should never be relinquished.

FOREIGN TRADE

4. The Federal Government has acquired by its merchant fleet and its War Trade Board in-

timate knowledge and capacity for mobilizing our resources for foreign trade. Factors which will be valuable in normal peace times should be retained.

NATIONAL RESOURCES

5. The Federal Government through its Food and Fuel Administrations and its War Industries Board has acquired command over basic resources which played a vital part in securing national efficiency. Every effort should be made to preserve the nucleus of these valuable agencies in such form and with such powers that we may achieve some part of that efficiency in peace.

PROFITEERING

6. The Federal Government has manifested grave interest and exerted its war powers to influence the cost of living and prevent profiteering. It should continue to exert its peace powers toward the same beneficent end.

HOUSING

7. The Federal Government has concerned itself effectively in the problem of housing industrial workers and has placed upon a new basis of prestige and authority the American movement for garden cities and suburbs. Its interest in this aspect of the welfare of the workers and the efficiency of industry should not now lapse, but the Labor Department's Bureau of Housing should be continued and its powers broadened to include educational work and research into our vast industrial housing problems.

MUNICIPAL PROBLEMS

8. As a measure of protecting the effectiveness of its soldiers and industrial workers the Federal Government has found it necessary to use its influence with local governments regarding moral and health conditions. Such Federal interest in local governments should not lapse, but should eventuate in the continued attack upon vice problems by the Public Health Service and in the formation of a Federal Bureau of Municipalities in the Department of the Interior to collect and distribute information on municipal problems.

In short, we, as a people during the next few months, must vigorously hold the ground we have gained during the war.

The National Municipal League at this conference adopted a resolution for the appointment of a committee with a paid secretary to deal with municipal reconstruction problems after the war.

The conference was attended by representatives of many civic and commercial organizations throughout the country. George E. Hooker, Civic Secretary of the City Club of Chicago, was one of those present.

NEW MEMBERS are coming in every week. Are you helping?

Notes on Some Books About

Peace and the New Society

By Aksel G. S. Josephson

(Continued from last issue)

Carl H. Grabo's little book *The World Peace and After* (N. Y.: A. A. Knopf) discusses the international question and the relations of various groups within the nation to each other and to the state, and closes with some practical proposals, among them arrangement for minority representation with the abolition of the two-party system and "the alliance of the professional and intellectual workers with the manual workers for the purpose of securing greater political power."

"When the great peoples championing the cause of democracy feel that their cause involves the polar extremes of human life, then we may be sure that the war is the birth throes of a nobler civilization," says John Firman Coar in *Democracy and the War* (N. Y.: G. P. Putnam's Sons).

In *Patriotism, National and International* (N. Y.: Longmans, Green & Co.) Sir Charles Waldstein tries to show "that German so-called patriotism, in the form of the corporate pride of the individual German citizen, has ultimately been most effective in producing this war." The purpose of the book is to help foster an opinion hostile to *this* kind of patriotism.—To guide public opinion in a rational direction is the expressed purpose of another book: *What is National Honor?* (N. Y.: Macmillan) by Leo Perla. Against national honor he places international. In this he sees the only sure guarantee for a future peace.

Lothrop Stoddard and Frank Glenn have published, under the title *Stakes of the War* (N. Y.: Century Co.), a "summary of the various problems, claims and interests of the nations at the peace table." The book is an examination of these claims and "those racial and territorial problems directly involved in the war at the time the book goes to press, and which are virtually certain to be treated at the peace table." There may be more problems coming; nothing is more uncertain in this crisis than the number of problems that will come up for solution. The opening sentences of the preface are significant: "Yesterday the detailed facts of European politics, trade, industry and religion were of primary importance to the scholar and foreign trader. Today they inject themselves into the discussions of every counting room, throw their shadow across the deliberation of every labor council, and stand as stubborn factors in the personal fortune and future of every American."

Walter E. Weyl writes about *The End of the War* (N. Y.: Macmillan Co.). It is not easy to say when the end will come, nor what its character will be. Pacifists and patriots are at log-

> # Bring Him to Lunch—
>
> That man whom you think would be a good member of the City Club — ask him to lunch when there is a speaker he would enjoy. Keep your mind open for possible new members of the Club. Invest in a lunch for his good, and Chicago's. Membership application blanks may be had at the cashier's desk.

gerheads, America must be converted from its isolation to take part in world politics, as arbiter. Militarism is the enemy. In the fight against it, liberals in all lands stand aligned against the forces of reaction that endeavor to gain the upper hand in all lands. Many obstacles stand in the way of the goal: internationalism. The struggle is not ended with the return of the delegates from the peace conference. Then first begins the struggle for democracy.

To show up the dogma of the sovereignty of the state, its right to act the bandit, as the enemy that must be fought, rather than any particular kind of organization of the state, is the purpose of David Jane Hill's *The Rebuilding of Europe* (N. Y.: Century Co.). This author sees the deepest cause of the war in the fact that peaceful development failed to create an effective international organization.

It is necessary that a high ideal be placed before the nations of the world, if such an organization shall be possible. It was such an ideal President Wilson presented in his second Address of acceptance, on the 2nd of September, 1916. On that occasion he uttered these following words: "No nation stands wholly apart in interest when the interest of all nations are thrown into confusion and peril. If hopeful and generous enterprise is to be renewed, if the healing and helpful arts of life are indeed to be revived when peace comes again, a new atmosphere of justice and friendship must be generated by means the world has never tried before. The nations of the world must unite in joint guarantees that whatever is done to disturb the whole world's life must first be tested in the court of the whole world's opinion before it is attempted."

President Wilson's speeches and public writings are a commentary to the part the United States has played in the world drama that now is brought to a close. Several editions have been published. I have the following before me: *President Wilson's Foreign Policy,* edited by John Brown Scott, with an introduction and notes by the editor and containing only those portions that deal with the relations with foreign powers (N. Y.: Oxford University Press); *President Wil-*

son's State Papers and Addresses, with an introduction by Albert Shaw (N. Y.: G. H. Doran Co.); and *President Wilson's Addresses* (N. Y.: H. Holt & Co.), an inexpensive edition, edited by George M. Harper, with an introduction by the editor dealing with Woodrow Wilson as a literary artist. Also *America's Attitude towards the War,* a collection of excerpts published by The Bankers' Trust Company in New York.

The question of the international organization of the states and peoples of the earth is closely connected with the peace settlement, is the opinion expressed by H. N. Brailsford in *A League of Nations* (N. Y.: Macmillan). The peace will be incomplete and temporary only if a single nation remains trammeled in its development. "When each nation turns to its fellow and speaks, though it be still in bewilderment and pain, the wish to create the co-operative world in which all may live and grow," then can the new league of nations be built up. This idea, of a new league of nations, built on the foundations of co-operation and democracy, has spread to all sections of the community. Even the men of the church, naturally so conservative, and not easily moved in the direction of new ideas, have taken it up and given it their support. See, e. g., the pamphlet of the bishop of Oxford, Charles Gore, entitled *The League of Nations and the Opportunity of the Church* (N. Y.: Doran). H. G. Wells *In the Fourth Year* (N. Y.: Macmillan) calls it "the most creative and hopeful of political ideas that has ever dawned upon the consciousness of mankind." He regards the British Empire as the nucleus of the League to come. It is, as it exists today, "a provisional thing," "an emergency arrangement." "Here we hold as trustees," he says, "and there on account of strategic considerations that may presently disappear, and though we will not contemplate the replacement of our flag anywhere by the flag of any other competing nation, though we do hope to hold together with our kin and with those who increasingly share our tradition and our language, nevertheless we are prepared to welcome great renunciations of our present ascendency and privileges in the interest of mankind as a whole." He greets with satisfaction the large number of books on the subject that have appeared. His own is one of the most important of them all.

Norman Angell, in his latest book *The Political Conditions of Allied Success* (N. Y.: Putnam), points to the two tendencies that will wrestle with each other during the peace settlement and after: the imperialistic and the democratic. Whether the thousands of young men of the allied nations that have been and will be sacrificed, will have died for a cause that is worth this sacrifice, depends, he says, on "the understanding which those who remain can manage to bring to bear upon our international problem."

This League of nations, or of *free* nations, as Wells calls it, is not to be confused with the *League to Enforce Peace* which was organized in Washington by a group of American men of affairs. The proceedings of the first annual meeting of that League, held in May, 1916, have been published under the title *Enforced Peace;* this volume contains the most authoritative statement about its program and ideals.

"Know thyself" was the admonition of the Delphic oracle to those who came there for advice. "To the American people, as they turn, in this momentous hour, to inquire what Destiny has in store for them, this injunction is particularly fitting," says H. P. Powers in the opening sentences of his new book *America Among the Nations* (N. Y.: Macmillan). To aid in this inquiry this author presents a survey of the relations of the United States to other states, large and small. The closing chapter is a forecast and here the author points out that "though the world must be subdued to order, humanity must somehow still be free."

"Every European will probably agree that at the close of the present war there ought to be, and, indeed, there must be, some reconstruction of the map of Europe. And every democratic European will certainly also agree that the basis of that reconstruction must be sought in the more ample recognition of the principle of nationality." Thus the Earl of Cromer in the introduction which he has supplied to Arnold J. Toynbee's "essays in reconstruction" published under the title *The New Europe* (N. Y.: E. P. Dutton & Co.). In the first of the seven essays composing this volume the author speaks of "Two Ideals of Nationality," the British "inward will to co-operate and the German demand for power over all the lands where German arms have at any time been victorious.' The question of nationality permeates the whole volume. The last essay, dealing with Ukraine "as a question taken at random," ends with these words: "If the settlement is to be wisely and justly accomplished (and if it is not, the future is unthinkable), it will need the fervent thought and the unweary-

ing goodwill, not only of the statesmen in council, but of every citizen of every country of Europe," and would add: of America.

"It is not enough to wish to end war. We must uproot the errors that foster it," is the admonition of G. Lowes Dickinson in *The Choice Before Us* (N. Y.: Dodd, Mead & Co.). If there shall be an end to war, if the present war shall really be a war against war, then the forces that cause war must be overcome. The principal among these is militarism, which, he states, is not only a military and political system, but a state of mind. And he points out how important it is not to lose from sight, in time of war, what it is that we are fighting for.

Winston Churchill's *A Traveler in War Time* (N. Y.: Macmillan Co.) is a vivid account of a few weeks' visit to France and what the author saw and heard there. To this he has added "An essay on the American contribution and the democratic idea" in which he emphasizes that "failure to recognize that the American is at heart an idealist is to lack understanding of our national character."

(To be continued)

This Club

The City Club is the best organized institution in Chicago to unite men who are interested in good government and a better city.

There are many problems facing the municipality following the war. Thousands of men in Chicago have had an impulse to help in making Chicago a better place in which to live. They don't know just how to make their efforts effective. They can accomplish much through the Club. Membership means that they are lining themselves up with the organized forces of civic betterment. The Club needs their counsel, their support. It cannot do its best work without the backing of every right-minded man who does business in Chicago.

The City Club seeks to give an opportunity for service. It is a club in which a man expects to give more than he gets if he will approximate the ideals upon which the Club is founded.

H. H. S.

DON'T FORGET to register your guests at the door. We want to know who is interested in coming to the Club.

WASH AWAY THE CARES of the day with a little spray from the shower at the City Club. Fourth floor!

DON'T EAT YOUR LUNCHEON in a corner. Be sociable this week!

CHARLES M. WILLIAMS is camp business secretary for the Y. M. C. A. at Fort Morgan, Ala.

The City Club Bulletin
A Journal of Active Citizenship

| VOLUME XI. | MONDAY, DECEMBER 23, 1918 | NUMBER 43 |

MERRY CHRISTMAS!

WEDNESDAY, DECEMBER 25 — Christmas
Club House closed all day

SATURDAY, DECEMBER 28, at Luncheon — Ladies' Day
Joint Meeting City Club of Chicago and "Corda Fratres"
Association of Cosmopolitan Clubs

INTERNATIONALISM

"Cosmopolitan America and Internationalism"
PROF. GRAHAM TAYLOR

"Internationalism and Industry"
JOHN J. ARNOLD
Vice-President First National Bank, Chicago

Corda Fratres Association of Cosmopolitan Clubs is the federation of the fifty local chapters known as Cosmopolitan Clubs in universities and colleges in the United States and Canada. These Cosmopolitan Clubs are composed of students of all nations, the majority of whom are natives of foreign countries.

At 2:30 the Association will hold another session at the City Club, to which all members of the Club who are interested are invited. The subject of this session will be "The Revival and Realization of National Aspirations." The program is printed more fully on another page.

An Exchange

The Directors have just completed arrangements for an exchange of privileges between the City Club of Cleveland and our own Club. Any member of this Club may, by presenting a membership card (which can be obtained from the Club office), avail himself of the privileges of the City Club of Cleveland.

The clubrooms of the City Club of Cleveland are on the third floor of the Hollenden Hotel. The Club has a large dining room, a comfortable lounge, writing room, library, reading room, game room, etc. Our members who visit Cleveland should make the acquaintance of the City Club there. The City Club of Chicago will be glad to welcome members of its brother organization of Cleveland.

The City Club of Chicago now has similar exchange arrangements with the City Clubs of Baltimore, Boston, Cincinnati, Kansas City, Milwaukee, Philadelphia, Portland and St. Louis, and also with the Duluth Commercial Club and the Civic Club of New York City.

IN THE EXCITEMENT of Christmas, don't forget to send your card pledging a new member. And, even more important, don't forget to get the new member. The Committee also asks you to send in the names and addresses of five men who would make good members.

The City Club Bulletin

A Journal of Active Citizenship

Published Weekly Except July, August and September;
bi-weekly during July, August and September

By the CITY CLUB OF CHICAGO

315 Plymouth Court   Telephone: Harrison 8278

DWIGHT L. AKERS, Editor

$1.00 per Year - - - - - - 10c per Copy

Entered as second class matter, December 3, 1917,
at the postoffice at Chicago, Illinois, under the act of
March 3, 1879.

Vol. XI.   Monday, December 23, 1918   No. 43

America's Wiseman

Since that far day in Palestine—
When in the East the star appeared—
And three wisemen
With gifts diverse and precious
Divined its meaning and set forth
To come at last, amazed and humble,
Among a throng of angels and of shepherds—
In a stable—prostrate—before Christ;
There has been no such Christmas time as this
So full of portent. This can fulfil that,
Or it can strangle once again, as Herod,
The hopes of little children and their like—
Whose welfare is the only guide we have
To any hope of any heaven anywhere.

And of the three who offer at Versailles,
Their lofty gifts of tested mind and heart,
America sends one
Who best the meaning and intent of Christmas
    day
Interprets to the world;
And we may rest content,
That man will render there,
Nothing to Cæsar that belongs to God.
    —Contributed by a member of the City Club.

Cosmopolitan Clubs to Meet

NEXT Saturday the City Club will join with the Corda Fratres Association of Cosmopolitan Clubs in a luncheon meeting devoted to the subject of "Internationalism." The speakers will be Graham Taylor and John J. Arnold. The meeing is in connection with a convention of the Association, whose sessions are divided between the University of Chicago, Hull House, and the City Club.

Corda Fratres Association of Cosmopolitan Clubs is a federation of about fifty college and university cosmopolitan clubs in the United States and Canada. "The main object of the 'Cosmopolitan Movement,'" according to the president of the Association, Prof. E. W. Burgess of the University of Chicago, "is to promote fellowship, brotherhood and mutual understanding among young people of all nations. The Association of Cosmopolitan Clubs believes that its highest service to the world will be in bringing into intimate friendly contact the young men who though now students in a foreign country are in the future destined to fill places of highest leadership in their native countries."

The convention opens Thursday night, at the University of Chicago, with an address by Prof. Shailer Mathews on "The Hope of Reconstruction." On Friday evening the session will be held at Hull House. Jane Addams will speak on "Woman and the New Social Order," Agnes Nestor on "The Woman Trade Union League, Industrial Democracy and the New World Order," and Mme. Raisa Lomonosoff on "Women and the New Russia."

The Saturday luncheon program at the City Club is announced on the first page of the Bulletin. At 2:30 at the City Club there will be a session on "The Revival and Realization of National Aspirations." Prof. Herbert A. Miller, a director of the Mid-European Union, will preside, and addresses will be made by the following persons: For Poland, Emily Napieralski; for Czecho-Slavia, Jakub Horak; for Jugo-Slavia, Theophile Yovanovitch; for Lithuania, Kleofas Jurgelionis; for India, A. C. Chakravasty; for the Philippine Islands, Aurelio L. Corcuera.

GEORGE R. HORTON of the Western Architect and F. Guy Davis, manager L. H. Crall Company, were appointed members of the editorial board of the City Club Bulletin last week.

MAKE A CHRISTMAS present to your Club by getting a new member. Names are now coming in as a result of the Committee's appeal. Are you helping?

Russia's Lesson to America

'NO country has more Bolshevism than it deserves," said an Englishman in Russia, uoted by Prof. Ralph B. Dennis of Northwest-rn University, at the City Club luncheon last ednesday. Does America deserve Bolshevism? oes the Russian Revolution have any lesson for merica? A large number of commissars in the irious towns in Russia, according to Professor ennis, have lived in America for periods of om three to fifteen years. It was the opinion : foreign residents in Moscow that among the :volutionists those who had lived in America ere the most bitter in opposition to "capital-m" and the most determined to eliminate the ourgeoisie.

A Good Life

In conversation with a group of soldiers of the ed Guard, three of whom had been in America, companion of Prof. Dennis, an Englishman, irning to one of these soldiers, said: "Why do)u not go back to America? You can earn more oney there." The soldier replied: "We want >mething more than money. We want the op-ortunity to live a good life. May be we can nd it here." "That boy," said Prof. Dennis, 'had come back from 'free America' to 'darkest Russia,' hoping to find a chance to lead a good ife. What was the matter with him? He had :ome to America a peasant. Where did he land? Probably in some great manufacturing city or :ome mining town. And what was he? He was ι 'hunkie.' Nobody 'cared a damn' what hap-)ened to him or tried to teach him about Amer-ca. He came a 'hunkie' and he left a 'hunkie.' And this is the history not only of the 'hunkie,')ut of the 'wop,' the 'sheeny' and the 'dago.'

When the "Hunkie" Marches Home

"The boys who fought our battles in France will be coming back soon. They will march lown the streets and in the parade will be autos :ontaining men whose legs or arms are gone or who perhaps are forever shut out from the light >f day. Among these men will be 'dagoes,' wops,' 'sheenies' and 'hunkies.' But they will)e hard to pick out from the others because they are all Americans.

"What are those soldiers coming back to? Are they coming back to the old pre-war antago-nisms? If they are, the men who are responsible for it are doing everything in their power to add to Bolshevism in this country. Bolshevism is a state of mind and must be met as such. During the war capital and labor buried the hatchet to lick the Kaiser and marched shoulder to shoul-der to make the world safe for the little de-mocracies. Are we going to do less for our own country?

"There are men in the employing group who stick out their jaws and say, 'we'll show 'em'—and they have pretty good jaws, too. This is not the time for that sort of thing. Many em-ployers have no conception of what is going on in the world. In the early days of the war a Japanese statesman said: 'This war ends Euro-pean civilization.' Nobody really knows that is happening in Europe today. On the one hand is starvation, on the other hand anarchy. This is a new world with new forces which must be met.

"I believe that the long reign of *selfish* indi-vidualism is over. The gap between capital and labor must be bridged by democracy—and by more and more democracy. The way to stop the spread of Bolshevism is to make, for every Bol-shevist ten thousand contented workmen. I be-lieve in America's brains, purpose and will to bring this about.

Hope for Russia

Prof. Dennis' analysis of the situation in Rus-sia was based on a year's stay there as American vice-consul. He arrived just after the Bol-shevist revolution of November, 1917. He trav-eled widely in Russia, chiefly second or third class or by box car, and had constant opportu-nity for rubbing elbows with Russian peasants, workingmen and soldiers. On two occasions, also, he lived with people of the upper class. Having this varied background of experience and this wide contact with Russian people, he said: "I like Russia and the Russian people and believe in their potentialities." "If you sympa-thized with the Russian people under the rule of the Czar, that sympathy you should give them today," he continued. He quoted, as summing up, his understanding of the Russian situation, this statement from a letter written by a Rus-sian shortly before the revolution: 'The time is by when nine-tenths of the people can be treated as manure with which to grow a few roses.' "

A Great Empire

"Russia owns one-seventh of this earth," con-tinued Prof. Dennis. "Her people number about two hundred million. One hundred and three languages and dialects are spoken within her borders. About thirty-five races and tribes are represented in her population.

"Russia's class divisions are most vital. Eighty-five per cent of the population is made up of peasants and workmen, and most of these are peasants. According to varying estimates from 75 per cent to 90 per cent of the people are illiterate. They have wrung a hard living from the soil and while they know little about political institutions and that sort of thing, they know much about the fundamental things of life.

THE DARK PEOPLE

"On top of this mass have been the fifteen per cent of the well-to-do—the intelligencia, the wealthy classes and the bureaucracy. The people on top called those below them 'the dark people.' The bureaucracy has always feared 'the dark people,' and intellectuals who tried to give them education, or to better their conditions, were sent to Siberia. These 'dark people' have thrown off their shackles and taken away the whip, but not knowing where to turn and with eyes unaccustomed to the light, they have staggered forward and brought down their own house on their heads.

THE BETRAYAL OF RUSSIA

"Why did Russia get out of the war? When I asked that question in Russia I always got the answer, 'we were tired.' But France and England were tired and they kept on fighting. When I told Russian people that, they told me of the betrayal of Russia by those who were in high places, from the Czarina down. Guns, food, everything for the army went wrong. No Russian warship was allowed to attack a German vessel without the permission of the admiral.

"At least fifteen million men were called to the colors, more than twice as many as Russia could equip and use. Most of them were illiterate peasants, not knowing who they were fighting, or why. They were like cattle driven down the street.

RUSSIA'S "REGENERATION"

"The revolution came and the Czar was no more. The people rejoiced. All political exiles were welcomed back. They came from Siberia, England, France and America by the thousands. These people during their exile had been thinking, had been developing a psychology of protest. When they returned they let loose this flood of ideas upon the Russian people. In the first days of rejoicing the sympathy was even extended to criminals. Prison doors were opened, the people seemed to believe that everybody would be regenerated by the revolution. At the same time Germany sent in hundreds of workers to spread certain doctrines in the Russian Army." Such influences could of course create only chaos.

"Among the political groups in Russia," said Prof. Dennis, "there are three which should be given special mention, the Constitutional Democrats, or Cadets, the Mensheviki and the Bolsheviki. The Cadets want to create a republic much like our own, with wealth and intelligence in control. The Mensheviki are the party of peasants. They want the peasant to control, but are willing to give the bourgeoisie a voice. The Bolsheviki believe in the nationalization of land and industry. They would leave neither in private hands. They are for the complete exclusion of the bourgeoisie from the government and the elimination and extermination of those who oppose their program.

"Kerensky was not a big enough man for the situation or he would be there yet. At one time he had Lenine and Trotzky arrested, but he let them go. Immediately after their release they went to the army and told the peasants to take their guns and to go back and take the land. They told the workingmen to take their guns and go back and take the factories. When that army started nothing could stop it.

THE TASK OF REBUILDING

"The difficulty of working out the new order was of course tremendous. Russia is vast and uneducated and communication is poor. It would not be easy to organize such a country even under the best conditions. With the Bolsheviki things did not come along according to schedule. I doubt if the peasant knows what nationalization means. When he settled down on the land, he said, It's mine. He was through with the revolution.

INDUSTRIAL PROGRAM FAILS

"In the cities factory owners were forced out and the workmen elected committees to run the plants." Prof. Dennis, by way of illustration, mentioned several instances of the dispossession of factory owners and the consequences. "In one case," he said, "the first thing which the committee did was to raise wages and shorten hours, but that committee lasted only a few days, because it did not go fast enough. In four months in that plant there were four different committees, because the men couldn't get committees which would go far enough to suit them. During these four months not a single finished machine was put out from that factory. There was no money coming in and the government paid the wages." In another plant mentioned by Prof. Dennis, production fell off 90 per cent. "It would be difficult," he said, "to find in Russia any factory which is running at peace-time capacity. Many factories are closed.

"The government is having many difficulties with the peasants. It placed fixed prices on food products below the prices for which the peasants could sell. I have seen the Red Guard, with machine guns, go out to farms and take food from the peasants by force. But the peasants also have guns—even machine guns which they brought back from the front—and in some districts they are organized to resist the Red Guard. The peasant has been ordered by the government to turn in a statment of his crops and to sell at prices fixed by the government. I doubt very much if he will do that."

Prof. Dennis said that he believed that a majority of the Russian people are not with the present government. It has given them neither peace nor food.

A GAME OF TAG

"Lenine and Trotzky," he said, "are probably honest in their belief that what they are doing is the way to better society. They took German money, but not to help Germany. It was their idea that after they had done their job in Russia, they were going to do the same job in Germany. Lenine and the Kaiser were trying to use each other. Which, in the light of history, saw the farthest? The laugh at this time seems to be with Lenine."

The Negro and Reconstruction

IN the great social awakening which we have been led to expect as a product of the war and of reconstruction, what improvement is to be hoped for in the status of the black citizen? Is he to be permanently of an inferior caste, or is he to be given political, social and educational opportunities more nearly like those with which his white brother is favored? John R. Shillady, Secretary of the National Association for the Advancement of Colored People, an organization of both whites and blacks, spoke on this subject at the City Club, Saturday, December 9th.

THE ARMY AND THE NEGRO

The negro was as much touched as any other citizen by the great cause in which America was engaged, said Mr. Shillady. Efforts of German propaganda to undermine his loyalty were futile. But in spite of his devotion to the cause, efforts were made to give him an inferior place in the army. It was first proposed that he be excluded from the draft on the ground that he was needed in agriculture. That plan was defeated, as was also the attempt to prevent negroes from becoming officers. There are in the army many negro officers, including two colonels, but there is a dead line of rank in the army which no negro has crossed. Colored men are not admitted to West Point or Annapolis.

Mr. Shillady told of discriminations against the negro in the federal departments at Washington. For the first time in history, he said, the black man has been "jim-crowed" by the federal government. Hitherto such discrimination had been confined to the states, but now the federal government, through its policy of segregation, has set the same seal of inferiority upon him. Colored men who have passed civil service examinations and gone to Washington to take their positions, have been told that no positions were open, although whites were appointed to such places immediately afterwards.

"THE DISTINCTIVE AMERICAN SPORT"

The most terrible indictment of the American people in their treatment of the negro is the record of lynchings. Henry Waterson called lynching the "distinctive American sport." During 1918, according to Mr. Shillady, there have been, in the United States, 58 lynchings, the authenticity of which has been established. There are undoubtedly others which have not been authenticated. Nineteen of these lynchings occurred in Georgia. Many of them have been accompanied by the most indescribable tortures.

In Tennessee, on Lincoln's birthday, Mr. Shillady said, two negroes were lynched. One of them was taken to the edge of town where a fire was built and irons heated. Red hot irons were forced down his throat, and other terrible and unmentionable things were done to him. He was placed alive upon the fire and died after twenty minutes of excruciating torture. A week later a committee from the association which Mr. Shillady represents visited the President. He had not heard of the incident. So common were lynchings, or so much was the veil of secrecy drawn around them that an incident such as this might occur and the President of the United States not even be aware of it. The President promised that he would speak out on the subject of lynchings and he did so last July.

FEAR AMONG NEGROES

It is very difficult, Mr. Shillady said, to get evidence on lynchings, because of fear that is created among the negroes. After the Georgia lynchings about five hundred left town. An investigator for the Association reported that in the

South apparently the only effect of Wilson's statement on lynchings was to create a conspiracy of silence. Generally the prosecution of lynchings has been left to local authorities. Under these conditions it is of course difficult to obtain action against the guilty. In only one state has the Attorney General been designated as the prosecuting officer. A great national conference will be held in New York on February 11th to arouse public sentiment on the subject of lynchings.

COMPULSORY WORK LAWS

Mr. Shillady discussed the many kinds of discrimination practiced against the negro, particularly in the South. In most southern states, he said, the negro is not allowed to sit on juries, and if he is charged with any offence against the laws he is tried by white men. The negro claims that there is not an equal administration of the laws as between negroes and the whites. An investigation of the enforcement of the compulsory work laws showed that in some southern states during the war, these laws have not been enforced equally against negroes and whites. They have been enforced with particular stringency against negro women, presumably because of the shortage of domestic servants. Cases have occurred in which negro women have been arrested and taken out of their homes on vagrancy charges because they were not in service.

"JIM CROW"

The "Jim Crow" car represents another type of discrimination against the negro. "It is not that the negro wants to associate with the white people," said Mr. Shillady, "but he wants to get what he pays for, and that is accommodations equal to those furnished white people." The "Jim Crow" car is usually the rear of a smoker. It is usually crowded and dirty and the toilet facilities are inadequate. When a negro enters a railroad station in the South to buy a ticket, he must usually wait until all the whites have been served. It is also almost impossible for him to get sleeper accommodations. In some cases negro officers of the United States Army traveling on government transportation have been forced out of sleeping cars as soon as they entered a southern state.

EDUCATION FOR THE BLACK CHILD

"The colored people have made great advance in education since the Civil War, in spite of the discrimination against them," said Mr. Shillady. At the close of the war ninety per cent of the colored people were illiterate. Illiteracy among them now has been reduced to about thirty per cent. "All that the negro asks," said Mr. Shillady, "is that in any appropriations for education the negro should have his fair share." Investigation shows that the average annual amount spent for teachers' salaries in the South is $10.32 for each white child and $2.89 for each colored child. In counties where the percentage of negroes is highest, the amount spent upon the white child exceeds $22, the amount spent upon the colored child is only $1.78.

"In some southern states the negro is practically disfranchised," Mr. Shillady continued. One means of depriving him of his privileges as a voter is the use of the so-called "understanding clause." The voter must be able to show an understanding of the provisions of the constitution. The colored man says that his white brother is asked some easy question, such as, "How many houses has Congress?" The colored man, on the other hand, is asked to define *ex post facto* laws, or to answer some very difficult question.

THE BLACK MAN IN INDUSTRY

The colored man is also subject to industrial disqualifications. He has been denied membership in certain trade unions, as for instance in the railroad brotherhoods. Not long ago, news was received that an entire colored regiment had been granted the *croix de guerre* by the French war authorities. On the same day word came that one of the regional directors of the railroad administration had issued an order against the employment of black men in positions to which they had formerly not been admitted. These two facts, so illuminating in their contrast, were called to Mr. McAdoo's attention and an investigation was made. It was learned that the order was due to objections of the railroad unions, whose members did not wish to work with colored men. On the instructions of Mr. McAdoo, the order was withdrawn.

"It is unfortunate in a democracy," Mr. Shillady concluded, "that a striving people, a people which is coming up in the scale of civilization, which is acquiring education and increasing in economic power, should thus be denied its opportunity of advancement." What the colored people are asking is, "Can the people of America include them in a democracy, or do they intend placing the colored people in a permanently inferior status. It is not simply a question of color, as the attitude of southern people toward their negro servants demonstrates, but they want to keep the negro in an inferior caste. It is not safe for America that such a condition should exist. In a democracy even the weakest member should be able to feel that he will have his day in court, and will be granted, if not social equality, at least justice."

Notes on Some Books About

Peace and the New Society

By Aksel G. S. Josephson

(Continued from last issue)

The international problem is not the only one to be solved in the spirit of democracy. The other great problem is the industrial. The reorganization of industry is a subject which all these writers emphasize as a task that demands the most careful consideration. A conference of representatives of industry and commerce, both employers and employees, was held at Ruskin College in Oxford in July, 1916, at which occasion the question was discussed from all sides. The papers read at the conference and the subsequent discussions have been published by the college in a pamphlet entitled *The Reorganization of Industry*. Another British institution, the Garton Foundation in London, has issued a *Memorandum on the Industrial Situation after the War*, the result of a conference of a number of anonymous leaders of industry, labor and other interests, which was held at its initiative during the months of May to September, 1916. Those that partook in the conference foresaw strife in the economic field after the war and the result of their deliberation may be expressed in a nutshell thus: "To hold the balance true between the economic and the human side of the problem—is a task as truly national as that of victory in war."

Industrial Reconstruction (N. Y.: E. P. Dutton & Co.) is the title of a symposium published in 1917, consisting of letters and other statements by leading Englishmen in reply to a questionnaire sent out by Huntley Carter asking: "1· What in your opinion will be the industrial situation after the War as regards (a) Labor; (b) Capital; (c) the Nation as a single commercial entity? 2. What in your view is the best policy to be pursued by (a) Labor; (b) Capital; (c) the State?" The editor speaks of the national interest as the compelling force in men's mind. "Men in this country (i. e. Great Britain) are indeed," he says, "seriously and deeply moved in the direction of uneasy yet hopeful speculation concerning the problems of the future, and the industrial problem most of all. Is it peace that the War will bring, or is it a worse war than that in which we are engaged? And if peace, how shall we find it? What new feeling and thought, what new energy, what taste and refinement, aided by extended knowledge, will announce the appearance of this healthy movement? What changes effected in the minds of industrialists will enable them to understand each other, and leave them

to felicitate themselves on the noble uses of harmony?"

Another English symposium, *Labour and Capital after the War* (London: John Murray), is edited by S. J. Chapman, a member of the Whitley Committee; it contains as an appendix the First Report of that Committee and has an introduction by Mr. Whitley himself. The various contributors discuss the general subject from their several points of view, but the editor remarks in his preface that on the labor question they all agree, no matter how divergent are their views on other subjects. The last essay is contributed by the editor. He speaks of the "greater solidarity," which was growing rapidly before the war and has since been accentuated and become more articulate. "A social structure bound together by serfdom," he points out, "is a ramshackle creation at best, devoid of any internal principle of cohesion. This is not far behind us, but the bare wage system repeats many of its inherent defects. At the other extreme, to which the civilization for which the Allies stand is working, lies the ideal of self-determination. In this, the ruling authority is not acquired by force, but is won by efficient leadership and the acceptance of responsibilities that go far beyond wages and profits concepts and the most obvious humanitarian obligations. Moreover, it is being increasingly borne in upon us that it is an authority which is not and should not be wholly centralized in the employer. To some extent it must be divided and distributed according to the capacities of the several human parts of the industrial organism to think wisely for more than personal objects."

American Problems of Reconstruction, edited by Elisha M. Friedman (N. Y.: E. P. Dutton & Co.), deals mainly with economic and financial aspects in the narrower sense of these words. Scientific management, Industrial research, International commerce, Stabilizing foreign trade, these are some of the subjects discussed in this symposium by business men and lawyers. The conservative nature of the discussion is well exemplified in the Foreword, by Franklin K. Lane. He writes: "The one danger of any period of reconstruction is not the inventiveness of the human mind,—throwing into the air for all men to gather by wireless new lines of thought, novel conceptions of society,—the danger is in letting go the old before the new is tested. The ship must not be allowed to drift. We must make sure that we have power to take us in the new direction before we let go the anchor. To reject tradition, to despise the warnings of history and to be superior to the limitations of human nature, is to drive without a chart into a Saragossa sea of water logged uselessness." Charles M. Schwab emphasizes the need of technical research because the cost of production must be lowered by other means than lowering the wages of the workers.

In Britain after the Peace: Revolution or Reconstruction (London: T. F. Unwin) Brougham Villiers endeavors to look "below the battle," as he says in the last chapter of the book. He discusses the various problems of reconstruction of society: demobilization, finance, industry, land, and the problem of development, intellectual, material and political, suggesting as the result of his considerations, a National Works Department. "To look beyond the welter of hate and destruction now proceeding in Europe to the serener atmosphere 'above the battle'," or "to peer below it, to see what the rapid changes going on beneath the surface of things portend, and what problems they are preparing for us after the war is over," either of these courses, he says, "is more profitable than to watch the fleeting incidents of the battle itself." What the statesmen and writers of the world have written and said during the war, is "for the most part only the outbreaks of its delirium." And the

author closes with the question: "Are we to take full advantage of the things that have been happening below the battle, the destruction which the war itself has brought not upon this or that army or Empire, but on the system of military Imperialism itself?"

The British Labor Party took up the question of reconstruction and outlined its views on this subject in a remarkable program which it placed before the country's electors and of which an American edition has been issued under the title *Towards a New World* (Wyoming, N. Y.: W. R. Browne). In its comprehensiveness and its definiteness it is the most remarkable document which to date any political party has issued. An allied victory will not be a democratic victory "if the result be merely a restoration of the capitalistic regime which the war has discredited and destroyed." The program which the party presents involves a complete recasting of the present foundations of society. And it reaches farther than any socialistic party ever did in that it wants to represent "all that work with hands or brain."* The leader of the party, Arthur Henderson, comments on the program in a pamphlet: *The Aims of Labour* (N. Y.: Huebsch). He sees clearly what the future has to offer: "an era of revolutionary change to which there is no parallel in history." *A Clean Peace* is the title of a pamphlet issued by Charles A. McCurdy (N. Y.: Doran) containing the official text of the memorandum in regard to the conditions of peace which were accepted at a conference between representatives of labor and socialist groups in the allied countries, held in London in February, 1918. It is nearly identical with the statement on the same subject which was made in December, 1917, by the British Labor Party and the Trade Union Congress.   *(To be concluded.)*

---

* Since this was written, the Chicago Federation of Labor has issued a leaflet containing an Independent Labor Party Program, embodying similar ideas.

Christmas Suggestion

Editor of the City Club Bulletin: Nobody has asked me, but if I were asked for a short, all-around 1919 motto for everybody—applicable internationally, nationally, industrially, politically, religiously, socially, in the home, in the club, and to myself—it would be

DON'T BE TOO SELFISH!

Written, but not signed, by a quiet, unobtrusive, humble, inarticulate, reserved, cowardly member of the City Club of Chicago.

Merry Christmas! Happy New Year!

Get a new member now!

The City Club Bulletin

A Journal of Active Citizenship

VOLUME XI.   MONDAY, DECEMBER 30, 1918   NUMBER 44

NEW YEAR'S WEEK
TUESDAY, DECEMBER 31, AT LUNCHEON

PROF. JAMES A. FIELD
Member American Shipping Mission

will speak on

"The Allied Control of Shipping"

Prof. Field has just returned from London where he has for ten months been engaged upon the problems of world shipping, in connection with the Allied Maritime Transport Council.

To what extent shall the international control of shipping be continued after the war? The answer to that question is vital in its bearing, not only upon commerce and industry, but upon the whole scheme of international organization after the war. Professor Field, fresh from his labors in London and Paris, will be able to throw light upon this most important question.

Speaking promptly at 1.

Clubhouse will be closed all day New Years.

Notes on Some Books about Peace and the New Society
By Aksel G. S. Josephson
(Concluded.)

"The war has profoundly altered the attitude of women toward public affairs,' says Marion Phillips in the Introduction to a small volume, *Women and the Labor Party* (N. Y.: Huebsch), written by some British women members of that party. "These hitherto unconsidered citizens," she says further on, "have begun to think on political issues: they naturally ask how they shall act." The essays contained in the book are intended to "describe the work which lies before the people when the world once more is at peace." They treat of woman's activities along various lines, in the home and the factory, as domestic workers and brainworkers, with a closing study of "Women and Internationalism" in which Mary Longman speaks of the work of the Women's International Council of Socialist and Labor Organizations, British Section, which was formed in 1910. She closes by saying that women "have had a share in sav'ng internationalism from being wrecked in the storms of war, and when peace comes they will have a large responsibility in the task of rebuilding a society in which international sentiment is expressed in terms of international organization."

Paul U. Kellogg's *British Labor and the*

The City Club Bulletin

A Journal of Active Citizenship

Published Weekly Except July, August and September;
bi-weekly during July, August and September

By the CITY CLUB OF CHICAGO

315 Plymouth Court   Telephone: Harrison 8278

$1.00 per Year - - - - - - - 10c per Copy

Entered as second class matter, December 3, 1917,
at the postoffice at Chicago, Illinois, under the act of
March 3, 1879.

Vol. XI.   Monday, December 30, 1918   No. 44

War (N. Y.: Boni & Liveright) deals very fully with the war-aims of the British Labor Party, and ideas of reconstruction, with a view on the American Federation of Labor and its standpoint in regard to the labor movement in England.

That the industrial problem must be solved in a way that is satisfactory to all parties, without being a compromise, is pointed out by Sidney Webb in his study of *The Restoration of Trade Union Conditions* (N. Y.: Huebsch). And J. A. Hobson says in *Democracy After the War* (N. Y.: Macmillan) that the problems of peace, democracy and internationalism are inseparable and at bottom one and that "with the triumph of this league is the problem of personal liberty, political and industrial, as well as spiritual, indissolubly joined."

Questions of pure science are treated in a collection of essays: *Science and the Nation* (Cambridge, England: University Press), edited by A. C. Seward and with an interesting introduction by Lord Moulton. The thesis of the collection is that it is to be feared that the industrial advancement that has been fostered by the war may lead to a neglect of pure science. Lord Moulton does not share this fear. These studies show how pure science, or, as he would call it, experimental research, has aided mankind in its everyday life. Its influence will not be diminished in the future.

Science has had its own peculiar problems as well, affected by the war. One of them is the question of publications of learned societies. There is much overlapping, a deplorable lack of proper co-operation, much resulting waste. This was brought before the English scientific public at the initiative of Sir Robert Hadfield, president of the Faraday Society. His address and the subsequent discussion have been reprinted from the *Transactions* of the Society under the title: *The Co-ordination of Scientific Publication.*

The spiritual and religious problems that have been aroused by the War also have their spokesmen, e. g. George Lansbury, the author of *Your Part in Poverty* (N. Y.: Huebsch), one of England's most prominent labor leaders, socialist and member of the Church of England. What we need is, he says, a new heart, a complete change of point of view. And he writes about the failure of Christendom to redeem the world; this is, he says, "writ large on the blood-stained battlefields which today stretch across Europe, Asia and Africa" and "still deeper on the social life of all those nations who profess to serve God and to believe in the teachings of his blessed Son." And he berates the idea that either individuals or nations can gain anything by dominating over others. The same standpoint takes Henry S. Coffin in a series of lectures on the ministry and the church: *In a Day of Social Rebuilding* (New Haven: Yale University Press). Without new motives, he says, social control is of small avail. A new heart, a new spirit must inspire the peoples, if not all attempts at international organization shall be in vain.

The World Significance of a Jewish State lies, according to A. A. Berle, in its being a link between the Asiatic and the European nations. The little book is also a contribution to the discussion of spiritual values. The author, a protestant theologian, sees in the establishment of a Jewish state in Palestine a matter of great interest to Christians as well as to Jews, because that country is the original home of both the Jewish and the Christian religion (N. Y.: M. Kennerley).

About ten years ago Ralph Adams Cram wrote an essay called *The Great Thousand Years,* in which he praised the Middle Ages and its civilization and prophesied the destruction of ours. He has now re-published it in book form with a supplementary chapter, "Ten Years After" (Boston: Marshall Jones). He sees the only salvation out of the coming revolution in a new kind of monasticism, "the instinctive gathering together of men into small units for defense and community development" and their further "assimilating into a larger unity without the surrender of independence and autonomy." In another booklet, *The Nemesis of Mediocrity* (same publ.), he deprecates the lack, in our generation, of leaders, without whom, he says, democracy is a danger and culture and even civilization will pass away.

Creative Impulse in Industry by Helen Marot (N. Y.: Dutton) is called "a proposition for educators"; it is a contribution to the discussion about industrial education, and the author speaks of "the impasse which we had apparently reached when the war occurred; it is where we still are," she says. Educators have opposed the control of education by business, because "industry under the influence of business prostitutes effort." But schools must work hand-in-hand with industry: "unattached to the human hive they are denied participation in life." On the basis of this idea Miss Marot has worked out a plan for an educational experiment which is here published under the auspices of the Bureau of

A New Year's Resolution for a City Club Member

I resolve —

TO SECURE at least one new member for the Club—the sooner, the better,

TO "BOOST" the City Club loyally and enthusiastically among my business and social associates,

TO SEND to the Membership Extension Committee the names and addresses of friends and acquaintances who should become members;

Because —

MORE CIVIC-MINDED men should share the advantages and support the ideals of the Club,

MORE NEW MEMBERS are needed to fill the places of those who are in military service,

MORE DOLLARS must be secured to meet the expenses of the Club inasmuch as members who are in service are exempt from dues, and cost of operation has increased.

Information, Literature, Co-operation upon application to the

MEMBERSHIP EXTENSION COMMITTEE

Educational Experiments. Such an experiment will be an important step in the work of reconstructing society after the war.

Two writers, an English university teacher and journalist and an American philosopher, have issued collections of their essays and addresses from the last four years. A reading of these two volumes will disclose the thoughts that have moved and still move the intellectual classes in both countries. The Englishman, Gilbert Murray, has, as he tells in the preface, had an American audience in mind in making up this particular collection of his essays; he calls it *Faith, War and Policy* (Boston: Houghton Mifflin Co.) and in the preface he makes the following significant confession of guilt of England and its allies: "We have none of us done our duty as free societies. We have oppressed the poor; we have accepted advertisement in the place of truth; we have given too much power to money; and we have been indifferent to the quality of human character." *Liberty and Democracy* is the title of Hartley B. Alexander's book (Boston: Jones). Never has clear thinking been more necessary, he says. His object in publishing the book has been to be of service to his fellow citizens, as far as is in his power. It is the duty of every man to express what he thinks in the most important questions of the day. It is particularly the duty of the teacher. The reconstruction of society, this author says, must be accomplished through the education of the individual citizen. It is worth while to quote the aphorism of Aristoteles which he has placed as motto for his book: "He who would duly inquire about the best form of a state, ought first to determine which is the most eligible life." He who wishes to make up his mind on this point will find an excellent guide in Bertrand Russell's two books: *Principles of Social Reconstruction*, published in this country under the more catching title *Why men fight*, and *Political Ideals* (both N. Y.: Century Co.). They both survey the most important political and social problems from an individualistic point of view. The last chapter of the former is called "What we can do." We can think the thoughts of the future, the author says: "Our expectations must not be for tomorrow, but for the time when what is thought now by a few shall have become the common thought of many. If we have courage and patience, we can think the thoughts and feel the hopes by which, sooner or later, men will be inspired, and weariness and discouragement will be turned into energy and ardor. For this reason, the first thing we have to do is to be clear in our own minds as to the kind of life we think good and the kind of change that we desire in the world." I close these notes with the opening words of *Political Ideals*: "In dark days, men need a clear faith and a well-grounded hope; and as the outcome of these, the calm courage which takes no account of hardships by the way."

Index to the City Club Bulletin —Vol. XI, 1918, Nos. 1-44

The titles listed below are the more important of those included in the Bulletin during the last year.